Introduction to Physical Anthropology

Robert Jurmain | Lynn Kilgore |
Wenda Trevathan | Russell L. Ciochon

Australia • Brazil • Japan • Korea • Mexico • Singapore • Spain • United Kingdom • United States

Introduction to Physical Anthropology

Senior Manager, Custom Production:
Donna Brown
Linda deStefano
Julie Dierig

Manager, Custom Production:
Terri Daley
Louis Schwartz

Marketing Manager:
Rachael Kloos

Manager, Premedia:
Kim Fry

Manager, Intellectual Property Project Management:
Brian Methe

Manager, Manufacturing & Inventory:
Spring Stephens

Introduction to Physical Anthropology, 2013-2014 Edition, 14th Edition
Robert Jurmain | Lynn Kilgore | Wenda Trevathan | Russell L. Ciochon

For product information and technology assistance, contact us at
Cengage Learning Customer & Sales Support, 1-800-354-9706
For permission to use material from this text or product,
submit all requests online at **cengage.com/permissions**
Further permissions questions can be emailed to
permissionrequest@cengage.com

This book contains select works from existing Cengage Learning resources and was produced by Cengage Learning Custom Solutions for collegiate use. As such, those adopting and/or contributing to this work are responsible for editorial content accuracy, continuity and completeness.

ISBN: 978-1-305-30058-3

WCN: 01-100-101

Cengage Learning
20 Channel Center Street
Boston, MA 02210
USA

Cengage Learning is a leading provider of customized learning solutions with office locations around the globe, including Singapore, the United Kingdom, Australia, Mexico, Brazil, and Japan. Locate your local office at: **www.international.cengage.com/region.**

Cengage Learning products are represented in Canada by Nelson Education, Ltd.

For your lifelong learning solutions, visit **www.cengage.com/custom.**

Visit our corporate website at **www.cengage.com.**

Acknowledgements

The content of this text has been adapted from the following product(s):

Source Title: Introduction to Physical Anthropology, 2013-2014 Edition
Authors: Jurmain/Kilgore/Trevathan/Ciochon
ISBN10: 1285061977
ISBN13: 9781285061979

Table Of Contents

Connections

Physical anthropology is a biological science that investigates how humans have evolved and continue to do so.

Evolutionary theory, particularly natural selection, explains how life forms have changed over time and how new species are produced.

Cristina G. Mittermeier

Introduction to Physical Anthropology

1

Student Learning Objectives

After mastering the material in this chapter, you should be able to:

- Describe the discipline of anthropology as it is practiced in the United States, its subfields, and the general anthropological perspective on how humans are biologically and behaviorally connected to other species.
- Provide a brief description of the major subfields of physical or biological anthropology.
- Understand the fundamentals of the scientific method and the importance of hypothesis testing.
- Explain why scientific theories are not simply guesses or hunches, as the term (theory) is often incorrectly used and interpreted.
- Appreciate how understanding the nature of scientific research can lead to the development of critical thinking skills, which, in turn, are an extremely important outcome of a college education.

Introduction

One day, perhaps during the rainy season some 3.7 million years ago, two or three animals walked across a grassland **savanna** in what is now northern Tanzania, in East Africa. These individuals were early **hominins**, members of the same evolutionary lineage that includes our own **species**, *Homo sapiens*. Fortunately for us, a record of their passage on that long-forgotten day remains in the form of fossilized footprints, preserved in hardened volcanic deposits. As chance would have it, shortly after heels and toes were pressed into the damp soil, a nearby volcano erupted. The ensuing ash fall blanketed everything on the ground. In time, the ash layer hardened into a deposit that remarkably preserved the tracks of numerous animals, including those early hominins, for nearly 4 million years (**Fig. 1-1**).

These now famous prints indicate that two individuals, one smaller than the other, perhaps walking side by side, left parallel sets of tracks. But because the larger individual's prints are obscured, possibly by those of a third, it's unclear how many actually made that journey so long ago. What is clear is that the prints were made by an animal that habitually walked **bipedally** (on two feet), and that fact tells us that those ancient travelers were hominins.

In addition to the footprints, scientists working at this site (called Laetoli) and at other locations have discovered many fossilized parts of skeletons of an animal we call *Australopithecus afarensis*. Because the remains have been extensively studied, we know that these hominins were anatomically similar to ourselves, although their brains were only about one-third the size of ours. They may have used stones and sticks as simple tools, but there is no evidence that they actually made stone tools. In fact, they were very much at the mercy of nature's whims. They certainly could not outrun most predators, and their canine teeth were fairly small, so compared to many other animals, they were pretty much defenseless.

We've asked hundreds of questions about the Laetoli hominins, but we will never be able to answer them all. They walked down a path into what became their future, and their journey ended so long ago that we cannot really grasp how much time has passed since that

savanna (also spelled savannah) A large flat grassland with scattered trees and shrubs. Savannas are found in many regions of the world with dry and warm-to-hot climates.

hominins Colloquial term for members of the evolutionary group that includes modern humans and now-extinct bipedal relatives.

species A group of organisms that can interbreed to produce fertile offspring. Members of one species are reproductively isolated from members of all other species (i.e., they cannot mate with them to produce fertile offspring).

bipedally On two feet; walking habitually on two legs.

day. But it remains for us to learn as much as we can about them, and as we continue to do this, their greater journey continues.

On July 20, 1969, a television audience numbering in the hundreds of millions watched as two human beings stepped out of a spacecraft onto the surface of the moon. People born after that date have always lived in an age of space exploration, and many may now take that first moon landing more or less for granted. But the significance of that first moonwalk can't be overstated, because it represents humankind's presumed mastery over the natural forces that govern our presence on earth. For the first time ever, people actually walked upon the surface of a celestial body that, as far as we know, has never given birth to biological life.

As the astronauts gathered geological specimens and frolicked in near weightlessness, they left traces of their fleeting presence in the form of footprints in the lunar dust (**Fig. 1-2**). On the surface of the moon, where no rain falls and no wind blows, the footprints remain undisturbed to this day. They survive as silent testimony to a brief visit by a medium-sized, big-brained creature that presumed to challenge the very forces that created it.

You may wonder why anyone would care about early hominin footprints and how they can possibly be relevant to your life. You may also wonder why a physical **anthropology** textbook would begin by discussing two such seemingly unrelated events as ancient hominins walking across an African savanna and a moonwalk. But the fact is, these two events are very closely connected.

Physical, or biological, anthropology (both terms are used) is a scientific discipline concerned with the biological and behavioral characteristics of human beings; our closest relatives, the nonhuman **primates** (apes, monkeys, tarsiers, lemurs, and lorises); and our ancestors. This kind of research helps us explain what it means to be human and how we came to be the way we are. This is an ambitious goal and it probably isn't fully attainable, but it's certainly worth pursuing. We're the only species to ponder our own existence and question how we fit into the spectrum of life on earth. Most people view

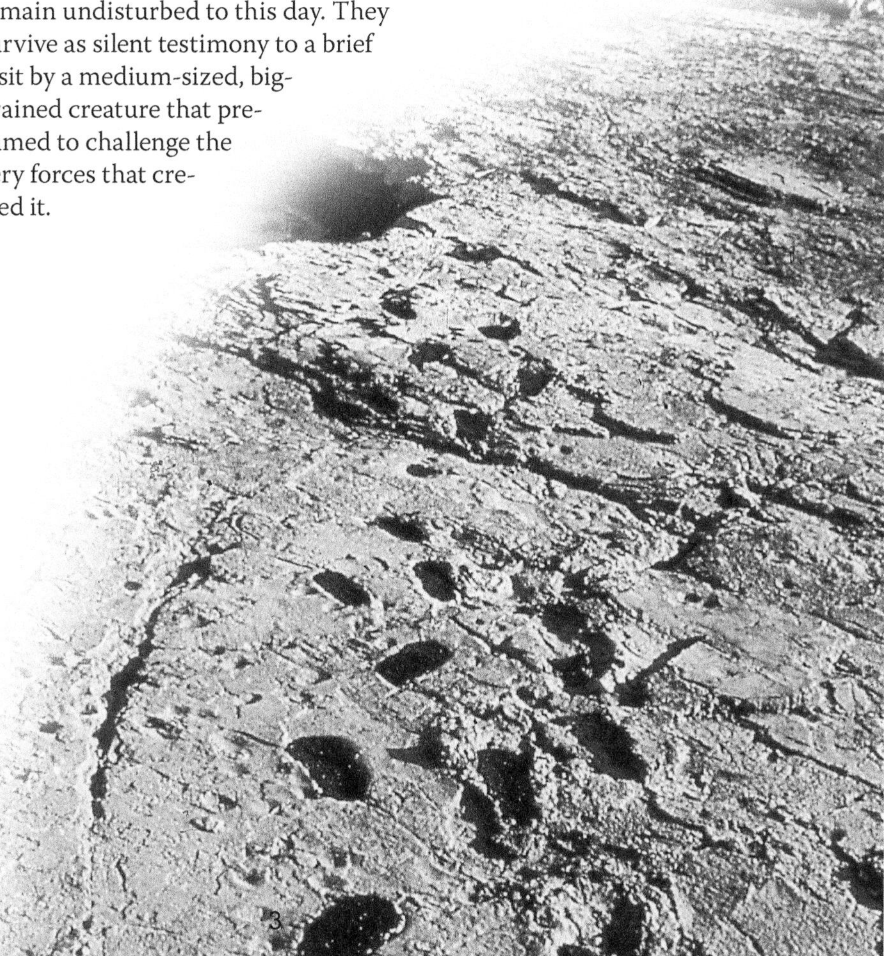

▸ **Figure 1-1** Early hominin footprints at Laetoli, Tanzania. The tracks to the left were made by one individual, while those to the right appear to have been made by two individuals, the second stepping in the tracks of the first.

Peter Jones

anthropology The field of inquiry that studies human culture and evolutionary aspects of human biology; includes cultural anthropology, archaeology, linguistics, and physical, or biological, anthropology.

primates Members of the mammalian order Primates (pronounced "pry-may´-tees"), which includes lemurs, lorises, tarsiers, monkeys, apes, and humans.

humanity as quite separate from the rest of the animal kingdom. But at the same time, many are curious about the similarities we share with other species. Maybe, as a child, you looked at your dog and tried to figure out how her front legs might correspond to your arms. Or perhaps during a visit to the zoo, you recognized the similarities between a chimpanzee's hands or facial expressions and your own. Maybe you wondered if he also shared your thoughts and feelings. If you've ever had thoughts and questions like these, then you've indeed been curious about humankind's place in nature.

How did *Homo sapiens*, a result of the same evolutionary forces that produced all other forms of life on this planet, gain the power to control the flow of rivers and even alter the climate on a global scale? As tropical animals, how were we able to leave the tropics and eventually occupy most of the earth's land surfaces? How did we adjust to different environmental conditions as we dispersed? How could our species, which numbered fewer than 1 billion until the mid-nineteenth century, come to number more than 7 billion worldwide today and, as we now do, add another billion people approximately every 11 years?

These are some of the many questions that physical anthropologists try to answer through the study of human **evolution**, variation, and **adaptation**. These issues, and many others, are covered in this textbook, because physical anthropology is, in large part, human biology seen from an evolutionary perspective. On hearing the term *evolution*, most people think of the appearance of new species. Certainly new species are one important consequence of evolution, but not the only one. Evolution is an ongoing biological process with more than one outcome. Simply stated, evolution is a change in the **genetic** makeup of a population from one generation to the next, and it can be defined and studied at two levels. Over time, some genetic changes in populations do result in the appearance of a new species (or *speciation*), especially when those populations are isolated from one another. Change at this level is called *macroevolution*. At the other level, there are genetic alterations *within* populations; and though this type of change may not lead to speciation, it does cause populations of a species to differ from one another in the frequency of certain traits. Evolution at this level is referred to as *microevolution*. Evolution at both these levels will be discussed in this book.

NASA

▲ **Figure 1-2** Human footprints left on the lunar surface during the *Apollo* mission.

The Human Connection

The unifying theme of this textbook is how human beings are linked to all other life on earth. We can see how we are connected to other organisms in countless ways, as you will learn throughout this book. For example, our DNA is structurally identical to that of every living thing. Indeed, we share genes that are involved in the most fundamental life processes with even the simplest of animals, such as sponges. These genes have changed very little over the course of several hundred million years of evolution. With few exceptions, our cells have the same structure and work the same way as in all life forms. Anatomically, we have the same muscles and bones as other animals. What's more, many aspects of our **behavior** have direct connections to nonhuman species, especially other primates.

The countless connections we share with other organisms show that

evolution A change in the genetic structure of a population. The term is also frequently used to refer to the appearance of a new species.

adaptation An anatomical, physiological, or behavioral response of organisms or populations to the environment. Adaptations result from evolutionary change (specifically as a result of natural selection).

genetic Having to do with the study of gene structure and action, and the patterns of inheritance of traits from parent to offspring. Genetic mechanisms are the foundation of evolutionary change.

behavior Anything organisms do that involves action in response to internal or external stimuli; the response of an individual, group, or species to its environment. Such responses may or may not be deliberate, and they aren't necessarily the result of conscious decision making (which is absent in single-celled organisms, insects, and many other species).

humans are a product of the same evolutionary forces that produced all living things. But, clearly we aren't identical to any other species. In fact, all species are unique in some ways. We humans are one contemporary component of a vast biological **continuum** at a particular point in time; and in this regard, we aren't really all that special. Stating that humans are part of a continuum doesn't imply that we're at the peak of development on that continuum. Depending on the criteria used, humans can be seen to exist at one end of the spectrum or the other, or somewhere in between, but we don't occupy a position of inherent superiority over other species (**Fig. 1-3**).

However, human beings are unquestionably unique regarding one highly significant characteristic, and that is intellect. After all, humans are the only species, born of earth, to stir the lunar dust. We're the only species to develop language and complex culture as a means of buffering nature's challenges, and by doing so we have gained the power to shape the planet's very destiny.

Biocultural Evolution

Biological anthropologists don't just study physiological and biological systems. When these topics are considered within the broader context of human evolution, another factor must be considered, and that is **culture**. Culture is an extremely important concept, not only as it relates to modern humans but also because of its critical role in human evolution. Quite simply, and in a very broad sense, culture can be defined as the strategy by which humans adapt to the natural environment. In fact, culture has so altered and dominated our world that it's become the environment in which we live. Culture includes technologies ranging from stone tools to computers; subsistence patterns, from hunting and gathering to global agribusiness; housing types, from thatched huts to skyscrapers; and clothing, from animal skins to high-tech synthetic fibers (**Fig. 1-4**). Technology, religion, values, social organization, language, kinship, marriage rules, gender roles, dietary practices, inheritance of property, and so on are all aspects of culture. Each culture shapes people's perceptions of the external environment, or **worldview**, in particular ways that distinguish a particular society from all others.

One important point to remember is that culture isn't genetically passed from one generation to the next. We aren't born with innate knowledge that leads us to behave in ways appropriate to our own culture. Culture is *learned*, and the process of learning one's culture begins, quite literally, at birth. All people are products of the culture they're raised in, and since most human behavior is learned, it follows that most human behaviors, perceptions, values, and reactions are shaped by culture.

It's important to emphasize that even though culture isn't genetically determined, the human predisposition to assimilate culture and function within it is very much influenced by biological factors. Most nonhuman animals rely to varying degrees on learned behavior. This is especially true of the great apes (gorillas, chimpanzees, bonobos, and orangutans), which exhibit several aspects of culture.

The predisposition for culture is perhaps the most critical component of human evolutionary history, and it was inherited from our early hominin or even prehominin ancestors. In fact, the common ancestor we share with chimpanzees may have had this predisposition. But during the course of human evolution, the role of culture became increasingly important. Over time, as you will see, culture influenced many aspects of our biological makeup; in turn, aspects of biology influenced cultural practices. For this reason, humans are the result of long-term interactions between biology and culture. We call these interactions **biocultural evolution**; and in this respect, humans are unique.

continuum A set of relationships in which all components fall along a single integrated spectrum (for example, color). All life reflects a single biological continuum.

culture Behavioral aspects of human adaptation, including technology, traditions, language, religion, marriage patterns, and social roles. Culture is a set of learned behaviors transmitted from one generation to the next by nonbiological (i.e., nongenetic) means.

worldview General cultural orientation or perspective shared by the members of a society.

biocultural evolution The mutual interactive evolution of human biology and culture; the concept that biology (anatomy, neurological attributes, etc.) makes culture possible and that developing culture further influences the direction of biological evolution; this is a basic concept in understanding the unique components of human evolution.

▸ **Figure 1-3** Traditional and recent technologies. (**a**) An early stone tool from East Africa. This artifact represents one of the oldest types of stone tools found anywhere. (**b**) The Hubble Space telescope, a late twentieth-century tool, orbits the earth every 96 minutes at an altitude of 360 miles. Because it is above the earth's atmosphere, it provides distortion-free images of objects in deep space. (**c**) A cuneiform tablet. Cuneiform, the earliest form of writing, involved pressing symbols into clay tablets. It originated in southern Iraq some 5,000 years ago. (**d**) Text messaging, a fairly recent innovation in satellite communication, has generated a new language of sorts. Today, more than 500 million text messages are sent every day worldwide. (**e**) A Samburu woman in East Africa building a traditional but complicated dwelling of stems, small branches, and mud. (**f**) These Hong Kong skyscrapers are typical of cities in industrialized countries today.

Lynn Kilgore

NASA / Space Telescope Science Institute

Museum of Primitive Art and Culture, Peace Dale, RI.

iStockphoto.com/Ravi Tahilramani

Lynn Kilgore

iStockphoto.com/Justin Horrocks

Connections

Figure 1-4
Humans are biologically connected to all forms of life. This central theme will be addressed in every chapter of this textbook as shown in this figure.

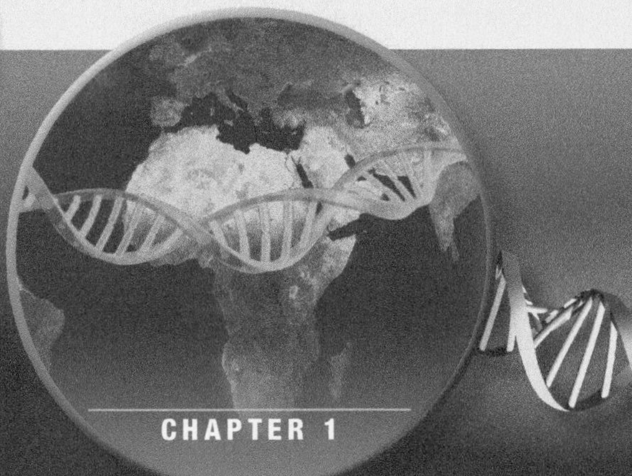

Physical anthropology is a biological science that investigates how humans have evolved and continue to do so.

Evolutionary theory, particularly natural selection, explains how life forms have changed over time and how new species are produced.

The immediate predecessors of modern humans, including the Neandertals, were much like us, but had some anatomical and behavioral differences.

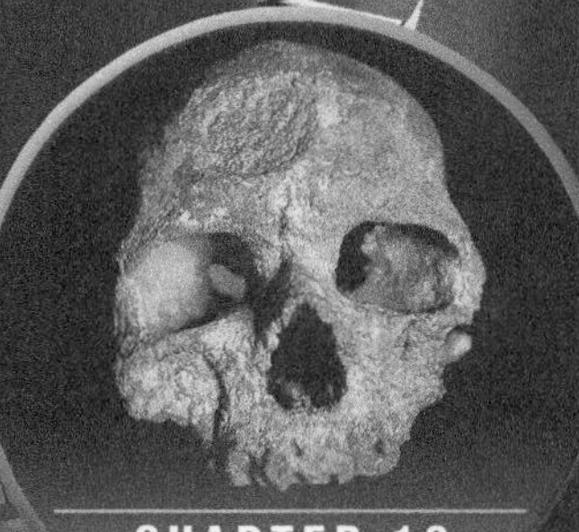

Modern humans first evolved in Africa and later spread to other areas of the world, where they occasionally interbred with Neandertals and other pre-modern humans.

Modern human variation is best understood by examining similarities and differences in DNA among populations.

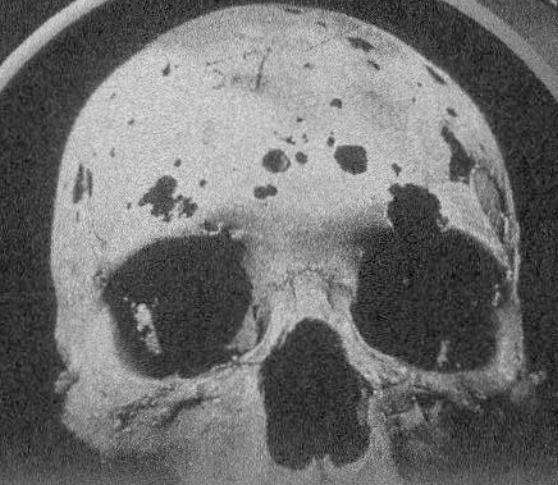

Through natural selection, humans have and continue to adapt to environmental factors including solar radiation, cold, altitude, and, most importantly, infectious disease.

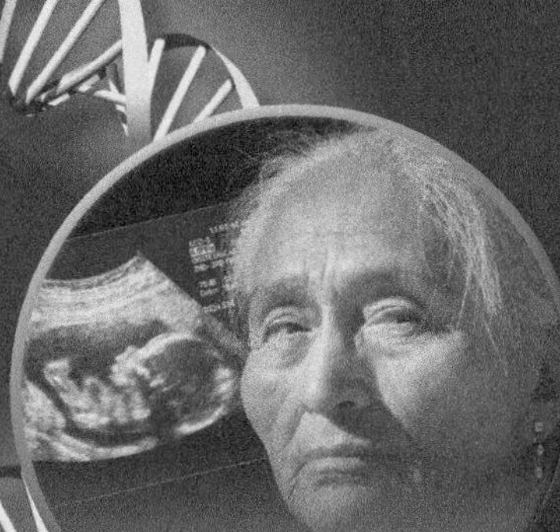

Human development and adaptation is best understood from an evolutionary perspective.

Humans have recently become disconnected from other life and are rapidly altering the planet.

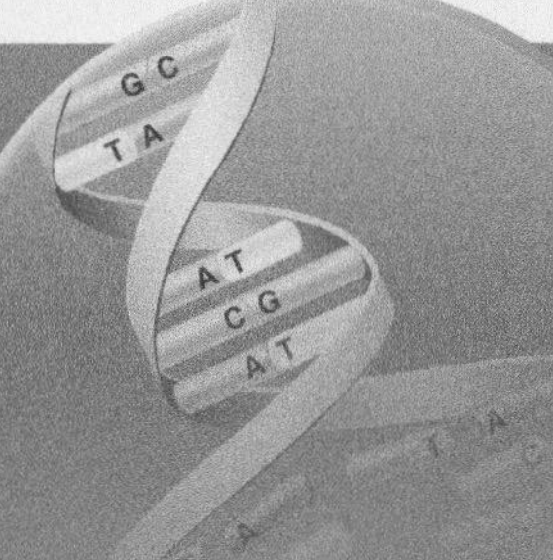

The DNA molecule is the basis of all life.

Evolution occurs when DNA changes and genetic variation is further influenced by natural selection and other factors.

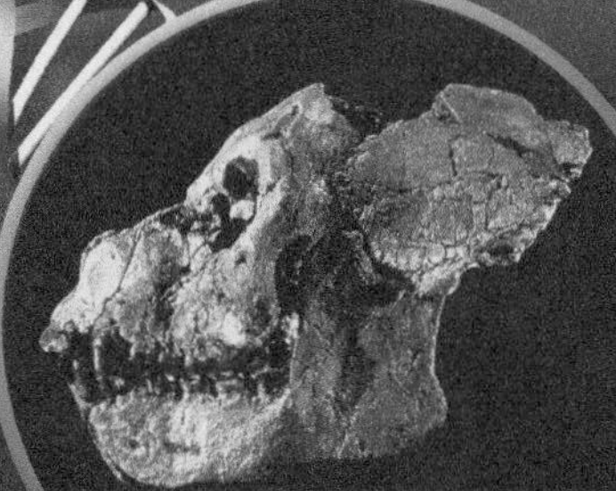

Humans are both vertebrates and mammals, and their evolutionary history over many millions of years explains our early roots.

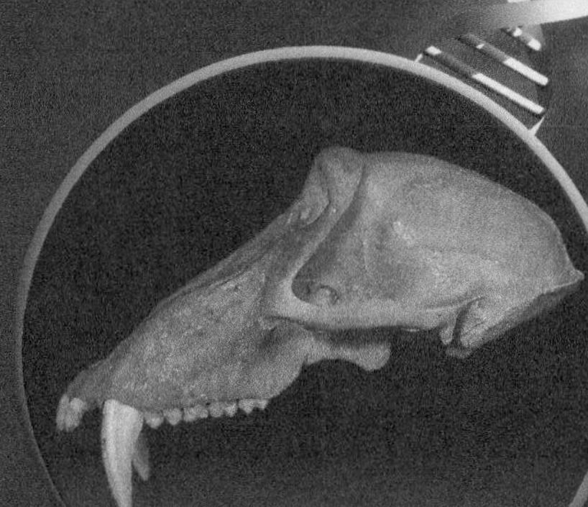

Humans are primates and share many biological characteristics with other primates.

Partly because of common evolutionary history, many human behaviors are also seen in other primates.

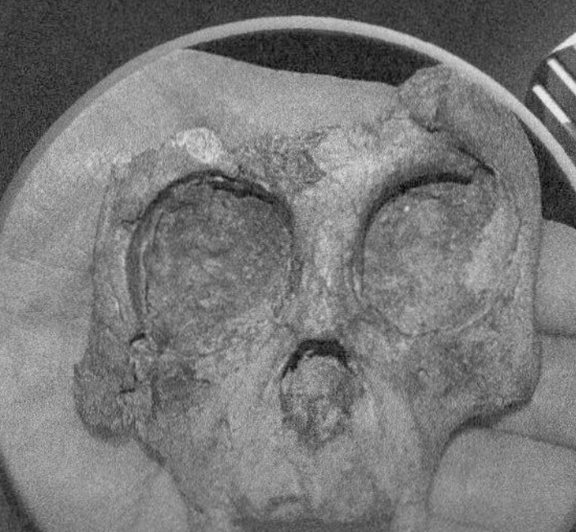

Fossil evidence indicates our primate origins date to at least 65 million years ago.

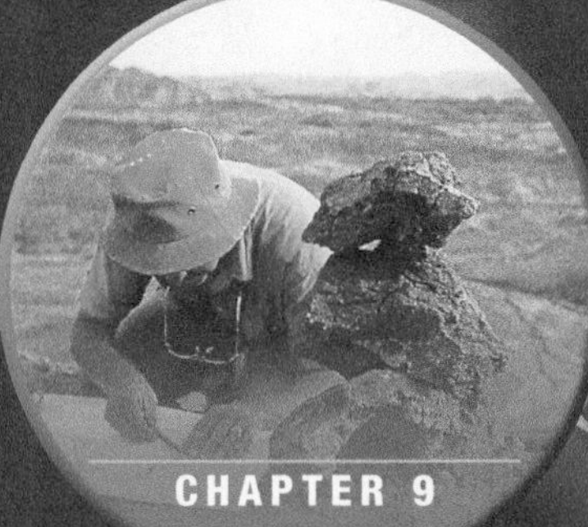

Paleoanthropology, which includes physical anthropology, archaeology, and geology, provides the scientific basis to understand hominin evolution.

The first more human-like animals (hominins) appeared in Africa around 6 mya ago and evolved into a variety of different species.

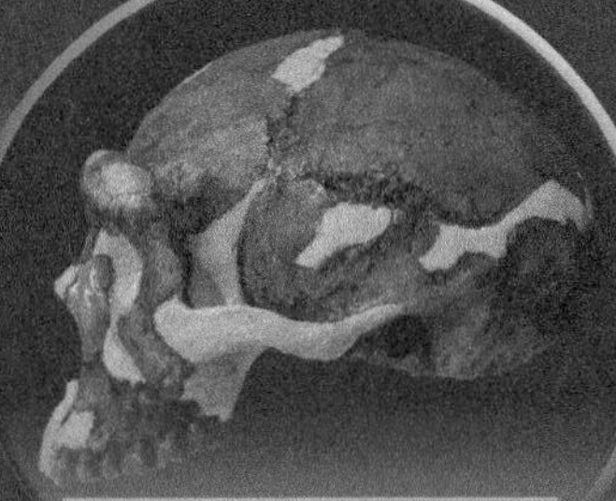

Hominins began to disperse out of Africa around 2 million years ago, and during the next 1 million years inhabited much of Eurasia.

Biocultural interactions have resulted in many anatomical, biological, and behavioral changes during the course of human evolution. Alterations in the shape of the pelvis, increased brain size, reorganization of neurological structures, smaller teeth, and the development of language are some of the results of the evolutionary process in our lineage. Today biocultural interactions are as important as ever, especially with regard to health and disease. Air pollution and exposure to dangerous chemicals have increased the prevalence of respiratory disease and cancer. While air travel makes it possible for people to travel thousands of miles in just a few hours, we aren't the only species that can do this. Millions of disease-causing organisms travel on airplanes with their human hosts, making it possible for infectious diseases to spread within hours across the globe.

Many human activities have changed the patterns of such infectious diseases as tuberculosis, influenza, and malaria. After the domestication of nonhuman animals, close contact with chickens, pigs, and cattle greatly increased human exposure to some of the diseases these animals carry. Through this contact we've also changed the genetic makeup of disease-causing microorganisms. For example, the H1N1 "swine flu" virus that caused the 2009 pandemic actually contains genetic material derived from bacteria that infect three different species: humans, birds, and pigs. As it turned out, that pandemic wasn't as serious as had originally been feared, but the next one could be. Because we have overused antibiotics, we've made many bacteria resistant to treatment and many are even deadly. Likewise, although we're making progress in treating malaria, the microorganism that causes it has developed resistance to some treatments and preventive medications. We've also increased the geographical distribution of malaria-carrying mosquitoes through agricultural practices and global climate change. But while it's clear that we humans have influenced the development and spread of infectious disease, we still don't know the many ways that changes in infectious disease patterns are affecting human biology and behavior. Anthropological research in this one area alone is extremely relevant to all of us, and there are many other critical topics that biological anthropologists explore.

What Is Anthropology?

Many anthropology students contemplate this question when their parents or friends ask, "What are you studying?" The answer is often followed by a blank stare or a comment about dinosaurs. So, what is anthropology, and how is it different from several related disciplines?

Like physical anthropologists, biologists investigate human adaptation and evolution. Similarly, historians and sociologists also study aspects of human societies past and present. But when biological or social research also considers the interactions between evolutionary and cultural factors, it's included in the discipline of anthropology.

In the United States, anthropology is divided into four main subfields: cultural, or social, anthropology; archaeology; linguistic anthropology; and physical, or biological, anthropology. Each of these, in turn, is divided into several specialized areas of interest. This four-field approach concerns all aspects of humanity across space and time. Each subdiscipline emphasizes different aspects of the human experience, but together they offer a means of explaining variation in human biological and behavioral adaptations. In addition, each of these subfields has practical applications, and many anthropologists pursue careers outside the university environment. This kind of anthropology is called **applied anthropology**, and it's extremely important today.

applied anthropology The practical application of anthropological and archaeological theories and techniques. For example, many biological anthropologists work in the public health sector.

Cultural Anthropology

Cultural, or social, anthropology is the study of patterns of belief and behavior found in modern and historical cultures. The origins of cultural anthropology can be traced to the nineteenth century, when travel and exploration brought Europeans into contact (and sometimes conflict) with various cultures in Africa, Asia, and the New World.

This contact sparked an interest in "traditional" societies and led many early anthropologists to study and record lifestyles that are now mostly extinct. These studies produced many descriptive **ethnographies** that covered a range of topics such as religion, ritual, myth, the use of symbols, diet, technology, gender roles, and child-rearing practices. Ethnographic accounts, in turn, formed the basis for comparative studies of numerous cultures. By examining the similarities and differences among cultures, cultural anthropologists have been able to formulate many hypotheses regarding fundamental aspects of human behavior.

The focus of cultural anthropology shifted over the course of the twentieth century. Cultural anthropologists still work in remote areas, but increasingly they've turned their gaze toward their own cultures and the people around them. Increasingly, ethnographic techniques have been applied to the study of diverse subcultures and their interactions with one another in contemporary metropolitan areas (urban anthropology). The population of any city is composed of many subgroups defined by economic status, religion, ethnic background, profession, age, level of education, and so on. Even the student body of your own college or university is made up of many subcultures, and as you walk across campus, you see students of many nationalities and diverse religious and ethnic backgrounds.

Archaeology

Archaeology is the study of earlier cultures by anthropologists who specialize in the scientific recovery, analysis, and interpretation of the material remains of past societies. Archaeologists obtain information from **artifacts** and structures left behind by earlier cultures. The remains of earlier societies, in the form of tools, structures, art, eating implements, fragments of writing, and so on, provide a great deal of information about many important aspects of a society, such as religion and social structure.

Unlike in the past, sites aren't excavated simply for the artifacts or "treasures" they may contain. Rather, they're excavated to gain information about human behavior. For example, patterns of behavior are reflected in the dispersal of human settlements across a landscape and in the distribution of cultural remains within them. Archaeological research may focus on specific localities or peoples and attempt to identify, for example, various aspects of social organization, subsistence techniques, or factors that led to the collapse of a civilization. Alternatively, inquiry may reflect an interest in broader issues relating to human culture in general, such as the development of agriculture or the rise of cities.

Linguistic Anthropology

Linguistic anthropology is the study of human speech and language, including the origins of language in general as well as specific languages. By examining similarities between contemporary languages, linguists have been able to trace historical ties between particular languages and groups of languages, thus facilitating the identification of language families and perhaps past relationships between human populations.

ethnographies Detailed descriptive studies of human societies. In cultural anthropology, an ethnography is traditionally the study of a non-Western society.

artifacts Objects or materials made or modified for use by hominins. The earliest artifacts are usually tools made of stone or occasionally bone.

Because the spontaneous acquisition and use of language is a uniquely human characteristic, it's an important topic for linguistic anthropologists, who, along with specialists in other fields, study the process of language acquisition in infants. Because insights into the process may well have implications for the development of language in human evolution as well as in growing children, it's also an important subject in physical anthropology.

Physical Anthropology

As we've already said, *physical anthropology* is the study of human biology within the framework of evolution with an emphasis on the interaction between biology and culture. This subdiscipline is also referred to as *biological anthropology*, and you'll find the terms used interchangeably. *Physical anthropology* is the original term, and it reflects the initial interests anthropologists had in describing human physical variation. The American Association of Physical Anthropologists, its journal, many college courses, and numerous publications retain this term. The designation *biological anthropology* reflects the shift in emphasis to more biologically oriented topics, such as genetics, evolutionary biology, nutrition, physiological adaptation, and growth and development. This shift occurred largely because of advances in the field of genetics and molecular biology since the late 1950s. Although we've continued to use the traditional term in the title of this textbook, you'll find that all of the major topics we discuss pertain to biological issues.

The origins of biological anthropology can be traced to two principal areas of interest among nineteenth-century European and American scholars: the ancestry of modern species, including humans; and human variation. Although most of these scholars held religious convictions, they were beginning to doubt the literal interpretation of the biblical account of creation and to support explanations that emphasized natural processes rather than supernatural phenomena. Eventually, the sparks of interest in biological change over time were fanned into flames by the publication of Charles Darwin's *On the Origin of Species* in 1859.

Today, **paleoanthropology**, the study of anatomical and behavioral human evolution as revealed in the fossil record, is a major subfield of physical anthropology (**Fig. 1-5**). Thousands of fossilized remains of early primates, including human ancestors, are now kept in research collections. Taken together, these fossils span at least 7 million years of human prehistory. Although most of these fossils are incomplete, they provide us with a significant wealth of knowledge that increases each year. It's the ultimate goal of paleoanthropological research to identify the various early human and humanlike species, establish a chronological sequence of relationships among them, and gain insights into their adaptation and behavior. Only then will we have a clear picture of how and when modern humans came into being.

To some extent, **primate paleontology** can be viewed as a subset of paleoanthropology. Primate paleontology is the study of the primate fossil record, which extends back to the beginning of primate evolution some 65 million years ago (mya). Virtually every year, fossil-bearing geological beds around the world yield important new discoveries. By studying fossil primates and comparing them with anatomically similar living species, primate paleontologists are learning a great deal about factors such as diet or locomotion in earlier forms. They can also try to identify aspects of behavior in some extinct primates and attempt to clarify what we know about evolutionary relationships between extinct and modern species, including ourselves.

paleoanthropology The interdisciplinary approach to the study of earlier hominins—their chronology, physical structure, archaeological remains, habitats, and so on.

primate paleontology The study of fossil primates, especially those that lived before the appearance of hominins.

▲ **Figure 1-5** (**a**) Paleoanthropologist Meave Leakey and crew excavate an early hominin skull at Lake Turkana in northern Kenya. (**b**) Primate paleontologist Russell L. Ciochon (left) and Le Trang Kha (right), a vertebrate paleontologist, examine the fossil remains of *Gigantopithecus* from a 450,000-year-old site in Vietnam. *Gigantopithecus* is the name given to the largest apes that have ever lived. In the background is a reconstruction of this enormous animal.

Visible physical variation was the other major area of interest for early physical anthropologists. Enormous effort was spent in measuring, describing, and explaining visible differences among various human populations, with particular attention being focused on skin color, body proportions, and the shape of the head and face. Although some approaches were misguided and even racist, they gave birth to many body measurements that are sometimes still used. They've been used to design everything from wheelchairs to office furniture. They have also been used to determine the absolute minimum amount of leg room a person needs in order to remain sane during a 3-hour flight on a commercial airliner. Lastly, they are also very important to the study of skeletal remains from archaeological sites (**Fig. 1-6**).

Today, physical anthropologists are concerned with human variation because of its possible *adaptive significance* and because they want to identify the factors that have produced not only visible physical variation but genetic variation as well. In other words, many traits that typify certain populations evolved as biological adaptations, or adjustments, to local environmental conditions such as sunlight, altitude, or infectious disease. Other characteristics may be the result of geographical isolation or the descent of populations from small founding groups.

Since the early 1990s, the focus of human variation studies has shifted completely away from the visible differences we see in people to the underlying genetic factors that influence these and many other traits. This shift occurred partly because the examination of genetic variation between populations and individuals of any species helps to explain biological change over time, which is precisely what the evolutionary process is all about.

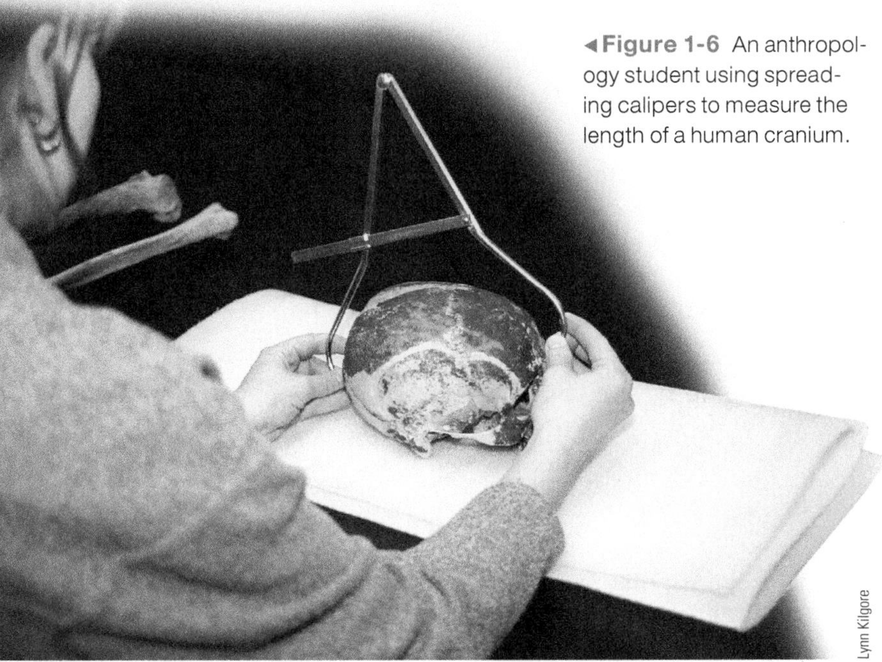

◀ **Figure 1-6** An anthropology student using spreading calipers to measure the length of a human cranium.

Lynn Kilgore

Modern population studies also examine other important aspects of human variation, including how different groups respond physiologically to different kinds of environmentally induced stress (**Fig. 1-7**). Such stresses may include high altitude, cold, or heat. *Nutritional anthropologists* study the relationships between various dietary components, cultural practices, physiology, and certain aspects of health and disease (**Fig. 1-8**). Investigations of human fertility, growth, and development are also closely related to the topic of nutrition. These fields of inquiry, which are fundamental to studies of adaptation in modern human populations, can also provide insights into hominin evolution.

It would be impossible to study evolutionary processes without some knowledge of how traits are inherited. For this reason and others, genetics is a crucial field for physical anthropologists. Modern physical anthropology wouldn't exist as an evolutionary science if it weren't for advances in the understanding of genetic mechanisms.

Molecular anthropologists use cutting-edge technologies to investigate evolutionary relationships between human populations as well as between humans and nonhuman primates. To do this, they examine similarities and differences in **DNA** sequences between individuals, populations, and species. What's more, by extracting DNA from certain fossils, these researchers have contributed to our understanding of evolutionary relationships between extinct and living species. As genetic technologies continue to be developed, molecular anthropologists will play a key role in explaining human evolution, adaptation, and our biological relationships with other species (**Fig. 1-9**).

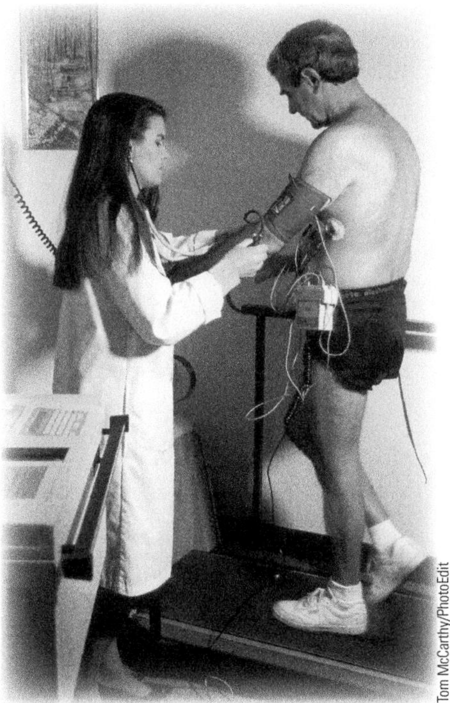

▶ **Figure 1-7** This researcher is using a treadmill test to assess a subject's heart rate, blood pressure, and oxygen consumption.

Tom McCarthy/PhotoEdit

DNA (deoxyribonucleic acid) The double-stranded molecule that contains the genetic code. DNA is a main component of chromosomes.

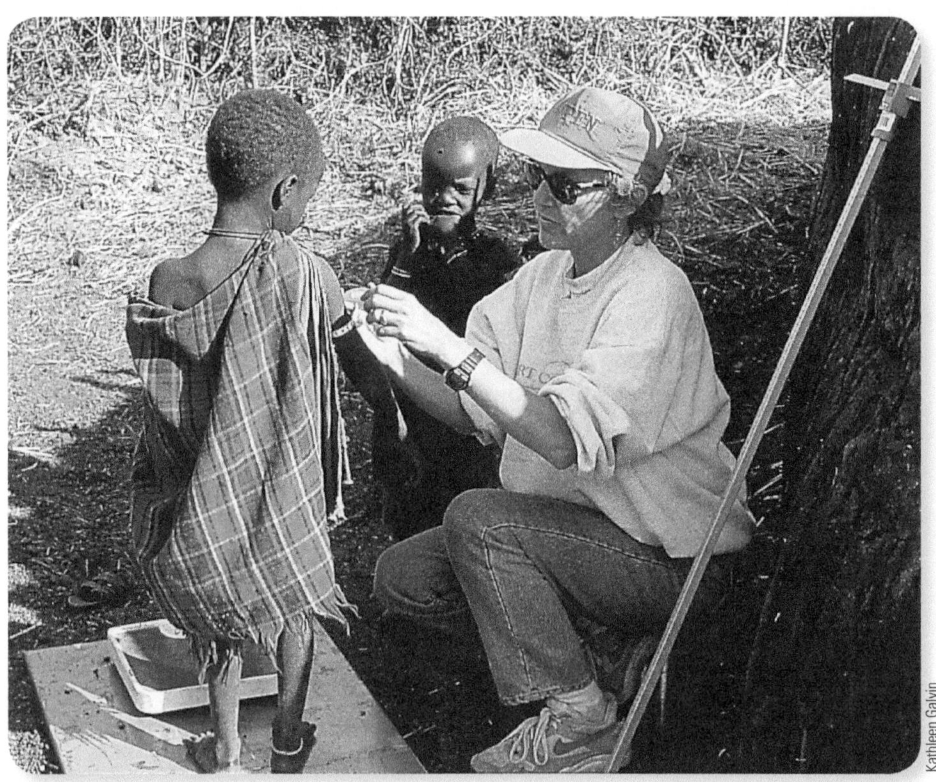

◄ **Figure 1-8** Dr. Kathleen Galvin measures the upper arm circumference of a young Maasai boy in Tanzania. Data derived from various body measurements, including height and weight, were used in a health and nutrition study of groups of Maasai cattle herders.

However, before genetic and molecular techniques became widespread, **osteology**, the study of the skeleton, was the only way that anthropologists could study our immediate ancestors. In fact, a thorough knowledge of skeletal structure and function is still critical to the interpretation of fossil material today. For this reason, osteology has long been viewed as central to physical anthropology. In fact, it's so important that when many people think of biological anthropology, the first thing that comes to mind is bones!

Bone biology and physiology are of major importance to many other

◄ **Figure 1-9** Molecular anthropologist Nelson Ting collecting red colobus fecal samples for a study of genetic variation in small groups of monkeys isolated from one another by agricultural clearing.

osteology The study of skeletal material. Human osteology focuses on the interpretation of skeletal remains from archaeological sites, skeletal anatomy, bone physiology, and growth and development. Some of the same techniques are used in paleoanthropology to study early hominins.

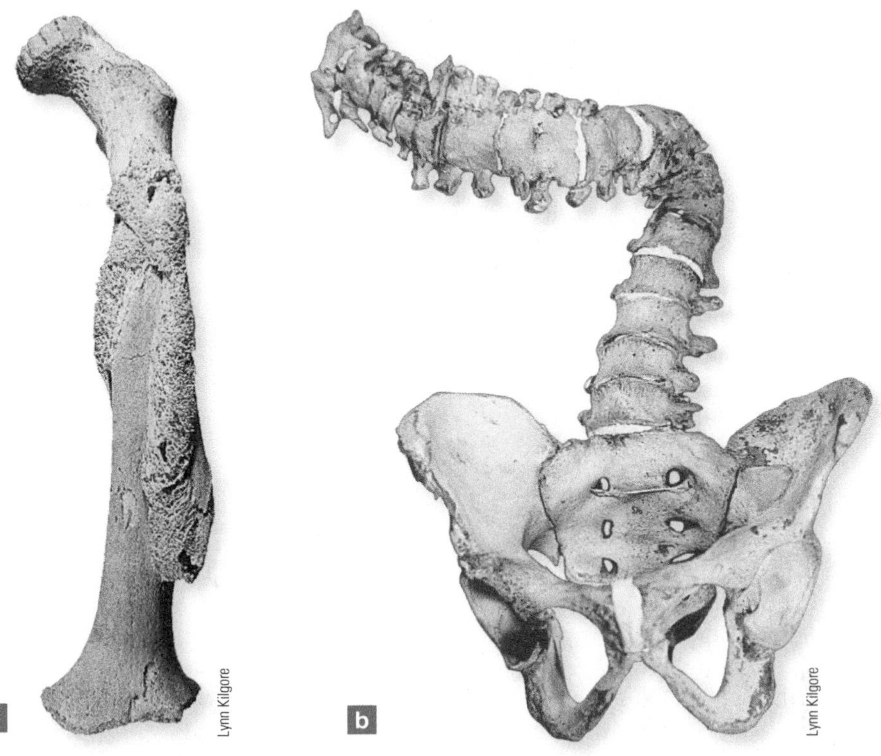

▶ **Figure 1-10** Two examples of pathological conditions in human skeletal remains from the Nubian site of Kulubnarti in Sudan. These remains are approximately 1,000 years old. (**a**) A partially healed fracture of a child's left femur (thigh bone). This child died around the age of 6, probably of an infection that resulted from this injury. (**b**) Very severe congenital scoliosis in an adult male. The curves are due to developmental defects in individual vertebrae. (This is not the most common form of scoliosis.)

aspects of physical anthropology besides human evolution. Many osteologists specialize in the measurement of skeletal elements, essential for identifying stature and growth patterns in archaeological populations. In the last 30 years or so, the study of human skeletal remains from archaeological sites has sometimes been called **bioarchaeology**.

Paleopathology, the study of disease and trauma in ancient skeletal populations, is a major component of bioarchaeology. Paleopathologists investigate the prevalence of trauma, certain infectious diseases (such as syphilis and tuberculosis), nutritional deficiencies, and numerous other conditions that may leave evidence in bone (**Fig. 1-10**). This research can tell us a great deal about the lives of individuals and populations in the past. Paleopathology also yields information regarding the history of certain disease processes, and for this reason it's of interest to scientists in biomedical fields.

Forensic anthropology is directly related to osteology and paleopathology and has become popular among the public because of forensic TV shows like *Bones* (based on a character created by a practicing forensic anthropologist) and *Crime Scene Investigation*. Technically, this approach is the application of anthropological (usually osteological and sometimes archaeological) techniques to legal issues. Forensic anthropologists help identify skeletal remains in mass disasters or other situations in which a human body has been found. They've been involved in numerous cases having important legal, historical, and human consequences (**Fig. 1-11**). They were instrumental in identifying the skeletons of most of the Russian imperial family, executed in 1918, and many participated in the overwhelming task of trying to identify the remains of victims of the September 11, 2001, terrorist attacks in the United States.

Anatomy is yet another important area of interest for physical anthropol-

bioarchaeology The study of skeletal remains from archaeological sites.

paleopathology The branch of osteology that studies the evidence of disease and injury in human skeletal (or, occasionally, mummified) remains from archaeological sites.

forensic anthropology An applied anthropological approach dealing with legal matters. Forensic anthropologists work with coroners and others in identifying and analyzing human remains.

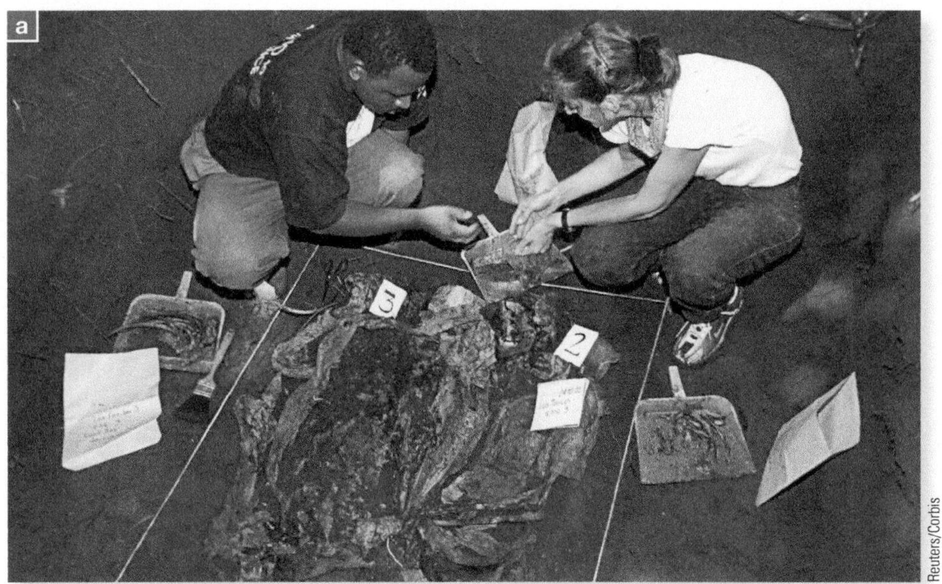

Reuters/Corbis

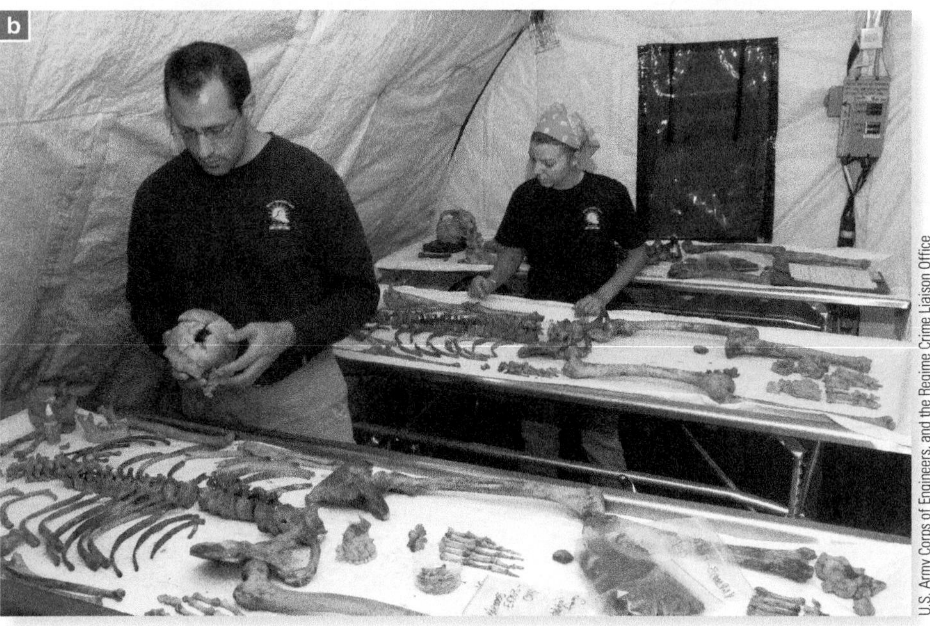

U.S. Army Corps of Engineers, and the Regime Crime Liaison Office

◀ **Figure 1-11** (**a**) Forensic anthropologists Vuzumusi Madasco (from Zimbabwe) and Patricia Bernardi (from Argentina) excavating the skeletal remains and clothing of one of many victims of a civil war massacre in El Salvador. The goal is to identify as many of the victims as possible. (**b**) These forensic anthropologists, working in a lab near Baghdad, are examining the skeletal remains of Kurdish victims of genocide. They cataloged the injuries of 114 individuals buried in a mass grave, and some of their evidence was used against Saddam Hussein during his trial in 2006.

ogists. In living organisms, bones and teeth are intimately linked to the soft tissues that surround and act on them. Consequently a thorough knowledge of soft tissue anatomy is essential to understanding the biomechanical relationships involved in movement. Such relationships are important in assessing the structure and function of limbs and other components of fossilized remains. For these reasons and others, many physical anthropologists specialize in anatomical studies. In fact, several physical anthropologists are professors in anatomy departments at universities and medical schools (**Fig. 1-12**).

Given our evolutionary focus and the fact that we ourselves are primates, it's natural that **primatology**, the study of the living nonhuman primates, has become increasingly important since the late 1950s (**Fig. 1-13**). Today, dozens of nonhuman primate species have been and are being studied. Because

primatology The study of the biology and behavior of nonhuman primates (lemurs, lorises, tarsiers, monkeys, and apes).

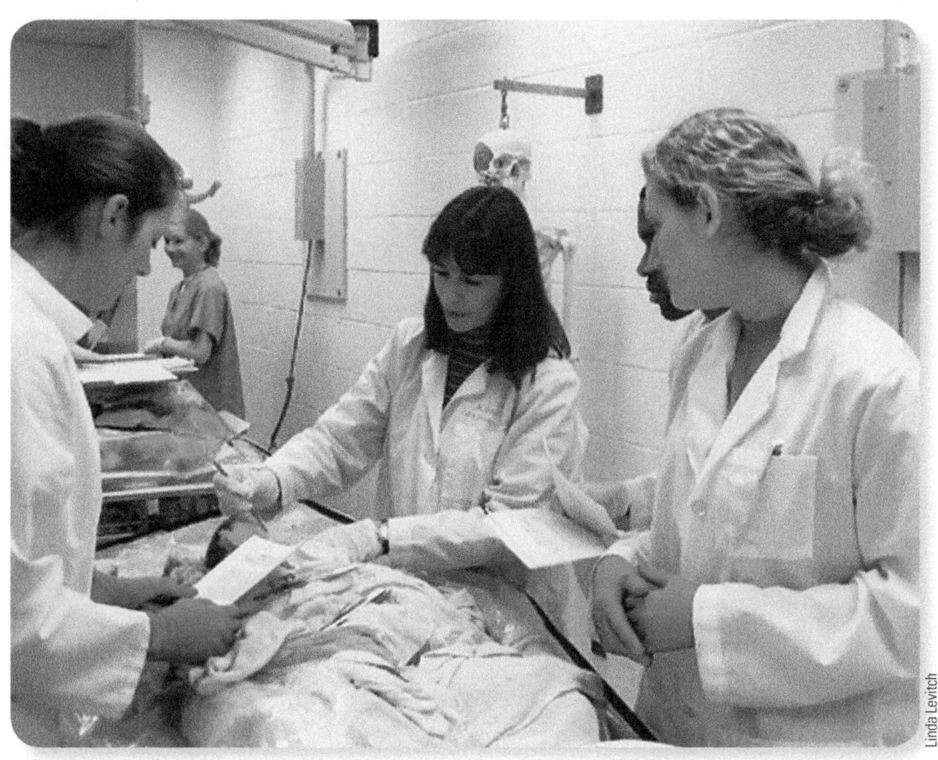

Linda Levitch

▶ **Figure 1-12** Dr. Linda Levitch teaching a human anatomy class at the University of North Carolina School of Medicine.

nonhuman primates are our closest living relatives, identifying the underlying factors related to their social behavior, communication, infant care, reproductive behavior, and so on helps us develop a better understanding of the natural forces that have shaped so many aspects of modern human behavior. Nonhuman primates are also important to study in their own right. This is particularly true today because the majority of primate species are threatened or seriously endangered. For this reason many primatologists have become actively involved in primate conservation. Only through study will scientists be able to recommend policies that can better ensure the survival of many nonhuman primates as well as thousands of other species.

Applied Anthropology

Applied anthropology is the practical use of anthropological theories and methods outside the academic setting, but applied and academic anthropology aren't mutually exclusive approaches. In fact, applied anthropology relies on the research and theories of academic anthropologists and at the same time has much to contribute to theory and techniques.

Within biological anthropology, forensic anthropology is a good example of the applied approach. But the practical application of the techniques of physical anthropology isn't new. During World War II, for example, physical anthropologists were extensively involved in designing gun turrets and airplane cockpits. Since then, many physical anthropologists have pursued careers in genetic and biomedical research, public health, evolutionary medicine, medical anthropology, and the conservation of nonhuman primates, and many hold positions in museums and zoos. In fact, a background in physical anthropology is excellent preparation for almost any career in the medical and biological fields (**Fig. 1-14**).

science A body of knowledge gained through observation and experimentation; from the Latin *scientia*, meaning "knowledge."

hypotheses (*sing.*, hypothesis) A provisional explanation of a phenomenon. Hypotheses require verification or falsification through testing.

empirical Relying on experiment or observation; from the Latin *empiricus*, meaning "experienced."

scientific method An approach to research whereby a problem is identified, a hypothesis (provisional explanation) is stated, and that hypothesis is tested by collecting and analyzing data.

data (*sing.*, datum) Facts from which conclusions can be drawn; scientific information.

▲ **Figure 1-13** (**a**) Primatologist Emmanuelle Grundmann using ropes and a harness to observe an orangutan in Borneo. (**b**) Primatologist Jill Pruetz follows a chimpanzee in Senegal, West Africa.

Physical Anthropology and the Scientific Method

Science is a method of explaining natural phenomena. It involves observation, developing **hypotheses** to explain what has been observed, and developing a research design or series of experiments to test these hypotheses. This is an **empirical** approach to gaining information. Because biological anthropologists are engaged in scientific research, they adhere to the principles of the **scientific method** by identifying a research problem and then gathering information to solve it.

Once a question or problem has been identified, the first step is usually to explore the existing literature (books and journals) to determine what other people have done to resolve the issue. Based on this preliminary research and other observations, one or even several tentative explanations (hypotheses) are then proposed. The next step is to develop a research design or methodology to test the hypothesis. These methods involve collecting information, or **data**, that can

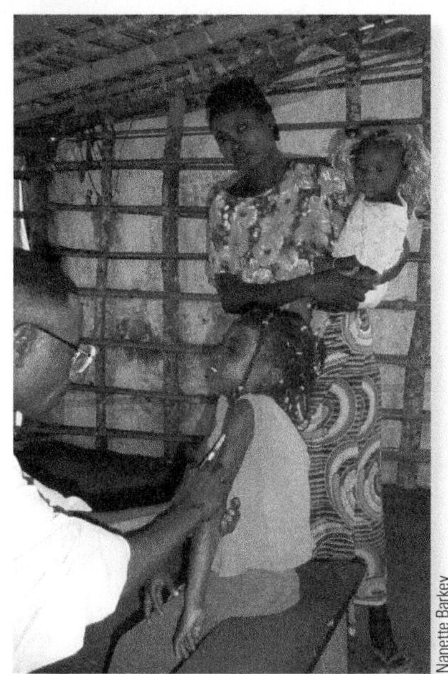

▲ **Figure 1-14** Nanette Barkey, a medical anthropologist involved in a repatriation project in Angola, photographed this little girl being vaccinated at a refugee transit camp. Vaccinations were being administered to Angolan refugees returning home in 2004 from the Democratic Republic of Congo, where they had fled to escape warfare in their own country.

then be studied and analyzed. Data can be analyzed in many ways, most of them involving various statistical tests. During the data collection and analysis phase, it's important for scientists to use a strictly controlled approach so that they can precisely describe their techniques and results. This precision is critical because it enables others to repeat the experiments and allows scientists to make comparisons between their study and the work of others.

For example, when scientists collect data on tooth size in hominin fossils, they must specify which teeth are measured, how they're measured, and the results of the measurements (expressed numerically, or **quantitatively**). Then, by analyzing the data, the investigators try to draw conclusions about the meaning and significance of their measurements. This body of information then becomes the basis of future studies, perhaps by other researchers, who can compare their own results with those already obtained.

Hypothesis testing is the very core of the scientific method, and although it may seem contradictory at first, it's based on the potential to *falsify* the hypothesis. Falsification doesn't mean that the entire hypothesis is untrue, but it does indicate that the hypothesis may need to be refined and subjected to further testing.

Eventually, if a hypothesis stands up to repeated testing, it may become part of a **theory** or perhaps a theory itself. There's a popular misconception that a theory is nothing more than conjecture, or a "hunch." But in science, theories are proposed explanations of relationships between natural phenomena. Theories usually concern broader, more universal views than hypotheses, which have a narrower focus and deal with more specific relationships between phenomena. But like hypotheses, theories aren't facts. *They are tested explanations of facts*. For example, it's a fact that when you drop an object, it falls to the ground. The explanation for this fact is the theory of gravity. But, like hypotheses, theories can be altered over time with further experimentation and by using newly developed technologies in testing. The theory of gravity has been tested many times and qualified by experiments showing how the mass of objects affects how they're attracted to one another. So far, the theory has held up.

Scientific testing of hypotheses may take several years (or longer) and may involve researchers who didn't participate in the original work. What's more, new methods may permit different kinds of testing that weren't previously possible; this is a strength, not a weakness, of scientific research. For example, since the 1970s, primatologists have reported that male nonhuman primates (as well as males of many other species) sometimes kill infants. One hypothesis has been that infanticidal males only killed the offspring of other males and not their own. But many scientists have objected to this hypothesis and have proposed several alternatives. For one thing, there was no way to know for certain that the males weren't killing their own offspring; if they were, this would argue against the hypothesis. However, in a fairly recent study, scientists collected DNA samples from dead infants and the males who killed them. The evidence showed that most of the time, the males were not related to their victims. This result doesn't prove that the original hypothesis is accurate but it does strengthen it. This study is described in more detail in Chapter 7, but we mention it here to emphasize that science is an ongoing process that builds on previous work and benefits from newly developed techniques (in this case, DNA testing) in ways that constantly expand our knowledge.

Throughout this book we present several examples of how different approaches to research and new technologies (especially in the field of genetics) have helped support or alter numerous hypotheses. Scientific research is frequently ridiculed and/or dismissed by the general public, politi-

quantitatively Pertaining to measurements of quantity and including such properties as size, number, and capacity. When data are quantified, they're expressed numerically and can be tested statistically.

theory A broad statement of scientific relationships or underlying principles that has been substantially verified through the testing of hypotheses.

scientific testing The precise repetition of an experiment or expansion of observed data to provide verification; the procedure by which hypotheses and theories are verified, modified, or discarded.

A Closer Look

Forensic Anthropology in Practice

Forensic anthropology is the application of the principles of physical anthropology and archaeology to the legal system, especially as they relate to the study of the human skeleton. Forensic anthropologists are often called on to assist local law enforcement with crime scene recovery and analysis of human remains. Because of their specialized knowledge and training in physical anthropology, archaeology, and forensic science, they are ideally suited to assist with cases involving badly decomposed or skeletonized remains. Although many forensic anthropologists are employed by universities, there is a growing number who work in museums, state and federal law enforcement agencies, human rights organizations, and for mass disaster agencies (Fig. 1).

The first step in a potential forensic investigation is to determine if the remains are human or nonhuman. If they are human it is then necessary to ascertain if they are of recent origin. A skeletal analysis initially begins with establishing a *biological profile* of the person whose remains are under investigation. This involves the estimation of the person's sex, age at death, ancestry, and living height (*stature*). These characteristics aid in narrowing down the pool of missing persons to consider for comparison. A positive identification of an unknown individual can be made through comparisons of antemortem (conditions that affected the skeleton during life) records, such as medical and dental x-rays, with unique biological characteristics observed on the skeleton. These may include genetic anomalies, such as unusual or atypical skeletal or dental features, or

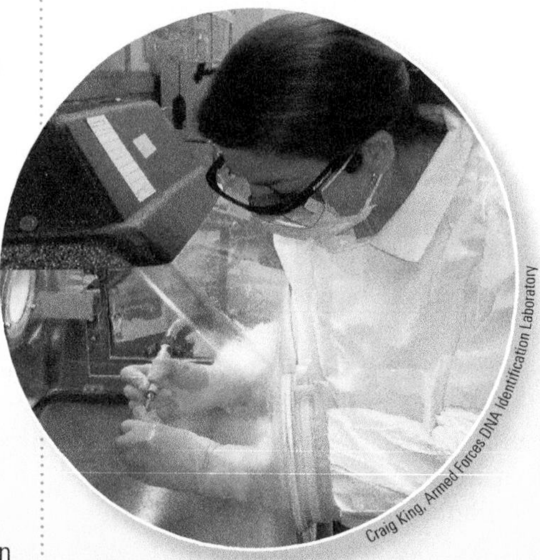
Craig King, Armed Forces DNA Identification Laboratory

▲ **Figure 1** Heather Thew, who was trained as an anthropologist, is shown working at the Armed Forces DNA Laboratory where remains of missing soldiers are identified.

pathological conditions, such as bone infections or healed fractures. Multiple points of similarity between antemortem and postmortem records (i.e., information collected on the deceased individual) can then help to establish identity. Finally, an analysis involves a comprehensive assessment of skeletal trauma, usually classified as blunt-force, sharp-force, or projectile trauma. Forensic anthropologists carefully document trauma that occurred at or around the time of death (*perimortem trauma*) to provide investigators with information regarding the circumstances of death. They also study postmortem alterations, such as damage to bone caused by exposure to the sun or by scavenging animals. It is critical to be able to differentiate this damage from trauma caused by interpersonal violence.

Ultimately, forensic anthropologists provide services that may help to resolve a case and provide closure to families. They are sometimes called into court as expert witnesses to testify regarding the identity of an individual and to describe traumatic injuries identified on skeletal remains that may pertain to the cause and manner of death. It is strongly recommended that people who wish to practice forensic anthropology receive a doctorate in physical anthropology and undergo certification through the American Board of Forensic Anthropology (see: www.theabfa.org). Currently there are over 70 active board certified forensic anthropologists in North America.

cians, and some members of the press. (Particularly good current examples of this relate to climate change research and evolution.) These anti-science positions have been quite successful because the majority of people don't understand the nature or goals of scientific research.

There's one more extremely important fact about hypotheses and theories: *Any proposition that is stated as absolute or does not allow the possibility of falsification is not a scientific hypothesis and should never be considered as such.* For a statement to be considered a scientific hypothesis, there must be a way to evaluate its validity. A statement such as "Heaven exists" may be true, but there is no rational, empirical means (based on experience or experiment) of testing it. Therefore acceptance of such a view is based on faith rather than scientific verification. *The purpose of scientific research is not to establish absolute truths; rather, it is to generate ever more accurate and consistent explanations of phenomena in our universe based on observation and testing.* At its very heart, scientific methodology is an exercise in rational thought and critical thinking.

The development of critical thinking skills is an extremely important benefit of a college education. Such skills enable people to evaluate, compare, analyze, critique, and synthesize information so that they won't accept everything they hear at face value. Critical thinking skills are perhaps most needed when it comes to advertising and politics. People spend billions of dollars every year on "natural" dietary supplements based on marketing claims that may not have even been tested. So when a salesperson tells you that, for example, echinacea helps prevent colds, you should ask if that statement has been scientifically tested, how it was tested, when, by whom, and where the results were published. Similarly, when politicians make claims in 30-second sound bites, check those claims before you accept them as truth. Be skeptical, and if you do check the validity of advertising and political statements, you'll find that frequently they're either misleading or just plain wrong.

The Anthropological Perspective

Perhaps the most important benefit you'll receive from this textbook and this course is a wider appreciation of the human experience. To understand human beings and how our species came to be, we must broaden our viewpoint through both time and space. All branches of anthropology fundamentally seek to do this in what we call the *anthropological perspective.*

Physical anthropologists, for example, are interested in how humans both differ from and are similar to other animals, especially nonhuman primates. For example, we've defined *hominins* as bipedal primates, but what are the major anatomical components of bipedal locomotion and how do they differ from, say, those in a **quadrupedal** ape? To answer these questions, biological anthropologists have studied the anatomical structures involved in human locomotion (muscles, hips, legs, and feet) and compared them with the same structures in various nonhuman primates.

Through a perspective that is broad in space and time, we can begin to grasp the diversity of the human experience within the context of biological and behavioral connections with other species. In this way, we may better understand the limits and potentials of humankind. And by extending our knowledge to include cultures other than our own, we may hope to avoid the **ethnocentric** pitfalls inherent in a more limited view of humanity.

This **relativistic** view of culture is perhaps more important now than ever before because, in our interdependent global community, it allows us to understand other people's concerns and to view our own culture from a broader perspective. Likewise, by examining our species as part of a wide spectrum of life, we realize that we can't judge other species using only human criteria. Each species is unique, with needs and a behavioral repertoire not exactly like that of any other. By recognizing that we share many similarities (both biological and behavioral) with other animals, perhaps we may come to recognize that they have a place in nature just as surely as we ourselves do.

We hope that after reading the following pages, you will have an increased understanding not only of the similarities we share with other biological organisms but also of the processes that have shaped the traits that make us unique. We live in what may well be the most crucial time for our planet in the past 65 million years. We are members of the one species

quadrupedal Using all four limbs to support the body during locomotion; the basic mammalian (and primate) form of locomotion.

ethnocentric Viewing other cultures from the inherently biased perspective of one's own culture. Ethnocentrism often causes other cultures to be seen as inferior to one's own.

relativistic Viewing entities as they relate to something else. Cultural relativism is the view that cultures have merits within their own historical and environmental contexts.

that, through the very agency of culture, has wrought such devastating changes in ecological systems that we must now alter our technologies or face potentially unspeakable consequences. In such a time, it's vital that we attempt to gain the best possible understanding of what it means to be human. We believe that the study of physical anthropology is one endeavor that aids in this attempt, and that is indeed the goal of this textbook.

Summary of Main Topics

- The major subfields of anthropology are cultural anthropology, linguistic anthropology, archaeology, and physical anthropology.
- Physical anthropology is a discipline that seeks to explain how and when human beings evolved. This requires a detailed examination of the primate and particularly the hominin fossil record (primate paleontology). Another major topic of physical anthropology is human biological variation, its genetic basis, and its adaptive significance. In addition, physical anthropologists study the behavior and biology of nonhuman primates, partly as a method of understanding humans but also because nonhuman primates are important in their own right.
- Because physical anthropology is a scientific approach to the investigation of all aspects of human evolution, variation, and adaptation, research in this field is based on the scientific method. The scientific method is a system of inquiry that involves the development of hypotheses to explain phenomena. To determine the validity of hypotheses, scientists develop research designs aimed at collecting information (data) and testing the data to see if they support the hypothesis. If the hypothesis is not supported by the data, it may be rejected or modified and retested. If it is supported, it may also be modified or refined over time and further tested. Further tests frequently use new technologies that have been developed since the original hypothesis was proposed. If a hypothesis stands up to continued testing, it may eventually be accepted as a theory or part of a theory.

Critical Thinking Questions

1. Given that you've only just been introduced to the field of physical anthropology, why do you think subjects such as anatomy, genetics, nonhuman primate behavior, and human evolution are integrated into a discussion of what it means to be human?
2. Is it important to you, personally, to know about human evolution? Why or why not?
3. Do you see a connection between hominin footprints that are almost 4 million years old and human footprints left on the moon in 1969? If so, do you think this relationship is important? What does the fact that there are human footprints on the moon say about human adaptation? (Consider both biological and cultural adaptation.)

Connections

Physical anthropology investigates how humans have evolved.

Evolutionary theory, particularly natural selection, explains how life forms have changed over time.

DNA molecule is the basis of all life.

Minden Pictures/Superstock

The Development of Evolutionary Theory

2

Student Learning Objectives

After mastering the material in this chapter, you should be able to:

- Trace the major developments in scientific thinking that led to the discovery of evolutionary processes.
- Compare Darwin's and Wallace's theory of natural selection to earlier explanations of how species came to exist.
- Understand how natural selection operates on biological variation in species to cause evolutionary change over time.
- Define the term *fitness* as it relates to reproductive success.
- Explain how science and religion differ in their explanations of natural phenomena.
- Discuss the history of opposition to the teaching of evolution in the United States.

Has anyone ever asked you, "If humans evolved from monkeys, why do we still have monkeys?" Or maybe, "If evolution happens, why don't we ever see new species?" These are the kinds of questions people sometimes ask if they don't understand evolutionary processes or don't believe that evolution occurs. Evolution is one of the most fundamental of all biological processes and one of the most misunderstood. The explanation for this misunderstanding is simple: Evolution is not taught in most primary and secondary schools. In fact, it's frequently avoided. Even in colleges and universities, it receives the most detailed treatment in biological anthropology. If you're not an anthropology or biology major and you're taking a class in biological anthropology mainly to fulfill a science requirement, you'll probably never study evolution again.

By the end of this course, you'll know the answers to the questions in the preceding paragraph. Briefly, no one who understands evolution would ever say that humans evolved from monkeys, because we didn't. We didn't evolve from chimpanzees either. The earliest human ancestors evolved from a species that lived some 6 to 8 million years ago (mya). That ancestral species was the *last common ancestor* we share with chimpanzees. In turn, the lineage that eventually gave rise to apes and humans separated from a monkey-like ancestor some 20 mya, and monkeys are still around because as early primate lineages diverged from one another, each went its separate way. Over millions of years, some of these groups became extinct while others evolved into the species we know today. Thus all living species are the current results of processes that go back millions of years. The evolution of new species takes time, a lot of time, which is why we don't witness the appearance of new species except microorganisms. But we do see *microevolutionary* changes in many species, including humans.

The subject of evolution is controversial, especially in the United States, because some religious views hold that evolutionary statements run counter to biblical teachings. In fact, as you're probably aware, there is strong opposition in the United States to the teaching of evolution in public schools. Opponents of teaching evolution often say, "It's just a theory," meaning that evolution is just an idea or hunch. As we pointed out in Chapter 1, scientific theories aren't just ideas, although that's how the word *theory* is commonly used in everyday conversation. But when dealing with scientific issues, referring to a concept as "theory" supports it. Theories have been tested and subjected to verification through accumulated evidence, and they have not been disproved, sometimes after decades of experimentation. It is absolutely true that evolution is a theory, one supported by a mounting body of genetic evidence that grows daily. It's a theory that explains how biological change occurs in species over time, and it has stood the test of time. Today, evolutionary theory stands as the most fundamental unifying force in biological science, and evolutionary biologists can explain many evolutionary processes in ways that were impossible even 10 years ago.

Because physical anthropology is concerned with all aspects of how humans came to be and how we adapt physiologically to the external environment, the details of the evolutionary process are crucial to the field. Given the central importance of evolution to biological anthropology, it's helpful to know how the mechanics of the process came to be discovered. Also, if we want to understand and make critical assessments of the controversy that surrounds the issue today, we need to explore the social and political events that influenced the discovery of evolutionary principles.

A Brief History of Evolutionary Thought

The discovery of evolutionary principles first took place in western Europe and was made possible by advances in scientific thinking that date back to the sixteenth century. Having said this, we must recognize that Western science borrowed many of its ideas from other cultures, especially the Arabs, Indians, and Chinese. In fact, intellectuals in these cultures and in ancient Greece had developed notions of biological evolution centuries before Charles Darwin did (Teresi, 2002), but they never formulated them into a cohesive theory.

Charles Darwin was the first person to explain the basic mechanics of the evolutionary process. But while he was developing his theory of **natural selection**, a Scottish naturalist named Alfred Russel Wallace independently reached the same conclusion. That natural selection, the single most important force of evolutionary change, was proposed at more or less the same time by two British men in the mid-nineteenth century may seem like a strange coincidence. But actually if Darwin and Wallace hadn't made their simultaneous discoveries, someone else soon would have, and that someone would probably have been British or French. That's because the groundwork had already been laid in Britain and France, and many scientists there were prepared to accept explanations of biological change that would have been unacceptable even 25 years before.

In science as in other human endeavors, knowledge is usually gained through a series of small steps rather than giant leaps. And just as technological change is based on past achievements, scientific knowledge builds on previously developed theories. Therefore, it's informative to examine the development of ideas that led Darwin and Wallace to independently arrive at the theory of evolution by natural selection.

Throughout the Middle Ages, one predominant feature of the European worldview was that all aspects of nature, including all forms of life and their relationships to one another, never changed. This view was partly shaped by a feudal society that was itself a rigid class system that had barely changed for centuries. But the most important influence was an extremely powerful religious system in which the teachings of Christianity

natural selection The most critical mechanism of evolutionary change, first described by Charles Darwin; the term refers to genetic change or changes in the frequencies of certain traits in populations due to differential reproductive success between individuals.

Bridgeman Art Culture History

◀ **Figure 2-1** Portion of a Renaissance painting that depicts the execution of Father Girolamo Savonarola in 1498 in Florence, Italy, (artist unknown). Savonarola wasn't promoting scientific arguments, but he did run afoul of church leaders. His execution by burning was a common punishment for those, including many scientists and philosophers, who promoted scientific explanations of natural phenomena.

were held to be the only "truth." Consequently it was generally accepted that all life on earth had been created by God exactly as it existed in the present and the belief that life-forms could not and did not change, came to be known as **fixity of species**. Anyone who questioned the assumptions of fixity, especially in the fifteenth and sixteenth centuries, could be accused of challenging God's perfection, which was heresy. Generally it was a good idea to avoid being accused of heresy, because this was a crime that could be punished by a particularly unpleasant and often fiery death (**Fig. 2-1**).

The plan of the entire universe was viewed as God's design. In what is called the "argument from design," anatomical structures were held to have been engineered to meet their intended purpose. Limbs, internal organs, and eyes all fit the functions they performed; and they, along with the rest of nature, were part of the Grand Designer's deliberate plan. Also, the Grand Designer was thought to have completed his works as recently as 4004 B.C. The prevailing belief in the earth's brief existence, together with fixity of species, was a virtually insurmountable obstacle to the development of evolutionary theory. The idea of immense geological time, which today we take for granted, simply didn't exist. In fact, until the concepts of fixity and time were fundamentally altered, it was impossible to conceive of evolution by means of natural selection.

The Scientific Revolution

So what transformed this centuries-old belief in a rigid, static universe into a view of worlds in continuous motion? How did the earth's brief history become an immense expanse of incomprehensible time? How did the scientific method as we know it today develop? These are important questions, but we could also ask why it took so long for Europe to break away from traditional beliefs. After all, scholars in India and the Arab world had developed concepts of planetary motion, for example, centuries earlier.

The development of evolutionary theory came about as a result of a

fixity of species The notion that species, once created, can never change is diametrically opposed to theories of biological evolution.

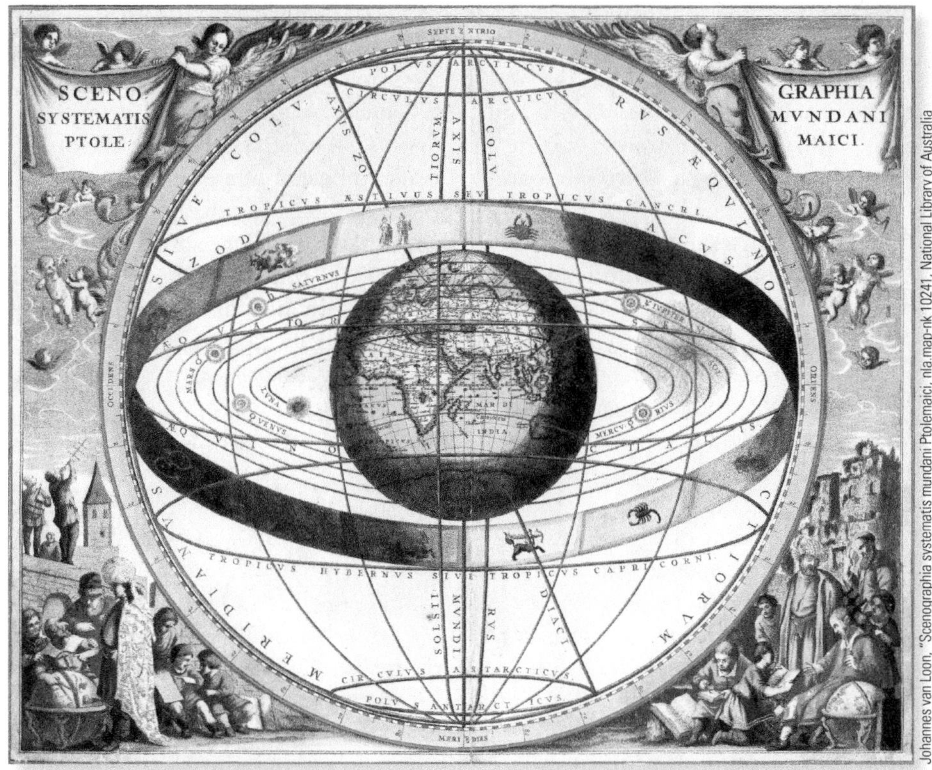

▶ **Figure 2-2** This beautifully illustrated seventeenth-century map shows the earth at the center of the solar system. Around it are seven concentric circles depicting the orbits of the moon, the sun, and the five planets that were known at the time. (Note also the signs of the zodiac.)

Johannes van Loon, "Scenographia systematis mundani Ptolemaici, nla.map-nk 10241, National Library of Australia

series of discoveries that led to major **paradigm shifts**. For example, the discovery of the New World and circumnavigation of the globe in the fifteenth century overturned some very basic European ideas about the planet. Among other things, the earth could no longer be thought of as flat. Also, as Europeans began to explore the New World, encountering plants and animals they'd never seen before, their awareness of biological diversity expanded.

There were other attacks on traditional beliefs. In 1514, a Polish mathematician named Copernicus challenged a notion proposed more than 1,500 years earlier, in the fourth-century B.C., by the Greek philosopher Aristotle. Aristotle had taught that the sun and planets existed in a series of concentric spheres that revolved around the earth (**Fig. 2-2**), a system that was, in turn, surrounded by the stars. Thus it came to be accepted that the earth was the center of the solar system. In fact, scholars in India had figured out that the earth orbited the sun long before Copernicus did; but Copernicus is generally credited with removing the earth as the center of all things.

Copernicus' theory was discussed in intellectual circles, but it didn't attract much attention from the Catholic Church. (Catholicism was the only form of Christianity until the 1520s.) Nevertheless, the theory did contradict a major premise of church doctrine, which at that time wholeheartedly embraced the teachings of Aristotle. By the 1300s, the church had accepted these teachings as dogma because they reinforced the notion that the earth, and the humans on it, were the central focus of God's creation and must therefore have a central position in the solar system.

However, in the early 1600s, an Italian mathematician named Galileo Galilei restated Copernicus' views, using logic and mathematics to support his claim. To his misfortune, Galileo was eventually confronted by the highest-ranking officials of the Catholic Church (including the pope, his onetime friend), who sentenced him to house arrest for the last nine years of

paradigm shift A transition from one conceptual framework or prevailing and widely accepted viewpoint to another. The acceptance of the discovery that the sun is the center of our solar system is an example of a paradigm shift.

his life. Nevertheless, in intellectual circles there had been a paradigm shift. The solar system had changed; the sun was now at its center, and the earth and other planets revolved around it as the entire system journeyed through space.

Throughout the sixteenth and seventeenth centuries, European scientists developed other methods and theories that revolutionized scientific thought. The seventeenth century, in particular, saw the discovery of the principles of physics (such as motion and gravity) and the invention of numerous scientific instruments, including the microscope. These advances made it possible to investigate many previously misunderstood natural phenomena. But even with these advances, the idea that living forms could change over time simply didn't occur to people.

Precursors of the Theory of Evolution

Before early naturalists could begin to understand the many forms of organic life, they had to list and describe them. And as research progressed, scholars were increasingly impressed with the amount of biological diversity they saw.

The concept of species, as we think of them today, wasn't proposed until the seventeenth century, when John Ray, a minister educated at the University of Cambridge, developed it. He recognized that groups of plants and animals could be differentiated from other groups by their ability to mate with one another and produce fertile offspring. He placed such groups of **reproductively isolated** organisms into categories, which he called species *(sing.,* species). Thus, by the late 1600s, the biological criterion of reproduction was used to define species, much as it is today (Young, 1992). Ray also recognized that species frequently share similarities with other species, and he grouped these together in a second level of classification he called the genus (*pl.*, genera). He was the first to use the labels *genus* and *species* in this way, and these terms are still in use today.

Carolus Linnaeus (1707–1778) was a Swedish naturalist who developed a method of classifying plants and animals. In his famous work *Systema Naturae* (The System of Nature), first published in 1735, he standardized Ray's use of genus and species terminology and established the system of **binomial nomenclature**. He also added two more categories: class and order. Linnaeus' four-level system became the basis for **taxonomy**, the system of classification we still use today.

Linnaeus also included humans in his classification of animals, placing them in the genus *Homo* and species *sapiens*. (Genus and species names are always italicized.) Including humans in this scheme was controversial because it defied the idea that humans should be considered unique and separate from the rest of the animal kingdom. Unfortunately for other species, most people still have this view, in spite of all the research that has demonstrated biological and behavioral continuity among all animals including ourselves.

For all his progressive tendencies, Linnaeus still believed in fixity of species, although in later years, faced with mounting evidence to the contrary, he came to question it. Indeed, fixity was being challenged on many fronts, especially in France, where voices were being raised in favor of a universe based on change and, more to the point, in favor of a biological relationship between similar species based on descent from a common ancestor.

Georges-Louis Leclerc de Buffon (1707–1788), a French naturalist, recognized the dynamic relationship between the external environment and living forms. In his *Natural History*, first published in 1749, he recognized that different regions have unique plants and animals. He also stressed that animals had come from a "center of origin," but he never discussed the diversification of life over time. Even so, Buffon recognized that alterations of the external

reproductively isolated Pertaining to groups of organisms that, mainly because of genetic differences, are prevented from mating and producing offspring with members of other such groups. For example, dogs cannot mate and produce offspring with cats.

binomial nomenclature (*binomial*, meaning "two names") In taxonomy, the convention established by Carolus Linnaeus whereby genus and species names are used to refer to living things. For example, *Homo sapiens* refers to human beings.

taxonomy The branch of science concerned with the rules of classifying organisms on the basis of evolutionary relationships.

▲ **Figure 2-3** Portrait of Jean-Baptiste Lamarck. Lamarck believed that species change was influenced by environmental change. He is best known for his theory of the inheritance of acquired characteristics.

Oil on canvas, Thevenin, Charles (1764–1838) / Private Collection / The Bridgeman Art Library International.

catastrophism The view that the earth's geological landscape is the result of violent cataclysmic events. Cuvier promoted this view, especially in opposition to Lamarck.

environment, including the climate, were agents of change in species.

Today, Erasmus Darwin (1731–1802) is best known as Charles Darwin's grandfather. But he was also a physician, poet, and leading member of an important intellectual community in England. In fact, Darwin counted among his friends some of the most important figures of the industrial revolution—a time of rapid technological and social change. In his most famous poem, Darwin expressed the view that life had originated in the seas and that all species had descended from a common ancestor. Thus he introduced many of the ideas that his grandson would propose 56 years later. These concepts include vast expanses of time for life to evolve, competition for resources, and the importance of the environment in evolutionary processes. From letters and other sources, we know that Charles Darwin read his grandfather's writings, but we don't know how much they influenced him.

Neither Buffon nor Erasmus Darwin attempted to *explain* the evolutionary process, but a French naturalist named Jean-Baptiste Lamarck (1744–1829) did. Lamarck (**Fig. 2-3**) suggested a dynamic relationship between species and the environment such that if the external environment changed, an animal's activity patterns would also change to accommodate the new circumstances. This would result in the increased or decreased use of certain body parts; consequently those body parts would be modified. According to Lamarck, the parts that weren't used would disappear over time. However, the parts that continued to be used, perhaps in different ways, would change. Such physical changes would occur in response to bodily "needs," so that if a particular part of the body felt a certain need, "fluids and forces" would be directed to that point, and the structure would be modified. Because the alteration would make the animal better suited to its habitat, the new trait would be passed on to offspring. This theory is known as the *inheritance of acquired characteristics*, or the *use-disuse* theory.

One of the most frequently given hypothetical examples of Lamarck's theory is the giraffe, which, having stripped all the leaves from the lower branches of a tree (environmental change), tries to reach the leaves on upper branches. As "vital forces" move to tissues of the neck, it becomes slightly longer and the giraffe can reach higher. The longer neck is then transmitted to offspring, with the eventual result that all giraffes have longer necks than their predecessors had (**Fig. 2-4**). So, according to this theory, *a trait acquired by an animal during its lifetime can be passed on to offspring.* Today we know that this explanation is wrong because only those traits that are influenced by genetic information contained within sex cells (eggs and sperm) can be inherited (see Chapter 3).

Because Lamarck's explanation of species change isn't genetically correct, he is frequently scorned even today. But in fact Lamarck deserves a great deal of credit because he emphasized the importance of interactions between organisms and the external environment in the evolutionary process. He also coined the term *biology* to refer to the study of living organisms, and a central feature of this new discipline was the idea of species change.

Lamarck's most vehement opponent was a French vertebrate paleontologist named Georges Cuvier (1769–1832). Cuvier introduced the concept of extinction to explain the disappearance of animals represented by fossils. Cuvier was a brilliant anatomist, but he never grasped the dynamic concept of nature and continued to insist on the fixity of species. So, rather than assuming that similarities between fossil forms and living species indicate evolutionary relationships, Cuvier proposed a variation of a doctrine known as **catastrophism**.

Catastrophism was the belief that the earth's geological features are the results of sudden, worldwide cataclys-

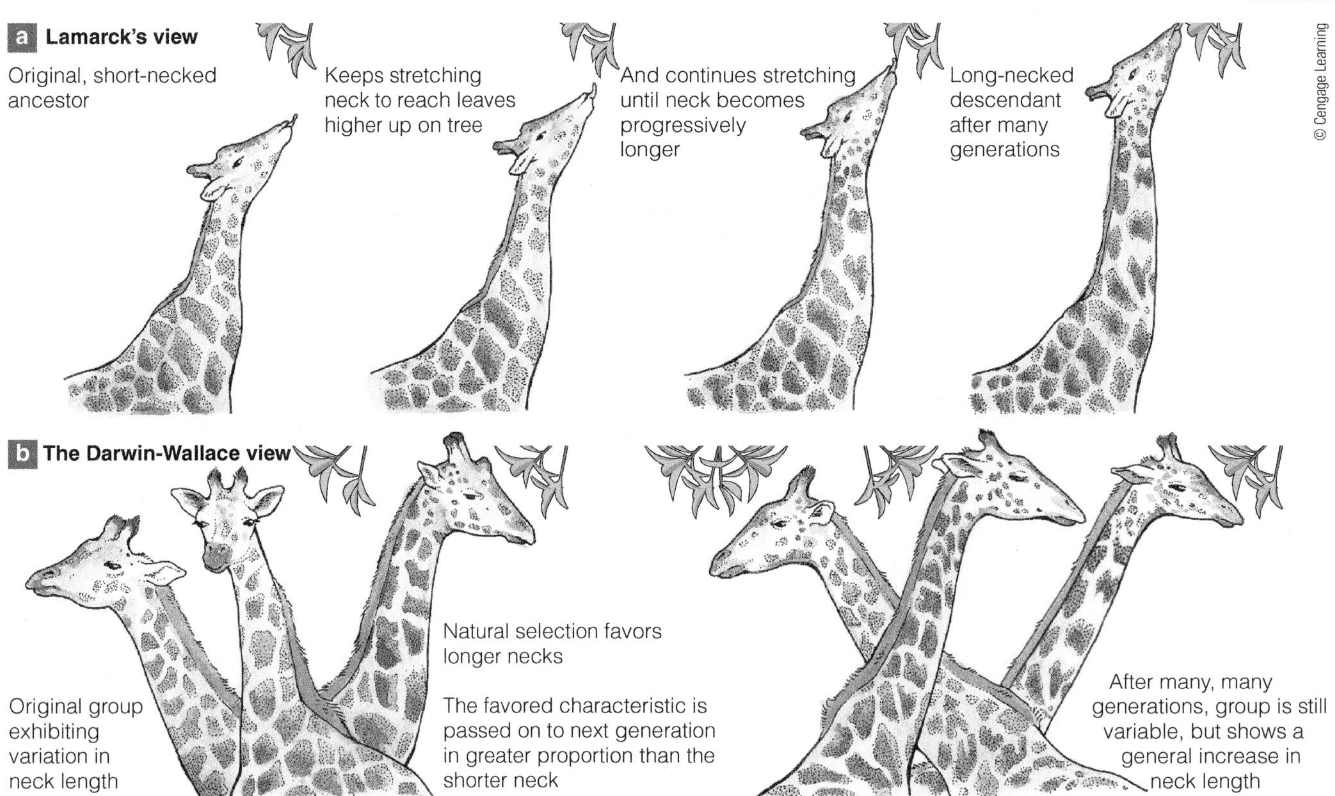
a Lamarck's view
Original, short-necked ancestor
Keeps stretching neck to reach leaves higher up on tree
And continues stretching until neck becomes progressively longer
Long-necked descendant after many generations
b The Darwin-Wallace view
Original group exhibiting variation in neck length
Natural selection favors longer necks
The favored characteristic is passed on to next generation in greater proportion than the shorter neck
After many, many generations, group is still variable, but shows a general increase in neck length
© Cengage Learning

▲ **Figure 2-4** Contrasting ideas about the mechanism of evolution. (**a**) Lamarck's theory held that acquired characteristics can be passed to offspring. Short-necked giraffes stretched to reach higher into trees for food; therefore their necks grew longer. According to Lamarck, this acquired trait was then passed on to offspring, who were born with longer necks. (**b**) The Darwin-Wallace theory of natural selection states that there is variation in neck length among giraffes. If having a longer neck provides an advantage for feeding, the trait will be passed on to a greater number of offspring, leading to an overall increase in the length of giraffe necks over many generations.

mic events. Cuvier's version of catastrophism suggested that a series of regional disasters had destroyed most or all of the local plant and animal life in many places. These areas were then restocked with new, similar forms that migrated in from unaffected regions. In order to be consistent with emerging fossil evidence, which indicated that organisms had become more complex over time, Cuvier proposed that after each disaster, the incoming migrants were more similar to living species because they had been produced by more recent creation events. In this way, Cuvier's explanation of increased complexity over time avoided any notion of evolution, but it still managed to account for the evidence of change so well preserved in the fossil record.

In 1798, an English economist named Thomas Malthus (1766–1834) wrote *An Essay on the Principle of Population*. This important essay inspired both Charles Darwin and Alfred Russel Wallace in their separate discoveries of natural selection. It's interesting that, although Malthus had an enormous influence on these two men, he wasn't interested in species change at all. Instead, he was arguing for limits to human population growth. He pointed out that in nature, there is a tendency for animal populations to increase in size, but the amount of resources (food and water) remains relatively the same. Therefore population size is held in check by resource availability. Even though humans can reduce constraints on population

▲ **Figure 2-5** Portrait of Charles Lyell.

size by producing more food, Malthus argued that the lack of sufficient food and water would always be a constant source of "misery" and famine for humankind if our numbers continued to increase. Unfortunately we are now testing Malthus' hypothesis, as the number of humans on earth reached 7 billion in 2011!

Both Darwin and Wallace extended Malthus' principles to all organisms, not just humans. Moreover, they recognized the important fact that when population size is limited by resource availability, there is constant competition. This is a crucial point, because competition among individuals is the ultimate key to understanding natural selection.

Charles Lyell (1797–1875) is considered the founder of modern geology (**Fig. 2-5**). He was a lawyer, a geologist, and, for many years, Charles Darwin's friend and mentor. Before meeting Darwin in 1836, Lyell had earned acceptance in Europe's most prestigious scientific circles, thanks to his highly praised *Principles of Geology*, first published during the years 1830–1833.

In this extremely important work, Lyell argued that the geological processes we see today are the same as those that existed in the past. This theory, called geological **uniformitarianism**, didn't originate entirely with Lyell, having been proposed by James Hutton in the late 1700s. Even so, it was Lyell who demonstrated that forces such as wind, water erosion, local flooding, frost, decomposition of vegetable matter, volcanoes, earthquakes, and glacial movements had all contributed in the past to produce the geological landscape that we see today. What's more, these processes were ongoing, indicating that geological change was still happening and that the forces driving such change were consistent, or *uniform*, over time. In other words, various aspects of the earth's surface (mountain ranges, rivers, the position of continents, and so forth) vary through time, but the *underlying processes* that influence them are constant.

Lyell also emphasized the obvious: namely, that for such slowly acting forces to produce momentous change, the earth must be far older than anyone had previously suspected. By providing an immense time scale and thereby changing perceptions of the earth's history from a few thousand to many millions of years, Lyell changed the framework within which scientists viewed the geological past. Thus the concept of "deep time" (Gould, 1987) remains one of Lyell's most significant contributions to the discovery of evolutionary principles, because the immensity of geological time permitted the necessary time depth for the inherently slow process of evolutionary change (**Fig. 2-6**).

As you can see, the roots of evolutionary theory are deeply embedded in the late eighteenth and early nineteenth centuries. During that time, many lesser-known but very important people also contributed to this intellectual movement. One such person was Mary Anning (1799–1847), who lived in the town of Lyme Regis on the south coast of England.

Anning's father died when she was 11 years old, leaving his wife and two children destitute. Fortunately, he had taught Mary to recognize marine fossils embedded in the cliffs near the town. Thus she began to earn a living by collecting and selling fossils to collectors who were becoming increasingly interested in the remains of creatures that many people believed had been killed in the Noah flood.

After Anning's discovery of the first *complete* fossil of *Ichthyosaurus*, a large marine reptile, and the first *Pleiosaurus* fossil (another ocean-dwelling reptile), some of the most famous scientists in England repeatedly visited her home. Eventually she became known as one of the world's leading "fossilists." And by sharing her extensive knowledge of fossil species with the leading scientists of the day, she contributed to the under-

uniformitarianism The theory that the earth's features are the result of long-term processes that continue to operate in the present just as they did in the past. Elaborated on by Lyell, this theory opposed catastrophism and greatly contributed to the concept of immense geological time.

◀ **Figure 2-6** (**a**) These limestone cliffs in southern France were formed around 300 million years ago from shells and the skeletal remains of countless sea creatures. (**b**) Part of a block of stone cut from the same limestone containing fossilized shells.

standing of the evolution of marine life, which spanned over 200 million years. But because she was a woman and of low social position, Anning wasn't acknowledged in the numerous scientific publications she facilitated. In recent years, however, she has achieved the recognition she deserves; her portrait hangs prominently in the British Museum (Natural History) in London.

The Discovery of Natural Selection

Having already been introduced to Erasmus Darwin, you shouldn't be surprised to learn that his grandson Charles grew up in an educated family with ties to the intellectual circles of the time. Charles Darwin (1809–1882) was one of six children of Dr. Robert and Susanna Darwin (**Fig. 2-7**). Being the grandson not only of Erasmus Darwin but also of the wealthy Josiah Wedgwood (of Wedgwood china fame), Charles grew up enjoying the comfortable lifestyle of the landed gentry in rural England.

As a boy, Darwin had a keen interest in nature, but this interest did little to dispel the generally held view among family and friends that he was in no way remarkable. In fact, his performance at school was no more than ordinary.

After his mother's death when he was 8 years old, Darwin was raised by his father and older sisters. Because he showed little interest in anything except hunting, shooting, and perhaps science, his father sent him to Edinburgh University to study medicine. It was there that Darwin first became acquainted with the evolutionary theories of Lamarck and others.

During that time (the 1820s), notions of evolution were becoming feared in England and elsewhere. Anything identified with postrevolutionary France was viewed with suspicion by the established order in England, and Lamarck, partly because he was French, was especially vilified by British scientists.

It was also a time of growing political unrest in Britain. The Reform Movement, which sought to undo the

▲ **Figure 2-7** Charles Darwin, photographed five years before the publication of *On the Origin of Species*.

many inequalities of the traditional class system, was under way, and like most social movements, it had a radical faction. Because many of the radicals were atheists and socialists who also supported Lamarck's ideas, many people came to associate evolution with atheism and political subversion. The growing fear of evolutionary ideas led many to believe that if these ideas were generally accepted, "the Church would crash, the moral fabric of society would be torn apart, and civilized man would return to savagery" (Desmond and Moore, 1991, p. 34). It's unfortunate that some of the most outspoken early proponents of species change were so vehemently anti-Christian, because their rhetoric helped to establish the entrenched suspicion and misunderstanding of evolutionary theory that persists today.

While at Edinburgh, Darwin studied with professors who were outspoken supporters of Lamarck. So, even though he hated medicine and left Edinburgh after two years, his experience there was a formative period in his intellectual development.

Although Darwin was fairly indifferent to religion, he next went to Cambridge to study theology. It was during his Cambridge years that he cultivated interests in natural science and immersed himself in botany and geology. Following his graduation in 1831, he was invited to join a scientific expedition that would circle the globe. And so it was that Darwin set sail aboard HMS *Beagle* on December 17, 1831 (**Fig. 2-8**). The famous voyage of the *Beagle* would take almost five years and would forever change not only the course of Darwin's life but also the history of biological science (**Fig. 2-9**).

Darwin went aboard the *Beagle* believing in the fixity of species. But during the voyage he privately began to have doubts. For one thing, he came across fossils of ancient giant animals that, except for size, looked very much like species that still lived in the same vicinity. The similarities he saw caused

▼ **Figure 2-8** The route of HMS *Beagle*.

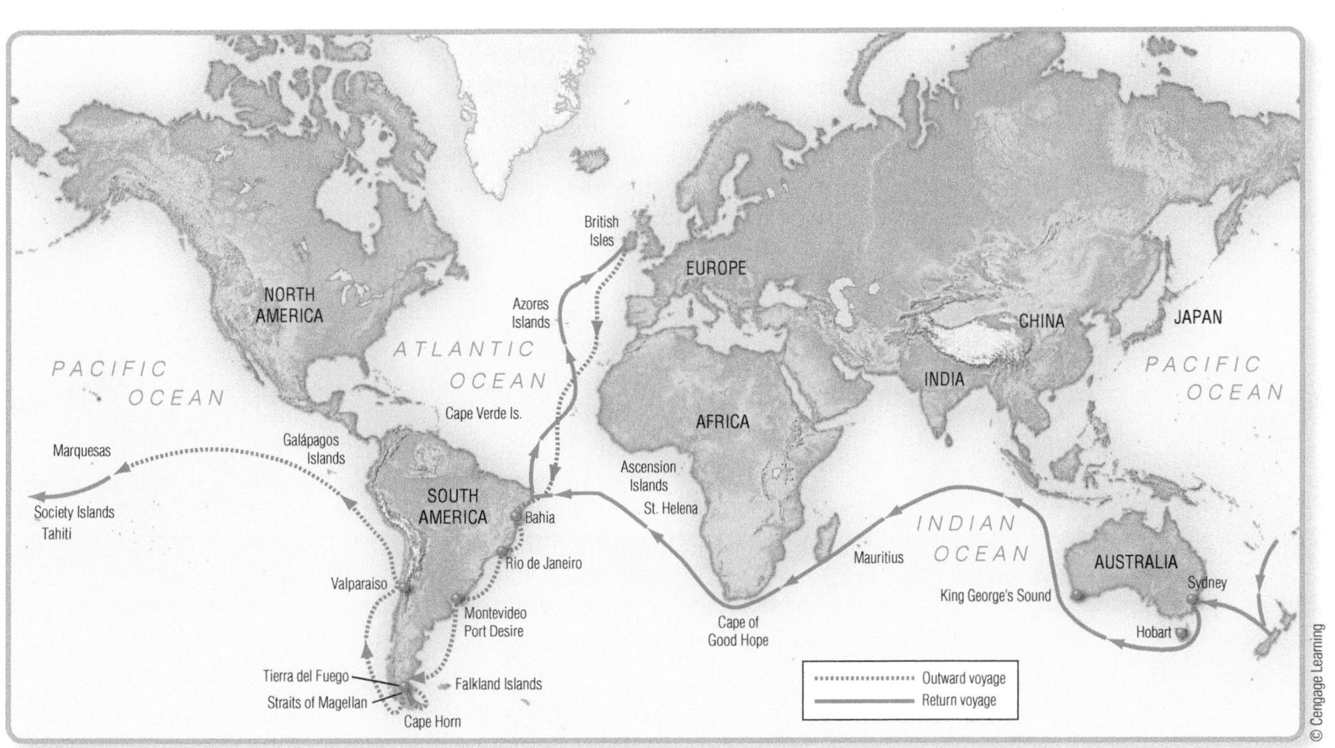

◀ **Figure 2-9** A painting by John Chancellor of HMS *Beagle* sailing through the Galápagos Islands in 1835.

him to speculate that the fossils represented ancestors of those living forms.

During the now famous stopover at the Galápagos Islands, off the coast of Ecuador, Darwin noticed that the vegetation and animals (especially birds) shared many similarities with those on the South American mainland. But they weren't identical to them. What's more, the birds varied from island to island. Darwin collected 13 varieties of Galápagos finches, and it was clear that they represented a closely related group; but some of their physical traits were different, particularly the shape and size of their beaks (**Fig. 2-10**). Darwin also collected finches from the mainland, and these appeared to represent only one group, or species.

The insight that Darwin gained from the finches is legendary. But, contrary to popular misconception, it wasn't until *after* he returned to England that he recognized the significance of the variation in beak structure. In fact, during the voyage, he had paid little attention to the finches. It was only later that he considered the

▼ **Figure 2-10** Beak variation in Darwin's Galápagos finches.

Ground finch	Tree finch	Tree finch (called woodpecker finch)	Ground finch (known as warbler finch)
Main Food: seeds	Main food: leaves, buds, blossoms, fruits	Main food: insects	Main food: insects
Beak: heavy	Beak: thick, short	Beak: stout, straight	Beak: slender

▶ **Figure 2-11** Down House as seen from the rear. Darwin wrote *On the Origin of Species* and numerous other publications here.

Robert Jurmain

factors that could lead to the modification of one species into many (Gould, 1985; Desmond and Moore, 1991). He realized that the various Galapagos finches had all descended from a common mainland ancestor and had been modified over time in response to different island habitats and dietary preferences.

Darwin returned to England in October 1836 and was immediately accepted into the most prestigious scientific circles. He married his cousin Emma Wedgwood and moved to the village of Down, near London, where he spent the rest of his life writing on topics ranging from fossils to orchids (**Fig. 2-11**). But the question of species change was his overriding passion.

At Down, Darwin began to develop his views on what he called *natural selection*. This concept was borrowed from animal breeders, who choose, or "select," as breeding stock those animals that possess certain traits that the breeders want to emphasize in offspring. Animals with undesirable traits are "selected against," or prevented from breeding. A dramatic example of the effects of selective breeding can be seen in the various domestic dog breeds shown in **Figure 2-12**. Darwin applied his knowledge of domesticated species to naturally occurring ones, and he recognized that in undomesticated organisms, the selective agent was nature, not humans.

By the late 1830s, Darwin had realized that biological variation within a species (that is, differences among individuals) was crucial. Furthermore, he realized that sexual reproduction increased variation, although he didn't know why. Then, in 1838, he read Malthus' essay; and there he found the answer to the question of how new species came to be. He accepted Malthus' idea that populations increase at a faster rate than resources do, and he recognized that in nonhuman animals, population size is always limited by the amount of available food and water. He also recognized that these two facts lead to a constant "struggle for existence." The idea that in each generation more offspring are born than survive to adulthood coupled with the notions of competition for resources and biological diversity was all Darwin needed to develop his theory of natural selection. He wrote: "It at once struck me that under these circumstances favourable variations would tend to be preserved, and unfavourable ones to be destroyed. The result of this would be the formation of a new species" (F. Darwin, 1950,

Wolf: Corbis/Superstock Dogs surrounding wolf: Lynn Kilgore and Lin Marshall; Great Dane, Eric Isselée/Shutterstock; Chihuahua, iStockphoto.com/Marcin Pikula; Yorkshire terrier, iStockphoto.com/Eriklam

▲ **Figure 2-12** All domestic dog breeds share a common ancestor, the wolf. The extreme variation exhibited by dog breeds today has been achieved in a relatively short time through artificial selection. In this situation, humans allow only certain dogs to breed in order to emphasize specific characteristics. (We should note that many traits desired by human breeders are detrimental to the dogs themselves.)

pp. 53–54). Basically, this quotation summarizes the entire theory of natural selection.

By 1844, Darwin had written a short summary of his natural selection hypothesis but he didn't think he had enough data to support it, so he continued his research without publishing. He also had other reasons for not publishing what he knew would be a highly controversial work. He was deeply troubled that his wife, Emma, saw his ideas as running counter to her strong religious convictions (Keynes, 2002). Also, as a member of the established order, he knew that many of his friends and associates were concerned with threats to the status quo, and evolutionary theory was viewed as a very serious threat indeed.

In Darwin's Shadow

Unlike Darwin, Alfred Russel Wallace (1823–1913) was born into a family of modest means (**Fig. 2-13**). He went to work at the age of 14 and, with little formal education, moved from one job to the next. Eventually he became interested in collecting plants and animals and joined expeditions to the Amazon and Southeast Asia, where he acquired firsthand knowledge of many natural phenomena.

In 1855, Wallace published an article suggesting that current species were descended from other species and that the appearance of new ones was influenced by environmental factors (Trinkaus and Shipman, 1992). This article caused Lyell and others to urge

English Heritage Photo Library/The Bridgeman Art Library

▲ **Figure 2-13** Alfred Russel Wallace independently identified natural selection as the key to the evolutionary process.

Oil on canvas by Evstafieff (19th century) Down House, Downe, Kent, UK/ © English Heritage Photo Library / The Bridgeman Art Library.

© Russell L. Ciochon

▲ **Figure 2-14** Charles Darwin's *Origin of Species*, the book that revolutionized biological science.

Darwin to publish, but he continued to hesitate.

Then, in 1858, Wallace sent Darwin another paper, "On the Tendency of Varieties to Depart Indefinitely from the Original Type." In it, Wallace described evolution as a process driven by competition and natural selection. When he received Wallace's paper, Darwin realized that if he continued to wait, Wallace might get credit for a theory (natural selection) that he himself had developed. He quickly wrote a paper presenting his ideas, and both papers were read before the Linnean Society of London. Neither author was present. Wallace was out of the country and Darwin was mourning the recent death of his young son.

The papers received little notice at the time. But in December 1859, when Darwin completed and published his greatest work, *On the Origin of Species*,* the storm broke, and it still hasn't abated (**Fig. 2-14**). Although public opinion was negative, there was much scholarly praise for the book, and scientific opinion gradually came to Darwin's support. The question of species was now explained: Species could change, they weren't fixed, and they evolved from other species through the mechanism of natural selection.

Natural Selection

Early in his research, Darwin had realized that natural selection was the key to evolution. With the help of Malthus' ideas, he saw *how* selection in nature could be explained. In the struggle for existence, those *individuals* with favorable variations would survive and reproduce, but those with unfavorable variations would not. For Darwin, the explanation of evolution was simple. The basic processes, as he understood them, are as follows:

1. All species are capable of producing offspring at a faster rate than food supplies increase.
2. There is biological variation in all species.
3. In each generation more offspring are produced than survive, and because of limited resources, there is competition among individuals. (*Note:* This statement does not mean that there is constant fierce fighting.)
4. Individuals who possess favorable variations or traits (for example, speed, resistance to disease, protective coloration) have an advantage over those who don't. In other words, they have greater **fitness**, because favorable traits increase the likelihood that they will survive to adulthood and reproduce.
5. The environmental context determines whether or not a trait is beneficial. What is favorable in one setting may be a liability in another. Consequently the traits that become most advantageous are the results of a natural process.
6. Traits are inherited and passed on to the next generation. Because individuals who possess favorable traits contribute more offspring to the next generation than do oth-

* The full title is *On the Origin of Species by Means of Natural Selection, or the Preservation of Favoured Races in the Struggle for Life.*

ers, over time those favorable traits become more common in the population. Less favorable characteristics aren't passed as frequently, so they become less common over time and are "weeded out." Individuals who produce more offspring in comparison to others are said to have greater **reproductive success**, or fitness.

7. Over long periods of time, successful variations accumulate in a population, so that later generations may be distinct from ancestral ones. Thus, in time, a new species may appear.
8. Geographical isolation also contributes to the formation of new species. As populations of a species become geographically isolated from one another, for whatever reasons (for example, distance or natural barriers such as rivers), they begin to adapt to different environments. Over time, as populations continue to respond to different **selective pressures** (that is, different ecological circumstances), they may become distinct species. The 13 species of Galápagos finches are presumably all descended from a common ancestor that lived on the South American mainland. Thus, they provide an example of the role of geographical isolation.

Before Darwin, individual members of species were not considered important, so they weren't studied. But as we've seen, Darwin recognized the uniqueness of individuals and realized that variation among them could explain how selection occurs. Favorable variations are selected, or chosen, for survival by nature; unfavorable ones are eliminated. *Natural selection operates on individuals*, either favorably or unfavorably, but *it's the population that evolves*. It's important to emphasize that the unit of natural selection is the individual; the unit of evolution is the population. This is because individuals don't change genetically but, over time, populations do.

Natural Selection in Action

One of the most frequently cited examples of natural selection relates to changes in the coloration of a species of moth. In recent years, the moth story has come under some criticism; but the premise remains valid, so we use it to illustrate how natural selection works.

Before the nineteenth century, the most common variety of the peppered moth in England was a mottled gray color. During the day, as the moths rested on lichen-covered tree trunks, their coloration provided camouflage (**Fig. 2-15**). There was also a dark gray variety of the same species, but because the dark moths were not as well camouflaged, they were more frequently eaten by birds; therefore they were less common. (In this example, the birds are the *selective agents*, and they apply *selective pressures* on the moths.) Yet by the end of the nineteenth century, the darker form had almost completely replaced the common gray one.

The cause of this change was the changing environment of industrialized nineteenth-century England. Coal dust from factories and fireplaces settled on the trees, turning them dark gray and killing the lichen. The moths continued to rest on the trees, but the light gray ones became more conspicuous as the trees became darker, and they were increasingly targeted by birds. Thus, the light gray moths began to contribute fewer genes to the next generation than the darker moths, and the proportion of lighter moths decreased while the dark moths became more common. A similar color shift also occurred in North America. But the introduction of clean air acts in both Britain and the United States reduced the amount of air pollution (at least from coal), and the predominant color of the peppered moth once again became the light mottled gray. This kind of evolutionary shift in response to environmental change is called *adaptation*.

fitness Pertaining to natural selection, a measure of the relative reproductive success of individuals. Fitness can be measured by an individual's genetic contribution to the next generation compared with that of other individuals. The terms *genetic fitness*, *reproductive fitness*, and *differential net reproductive success* are also used.

reproductive success The number of offspring an individual produces and rears to reproductive age, or an individual's genetic contribution to the next generation.

selective pressures Forces in the environment that influence reproductive success in individuals.

Perennou Nuridsany/Photo Researchers, Inc.

Michael Willmer Forbes Tweedie/Photo Researchers, Inc.

▶ Figure 2-15
Variation in the peppered moth. (**a**) The dark form is more visible on the light, lichen-covered tree. (**b**) On trees darkened by pollution, the lighter form is more visible.

The medium ground finch of the Galápagos Islands provides another example of natural selection. In 1977, drought killed many of the plants that produced the smaller, softer seeds favored by these birds. This forced a population of finches on one of the islands to feed on larger, harder seeds. Even before 1977, some birds had smaller, less robust beaks than others (that is, there was variation). During the drought, because they were less able to process the larger seeds, more smaller-beaked birds died than larger-beaked birds. So, although overall population size declined, average beak thickness in the survivors and their offspring increased, simply because larger-beaked individuals were surviving in greater numbers and producing more offspring. In other words, they had greater reproductive success. But during heavy rains in 1982–1983, smaller seeds became more plentiful again and the pattern in beak size reversed itself, demonstrating again how reproductive success is related to environmental conditions (Boag and Grant, 1981; Ridley, 1993).

The best illustration of natural selection, however—and certainly one with potentially grave consequences for humans—is the recent increase in resistant strains of disease-causing microorganisms. When antibiotics were first introduced in the 1940s, they were seen as the cure for bacterial disease. But that optimistic view didn't take into account that bacteria, like other organisms, possess genetic variability. Consequently, though an antibiotic will kill most bacteria in an infected person, any bacterium with an inherited resistance to that particular therapy will survive. In turn, the survivors reproduce and pass their drug resistance to future generations, so that eventually, the population is mostly made up of bacteria that don't respond to treatment. What's more, because bacteria produce new generations every few hours, antibiotic-resistant strains are continuously appearing. As a result, many types of infection no longer respond to treatment. For example, tuberculosis was once thought to be well controlled, but there's been a resurgence of TB in recent years because some strains of the bacterium that causes it are resistant to most of the antibiotics used to treat it.

These examples (moths, finches, and bacteria) provide the following insights into the fundamentals of evolutionary change produced by natural selection:

1. *A trait must be inherited if natural selection is to act on it.* A charac-

teristic that isn't hereditary (such as a temporary change in hair color produced by the hairdresser) won't be passed on to offspring. In finches, for example, beak size is a hereditary trait.

2. *Natural selection cannot occur without population variation in inherited characteristics.* If, for example, all the peppered moths had initially been light gray and the trees had become darker, the survival and reproduction of the moths could have been so low that the population might have become extinct. *Selection can work only with variation that already exists.*
3. *Fitness is a relative measure that changes as the environment changes.* Fitness is simply differential net reproductive success. In the initial stage, the lighter moths were more fit because they produced more offspring. But as the environment changed, the dark gray moths became more fit. Later, a further change reversed the pattern again. Likewise, the majority of Galápagos finches will have larger or smaller beaks, depending on external conditions. So it should be obvious that statements regarding the "most fit" don't mean anything without reference to specific environments.
4. *Natural selection can act only on traits that affect reproduction.* If a characteristic isn't expressed until later in life, after organisms have reproduced, natural selection can't influence it. This is because the trait's inherited components have already been passed on to offspring. Many forms of cancer and cardiovascular disease are influenced by hereditary factors, but because these diseases usually affect people after they've had children, natural selection can't act against them. By the same token, if a condition usually kills or compromises the individual before he or she reproduces, natural selection is able to act against it because the trait won't be passed on.

So far, our examples have shown how different death rates influence natural selection (for example, moths or finches that die early leave fewer offspring). But mortality is only part of the picture. Another important aspect of natural selection is **fertility**, because an animal that gives birth to more young contributes more genes to the next generation than an animal that produces fewer. But fertility isn't the entire story either, because the crucial element is the number of young raised successfully to the point where they themselves reproduce. We call this *differential net reproductive success.* The way this mechanism works can be demonstrated through another example.

In swifts (small birds that resemble swallows), data show that producing more offspring doesn't necessarily guarantee that more young will be successfully raised. The number of eggs hatched in a breeding season is a measure of fertility. The number of birds that mature and are eventually able to leave the nest is a measure of net reproductive success, or successfully raised offspring. The following table shows the correlation between the number of eggs hatched (fertility) and the number of young that leave the nest (reproductive success), averaged over four breeding seasons (Lack, 1966):

Number of eggs hatched (fertility)	**2 eggs**	**3 eggs**	**4 eggs**
Average number of young raised (reproductive success)	1.92	2.54	1.76
Sample size (number of nests)	72	20	16

As you can see, the most efficient number of eggs is three, because that number yields the highest reproductive

fertility The ability to conceive and produce healthy offspring.

success. Raising two offspring is less beneficial to the parents, because the end result isn't as successful as with three eggs. Trying to raise more than three is actually detrimental, as the parents may not be able to provide enough nourishment for any of the offspring. Offspring that die before reaching reproductive age are, in evolutionary terms, equivalent to never being born. Moreover, an offspring that dies can be a minus to the parents, because before it dies it drains parental resources. It may even inhibit their ability to raise other offspring, thus reducing their reproductive success even further. Selection favors those genetic traits that yield the maximum net reproductive success. If the number of eggs laid is a genetic trait in birds (and it seems to be), natural selection in swifts should act to favor laying three eggs as opposed to two or four.

Constraints on Nineteenth-Century Evolutionary Theory

Darwin argued for the concept of evolution in general and the role of natural selection in particular. But he didn't understand the exact mechanisms of evolutionary change. As we've already seen, natural selection acts on *variation* within species; but what Darwin didn't understand was where the variation came from. In the nineteenth century, this remained an unanswered question, plus no one understood how offspring inherited traits from their parents. Almost without exception, nineteenth-century scientists believed inheritance to be a *blending* process in which parental characteristics were mixed together to produce intermediate expressions in offspring. Given this notion, we can see why the true nature of genes was unimaginable; and, with no alternative explanation, Darwin accepted the blending theory of inheritance. As it turns out, a contemporary of Darwin's had actually worked out the rules of heredity. However, the work of this Augustinian monk, named Gregor Mendel (whom you'll meet in Chapter 4), wasn't recognized until the beginning of the twentieth century.

The first three decades of the twentieth century saw the merger of natural selection theory and Mendel's discoveries. This was a crucial development because until then, scientists thought these concepts were unrelated. Then, in 1953, the structure of DNA was discovered. This landmark achievement has been followed by even more amazing advances in the field of genetics. The human **genome** was sequenced in 2003, followed by the chimpanzee genome in 2005. The genomes of many other species have also now been sequenced. By comparing the genomes of different species (a field called comparative genomics), scientists can examine how genetically similar or different they are. This can explain many aspects of how these species evolved. Also, since the early 1990s, several scientists have merged the fields of evolutionary and developmental biology into a new field called "evo-devo." This approach, which compares the actions of different developmental genes and the factors that regulate them, is making it possible to explain evolution in ways that were impossible even 15 years ago. Scientists are truly on the threshold of revealing many secrets of the evolutionary process. If only Darwin could know!

Opposition to Evolution Today

More than 150 years after the publication of *Origin of Species*, the debate over evolution is far from over, especially in the United States and, increasingly, in several Muslim countries. For most biologists, evolution is indisputable. The genetic evidence for it is solid and accumulates daily. Anyone who appreciates and understands

genome The entire genetic makeup of an individual or species.

genetic mechanisms can't avoid the conclusion that populations and species evolve. What's more, the majority of Christians don't believe that biblical depictions should be taken literally. But at the same time, some surveys show that about half of all Americans don't believe that evolution occurs. There are a number of reasons for this.

The mechanisms of evolution are complex and do not lend themselves to simple explanations. Understanding them requires some familiarity with genetics and biology, a familiarity that most people don't have unless they took related courses in school. What is more, many people want definitive, clear-cut answers to complex questions. But as you learned in Chapter 1, science doesn't always provide definitive answers to questions; it doesn't establish absolute truths; and it doesn't *prove* facts. Another thing to consider is that regardless of their culture, most people are raised in belief systems that don't emphasize **biological continuity** between species or offer scientific explanations for natural phenomena.

The relationship between science and religion has never been easy (remember Galileo), even though both serve in their own ways to explain natural phenomena. As you read in Chapter 1, scientific explanations are based on data analysis, hypothesis testing, and interpretation. Religions, meanwhile, are systems of faith-based beliefs. A major difference between science and religion is that religious explanations aren't amenable to scientific testing. Religion and science concern different aspects of the human experience, but they aren't inherently mutually exclusive approaches. That is, belief in God doesn't exclude the occurrence of biological evolution; and acknowledgment of evolutionary processes doesn't preclude the existence of God. What's more, evolutionary theories aren't rejected by all religions or by most forms of Christianity.

Some years ago, the Vatican hosted an international conference on human evolution; in 1996, Pope John Paul II issued a statement that "fresh knowledge leads to recognition of the theory of evolution as more than just a hypothesis." Today, the official position of the Catholic Church is that evolutionary processes do occur, but that the human soul is of divine creation and not subject to evolutionary processes. Likewise, mainstream Protestants don't generally see a conflict. Unfortunately those who believe in an absolutely literal interpretation of the Bible (called *fundamentalists*) accept no compromise.

A Brief History of Opposition to Evolution in the United States

There are historical reasons for the opposition to the teaching of evolution in the United States. Reacting to rapid cultural change after World War I, conservative Christians sought a revival of what they considered to be "traditional values." In their view, one way to achieve this was to prevent any mention of Darwinism in public schools. One result of this effort was a state law, passed in Tennessee in 1925, that banned the teaching of any theory (particularly evolution) that did not support the biblical version of the creation of humankind. To test the validity of this law, the American Civil Liberties Union persuaded a high school teacher named John Scopes to submit to being arrested and tried for teaching evolution (**Fig. 2-16**). The subsequent trial, called the "Scopes Monkey Trial" was a 1920s equivalent of current celebrity trials. In the end, Scopes was convicted and fined $100, though the conviction was later overturned. Although most states didn't actually forbid the teaching of evolution, Arkansas, Tennessee, and a few others continued to prohibit any mention of it until 1968, when the U.S. Supreme Court struck down the ban against teaching evolution in public schools. (One coauthor of this textbook remembers when her junior high

biological continuity A biological continuum. When expressions of a phenomenon continuously grade into one another so that there are no discrete categories, they exist on a continuum. Color is one such phenomenon, and life-forms are another.

▶ **Figure 2-16** Photo taken at the "Scopes Monkey Trial." The well-known defense attorney Clarence Darrow is sitting on the edge of the table. John Scopes, wearing a white shirt, is sitting with his arms folded behind Darrow.

Bettmann/Corbis

school science teacher was fired for mentioning evolution in Little Rock, Arkansas.)

By the mid-1960s, coverage of evolution in textbooks had increased. As a result, **Christian fundamentalists** renewed their campaign to eliminate evolution from public school curricula and to introduce antievolutionary material into public school classes. The *creation science* movement was born out of this effort.

Proponents of creation science are called "creationists" because they explain the existence of the universe as the result of a sudden creation event that occurred over the course of six 24-hour days, as described in the book of Genesis. The premise of creation science is that the biblical account of the earth's origins and the story of Noah and the flood can be supported by scientific evidence.

Creationists have insisted that what they used to call "creation science" and now call "intelligent design" (ID) is a valid scientific explanation of the earth's origins. They've argued that in the interest of fairness, a balanced view should be offered in public schools: If evolution is taught as science, then creationism should also be taught as science. Sounds fair, doesn't it? But ID isn't science at all, for the simple reason that creationists insist that their view is absolute and infallible. Therefore creationism is not a hypothesis that can be tested, nor is it amenable to falsification. And because hypothesis testing is the basis of all science, creationism by its very nature cannot be considered science.

Since the 1970s, creationists have become increasingly active on local school boards and in state legislatures, promoting laws that mandate the teaching of creationism in public schools. However, state and federal courts have consistently overruled these laws because they violate the "establishment clause" of the First Amendment of the U.S. Constitution, which states that "Congress shall make no law respecting an establishment of

Christian fundamentalists Adherents to a movement in American Protestantism that began in the early twentieth century. This group holds that the teachings of the Bible are infallible and should be taken literally.

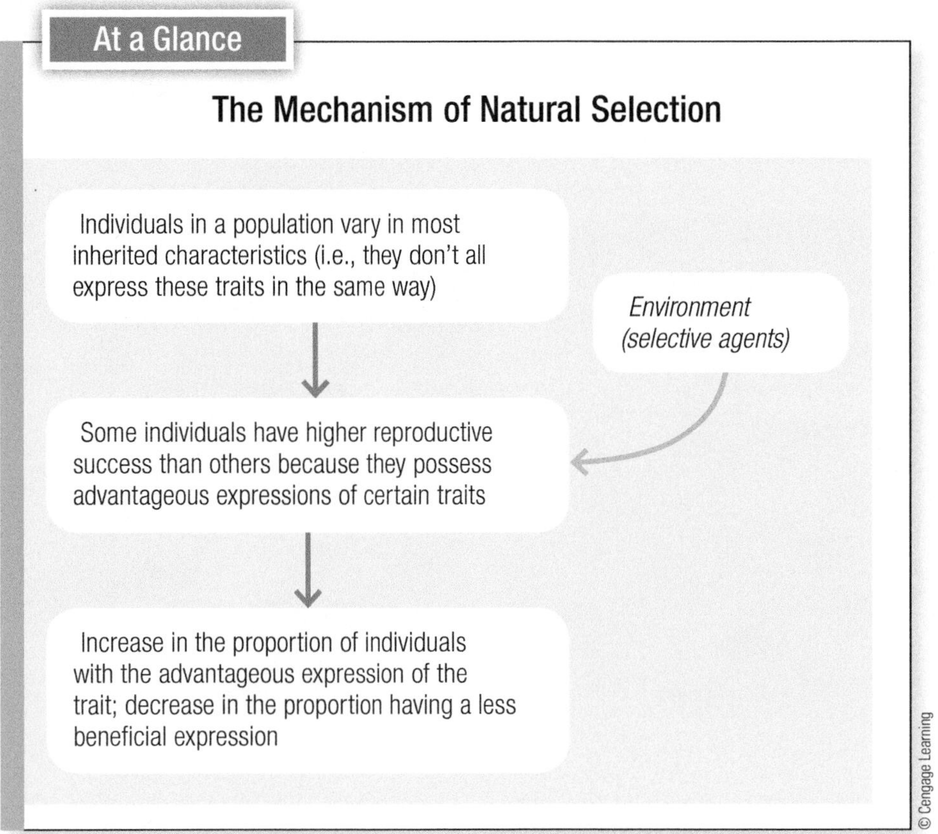

religion, or prohibiting the free exercise thereof." This statement guarantees the separation of church and state, and it means that the government can neither promote nor inhibit the practice of any religion. Therefore the use of public institutions (including schools), paid for by taxes, to promote any particular religion is unconstitutional. Of course this does not mean that individuals can't have private religious discussions or pray in publicly funded institutions; but it does mean that such places can't be used for organized religious events. This hasn't stopped creationists, who encourage teachers to claim "academic freedom" to teach creationism. To avoid objections based on the guarantee of separation of church and state, proponents of ID claim that they don't emphasize any particular religion. But this argument doesn't address the essential point that teaching *any* religious views in a way that promotes them in publicly funded schools is a violation of the U.S. Constitution.

It is curious that the biological process that has led to the appearance of millions of plants and animals on our planet should generate such controversy. Our current understanding of evolution is directly traceable to developments in intellectual thought over the past 400 years. Many people contributed to this shift in perspective; we've named only a few to provide a short historical view. It is quite likely that, in the next 20 years, scientists will identify many of the secrets of our evolutionary past through advances in genetic technologies and the continued discovery of fossil material. For evolutionary science, the early twenty-first century is indeed an exciting time.

How Do We Know?

During the last 150 years, biologists have gathered overwhelming evidence to support evolutionary theory. In this chapter we have emphasized the role of natural selection, which is demonstrated by studying the effects of human selective breeding on such species as domestic dogs. We can see how natural selection causes microevolutionary change by observing alterations over a few decades in many species. And evolutionary change, including speciation, can also be documented much faster (just a few weeks) in rapidly reproducing species such as bacteria.

Within the past 20 years, scientists have developed many techniques that allow them to directly compare different species genetically. In fact, they can now provide reliable estimates as to when two related species last shared a common ancestor, or when they became separate species. For example, Hailer et al (2012) used genetic evidence to suggest that polar bears diverged from their close relative, the European brown bear around 600 kya.*

Prior to the development of recent innovations in genetic research, it was impossible to estimate when speciation events occurred. But by combining fossil and genetic evidence we are now in a position to explain microevolution and the appearance of new species (speciation) in ways that, until recently, were only dreamed of.

*kya = thousand years ago

Summary of Main Topics

- Our current understanding of evolutionary processes is directly traceable to developments in intellectual thought in western Europe and the East over the past 400 years. Darwin and Wallace were able to discover the process of natural selection and evolution because of the discoveries of numerous scientists who had laid the groundwork for them. Among others, Galileo, Lyell, Lamarck, Linnaeus, and Malthus all contributed to a dramatic shift in how people viewed the planet and themselves as part of a system governed by natural processes.
- Charles Darwin and Alfred Russel Wallace recognized that there was variation among individuals in any population (human or nonhuman). Having come to understand how animal breeders selected for certain traits in cattle, pigeons, and other species, Darwin was able to formulate the theory of natural selection. Stated in the simplest terms, natural selection is a process whereby individuals who possess favorable traits (characteristics that permit them to survive and reproduce in a specific environment) will produce more offspring than individuals who have less favorable traits. Over time, the beneficial characteristics will become more frequent in the population, and the makeup of the population (or even a species) will change.
- As populations of a species become reproductively isolated from one another (perhaps because of distance or geographical barriers), they become increasingly different as each population adapts, by means of natural selection, to its own environment. Eventually, the populations may become distinct enough that they can no longer interbreed; at this point, they are considered separate species.
- In the United States, and increasingly in some Muslim countries, the teaching of evolutionary processes is denounced because they are seen as contradictory to certain religious views. In recent years, Christian fundamentalists in the United States have argued in favor of teaching "creation science" or "intelligent design" in public schools. So far, courts have ruled against various attempts to promote "creation science" because the U.S. Constitution provides for the separation of church and state.

Critical Thinking Questions

1. After having read this chapter, how would you respond to the question, "If humans evolved from monkeys, why do we still have monkeys?"
2. We live in an age of unprecedented technological change that is rapidly altering almost all aspects of our lives. Can you think of a paradigm shift that has occurred because of technological innovations in the past 30 years or so?
3. Given what you've read about the scientific method in Chapter 1, how would you explain the differences between science and religion as methods of explaining natural phenomena? Do you personally see a conflict between evolutionary and religious explanations of how species came to be?
4. Can you think of some examples of artificial and natural selection that were not discussed in this chapter? For your examples, what traits have been selected for? In the case of natural selection, what was the selective agent?

Media Resources

Video

See the video "Natural Selection" to learn more about topics covered in this chapter.

Login to your Anthropology CourseMate at www.cengagebrain.com to access videos.

Connections
Evolutionary theory, particularly natural selection, explains how life forms have changed over time.
DNA is the basis of all life.
Heredity is based on the transmission of DNA from one generation to the next.

MedicalRF/Science Source/Photo Researchers

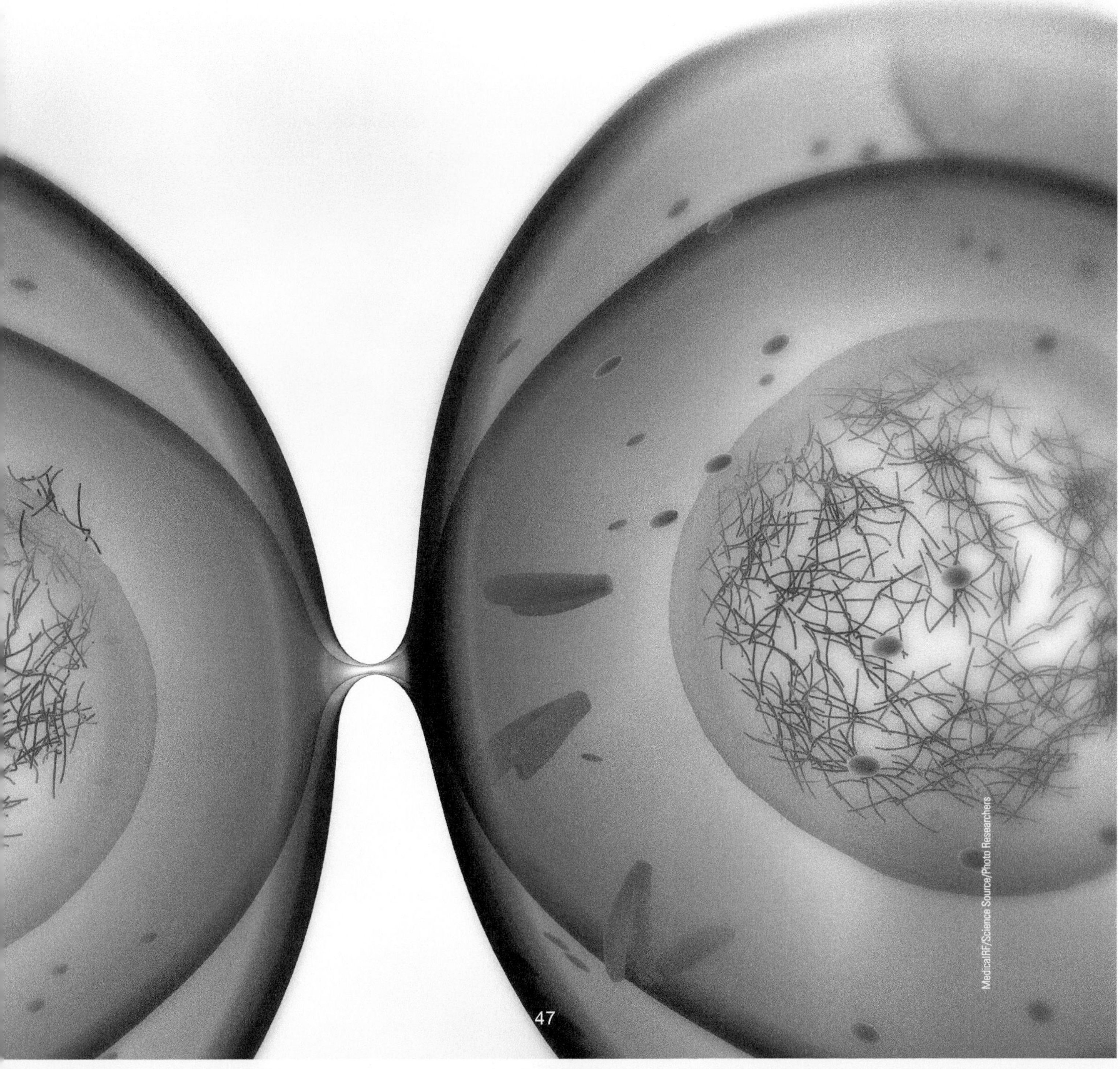

The Biological Basis of Life

3

Student Learning Objectives

After mastering the material in this chapter, you should be able to:

- Discuss why DNA is the biological basis of life and explain some of the scientific evidence showing how all species are ultimately related to one another.
- Understand in general what DNA does.
- Explain why DNA replication has been important to evolutionary processes.
- Discuss what genes do.
- Outline the steps involved in DNA replication and protein synthesis.
- Understand why regulatory genes are important to the evolutionary process.
- Discuss the genetic evidence demonstrating how humans are connected to other species, that is, how we are part of a biological continuum.
- Understand why the study of genetics is critical to biological anthropology today.

You've just gotten home after a rotten day, and you're watching the news on TV. The first story, after around 20 minutes of commercials, is about genetically modified foods, synthetic DNA, or the controversy over stem cell research. What do you do? Change the channel? Press the mute button? Go to sleep? Or do you follow the story? If you watch it, do you understand it, and do you think it's important to you personally? In fact, all of these topics are important to you because you live in an age when genetic discoveries and genetically based technologies are advancing daily, and one way or another, they're going to profoundly affect your life.

At some point, you or someone you love will probably need lifesaving medical treatment, perhaps for cancer, and this treatment will almost certainly be based on genetic research. Like it or not, you already eat genetically modified foods, and you may eventually take advantage of developing reproductive technologies. Sadly, you may also see the development of biological weapons based on genetically altered bacteria and viruses. But fortunately, you'll also live to see many of the secrets of evolution revealed through genetic research. So even if you haven't been particularly interested in genetic issues, you should be aware that they affect your life every day.

As you already know, this book is about human evolution, variation, and adaptation, all of which are ultimately linked to life processes that involve cells, the duplication and decoding of genetic information, and the transmission of this information between generations. So before we go any further, we must examine the basic principles of genetics. Genetics is the study of how genes work and how traits are passed from one generation to the next. Although most physical anthropologists don't specialize in this field, they're very familiar with it because the various subdisciplines of biological anthropology are ultimately connected by genetics.

Cells

In order to discuss genetic and evolutionary principles, it's first necessary to understand the basic functions of cells. Cells are the fundamental units of life in all organisms. In some life-forms, such as bacteria, the entire organism consists of only a single cell (**Fig. 3-1**). However, more complex *multicellular* forms, such as plants, insects, birds, and mammals, are composed of billions of cells. In fact, an adult human body may be composed of as many as 1 trillion (1,000,000,000,000) cells, all functioning in complex ways that ultimately promote the survival of the individual.

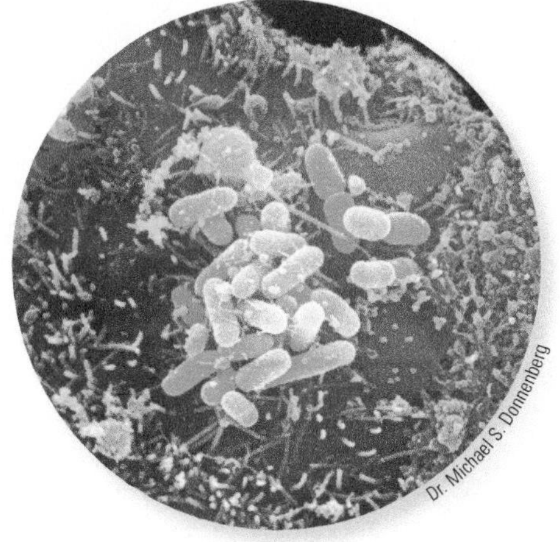

▲ **Figure 3-1** Each one of these pink sausage-shaped structures is a single-celled bacterium.

Life on earth began more than 3.5 billion years ago in the form of single-celled organisms, represented today by bacteria and blue-green algae. Structurally more complex cells, called *eukaryotic* cells, appeared approximately 1.2 billion years ago, and because they are the kind of cell found in multicellular organisms, they will be the focus of this chapter. Despite the numerous differences among various forms of life, it's important to understand that the cells of all living organisms share many similarities because of their common evolutionary past. In this way, all living things are ultimately connected.

In general, a eukaryotic cell is a three-dimensional structure composed of carbohydrates, lipids (fats), nucleic acids, and **proteins**. It also contains several kinds of substructures called *organelles*, one of which is the **nucleus** (*pl.*, nuclei), a discrete unit surrounded by a thin membrane called the *nuclear membrane* (**Fig. 3-2**). Inside the nucleus are two kinds of **molecules** that contain the genetic information that controls the cell's functions.

▶ **Figure 3-2** Structure of a generalized eukaryotic cell, illustrating its three-dimensional nature. Various organelles are shown; but for simplicity, only those we discuss are labeled.

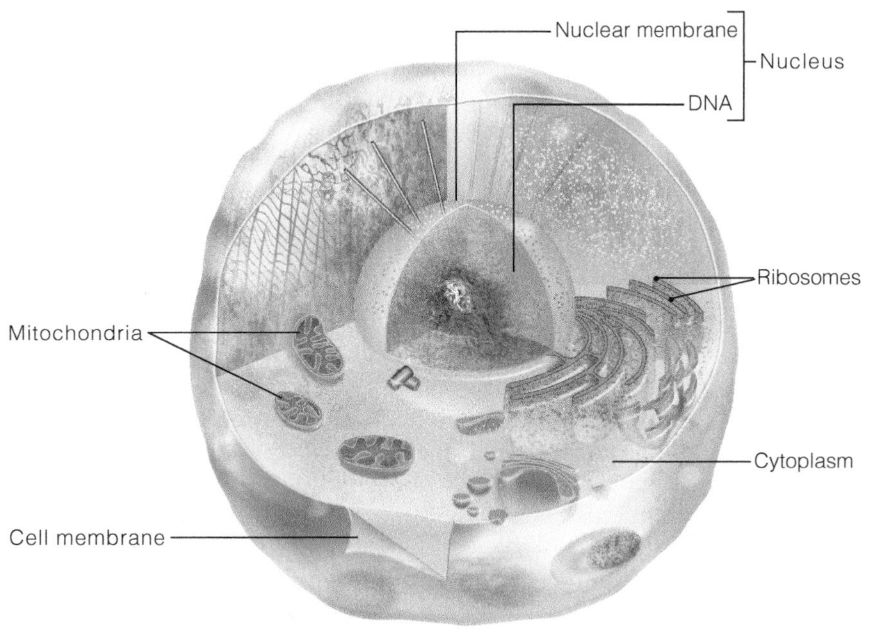

proteins Three-dimensional molecules that serve a wide variety of functions through their ability to bind to other molecules.

nucleus A structure (organelle) found in all eukaryotic cells. The nucleus contains DNA and RNA, among other things.

molecules Structures made up of two or more atoms. Molecules can combine with other molecules to form more complex structures.

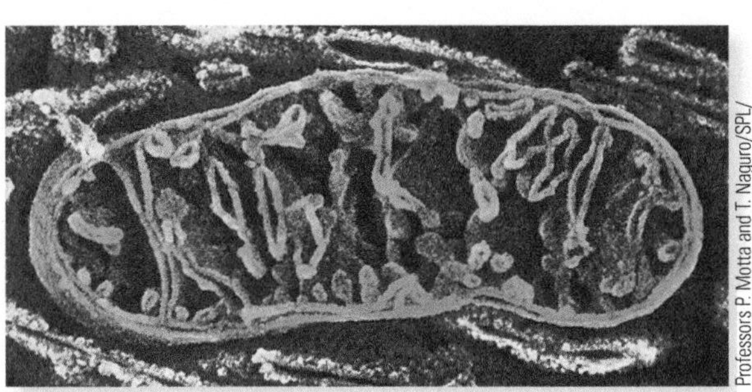

Professors P. Motta and T. Naguro/SPL/ Photo Researchers, Inc.

◄**Figure 3-3** Scanning electron micrograph of a mitochondrion.

Actually, these two molecules, **DNA (deoxyribonucleic acid)** and **RNA (ribonucleic acid)**, are fundamental not only to cellular activities but also to life itself.

The nucleus is surrounded by a gel-like substance called **cytoplasm**, which contains many other types of organelles involved in activities related to the function of the cell and organism. These activities include breaking down nutrients and converting them to other substances, storing and releasing energy, eliminating waste, and manufacturing proteins through a process called **protein synthesis**.

Two of these organelles, **mitochondria** (*sing.*, mitochondrion) and **ribosomes**, require further mention. Mitochondria (**Fig. 3-3**) produce energy and can be thought of as the cell's engines. Mitochondria are structures enclosed within a folded membrane and contain their own distinct DNA, called **mitochondrial DNA (mtDNA)**, which directs mitochondrial activities. Mitochondrial DNA has the same molecular structure and function as nuclear DNA (that is, DNA found in the nucleus), but it's organized somewhat differently. In recent years, mtDNA has attracted a lot of attention because of the traits it influences and because it can be used to study certain evolutionary processes. For these reasons, we'll discuss mitochondrial inheritance in more detail later. Ribosomes, which will also be discussed later, are partly composed of RNA. They're important because they're essential to protein synthesis.

There are basically two types of cells: **somatic cells** and **gametes**. Somatic cells make up the body tissues, such as muscles, bones, organs, and the brain. Gametes, or sex cells, are specifically involved in reproduction and are not important as structural components of the body. There are two types of gametes: egg cells, produced in female ovaries, and sperm cells, which develop in male testes. The sole function of a sex cell is to unite with a gamete from another individual to form a **zygote**, which has the potential of developing into a new individual. In this way, gametes transmit genetic information from parent to offspring.

The Structure of DNA

DNA is the very basis of life because it directs all cellular activities. So if we want to understand these activities and how traits are inherited, we must know something about the structure and function of DNA. The exact physical and chemical properties of DNA were unknown until 1953, when, at the University of Cambridge, in England, an American researcher named James Watson and three British scientists, Francis Crick, Maurice Wilkins, and Rosalind Franklin, developed a structural and functional model of DNA (Watson and Crick, 1953a, b). It's impossible to overstate the importance of this achievement because it completely revolutionized the fields of biology and medicine and forever altered our understanding of biological and evolutionary mechanisms (see "A Closer Look: Rosalind Franklin: The Fourth [but Invisible] Member of the Double Helix Team").

The DNA molecule is composed of two chains of even smaller units called **nucleotides**. A nucleotide, in turn, is made up of three components: a sugar molecule (deoxyribose), a phosphate group (a molecule composed of phosphorus and oxygen), and one of four nitrogenous *bases* (**Fig. 3-4**). In DNA, nucleotides are stacked on top of one

DNA (deoxyribonucleic acid) The double-stranded molecule that contains the genetic code. DNA is a main component of chromosomes.

RNA (ribonucleic acid) A single-stranded molecule similar in structure to DNA. Three forms of RNA are essential to protein synthesis: messenger RNA (mRNA), transfer RNA (tRNA), and ribosomal RNA (rRNA)

cytoplasm The semifluid, gel-like substance contained within the cell membrane. The nucleus and numerous structures involved with cell function are found within the cytoplasm.

protein synthesis The manufacture of proteins; that is, the assembly of chains of amino acids into functional protein molecules. Protein synthesis is directed by DNA.

mitochondria (*sing.*, mitochondrion) Structures contained within the cytoplasm of eukaryotic cells that convert energy, derived from nutrients, to a form that can be used by the cell.

ribosomes Structures composed of a form of RNA called ribosomal RNA (rRNA) and protein. Ribosomes are found in a cell's cytoplasm and are essential to the manufacture of proteins.

mitochondrial DNA (mtDNA) DNA found in the mitochondria. Mitochondrial DNA is inherited only from the mother.

somatic cells Basically, all the cells in the body except those involved with reproduction.

gametes Reproductive cells (eggs and sperm in animals) developed from precursor cells in ovaries and testes.

zygote A cell formed by the union of an egg cell and a sperm cell. It contains the full complement of chromosomes (in humans, 46) and has the potential of developing into an entire organism.

nucleotides Basic units of the DNA molecule, composed of a sugar, a phosphate, and one of four DNA bases.

A Closer Look

Rosalind Franklin: The Fourth (but Invisible) Member of the Double Helix Team

In 1962, three men, James Watson, Francis Crick, and Maurice Wilkins, won the Nobel Prize for medicine and physiology. They earned this most prestigious of all scientific honors for their discovery of the structure of the DNA molecule, which they had published in 1953. But due credit was not given to a fourth, equally deserving but unacknowledged person named Rosalind Franklin, who had died of ovarian cancer in 1958. But even if she had been acknowledged in 1962, Franklin still wouldn't have been a Nobel recipient because the Nobel Prize isn't awarded posthumously.

Franklin was a chemist who went to the University of Cambridge in 1951, after being invited to study the structure of DNA. Before that, she'd been in Paris using a technique called x-ray diffraction, a process that reveals the positions of atoms in crystalline structures. What Franklin didn't know was that a colleague in her Cambridge lab, Maurice Wilkins, was working on the same DNA project. To make matters worse, Wilkins hadn't been told what her position was, so he thought she'd been hired as his assistant. Needless to say, this was hardly a good way to begin a working relationship, and as you might expect, there were a few tense moments between them.

Franklin soon produced some excellent x-ray diffraction images of some DNA fibers that Wilkins had provided, and the images clearly showed that the structure was helical. Furthermore, she worked out that there were two strands, not one. Wilkins innocently (but without Franklin's knowledge) showed the images to Watson and Crick, who were working in another laboratory, also at Cambridge. Within 2 weeks, Watson and Crick had developed their now famous model of a double-stranded helix without Franklin's knowledge.

▲ **Figure 1** Rosalind Franklin

Desperately unhappy at Cambridge, Franklin took a position at King's College, London, in 1953. In April of that year, she and a student published an article in the journal *Nature* that dealt indirectly with the helical structure of DNA. The article by Watson and Crick was published in the same issue.

During her lifetime, Franklin gained recognition for her work in carbons, coal, and viruses, topics on which she published many articles; and she was happy with the reputation she achieved. After her death, Watson made many derogative comments about Rosalind Franklin, including several in print. Even so, it appears that they remained on friendly terms until she died at the age of 37. She also remained friendly with Crick, but she never knew that their revolutionary discovery was partly made possible by her photographic images.

another to form a chain that is bonded by its bases to another nucleotide chain. Together the two chains twist to form a spiral, or helical shape. Thus, the DNA molecule is double-stranded and is described as forming a *double helix* that resembles a twisted ladder. If we follow the twisted ladder analogy, the sugars and phosphates represent the two sides while the bases and the bonds that join them form the rungs.

The four bases are the key to how DNA works. These bases are *adenine, guanine, thymine,* and *cytosine,* usually referred to by their initial letters: A, G, T, and C. When the double helix is formed, one type of base is able to pair, or bond, with only one other type: A can pair only with T, and G can pair only with C (**Fig. 3-4**). This specificity is absolutely essential to the DNA molecule's ability to **replicate**, or make an exact copy of itself.

replicate To duplicate. The DNA molecule is able to make copies of itself.

DNA Replication

Cells multiply by dividing to make exact copies of themselves. This, in turn, enables organisms to grow and injured tissues to heal. There are two kinds of cell division. In the simpler

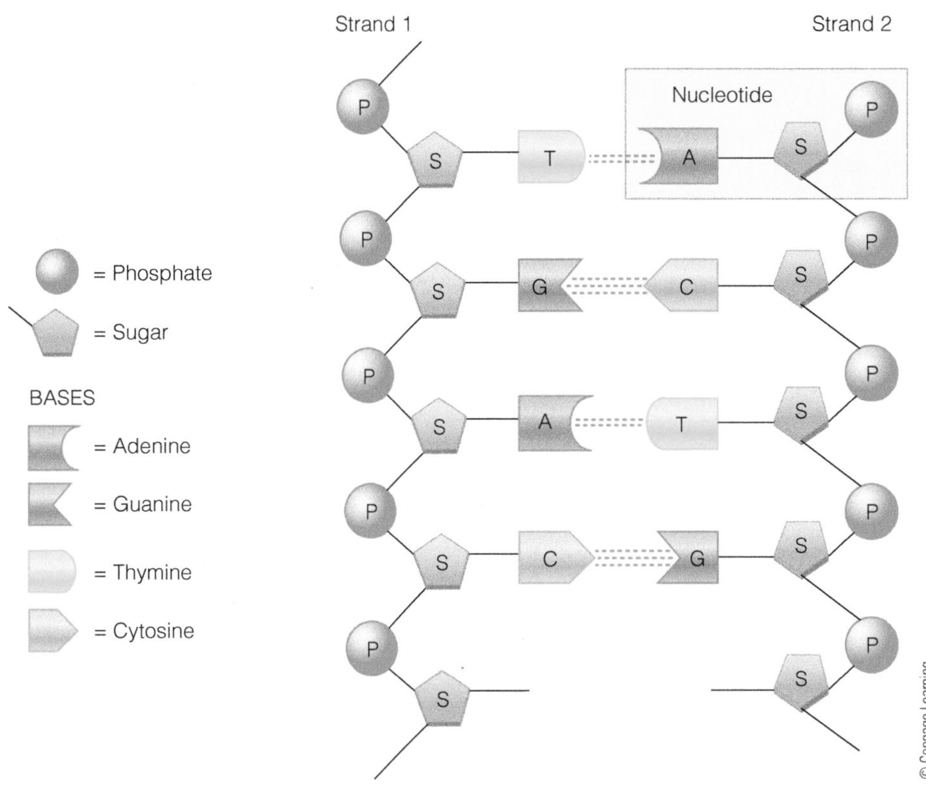

◄ **Figure 3-4** Part of a DNA molecule. The illustration shows the two DNA strands with the sugar (green) and phosphate (purple) molecules forming the sides of the strands and the bases (labeled T, A, G, and C) joined together in the middle.

form, a cell divides one time to produce two "daughter" cells, each of which receives a full set of genetic material. This is important, because a cell can't function properly without the right amount of DNA. But before a cell can divide, its DNA must replicate.

Replication begins when **enzymes** break the bonds between bases throughout the DNA molecule, separating the two previously joined strands of nucleotides and leaving their bases exposed (**Fig. 3-5**). These exposed bases then attract unattached DNA nucleotides that have been made by DNA elsewhere in the cell nucleus. Because each base can pair with only one other, the attraction between bases occurs in a **complementary** way. This means that the two previously joined parental nucleotide chains serve as models, or templates, for forming new strands of nucleotides. As each new strand is formed, its bases are joined to the bases of an original strand. When the process is complete, there are two double-stranded DNA molecules exactly like the original one. Importantly, each newly formed molecule consists of one original nucleotide chain joined to a newly formed chain.

Protein Synthesis

One of the most important activities of DNA is to direct the assembly of proteins (protein synthesis) within cells. Proteins are complex three-dimensional molecules that function through their ability to bind to other molecules. For example, the protein **hemoglobin** (**Fig. 3-6**), found in red blood cells, is able to bind to oxygen, which it carries to cells throughout the body.

Proteins function in countless ways. Some, such as collagen (the most common protein in the body), are structural components of tissues. Enzymes are also proteins, which regulate chemical reactions. For example, a digestive enzyme called *lactase* breaks down *lactose*, or milk sugar, into two simpler sugars. Another class of proteins

enzymes Specialized proteins that initiate and direct chemical reactions in the body.

complementary In genetics, referring to the fact that DNA bases form pairs (called base pairs) in a precise manner. For example, adenine can bond only to thymine. These two bases are said to be complementary because one requires the other to form a complete DNA base pair.

hemoglobin A protein molecule that occurs in red blood cells and binds to oxygen molecules.

hormones Substances (usually proteins) that are produced by specialized cells and that travel to other parts of the body, where they influence chemical reactions and regulate various cellular functions.

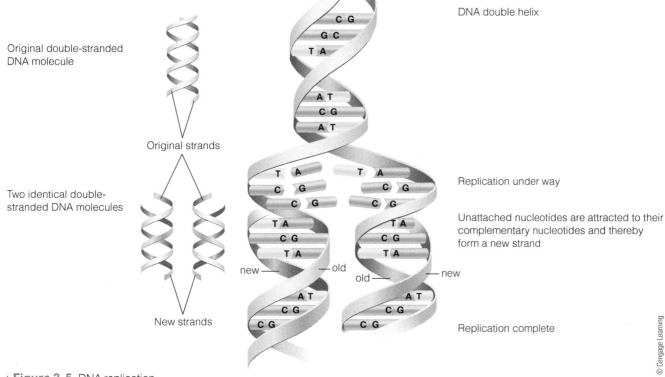

Original double-stranded DNA molecule
Original strands
Two identical double-stranded DNA molecules
New strands
DNA double helix
Replication under way
Unattached nucleotides are attracted to their complementary nucleotides and thereby form a new strand
Replication complete
© Cengage Learning

▲**Figure 3-5** DNA replication. During DNA replication, the two strands of the DNA molecule (purple) are separated, and each strand serves as a template for the formation of a new strand (brown). When replication is complete, there are two DNA molecules, each consisting of one new strand and one original strand.

includes many types of **hormones**. Hormones are produced by specialized cells and then released into the bloodstream to circulate to other parts of the body, where they produce specific effects in tissues and organs. Insulin, for example, is a hormone produced by cells in the pancreas, but it functions in the liver where it causes cells in the liver to absorb energy-producing glucose (sugar) from the blood. People whose pancreatic cells fail to produce sufficient amounts of insulin have one of the two types of diabetes. Lastly, many kinds of proteins can enter a cell's nucleus and attach directly to its DNA. This is very important because when these proteins bind to the DNA, they can regulate its activity. From this brief description, you can see that proteins make us what we are. So protein synthesis must occur accurately, because if it doesn't, physiological development and cellular activities can be disrupted or even prevented.

Proteins are made up of chains of smaller molecules called **amino acids**. In all, there are 20 amino acids, 8 of which must be obtained from foods (see Chapter 16). The remaining 12 are produced in cells. These 20 amino acids are combined in different amounts and sequences to produce at least 90,000 different proteins. What makes proteins different from one another is the number and sequence of their amino acids.

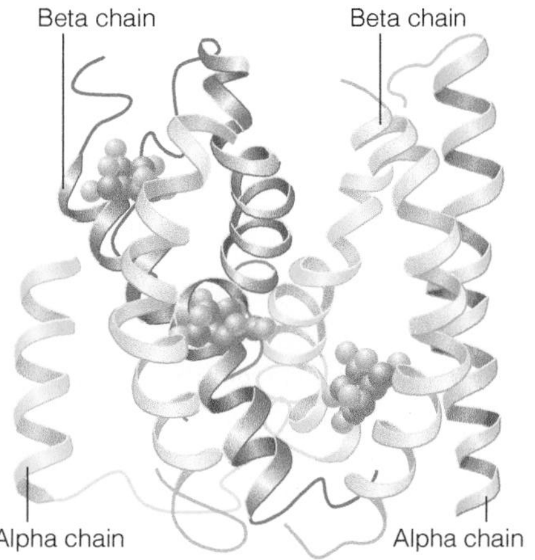

▶**Figure 3-6** Diagrammatic representation of a hemoglobin molecule. Hemoglobin molecules are composed of four chains of amino acids (two alpha chains and two beta chains).

amino acids Small molecules that are the components of proteins.

Table 3.1 **The Genetic Code**

Amino Acid Symbol	Amino Acid	mRNA Codon	DNA Triplet
Ala	Alanine	GCU, GCC, GCA, GCG	CGA, CGG, CGT, CGC
Arg	Arginine	CGU, CGC, CGA, CGG, AGA, AGG	GCA, GCG, GCT, GCC, TCT, TCC
Asn	Asparagine	AAU, AAC	TTA, TTG
Asp	Aspartic acid	GAU, GAC	CTA, CTG
Cys	Cysteine	UGU, UGC	ACA, ACG
Gln	Glutamine	CAA, CAG	GTT, GTC
Glu	Glutamic acid	GAA, GAG	CTT, CTC
Gly	Glycine	GGU, GGC, GGA, GGG	CCA, CCG, CCT, CCC
His	Histidine	CAU, CAC	GTA, GTG
Ile	Isoleucine	AUU, AUC, AUA	TAA, TAG, TAT
Leu	Leucine	UUA, UUG, CUU, CUC, CUA, CUG	AAT, AAC, GAA, GAG, GAT, GAC
Lys	Lysine	AAA, AAG	TTT, TTC
Met	Methionine	AUG	TAC
Phe	Phenylalanine	UUU, UUC	AAA, AAG
Pro	Proline	CCU, CCC, CCA, CCG	GGA, GGG, GGT, GGC
Ser	Serine	UCU, UCC, UCA, UCG, AGU, AGC	AGA, AGG, AGT, AGC, TCA, TCG
Thr	Threonine	ACU, ACC, ACA, ACG	TGA, TGG, TGT, TGC
Trp	Tryptophan	UGG	ACC
Tyr	Tyrosine	UAU, UAC	ATA, ATG
Val	Valine	GUU, GUC, GUA, GUG	CAA, CAG, CAT, CAC
Terminating triplets		UAA, UAG, UGA	ATT, ATC, ACT

In part, DNA is a recipe for making a protein, because it's the sequence of DNA bases that ultimately determines the order of amino acids in a protein. In the DNA instructions, a *triplet*, or group of three bases, specifies a particular amino acid. For example, if a triplet consists of the base sequence cytosine, guanine, and adenine (CGA), it specifies the amino acid arginine (**Table 3.1**). Therefore, a small portion of a DNA recipe might look like this (except that there would be no spaces between the triplets): AGA CGA ACA ACC TAC TTT TTC CTT AAG GTC.

Protein synthesis actually takes place outside the cell nucleus, in the cytoplasm at the ribosomes. But the DNA molecule can't leave the cell's nucleus. Therefore the first step in protein synthesis is to copy the DNA message into a form of RNA called **messenger RNA (mRNA)**, which can pass through the nuclear membrane into the cytoplasm. RNA is similar to DNA but it differs in some important ways:

1. It's single-stranded. (This is true for the forms we discuss here but not true for all forms of RNA.)
2. It contains a different type of sugar.
3. It contains the base uracil as a substitute for the DNA base thymine. (Uracil binds to adenine in the same way thymine does.)

The mRNA molecule forms on the DNA template in pretty much the same way that new DNA molecules do. As

messenger RNA (mRNA) A form of RNA that's assembled on a sequence of DNA bases. It carries the DNA code to the ribosome during protein synthesis.

in DNA replication, the two DNA strands separate, but only partially, and one of these strands attracts free-floating RNA nucleotides (also produced in the cell), which are joined together on the DNA template. The formation of mRNA is called *transcription* because, in fact, the DNA code is being copied, or transcribed (**Fig. 3-7**). Transcription continues until a section of DNA called a terminator region (composed of one of three specific DNA triplets) is reached and the process stops (see Table 3-1). At this point, the mRNA strand, comprising anywhere from 5,000 to perhaps as many as 200,000 nucleotides, peels away from the DNA model, and a portion of it travels through the nuclear membrane to the ribosome. Meanwhile, the bonds between the DNA bases are reestablished and the DNA molecule is once more intact.

As the mRNA strand arrives at the ribosome, its message is translated, or decoded (**Fig. 3-8**). Just as each DNA triplet specifies

▼**Figure 3-7** Transcription. In this illustration, the two DNA strands have partly separated. Messenger RNA (mRNA) nucleotides have been drawn to the template strand and a strand of mRNA is being made. Note that the mRNA strand will exactly complement the DNA template strand except that uracil (U) replaces thymine (T).

a As the ribosome binds to the mRNA, tRNA brings a particular amino acid, specified by the mRNA codon, to the ribosome.

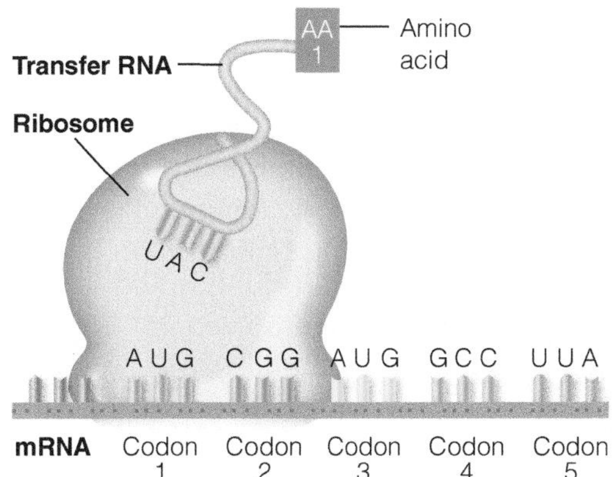

b The tRNA binds to the first codon while a second tRNA–amino acid complex arrives at the ribosome.

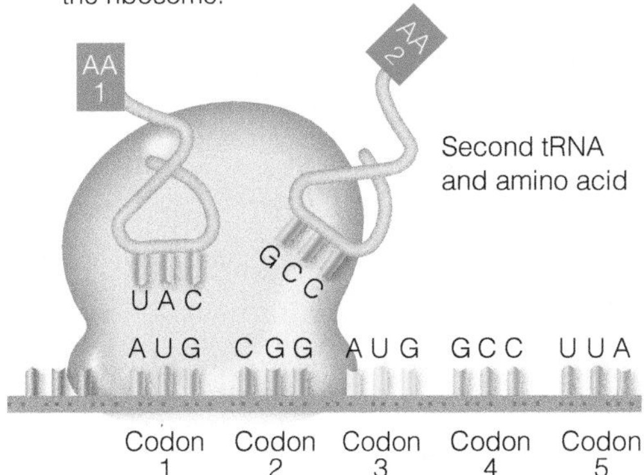

c The ribosome moves down the mRNA, allowing a third amino acid to be brought into position by another tRNA molecule. Note that the first two amino acids are now joined together.

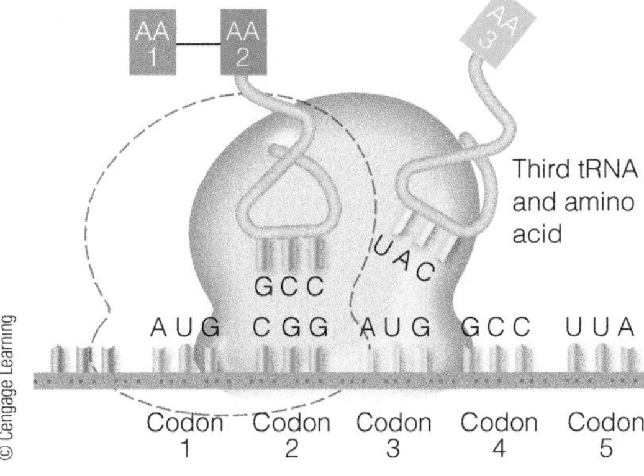

▲**Figure 3-8** Assembly of an amino acid chain in protein synthesis.

one amino acid, so do mRNA triplets, which are called **codons**. Therefore the mRNA strand is "read" in codons, or groups of three mRNA bases at a time (see Table 3-1). Subsequently, another form of RNA, called **transfer RNA (tRNA)**, brings each amino acid to the ribosome. The ribosome then joins that amino acid to another amino acid in the order dictated by the sequence of mRNA codons (or, ultimately, DNA triplets). In this way, amino acids are linked together to form a molecule that will eventually be a protein or part of a protein. But it's important to mention that if a DNA base or sequence of bases is changed through **mutation**, some proteins may not be made or they may be defective. In this case, cells won't function properly, or they may not function at all.

What Is a Gene?

The answer to this question is complicated, and the definition of the term **gene** is currently the subject of some debate. In the past, textbooks compared genes to a string of beads, with each bead representing one gene on a chromosome. For 50 years or so, biologists considered a gene to be an uninterrupted sequence of DNA bases responsible for the manufacture of a protein or part of a protein. Or, put another way, a gene could be defined as *a segment of DNA that specifies the sequence of amino acids in a particular protein*. This definition, based on the concept of a one gene–one protein relationship, was a core principle in biology for decades, but it's been substantially modified, partly in recognition of the fact that DNA codes not only for proteins but also for RNA and other DNA nucleotides.

Moreover, when the human **genome** was sequenced in 2001, scientists determined that humans have only about 25,000 genes (International Human Genome Sequencing Consortium, 2001; Venter et al., 2001). This number has now been revised to approximately 21,000 (Pennisi, 2012). Yet we produce as many as 90,000 proteins! Furthermore, protein-coding genes (also called *coding sequences*), the DNA segments that are transcribed into proteins, make up only about 2 to 3 percent of the entire human genome! The rest is composed of **noncoding DNA**, or what used to be called "junk DNA" (see A Closer Look: Noncoding DNA—Not Junk After All). Thus gene action is much more complicated than previously believed and it's impossible for every protein to be coded for by a specific gene. This shift in perspective is a good example of something we discussed in Chapter 1, that hypotheses and theories can and do change over time as we continue to acquire new knowledge.

Geneticists have also learned that only some parts of genes, called **exons**, are actually transcribed into mRNA and thus code for specific amino acids. In fact, most of the nucleotide sequences in genes are not expressed during protein synthesis. (By *expressed* we mean that the DNA sequence is actually making a product.) Many sequences, called **introns**, are initially transcribed into mRNA and then clipped out (Fig. 3-9). Therefore introns aren't translated into amino acid sequences. Moreover, the intron segments that are snipped out of a gene aren't always the same ones. This means that the exons can be combined in different ways to make segments that code for more than one protein. That's how 21,000 coding sequences can make 90,000 proteins. Genes can also overlap one another, and there can be genes within genes (Fig. 3-10). But they're still a part of the DNA molecule, and it's the combination of introns

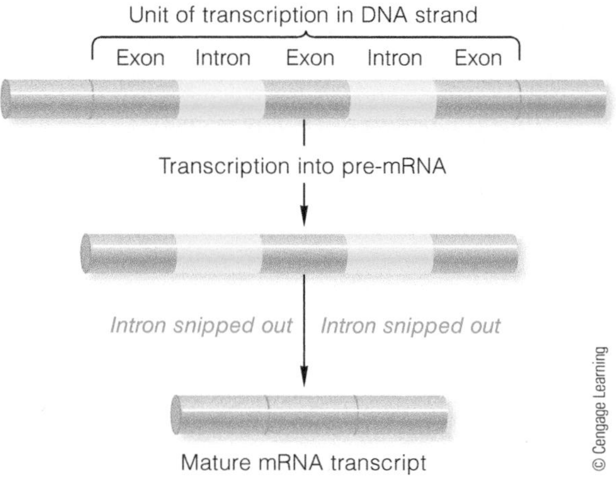

▲ **Figure 3-9** Diagram of a DNA sequence being transcribed. The introns are deleted from pre-mRNA before it leaves the cell's nucleus. The remaining mature RNA contains only exons, which will code for a protein or part of a protein.

codons Triplets of messenger RNA bases that code for specific amino acids during protein synthesis.

transfer RNA (tRNA) A type of RNA that binds to specific amino acids and transports them to the ribosome during protein synthesis.

mutation A change in DNA. The term can refer to changes in DNA bases (specifically called point mutations) as well as to changes in chromosome number and/or structure.

gene A sequence of DNA bases that specifies the order of amino acids in an entire protein, a portion of a protein, or any functional product, such as RNA. A gene may be composed of thousands of DNA bases.

genome The entire genetic makeup of an individual or species. In humans, it's estimated that the human genome comprises about 3 billion DNA bases.

noncoding DNA DNA that does not direct the production of proteins. However, such DNA segments produce thousands of molecules (for example, RNA) that are involved in gene regulation. Thus the term noncoding DNA is misleading.

exons Segments of genes that are transcribed and are involved in protein synthesis. (The prefix *ex* denotes that these segments are expressed.)

introns Segments of genes that are initially transcribed and then deleted. Because introns are not expressed, they aren't involved in protein synthesis.

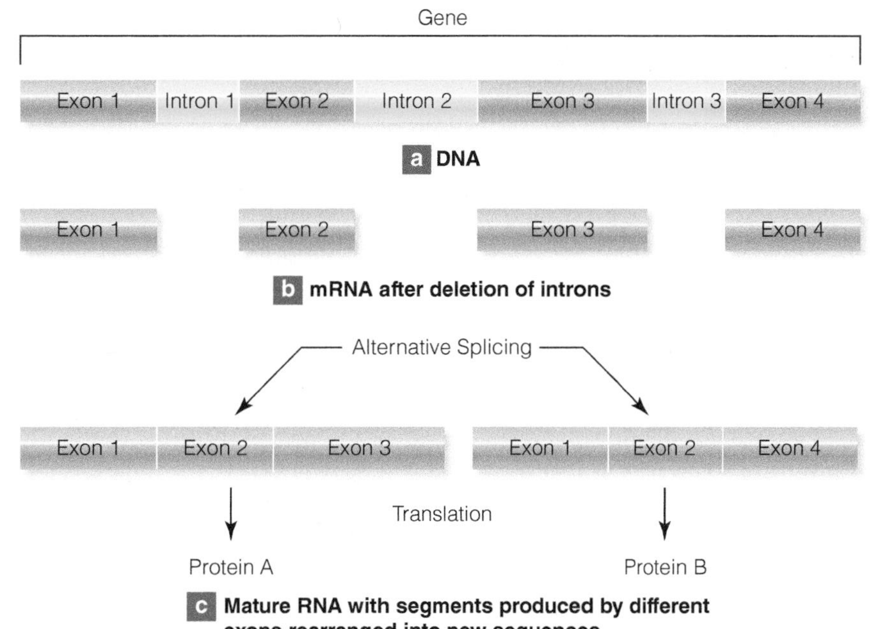

▶ **Figure 3-10** Diagrammatic representation of how our views of gene function have changed. According to the traditional view, genes are discrete segments of DNA, each coding for a specific protein. (**a**) We now know that genes are composed of some DNA segments that are expressed (exons), and others that are not (introns). (**b**) Introns aren't expressed because they're deleted during the formation of mRNA. (**c**) The remaining exons can be rearranged to form several different coding sequences, each of which produces a different protein.

and exons, interspersed along a DNA strand, that makes up the unit we call a gene. So much for beads on a string.

Clearly, the answer to the question "What is a gene?" is complicated, and a completely accurate definition may be a long time coming. However, a proposed and more inclusive definition simply states that a gene is "a complete chromosomal segment responsible for making a functional product" (Snyder and Gerstein, 2003).

In spite of all the recently obtained information that has changed some of our views and expanded our knowledge of DNA, there is one fact that doesn't change. The genetic code is *universal*, and at least on earth, DNA is the molecule that governs the expression, inheritance, and evolution of biological traits in all forms of life. The DNA of all organisms, from bacteria to oak trees to fruit flies to human beings, is composed of the same molecules using the same kinds of instructions. The DNA triplet CGA, for example, specifies the amino acid alanine regardless of species. These similarities imply biological relationships between all forms of life—and a common ancestry as well. What makes fruit flies distinct from humans isn't differences in the DNA material itself, but differences in how that material is arranged and regulated.

regulatory genes Genes that influence the activity of other genes. Regulatory genes direct embryonic development and are involved in physiological processes throughout life. They are critically important to the evolutionary process.

Regulatory Genes

Some genes act solely to control the expression of other genes. Basically these **regulatory genes** make various kinds of RNA, proteins, and other molecules that switch other DNA segments (genes) on or off. Also, many regulatory genes diminish or enhance the expression of other genes. They play a fundamental role in embryological development, cellular function, and evolution. In fact, without them, life as we know it could not exist. The study of regulatory genes and their role in evolution is still in its infancy; but as information about them continues to accumulate, we will eventually be able to answer many of the questions we still have about the evolution of species.

DNA deactivation during embryonic development is one good example of how regulatory genes work. As you know, all somatic cells contain the same genetic information; but in any given cell, only a fraction of the DNA is actually involved in protein synthesis. For example, like the cells of the stomach lining, bone cells have DNA that codes for the production of digestive enzymes. But bone cells don't produce digestive enzymes. Instead, they make collagen, the main organic component of bone. This is because cells become

A Closer Look

Noncoding DNA—Not Junk After All

In all fields of inquiry, important discoveries always raise new questions that eventually lead to further revelations. There's probably no statement that could be more appropriately applied to the field of genetics. For example, in 1977, geneticists recognized that during protein synthesis, the initially formed mRNA molecule contains many more nucleotides than are represented in the subsequently produced protein. This finding led to the discovery of *introns*, portions of genes that don't code for proteins. In the 1980s, geneticists learned that only about 2 percent of human DNA is contained within exons, the segments that actually provide the code for protein synthesis. We also know that a human gene can specify the production of as many as three different proteins by using different combinations of the exons interspersed within it (Pennisi, 2005).

As discussed earlier, with only 2 percent of the human genome directing protein synthesis, humans have more non-protein coding DNA than any other species so far studied. Invertebrates and some vertebrates have only small amounts of noncoding sequences, and yet they're fully functional organisms. So just what does all this noncoding DNA (originally called "junk DNA") do in humans? Apparently much of it codes for different forms of RNA that act to regulate gene function, but it does not directly participate in protein synthesis (Pennisi, 2012; the ENCODE Project Consortium, 2012).

Almost half of all human DNA consists of noncoding segments that are repeated over and over and over. Depending on their length, these segments have been referred to as tandem repeats, satellites, or microsatellites, but now they're frequently lumped together and called copy number variants (CNVs). Microsatellites have an extremely high mutation rate and can gain or lose repeated segments and then return to their former length. But this tendency to mutate means that the number of repeats in a given microsatellite varies between individuals. And this tremendous variation has been the basis for DNA fingerprinting, a technique commonly used to provide evidence in criminal cases. Actually, anthropologists are now using microsatellite variation for all kinds of research, from tracing migrations of populations to paternity testing in nonhuman primates.

Some of the variations in microsatellite composition are associated with various disorders, so we can't help wondering why these variations exist. One answer is that some microsatellites influence the activities of protein coding DNA sequences. Also, by losing or adding material, they can alter the sequences of bases in genes, thus becoming a source of mutation in functional genes. And these mutations are a source of genetic variation.

Lastly, there are transposable elements (TEs), the so-called *jumping genes*. These are DNA sequences that can make thousands of copies of themselves, which are then scattered throughout the genome. One family of TEs, called Alu, is found only in primates. About 5 percent of the human genome is made up of Alu sequences, and although most of these are shared with other primates, about 7,000 are unique to humans (Chimpanzee Sequencing and Analysis Consortium, 2005).

TEs mainly code for proteins that enable them to move about, and because they can land right in the middle of coding sequences (exons), TEs cause mutations. Some of these mutations are harmful, and TEs have been associated with numerous disease conditions, including some forms of cancer (Deragon and Capy, 2000). But at the same time, TEs essentially create new exons, thereby generating variations on which natural selection can act. Moreover, they also regulate the activities of many genes, including those involved in development. So rather than being junk, TEs are increasingly being recognized as serving extremely important functions in the evolutionary process, including the introduction of genetic changes that have led to the origin of new lineages.

specialized during embryonic development to perform only certain functions, and most of their DNA is permanently switched off by regulatory genes. In other words, they become specific types of cells, such as bone cells.

There are thousands of kinds of regulatory genes and one crucially important group is referred to as **homeobox genes**. The best known homeobox genes are the *Hox* genes, which direct the early segmentation of embryonic tissues. They also determine the identity of individual segments, by specifying what they will become, such as part of the head or thorax. *Hox* genes interact with other genes to determine the characteristics of developing body segments and structures but not their actual development. For example, they determine where, in a developing embryo, limb buds will appear; and they establish the number and overall pattern of the different types of vertebrae, the bones that make up the spine (**Fig. 3-11**).

homeobox genes An evolutionarily ancient family of regulatory genes that directs the development of the overall body plan and the segmentation of body tissues. There are at least 20 families of homeobox genes.

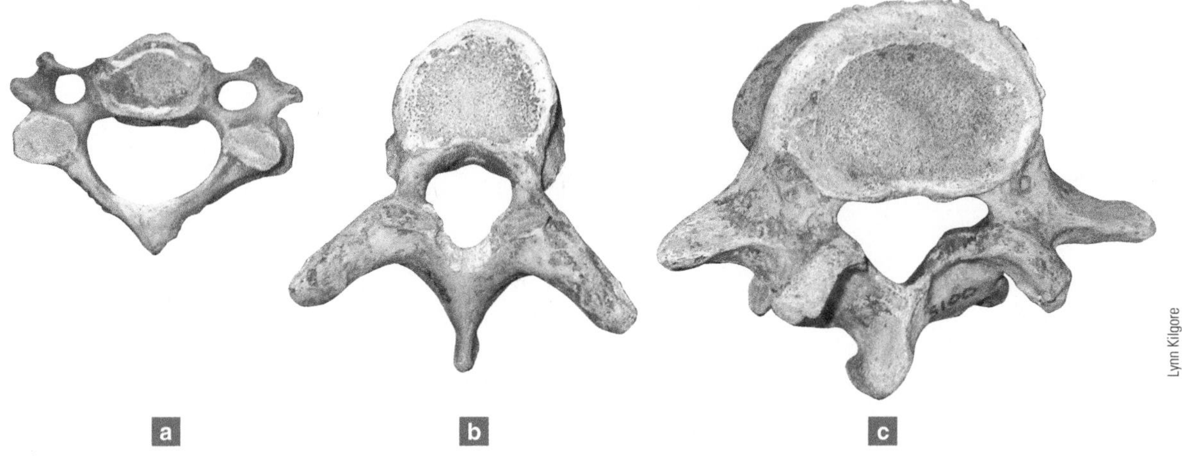

▲ **Figure 3-11** The differences in these three vertebrae, from different regions of the spine, are caused by the action of *Hox* genes during embryonic development. (**a**) The cervical (neck) vertebrae have characteristics that differentiate them from (**b**) thoracic vertebrae, which are attached to the ribs, and also from (**c**) lumbar vertebrae of the lower back. *Hox* genes determine the overall pattern not only of each type of vertebra but also of each individual vertebra.

All homeobox genes are highly conserved, meaning that they've been maintained throughout much of evolutionary history. They're present in all invertebrates (such as worms and insects) and vertebrates, and they don't vary greatly from species to species. This type of conservation means not only that these genes are vitally important but also that they evolved from genes that were present in some of the earliest forms of life. Moreover, changes in the behavior of homeobox genes are responsible for various physical differences between closely related species or different breeds of domesticated animals. For these reasons, homeobox genes, and the many other kinds of regulatory genes, are now a critical area of research in evolutionary and developmental biology.

The finches of the Galápagos Islands provide an excellent example of how regulatory genes influence evolutionary change. In Chapter 2, we saw how Charles Darwin came to recognize that variation in these finches was an example of natural selection. Scientists have now explained the genetic basis for some of the finch variation by identifying two of the regulatory genes involved in the shape and size of bird beaks (Abzhanov et al., 2004, 2006). One of these genes (also involved in bone formation) is expressed to a greater degree during the embryonic development of wide-beaked ground fiches than in that of finches with narrower beaks. Likewise, another gene is more active during beak development in finches that have longer, narrower beaks. Therefore the length and width of bird beaks are controlled by the activity of at least two different regulatory genes, allowing each aspect of beak size to evolve separately.

There are many other types of highly conserved genes as well. For example, recent sequencing of the sea sponge genome has shown that humans share many genes with sea sponges (Srivastava et al., 2010). This doesn't mean that sponges were ancestral to humans, but it does mean that we have genes that were already in existence some 600 mya. These genes ultimately laid the foundation for the evolution of complex animals, and they're crucial to many of the basic cellular processes that are fundamental to life today. These processes include a cell's ability to recognize foreign cells (immunity), the development of specific cell types, and signaling between cells during growth and development.

We cannot overstate the importance of regulatory genes in evolution. The fact that these genes, with little modification, are present in all complex (as well as in some not so complex) organisms, including humans, is the basis of biological continuity between species.

At a Glance

Coding and Noncoding DNA

Coding DNA	Noncoding DNA
Codes for sequences of amino acids (i.e., functional proteins) or RNA molecules	Function not well known, but some (perhaps many) noncoding segments regulate the activities of protein-coding genes. This terminology may change as more discoveries are made.
Comprises approximately 2% of human nuclear DNA	Comprises about 98% of human nuclear DNA
Includes exons within functional genes	Includes introns within functional genes and multiple repeated segments elsewhere on chromosomes

Mutation: When Genes Change

The best way to understand how genes function is to see what happens when they change, or mutate. Normal adult hemoglobin is made up of four amino acid chains (two *alpha* chains and two *beta* chains) that are the direct products of gene action. Each beta chain is in turn composed of 146 amino acids. There are several hemoglobin disorders with genetic origins, and perhaps the best known of these is **sickle-cell anemia**, which results from a defect in the beta chain. People with sickle-cell anemia inherit, from both parents, a mutated form of the gene that directs the formation of the beta chain. This mutation is caused by the substitution of one amino acid (*valine*) for the amino acid that's normally present (*glutamic acid*). This single amino acid substitution on the beta chain results in the production of a less efficient form of hemoglobin called hemoglobin S (Hb^S) instead of the normal form, which is called hemoglobin A (Hb^A). In situations where the availability of oxygen is reduced, such as at high altitude or when oxygen requirements are increased through exercise, red blood cells with Hb^S collapse and become sickle-shaped (**Fig. 3-12**). What follows is a cascade of events, all of which result in severe anemia and its consequences (**Fig. 3-13**). Briefly, these consequences include impaired circulation from blocked capillaries, red blood cell destruction, oxygen deprivation to vital organs (including the brain), and, without treatment, death.

People who inherit the altered form of the gene from only one parent don't have sickle-cell anemia, but they do have what's called *sickle-cell trait.* Fortunately for them, they're much less severely affected because only about 40 percent of their hemoglobin is abnormal.

The cause of sickle-cell anemia is a very slight change in the *Hb* gene. Remember that hemoglobin beta chains each have 146 amino acids. What's more, to emphasize the

sickle-cell anemia A severe inherited hemoglobin disorder in which red blood cells collapse when deprived of oxygen. It results from inheriting two copies of a mutant allele. The type of mutation that produces the sickle-cell allele is a point mutation.

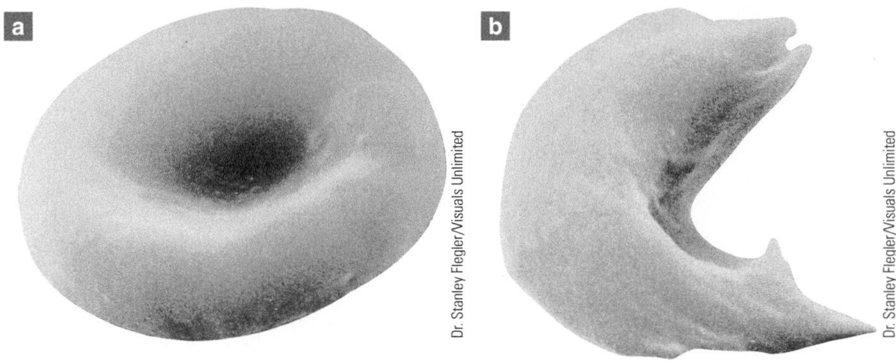

▸ **Figure 3-12** Scanning electron micrographs of (**a**) a normal, fully oxygenated red blood cell and (**b**) a collapsed, sickle-shaped red blood cell that contains Hb^S.

importance of a seemingly minor alteration, consider that triplets of DNA bases are required to specify amino acids. Therefore it takes 438 bases (146 × 3) to produce the chain of 146 amino acids that forms the adult hemoglobin beta chain. But a change in only one of these 438 bases produces the life-threatening complications seen in sickle-cell anemia. **Figure 3-14** shows the DNA base sequence and the resulting amino acid products for both normal and sickling hemoglobin. As you can see, a single base substitution (from CTC to CAC) can result in an altered amino acid sequence, from

. . . proline—*glutamic acid*—glutamic acid . . .

to

. . . proline—*valine*—glutamic acid . . .

This kind of change in the genetic code is referred to as a **point mutation** or *base substitution*. In evolution, these changes are important sources of new genetic variation in populations. Point mutations, like the one that causes sickle-cell anemia, probably occur fairly frequently. But for a new mutation to be evolutionarily significant, it must be passed on to offspring and eventually become more common in a population.

▾ **Figure 3-13** Diagram showing the cascade of symptoms that can occur in people with sickle-cell anemia.

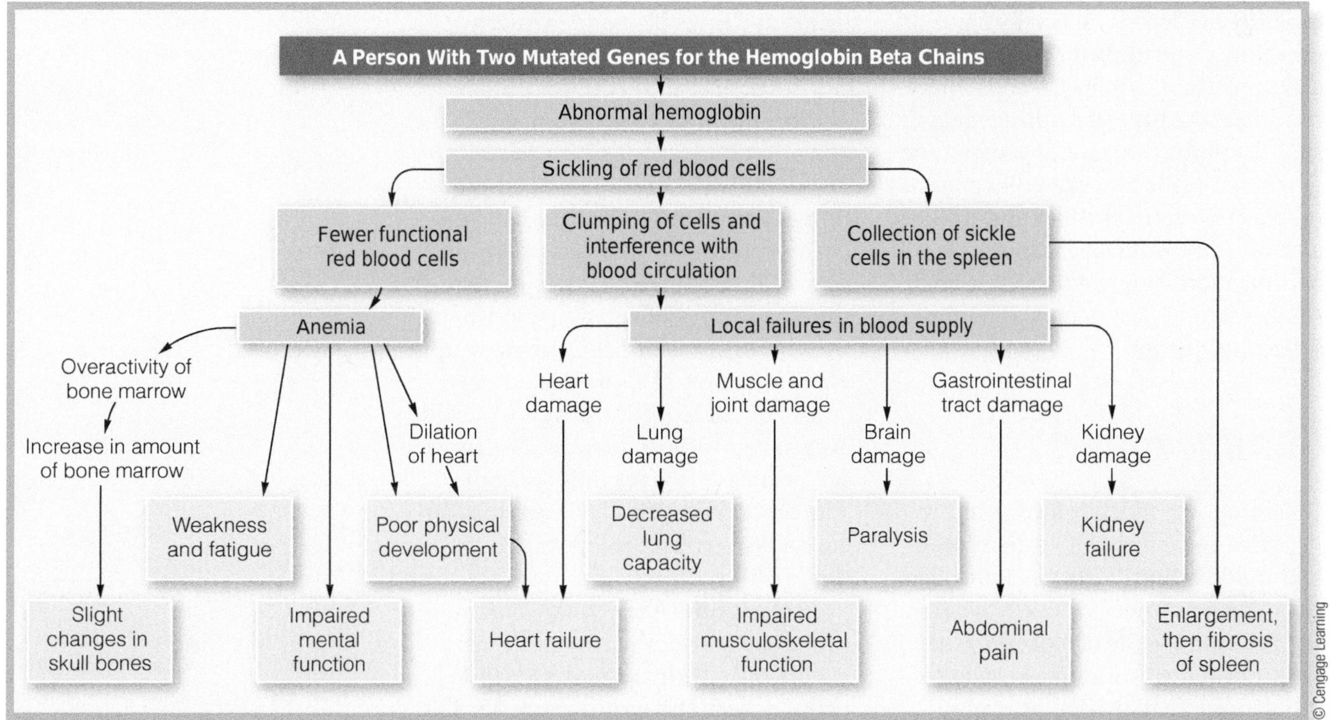

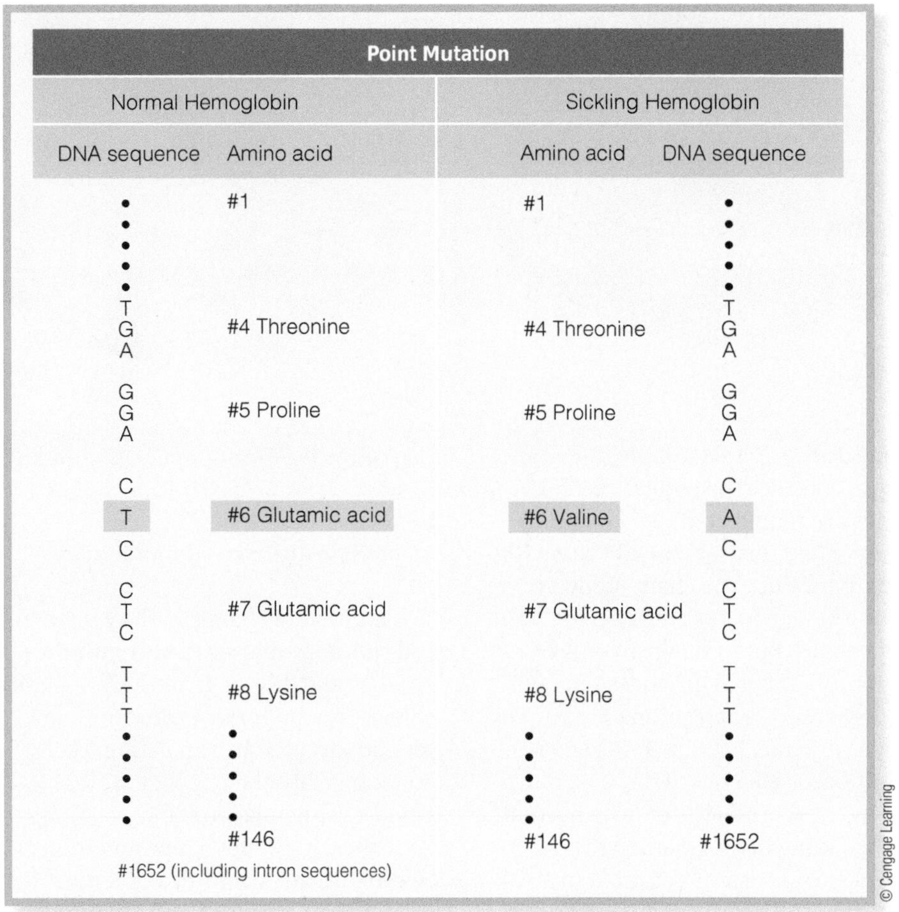

Point Mutation

Normal Hemoglobin		Sickling Hemoglobin	
DNA sequence	Amino acid	Amino acid	DNA sequence
• • • • •	#1	#1	• • • • •
T G A	#4 Threonine	#4 Threonine	T G A
G G A	#5 Proline	#5 Proline	G G A
C **T** C	**#6 Glutamic acid**	**#6 Valine**	C **A** C
C T C	#7 Glutamic acid	#7 Glutamic acid	C T C
T T T	#8 Lysine	#8 Lysine	T T T
• • • • •	• • • • •	• • • • •	• • • • •
#1652 (including intron sequences)	#146	#146	#1652

◄ **Figure 3-14** Substitution of one base at position 6 produces sickling hemoglobin.

Once point mutations occur, their fate in populations depends on the other evolutionary forces, especially natural selection. Depending on how beneficial a mutation is, it may become more common over time; if it's disadvantageous, it probably won't. Sickle-cell anemia is one of the best examples of natural selection acting on humans; it shows us how a disadvantageous mutation can become more frequent in certain environments. This last point will be considered in Chapter 4.

Chromosomes

Throughout much of a cell's life, its DNA (all 6 feet of it!) directs cellular functions and exists as an uncoiled, granular substance. However, at various times in the life of most types of cells, normal activities cease and the cell divides. Cell division produces new cells, and at the beginning of this process, the DNA becomes tightly coiled and is visible under a microscope as a set of discrete structures called **chromosomes** (**Fig. 3-15**).

Chromosomes are composed of a DNA molecule and proteins (**Fig. 3-16**). During normal cell function, if the DNA were organized into chromosomes, they would be single-stranded structures. However, during the early stages of cell division when they become visible, they're made up of two strands, or two DNA molecules, joined together at a constricted area called the *centromere*. The reason there are two strands is simple: The DNA molecules have replicated, and one strand is an exact copy of the other.

Every species has a specific number of chromosomes in somatic cells (**Table 3.2**). Humans have 46, while chimpanzees and gorillas have 48. This

point mutation A change in one of the four DNA bases.

chromosomes Discrete structures composed of DNA and proteins found only in the nuclei of cells. Chromosomes are visible under magnification only during certain phases of cell division.

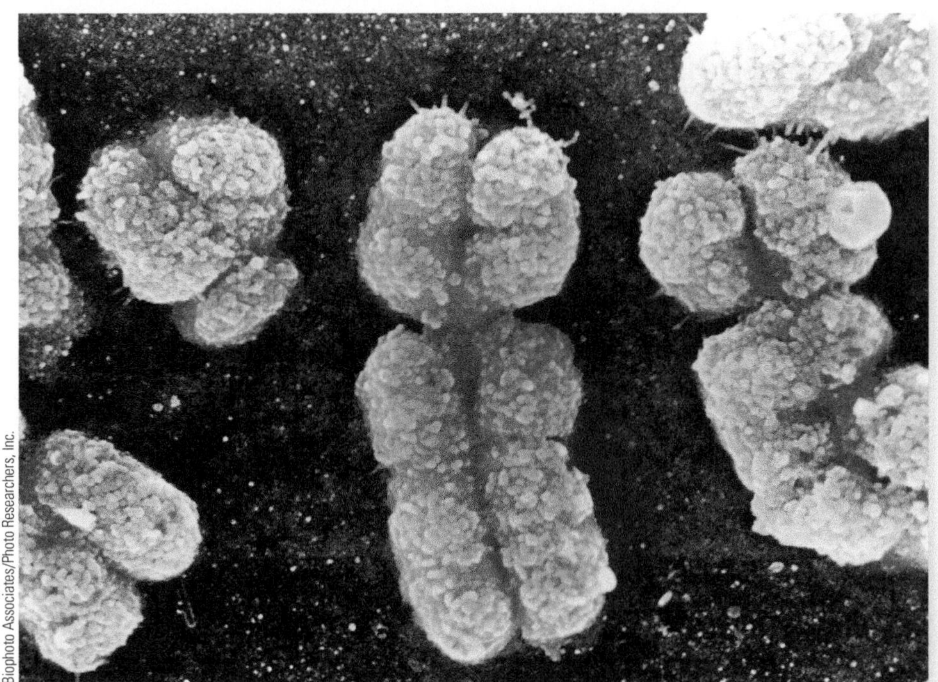

Biophoto Associates/Photo Researchers, Inc.

▶ **Figure 3-15** Colorized scanning electronmicrograph of human chromosomes.

doesn't mean that humans have less DNA than chimpanzees and gorillas. It just means that the DNA is packaged differently.

There are two basic types of chromosomes: **autosomes** and **sex chromosomes**. Autosomes carry information that governs all physical characteristics except primary sex determination. The two sex chromosomes are the X and Y chromosomes; in mammals, the Y chromosome is directly involved in determining maleness. Although the X chromosome is called a sex chromosome, it actually functions more like an autosome

autosomes All chromosomes except the sex chromosomes.

sex chromosomes In mammals, the X and Y chromosomes.

Table 3.2 Standard Chromosomal Complement in Various Organisms

Organism	Chromosome Number in Somatic Cells	Chromosome Number in Gametes
Human (*Homo sapiens*)	46	23
Chimpanzee (*Pan troglodytes*)	48	24
Gorilla (*Gorilla gorilla*)	48	24
Dog (*Canis familiaris*)	78	39
Chicken (*Gallus domesticus*)	78	39
Frog (*Rana pipiens*)	26	13
Housefly (*Musca domestica*)	12	6
Onion (*Allium cepa*)	16	8
Corn (*Zea mays*)	20	10
Tobacco (*Nicotiana tabacum*)	48	24

Source: Cummings, 2000, p. 16.

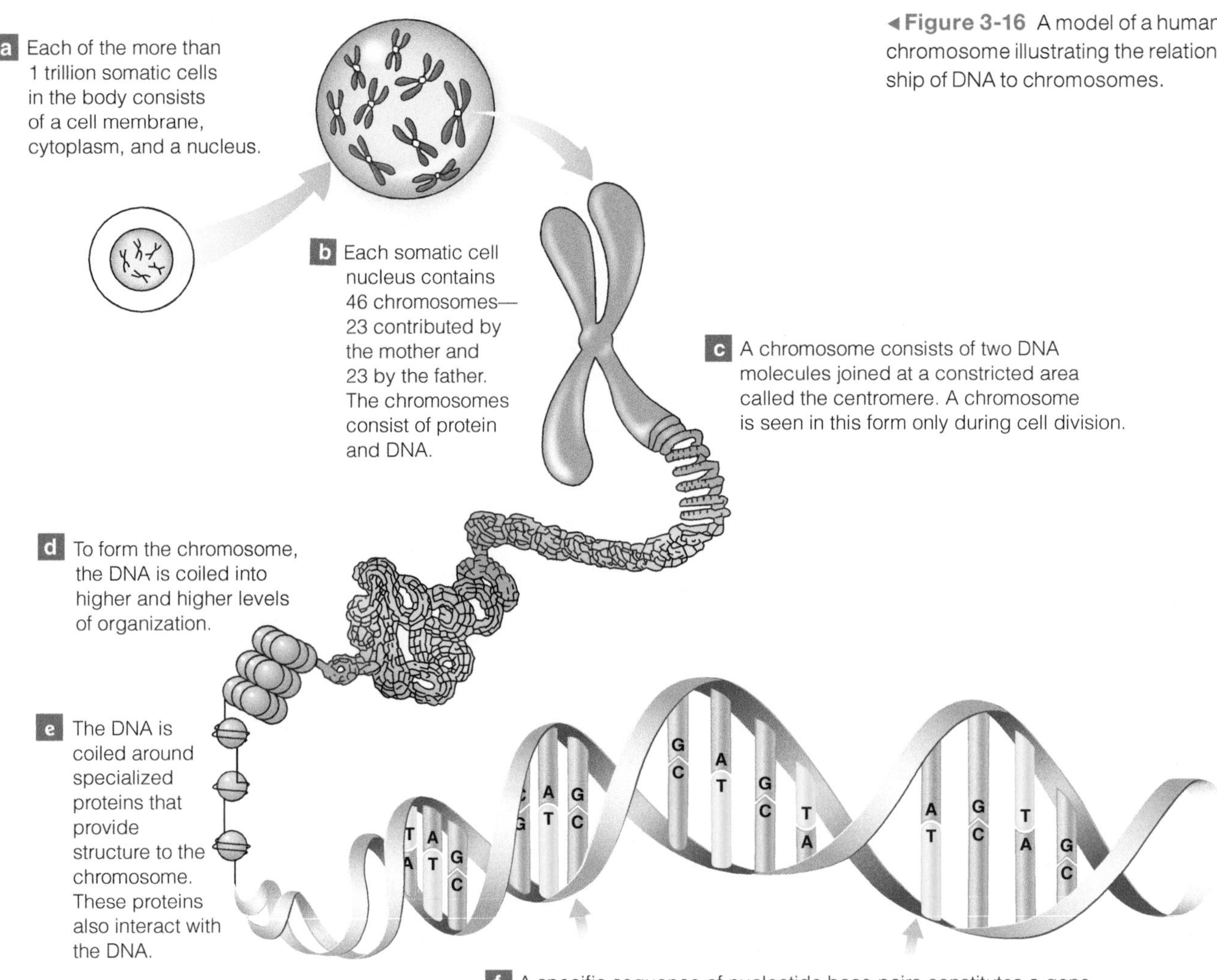

a Each of the more than 1 trillion somatic cells in the body consists of a cell membrane, cytoplasm, and a nucleus.
b Each somatic cell nucleus contains 46 chromosomes—23 contributed by the mother and 23 by the father. The chromosomes consist of protein and DNA.
c A chromosome consists of two DNA molecules joined at a constricted area called the centromere. A chromosome is seen in this form only during cell division.
d To form the chromosome, the DNA is coiled into higher and higher levels of organization.
e The DNA is coiled around specialized proteins that provide structure to the chromosome. These proteins also interact with the DNA.
f A specific sequence of nucleotide base pairs constitutes a gene.
© Cengage Learning

◄**Figure 3-16** A model of a human chromosome illustrating the relationship of DNA to chromosomes.

because it's not involved in primary sex determination and it influences several other traits. Among mammals, all genetically normal females have two X chromosomes (XX), and they're female only because they don't have a Y chromosome. (Female is the default setting.) All genetically normal males have one X and one Y chromosome (XY).

Chromosomes occur in pairs, so all normal human somatic cells have 22 pairs of autosomes and one pair of sex chromosomes (23 pairs in all). With few exceptions, abnormal numbers of autosomes are fatal—usually soon after conception. Although abnormal numbers of sex chromosomes aren't usually fatal, they may result in sterility and frequently have other consequences. So to function normally, it's essential for a human cell to possess both members of each chromosomal pair, or a total of 46 chromosomes.

Offspring inherit one member of each chromosomal pair from the father (the paternal chromosome) and one member from the mother (the maternal chromosome). Members of chromosomal pairs are alike in size and position of the centromere, and they carry genetic information governing the same traits. However, this doesn't mean that partner chromosomes are genetically identical; it just means that they influence the same traits. For example, on both copies of a person's ninth chromosome, there's a **locus**, or gene position, that determines which of the four ABO blood types (A, B, AB, or O) he or she will have. However, these

locus (*pl.*, loci) (lo'-kus, lo-sigh') The position or location on a chromosome where a given gene occurs. The term is sometimes used interchangeably with *gene*.

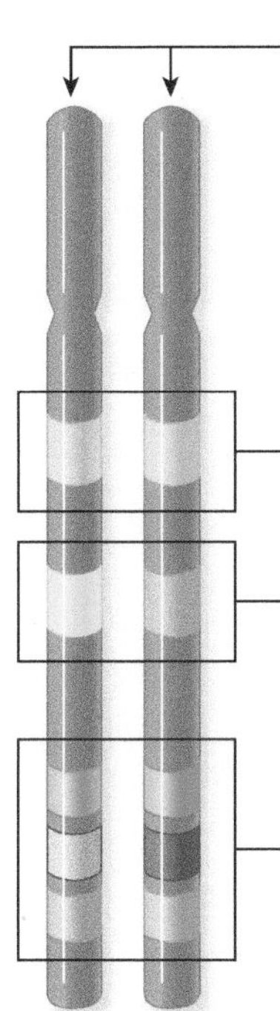

Members of a pair of chromosomes. One chromosome is from a male parent, and its partner is from a female parent.
Gene locus. The location for a specific gene on a chromosome.
Pair of alleles. Although they influence the same characteristic, their DNA varies slightly, so they produce somewhat different expressions of the same trait.
Three pairs of alleles (at three loci on this pair of chomosomes). Note that at two loci the alleles are identical (homozygous), and at one locus they are different (heterozygous).

▶ **Figure 3-17** As this diagram illustrates, alleles are located at the same locus on paired chromosomes, but they aren't always identical.

© Cengage Learning

two ninth chromosomes might not have identical DNA segments at the ABO locus. In other words, at numerous genetic loci, there may be more than one possible form of a gene, and these different forms are called **alleles** (**Fig 3-17**).

Alleles are alternate forms of a gene that can direct the cell to produce slightly different forms of a product, and ultimately, different expressions of a trait—as in the hemoglobin S (Hb^S) example. At the ABO locus, there are three possible alleles: *A*, *B*, and *O*. However, since individuals have only two ninth chromosomes, only two alleles are present in any one person. And the variation in alleles at the ABO locus is what accounts for the variation among humans in ABO blood type.

Karyotyping Chromosomes

One method frequently used to examine chromosomes in an individual is to produce a **karyotype**. (An example of a human karyotype is shown in **Fig. 3-18**.) The chromosomes used in karyotypes are obtained from dividing cells. White blood cells can be cultured, chemically treated, and microscopically examined to identify the ones that are dividing. These cells are then photographed through a microscope to produce *photomicrographs* of intact, double-stranded chromosomes. Partner chromosomes are then matched up, and the entire set is arranged in descending order by size so that the largest chromosome appears first.

Karyotyping has had numerous practical applications. Physicians and

▼ **Figure 3-18** A karyotype of a human male with the chromosomes arranged by size, position of the centromere, and banding patterns.

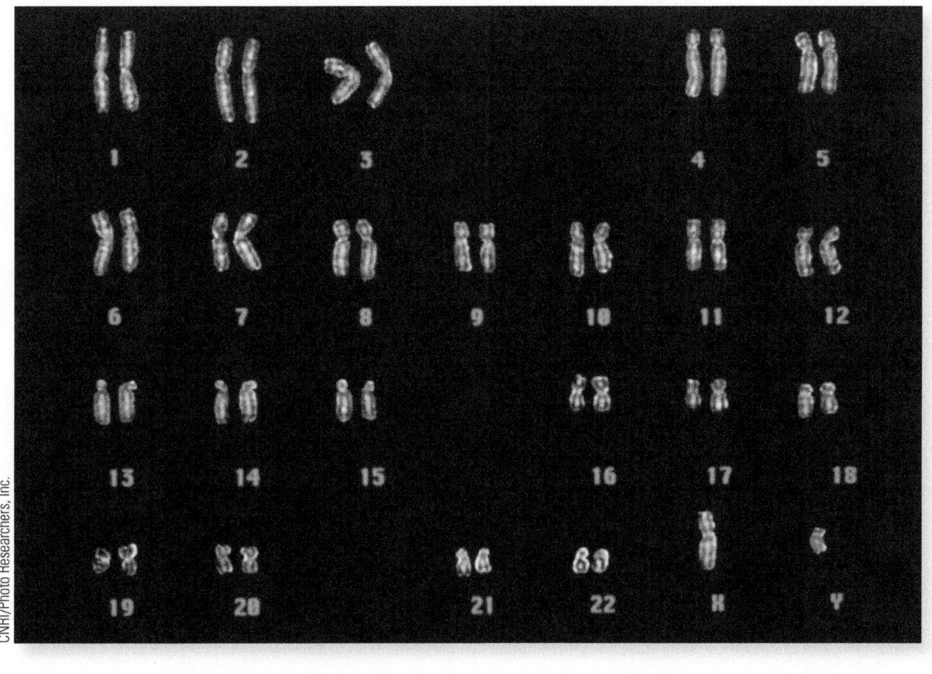

CNRI/Photo Researchers, Inc.

alleles Alternate forms of a gene. Alleles occur at the same locus on paired chromosomes and thus govern the same trait, but because they're different, their action may result in different expressions of that trait.

karyotype The chromosomes of an individual, or what is typical of a species, viewed microscopically and displayed in a photograph. The chromosomes are arranged in pairs and according to size and position of the centromere.

mitosis Simple cell division; the process by which somatic cells divide to produce two identical daughter cells.

meiosis Cell division in specialized cells in ovaries and testes. Meiosis involves two divisions and results in four daughter cells, each containing only half the original number of chromosomes. These cells can develop into gametes.

genetic counselors use karyotypes to help diagnose chromosomal disorders in patients, and they're used in prenatal testing to identify chromosomal abnormalities in developing fetuses. Karyotype analysis has also revealed many chromosomal similarities shared by different species, including humans and nonhuman primates. But, now that scientists can directly compare the genomes of species, karyotyping probably won't continue being used for this or several other purposes.

Cell Division

As we mentioned earlier, normal cellular function is periodically interrupted so that the cell can divide. Cell division in somatic cells is called **mitosis**, and it's the way somatic cells reproduce. Mitosis occurs during growth and development; it also plays a role in the repair of injured tissues; and it replaces older cells with newer ones. But while mitosis produces new somatic cells, another type of cell division, called **meiosis**, may lead to the development of new individuals, since it produces reproductive cells, or gametes.

Mitosis

In the early stages of mitosis, a human somatic cell has 46 double-stranded chromosomes, and as the cell begins to divide, these chromosomes line up along its center and split apart so that the two strands separate (**Fig. 3-19**). Once the two strands are apart, they pull away from each other and move to opposite ends of the dividing cell. At this point, each strand is a distinct chromosome, *composed of one DNA molecule*. Following the separation of chromosome strands, the cell membrane pinches in and seals, so that there are two new cells, each with a full complement of DNA, or 46 chromosomes.

Mitosis is referred to as "simple cell division" because a somatic cell divides

a The cell is involved in metabolic activities. DNA replication occurs, but chromosomes are not visible.

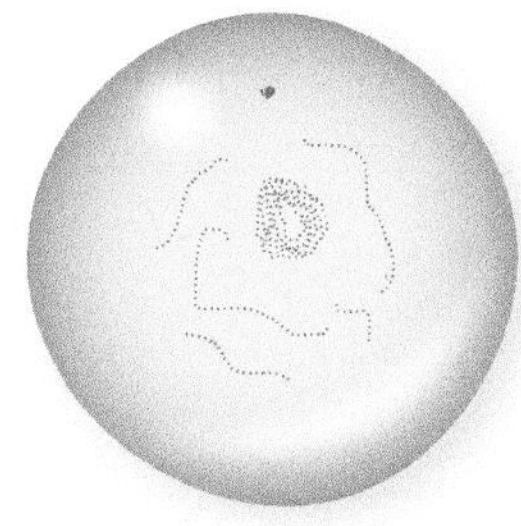

b The nuclear membrane disappears, and double-stranded chromosomes are visible.

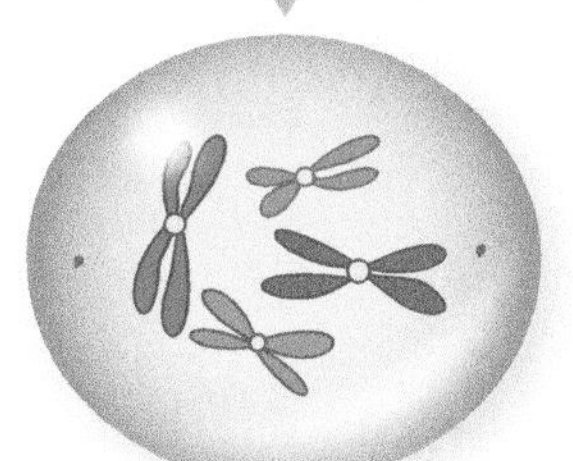

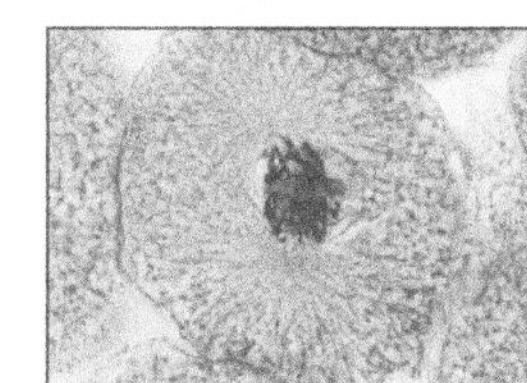

c The chromosomes align themselves at the center of the cell.

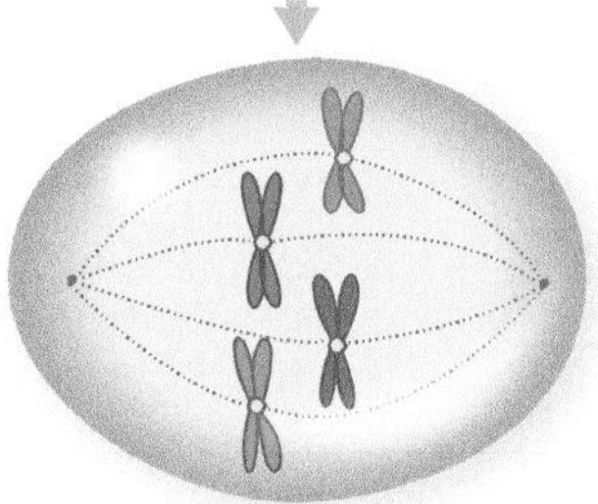

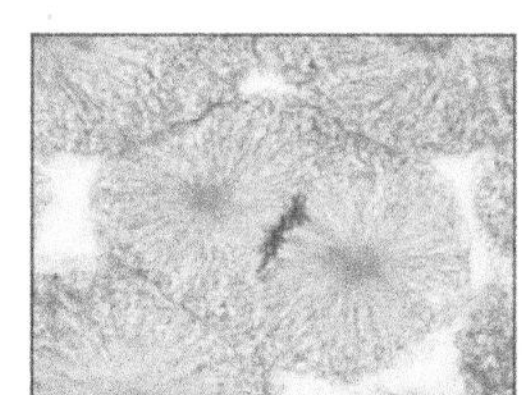

d The chromosomes split at the centromere, and the strands separate and move to opposite ends of the dividing cell.

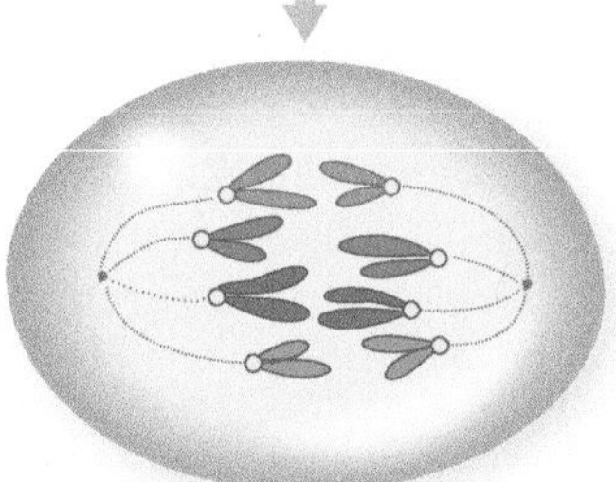

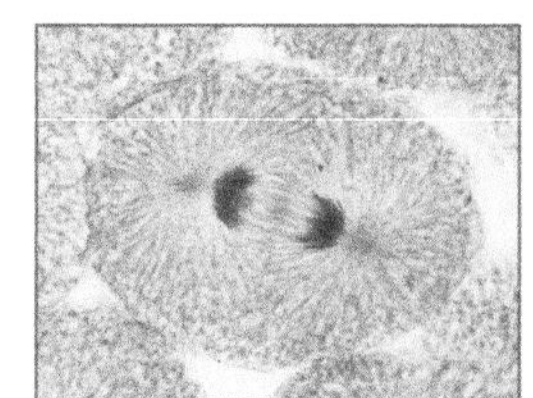

e The cell membrane pinches in as the cell continues to divide. The chromosomes begin to uncoil (not shown here).

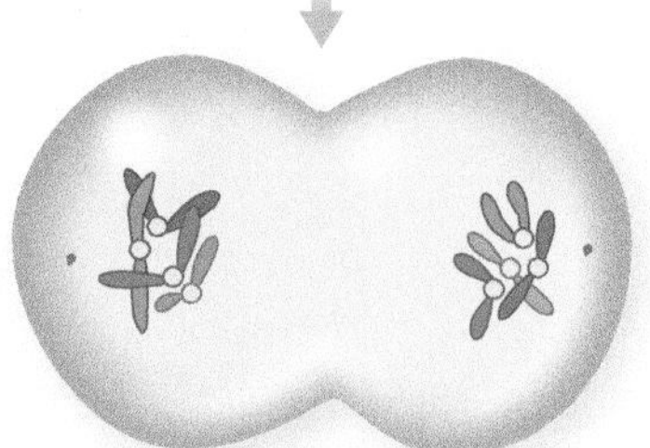

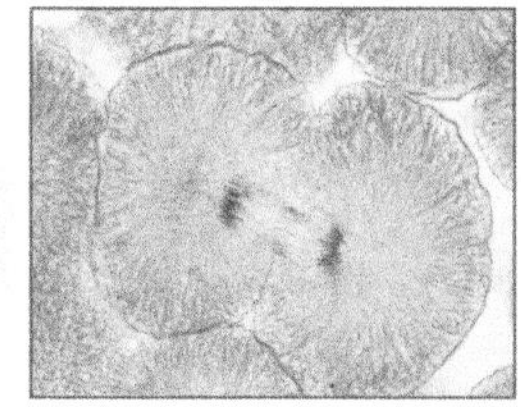

f After mitosis is complete, there are two identical daughter cells. The nuclear membrane is present, and chromosomes are no longer visible.

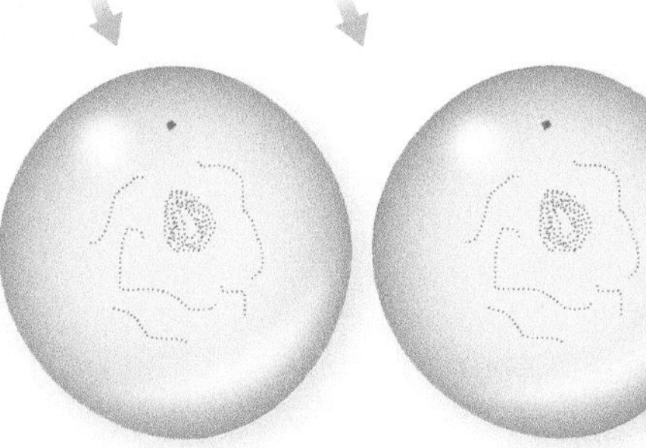

◄ **Figure 3-19** Diagrammatic representation of mitosis. The blue images next to some of these illustrations are photomicrographs of actual chromosomes in a dividing cell.

one time to produce two daughter cells that are genetically identical to each other and to the original cell. In mitosis, the original cell possesses 46 chromosomes, and each new daughter cell inherits an exact copy of all 46. This precision is made possible by the DNA molecule's ability to replicate. Therefore DNA replication ensures that the amount of genetic material remains constant from one generation of cells to the next.

We should mention here that certain types of somatic cells don't divide. Red blood cells are produced continuously by specialized cells in bone marrow, but they can't divide because they have no nucleus and no nuclear DNA. Once the brain and nervous system are fully developed, brain and nerve cells (neurons) stop dividing, although there is some debate about this issue. Liver cells also do not divide after growth has stopped unless this vital organ is damaged through injury or disease. With these three exceptions (red blood cells, mature neurons, and liver cells), somatic cells are regularly duplicated through the process of mitosis.

Meiosis

While mitosis produces new cells, meiosis can lead to the development of a new organism because it produces reproductive cells (gametes). Although meiosis is similar to mitosis, it's more complicated. In meiosis, there are two divisions instead of one. Also, meiosis produces four daughter cells, not two, and each of these four cells contains only half the original number of chromosomes.

During meiosis, specialized cells in male testes and female ovaries divide and eventually develop into sperm and egg cells. Initially, these cells contain the full complement of chromosomes (46 in humans); but after the first division (called *reduction division*), the number of chromosomes in the two daughter cells is 23, or half the original number (**Fig. 3-20**). This reduction of chromosome number is crucial because the resulting gamete, with its 23 chromosomes, may eventually unite with another gamete that also has 23 chromosomes. The product of this union is a *zygote*, or fertilized egg, in which the original number of chromosomes (46) has been restored. In other words, a zygote inherits the exact amount of DNA it needs (half from each parent) to develop and function normally. If it weren't for reduction division in meiosis, it wouldn't be possible to maintain the correct number of chromosomes from one generation to the next.

During the first division, partner chromosomes come together to form pairs of double-stranded chromosomes that line up along the cell's center. Pairing of partner chromosomes is essential because while they're together, members of pairs exchange genetic information in a process called **recombination**. Pairing is also important because it ensures that each new daughter cell receives only one member of each pair.

As the cell begins to divide, the chromosomes themselves remain intact (that is, double-stranded), but *members of pairs* pull apart and move to opposite ends of the cell. After the first division, there are two new daughter cells, but they aren't identical to each other or to the parental cell. They're different because each cell contains only one member of each chromosome pair (that is, only 23 chromosomes), each of which still has two strands. Also, because of recombination, each chromosome now contains some combinations of alleles it didn't have before.

The second meiotic division is similar to division in mitosis. (For a comparison of mitosis and meiosis, see **Fig. 3-21**.) In the two newly formed cells, the 23 double-stranded chromosomes line up at the cell's center and, as in mitosis, the strands of each chromosome separate and move apart. Once this second division is completed, there are four daughter cells, each with 23 single-stranded chromosomes, or 23 DNA molecules.

recombination The exchange of genetic material between paired chromosomes during meiosis; also called *crossing over*.

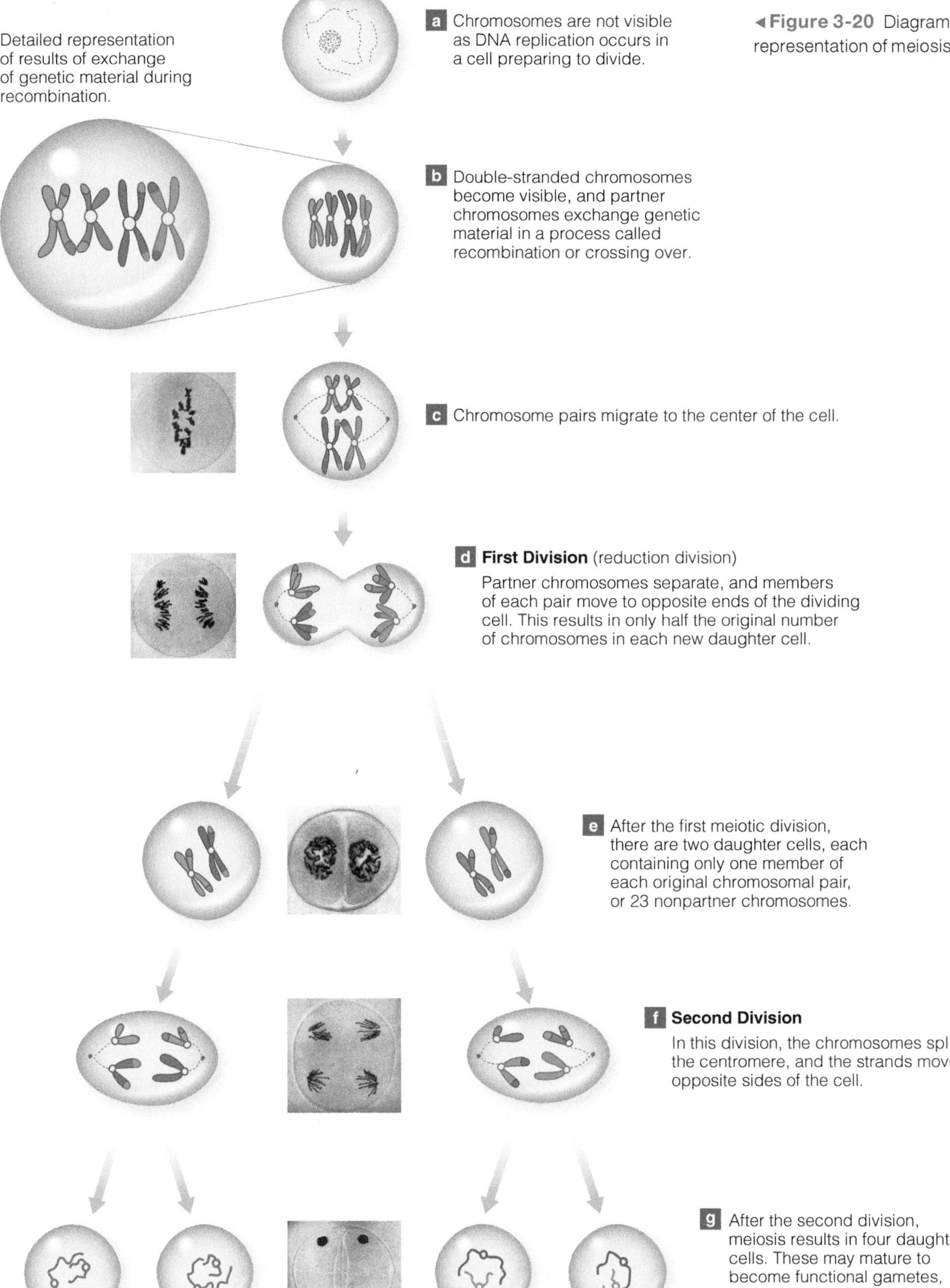

Detailed representation of results of exchange of genetic material during recombination.
a Chromosomes are not visible as DNA replication occurs in a cell preparing to divide.
b Double-stranded chromosomes become visible, and partner chromosomes exchange genetic material in a process called recombination or crossing over.
c Chromosome pairs migrate to the center of the cell.
d **First Division** (reduction division)
Partner chromosomes separate, and members of each pair move to opposite ends of the dividing cell. This results in only half the original number of chromosomes in each new daughter cell.
e After the first meiotic division, there are two daughter cells, each containing only one member of each original chromosomal pair, or 23 nonpartner chromosomes.
f **Second Division**
In this division, the chromosomes split at the centromere, and the strands move to opposite sides of the cell.
g After the second division, meiosis results in four daughter cells. These may mature to become functional gametes, containing only half the DNA in the original cell.

◂**Figure 3-20** Diagrammatic representation of meiosis.

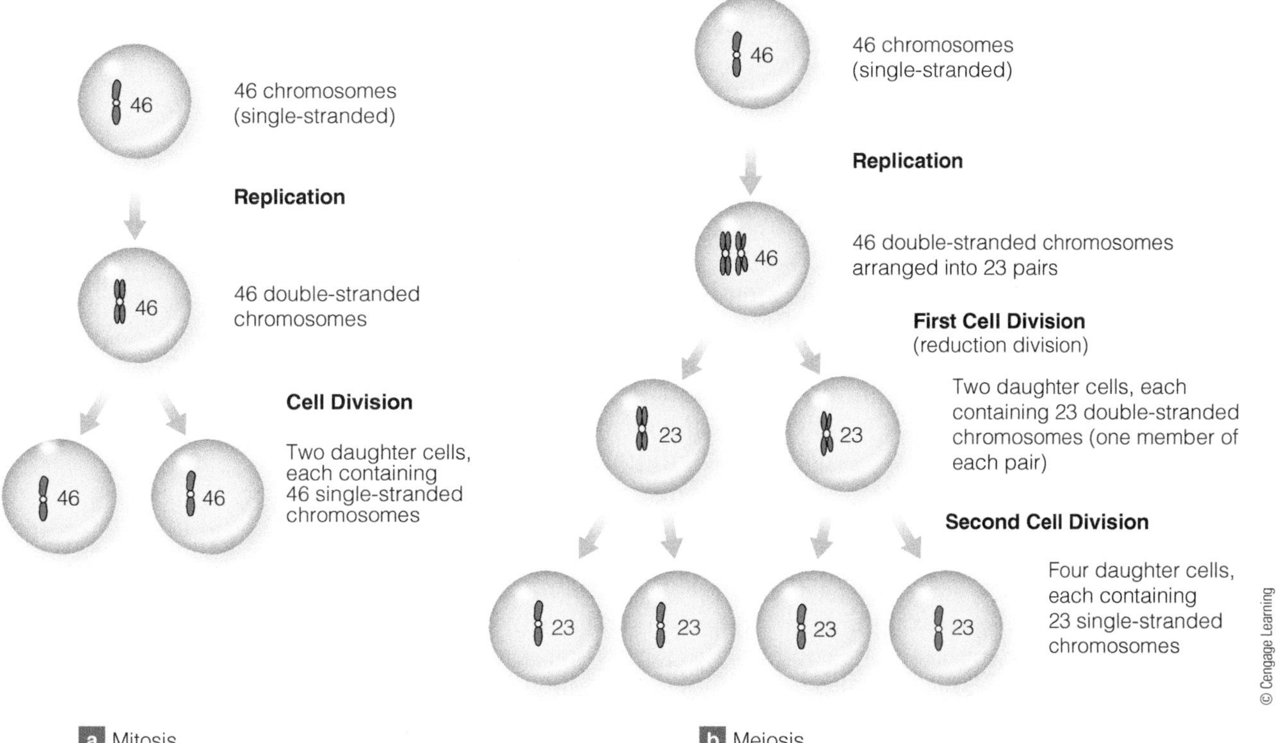

▲ **Figure 3-21** Mitosis and meiosis compared. In mitosis, one division produces two daughter cells, each of which contains 46 chromosomes. In meiosis, there are two divisions. After the first, there are two cells, each containing only 23 chromosomes (one member of each original chromosome pair). Each daughter cell divides again, so that the final result is four cells, each with only half the original number of chromosomes.

The Evolutionary Significance of Meiosis Meiosis occurs in all sexually reproducing organisms and is an extremely important evolutionary innovation because it increases genetic variation in populations. Members of sexually reproducing species aren't genetically identical **clones** of other individuals because they receive genetic contributions from two parents. Just from the **random assortment** of chromosome pairs during the first division of meiosis, each parent can produce around 8 million genetically different gametes. In human matings, literally trillions of genetic combinations can result in the offspring of two parents. Consequently every individual represents a unique combination of genes that, in all likelihood, has never occurred before and will never occur again.

As you can see, genetic diversity is considerably enhanced by meiosis, and this diversity is essential if species are to adapt to changing selective pressures. As we mentioned in Chapter 2, natural selection acts on genetic variation in populations; thus if all individuals were genetically identical, natural selection would have nothing to act upon and evolution couldn't occur. In all species, *mutation* is the only source of new genetic variation because it produces new alleles. But sexually reproducing species have an additional advantage because recombination produces new *arrangements* of genetic information, potentially providing additional material for selection to act on. In fact, the influence of meiosis on genetic variation is the main advantage of sexual reproduction. Thus, sexual reproduction and meiosis are of major evolutionary importance because they contribute to the role of natural selection in populations.

Problems with Meiosis For fetal development to occur normally, the process of meiosis must be exact. If chromosomes or chromosome strands don't separate during either of the two divisions, serious problems can develop. This failure to separate is called *nondisjunction*; when it happens, one of the daughter cells receives two copies of the affected chromosome while the other daughter cell receives none. If such an affected gamete unites with a normal gamete containing 23 chromo-

clones Organisms that are genetically identical to another organism. The term may also be used to refer to genetically identical DNA segments, molecules, or cells.

random assortment The chance distribution of chromosomes to daughter cells during meiosis. Along with recombination, random assortment is an important source of genetic variation (but not new alleles).

somes, the resulting zygote will have either 45 or 47 chromosomes. If there are 47, then there will be three copies of one chromosome instead of two, a situation called *trisomy*.

You can appreciate the potential effects of an abnormal number of chromosomes if you remember that the zygote, by means of mitosis, ultimately gives rise to all the cells in the developing body. Consequently every one of those cells will inherit an incorrect number of chromosomes. And since most abnormal numbers of autosomes are lethal, the embryo is usually spontaneously aborted, frequently before the pregnancy is even recognized.

Trisomy 21 (formerly called Down syndrome) is the only example of an incorrect number of autosomes that's compatible with life beyond the first few years after birth. Trisomy 21 is caused by the presence of three copies of chromosome 21. It occurs in approximately 1 out of every 1,000 live births and is associated with various developmental and health problems. These problems include congenital heart defects (seen in about 40 percent of affected newborns) as well as increased susceptibility to respiratory infections and leukemia. However, the most widely recognized effect is mental impairment, which is variably expressed and ranges from mild to severe.

Trisomy 21 is partly associated with advanced maternal age. For example, the risk of a 20-year-old woman giving birth to an affected infant is just 0.05 percent (5 in 10,000). However, 3 percent of babies born to mothers aged 45 and older are affected (a 60-fold increase). Actually, most affected infants are born to women under the age of 35, but that's because the majority of women who have babies are less than 35 years old. The increased prevalence of trisomy 21 with maternal age is thought to be related to the fact that meiosis actually begins in females during their own fetal development and then stops, only to be resumed and completed at ovulation. This means that a woman's gametes are as old as she is, and age-related changes in the chromosomes themselves appear to increase the risk of nondisjunction, at least for some chromosomes.

Nondisjunction also occurs in sex chromosomes (see **Table 3.3**). For example, a man may have two X chromosomes and one Y chromosome (XXY) or one X chromosome and two Y chromosomes (XYY). Likewise, a woman may have only one X chromosome (X0), or she may have more than two (XXX). Although abnormal numbers of sex chromosomes don't always result in spontaneous abortion or death, they can cause sterility, some mental impairment, and other problems. And while it's possible to live without a Y chromosome (roughly half of all people do), it's impossible for an embryo to survive without an X chromosome. (Remember, X chromosomes carry genes that influence many traits.) Clearly normal development depends on having the correct number of chromosomes.

New Frontiers

Since the discovery of DNA structure and function in the 1950s, the field of genetics has revolutionized biological science and reshaped our understanding of inheritance, genetic disease, and evolutionary processes. For example, a technique developed in 1986, called **polymerase chain reaction (PCR)**, enables scientists to make thousands of copies of small samples of DNA, which can then be analyzed. In the past, DNA samples from crime scenes or fossils were usually too small to be studied. But PCR makes it possible to examine DNA sequences in, for example, Neandertal fossils and Egyptian mummies, and it has limitless potential for many disciplines, including forensic science, medicine, and paleoanthropology.

Another application of PCR allows scientists to identify *DNA fingerprints*, so called because they appear as patterns of repeated DNA sequences that are unique to each individual (**Fig. 3-22** on p. 73). For example, one person

polymerase chain reaction (PCR) A method of producing thousands of copies of a DNA sample.

Table 3.3 Examples of Nondisjunction in Sex Chromosomes

Chromosomal Complement	Condition	Estimated Incidence	Manifestations
XXX	Trisomy X	1 per 1,000 female births	Affected women are usually clinically normal, but there is a slight increase in sterility and mental impairment compared to the general population. In cases with more than three X chromosomes, mental impairment can be severe.
XYY	XYY syndrome	1 per 1,000 male births	Affected males are fertile and tend to be taller than average.
XO	Turner syndrome	1 per 10,000 female births	Affected females are short-statured, have broad chests and webbed necks, and are sterile. There is usually no mental impairment, but concepts relating to spatial relationships, including mathematics, can pose difficulties. Between 95 and 99 percent of affected fetuses die before birth.
XXY	Klinefelter syndrome	1 per 1,000 male births	Symptoms are noticeable by puberty: reduced testicular development, reduced facial and body hair, some breast development in about half of all cases, and reduced fertility or sterility. Some individuals exhibit lowered intelligence. Additional X chromosomes (XXXY) are associated with mental impairment.

might have a segment of six bases such as ATTCTA repeated 3 times, while another person might have 20 copies of the same sequence. DNA fingerprinting is perhaps the most powerful tool available for human identification. Scientists have used it to identify scores of remains, including members of the Russian royal family murdered in 1918 and victims of the September 11, 2001, terrorist attacks. Moreover, the technique has been used to exonerate many innocent people wrongly convicted of crimes, in some cases decades after they were imprisoned.

Over the last two decades, scientists have used the techniques of *recombinant DNA technology* to transfer genes from the cells of one species into those of another. One common method has been to insert human genes that direct the production of various proteins into bacterial cells in laboratories. The altered bacteria can then produce human gene products, such as insulin. Until the early 1980s, people with diabetes relied on insulin derived from nonhuman animals. However, this insulin wasn't plentiful, and some patients became allergic to it. But since 1982, abundant supplies of human insulin, produced by bacteria, have been available, and insulin derived from bacteria doesn't cause allergic reactions.

In recent years, genetic manipulation has become increasingly controversial owing to questions related to product safety, environmental concerns, animal welfare, and concern over the experimental use of human embryos. For example, the insertion of bacterial DNA into certain crops has made them toxic to leaf-eating insects, thus reducing the need for pesticides. Cattle and pigs are commonly treated with antibiotics and genetically engineered growth hormone to increase growth rates. (There's no concrete evidence that humans are susceptible to the insect-repelling bacterial DNA or harmed by consuming meat and dairy products from animals treated with growth hormone. But there are concerns over the unknown effects of long-term exposure.)

Cloning has been one of the most controversial of all the new genetic technologies. But cloning isn't as new as you might think. Anyone who has ever taken a cutting from a plant and rooted it to grow a new one has produced a clone. Many mammalian species have now been cloned, and researchers have even produced clones of dead mice that were frozen for as long as 16 years. This gives rise to hopes that eventually it may be possible to clone extinct animals, such as mammoths, from the frozen bodies of animals that died several thousand years ago (Wakayama et al., 2008). But don't count on visiting a *Jurassic Park* type zoo anytime soon.

As exciting as these innovations are, probably the single most important advance in genetics has been the progress made by the **Human Genome Project** (International Human Genome Sequencing Consortium, 2001; Venter et al., 2001). The goal of this international effort, begun in 1990, was to sequence the entire human genome, which consists of some 3 billion bases making up approximately 21,000 protein-coding genes. This extremely important project was completed in 2003. Since that time, the genomes of hundreds of species have been sequenced, including those of chimpanzees (Chimpanzee Sequencing and Analysis Consortium, 2005), rhesus macaques (Rhesus Macaque Genome Sequencing and Analysis Consortium, 2007), western lowland gorillas (Scally et al., 2012), Orangutans (Locke et al., 2011), and bonobos (Prüfer et al., 2012). By comparing different primate genomes, including that of humans, molecular anthropologists are revealing more details regarding phylogenetic relationships among all primate species.

Since the publication of the human genome, DNA sequencing technologies have become increasingly inexpensive, more widely available, and much faster. In May 2010, researchers finished sequencing the entire Neandertal genome (Green et al., 2010). To date, the most exciting announcement stemming from this research is that modern Europeans and Asians (but not Africans) inherited 1 to 4 percent of their genes from ancient Neandertal ancestors. This finding sheds light on debates concerning whether or not early modern humans interbred with Neandertals. These debates have been ongoing in physical anthropology for more than 50 years, and while this new genetic evidence does not conclusively end the discussion, it strongly supports the argument that interbreeding did indeed take place and that many of us carry a few Neandertal genes (see Chapter 13).

Equally exciting was the sequencing of the entire genome of another pre-modern human group called the Denisovans (Reich et al., 2010; Meyer et al., 2012). This group is dated to around 50,000 ya and the entire col-lection of Denisovan skeletal remains consists of a tiny finger bone and two teeth discovered in Siberia. Yet, in a feat that would have been unimaginable just ten years ago, researchers have been able to obtain high quality DNA from the finger bone and sequence the entire genome of this population! The Denisovan genome has now been compared to that of their Neandertal cousins and to the genomes of modern human populations (see Chapter 12).

Eventually, comparative genome analysis should provide a thorough assessment of genetic similarities and differences and thus of the evolutionary relationships between humans and other primates. What's more, we can already look at human variation in an entirely different light than was possible just 10 years ago (see Chapter 15). Among other things, genetic comparisons between human groups can inform us about population movements in the past and what selective pressures may have been exerted on different populations to produce some of the variability we see.

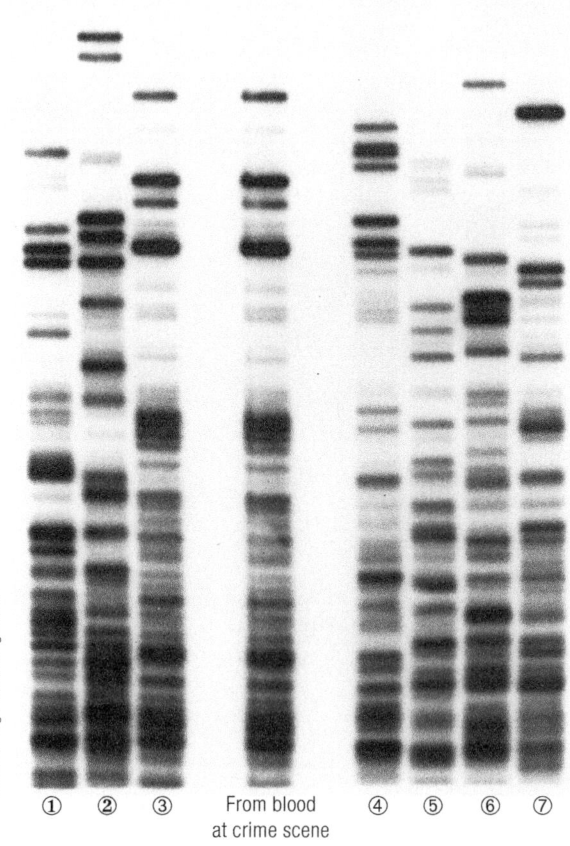

Cellmark Diagnostics, Abingdon, UK

▲ **Figure 3-22** Eight DNA fingerprints, one of which is from a blood sample left at an actual crime scene. The other seven are from suspects. By comparing the banding patterns, it's easy to identify the guilty person.

Human Genome Project An international effort aimed at sequencing and mapping the entire human genome, completed in 2003.

The Encyclopedia of DNA Elements, or ENCODE, is a project initially conceived to follow up on the progress made by the Human Genome Project. This huge study, begun in 2003, now involves an international consortium of more than 400 researchers who, in September 2012, simultaneously published 30 articles in several scientific journals. Initially, the project set out to catalog the functional DNA sequences contained within the vast stretches of non-protein coding DNA, determine what they do, and examine how the human genome is regulated (Maher, 2012; Pennisi, 2012; The ENCODE Project Consortium, 2012).

The current results of the ENCODE project are far too numerous to mention here. But the some of the most important ones include the discovery that as much as 80 percent of the human genome is involved in some form of biochemical function. That estimate may be high and most of the biochemical functions have not been identified. In fact, some of them are probably not even important. But some of these activities include the manufacture of non-coding RNA (RNA that is not involved in protein synthesis but that regulates gene function), and binding sites where regulatory proteins attach, In short, some of what used to be called "junk DNA" is active in gene regulation. It is also of great interest that many regulatory factors have been shown to be involved in disease, including autoimmune conditions such as rheumatoid arthritis, Crohn's disease, and multiple sclerosis (Maurano, et al., 2012). This discovery will radically alter future approaches to the diagnosis and treatment of genetically caused diseases.

The ENCODE project has determined that at least 9 percent (and probably much more) of the human genome has regulatory functions. It has also determined that the regulation of protein coding genes is more complex and has evolved more quickly in humans than in most other species. Moreover, evolution occurs more rapidly in regulatory elements. These facts may partly explain the accelerated pace of evolutionary change in modern humans compared to that of other animals. Ultimately the detailed understanding of how gene regulation works will revolutionize how we view evolutionary processes. The focus of many genetic and evolutionary studies will shift away from protein coding genes and toward regulatory elements. The factors that regulate gene activity in embryonic development are also the basis of evolutionary change. It follows that if we are going to reveal the secrets of our evolutionary past, we must first examine how DNA function is regulated in the present. Certainly the term "junk DNA" will be laid to rest.

How Do We Know?

There are thousands of DNA coding sequences (genes) that have functions which have not been identified. One way geneticists determine what specific genes do is to study what happens when they aren't functioning. Using various techniques, scientists can insert products into mouse embryos very early in development. These products can then "knock out" a target gene so that it doesn't function. This means that virtually every cell in the developing embryo will have a disabled gene at the locus under investigation. Then, when these knockout mice are born, the results can be detected.

One of the many uses of knockout mice has been to identify which *Hox* genes influence the development of specific vertebrae. This information has many clinical applications because the *Hox* genes that determine vertebral identity in mice have human counterparts. Therefore many defects of the spine can now be traced to the gain, loss, or alteration of the function of specific genes during early embryonic development. Subsequent investigations can then search for causes of gene malfunction, including substances in the environment or in food that might influence DNA activity in embryos. For example, it is known that vitamin A can attach to DNA and cause vertebral anomalies. In the future, it is likely that many developmental defects will be detected and treated very early in embryonic development, partly because of the use of knockout techniques.

Summary of Main Topics

- Cells are the fundamental units of life, and in multicellular organisms, there are basically two types. Somatic cells make up body tissues, while gametes (eggs and sperm) are reproductive cells that transmit genetic information from parents to offspring.
- Genetic information is contained in the DNA molecule, found in the nucleus of cells and in mitochondria. The DNA molecule is capable of replication, or making copies of itself. Replication makes it possible for daughter cells to receive a full complement of DNA (contained in chromosomes). DNA also controls protein synthesis by directing the cell to arrange amino acids in the proper sequence for each protein. Also involved in the process of protein synthesis is another, similar molecule called RNA.
- There are many genes that regulate the function of other genes. One class of regulatory genes, the homeobox genes, direct the development of the overall body plan. Other regulatory genes turn genes on and off.
- Cells multiply by dividing and when they do, the DNA within them is visible microscopically in the form of chromosomes. In humans, there are 46 chromosomes (23 pairs). If the full complement isn't precisely distributed to succeeding generations of cells, there can be serious consequences.
- Somatic cells divide during growth or tissue repair or to replace old worn-out cells. Somatic cell division is called mitosis. A cell divides one time to produce two daughter cells, each possessing a full and identical set of chromosomes.
- Sex cells are produced when specialized cells in the ovaries and testes divide during meiosis. Unlike mitosis, meiosis is characterized by two divisions that produce four nonidentical daughter cells, each containing only half the amount of DNA (23 chromosomes).
- About 98 percent of our DNA doesn't actually code for protein production.
- Some noncoding sequences, called introns, are contained within genes. Introns are initially transcribed into mRNA but are then deleted before the mRNA leaves the cell nucleus.
- A high percentage of nonprotein coding DNA is involved in gene regulation. In fact, humans have more regulatory DNA than any other species so far studied.

Critical Thinking Questions

1. Before you read this chapter, were you aware that the DNA in your body is structurally the same as that in all other organisms? Do you see this fact as having potential to clarify some of the many questions we still have regarding biological evolution? Why?
2. Do you think proteins are exactly the same in all species? If not, how do you think they would differ in terms of their composition, and why might these differences be important to biological anthropologists?
3. How can regulatory genes, especially *Hox* genes, play an important role in biological evolution?

Media Resources

Video

See the video "Natural Selection in Action" to learn more about topics covered in this chapter.

Login to your Anthropology CourseMate at www.cengagebrain.com to access videos.

Connections

DNA is the basis of all life.

Evolution occurs when DNA changes and genetic variation is further influenced by natural selection and other factors.

Humans are both vertebrates and mammals and we've shared evolutionary history for millions of years.

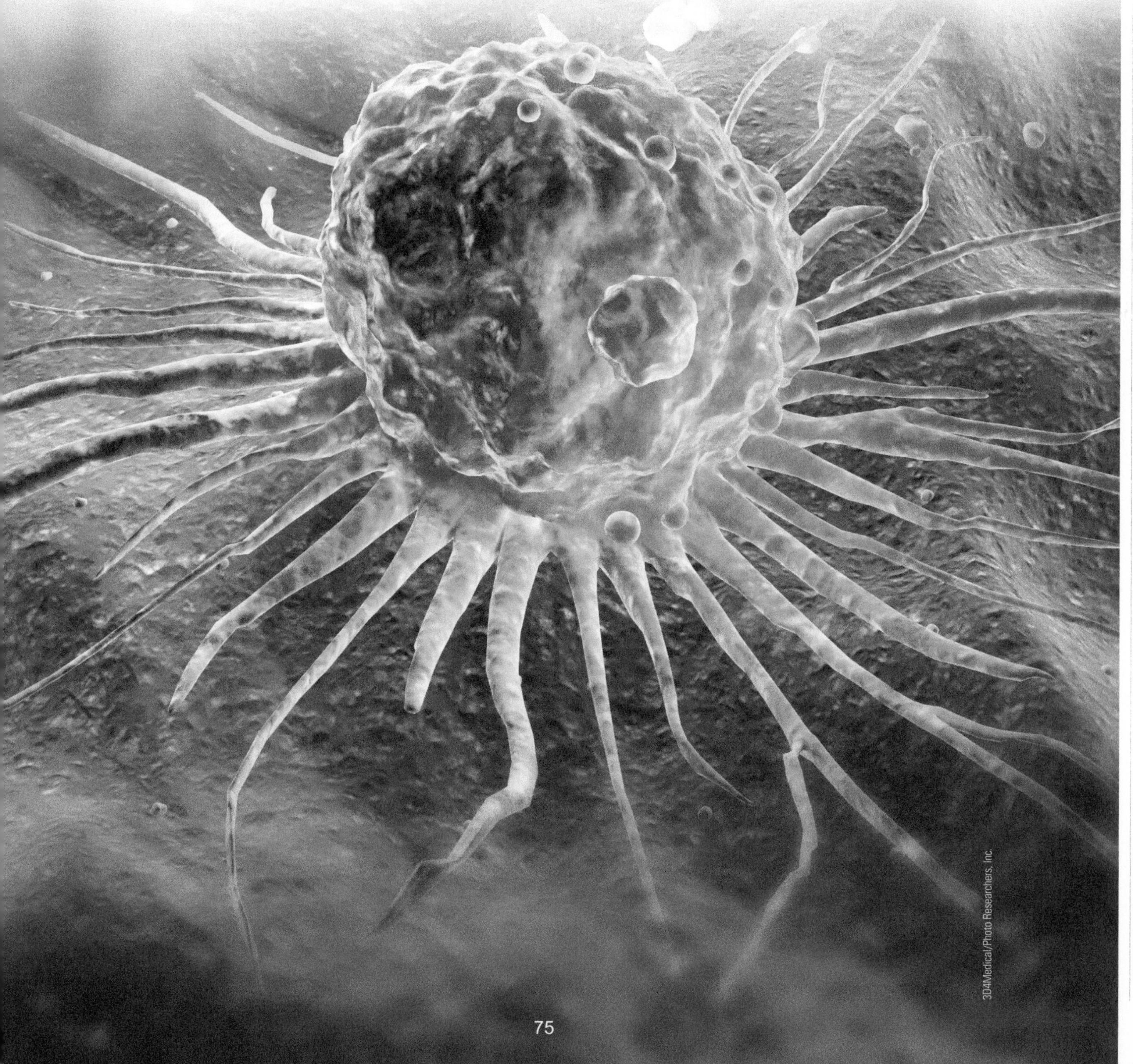

3D4Medical/Photo Researchers, Inc.

Heredity and Evolution

4

Student Learning Objectives

After mastering the material in this chapter, you should be able to:

- Explain the principles of inheritance, first discovered by Gregor Mendel.
- Explain why, when Mendel did his experiments with pea plants, he observed three tall plants for every short plant in the F_2 generation.
- Describe how dominant and recessive traits are inherited and how these modes of inheritance differ from one another.
- Summarize why mutation is important to the evolutionary process.
- Discuss how natural selection works and why there must be genetic variation in a population for natural selection to occur. You should also be able to provide some examples of natural selection in humans.
- Discuss how mutation, genetic drift, gene flow, and natural selection interact over time to produce evolutionary change in populations and species.

Have you ever had a cat with five, six, or even seven toes? Even if you haven't, you may have seen one, because extra toes are fairly common in cats. Or, maybe you've known someone with an extra finger or toe, because some people have extra digits too. Anne Boleyn, mother of England's Queen Elizabeth I and the first of Henry VIII's wives to lose her head, apparently had at least part of an extra little finger. (Of course, this had nothing to do with her early demise; that's another story.)

Having extra digits (fingers and toes) is called *polydactyly*, and it's pretty certain that one of Anne Boleyn's parents was also polydactylous (**Fig. 4-1**). It's also likely that any polydactylous cat has a parent with extra toes. But how do we know this? Actually, it's fairly simple. It's because polydactyly is a Mendelian trait inherited in a predictable way, and its pattern of inheritance, among others, was discovered almost 150 years ago by a monk named Gregor Mendel (**Fig. 4-2**).

For at least 10,000 years, people have raised domesticated plants and animals. However, it wasn't until the twentieth century that scientists understood *how* **selective breeding** could increase the frequency of desirable characteristics. From the time when ancient Greek philosophers considered the question of how traits were inherited until well into the nineteenth century, the most common belief was that the traits seen in offspring resulted from the *blending* of parental traits. There were different explanations of how this happened, but numerous scholars, including Charles Darwin, accepted some aspects of this explanation focused on blending.

selective breeding A practice whereby animal or plant breeders choose which individual animals or plants will be allowed to mate based on the traits (such as coat color or body size) they hope to produce in the offspring. Animals or plants that don't have the desirable traits aren't allowed to breed.

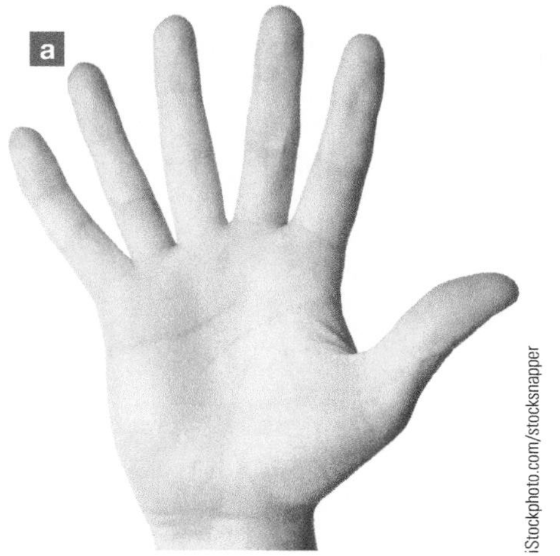

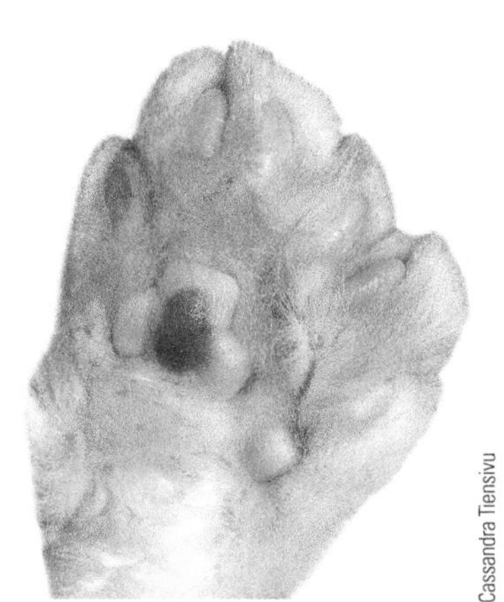

▶ **Figure 4-1** (**a**) Hand of a person with polydactyly. (**b**) Front foot of a polydactylous cat.

The Genetic Principles Discovered by Mendel

It may seem strange that, after discussing recent discoveries about DNA, we now turn our attention to the middle of the nineteenth century, but that's when the science of genetics was born. By examining how the basic principles of inheritance were discovered, we can more easily understand them. It wasn't until Gregor Mendel (1822–1884) considered the question of heredity that it began to be resolved. Mendel was living in an abbey in what is now the Czech Republic. At the time he began his research, he'd already studied botany at the University of Vienna. He had also performed various experiments in the monastery gardens, and this background led him to investigate how physical traits, such as color or height, could be expressed in plant **hybrids**.

▲ **Figure 4-2** Portrait of Gregor Mendel.

hybrids Offspring of parents who differ from each other with regard to certain traits or certain aspects of genetic makeup; also known as heterozygotes.

Mendel worked with garden peas, concentrating on seven different traits, each of which could be expressed in two ways (**Fig. 4-3**). You may think it's unusual that we're discussing peas in an anthropology book, but they provide a simple example of the basic rules of inheritance. The principles Mendel discovered apply to all biological organisms, including humans—another fact illustrating the biological connections among all living things.

Segregation

First, Mendel grew groups of pea plants that were different from one another with regard to at least one trait. For example, in one group all the plants were tall, while in another all were short. To see how the expression of height would change from one generation to the next, he crossed tall plants with short plants, calling them the *parental* generation. According to traditional views, all the hybrid offspring, which he called the *F_1 generation*, should have been intermediate in height. But they weren't. Instead they were all tall (**Fig. 4-4**).

Next, Mendel let the F_1 plants self-fertilize to produce a second generation (the F_2 generation). But this time, only about three quarters of the offspring were tall; the remaining one quarter were short. One expression (short) of the trait (height) had completely disappeared in the F_1 generation and then reappeared in the F_2 generation. Moreover, the expression that was present in all the F_1 plants was more common in the F_2 plants, occurring in

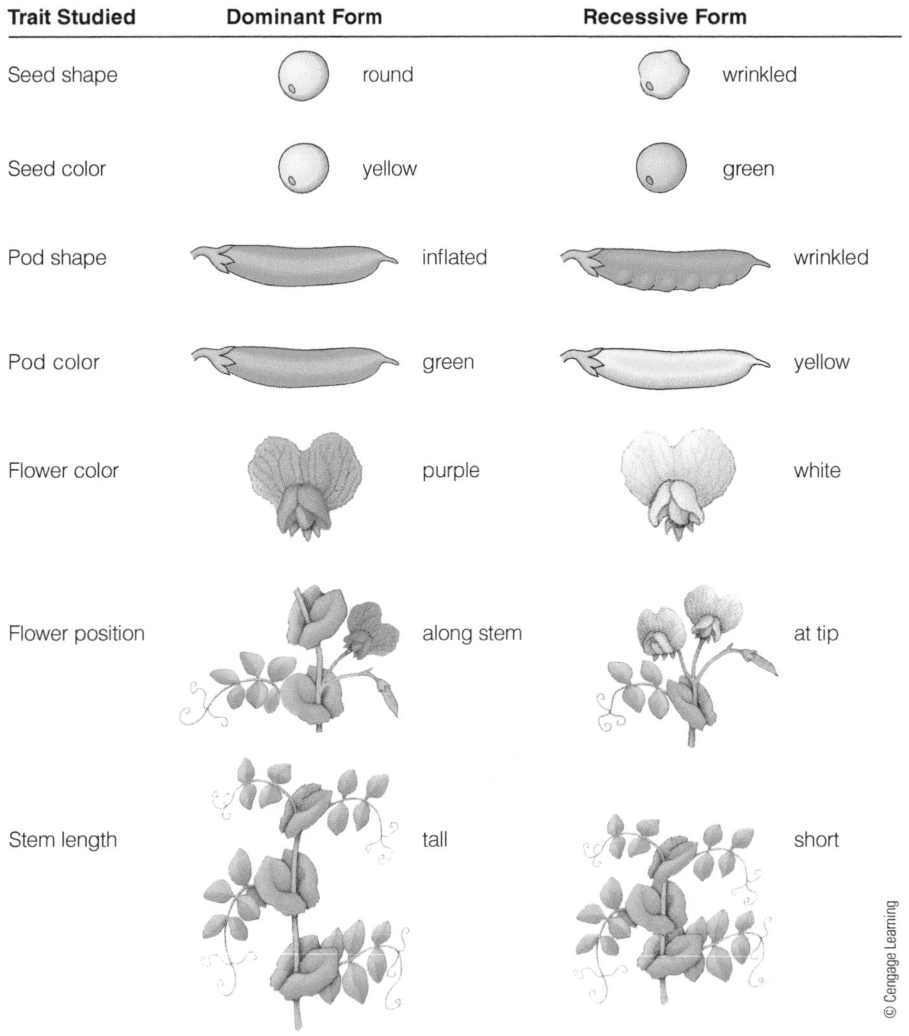

Trait Studied	Dominant Form	Recessive Form
Seed shape	round	wrinkled
Seed color	yellow	green
Pod shape	inflated	wrinkled
Pod color	green	yellow
Flower color	purple	white
Flower position	along stem	at tip
Stem length	tall	short

© Cengage Learning

◄ **Figure 4-3** The traits Mendel studied in peas.

a ratio of approximately 3:1 (three tall plants for every short one).

These results suggested that different expressions of a trait were controlled by discrete *units* (we would call them genes) occurring in pairs and that offspring inherited one unit from each parent. Mendel realized that the members of a pair of units controlling a trait somehow separated into different sex cells and were again united with another member during fertilization of the egg. This is Mendel's *first principle of inheritance,* known as the **principle of segregation.**

Today we know that meiosis explains Mendel's principle of segregation. During meiosis, paired chromosomes, and the genes they carry, separate from each other and end up in different gametes. However, in the zygote, the full complement of chromosomes is restored, and both members of each chromosome pair are present in the offspring.

Dominance and Recessiveness

Mendel also realized that the "unit" for the absent characteristic (shortness) in the F_1 plants hadn't actually disappeared. It was still there, but for some reason it wasn't expressed. Mendel described the expression that seemed to be lost as "**recessive,**" and the expressed trait "**dominant.**" Thus,

principle of segregation Genes (alleles) occur in pairs because chromosomes occur in pairs. During gamete formation, the members of each pair of alleles separate, so that each gamete contains one member of each pair.

recessive Describing a trait that isn't expressed in heterozygotes; it also refers to the allele that governs the trait. For a recessive allele to be expressed, an individual must have two copies of it (i.e., the individual must be homozygous).

dominant In genetics, describing a trait governed by an allele that's expressed in the presence of another allele (i.e., in heterozygotes). Dominant alleles prevent the expression of recessive alleles in heterozygotes. (This is the definition of *complete* dominance.)

▶ **Figure 4-4** Results of crosses when only one trait (height) at a time is considered.

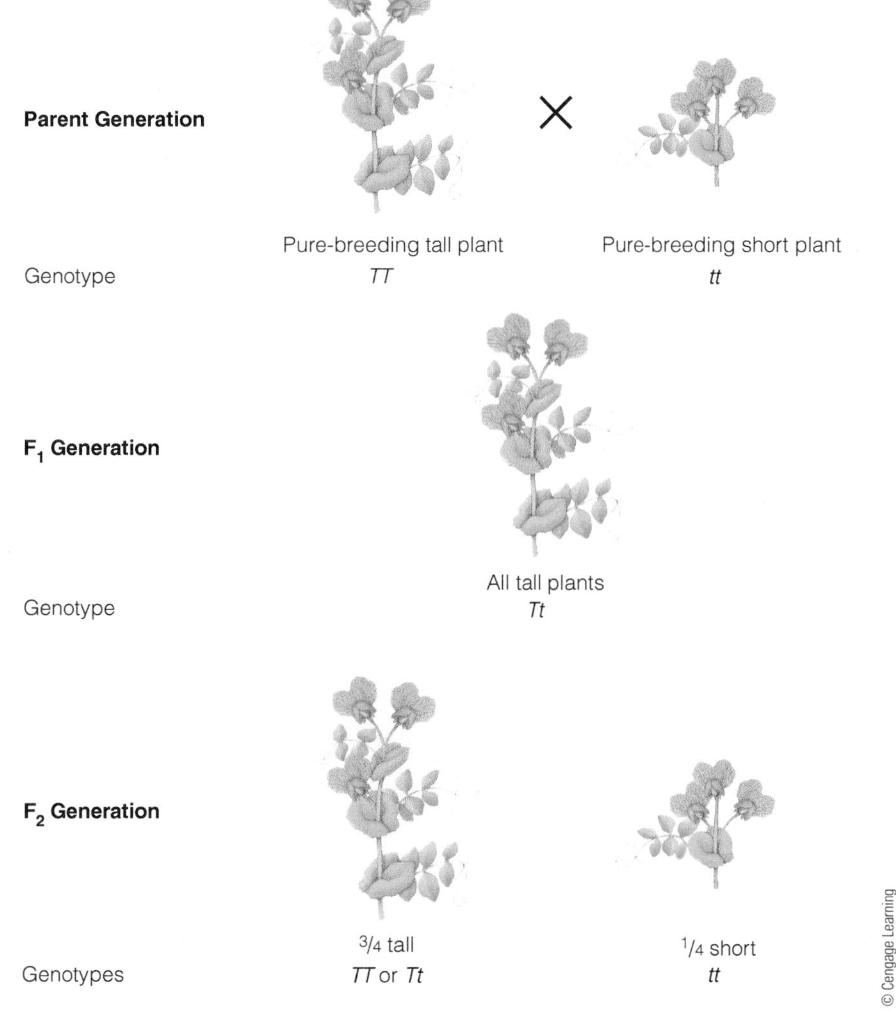

the principles of *dominance* and *recessiveness* were developed, and they remain important concepts in genetics today.

As it turns out, height in garden peas is controlled by two different alleles at the same genetic locus; we'll call it the height locus. The allele that specifies tall is dominant to the allele for short. (It's worth mentioning that height isn't controlled this way in all plants.) In Mendel's experiments, all the parent plants had two copies of the same allele, either dominant or recessive, depending on whether they were tall or short. When two copies of the same allele are present, the individual is said to be **homozygous**. Thus all the tall parent plants were homozygous for the dominant allele and all the short parent plants were homozygous for the recessive allele. This explains why crossing tall plants with tall plants produced only tall offspring. Likewise, all the crosses between short plants produced only short offspring. All the plants in the parent generation had the same allele—that is, they lacked genetic variation at the height locus. However, all the F_1 plants (hybrids) inherited one allele from each parent plant: a tall allele from one parent and a short allele from the other. Therefore they all inherited two different alleles at the height locus. Individuals that have two different alleles at a locus are **heterozygous**.

Figure 4-5 illustrates the crosses that Mendel initially performed. By convention, letters that represent

homozygous Having the same allele at the same locus on both members of a pair of chromosomes.

heterozygous Having different alleles at the same locus on members of a pair of chromosomes.

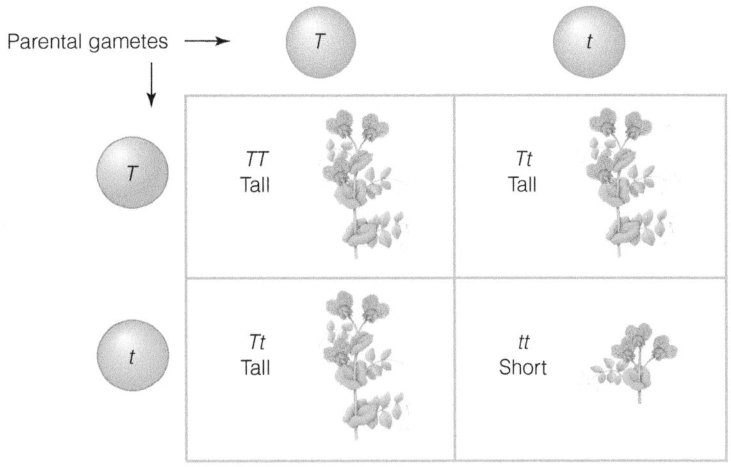

◄ **Figure 4-5** Punnett square representing possible genotypes and phenotypes and their proportions in the F_2 generation. The circles across the top and at the left of the Punnett square represent the gametes of the F_1 parents. Each square receives one allele from the gamete above it and another from the gamete to the left. Thus the square at the upper left has two dominant (*T*) alleles. Likewise the upper right square receives a recessive (*t*) allele from the blue gamete above it and a dominant (*T*) allele from the orange gamete to its left. In this way, the four squares illustrate that, statistically, one quarter of the F_2 plants can be expected to be homozygous tall (*TT*); another half of the plants can also be expected to be tall but will be heterozygous (*Tt*); and the remaining quarter can be expected to be short because they are homozygous for the recessive "short" allele (*tt*). Thus, three quarters of the plants can be expected to be tall and one quarter short.

alleles or genes are italicized, with uppercase letters referring to dominant alleles (or dominant traits) and lowercase letters referring to recessive alleles (or recessive traits). Therefore,

T = the allele for tallness
t = the allele for shortness

The same symbols are combined to describe an individual's actual genetic makeup, or **genotype**. The term *genotype* usually refers to the alleles at a specific genetic locus in an organism. Thus the genotypes of the plants in Mendel's experiments were

TT = homozygous tall plants
Tt = heterozygous tall plants
tt = homozygous short plants

Figure 4-5 also shows the different ways alleles can be combined when the F_1 plants are self-fertilized to produce an F_2 generation. Therefore the figure shows all the *genotypes* that are possible in the F_2 generation and, statistically speaking, it shows that we would expect one quarter of the F_2 plants to be homozygous dominant (*TT*), half to be heterozygous (*Tt*), and the remaining one quarter to be homozygous recessive (*tt*).

You can also see the proportions of F_2 **phenotypes**, the observed physical manifestations of genes, illustrating why Mendel saw approximately three tall plants for every short plant in the F_2 generation. One quarter of the F_2 plants are tall because they have the *TT* genotype. Furthermore, an additional half, which are heterozygous (*Tt*), are also tall because *T* is dominant to *t*, so it's expressed in the phenotype. The remaining one quarter are homozygous recessive (*tt*), and they're short because no dominant allele is present. It's important to understand that the *only* way a recessive allele can be expressed is if it occurs with another recessive allele—that is, if the individual is homozygous recessive at the particular locus in question.

Independent Assortment Mendel also demonstrated that different characteristics aren't necessarily inherited together by showing that plant height and seed color are independent of each other. That is, any tall pea plant had a 50-50 chance of producing either yellow or green peas. Because of this fact, he developed the **principle of independent assortment**. According to this principle, the units (genes) that code for different traits (in this example, plant height and seed color) sort out independently of each other during gamete formation (**Fig. 4-6**). Today we know that this happens because the genes that control plant height and seed color are located on different, nonpartner chromosomes and, during meiosis, the chromosomes travel to newly forming cells independently

genotype The genetic makeup of an individual. Genotype usually refers to an organism's genetic makeup (or alleles) at a particular locus.

phenotypes The observable or detectable physical characteristics of an organism; the detectable expressions of genotypes, frequently influenced by environmental factors.

principle of independent assortment The distribution of one pair of alleles into gametes does not influence the distribution of another pair. The genes controlling different traits are inherited independently of one another.

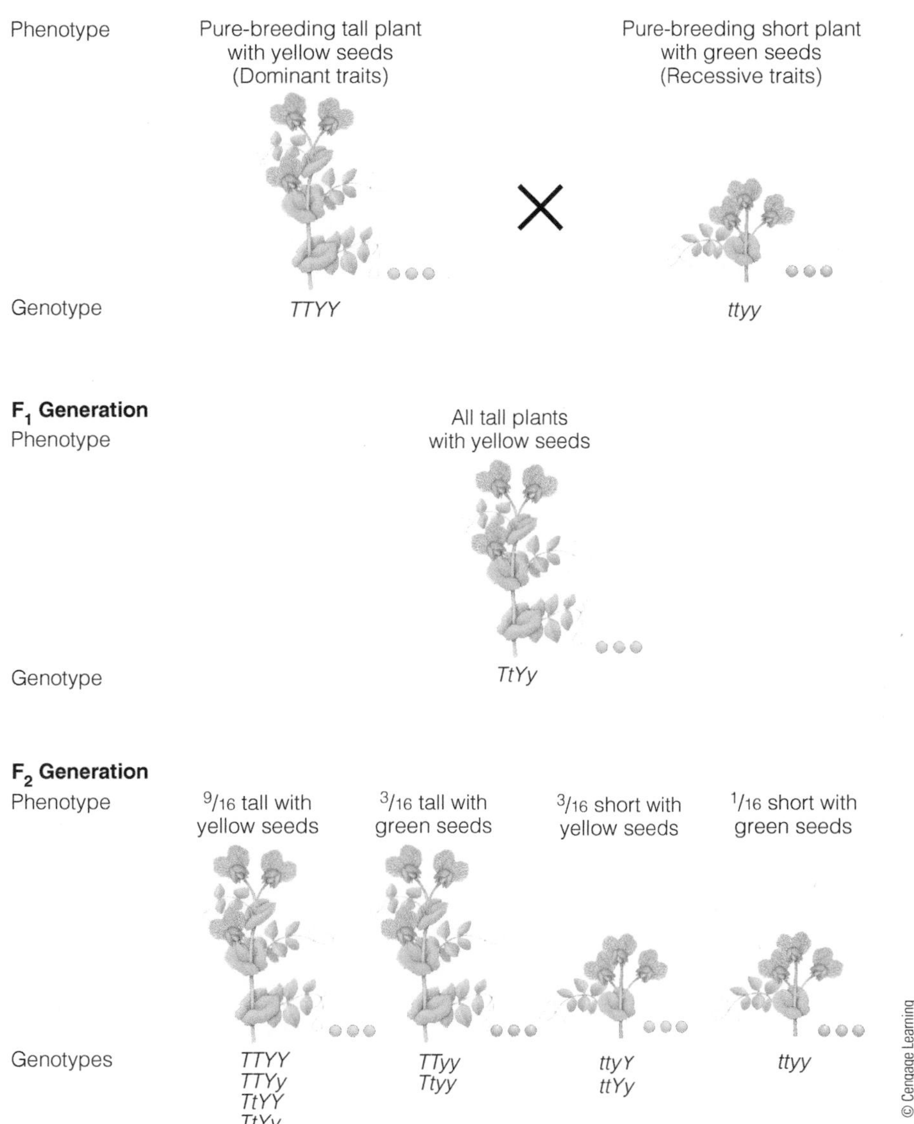

▶ **Figure 4-6** Results of a cross when two traits (height and seed color) are considered simultaneously. These two traits are independent of each other; that is, they aren't necessarily inherited together. Also shown are the genotypes associated with each phenotype. Notice that the ratio of tall plants to short plants is three quarters to one quarter, or 3:1, the same as in Figure 4-4. Likewise, the ratio of yellow seeds to green seeds is 3:1. Thus, the phenotypic ratio in the F_2 generation is 9:3:3:1.

of one another in a process called **random assortment**.

But if Mendel had used just *any* two traits, his results would have been different at least some of the time. This is because genes on the same chromosome aren't independent of each other, and they usually stay together during meiosis. Even though Mendel didn't know about chromosomes, he certainly knew that all characteristics weren't independent of one another. But because he wanted to emphasize independence, he reported only on those traits that illustrated independent assortment.

Mendel's results were published in 1866, but the methodology and statistical nature of the research were beyond the thinking of the time and their significance was overlooked and unappreciated. However, by the end of the nineteenth century, several investigators had made important contributions to the understanding of chromosomes and cell division. These discoveries paved the way for the acceptance of Mendel's work in 1900, when three different groups of scientists came across his paper. Regrettably, Mendel had died 16 years earlier and never knew how greatly his work came to be appreciated.

random assortment The chance distribution of chromosomes to daughter cells during meiosis. Along with recombination, random assortment is an important source of genetic variation (but not new alleles).

Mendelian Inheritance in Humans

Mendelian traits, also called *discrete traits*, are controlled by alleles at only one genetic locus (or, in some cases, two or more very closely linked loci). The most comprehensive listing of Mendelian traits in humans is available on the Internet. *Online Mendelian Inheritance in Man* (www.ncbi.nlm.nih.gov/omim/) currently lists more than 21,000 human characteristics that are inherited according to Mendelian principles.

Although some Mendelian characteristics have readily visible phenotypic expressions (such as polydactyly), most don't. The majority of Mendelian traits are biochemical in nature, and many genetic disorders result from harmful alleles inherited in Mendelian fashion (**Table 4.1** on page 84). So if it seems as though textbooks overly emphasize genetic disease in discussions of Mendelian traits, it's because many of the known Mendelian characteristics result from harmful alleles.

A number of genetic disorders are caused by dominant alleles (see Table 4-1). This means that if a person inherits only one copy of a harmful dominant allele, the condition it causes will be present regardless of the presence of a different, recessive allele on the partner chromosome.

Recessive conditions are commonly associated with the lack of a substance, usually an enzyme (see Table 4-1). For a person actually to have a recessive disorder, he or she must have two copies of the recessive allele causing it. People who have only one copy of a harmful recessive allele are unaffected. But even though they don't actually have the recessive condition, they can still pass the allele that causes it on to their children. For this reason they're frequently called *carriers*. (Remember, half their gametes will carry the recessive allele.) If such a person's mate is also a carrier, it's possible for them to have a child who will be homozygous for the allele, and that child will be affected. In fact, in a mating between two carriers, the risk of having an affected child is 25 percent (refer back to Fig. 4-5).

Blood groups, such as the ABO system, provide some of the best examples of Mendelian traits in humans. The ABO system is governed by three alleles, *A*, *B*, and *O*, found at the *ABO* locus on the ninth chromosome. These alleles determine a person's ABO blood type by coding for the production of molecules called **antigens** on the surface of red blood cells. If only antigen A is present, the blood type (phenotype) is A; if only B is present, the blood type is B; if both are present, the blood type is AB; and when neither is present, the blood type is O (**Table 4.2** on page 85).

The *O* allele is recessive to both *A* and *B*; therefore if a person has type O blood, he or she must have two copies of the *O* allele. However, since both *A* and *B* are dominant to *O*, an individual with blood type A can actually have one of two genotypes: *AA* or *AO*. The same is true of type B, which results from the genotypes *BB* and *BO* (see Table 4-2). However, type AB presents a slightly different situation, called **codominance**, where two different alleles are present and both are expressed. Therefore when both *A* and *B* alleles are present, both A and B antigens can be detected on the surface of red blood cells.

Misconceptions about Dominance and Recessiveness

Most people have the impression that dominance and recessiveness are all-or-nothing situations. This misconception especially pertains to recessive alleles. The general view is that when these alleles occur in carriers (heterozygotes), they have no effect on the phenotype; that is, they are completely inactivated by the presence of another (dominant) allele. Certainly this is how it appeared to Gregor Mendel.

Mendelian traits Characteristics that are influenced by alleles at only one genetic locus. Examples include many blood types, such as ABO. Many genetic disorders, including sickle-cell anemia and Tay-Sachs disease, are also Mendelian traits.

antigens Large molecules found on the surface of cells. Several different loci govern various antigens on red and white blood cells. (Foreign antigens provoke an immune response.)

codominance The expression of two alleles in heterozygotes. In this situation, neither allele is dominant or recessive, so they both influence the phenotype.

Table 4.1 Some Mendelian Traits in Humans

Dominant Traits Condition	Manifestations	Recessive Traits Condition	Manifestations
Achondroplasia	Dwarfism due to growth defects involving the long bones of the arms and legs; trunk and head size usually normal.	Cystic fibrosis	Among the most common genetic (Mendelian) disorders among European Americans; abnormal secretions of the exocrine glands, with pronounced involvement of the pancreas; most patients develop obstructive lung disease. Until the recent development of new treatments, only about half of all patients survived to early adulthood.
Brachydactyly	Shortened fingers and toes.		
Familial hyper-cholesterolemia	Elevated cholesterol levels and cholesterol plaque deposition; a leading cause of heart disease, with death frequently occurring by middle age.		
Neurofibromatosis	Symptoms range from the appearance of abnormal skin pigmentation to large tumors resulting in severe deformities; can, in extreme cases, lead to paralysis, blindness, and death.	Tay-Sachs disease	Most common among Ashkenazi Jews; degeneration of the nervous system beginning at about 6 months of age; lethal by age 2 or 3 years.
Marfan syndrome	The eyes and cardiovascular and skeletal systems are affected; symptoms include greater than average height, long arms and legs, eye problems, and enlargement of the aorta; death due to rupture of the aorta is common. Abraham Lincoln may have had Marfan syndrome.	Phenylketonuria (PKU)	Inability to metabolize the amino acid phenylalanine; results in mental impairment if left untreated during childhood; treatment involves strict dietary management and some supplementation.
Huntington disease	Progressive degeneration of the nervous system accompanied by dementia and seizures; age of onset variable but commonly between 30 and 40 years.	Albinism	Inability to produce normal amounts of the pigment melanin; results in very fair, untannable skin, light blond hair, and light eyes; may also be associated with vision problems. (There is more than one form of albinism.)
Camptodactyly	Malformation of the hands whereby the fingers, usually the little finger, is permanently contracted.	Sickle-cell anemia	Abnormal form of hemoglobin (Hb^S) that results in collapsed red blood cells, blockage of capillaries, reduced blood flow to organs, and, without treatment, death.
Hypodontia of upper lateral incisors	Upper lateral incisors are absent or only partially formed (peg-shaped). Pegged incisors are a partial expression of the allele.	Thalassemia	A group of disorders characterized by reduced or absent alpha or beta chains in the hemoglobin molecule; results in severe anemia and, in some forms, death.
Cleft chin	Dimple or depression in the middle of the chin; less prominent in females than in males.		
PTC tasting	The ability to taste the bitter substance phenylthiocarbamide (PTC). Tasting thresholds vary, suggesting that alleles at another locus may also exert an influence.	Absence of permanent dentition	Failure of the permanent dentition to erupt. The primary dentition is not affected.

However, various biochemical techniques available today show that many recessive alleles actually do have some effect on the phenotype, although these effects aren't usually detectable through simple observation. It turns out that in heterozygotes, the products of many recessive alleles are reduced but not completely eliminated. Therefore our perception of recessive alleles greatly depends on whether we examine them at the directly observable phenotypic level or the biochemical level.

There are also a number of misconceptions about dominant alleles.

Table 4.2 ABO Genotypes and Associated Phenotypes

Genotypes	Antigens on Red Blood Cells	ABO Blood Type (Phenotype)
AA, AO	A	A
BB, BO	B	B
AB	A and B	AB
OO	None	O

Many people think of dominant alleles as somehow "stronger" or "better," and there is always the mistaken notion that dominant alleles are more common in populations because natural selection favors them. These misconceptions undoubtedly stem from the label "dominant" and its connotations of power or control. But in genetic usage, this view is misleading. Just think about it. If dominant alleles were always more common, then a majority of people would have conditions such as achondroplasia and Marfan syndrome (see Table 4-1). But obviously that's not true.

Previously held views of dominance and recessiveness were influenced by available technologies, and as genetic technologies continue to change, new theories will emerge and our perceptions will be further altered. (This is another example of how new techniques and continued hypothesis testing can lead to a revision of hypotheses and theories.) In fact, although dominance and recessiveness will remain important factors in genetics, it's clear that the ways in which these concepts will be taught will be adapted to accommodate new discoveries.

Patterns of Mendelian Inheritance

It's important to be able to establish the pattern of inheritance of genetic traits, especially those that cause serious disease. Also, in families with a history of inherited disorders, it's important to determine an individual's risk of inheriting harmful alleles or expressing symptoms. The technique traditionally used to assess risk of genetic disease has been the construction of a **pedigree chart**, a diagram of matings and offspring in a family over the span of a few generations. Pedigree analysis helps researchers determine if a trait is Mendelian and also helps establish the mode of inheritance. By determining whether the gene that influences a particular trait is located on an autosome or sex chromosome and whether a particular allele is dominant or recessive, researchers have identified six different modes of Mendelian inheritance in humans: *autosomal dominant, autosomal recessive, X-linked recessive, X-linked dominant, Y-linked,* and *mitochondrial.* We'll discuss the first three in some detail.

Standardized symbols are used in pedigree charts. Squares and circles represent males and females, respectively. Horizontal lines connecting individuals indicate matings, and offspring are connected to horizontal mating lines by vertical lines. Siblings are joined by a horizontal line connected to a vertical line that descends from the parents (**Fig. 4-7**).

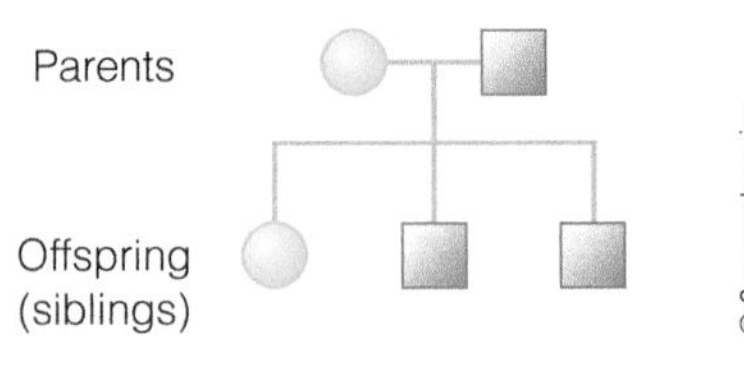

▲**Figure 4-7** Typical symbols used in pedigree charts. Circles and squares represent females and males respectively. Horizontal lines connecting two individuals indicate mating. Vertical lines connect generations.

Autosomal Dominant Traits As the term implies, autosomal dominant traits are governed by dominant alleles located on autosomes (that is, any chromosome except X or Y). One example of an autosomal dominant trait is achondroplasia, a form of dwarfism characterized by a normal-sized trunk and head but shortened arms and legs (see Table

pedigree chart A diagram showing family relationships. It's used to trace the hereditary pattern of particular genetic (usually Mendelian) traits.

Gareth Copley/Getty Images

▲ **Figure 4-8** Ellie Simmonds who has achondroplasia, won two gold medals for Great Britain in swimming events at both the 2008 and 2012 Paralympic Games. She inherited one copy of the dominant allele that causes achondroplasia by inhibiting bone growth during fetal development. As a result, her legs and arms are disproportionally short. People with achondroplasia are also unable to fully extend their arms—something that has not inhibited her swimming abilities.

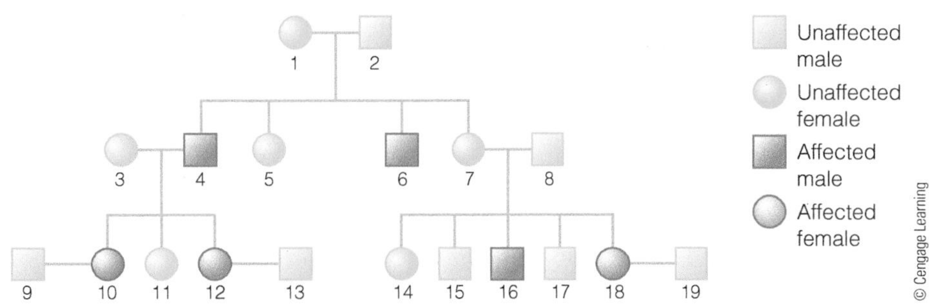

▲ **Figure 4-9** Inheritance of an autosomal dominant trait as illustrated by a human pedigree for achondroplasia. How can individuals 5, 11, 14, 15, and 17 be unaffected? What is the genotype of all affected individuals? (To answer the second question, let *A* = the dominant allele and *a* = the recessive allele.)

4-1 and **Fig. 4-8**). Achondroplasia occurs in approximately 1 out of every 10,000 live births. It is usually caused by a spontaneous point mutation in a gene that influences the development of cartilage and thus bone growth.

Because achondroplasia is caused by a dominant allele, anyone who inherits just one copy of it will have the trait. In this discussion, the symbol *A* refers to the dominant allele that causes the condition and *a* represents the recessive, normal allele. Since the allele is rare, virtually everyone who has achondroplasia is a heterozygote (*Aa*). Unaffected individuals (that is, almost everybody) are homozygous recessive (*aa*).

Figure 4-9 is a partial pedigree chart for achondroplasia. It's apparent from this pedigree that all affected members have at least one affected parent, so the condition doesn't skip generations. This pattern is true for all autosomal dominant traits. Another characteristic of autosomal dominant traits is that males and females are more or less equally affected. Also important regarding dominant traits is that approximately half the offspring of affected parents are also affected (**Fig. 4-10**). This proportion is what we

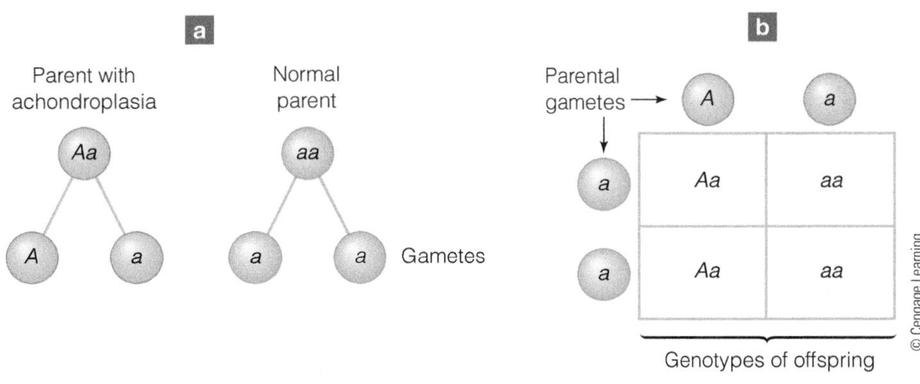

▲ **Figure 4-10** The pattern of inheritance of autosomal dominant traits is the direct result of the distribution of chromosomes and the alleles they carry into gametes during meiosis. (**a**) A diagram of possible gametes produced by two parents, one with achondroplasia and another with normal development of the extremities. The achondroplastic individual can produce two types of gametes: half with the dominant allele (*A*) and half with the recessive allele (*a*). All gametes produced by the normal-height parent will carry the recessive allele. (**b**) A Punnett square depicting the possible genotypes in the offspring of one parent with achondroplasia (*Aa*) and one with normal extremities (*aa*). Statistically, we would expect half the offspring to have the Aa genotype and thus have achondroplasia. The other half would be homozygous recessive (*aa*) and their extremities would grow normally.

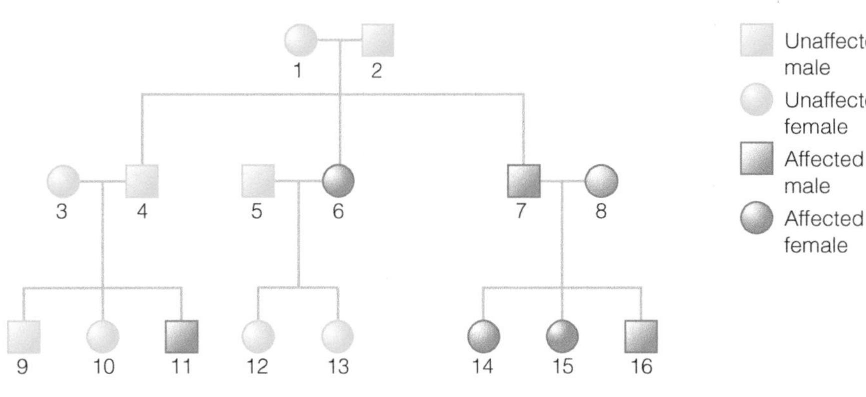

1
2
3
4
5
6
7
8
9
10
11
12
13
14
15
16
Unaffected male
Unaffected female
Affected male
Affected female
© Cengage Learning

◂**Figure 4-11** Partial pedigree for albinism, an autosomal recessive trait. Why are some of the offspring of affected individuals unaffected? Individuals 6 and 7, children of unaffected parents, are affected. Why? Four individuals are definitely unaffected carriers. Which ones are they? Why is individual 11 affected when his parents aren't?

would predict for an autosomal dominant trait where only one parent is affected, because half of that parent's gametes will have the dominant but harmful allele.

Autosomal Recessive Traits Autosomal recessive traits are also influenced by genes on autosomes, but they show a different pattern of inheritance. A good example is shown in **Figure 4-11**, a pedigree chart for albinism. The most common form of albinism is a metabolic disorder caused by an autosomal recessive allele that prevents the production of a pigment called melanin (see Chapter 15). Thus albinos have unusually light hair, skin, and eyes (**Fig. 4-12**). The frequency of this type of albinism varies widely among populations, with a prevalence of about 1 in 37,000 people of European ancestry; but approximately 1 in 200 Hopi Indians are affected.

Pedigrees for autosomal recessive traits show obvious differences from those for autosomal dominant characteristics. For one thing, an affected offspring can be produced by two phenotypically normal parents. In fact,

▾**Figure 4-12** (**a**) A Tanzanian woman with her young albino son. (Because of the social stigma attached to albinism, there has been, since the mid-2000s, a dramatic increase in the trade of albino body parts, which are used in witchcraft, especially in Tanzania.) (**b**) This albino horse may be beautiful, but it should not be kept outdoors all the time. With virtually no pigmentation, it would be highly susceptible to sunburn and various forms of skin cancer, including melanoma.

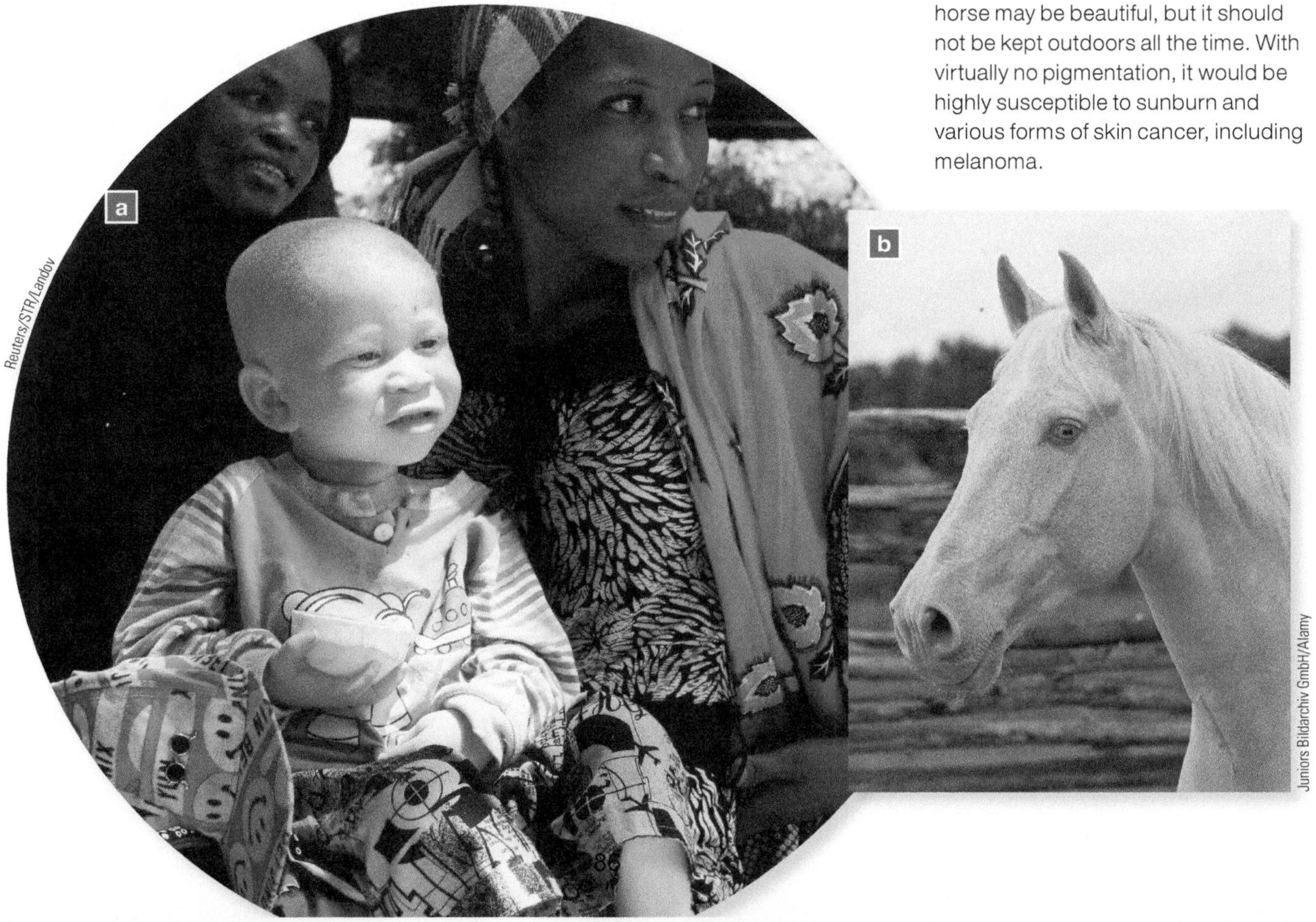

a
Reuters/STR/Landov
b
Juniors Bildarchiv GmbH/Alamy

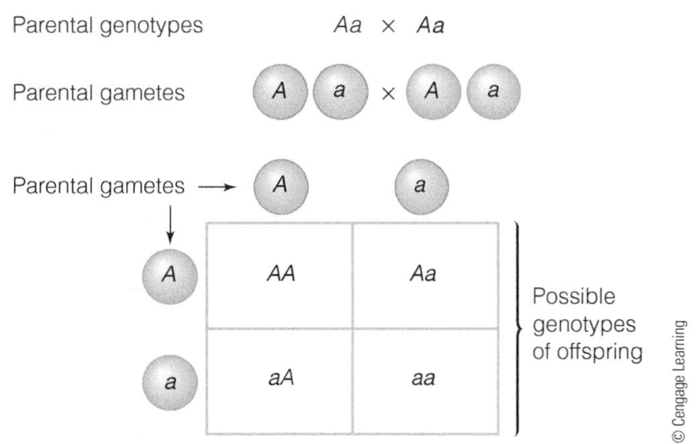

▶ **Figure 4-13** A cross between two phenotypically normal parents, both carriers of the albinism allele. From a mating such as this between two carriers, statistically we would expect the following possible proportions of genotypes and phenotypes in the offspring: homozygous dominants (*AA*) with normal phenotype, 25 percent; heterozygotes, or carriers (*Aa*) with normal phenotype, 50 percent; and homozygous recessives (*aa*) with albinism, 25 percent. This yields the phenotypic ratio of three with normal pigmentation to one albino.

most people who express recessive conditions have unaffected parents. In addition, the proportion of affected offspring from most matings is less than half. But when both parents have the trait, all their offspring will be affected. As in the pattern for autosomal dominant traits, males and females are equally affected.

The Mendelian principle of segregation explains the pattern of inheritance of autosomal recessive traits. In fact, this pattern is the very one Mendel first described in his pea experiments (look back at Fig. 4-5). Unaffected parents who produce an albino child *must both be carriers,* and their child will be homozygous for the recessive allele causing the abnormality. The Punnett square in **Figure 4-13** shows how such a mating produces both unaffected and affected offspring in predictable proportions—the typical *phenotypic ratio* of 3:1.

Sex-Linked Traits Sex-linked traits are controlled by genes located on the X and Y chromosomes. Almost all of the more than 1,000 sex-linked traits listed in *Online Mendelian Inheritance in Man* are influenced by genes on the X chromosome (**Table 4.3**). Most of the

Table 4.3 Some Mendelian Disorders Inherited as X-linked Recessive Traits in Humans

Condition	Manifestations
G-6-PD (glucose-6-phosphate) deficiency	Lack of an enzyme (G-6-PD) in red blood cells; produces severe, sometimes fatal anemia in the presence of certain foods (e.g., fava beans) and/or drugs (e.g., the antimalarial drug primaquin).
Muscular dystrophy	One form is X-linked; other forms can be inherited as autosomal recessives. Progressive weakness and atrophy of muscles beginning in early childhood; continues to progress throughout life; some female carriers may develop heart problems.
Red-green color blindness	Actually, there are two separate forms, one involving the perception of red and the other involving the perception of green. About 8 percent of European males have an impaired ability to distinguish green.
Lesch-Nyhan disease	Impaired motor development noticeable by 5 months; progressive motor impairment, diminished kidney function, self-mutilation, and early death.
Hemophilia	There are three forms; two (hemophilia A and B) are X-linked. In hemophilia A, a clotting factor is missing; hemophilia B is caused by a defective clotting factor. Both produce abnormal internal and external bleeding from minor injuries; severe pain is a frequent accompaniment; without treatment, death usually occurs before adulthood.
Ichthyosis	There are several forms; one is X-linked. A skin condition due to lack of an enzyme; characterized by scaly, brown lesions on the extremities and trunk. In the past, people with this condition were sometimes exhibited in circuses and sideshows as "the alligator man."

coding sequences (that is, those segments that actually specify a protein) on the Y chromosome are involved in determining maleness and testis function.

Hemophilia, one of the best known of the X-linked traits, is caused by a recessive allele on the X chromosome. This allele prevents the formation of a clotting factor in the blood, and affected individuals suffer bleeding episodes and may actually bleed to death from injuries that most of us would consider trivial.

The most famous pedigree illustrating this condition is that of Queen Victoria (1820–1901) of England and her descendants (**Fig. 4-14**). The most striking feature shown by this pattern of inheritance is that almost all affected people are males, because males have only one X chromosome and therefore only one copy of X-linked genes. This means that *any allele*, even a recessive one, located on their X chromosome will be expressed, because there's no possibility of a dominant allele on a partner chromosome to block it. Females, on the other hand, show the same pattern of expression of X-linked traits as for autosomal traits, because they have two X chromosomes. That is, just as with any other pair of chromosomes, the only way an X-linked recessive allele can be expressed in a female is if she has two copies of it. However, females who have one copy of the hemophilia allele are carriers, and they may have some tendency toward bleeding, even though they aren't severely affected.

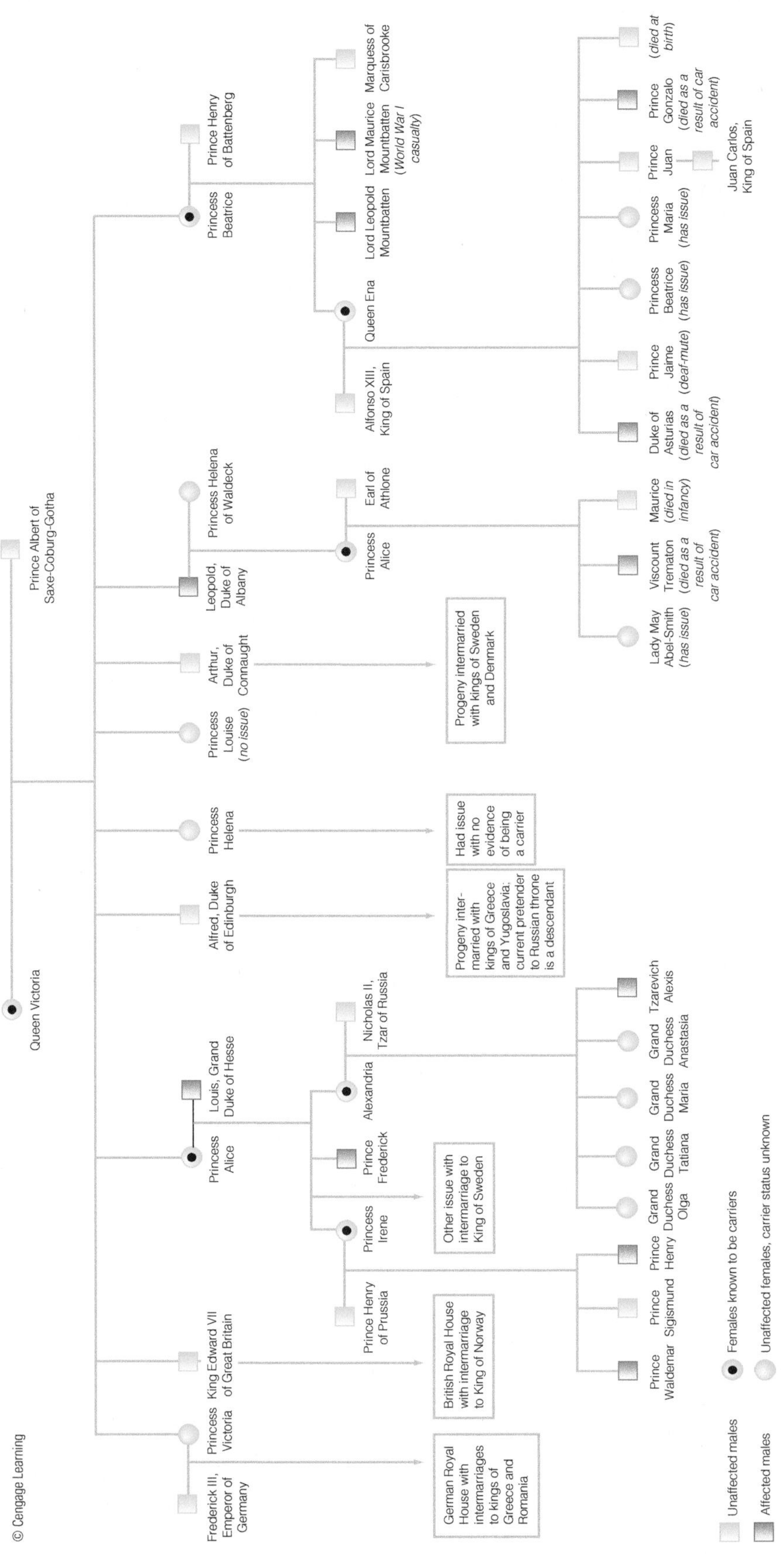

▲**Figure 4-14** Pedigree for Queen Victoria and some of her descendants, showing the inheritance of hemophilia, an X-linked recessive trait in humans.

Non-Mendelian Inheritance

Polygenic Inheritance

Mendelian traits are described as *discrete*, or *discontinuous*, because their phenotypic expressions don't overlap; instead, they fall into clearly defined categories (**Fig. 4-15a**). For example,

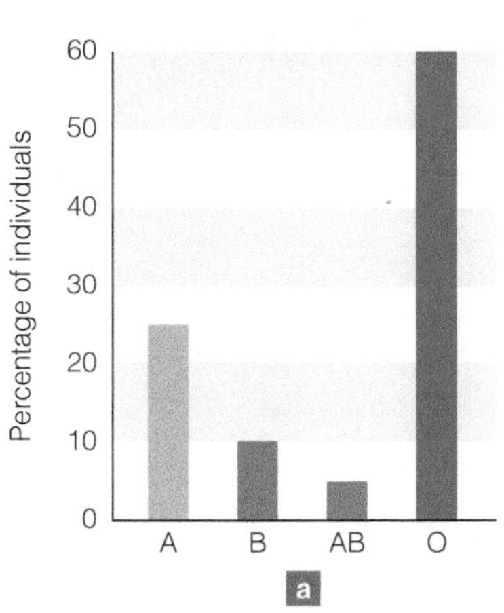

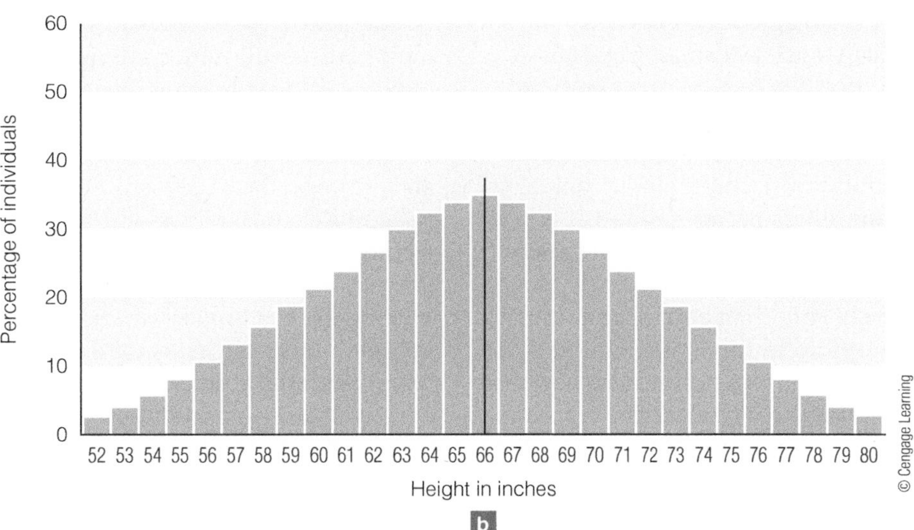

▲ **Figure 4-15** (**a**) This bar graph shows the discontinuous distribution of a Mendelian trait (ABO blood type) in a hypothetical population. Expression of the trait is described in terms of frequencies. (**b**) This histogram represents the continuous expression of a polygenic trait (height) in a large group of people. Notice that the percentage of extremely short or tall individuals is low; most people are closer to the mean, or average height, represented by the vertical line at the center of the distribution. (**c**) A group of male students arranged according to height. The most common height is 70 inches, which is the mean, or average, for this group.

in the ABO system, the four phenotypes are completely distinct from one another; that is, there is no intermediate form between type A and type B. In other words, Mendelian traits don't show *continuous* variation.

However, many traits do have a wide range of phenotypic expressions, which form a graded series. These are called **polygenic**, or *continuous*, traits (**Fig. 4-15b** and **c**). While Mendelian traits are governed by only one genetic locus, polygenic characteristics are governed by alleles at two or more loci, and each locus has some influence on the phenotype. Throughout the history of biological anthropology, the most frequently discussed examples of polygenic inheritance in humans have been skin, hair, and eye color (**Fig. 4-16**).

Coloration is determined by melanin, a **pigment** produced by specialized cells called melanocytes (see Chapter 16), and the amount of melanin that is produced determines how dark or light a person's skin will be. Melanin production is influenced by interactions between several differ-

polygenic Referring to traits influenced by genes at two or more loci. Examples include stature, skin color, eye color, and hair color. Many polygenic traits are influenced by environmental factors such as nutrition and exposure to sunlight.

pigment In this context, molecules that influence the color of skin, hair, and eyes.

ent loci that have now been identified. A study by Lamason and colleagues (2005) showed that one single, highly *conserved* gene (called *MC1R*) with two alleles makes a greater contribution to melanin production than some other melanin-producing genes. Moreover, geneticists know of at least four other pigmentation genes. This is very important because they can now examine the complex interactions between these genes and also how their functions are influenced by regulatory genes. So the story of melanin production is a complicated one, but it's exciting that many long-standing questions about variation in human skin color will be answered in the not too distant future.

As we stated earlier, eye color is influenced by more than one gene, and some of the genes that influence skin color are also involved. However, a gene called *OCA2*, located on chromosome 15, is apparently the most important gene in the development of blue eyes (Fig. 4-16). *OCA2* is involved in pigmentation of the iris of the eye, and mutations in this gene lead to a form of albinism. Sturm and colleagues (2008) demonstrated that this gene accounts for 74 percent of the variation in human eye color in European populations. (Northern European populations and their descendants exhibit more variability in eye color than is seen in any other human populations, and they're the only ones in which significant numbers of people have blue eyes.) Moreover, specific variations of the *OCA2* gene were found in virtually 100 percent of blue-eyed people from Denmark, Turkey, and Jordan. In addition, point mutations in one of several genes that regulate *OCA2* are also "perfectly associated" with blue eyes (Eiberg et al., 2007). Thus when we examine any trait, we must look not only at the genes traditionally associated with it but *also at the DNA sequences that regulate it*. Indeed, it's looking more and more like genes don't really do much by themselves; they just follow orders, and if the orders vary, their effects will also vary.

Polygenic traits actually account for most of the readily observable phenotypic variation in humans, and they've traditionally served as a basis for racial classification. In addition to skin, hair, and eye color, there are many other polygenic characteristics—including stature, shape of the face, and fingerprint pattern—to name a few. Because they exhibit continuous variation, most polygenic traits can be measured on a scale composed of equal increments. For example, height (stature) is measured in feet and inches (or meters and centimeters). If we were to measure height in a large number of individuals, the distribution of measurements would continue uninterrupted from the shortest extreme to the tallest (see Fig. 4-15b and c). That's what is meant by the term *continuous traits*.

Because polygenic traits can usually be measured, physical anthropologists can analyze them using certain statistical tests. The use of simple summary statistics, such as the *mean* (average) or *standard deviation* (a measure of variation within a group), permits basic descriptions of populations and comparisons between them. For example, a physical anthropologist might be interested in average height in two different populations, whether or not differences between the two are statistically significant, and if so, why. (Incidentally, *all* physical traits measured and statistically treated in fossils are polygenic in nature.)

Mendelian traits can't be measured in the same way because they're either present or absent—expressed one way or another. But this doesn't mean that they provide less information about genetic processes. They can be described in terms of frequency within populations, which makes it possible to compare groups for differences in prevalence. For example, one population may have a high frequency of blood type A while type A may be almost completely absent in another group. Also, Mendelian traits can be analyzed for mode of inheritance (dominant or recessive).

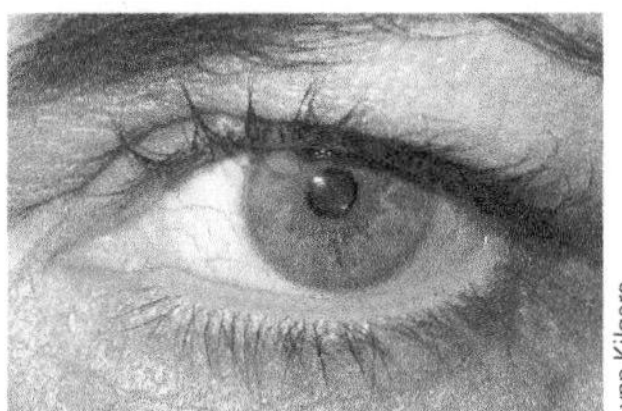
Lynn Kilgore

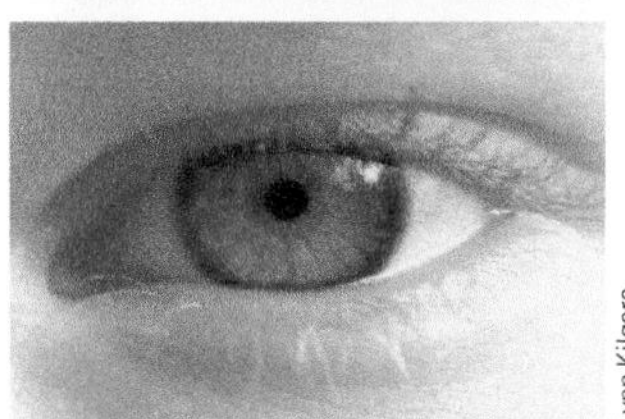
Lynn Kilgore

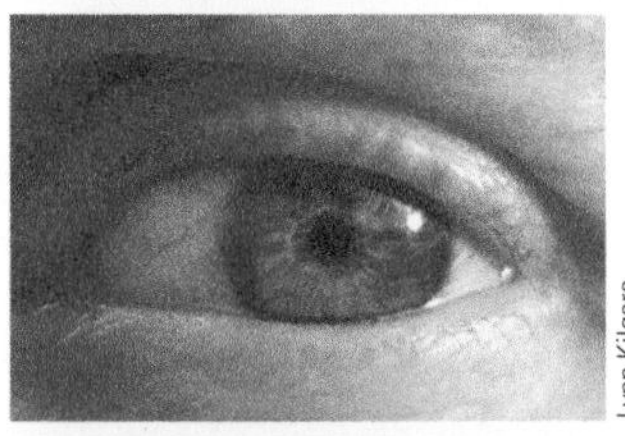
Lynn Kilgore

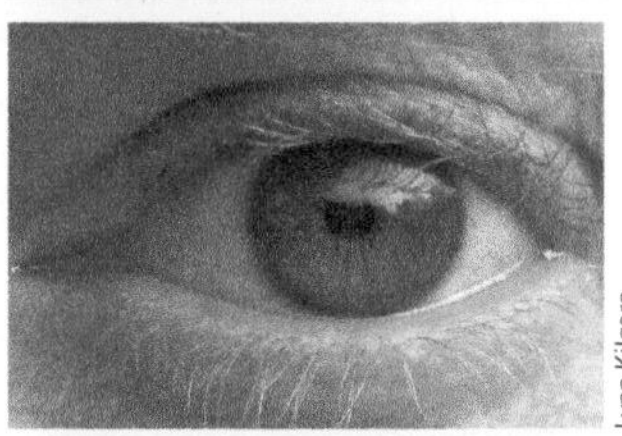
Lynn Kilgore

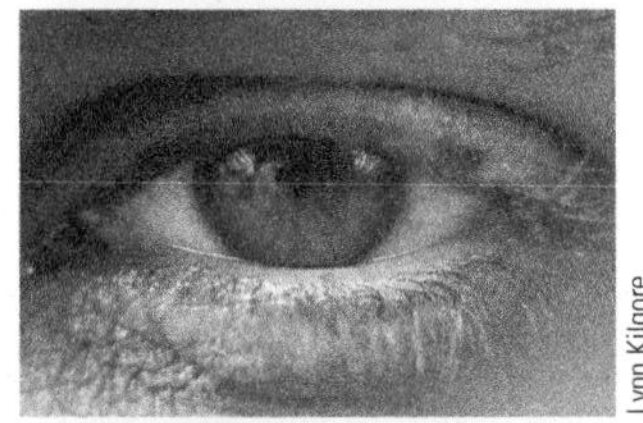
Lynn Kilgore

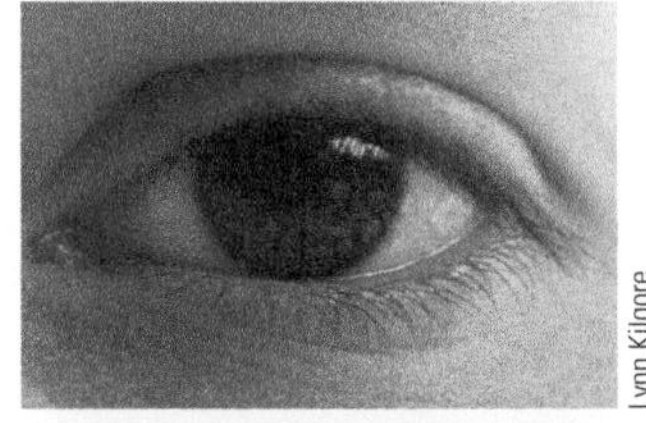
Lynn Kilgore

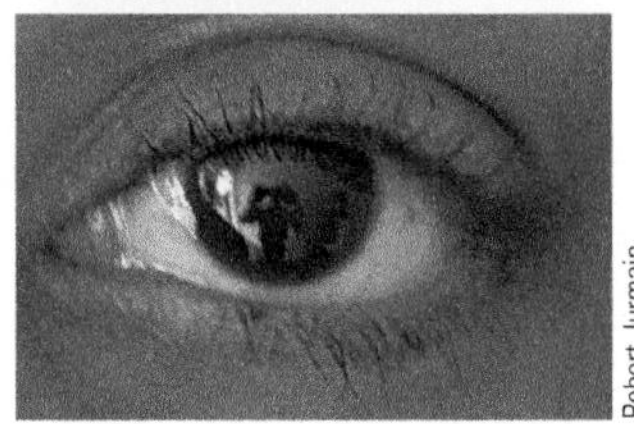
Robert Jurmain

▲ **Figure 4-16** Eye color is a polygenic characteristic and is a good example of continuous variation.

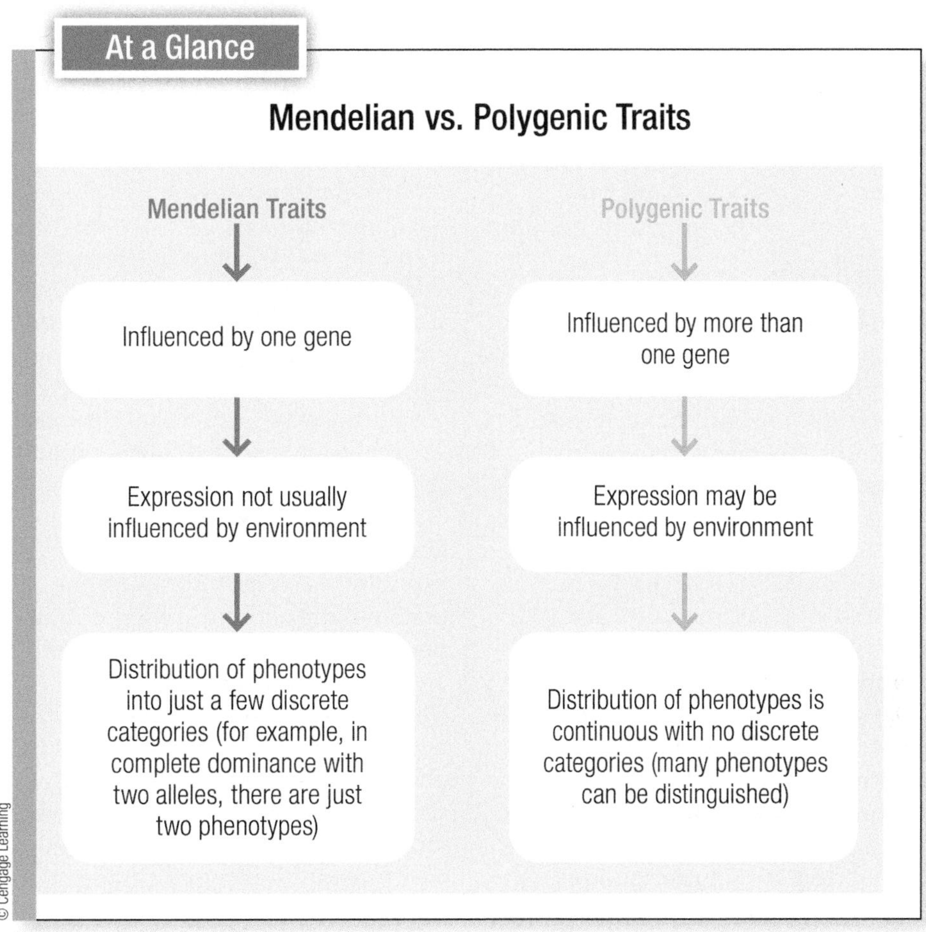

At a Glance
Mendelian vs. Polygenic Traits
Mendelian Traits
Influenced by one gene
Expression not usually influenced by environment
Distribution of phenotypes into just a few discrete categories (for example, in complete dominance with two alleles, there are just two phenotypes)
Polygenic Traits
Influenced by more than one gene
Expression may be influenced by environment
Distribution of phenotypes is continuous with no discrete categories (many phenotypes can be distinguished)
© Cengage Learning

Last, for many Mendelian traits, the approximate or exact positions of genetic loci are known, which makes it possible to examine the mechanisms and patterns of inheritance at these loci. This type of study isn't yet possible for polygenic traits because they're influenced by several genes that are only now being traced to specific loci.

Mitochondrial Inheritance

Another component of inheritance involves the organelles called *mitochondria* (see Chapter 3). All cells contain several hundred of these oval structures, which convert energy (derived from the breakdown of nutrients) to a form that can be used to perform cellular functions.

Each mitochondrion contains several copies of a ring-shaped DNA molecule, or chromosome. While *mitochondrial DNA (mtDNA)* is distinct from chromosomal DNA, its molecular structure and functions are the same. The entire molecule has been sequenced and is known to contain around 40 genes that direct the conversion of energy within the cell.

Like the DNA in a cell's nucleus, mtDNA is subject to mutations, some of which cause certain genetic disorders resulting from impaired energy conversion. Importantly, animals of both sexes inherit all their mtDNA, and thus the expression of all mitochondrial traits, from their mothers. Because mtDNA is inherited from only one parent, meiosis and recombination don't occur. This means that all the variation in mtDNA among individuals is caused by mutation, which makes mtDNA extremely useful for studying genetic change over time. So far, geneticists have used mutation rates in mtDNA to investigate evolutionary relationships between species, to trace ancestral relationships within the human lineage, and to study genetic variability among individuals and/or populations. While these techniques are still being refined, it's clear that we have a lot to learn from mtDNA.

Pleiotropy

While polygenic traits are governed by the actions of several genes, **pleiotropy** is a situation where a single gene influences more than one characteristic. Although this might seem unusual, pleiotropic effects are probably the rule rather than the exception.

The autosomal recessive disorder phenylketonuria (PKU) provides one example of pleiotropy (see Table 4-1). Individuals who are homozygous for the *PKU* allele don't produce the enzyme involved in the initial conversion of the amino acid *phenylalanine* to another amino acid, *tyrosine*. Because of this block in the metabolic pathway, phenylalanine breaks down into substances that accumulate in the central nervous system; without dietary management, these substances lead to mental deficiencies and several other consequences. Tyrosine is ultimately converted to several other substances, including the pigment melanin; therefore numerous other systems can also be affected. Thus another manifestation of PKU, owing to a diminished ability to produce melanin, is that affected people usually have blue eyes, fair skin, and light hair. There are many examples of pleiotropic genes, including the allele that causes sickle-cell anemia. Thus the action of one gene can influence a number of seemingly unrelated traits.

Genetic and Environmental Factors

By now you may have the impression that phenotypes are entirely the expressions of genotypes; but that's not true. (Here the terms *genotype* and *phenotype* are used in a broader sense to refer to an individual's *entire* genetic makeup and *all* observable or detectable characteristics.) Genotypes set limits and potentials for development, but they also interact with the environment, and many (but not all) aspects of the phenotype are influenced by this genetic-environmental interaction. For example, adult stature is influenced by both genes and the environment. Even though the maximum height a person can achieve is genetically determined, childhood nutrition (an environmental factor) is also important. Other important environmental factors include exposure to sunlight, altitude, temperature, and both toxic waste and airborne pollutants, which unfortunately are increasing almost everywhere. These and many other factors contribute in complex ways to the continuous phenotypic variation seen in traits governed by several genetic loci. However, for many characteristics, it's not possible to identify the *specific* environmental components that influence the phenotype.

Mendelian traits are less likely to be influenced by environmental factors. For example, ABO blood type is determined at fertilization and remains fixed throughout an individual's lifetime, regardless of diet, exposure to ultraviolet radiation, temperature, and so forth.

Mendelian and polygenic inheritance show different patterns of phenotypic variation. In the former, variation occurs in discrete categories, while in the latter, it's continuous. However, it's important to understand that even for polygenic characteristics, Mendelian principles still apply at individual loci. In other words, if a trait is influenced by six loci, each one of those loci may have two or more alleles, with some perhaps being dominant to others. It's the combined action of the alleles at all six loci, interacting with the environment, that produces the phenotype.

pleiotropy A situation where the action of one gene affects several different traits.

Modern Evolutionary Theory

By the beginning of the twentieth century, the foundations for evolutionary theory had already been developed. Darwin and Wallace had described natural selection 40 years earlier, and the rediscovery of Mendelian genetics in 1900 contributed the other major component: a mechanism for inheritance. We might expect that these two basic contributions would have been combined into a consistent theory of evolution, but they weren't. For the first 30 years of the twentieth century, some scientists argued that mutation was the main factor in evolution, while others emphasized natural selection. What they really needed was a merger of the two views rather than an either-or situation, but this didn't happen until the mid-1930s.

The Modern Synthesis

In the late 1920s and early 1930s, biologists realized that mutation and natural selection weren't opposing processes: They *both* contributed to biological evolution. The two major foundations of the biological sciences had finally been brought together in what is called the Modern Synthesis. From such a "modern" (that is, the middle of the twentieth century onward) perspective, evolution is defined as a two-stage process:

1. The production and redistribution of **variation** (inherited differences among organisms)
2. *Natural selection* acting on this variation, whereby inherited differences, or variations, among individuals differentially affect their ability to successfully reproduce

A Current Definition of Evolution

As we discussed in Chapter 2, Darwin saw evolution as the gradual unfolding of new varieties of life from preexisting ones. Certainly this is one result of the evolutionary process. But these long-term effects can come about only through the accumulation of many small genetic changes occurring over the generations. Today we can demonstrate how evolution works by examining some of the small genetic changes seen in populations and how they increase or decrease in frequency. From this perspective, we define evolution as *a change in* ***allele frequency*** *from one generation to the next.*

Allele frequencies are indicators of the genetic makeup of a **population**, the members of which share a common **gene pool**. To show how allele frequencies change, we'll use a simplified example of an inherited trait, again the ABO blood types. (*Note*: There are several blood groups, not just the ABO system, and they're all controlled by different genes.)

Let's assume that the students in your anthropology class represent a population and that we've determined everyone's ABO blood type. (To be considered a population, individuals must choose mates more often from *within* the group than from outside it. Obviously your class won't meet this requirement, but we'll overlook that.) The proportions of the *A*, *B*, and *O* alleles are the allele frequencies for this trait. If 50 percent of all the *ABO* alleles in your class are *A*, 40 percent are *B*, and 10 percent are *O*, the frequencies of these alleles are $A = 0.50$, $B = 0.40$, and $O = 0.10$.

Since the frequencies of these alleles represent proportions of a total, it's obvious that allele frequencies can refer only to groups of individuals, or populations. Individuals don't have allele frequencies; they have either *A*, *B*, or *O* in any combination of two. Also, from conception onward, a person's genetic makeup is fixed.* If you start out with blood type A, you will

* Although a person's genetic makeup is determined at conception, certain environmental factors, over time, can alter gene expression. However the nucleotide sequences themselves remain the same.

variation In genetics, inherited differences among individuals; the basis of all evolutionary change.

allele frequency In a population, the percentage of all the alleles at a locus accounted for by one specific allele.

population Within a species, a community of individuals where mates are usually found.

gene pool All of the genes shared by the reproductive members of a population.

always have type A. Therefore only a population can evolve over time; individuals can't.

Assume that 20 years from now we calculate the frequencies of the *ABO* alleles for the offspring of our classroom population and find the following: *A* = 0.30, *B* = 0.40, and *O* = 0.30. We can see that the relative proportions have changed: *A* has decreased, *O* has increased, and *B* has remained the same. This would not be a big deal, but in a biological sense, minor changes such as this constitute evolution. Over the short span of just a few generations, changes in the frequencies of inherited traits may be very small; but if they continue to happen, and particularly if they go in one direction as a result of natural selection, they can produce new adaptations and even new species.

Whether we're talking about the short-term effects (as in our classroom population) from one generation to the next, which is sometimes called **microevolution**, or the long-term effects through time, called speciation or **macroevolution**, the basic evolutionary mechanisms are similar. But how do allele frequencies change? Or, to put it another way, what causes evolution? As we've already said, evolution is a two-stage process. Genetic variation must first be produced by mutation, so that natural selection can then act upon it.

Factors That Produce and Redistribute Variation

Mutation

You've already learned that a mutation is a change in DNA. There are many kinds of mutations, but here we focus on point mutations, or substitutions of one DNA base for another. (Actually, alleles are the results of point mutations.) Point mutations must occur in sex cells if they're to have evolutionary consequences. This is because, in order for evolutionary change to occur, the mutation must be passed from one generation to the next. If a mutation takes place in a person's somatic cells but not in gametes, it won't be passed on to offspring. If, however, a genetic change occurs in the sperm or egg of one of the students in our classroom (*A* mutates to *B*, for instance), the offspring's blood type will be different from that of the parent, causing a minute shift in the allele frequencies of the next generation.

Actually, except in microorganisms, it's rare for evolution to take place solely because of mutations. Mutation rates for any given trait are usually low, so we wouldn't really expect to see a mutation at the *ABO* locus in a population as small as your class. In larger populations, mutations might be observed in 1 individual out of 10,000, but by themselves they would have no impact on allele frequencies. However, when mutation is combined with natural selection, evolutionary changes can occur more rapidly.

It's important to remember that mutation is the basic creative force in evolution, because it's the *only* way to produce *new* genes (that is, variation). Its role in the production of variation is key to the first stage of the evolutionary process.

In Chapter 3, we discussed the importance to the evolutionary process of mutations in regulatory genes. We also mentioned that many DNA sequences contain variable numbers of certain segments called *copy number variants* (CNVs) (see A Closer Look: "Noncoding DNA—Not Junk After All" in Chapter 3). Individuals and species have different numbers of certain segments within their genes, and these differences influence a gene's overall effect. When CNVs occur in regulatory genes, particularly those involved in development, they can cause dramatic phenotypic changes.

CNVs occur as a result of deletions or duplications of DNA segments within a gene. **Tandem repeats** are a type of duplication that has attracted a great deal of attention in recent years because they have much higher mutation rates than single alleles do

microevolution Small changes occurring within species, such as changes in allele frequencies.

macroevolution Changes produced only after many generations, such as the appearance of a new species.

tandem repeats Short, adjacent segments of DNA within a gene that are repeated several times.

iStockphoto.com/Waldemar Dabrowski

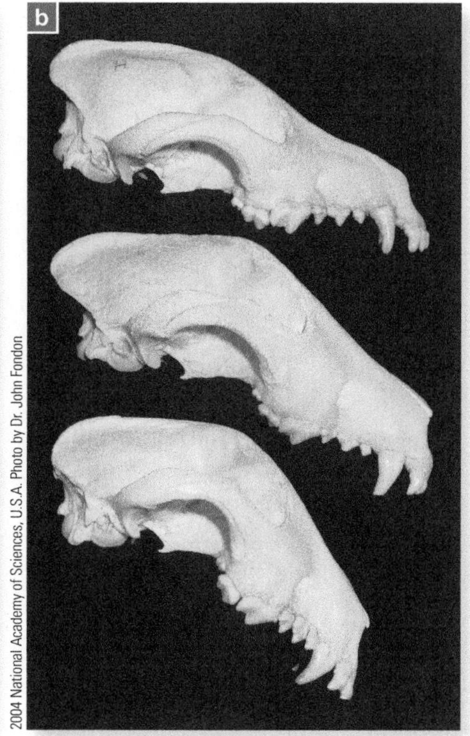

2004 National Academy of Sciences, U.S.A. Photo by Dr. John Fondon

▸ **Figure 4-17** (**a**) Selective breeding in bull terriers has produced dramatic changes in the shape of the head, resulting in a concave profile and downward-turning nose. (**b**) These three purebred bull terrier crania clearly illustrate how the shape of the head changed in this breed in just 35 years. The dates for the crania, from top to bottom, are 1931, 1950, and 1976. (The 1931 specimen, from a Swiss lab, provided DNA for use in comparisons with modern bull terriers DNA.)

and therefore could have a significant influence on rates of evolution. In one study, Fondon and Garner (2004) examined the relationship between tandem repeats in regulatory genes and phenotypic expression. Among other things, they showed how a tandem repeat in a regulatory gene involved in bone growth has dramatically influenced the shape of the cranium of bull terriers (**Fig. 4-17**).

The changes in bull terrier crania are the results of artificial selection for a specific trait (the long drooping snout), influenced by variation in a regulatory gene. While this is not speciation, it is dramatic evidence of how tandem repeats in protein-coding genes can produce significant phenotypic variation for natural selection to act on. Indeed, tandem repeats have played, and continue to play, a highly significant role in evolution.

Gene Flow

Gene flow is the exchange of genes between populations. The term *migration* is also sometimes used; but strictly speaking, *migration* refers to the movement of people. In contrast, *gene flow* refers to the exchange of genes between groups, which can happen only if the migrants interbreed. Also, even if individuals move temporarily and have offspring in the new population, they don't necessarily stay there. For example, the children of U.S. soldiers and Vietnamese women represent gene flow. Even though the fathers returned to the United States after the Vietnam War, some of their genes remained behind, although not in sufficient numbers to appreciably change allele frequencies.

In humans, mating patterns are mostly determined by social factors, and cultural anthropologists can work closely with biological anthropologists to isolate and measure this aspect of evolutionary change. Human population movements (particularly in the last 500 years) have reached previously unheard of proportions, and very few breeding isolates remain. But migration on a smaller scale has been a consistent feature of human evolution since the first dispersal of our genus,

gene flow Exchange of genes between populations.

and gene flow between populations (even though sometimes limited) helps explain why speciation has been rare during the past million years or so.

An interesting example of how gene flow influences microevolutionary changes in modern human populations is seen in African Americans. African Americans are largely of West African descent, but there has also been considerable genetic admixture with European Americans. By measuring allele frequencies for specific genetic loci, we can estimate the amount of migration of European alleles into the African American gene pool. Data from northern and western U.S. cities (including New York, Detroit, and Oakland) have shown that the proportion of *non*-African genes in the African American gene pool is 20 to 25 percent (Cummings, 2000).

Gene flow occurs for reasons other than large-scale movements of populations. In fact, significant changes in allele frequencies can come about through long-term patterns of mate selection whereby members of a group traditionally obtain mates from certain other groups. This is especially true if mate exchange consistently occurs in one direction over a long period of time. For example, if group A chooses mates from group B but group B doesn't reciprocate, eventually group A will have an increased proportion of group B alleles. If, however, mate exchange between groups is reciprocal, over time the two groups will become more alike genetically (**Fig. 4-18**).

Genetic Drift and Founder Effect

Genetic drift is the random factor in evolution, and it's a function of population size. *Drift occurs solely because the population is small.* If an allele is rare in a small population, it may disappear because, just by chance, it isn't passed on to offspring (**Fig. 4-19a**). Thus genetic drift reduces genetic variability in small populations.

One particular kind of genetic drift, called **founder effect**, is seen in many modern human and nonhuman populations. Founder effect can occur when a small band of "founders" leaves its parent group and forms a colony somewhere else. Over time, a new population will be established, and as long as mates are chosen only from within this population, all of its members will be descended from the small original group of founders. Therefore all the genes in the expanding group will have come from the original colonists. In such a case, an allele that was rare in the founders' parent population but was carried by even one of the founders can eventually become common among the founders' descendants (**Fig. 4-19b**). This is because a high proportion of people in later generations will all be descended from that one founder.

Colonization isn't the only way founder effect can happen. Small founding groups may be the survivors of a larger group that was mostly wiped out by some type of disaster. But like the small group of colonists, the survivors possess only a sample of all the alleles that were present in the original population.

Therefore, just by chance alone, some alleles may be completely lost from a population's gene pool while others may become the only alleles at loci that previously had two or more. Whatever the cause, the outcome is a reduction in genetic diversity, and the allele frequencies of succeeding generations may be substantially different from those of the original, larger population. The loss of genetic diversity in this type of situation is called a *genetic bottleneck*, and the effects can be highly detrimental to a species.

There are many known examples (both human and nonhuman) of species or populations that have passed through genetic bottlenecks. (In fact, many species are going through genetic bottlenecks right now.)

genetic drift Evolutionary changes, or changes in allele frequencies, produced by random factors in small populations. Genetic drift is a result of small population size.

founder effect A type of genetic drift in which allele frequencies are altered in small populations that are taken from larger populations or are remnants of the latter.

▶ **Figure 4-18** Gene flow. In this illustration, the colored dots represent different alleles and the circles that contain them represent two populations.

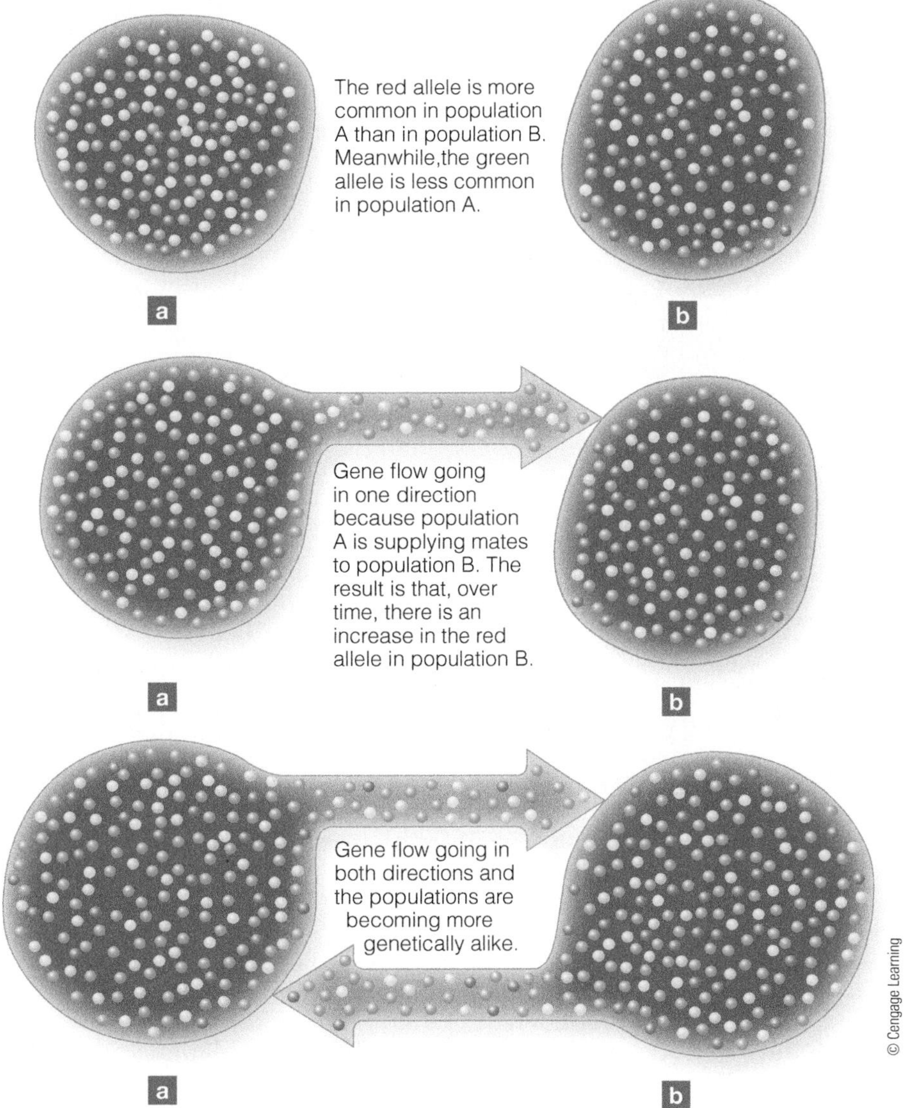

The red allele is more common in population A than in population B. Meanwhile,the green allele is less common in population A.
a
b
Gene flow going in one direction because population A is supplying mates to population B. The result is that, over time, there is an increase in the red allele in population B.
a
b
Gene flow going in both directions and the populations are becoming more genetically alike.
a
b
© Cengage Learning

Genetically, cheetahs (**Fig. 4-20**) are an extremely uniform species, and biologists believe that at some point in the past these magnificent cats suffered a catastrophic decline in numbers. For unknown reasons related to the species-wide loss of numerous alleles, male cheetahs produce a high percentage of defective sperm compared to other cat species. Decreased reproductive potential, greatly reduced genetic diversity, and other factors (including human hunting) have combined to jeopardize the continued existence of this species. Other species that have passed through genetic bottlenecks include California elephant seals, sea otters, and condors. Indeed, humans are much more genetically uniform than chimpanzees, and it appears that all modern human populations are the descendants of a few small groups.

One human example of genetic drift is provided by a fatal recessive condition called Amish microcephaly, in which a mutation results in abnormally small brains and heads in fetuses. The disorder is found only in the Old Order Amish community of Lancaster County, Pennsylvania, where it occurs in approximately 1 in 500 births (Kelley et al., 2002; Rosenberg et al., 2002). Genealogical research showed that affected families have all been traced

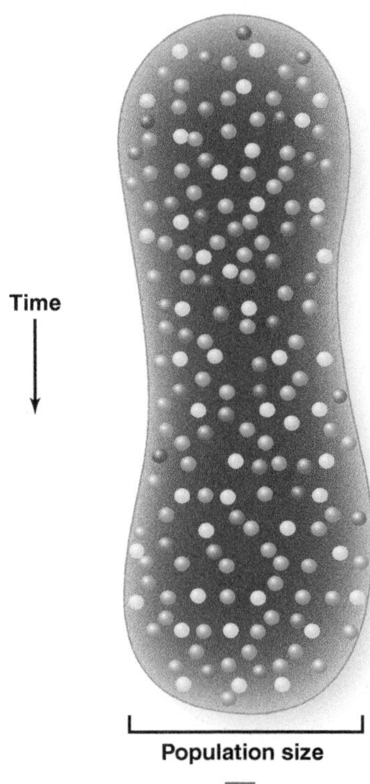

Time
A small population with considerable genetic variability. Note that the dark green and blue alleles are less common than the other alleles.
After just a few generations, the population is approximately the same size but genetic variation has been reduced. Both the dark green and blue alleles have been lost. Also, the red allele is less common and the frequency of the light green allele has increased.
Population size
a

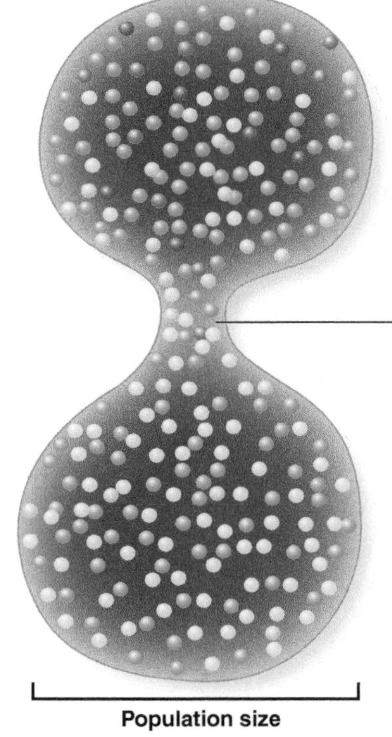

Original population with considerable genetic variation
A small group leaves to colonize a new area, or a bottleneck occurs, so that population size decreases and genetic variation is reduced.
Population size restored but the dark green and purple alleles have been lost. The frequencies of the red and yellow alleles have also changed.
Population size
b

▲ **Figure 4-19** Small populations are subject to genetic drift, where rare alleles can be lost because, just by chance, they weren't passed to offspring. Also, although more common alleles may not be lost, their frequencies may change for the same reason. (**a**) This diagram represents six alleles (different-colored dots) that occur at one genetic locus in a small population. You can see that in a fairly short period of time (three or four generations), rare alleles can be lost and genetic diversity consequently reduced. (**b**) This diagram illustrates the founder effect, a form of genetic drift where diversity is lost because a large population is drastically reduced in size and consequently passes through a genetic "bottleneck." Founder effect also happens when a small group leaves the larger group and "founds" a new population elsewhere. (In this case, the group of founders is represented by the bottleneck.) Those individuals that survive (the founders) and the alleles they carry represent only a sample of the variation that was present in the original population. And future generations, all descended from the survivors, will therefore have less variability.

back nine generations to a single couple. One member of this couple carried the deleterious recessive allele that, because of customs promoting marriage within (what was then) a small group, has greatly increased in frequency with very serious consequences.

Much insight into the evolutionary factors that have acted in the past can be gained by understanding how such mechanisms continue to operate on human populations today. In small populations, drift plays an important evolutionary role because fairly sudden fluctuations in allele frequency occur solely because of small population size. Likewise, throughout a good deal of human evolution, at least the last 4 to 5 million years, hominins probably lived in small groups, and drift probably had a significant impact.

Additional insight concerning the relative influences of the different evolutionary factors has emerged in recent studies of the early dispersal of modern *Homo sapiens*. Evidence suggests that in the last 100,000 to 200,000 years, our species experienced a genetic bottleneck that considerably influenced the pattern of genetic variation seen in all human populations today.

As we've seen, both gene flow and genetic drift can produce some evolutionary changes by themselves.

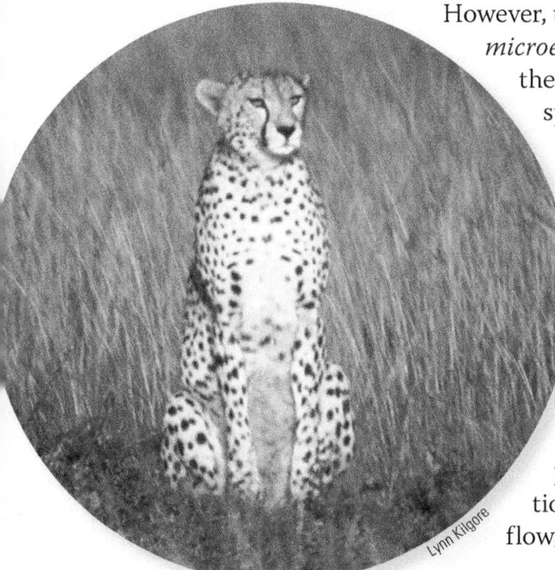

▲**Figure 4-20** Cheetahs, like many other species, have passed through a genetic bottleneck. Consequently they have little genetic variation as a species.

However, these changes are usually *microevolutionary* ones; that is, they produce changes within species over the short term. To produce the kind of evolutionary changes that ultimately result in new species (for example, the diversification of the first primates or the appearance of the earliest hominins), natural selection is necessary. But natural selection can't operate independently of the other evolutionary factors: mutation, gene flow, and genetic drift.

Recombination As we saw in Chapter 3, members of chromosome pairs exchange segments of DNA during meiosis. By itself, recombination doesn't change allele frequencies or cause evolution. However, when paired chromosomes exchange DNA, genes sometimes find themselves in different genetic environments. (It's as if they had moved to a new neighborhood.) This fact can be important because the functions of some genes can be influenced simply by the alleles they're close to. Thus recombination not only changes the composition of parts of chromosomes but can also affect how some genes act, and slight changes of gene function can become material for natural selection to act on. (The levels of organization in the evolutionary process are summarized in **Table 4.4**.)

Natural Selection Is Directional and Acts on Variation

The evolutionary factors just discussed (mutation, gene flow, genetic drift, and recombination) interact to produce variation and to distribute genes within and between populations. But there is no long-term *direction* to any of these factors, and for adaptation and evolution to occur, a population's gene pool must change in a specific direction. This means that some alleles must consistently become more common while others become less common, and natural selection is the one factor that can cause this kind of directional change in allele frequency *relative to specific environmental factors.* If the environment changes, selection pressures change and allele

Table 4.4 Levels of Organization in the Evolutionary Process

Evolutionary Factor	Level	Evolutionary Process	Technique of Study
Mutation	DNA	Storage of genetic information; ability to replicate; influences phenotype by production of proteins	Biochemistry, recombinant DNA
Mutation	Chromosomes	A vehicle for packaging and transmitting genetic material (DNA)	Light or electron microscope
Recombination (sex cells only)	Cell	The basic unit of life that contains the chromosomes and divides for growth and for production of sex cells	Light or electron microscope
Natural selection	Organism	The unit, composed of cells, that reproduces and that we observe for phenotypic traits	Visual study, biochemistry
Drift, gene flow	Population	A group of interbreeding organisms; changes in allele frequencies between generations; it's the population that evolves	Statistical analysis

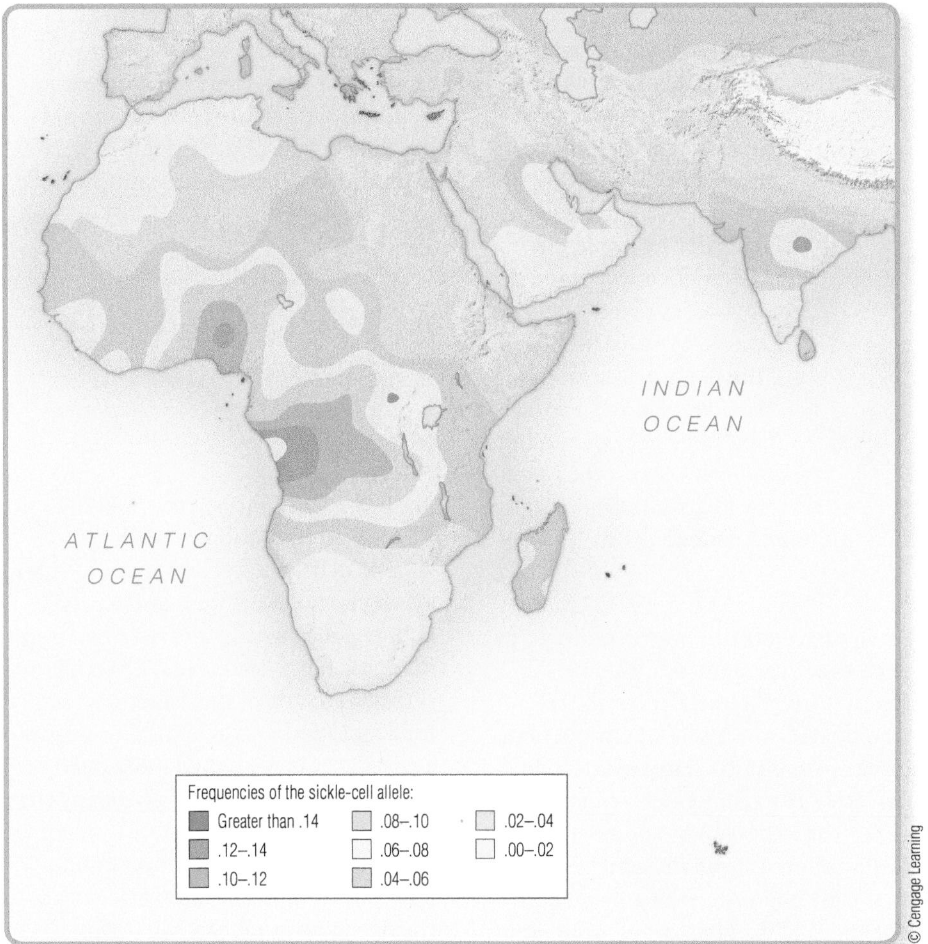

◀ **Figure 4-21** The distribution of the sickle-cell allele in the Old World.

frequencies shift. Such shifts in allele frequencies are called *adaptation.*

In humans, the best-documented example of natural selection involves hemoglobin S (Hb^S), an abnormal form of hemoglobin that results from a point mutation in the gene that produces part of the hemoglobin molecule. As you learned in Chapter 3, if an individual inherits the hemoglobin S (Hb^S) allele from both parents, he or she will have sickle-cell anemia. Worldwide, sickle-cell anemia causes an estimated 100,000 deaths each year; in the United States, approximately 40,000 to 50,000 people, mostly of African descent, have this disease (Ashley-Koch et al., 2000).

The Hb^S mutation (see Chapter 3) occurs occasionally in all human populations, but usually the allele is rare. However, in some populations, especially in western and central Africa, it's more common than elsewhere, with frequencies as high as 20 percent. The Hb^S allele is also fairly common in parts of Greece and India (**Fig. 4-21**). Given the devastating effects of hemoglobin S in homozygotes, you may wonder why it's so common in some populations. It seems as though natural selection would eliminate it, but it doesn't. In fact, natural selection has actually increased its frequency, and the explanation for this situation can be summed up in one word: malaria.

Malaria is an infectious disease caused by a single-celled parasitic organism known as *Plasmodium* (its genus name). It is transmitted to humans by mosquitoes, and it kills an estimated 1 to 3 million people worldwide every year. After an infected mosquito bite, plasmodial parasites invade red blood cells, where they obtain the oxygen they need for reproduction (**Fig. 4-22**). The

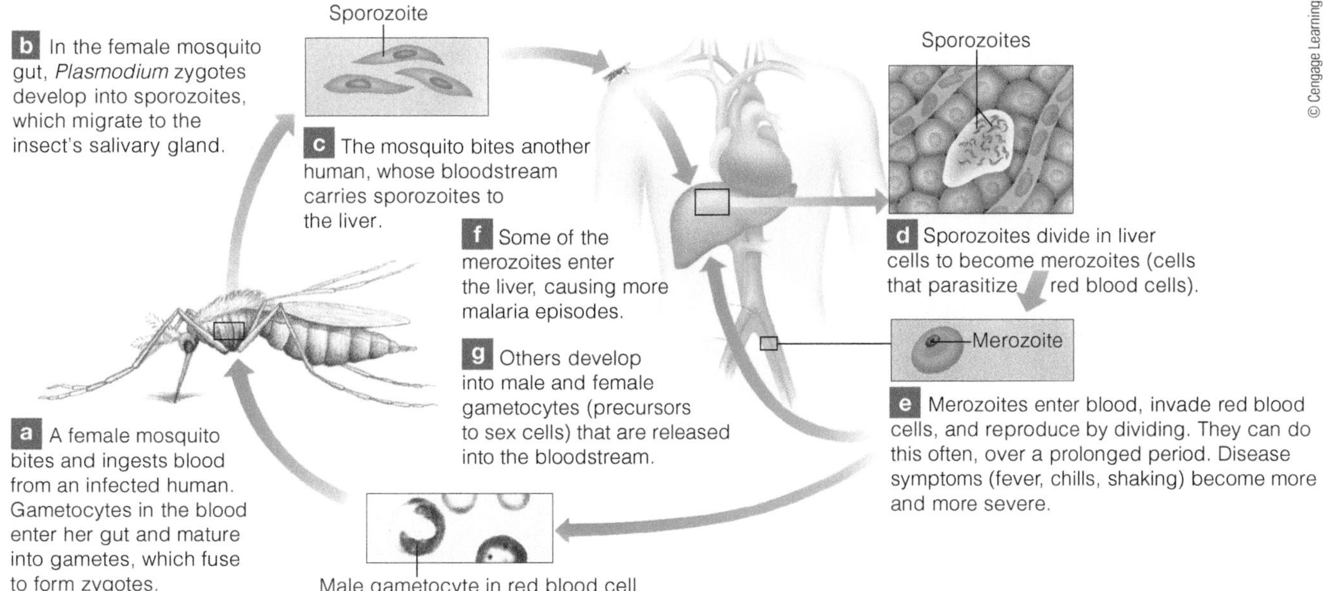

Sporozoite
b In the female mosquito gut, Plasmodium zygotes develop into sporozoites, which migrate to the insect's salivary gland.
c The mosquito bites another human, whose bloodstream carries sporozoites to the liver.
Sporozoites
d Sporozoites divide in liver cells to become merozoites (cells that parasitize red blood cells).
f Some of the merozoites enter the liver, causing more malaria episodes.
g Others develop into male and female gametocytes (precursors to sex cells) that are released into the bloodstream.
Merozoite
e Merozoites enter blood, invade red blood cells, and reproduce by dividing. They can do this often, over a prolonged period. Disease symptoms (fever, chills, shaking) become more and more severe.
a A female mosquito bites and ingests blood from an infected human. Gametocytes in the blood enter her gut and mature into gametes, which fuse to form zygotes.
Male gametocyte in red blood cell
© Cengage Learning

▲ **Figure 4-22** The life cycle of the parasite that causes malaria.

consequences of this infection to the human host include fever, chills, headache, nausea, vomiting, and frequently death. In parts of western and central Africa, where malaria is always present, as many as 50 to 75 percent of 2- to 9-year-olds are afflicted.

In the mid-twentieth century, the geographical correlation between malaria and the distribution of the sickle-cell allele (Hb^S) was the only evidence of a biological relationship between the two. But now we know that people (heterozygotes) with **sickle-cell trait** have greater resistance to malaria than people with only normal hemoglobin. This is because people with sickle-cell trait have some red blood cells that contain hemoglobin S, and these cells don't provide a suitable environment for the malarial parasite. In other words, having some hemoglobin S is beneficial because it affords some protection from malaria. So in areas where malaria is present, it acts as a selective agent favoring the heterozygous phenotype because people with sickle-cell trait have higher net reproductive success than those with only normal hemoglobin, who often die of malaria. But selection for heterozygotes means that the Hb^S allele will be maintained in the population. Thus there will always be some people with sickle-cell anemia, and they, of course, will have the lowest reproductive success, since most, without treatment, will die before reaching adulthood.

Review of Genetics and Evolutionary Factors

In this chapter, discussion focused on how genetic information is passed from one generation to the next. We also reviewed evolutionary theory, emphasizing the crucial role of natural selection. The various levels (molecular, cellular, individual, and populational) are different components of the evolutionary process, and they're related to each other in a way that can eventually produce evolutionary change. A step-by-step example will make this clear.

Consider a population in which almost everyone has hemoglobin A. For all practical purposes, there's almost no variation regarding this trait, and without some source of new variation, evolution is not possible.

sickle-cell trait Heterozygous condition where a person has one Hb^A allele and one Hb^S allele. Thus they have some normal hemoglobin.

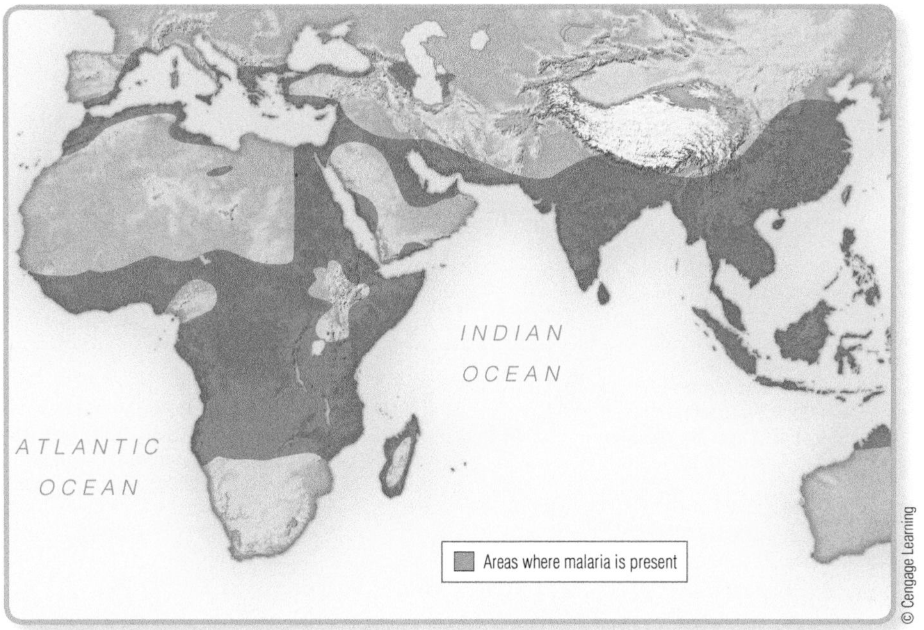

◀ **Figure 4-23** The distribution of malaria in the Old World.

However, in every generation, a few people carry a spontaneous mutation that changes just one DNA base in the Hb^A gene. This single point mutation, or base substitution, actually creates a new allele (Hb^S) in the DNA sequence, slightly altering the protein product (the hemoglobin molecule) and ultimately the phenotype of the individual. But for the mutated allele to have any evolutionary potential, it must be present in the gametes and transmitted to offspring.

Once a mutation has occurred, it will exist within a chromosome, which, along with other chromosomes, may be inherited by offspring. And if a person has the mutation on only one member of a pair of chromosomes, there's a 50-50 chance that the mutation will be passed on to each child he or she has.

But what does all this have to do with evolution? To repeat an earlier definition, evolution is based on a change in allele frequency in a population from one generation to the next. The key point here is that we are considering populations, because it's the populations that change over time.

We can determine if allele frequencies have changed in a population where sickle-cell hemoglobin is found by determining the percentage of individuals with the Hb^S allele versus those with the normal allele (Hb^A). If the relative proportions of these alleles change with time, the population is evolving at the Hb^A locus. But in addition to knowing that evolution is occuring, it's important to know why, and there are several possible explanations. First, the only way the new Hb^S allele could have arisen is by mutation, and we've shown how this can happen in a single individual. But this isn't an evolutionary change, since the alteration of one person's genes in a relatively large population won't change the allele frequencies of the entire population. Somehow, this new allele must *spread* in the population; and in the case of Hb^S, the allele spread because it was favored by natural selection. And the reason it was favored is because it conferred some advantage in an environment where malaria was present.

As you learned earlier, genetic drift can also greatly alter the frequencies of alleles in small populations. Just by chance, some alleles may not be passed on, and after a few generations, they're completely lost. Other alleles, meanwhile, may end up being the only allele at a particular locus. This situation represents a loss of variation in the population.

In the course of human evolution, drift has probably played a significant role; it's important to remember that at this microevolutionary level, drift and/or gene flow can (and will) produce evolutionary change, even in the absence of natural selection. However, such change will be random because natural selection is the only factor that can cause allele frequencies to change in a particular direction.

The way natural selection has worked in the past and still operates today (as with sickle-cell hemoglobin) is through differential net reproductive success. That is, individuals who carry a particular allele or combination of alleles produce more offspring than other individuals with different alleles. Hence if a certain allele is beneficial in a particular environment, its frequency should increase slowly from generation to generation. Likewise alleles that are detrimental should become less common. When this process is compounded over hundreds of generations at numerous loci, the result is significant evolutionary change. The levels of organization in the evolutionary process are summarized in Table 4-3.

How Do We Know?

In Table 4-1 we listed Tay-Sachs disease as an example of an autosomal recessive trait, most commonly seen in Ashkenazi Jews (Jews of eastern European descent). Tay-Sachs is actually a good example of why the inheritance and expression of dominant and recessive characteristics in populations is not as simple as textbooks (including this one) sometimes make it seem.

Tay-Sachs disease is a fatal disorder caused by the lack of an enzyme produced by the *HEXA* gene—an enzyme that breaks down lipids (molecules made of fats and other substances). In the absence of the enzyme, these substances accumulate in the brain. Resulting neurological symptoms usually appear by the age of 6 months and include blindness, deafness, paralysis, and death, usually before the age of 3 years. This description applies to the most common manifestation of the disease, infantile Tay-Sachs disease. The other two forms, juvenile and late onset, are much less common and are caused by other mutations in the *HEXA* gene. In fact there are more than 100 mutations in the gene; all of them affect how the enzyme functions (Kaback, 2000) and they cause different expressions of the disease. But scientists began to be aware of the many different mutations only in the 1970s, and more are still being discovered.

As we stated, infantile Tay-Sachs is most commonly seen in Ashkenazi Jews. But Cajun populations of southern Louisiana also exhibit Tay-Sachs in much higher frequencies than other populations. As it turns out, the cause is the same mutation in both populations. A different mutation causes higher than normal frequencies in French Canadians. In all three groups, founder effect is the principal explanation for the increased frequency of the mutations in the *HEXA* gene. Indeed, researchers have traced the Cajun mutation back to a single couple that lived in France in the eighteenth century (McDowell et al, 1992).

Likewise, French Canadians are mostly descendants of a small founder population. In addition, they tended to marry other French Canadians because they were isolated from the general population by geographic, language, and cultural differences.

As you can see from this one briefly described condition, patterns of genetic disease result from the interactions of several factors. In the case of Tay-Sachs, multiple recessive mutations in one gene have interacted with population movement and social factors to produce the distribution of Tay-Sachs disease we see today.

Summary of Main Topics

- In the mid-nineteenth century, a monk named Gregor Mendel discovered the principles of segregation, independent assortment, and dominance and recessiveness by doing experiments with pea plants. Although the field of genetics progressed exponentially during the twentieth century, the concepts first put forth by Mendel remain the basis of our current knowledge of how traits are inherited.
- Basic Mendelian principles are applied to the study of the various modes of inheritance we're familiar with today. The most important factor in all the Mendelian modes of inheritance is the role of segregation of chromosomes and the alleles they carry during meiosis.
- Building on fundamental nineteenth-century contributions by Charles Darwin and the rediscovery of Mendel's work in 1900, advances in genetics throughout the twentieth century contributed to contemporary evolutionary thought. In particular, the combination of natural selection with Mendel's principles of inheritance and experimental evidence concerning the nature of mutation have all been synthesized into a modern understanding of evolutionary change. In this contemporary theory of evolution, evolutionary change is seen as a two-stage process. The first stage is the production and redistribution of variation. The second stage is the process whereby natural selection acts on the accumulated genetic variation.
- Mutation is crucial to all evolutionary change because it's the only source of completely new genetic material (that is, new alleles), which increases variation. In addition, recombination, genetic drift, and gene flow redistribute variation within individuals (recombination), within populations (genetic drift), and between populations (gene flow).
- Natural selection is the central determining factor influencing the long-term direction of evolutionary change. How natural selection works can best be explained as differential net reproductive success, or how successful individuals are compared to others, in leaving offspring to succeeding generations. The detailed history of the evolutionary spread of the sickle-cell allele provides the best-documented example of natural selection among recent human populations. It must be remembered that evolution is an integrated process, and this chapter concluded with a discussion of how the various evolutionary factors can be integrated into a single comprehensive view of evolutionary change.

Critical Thinking Questions

1. If two people with blood type A, both with the *AO* genotype, have children, what *proportion* of their children would be expected to have blood type O? Why? Can these two parents have a child with AB blood? Why or why not?
2. After having read this chapter, do you understand evolutionary processes more completely? What questions do you still have?
3. Sickle-cell anemia is frequently described as affecting only Africans or people of African descent; it's considered a "racial" disease that doesn't affect other populations. How would you explain to someone that this view is wrong?
4. Give some examples of how selection, gene flow, genetic drift, and mutation have acted on populations or species in the past. Try to think of at least one human and one nonhuman example. Why do you think genetic drift might be important to endangered species today?

Connections

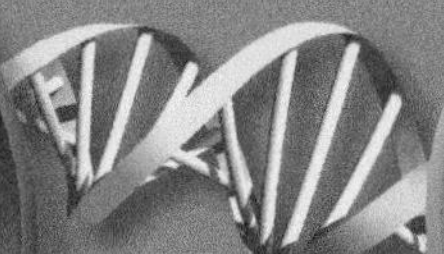

Evolution results from DNA changes and the action of other evolutionary factors.

Humans are both vertebrates and mammals, and we've shared evolutionary history for millions of years.

Humans are primates and share many biological characteristics with other primates.

Louie Psihoyos/Corbis

Macroevolution: Processes of Vertebrate and Mammalian Evolution 5

Student Learning Objectives

After mastering the material in this chapter, you should be able to:

- Compare microevolution and macroevolution and explain how they are similar and how they differ.
- Describe the main animal classifications and explain how humans fit into such classifications as vertebrates and as mammals.
- Compare and contrast the more traditional classification approach (evolutionary systematics) with that of cladistics.
- Explain what a fossil is and describe how different kinds of fossils are formed.
- Define the major characteristics of mammals, especially those of placental mammals.
- Explain how species are defined by biologists and how they originate from prior species.

Many people think of paleontology as a pretty dreary subject of interest only to overly serious academics. But have you ever been to a natural history museum—or perhaps to one of the larger, more elaborate toy stores? If so, you may have seen a full-size mock-up of *Tyrannosaurus rex*, one that might even move its head and arms and scream threateningly. These displays are usually encircled by enthralled adults and flocks of noisy, excited children. These same onlookers, however, show almost no interest in the display cases containing fossils of early marine organisms. Yet every trace of early life has a fascinating story to tell.

The study of the history of life on earth is full of mystery and adventure. The bits and pieces of fossils are the remains of once living, breathing animals (some of them extremely large and dangerous). Searching for these fossils in remote corners of the globe—from the Gobi Desert in Mongolia, to the rocky outcrops of Madagascar, to the badlands of South Dakota—is not a task for the faint of heart. Piecing together the tiny clues and ultimately reconstructing what *Tyrannosaurus rex* or a small, 50-million-year-old primate looked like and how it might have behaved is really much like detective work. Sure, it can be serious; but it's also a lot of fun.

In this chapter, we review the evolution of vertebrates—more specifically, mammals. It's important to understand these more general aspects of evolutionary history so that we can place our species in its proper biological context. *Homo sapiens* is only one of millions of species that have evolved. More than that, people have been around for just an instant in the vast expanse of time that life has existed, and we want to know where we fit in this long and complex story of life on earth. To discover how humans connect within this incredibly long story of life on earth, we also discuss some contemporary issues relating to evolutionary theory. In particular, we emphasize concepts relating to large-scale evolutionary processes—that is, *macroevolution* (in contrast to the microevolutionary focus of Chapter 4). The fundamental perspectives reviewed here concern geological history, principles of classification, and the nature of evolutionary change. These perspectives will serve as a basis for topics covered throughout much of the remainder of this book.

How We Connect: Discovering the Human Place in the Organic World

There are millions of species living today; if we were to include microorganisms, the total would likely exceed tens of millions. And if we added in the multitudes of species that are now extinct, the total would be staggering—perhaps *hundreds* of millions! Where do we fit in, and what types of evidence do scientists use to answer this question?

Biologists need methods to deal scientifically with all this diversity. One way to do this is to use a system of **classification** that organizes diversity into categories and at the same time indicates evolutionary relationships.

Multicellular organisms that move about and ingest food are called animals (**Fig. 5-1**). Within the kingdom Animalia, there are more than 20 major groups called *phyla* (*sing.*, phylum). **Chordata** is one of these phyla; it includes all animals with a nerve cord, gill slits (at some stage of development), and a supporting cord along the back. In turn, most chordates are **vertebrates**—so called because they have a vertebral column. Vertebrates also have a developed brain and paired sensory structures for sight, smell, and balance.

The vertebrates themselves are subdivided into five classes: cartilaginous fishes, bony fishes, amphibians, reptiles/birds, and mammals. We'll discuss mammalian classification later in this chapter.

By putting organisms into increasingly narrow groupings, we organize diversity into categories and also make statements about evolutionary and genetic relationships between species and groups of species. Further dividing mammals into orders makes the statement that, for example, all carnivores (Carnivora) are more closely related to each other than they are to any species placed in another order. Consequently bears, dogs, and cats (Carnivora) are more closely related to each other than they are to cattle, pigs, or deer (Artiodactyla). At each succeeding level (suborder, superfamily, family, subfamily, genus, and species), finer distinctions are made between categories until, at the species level, only those animals that can potentially interbreed and produce viable offspring are included.

Principles of Classification

Before we go any further, we must discuss the basis of animal classification. The field that specializes in establishing the rules of classification is called *taxonomy*. Most traditionally, organisms are classified first according to their physical similarities. This was the basis of the first systematic classification devised by Linnaeus in the eighteenth century (see Chapter 2).

Today, basic physical similarities are still considered a good starting point. But for similarities to be useful, they *must* reflect evolutionary descent. For example, the bones of the forelimb of all air-breathing vertebrates initially adapted to terrestrial (land) environments are so similar in number and form (**Fig. 5-2**) that the obvious explanation for the striking resemblance is that all four kinds of these "four-footed" (tetrapod) vertebrates ultimately derived their forelimb structure from a common ancestor. What's more, recent discoveries of remarkably well-preserved fossils from Canada have provided exciting new evidence of how the transition from aquatic to land living took place and what the earliest land vertebrates looked like (Daeschler et al., 2006; Shubin et al., 2006).

How could such seemingly major evolutionary modifications in structure occur? They quite likely began

classification In biology, the ordering of organisms into categories, such as orders, families, and genera, to show evolutionary relationships.

Chordata The phylum of the animal kingdom that includes vertebrates.

vertebrates Animals with segmented, bony spinal columns; these include fishes, amphibians, reptiles (including birds), and mammals.

▾ **Figure 5-1** In this classification chart, modified from Linnaeus, all animals are placed in certain categories based on structural similarities. Not all members of categories are shown; for example, there are up to 20 orders of placental mammals (8 are depicted). Chapter 6 presents a more comprehensive classification of the primate order.

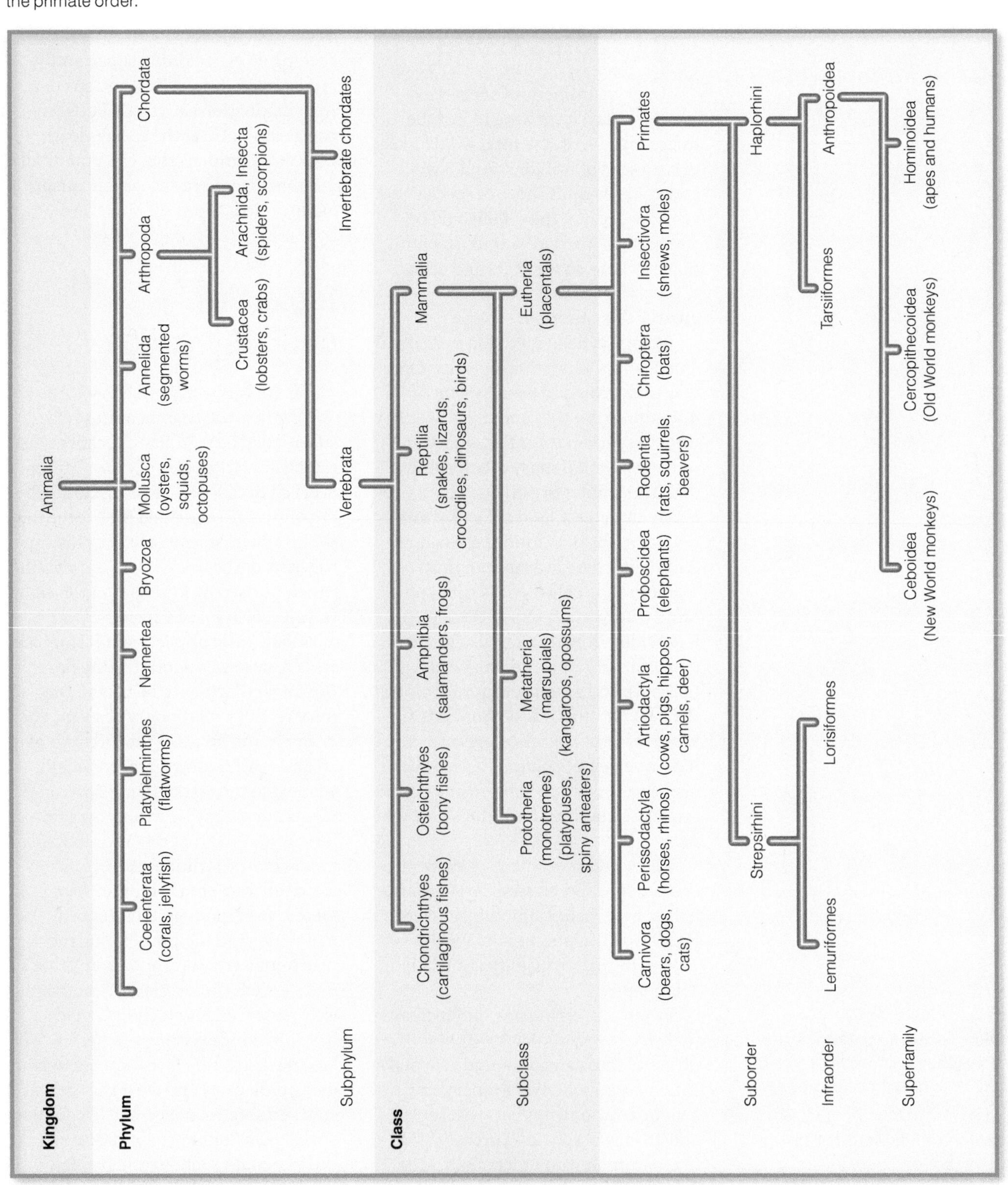

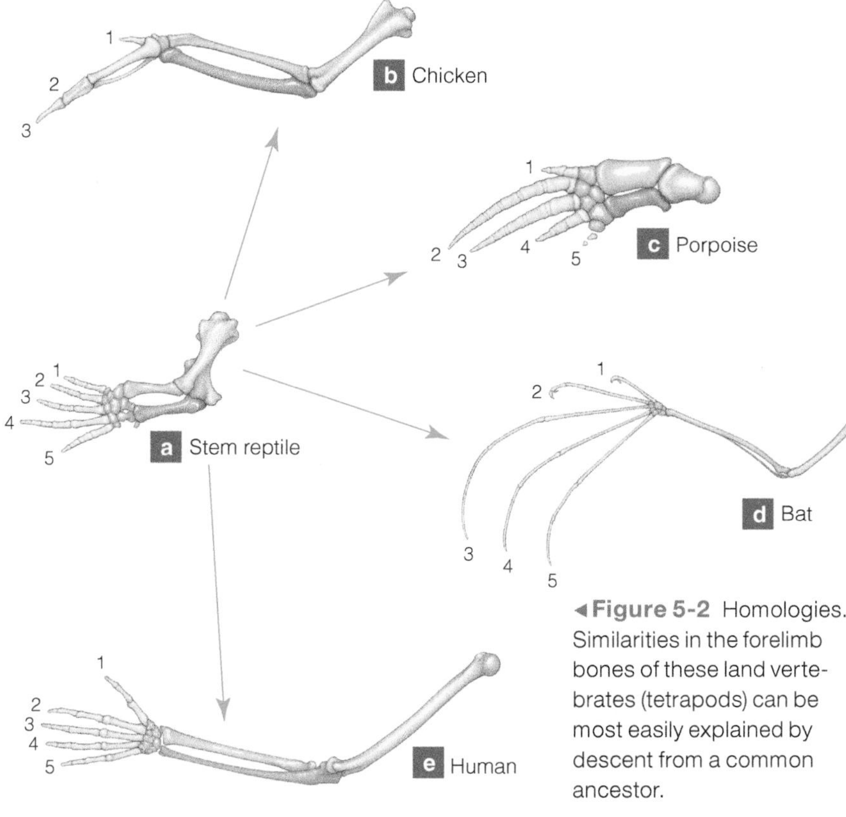

◄ **Figure 5-2** Homologies. Similarities in the forelimb bones of these land vertebrates (tetrapods) can be most easily explained by descent from a common ancestor.

with only relatively minor genetic changes. For example, recent research shows that forelimb development in all vertebrates is directed by just a few regulatory genes, called *Hox* genes (see Chapter 3; Shubin et al., 1997; Riddle and Tabin, 1999). A few mutations in certain *Hox* genes in early vertebrates led to the basic limb plan seen in all subsequent vertebrates. With further small mutations in these genes or in the genes they regulate, the varied structures that make up the wing of a chicken, the flipper of a porpoise, or the upper limb of a human developed. You should recognize that *basic* genetic regulatory mechanisms are highly conserved in animals; that is, they've been maintained relatively unchanged for hundreds of millions of years. Like a musical score with a basic theme, small variations on the pattern can produce the various "tunes" that differentiate one organism from another. This is the essential genetic foundation for most macroevolutionary change; it is a crucial point, showing how we quite easily connect biologically with other life-forms and how our and their evolutionary histories are part of the same grand story of life on earth (see "A Closer Look, Evo-Devo: The Evolution Revolution" on pages 82–83).

Structures that are shared by species on the basis of descent from a common ancestor are called **homologies**. Homologies alone are reliable indicators of evolutionary relationship, but we have to be careful not to draw hasty conclusions from superficial similarities. For example, both birds and butterflies have wings, but they shouldn't be grouped together on the basis of this single characteristic; butterflies (as insects) differ dramatically from birds in several other, even more fundamental ways. (For example, birds have an internal skeleton, central nervous system, and four limbs; insects don't.)

Here's what's happened in evolutionary history: From quite distant ancestors, both butterflies and birds developed wings *independently*. So their (superficial) similarities are a product of separate evolutionary responses to roughly similar functional demands. Such similarities, based on independent functional adaptation and not on shared evolutionary descent, are called **analogies**. The process that leads to the development of analogies (also called analogous structures) such as wings in birds and butterflies is termed **homoplasy**.

Making Connections: Constructing Classifications and Interpreting Evolutionary Relationships

Evolutionary biologists typically use two major approaches, or "schools," when they interpret evolutionary relationships with the goal

homologies Similarities between organisms based on descent from a common ancestor.

analogies Similarities between organisms based strictly on common function, with no assumed common evolutionary descent.

homoplasy (*homo*, meaning "same," and *plasy*, meaning "growth") The separate evolutionary development of similar characteristics in different groups of organisms.

of producing classifications. The first approach, called **evolutionary systematics**, is the more traditional. The second approach, called **cladistics**, has emerged primarily in the last three decades. Although aspects of both approaches are still used by most evolutionary biologists, in recent years cladistic methodologies have predominated among anthropologists. Indeed, one noted primate evolutionist commented that "virtually all current studies of primate phylogeny involve the methods and terminology" of cladistics (Fleagle, 1999, p. 1).

Comparing Evolutionary Systematics with Cladistics

Before we begin drawing distinctions between these two approaches, it's first helpful to note features shared by both evolutionary systematics and cladistics. First, both schools are interested in tracing evolutionary relationships and in constructing classifications that reflect these relationships. Second, both schools recognize that organisms must be compared using specific features (called *characters*) and that some of these characters are more informative than others. And third (deriving directly from the previous two points), both approaches focus exclusively on homologies.

But these approaches also have some significant differences—in how characters are chosen, which groups are compared, and how the results are interpreted and eventually incorporated into evolutionary schemes and classifications. The primary difference is that cladistics more explicitly and rigorously defines the kinds of homologies that yield the most useful information. For example, at a very basic level, all life (except for some viruses) shares DNA as the molecule underlying all organic processes. However, beyond inferring that all life most likely derives from a single origin, the mere presence of DNA tells us nothing further regarding more specific relationships among different kinds of life-forms. To draw further conclusions, we must look at particular characters that certain groups share as the result of more recent ancestry.

This perspective emphasizes an important point: Some homologous characters are much more informative than others. We saw earlier that all terrestrial vertebrates share homologies in the number and basic arrangement of bones in the forelimb. Even though these similarities are broadly useful in showing that these large evolutionary groups (amphibians, reptiles, and mammals) are all related through a distant ancestor, they don't provide information we can use to distinguish one group from another (a reptile from a mammal, for example). These kinds of characters (also called traits) that are shared through such remote ancestry are said to be **ancestral**, or primitive. We prefer the term *ancestral* because it doesn't reflect negatively on the evolutionary value of the character in question. In biological anthropology, the term *primitive* or *ancestral* simply means that a character seen in two organisms is inherited in both of them from a distant ancestor.

In most cases, analyzing ancestral characters doesn't supply enough information to make accurate evolutionary interpretations of relationships between different groups. In fact, misinterpretation of ancestral characters can easily lead to quite inaccurate evolutionary conclusions. Cladistics focuses on traits that distinguish particular evolutionary lineages; such traits are far more informative than ancestral traits. Lineages that share a common ancestor are called a **clade**, giving the name *cladistics* to the field that seeks to identify and interpret these groups. It is perhaps the most fundamental point of cladistics that evolutionary groups (that is, clades) all share one common ancestor and are thus said to be **monophyletic**. If a proposed evolutionary grouping is found to have more than one ancestor (rather than a single one shared by *all* members), it is said to be **polyphyletic**, and

evolutionary systematics A traditional approach to classification (and evolutionary interpretation) in which presumed ancestors and descendants are traced in time by analysis of homologous characters.

cladistics An approach to classification that attempts to make rigorous evolutionary interpretations based solely on analysis of certain types of homologous characters (those considered to be derived characters).

ancestral Referring to characters inherited by a group of organisms from a remote ancestor and thus not diagnostic of groups (lineages) that diverged after the character first appeared; also called primitive.

clade A group of organisms sharing a common ancestor. The group includes the common ancestor and all descendants.

monophyletic Referring to an evolutionary group (clade) composed of descendants all sharing a common ancestor.

polyphyletic Referring to an evolutionary group composed of descendants with more than one common ancestor (and thus not a true clade).

A Closer Look

Evo-Devo: The Evolution Revolution

In Chapter 4, you learned how, in the 1930s, scientists came to a better understanding of evolution once they realized that Mendel's principles and natural selection were both essential components of the process. This merger of ideas was a major step in evolutionary science, and with the discovery of the structure of DNA in 1953, the foundations of evolutionary biology were firmly established.

Almost half a century after the structure of the DNA molecule was revealed, another merger of disciplines occurred (Goodman and Coughlin, 2000). In 1999, the field of evolutionary developmental biology, or evo-devo, was created by uniting evolutionary biology with developmental biology. This combination resulted directly from research demonstrating that major evolutionary transformations involve changes in the very same regulatory genes that direct embryological development. The main goals of evo-devo are to discover how animals are put together and how the genes that control their development can, over time, produce new species.

Right now, there are millions of animal species (including insects and marine life), but they probably represent less than 1 percent of all the species that have ever existed on earth (Carroll et al., 2001). In spite of how diverse these species are, they share many anatomical similarities. They're all bilaterally symmetrical, meaning that one side is like the other except for certain aspects of internal organs. Also, and this is important, they all have a modular body plan made up of repeated segments. Arthropods (invertebrates with jointed feet, including all insects, spiders, and crustaceans) have segmented bodies and legs; and many have segmented wings, which are ultimately derived from leg-like appendages (**Fig. 1**).

Vertebrates also have segmented body parts, and this segmentation begins with the development of the head and vertebral column. Although the number of vertebrae and the number of each type of vertebra vary among species, the spine is made of repeated segments (**Fig. 2**).

Individual body parts are also modular. In humans, upper arms and thighs have one bone; forearms and lower legs have two; wrists and ankles have eight and seven, respectively; and hands and feet have five digits (see Fig. 5-2 and Appendix A). While snakes, whales, and dolphins don't have legs and feet, they're descended from animals that did. Moreover, some of these species, such as pythons and whales, have skeletal pelvic remnants.

We know that during embryonic development, bodies are formed according to a pattern that characterizes each species; and that pattern is dictated by a species' genome. Because of advances in comparative genomics, we also now know that the coding sequences of even distantly related species are very similar. For example, around 99 percent of mouse genes have a human counterpart (Mouse Genome Sequencing Consortium, 2002). So, what is it that makes us so different from mice?

Until about 25 years ago, biologists thought that changes in protein-coding genes were the key to evolutionary change, but now it's clear that changes in regulatory genes are the real answer to the question of how macroevolution occurs. DNA sequences of regulatory genes don't differ greatly among species; however (and this is key), these genes do differ when it comes to when, where, and how long they function. And these differences lead to major physical differences, because anatomical development depends on genes turning on and off at different times and in different places. There are many different kinds of regulatory genes, and they all instruct cells to make proteins (and different kinds of RNA) that in turn modulate the activity of yet other genes. Regulatory genes can be thought of as switches that turn other genes on or off at specific times in specific parts of the body (Carroll et al., 2008).

Many evolutionary biologists refer to the group of body-building regulatory genes as the *genetic tool kit*. It is highly conserved and is shared by all vertebrates and invertebrates. Through the roughly 600 million years of animal evolution, many of the genes that make up the tool kit have been somewhat changed by mutation and many have duplicated to produce families of genes. But given the amount of time and the huge array of descendant species, changes in the DNA sequences of tool kit genes have been extraordinarily minimal. Consequently, the roughly 10 percent of your genome that consists of regulatory genes has almost

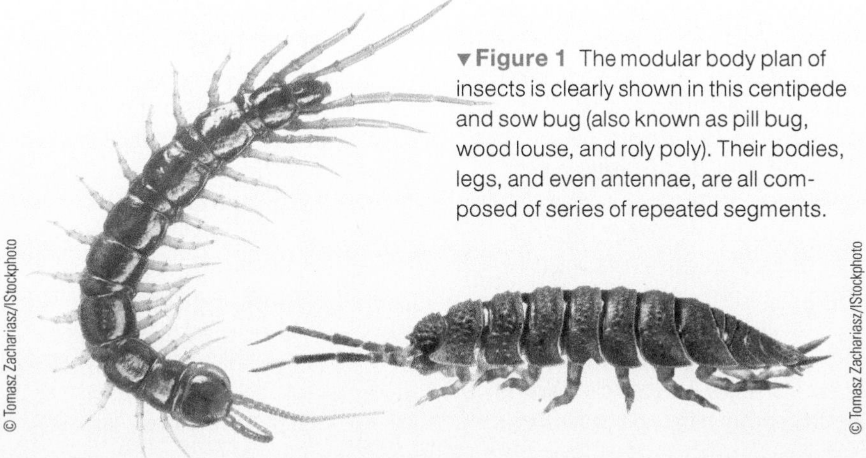

▼ **Figure 1** The modular body plan of insects is clearly shown in this centipede and sow bug (also known as pill bug, wood louse, and roly poly). Their bodies, legs, and even antennae, are all composed of series of repeated segments.

exactly the same DNA sequences as the regulatory genes of mice. It goes without saying that the tool kit genes serve as the best example of biological continuity among all animals, living and extinct. You should now be able to appreciate these most basic connections that link all animals, including us, with one another.

The genetic tool kit is composed of genes that make two basic kinds of proteins: *transcription factors* and *signaling molecules*. Here we're focusing on transcription factors, protein molecules that bind to specific DNA segments called *enhancers* or *promoters*. By binding to enhancers, transcription factors switch genes on and off, and they also determine how long those genes produce proteins.

Many transcription factors are produced by homeobox genes. These genes contain a highly conserved region of 180 nucleotides called the homeobox, and this sequence codes for the proteins that bind to enhancers. There are several families of genes that contain homeoboxes; the most familiar one is called *Hox* for short.

As we discussed in Chapter 3, *Hox* genes direct the early stages of embryonic development. Initially, they establish the identity of regions of the body and the pattern of structures along the main body axis that runs lengthwise through the embryo. These structures are actually early precursors to the head and vertebral column. Later in development, these same genes establish where limb buds will form and also determine limb polarity (that is, front, back, and sides). Mutations in these genes cause the transformation of one body part to another; we've learned about the most famous of these transformations from experiments on fruit flies, in which induced mutations cause all sorts of bizarre phenotypes (such as legs where antennae should be).

Most invertebrates have 10 *Hox* genes, fruit flies have 8, but vertebrates have more. Mammals, for example, have 39, located on four different chromosomes.

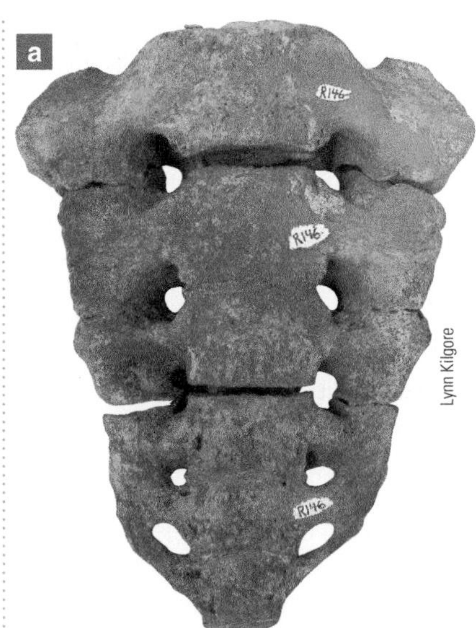

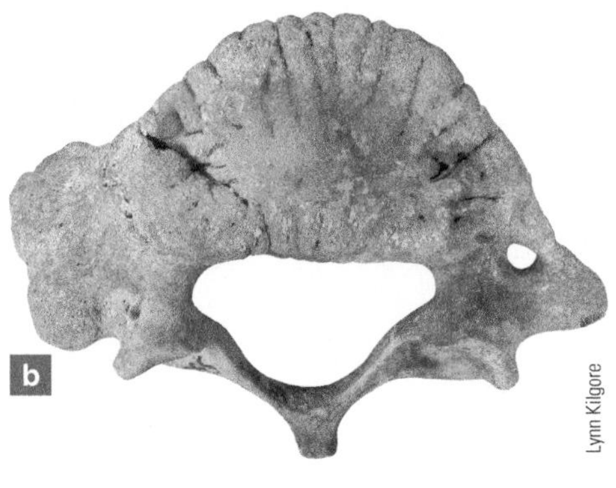

▲ **Figure 2** Two examples of *Hox* transformations. (**a**) This sacrum, seen from the front, is composed of six vertebrae when there should be only five. This was caused by the malfunction of one of the *Hox* genes involved in the initial patterning of the sacral vertebrae. (**b**) Top view of a sixth lumbar vertebra, the presence of which, in itself, is the result of a *Hox* malfunction. In addition, the left side has the morphology of a first sacral vertebra, and the opening on the right side is typical only of cervical (neck) vertebrae.

The reason vertebrates have more *Hox* genes than insects do is that, over time, the invertebrate versions have duplicated in vertebrates. From these observations, we can see that vertebrate *Hox* genes are descended from invertebrate *Hox* genes. Just to illustrate how conserved these genes are, many experiments have shown them to be interchangeable between species. For example, one study showed that fruit flies can function normally with *Hox* proteins derived from chick embryos (Lutz et al., 1996). This remarkable similarity indicates that these genes haven't changed much since fruit flies and chickens last shared a common ancestor some 600 millions years ago (Ayala and Rzhetskydagger, 1998).

The science of evo-devo allows us, for the first time, to understand how morphological change and macroevolution can occur through the action of the genes that make up the genetic tool kit. This understanding has been made possible through the recently developed techniques of gene cloning and comparative genomics. By adding the evidence provided by evo-devo to comparative anatomy and fossil studies, scientists are on the threshold of demonstrating how evolution has worked to produce the spectacular biological diversity we see today. The key to this great puzzle is to understand that it all derives from simple beginnings with a set of genes that have been shared by all animals for hundreds of millions of years. As Charles Darwin said in the last paragraph of *Origin of Species*, "There is grandeur in this view of life . . . from so simple a beginning endless forms most beautiful and most wonderful have been, and are being evolved." This quotation has been a favorite of biologists and anthropologists, not only for its eloquence, but also because we've long known that over many millions of years, life-forms have become more complex. For 150 years, we've explained this increased complexity in terms of natural selection, and we still do. But now we have the tools we need to reveal the very mechanism that allowed complexity to develop in the first place.

it represents neither a well-defined clade nor an evolutionary group actually separate from other ones. We'll encounter problems of exactly this nature in Chapter 6, when we tackle the classification of a small primate called a tarsier as well as that of the great apes.

When we try to identify a clade, the characters of interest are said to be **derived**, or **modified**. Thus, while the general ancestral bony pattern of the forelimb in land vertebrates doesn't allow us to distinguish among them, the further modification of this pattern in certain groups (as hooves, flippers, or wings, for instance) does.

An Example of Cladistic Analysis: The Evolutionary History of Cars and Trucks

A simplified example might help clarify the basic principles used in cladistic analysis. **Figure 5-3a** shows a hypothetical "lineage" of passenger vehicles. All of the "descendant" vehicles share a common ancestor, the prototype passenger vehicle. The first major division (I) differentiates passenger cars from trucks. The second split/diversification (II) is between luxury cars and sports cars (you could, of course, imagine many other subcategories). Derived characters that might distinguish trucks from cars could include type of frame, suspension, wheel size, and, in some forms, an open cargo bed. Derived characters that might distinguish sports cars from luxury cars could include engine size and type, wheel base size, and a decorative racing stripe.

Now let's assume that you're presented with an "unknown" vehicle (that is, one as yet unclassified). How do you decide what kind of vehicle it is? You might note such features as four wheels, a steering wheel, and a seat for the driver, but these are *ancestral* characters (found in the common ancestor) of all passenger vehicles. If, however, you note that the vehicle lacks a cargo bed and raised suspension (so it's not a truck) but has a racing stripe, you might conclude that it's a car, and more than that, a sports car (since it has a derived feature presumably of *only* that group).

All this seems fairly obvious, and you've probably noticed that this simple type of decision making characterizes much of human mental organization. Still, we frequently deal with complications that aren't so obvious. What if you're presented with a sports utility vehicle (SUV) with a racing stripe (**Fig. 5-3b**)? SUVs are basically trucks; the presence of the racing stripe could be seen as a homoplasy with sports cars. The lesson here is that we need to be careful, look at several traits, decide which are ancestral and which are derived, and finally try to recognize the complexity (and confusion) introduced by homoplasy.

Our example of passenger vehicles is useful up to a point. Because it concerns human inventions, the groupings possess characters that humans can add and delete in almost any combination. Naturally occurring organic systems are more limited in this respect. Any species can possess only those characters that have been inherited from its ancestor or that have been subsequently modified (derived) from those shared with the ancestor. So any modification in *any* species is constrained by that species' evolutionary legacy—that is, what the species starts out with.

Using Cladistics to Interpret Real Organisms

Another example, one drawn from paleontological (fossil) evidence of actual organisms, can help clarify these points. Most people know something about dinosaur evolution, and some of you may know about the recent controversies surrounding this topic. There are several intriguing issues concerning the evolutionary history of dinosaurs, and recent fossil discoveries have shed considerable light on them. Here we consider one of the more fascinat-

derived (modified) Referring to characters that are modified from the ancestral condition and thus diagnostic of particular evolutionary lineages.

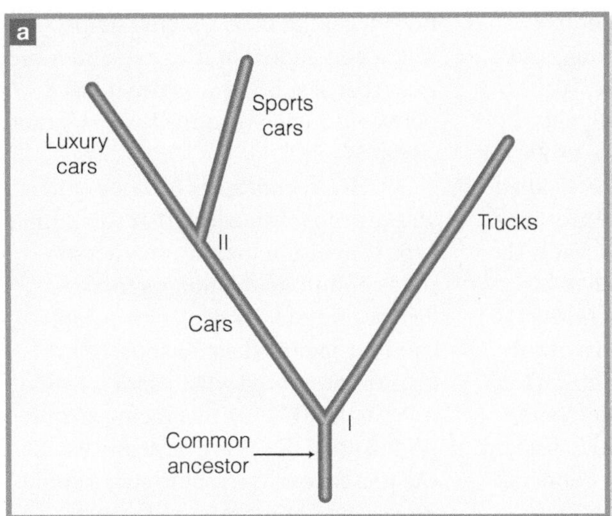

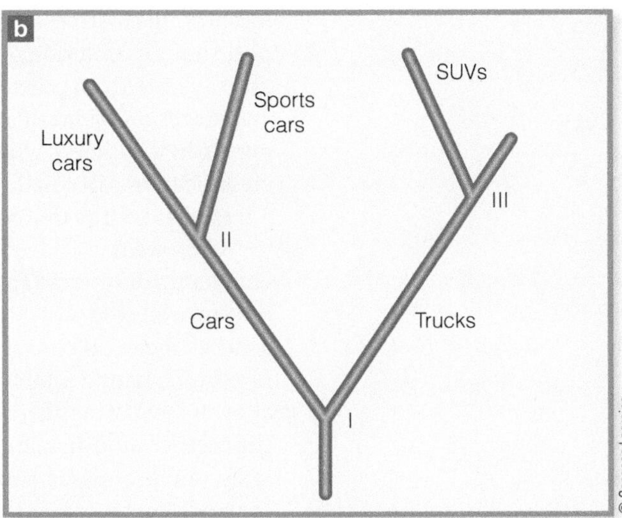

▲ **Figure 5-3** Evolutionary "trees" showing the development of passenger vehicles.

ing questions: the relationship of dinosaurs to birds.

Traditionally, it was thought that birds were a quite distinct group from reptiles and not especially closely related to any of them (including extinct forms, such as the dinosaurs; **Fig. 5-4a**). Still, the early origins of birds were clouded in mystery and have been much debated for more than a century. In fact, the first fossil evidence of a very primitive bird (now known to be about 150 million years old) was discovered in 1861, just two years following Darwin's publication of *Origin of Species*. Despite some initial and quite remarkably accurate interpretations linking these early birds to dinosaurs, most experts concluded that there was no close relationship. This view persisted through most of the twentieth century. But discoveries made in the last two decades have supported the hypothesis that birds *are* closely related to some dinosaurs. Two developments in particular have influenced this change of opinion: the remarkable discoveries in the 1990s from China, Madagascar, and elsewhere and the application of cladistic methods to the interpretation of these and other fossils. (Here's another example of how new discoveries as well as new approaches can become the basis for changing hypotheses.)

Recent finds from Madagascar of chicken-sized, primitive birds dated to 70–65 million years ago (mya) show an elongated second toe (similar, in fact, to that in the dinosaur *Velociraptor*, made infamous in the film *Jurassic Park*). Indeed, these primitive birds from Madagascar show many other similarities to *Velociraptor* and its close cousins, which together comprise a group of small- to medium-sized ground-living, carnivorous dinosaurs called **theropods**. Even more extraordinary finds have been unearthed recently in China, where the traces of what were once *feathers* have been found embossed in fossilized sediments! For many researchers, these new finds have finally solved the mystery of bird origins (**Fig. 5-4b**), leading them to conclude that "birds are not only *descended* from dinosaurs, they *are* dinosaurs (and reptiles)—just as humans are mammals, even though people are as different from other mammals as birds are from other reptiles" (Padian and Chiappe, 1998, p. 43).

There are some doubters who remain concerned that the presence of feathers in dinosaurs (145–125 mya) might simply be a homoplasy (that is, these creatures may have developed the trait independently from its appearance in birds). Certainly, the possibility of homoplasy must always be considered, as it can add considerably to the complexity of what seems like a straightforward evolutionary

theropods Small- to medium-sized ground-living dinosaurs, dated to approximately 150 mya and thought to be related to birds.

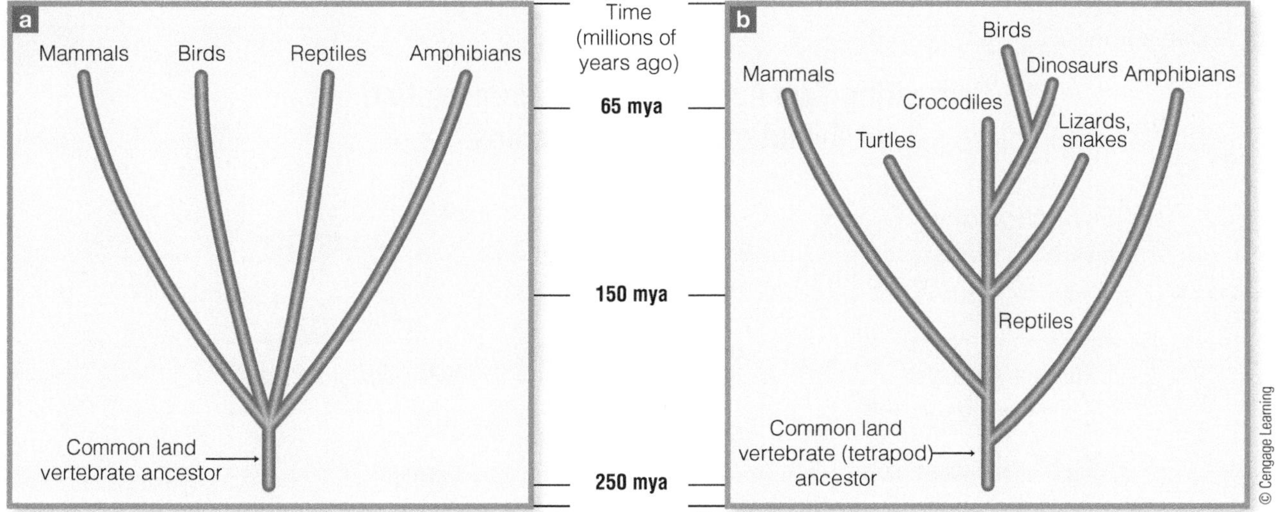

▲ **Figure 5-4** Evolutionary relationships of birds and dinosaurs. (**a**) Traditional view, showing no close relationship. (**b**) Revised view, showing common ancestry of birds and dinosaurs.

▼ **Figure 5-5** This cladogram shows the relationships of birds, dinosaurs, and other terrestrial vertebrates. Notice that there's no time scale, and both living and fossil forms are shown along the same dimension—that is, ancestor-descendant relationships aren't indicated. The chart is slightly simplified, as there are other branches (not shown) within the reptiles (with birds slightly more closely related to crocodiles than to other reptiles, such as snakes and lizards).

shared derived Relating to specific character traits shared in common between two life-forms and considered the most useful for making evolutionary interpretations.

phylogenetic tree A chart showing evolutionary relationships as determined by evolutionary systematics. It contains a time component and implies ancestor-descendant relationships.

cladogram A chart showing evolutionary relationships as determined by cladistic analysis. It's based solely on interpretation of shared derived characters. It contains no time component and does not imply ancestor-descendant relationships.

interpretation. Indeed, strict cladistic analysis assumes that homoplasy is not a common occurrence; if it were, perhaps no evolutionary interpretation could be very straightforward! In the case of the proposed relationship between some (theropod) dinosaurs and birds, the presence of feathers looks like an excellent example of a **shared derived** characteristic, which therefore *does* link the forms. What's more, cladistic analysis emphasizes that several characteristics should be examined, since homoplasy might muddle an interpretation based on just one or two shared traits. In the bird/dinosaur case, several other characteristics further suggest their evolutionary relationship.

One last point must be mentioned. Traditional evolutionary systematics illustrates the hypothesized evolutionary relationships using a *phylogeny*, more properly called a **phylogenetic tree**. Strict cladistic analysis, however, shows relationships in a **cladogram** (**Fig. 5-5**). If you examine the charts in Figures 5-4 and 5-5, you'll see some obvious differences. A phylogenetic tree incorporates the dimension of time, as shown in Figure 5-4 (you can find many other examples in this and upcoming chapters). A cladogram doesn't indicate time; all forms

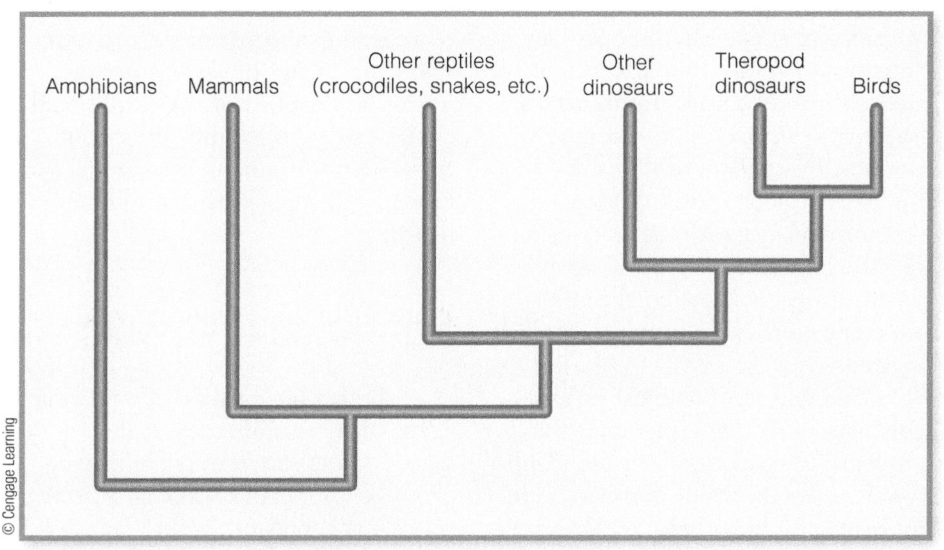

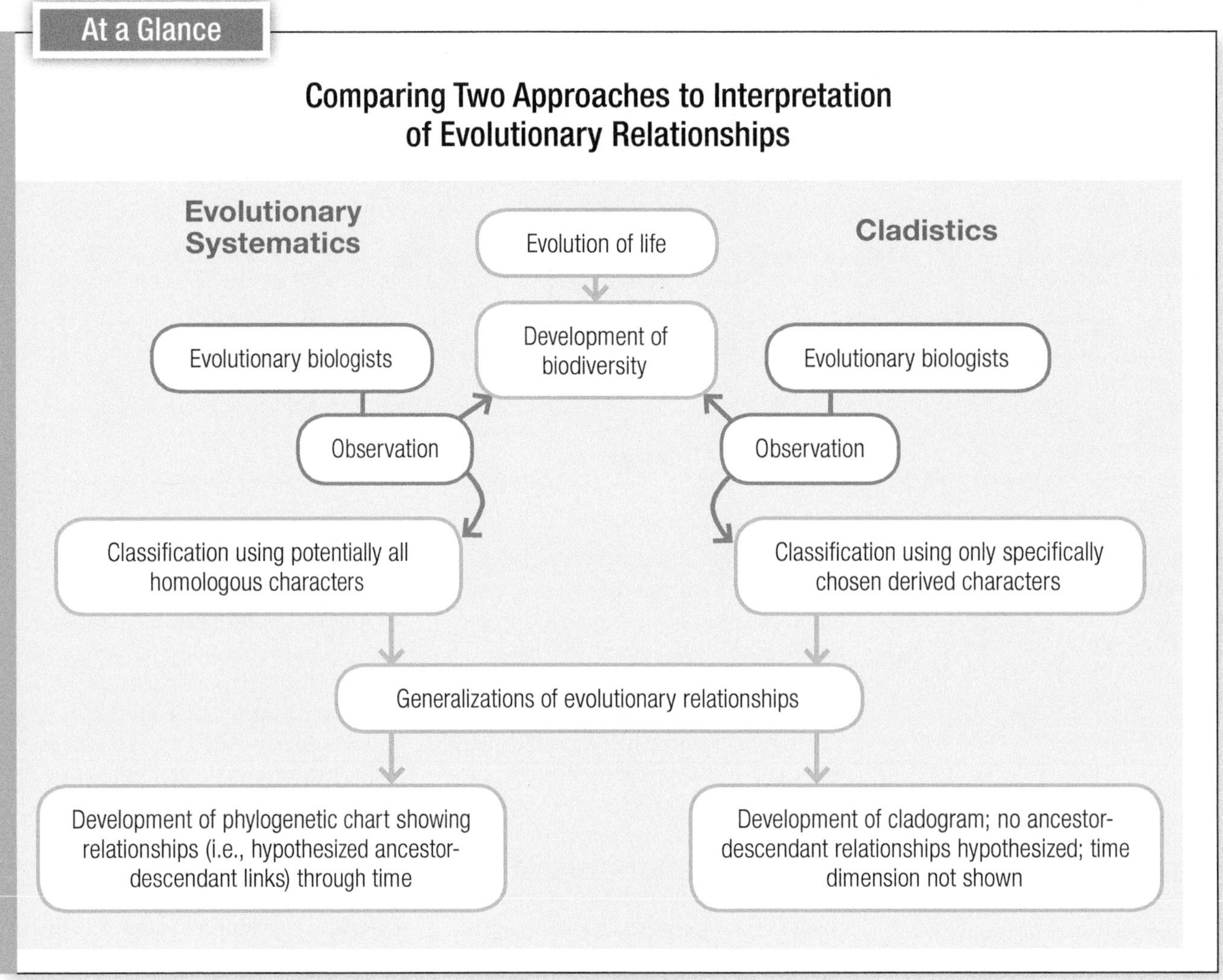

(fossil and modern) are shown along one dimension. Phylogenetic trees usually attempt to make some hypotheses regarding ancestor-descendant relationships (for example, theropods are ancestral to modern birds). Cladistic analysis (through cladograms) makes no attempt whatsoever to discern ancestor-descendant relationships. In fact, strict cladists are quite skeptical that the evidence really permits such specific evolutionary hypotheses to be scientifically confirmed (because there are many more extinct species than living ones).

In practice, most physical anthropologists (and other evolutionary biologists) utilize cladistic analysis to identify and assess the utility of traits and to make testable hypotheses regarding the relationships between groups of organisms. They also frequently extend this basic cladistic methodology to further hypothesize likely ancestor-descendant relationships shown relative to a time scale (that is, in a phylogenetic tree). In this way, aspects of both traditional evolutionary systematics and cladistic analysis are combined to produce a more complete picture of evolutionary history.

Definition of Species

Whether biologists are doing a cladistic or more traditional phylogenetic analysis, they're comparing groups of organisms—that is, different species, genera (*sing.*, genus), families,

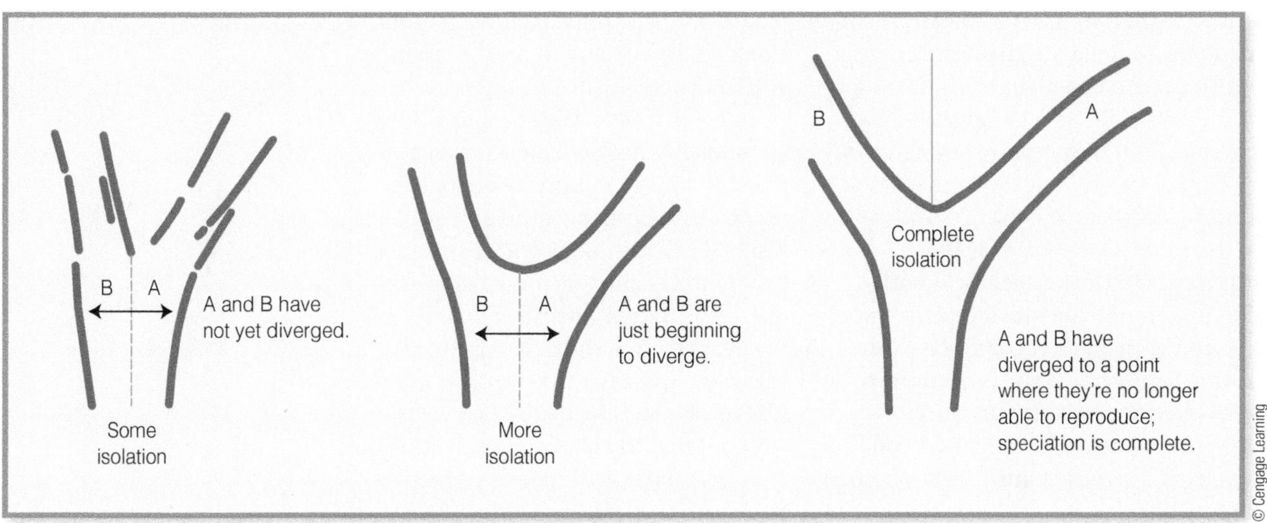
B
A
A and B have
not yet diverged.
Some
isolation
B
A
A and B are
just beginning
to diverge.
More
isolation
B
A
Complete
isolation
A and B have
diverged to a point
where they're no longer
able to reproduce;
speciation is complete.
© Cengage Learning

▲ **Figure 5-6** This speciation model illustrates branching evolution, or cladogenesis, which is caused by increasing reproductive isolation.

orders, and so forth. Fundamental to all these levels of classification is the most basic, the species. It's appropriate, then, to ask how biologists define species. We addressed this issue briefly in Chapter 1, where we used the most common definition, one that emphasizes interbreeding and reproductive isolation. While it's not the only definition of species (others are discussed shortly), this view, called the **biological species concept** (Mayr, 1970), is the one preferred by most zoologists.

To understand what species are, you might consider how they come about in the first place—what Darwin called the "origin of species." This most fundamental of macroevolutionary processes is called **speciation**. According to the biological species concept, the way new species are first produced involves some form of isolation. Picture a single species (baboons, for example) composed of several populations distributed over a wide geographical area. Gene exchange between populations (gene flow) will be limited if a geographical barrier, such as an ocean or a large river, effectively separates these populations. This extremely important form of isolating mechanism is called *geographical isolation*.

If one baboon population (A) is separated from another baboon population (B) by a river that has changed course, individual baboons of population A will not mate with individuals from B (**Fig. 5-6**). As time passes (perhaps hundreds or thousands of generations), genetic differences will accumulate in both populations. If population size is small, we can assume that genetic drift will also cause allele frequencies to change in both populations. And because drift is *random*, we wouldn't expect the effects to be the same. Consequently the two populations will begin to diverge genetically.

As long as gene exchange is limited, the populations can only become more genetically different over time. What's more, further difference can be expected if the baboon groups are occupying slightly different habitats. These additional genetic differences would be incorporated through the process of natural selection. Certain individuals in population A would be more reproductively fit in their own environment, but they would show less reproductive success in the environment occupied by population B. So allele frequencies will shift further, resulting in even greater divergence between the two groups.

With the cumulative effects of genetic drift and natural selection acting over many generations, the result will be two populations that—even if they were to come back into geographical contact—could no longer interbreed. More than just geographical iso-

biological species concept A depiction of species as groups of individuals capable of fertile interbreeding but reproductively isolated from other such groups.

speciation The process by which a new species evolves from an earlier species. Speciation is the most basic process in macroevolution.

lation might now apply. There may, for instance, be behavioral differences that interfere with courtship—what we call *behavioral isolation.* Using our *biological* definition of species, we would now recognize two distinct species where initially only one existed.

Another related process that can contribute to the further differentiation of populations into incipient species concerns mate recognition. This is sometimes called the **recognition species concept**, though the crucial process, again, concerns reproduction (that is, who's mating with whom; Ridley, 1993).

Assume, in our baboon example, that some isolation has already occurred and that phenotypic (and genotypic) differences are beginning to be established between two populations. In this situation, coloration patterns of faces or the size, location, coloration, or even smell of the female genital swelling might vary from group to group. If so, then a female from population A might not recognize a male from population B as an appropriate mate (and vice versa, of course). Natural selection would quickly favor such discrimination if hybrids were less reproductively successful than within-population crosses. Indeed, once such "selective breeding" became established, speciation would be accelerated considerably.

Another definition of species focuses primarily on natural selection and emphasizes that speciation is the result of influences of varied habitats. In this view, called the **ecological species concept**, a species is defined as a group of organisms exploiting a single niche. Also called an **ecological niche**, this is the physical as well as biological position of an organism within the biological world (that is, within the full ecosystem).

For each population, the ecological niche will vary slightly, and different phenotypes will be slightly more advantageous in each. For example, one population might be more arboreal and another more terrestrial; but there would not be an intermediate population equally successful on the ground and in the trees.

In recent years, the ecological species concept has attracted support from several evolutionary biologists, especially among physical anthropologists. While the biological species concept emphasizes gene flow and reproductive isolation, the ecological species concept stresses the role of natural selection. Clearly, our approach in this text has been to focus on the evolutionary contribution of natural selection; thus, the ecological species concept has much to offer here. Nevertheless, our understanding of species need not entail an either-or choice between the biological species concept and the ecological species concept. Some population isolation could indeed *begin* the process of speciation, and at this stage, the influence of genetic drift could be crucial. The process might then be further influenced by mate recognition as well as by natural selection as individuals in different populations adapt to varying environments.

Interpreting Species and Other Groups in the Fossil Record

Throughout much of this text, we'll be using various taxonomic terms for fossil primates (including fossil hominins). You'll be introduced to such terms as *Proconsul, Sivapithecus, Australopithecus,* and *Homo.* Of course, *Homo* is still a living primate. But it's especially difficult to make these types of designations from remains of animals that are long dead (and only partially preserved as skeletal remains). In these contexts, what do such names mean in evolutionary terms?

Our goal in applying species, genus, or other taxonomic labels to groups of organisms is to make meaningful biological statements about the variation that's represented. As we look at

recognition species concept A depiction of species in which the key aspect is the ability of individuals to identify members of their own species for purposes of mating (and to avoid mating with members of other species). In theory, this type of selective mating is a component of a species concept emphasizing mating and is therefore compatible with the biological species concept.

ecological species concept The concept that a species is a group of organisms exploiting a single niche. This view emphasizes the role of natural selection in separating species from one another.

ecological niche The position of a species within its physical and biological environments. A species' ecological niche is defined by such components as diet, terrain, vegetation, type of predators, relationships with other species, and activity patterns, and each niche is unique to a given species. Together, ecological niches make up an ecosystem.

populations of living or long-extinct animals, we are certainly going to see variation; this happens in *any* sexually reproducing organism due to recombination (see Chapter 3). As a result of recombination, each individual organism is a unique combination of genetic material, and the uniqueness is often reflected to some extent in the phenotype.

Besides such *individual variation*, we see other kinds of systematic variation in all biological populations. *Age changes* alter overall body size, as well as shape, in many mammals. One pertinent example for fossil human and ape studies is the change in number, size, and shape of teeth from deciduous teeth, also known as baby or milk teeth (only 20 teeth are present) to the permanent dentition (32 are present). It would be an obvious error to distinguish two fossil forms based solely on such age-dependent criteria. If one individual were represented just by milk teeth and another (seemingly very different) individual just by adult teeth, they could easily be different-aged individuals from the *same* population. Researchers dealing with fragmentary remains must be alert to variation of this sort. Otherwise, one could make such a silly mistake as thinking that pieces of a two-year-old were from a different species than his or her mother!

Variation due to sex also plays an important role. Differences in physical characteristics between males and females of the same species, called **sexual dimorphism**, can result in marked variation in body size and proportions in adults of the same species (we'll discuss this important topic in more detail in Chapter 6).

sexual dimorphism Differences in physical characteristics between males and females of the same species. For example, humans are slightly sexually dimorphic for body size, with males being taller, on average, than females of the same population. Sexual dimorphism is very pronounced in many species, such as gorillas.

intraspecific Within species; refers to variation seen within the same species.

interspecific Between species; refers to variation beyond that seen within the same species to include additional aspects seen between two different species.

paleospecies Species defined from fossil evidence, often covering a long time span.

Recognition of Fossil Species

Keeping in mind all the types of variation present within interbreeding groups of organisms, the minimum biological category we'd like to define in fossil primate samples is the *species*. As already defined (according to the biological species concept), a species is a group of interbreeding or potentially interbreeding organisms that is reproductively isolated from other such groups. In modern organisms, this concept is theoretically testable by observations of reproductive behavior. In animals long extinct, such observations are obviously impossible. Our only way, then, of getting a handle on the variation we see in fossil groups is to refer to living animals.

In studying a fossil group, we may observe obvious variation, such as some individuals being larger and with bigger teeth than others. The question then becomes: What's the biological significance of this variation? Two possibilities come to mind. Either the variation is accounted for by individual, age, and sex differences seen *within* every biological species (that is, it is **intraspecific**), or the variation represents differences *between* reproductively isolated groups (that is, it is **interspecific**). To decide which answer is correct, we have to look at contemporary species.

If the amount of variation we observe in fossil samples is comparable to that seen today *within species of closely related forms*, then we shouldn't "split" our sample into more than one species. We must, however, be careful in choosing modern analogues because rates of evolution vary among different groups of mammals. So, for example, in studying extinct fossil primates, we must compare them with well-known modern primates. Even so, studies of living groups have shown that defining exactly where species boundaries begin and end is often difficult. In dealing with extinct species, the uncertainties are even greater. In addition to the overlapping patterns of variation *spatially* (over space), variation also occurs *temporally* (through time). In other words, even more variation will be seen in **paleospecies**, since individuals may be separated by thousands or even millions of years. Applying a strict Linnaean taxonomy to such a situation presents an unavoidable dilemma. Standard Linnaean classification, designed to take account of variation present at any given time, describes a static situation. But when we deal with paleospecies, the time frame is expanded and the situation can be dynamic (that is, later forms might differ from earlier forms). In such a dynamic situation, taxonomic decisions (where to draw species boundaries) are ultimately going to be somewhat arbitrary.

Because the task of interpreting paleospecies is so difficult, paleoanthropologists have sought various solutions. Most researchers today define species using clusters of derived traits (identified cladistically). But owing to the ambiguity of how many derived characters are required to identify a fully distinct species (as opposed to a subspecies), the frequent mixing of characters into novel combinations, and the always difficult problem of homoplasy, there continues to be disagreement. A good deal of the dispute is driven by philosophical orientation. Exactly how much diversity should one expect among fossil primates, especially among fossil hominins?

Some researchers, called "splitters," claim that speciation occurred frequently during hominin evolution, and they often identify numerous fossil hominin species in a sample being studied. As the nickname suggests, these scientists are inclined to split groups into many species. Others, called "lumpers," assume that speciation was less common and see much variation as being intraspecific. These scientists lump groups together, so that fewer hominin species are identified, named, and eventually plugged into evolutionary schemes. As you'll see in the following chapters, debates of this sort pervade paleoanthropology, perhaps more than in any other branch of evolutionary biology.

Recognition of Fossil Genera

The next and broader level of taxonomic classification, the **genus** (*pl.*, genera), presents another challenge for biologists. To have more than one genus, we obviously must have at least two species (reproductively isolated groups), and the species of one genus must differ in a basic way from the species of another genus. A genus is therefore defined as a group of species composed of members more closely related to each other than they are to species from any other genus.

Grouping species into genera can be quite subjective and is often much debated by biologists. One possible test for contemporary animals is to check for results of hybridization between individuals of different species—rare in nature but quite common in captivity. If members of two normally separate species interbreed and produce live (though not necessarily fertile) offspring, the two parental species are probably not too different genetically and should therefore be grouped in the same genus. A well-known example of such a cross is horses with donkeys (*Equus caballus* × *Equus asinus*), which normally produces live but sterile offspring (mules).

As previously mentioned, we can't perform breeding experiments with extinct animals, which is why another definition of genus becomes highly relevant. Species that are members of the same genus share the same broad adaptive zone. An adaptive zone represents a general ecological lifestyle more basic than the narrower ecological niches characteristic of individual species. This ecological definition of genus can be an immense aid in interpreting fossil primates. Teeth are the most frequently preserved parts, and they often can provide excellent general ecological inferences. Cladistic analysis also helps scientists to make judgments about evolutionary relationships. That is, members of the same genus should

genus (*pl.*, genera) A group of closely related species.

all share derived characters not seen in members of other genera.

As a final comment, we should stress that classification by genus is not always a straightforward decision. For instance, in emphasizing the very close genetic similarities between humans (*Homo sapiens*) and chimpanzees (*Pan troglodytes*), some current researchers (Wildman et al., 2003) place both in the same genus (*Homo sapiens, Homo troglodytes*). This philosophy has caused some to advocate for extension of basic human rights to great apes (as proposed by members of the Great Ape Project). Such thinking might startle you. Of course when it gets this close to home, it's often difficult to remain objective!

What Are Fossils and How Do They Form?

Much of what we know about the history of life comes from studying **fossils**, which are traces of ancient organisms and can be formed in many ways. The oldest fossils found thus far date back more than 3 billion years; because they are the remains of microorganisms, they are extremely small and are called *microfossils*.

These very early traces of life are fragile and very rare. Most of our evidence comes from later in time and usually in the form of pieces of shells, bones, or teeth, all of which, even in a living animal, were already partly made of mineral, giving them a head start in the fossilization process. After the organism died, these "hard" tissues were further impregnated with other minerals, being eventually transformed into a stonelike composition in a process called **mineralization** (Fig. 5-7).

There are, however, many other ways in which life-forms have left traces of their existence. Sometimes insects were trapped in tree sap, which later became hardened and chemically altered. Because there was little or no oxygen inside the hardened amber, the insects have remained remarkably well preserved for millions of years, even with soft tissue and DNA still present (Fig. 5-8). This fascinating circumstance led author Michael Crichton to conjure the events depicted in the novel (and motion picture) *Jurassic Park.*

Dinosaur footprints as well as much more recent hominin tracks, leaf imprints in hardened mud or similar impressions of small organisms, and even the traces of dinosaur feathers—all of these are fossils. Recently, beautifully preserved theropod dinosaur feathers have been discovered in northeastern China (dated to approximately 125 mya). These remains are so superbly preserved that even microscopic cell structures have been indentified. These tiny structures directly influenced feather color in ancient dinosaurs; what's more, these same structures influence feather color in modern birds. Researchers are now able to deduce that some stripes in the feathers of one dinosaur were chestnut/reddish brown in color (Zhang et al., 2010)!

A spectacular discovery of a 47-million-year-old early primate fossil was widely publicized in 2009. This fossil is remarkable, preserving more than 95 percent of the skeleton as well as outlines of soft tissue and even fossilized remains of digestive tract contents (see Chapter 8) (Franzen et al., 2009). The amazing preservation of this small primate occurred because it died on the edge of a volcanic lake and was quickly covered with sediment. It reminds us that whether a dead animal will become fossilized and how much of it will be preserved depends partly on *how* it dies, but even more on *where* it dies.

Some ancient organisms have left vast amounts of fossil remains. Indeed, limestone deposits can be hundreds of feet thick and are largely made up of fossilized remains of marine shellfish (see Chapter 2). However, fossils of land animals are not nearly so com-

fossils Traces or remnants of organisms found in geological beds on the earth's surface.

mineralization The process in which parts of animals (or some plants) become transformed into stonelike structures. Mineralization usually occurs very slowly, as water carrying minerals—such as silica or iron—seeps into the tiny spaces within a bone. In some cases, the original minerals within the bone or tooth can be completely replaced, molecule by molecule, with other minerals.

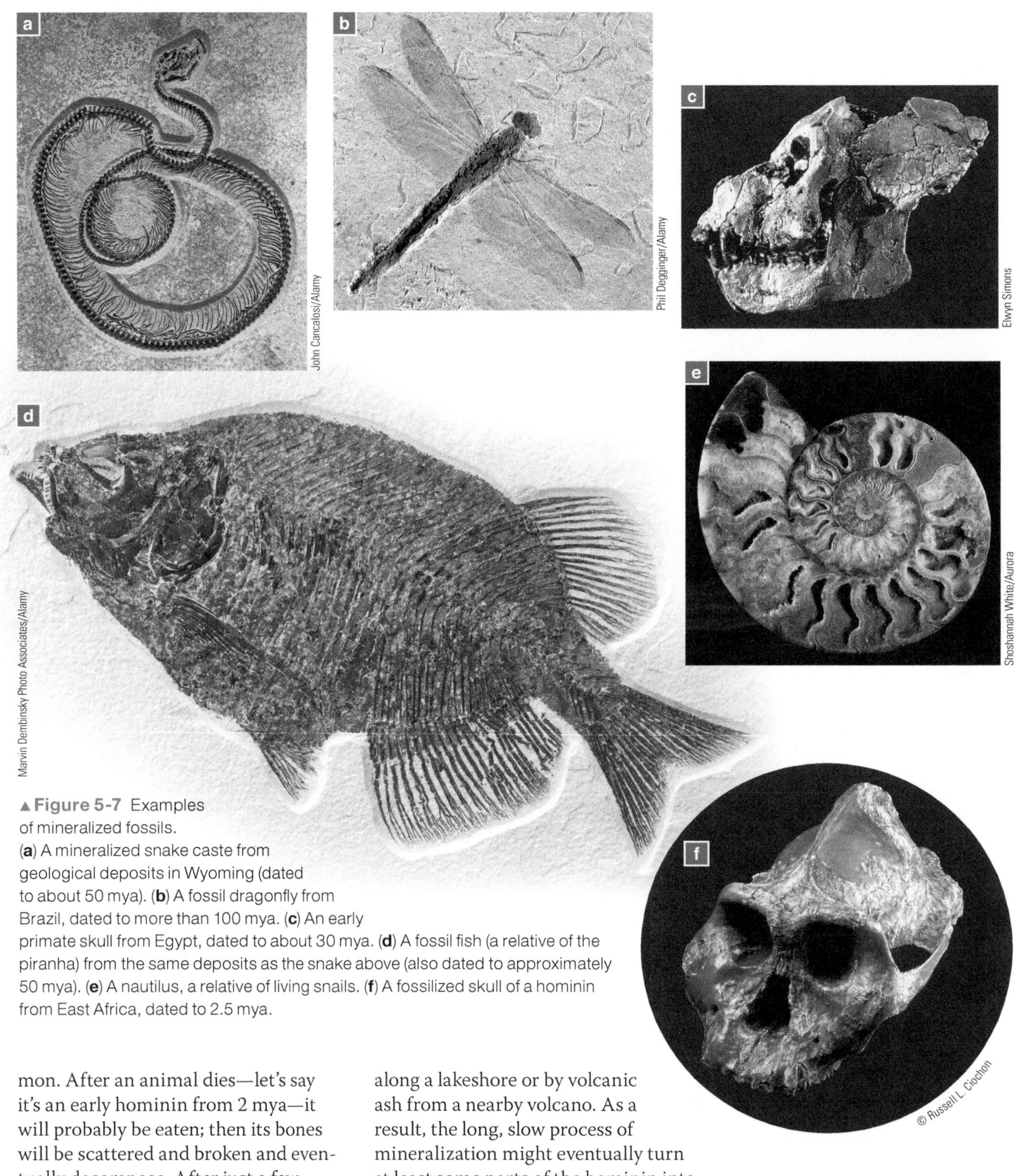

▲ **Figure 5-7** Examples of mineralized fossils. (**a**) A mineralized snake caste from geological deposits in Wyoming (dated to about 50 mya). (**b**) A fossil dragonfly from Brazil, dated to more than 100 mya. (**c**) An early primate skull from Egypt, dated to about 30 mya. (**d**) A fossil fish (a relative of the piranha) from the same deposits as the snake above (also dated to approximately 50 mya). (**e**) A nautilus, a relative of living snails. (**f**) A fossilized skull of a hominin from East Africa, dated to 2.5 mya.

mon. After an animal dies—let's say it's an early hominin from 2 mya—it will probably be eaten; then its bones will be scattered and broken and eventually decompose. After just a few weeks, there will be hardly anything left to fossilize. But suppose, by chance, this recently deceased hominin were quickly covered by sediment, perhaps by sand and mud in a streambed or along a lakeshore or by volcanic ash from a nearby volcano. As a result, the long, slow process of mineralization might eventually turn at least some parts of the hominin into a fossil.

The study of how bones and other materials come to be buried in the earth and preserved as fossils is called **taphonomy** (from the Greek *taphos*,

taphonomy The study of how bones and other materials come to be buried in the earth and preserved as fossils.

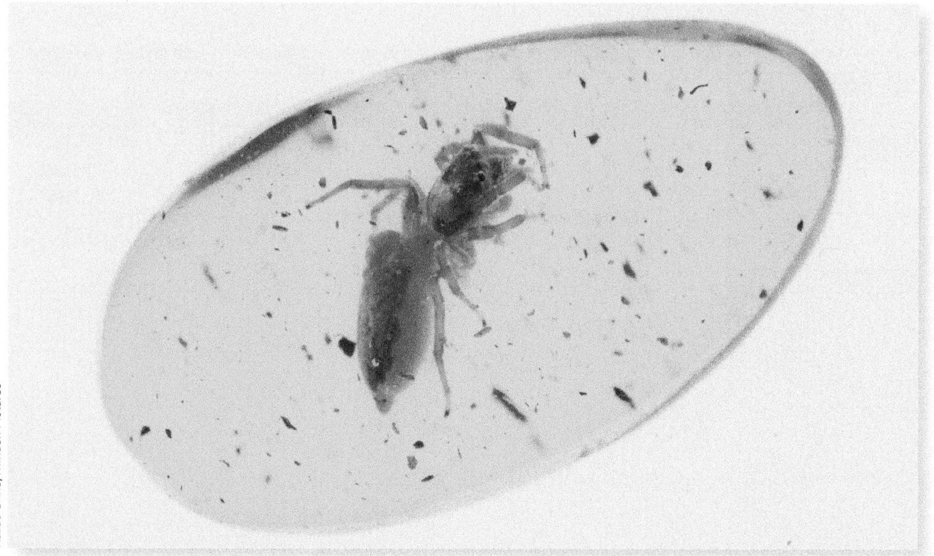

▶ **Figure 5-8** A spider fossilized in amber.

Kazuo Unno/Minden Pictures

meaning "study of the grave"). Such studies focus on everything that happens to an organism once it has died, making it the life history of the dead, so to speak. Among the topics that taphonomists try to understand are processes of sedimentation and burial, including the action of streams, preservation properties of bone, and carnivore disturbance factors.

Humans Are Vertebrates: Distant Connections

Biologists must contend with not only the staggering array of living and extinct life-forms but also the vast amount of time that life has been evolving on earth. Again, scientists have devised simplified schemes—but in this case to organize *time*, not biological diversity.

Geologists have formulated the **geological time scale** (**Fig. 5-9**), in which very large time spans are organized into eras that include one or more periods. Periods, in turn, can be broken down into epochs. For the time span encompassing vertebrate evolution, there are three eras: the Paleozoic, Mesozoic, and Cenozoic. The earliest vertebrates are present in the fossil record dating to early in the Paleozoic at 500 mya, and their origins are probably much older. It's the vertebrates' capacity to form bone that accounts for their more complete fossil record *after* 500 mya.

During the Paleozoic, several varieties of fishes (including the ancestors of modern sharks and bony fishes), amphibians, and reptiles appeared. At the end of the Paleozoic, close to 250 mya, several varieties of mammal-like reptiles were also diversifying. It's generally thought that some of these forms ultimately gave rise to the mammals.

The evolutionary history of vertebrates and other organisms during the Paleozoic and Mesozoic was profoundly influenced by geographical events. We know that the positions of the earth's continents shifted dramatically during the last several hundred million years. This process, called **continental drift**, is explained by the geological theory of *plate tectonics*, which states that the earth's crust is a series of gigantic moving and colliding plates. Such massive geological movements can induce volcanic activity (as, for example, all around the Pacific Rim), mountain building (for example, the Himalayas), and earthquakes.

geological time scale The organization of earth history into eras, periods, and epochs; commonly used by geologists and paleoanthropologists.

continental drift The movement of continents on sliding plates of the earth's surface. As a result, the positions of large landmasses have shifted drastically during the earth's history.

▼ **Figure 5-9** Geological time scale.

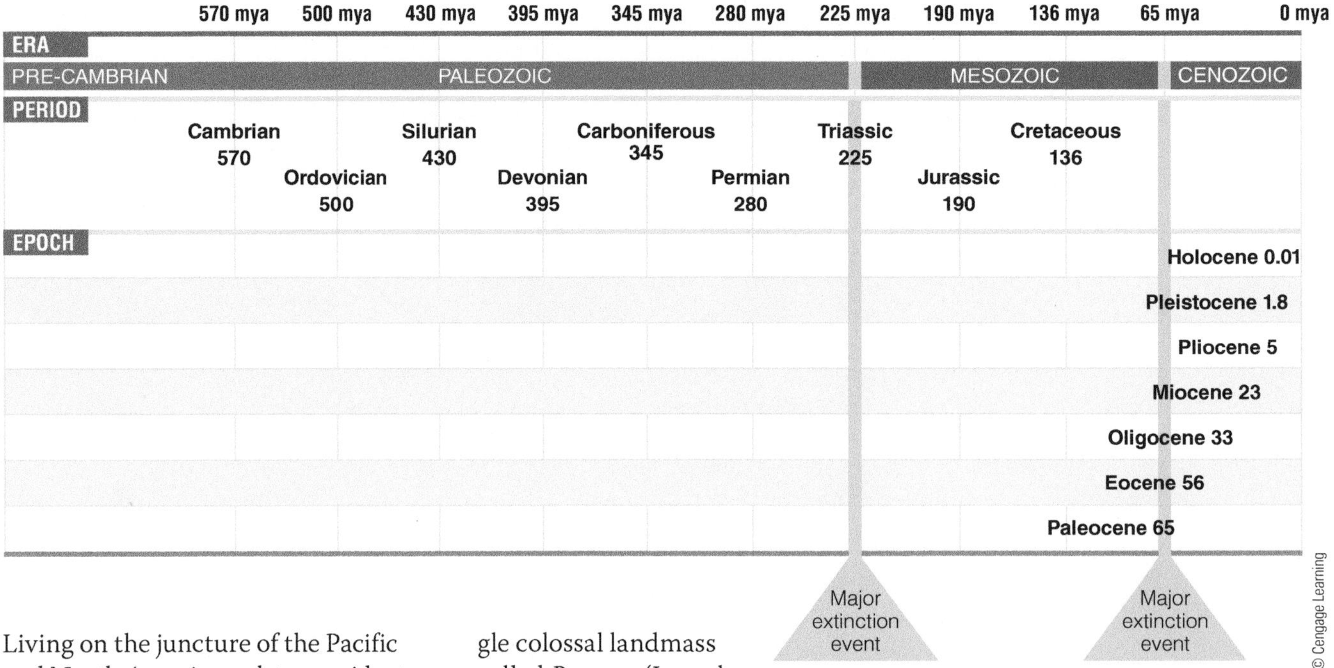

570 mya
500 mya
430 mya
395 mya
345 mya
280 mya
225 mya
190 mya
136 mya
65 mya
0 mya
ERA
PRE-CAMBRIAN
PALEOZOIC
MESOZOIC
CENOZOIC
PERIOD
Cambrian 570
Ordovician 500
Silurian 430
Devonian 395
Carboniferous 345
Permian 280
Triassic 225
Jurassic 190
Cretaceous 136
EPOCH
Holocene 0.01
Pleistocene 1.8
Pliocene 5
Miocene 23
Oligocene 33
Eocene 56
Paleocene 65
Major extinction event
Major extinction event
© Cengage Learning

Living on the juncture of the Pacific and North American plates, residents of the Pacific coast of the United States are acutely aware of some of these consequences, as illustrated by the explosive volcanic eruption of Mt. St. Helens and the frequent earthquakes in Alaska and California.

While reconstructing the earth's physical history, geologists have determined the earlier, much altered positions of major continental landmasses. During the late Paleozoic, the continents came together to form a single colossal landmass called *Pangea*. (In reality, the continents had been drifting on plates, coming together and separating, long before the end of the Paleozoic around 225 mya.) During the early Mesozoic, the southern continents (South America, Africa, Antarctica, Australia, and India) began to split off from Pangea, forming a large southern continent called *Gondwanaland* (**Fig. 5-10a**). Similarly, the northern continents (North America, Greenland, Europe,

LAURASIA
GONDWANALAND
NORTH AMERICA
EURASIA
AFRICA
SOUTH AMERICA
INDIA
MADAGASCAR
AUSTRALIA
ANTARCTICA
a
b
© Cengage Learning

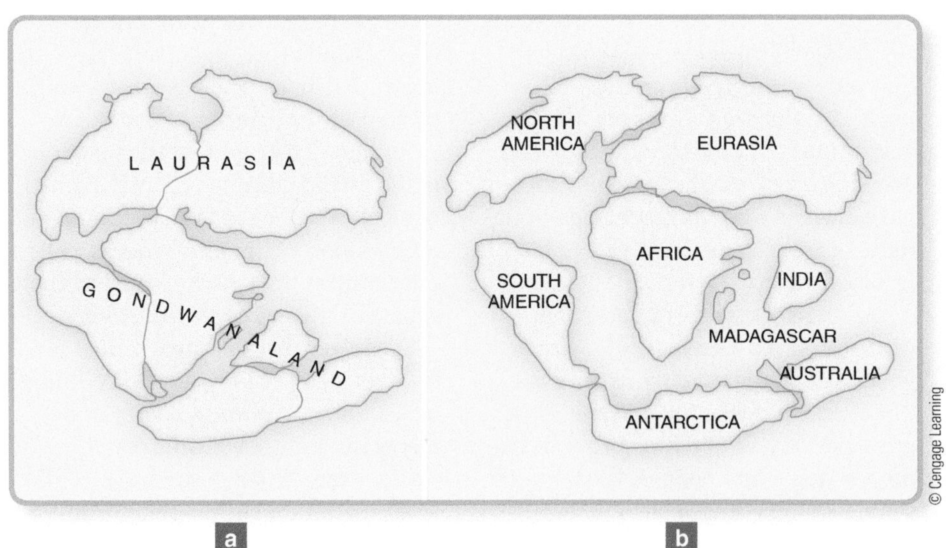

◀ **Figure 5-10** Continental drift. (**a**) Positions of the continents during the Mesozoic (ca. 125 mya). Pangea is breaking up into a northern landmass (Laurasia) and a southern landmass (Gondwanaland). (**b**) Positions of the continents at the beginning of the Cenozoic (ca. 65 mya).

A Closer Look

Deep Time

The vast expanse of time during which evolution has occurred on earth staggers the imagination. Indeed, this fundamental notion of what John McPhee has termed "deep time" is not really understood or, in fact, widely believed. Of course as we've emphasized beginning in Chapter 1, *belief*, as such, is not part of science. But observation, theory building, and testing are. Still, in a world populated mostly by nonscientists, the concept of deep time, crucial as it is to geology and anthropology, is resisted by many people. This situation really isn't surprising; the very notion of deep time is in many ways counterintuitive. Human beings tend to measure their existence in months, years, and the span of human lifetimes.

But what are these durations as measured against geological or galactic phenomena? In a real sense, these vast time expanses are beyond human comprehension. We can reasonably fathom the reaches of human history stretching to about 5,000 years ago. In a leap of imagination, we can perhaps even begin to grasp the stretch of time back to the cave painters of France and Spain, approximately 17,000 to 25,000 years ago. How do we relate, then, to a temporal span that's 10 times this one, back to 250,000 years ago, about the time of the earliest *Homo sapiens*—or to 10 times this span to 2,500,000 years ago (about the time of the appearance of our genus, *Homo*)? And when we multiply this last duration another 1,000 times (to 2,500,000,000), we're back to a time of fairly early lifeforms. We'd have to reach still further into earth's past, another 1.5 billion years, to approach the *earliest* documented life.

▲ **Figure 1** Geological exposures at the Grand Canyon. Some of the sediments are almost 2 billion years old and have been cut through by the Colorado River over the last 6 million years.

The dimensions of these intervals are humbling to say the least. The discovery in the nineteenth century of deep time (see Chapter 2), what the late Stephen Jay Gould called "geology's greatest contribution to human thought," plunged one more dagger into humanity's long-cherished view of itself as something special. Astronomers had previously established how puny our world was in the physical expanse of space, and then geologists showed that even on our own small planet we were but residues dwarfed within a river of time "without a vestige of a beginning or prospect of an end" (from James Hutton, a founder of modern geology and one of the discoverers of deep time). It's no wonder that people resist the concept of deep time; it not only stupefies our reason but implies a sense of collective meaninglessness and reinforces our individual mortality. Geologists, astronomers, and other scholars have struggled for over a century, with modest success, to

and Asia) were consolidated into a northern landmass called *Laurasia*. During the Mesozoic, Gondwanaland and Laurasia continued to drift apart and to break up into smaller segments. By the end of the Mesozoic (about 65 mya), the continents were beginning to assume their current positions (**Fig. 5-10b**).

The evolutionary ramifications of this long-term continental drift were profound. Groups of animals became effectively isolated from each other by oceans, significantly influencing the distribution of mammals and other land vertebrates. These continental movements continued in the Cenozoic and indeed are still happening, although without such dramatic results.

During most of the Mesozoic, reptiles were the dominant land vertebrates; they exhibited a broad expansion into a variety of *ecological niches*, which included aerial and marine habitats. The most famous of these highly successful Mesozoic reptiles were the dinosaurs, which themselves evolved into a wide array of sizes and species and adapted to a variety of lifestyles.

translate the tales told in rocks and hurtling stars into terms that everyone could understand. Various analogies have been attempted—metaphors, really—drawn from common experience. Among the most successful of these attempts is a "cosmic calendar" devised by eminent astronomer Carl Sagan in his book *Dragons of Eden* (1977). In this version of time's immensity, Sagan likens the passage of geological time to that of one calendar year. The year begins on January 1 with the Big Bang, the cosmic explosion marking the beginning of the universe and the beginning of time. In this version, the Big Bang is set at 15 billion years ago,* with some of the major events in the geological past as follows:

Time Unit Conversion Using the Cosmic Calendar

1 year = 15,000,000,000 years	1 hour = 1,740,000 years
1 month = 1,250,000,000 years	1 minute = 29,000 years
1 day = 41,000,000 years	1 second = 475 years

Big Bang	January 1
Formation of the earth	September 14
Origin of life on earth (approx.)	September 25
Significant oxygen atmosphere begins to develop	December 1
Precambrian ends; Paleozoic begins; invertebrates flourish	December 17
Paleozoic ends and Mesozoic begins	December 25
Cretaceous period: first flowers; dinosaurs become extinct	December 28
Mesozoic ends; Cenozoic begins; adaptive radiation of placental mammals	December 29

	December 31 Events
Appearance of early hominoids (apes and humans)	12:30 P.M.
First hominins	9:30 P.M.
Extensive cave painting in Europe	11:59 P.M.
Invention of agriculture	11:59:20 P.M.
Renaissance in Europe; Ming dynasty in China; emergence of scientific method	11:59:59 P.M.
Widespread development of science and technology; emergence of a global culture; first steps in space exploration; mass extinctions caused by humans	NOW: the first second of the New Year

* Recent evidence gathered by the Hubble Space Telescope has questioned the established date for the Big Bang. However, even the most recent data are somewhat contradictory, suggesting a date from as early as 16 billion years ago (indicated by the age of the oldest stars) to as recent as 8 billion years ago (indicated by the rate of expansion of the universe). Here we'll follow the conventional dating of 15 billion years; if you apply the most conservative approximation (8 billion years), the calibrations shift as follows: 1 day = 22,000,000 years; 1 hour = 913,000 years; 1 minute = 15,000 years. Using these calculations, for example, the first hominins appear on December 31 at 7:37 p.m., and modern humans (*Homo sapiens*) are on the scene at 11:42 p.m.

Dinosaur paleontology, never a boring field, has advanced several startling notions in recent years: that many dinosaurs were "warm-blooded"; that some varieties were quite social and probably also engaged in considerable parental care; that many forms became extinct because of major climate changes to the earth's atmosphere from collisions with comets or asteroids; and, finally, that not all dinosaurs became entirely extinct and have many descendants still living today (that is, all modern birds). (See **Fig. 5-11** for a summary of major events in early vertebrate evolutionary history.)

The Cenozoic is divided into two periods, the Tertiary (about 63 million years in duration) and the Quaternary, from about 1.8 mya up to and including the present (see Fig. 5-9). Paleontologists often refer to the next, more precise level of subdivision within the Cenozoic as the **epochs**. There are seven epochs within the Cenozoic: the Paleocene, Eocene, Oligocene, Miocene, Pliocene, Pleistocene, and Holocene, the last often referred to as the Recent epoch.

epochs Categories of the geological time scale; subdivisions of periods. In the Cenozoic era, epochs include the Paleocene, Eocene, Oligocene, Miocene, and Pliocene (from the Tertiary Period) and the Pleistocene and Holocene (from the Quaternary Period).

	570 mya	500 mya	430 mya	395 mya	345 mya
ERA	PALEOZOIC				
PERIOD	**Cambrian** Trilobites abundant; also brachiopods, jellyfish, worms, and other invertebrates	**Ordovician** First fishes; trilobites still abundant; graptolites and corals become plentiful; possible land plants	**Silurian** Jawed fishes appear; first air-breathing animals; definite land plants	**Devonian** Age of Fishes; first amphibians and first forests appear	**Carboniferous** First reptiles; radiation of amphibians; modern insects diversify

▲**Figure 5-11** This time line depicts major events in early vertebrate evolution.

Humans Are Also Mammals: Closer Connections

We can learn about mammalian evolution from fossils as well as from studying the DNA of living species (Bininda-Emonds et al., 2007). Studies using both of these approaches suggest that all the living groups of mammals (that is, all the orders) had diverged by 75 mya. Only later, several million years following the beginning of the Cenozoic, did the various current mammalian subgroups (that is, the particular families) begin to diversify.

Today there are over 4,000 species of mammals, and we could call the Cenozoic the Age of Mammals. It is during this era that, along with birds, mammals replaced earlier reptiles as the dominant land-living vertebrates.

How do we account for the relatively rapid success of the mammals during the late Mesozoic and early Cenozoic? Several characteristics relating to learning and general flexibility of behavior are of prime importance. Mammals were selected for larger brains than those typically found in reptiles, making them better equipped to process information. In particular, the cerebrum became generally enlarged, especially the outer covering, the **neocortex**, which controls higher brain functions (**Fig. 5-12**). In some mammals, the cerebrum expanded so much that it came to constitute most of the brain volume; the number of surface convolutions also increased, creating more surface area and thus providing space for even more nerve cells (neurons). As we'll see in Chapter 6, this trend is even further emphasized among the primates.

For such a large and complex organ as the mammalian brain to develop, a longer, more intense period of growth is required. Slower development can occur internally (*in utero*) as well as after birth. Internal fertilization and internal development aren't unique to mammals, but the latter was a major innovation among terrestrial vertebrates. Other forms (most fishes and reptiles—including birds) lay eggs, and "prenatal" development occurs externally, outside the mother's body. Mammals, with very few exceptions, give birth to live young. Even among mammals, however, there's considerable variation among the major groups in how mature the young are at birth; in **placental** mammals, including ourselves, *in utero* development goes farthest.

Another distinctive feature of mammals is the dentition. While many living reptiles (such as lizards and snakes) consistently have similarly shaped teeth (called a *homodont* dentition), mammals have differently shaped teeth (**Fig. 5-13**). This varied pattern, termed a **heterodont** dentition, is reflected in the ancestral (primitive) mammalian arrangement of teeth, which includes three incisors, one canine, four premolars, and three molars in each quarter of the mouth. So, with 11 teeth in each

neocortex The more recently evolved portions of the cortex of the brain that are involved with higher mental functions and composed of areas that integrate incoming information from different sensory organs.

placental A type (subclass) of mammal. During the Cenozoic, placentals became the most widespread and numerous mammals and today are represented by upward of 20 orders, including the primates.

heterodont Having different kinds of teeth; characteristic of mammals, whose teeth consist of incisors, canines, premolars, and molars.

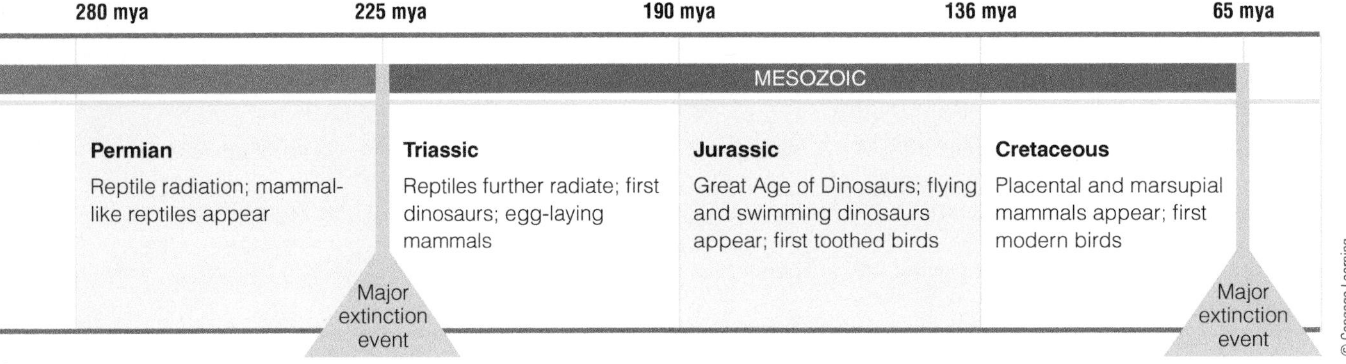

quarter of the mouth, the ancestral mammalian dental complement includes a total of 44 teeth. Such a heterodont arrangement allows mammals to process a wide variety of foods. Incisors are used for cutting, canines for grasping and piercing, and premolars and molars for crushing and grinding.

A final point regarding teeth relates to their disproportionate representation in the fossil record. As the hardest, most durable portion of a vertebrate skeleton, teeth have the greatest likelihood of becoming fossilized (that is, mineralized), because teeth are predominantly composed of mineral to begin with. As a result, the vast majority of available fossil data for most vertebrates, including primates, consists of teeth.

Another major adaptive complex that distinguishes contemporary mammals from reptiles (except birds) is the maintenance of a constant internal body temperature. Known colloquially (and incorrectly) as warm-bloodedness, this crucial physiological adaptation is also seen in contemporary birds and may have characterized many dinosaurs as well. Except for birds, reptiles maintain a constant internal body temperature through exposure to the sun; these reptiles are said to be *ectothermic*. In mammals and birds, however, energy is generated *internally* through metabolic activity (by processing food or by muscle action); for this reason, mammals and birds are said to be **endothermic**.

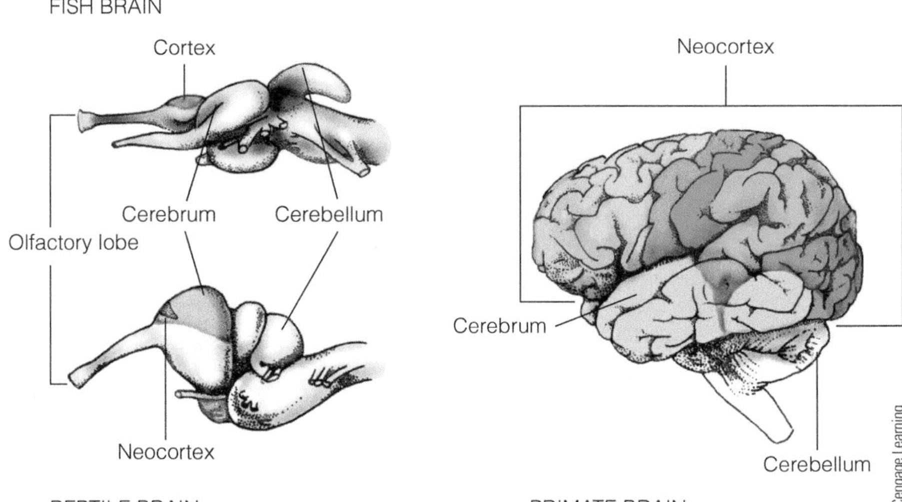

▲ **Figure 5-12** Lateral view of the brain in fishes, reptiles, and primates. You can see the increased size of the cerebral cortex (neocortex) of the primate brain. The cerebral cortex integrates sensory information and selects responses.

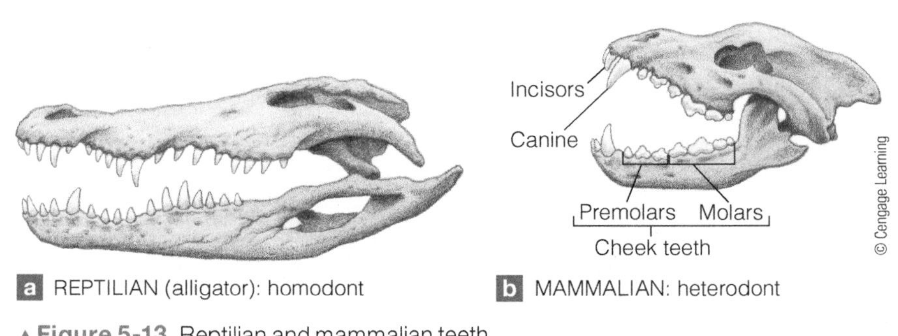

a REPTILIAN (alligator): homodont

b MAMMALIAN: heterodont

▲ **Figure 5-13** Reptilian and mammalian teeth.

endothermic (*endo*, meaning "within" or "internal") Able to maintain internal body temperature by producing energy through metabolic processes within cells; characteristic of mammals, birds, and perhaps some dinosaurs.

The Emergence of Major Mammalian Groups

There are three major subgroups of living mammals: the egg-laying mammals, or monotremes; the pouched mammals, or marsupials; and the placental mammals. The monotremes, of which the platypus is one example (**Fig. 5-14**), are extremely primitive and are considered more distinct from marsupials or placentals than these two subgroups are from each other. The recent sequencing of the full genome of the platypus (Warren et al., 2008) has confirmed the very ancient orgins of the monotremes and their distinctiveness from other mammals.

The most notable difference between marsupials and placentals concerns fetal development. In marsupials, the young are born extremely immature and must complete development in an external pouch (**Fig. 5-15**). But placental mammals develop over a longer period of time *in utero*, made possible by the evolutionary development of a specialized tissue (the placenta) that provides for fetal nourishment.

Tom McHugh/Photo Researchers, Inc.

▲ **Figure 5-14** A duck-billed platypus (monotreme).

© iStockphoto.com / Michael Sacco

▲ **Figure 5-15** A wallaby with an infant in its pouch (marsupials).

With a longer gestation period, the central nervous system develops more completely in the placental fetus. What's more, after birth, the "bond of milk" between mother and young allows more time for complex neural structures to form. We should also emphasize that from a *biosocial* perspective, this dependency period not only allows for adequate physiological development but also provides for a wider range of learning stimuli. That is, a vast amount of information is channeled to the young mammalian brain through observation of the mother's behavior and play with age-mates. It's not enough to have evolved a brain capable of learning. Collateral evolution of mammalian social systems has ensured that young mammallian brains are provided with ample learning opportunities and are thus put to good use.

Processes of Macroevolution

As we noted earlier, evolution operates at both micro- and macroevolutionary levels. We discussed evolution primarily from a microevolutionary perspective in Chapter 4; in this chapter, our focus is on macroevolution. Macroevolutionary mechanisms operate more on the whole species than on individuals or populations, and they take much longer than microevolutionary processes to have a noticeable impact.

Adaptive Radiation

As we mentioned in Chapter 2, the potential capacity of a group of organisms to multiply is practically unlimited, but its ability to increase its numbers is regulated largely by the availability of resources (food, water, shelter, mates, and space). As population size increases, access to resources decreases, and the environment will ultimately prove inadequate. Depleted resources induce some members of a population to seek an environment in which competition is reduced and the opportunities for survival and reproductive success are increased. This evolutionary tendency to exploit unoccupied habitats can eventually produce an abundance of diverse species.

This story has been played out countless times during the history of life, and some groups have expanded extremely rapidly. Known as **adaptive radiation**, this evolutionary process can be seen in the divergence of the stem reptiles into the profusion of different forms of the late Paleozoic and especially those of the Mesozoic. It's a process that takes place when a life-form rapidly takes advantage, so to speak, of the many newly available ecological niches.

The principle of evolution illustrated by adaptive radiation is fairly simple, but important. It may be stated this way: A species or group of species will diverge into as many variations as two factors allow. These factors are (1) its adaptive potential and (2) the adaptive opportunities of the available niches.

In the case of reptiles, there was little divergence in the very early stages of evolution, when the ancestral form was little more than one among a variety of amphibian water dwellers. Later, a more efficient egg (one that could incubate out of water) developed in reptiles; this new egg, with a hard, watertight shell, had great adaptive potential, but initially there were few zones to invade. When reptiles became fully terrestrial, however, a wide array of ecological niches became accessible to them. Once freed from their attachment to water, reptiles were able to exploit landmasses with no serious competition from any other animal. They moved into the many different ecological niches on land (and to some extent in the air and sea), and as they adapted to these areas, they diversified into a large number of species. This spectacular radiation burst forth with such evolutionary speed that it may well be termed an adaptive explosion.

Of course, the rapid expansion of placental mammals during the late Mesozoic and throughout the Cenozoic is another excellent example of adaptive radiation. The worldwide major extinction event at the end of the Mesozoic, as the dinosaurs disappeared, left thousands of econiches vacant. Small-bodied, mostly nocturnal mammals had been around for at least 70 million years, and once they were no longer in competition with the dinosaurs, they were free to move into previously occupied habitats. Thus, over the course of several million years, there was a major adaptive radiation of mammals as they diversified to exploit previously unavailable habitats.

Generalized and Specialized Characteristics

Another aspect of evolution closely related to adaptive radiation involves the transition from *generalized* characteristics to *specialized* characteristics. These two terms refer to the adaptive potential of a particular trait. A trait that's adapted for many functions is said to be generalized, whereas one that's limited to a narrow set of functions is said to be specialized.

For example, a generalized mammalian limb has five fairly flexible digits adapted for many possible functions (grasping, weight support, and digging). In this respect, human hands are still quite generalized. On the other hand (or foot), there have been many structural modifications in our feet to make them suited for the specialized function of stable weight support in an upright posture.

The terms *generalized* and *specialized* are also sometimes used when speaking of the adaptive potential of whole organisms. Consider, for example, the aye-aye of Madagascar, an unusual primate species. The aye-aye

adaptive radiation The relatively rapid expansion and diversification of life-forms into new ecological niches.

▲ **Figure 5-16** An aye-aye, a specialized primate native to Madagascar. Note the elongated middle finger, which is used to probe under bark for insects.

is a highly specialized animal, structurally adapted to a narrow, rodent/woodpecker-like econiche—digging holes with prominent incisors and removing insect larvae with an elongated bony finger (**Fig. 5-16**).

It's important to note that only a generalized ancestor can provide the flexible evolutionary basis for rapid diversification. Only a generalized species with potential for adaptation to varied ecological niches can lead to all the later diversification and specialization of forms into particular ecological niches.

An issue that we've already raised also bears on this discussion: the relationship of ancestral and derived characters. It's not always the case, but ancestral characters *usually* tend to be more generalized. And specialized characteristics are nearly always derived as well.

Working Together: Microevolution and Macroevolution

For many years, evolutionary biologists generally agreed that microevolutionary mechanisms could be translated directly into the larger-scale macroevolutionary changes, especially the most central of all macroevolutionary processes, speciation. However, four decades ago, some leading evolutionary biologists challenged this traditional view.

Over the last 40 years evolutionary biologists have debated whether there are fundamental differences between the processes of micro- as compared with macroevolution. This discussion continues, and divergent views, framed as specific hypotheses, are further tested against new evidence. At present, the major difference seems to be one of *scale*. That is, both processes are driven by similar factors; however, macroevolution takes much longer than microevolution to occur.

For example, several species of very early hominins evolved over more than 4 million years, initially separating from their common ancestor with chimpanzees, and some of these species eventually adapted to more ground-living niches. These changes clearly reflect macroevolutionary processes. Much more recently, some modern human populations adapted in just a couple of thousand years to living at high altitudes, which was made possible by changes in particular genes. This is a good example of microevolution.

We should note that rates of evolutionary change can speed up at certain times and slow down during others. Most crucially, natural selection is influenced by how fast the environment is changing (and how fast genetic changes appear and spread within a species). Both fossil and molecular evidence (Pagel et al., 2006) indicate that both gradual (slow) and rapid (also called "punctuated") changes have occurred in the evolution of both plant and animal species.

In all lineages, the pace assuredly speeds up and slows down due to factors that influence the size and relative isolation of populations. As we've said, environmental changes that influence the pace and direction of natural selection must also be considered. So, in general accordance with the Modern Synthesis and as indicated by molecular evidence, microevolution and macroevolution needn't be considered separately, as some evolutionary biologists have suggested. Some groups of primates, for instance, simply have slower or faster durations of speciation, which is why Old World monkeys typically speciate more slowly than the great apes.

How Do We Know?

We know about earlier life-forms directly from fossils, of which tens of trillions have formed over the vast time that life has existed on earth. We also know about "deep time" in earth's geological history, and the age when fossils formed over the last 3 billion years, from studies made by geologists who use precise dating techniques (the latter to be discussed in Chapter 9). Connections among all these life forms and how humans fit in are interpreted from the analysis of specific types of similarities called shared derived characteristics. From such data, hypotheses regarding evolutionary relationships are proposed and tested.

Summary of Main Topics

- Evolutionary systematics and cladistics are the two major types of classification. Evolutionary systematics uses homologous characteristics to make hypotheses regarding evolutionary relationships as well as ancestor-descendant relationships and shows the latter through time as a phylogenetic tree. Cladistics more rigorously uses only specific sorts of homologous characteristics (derived ones) and doesn't attempt to draw ancestor-descendant conclusions or show evolutionary relationships through time; conclusions are shown in a cladogram.
- According to the biological species concept, species are groups of individuals capable of fertile interbreeding but are reproductively isolated from other such groups. There are also other definitions of species suggested by biologists, but this one is the most widely used.
- Vertebrates are animals with a segmented backbone (vertebral column), a developed brain, and paired sensory structures. Vertebrates include fishes, amphibians, reptiles (including birds), and mammals.
- Humans are placental mammals that (along with some other mammals) are characterized by development *in utero* (that is, live birth), differently shaped (heterodont) teeth, more complex brains, and maintenance of a constant internal body temperature (endothermic). Placental mammals in particular have even more complex brains (with a large neocortex), longer periods of development, and more complex social behavior.
- Macroevolution takes many hundreds or thousands of generations and can result in the appearance of new species (a process called *speciation*). Microevolution can occur within just a few generations and results in small genetic differences between populations of a species.

Critical Thinking Questions

1. Remains of a fossil mammal have been found on your campus. If you adopt a cladistic approach, how would you determine (a) that it's a mammal rather than some other kind of vertebrate, (b) what kind of mammal it is, and (c) how it *might* be related to one or more living mammals?
2. For the same fossil find (and your interpretation) in question 2, draw an interpretive figure using cladistic analysis (that is, draw a cladogram). Next, using more traditional evolutionary systematics, construct a phylogenetic tree. Last, explain the differences between the cladogram and the phylogenetic tree (be sure to emphasize the fundamental ways in which the two schemes differ).
3. a. Humans are fairly generalized mammals. What do we mean by this, and what specific features (characters) would you select to illustrate this statement?

   b. More precisely, humans are *placental* mammals. How do humans and all other placental mammals differ from the other two major groups of mammals?

Connections

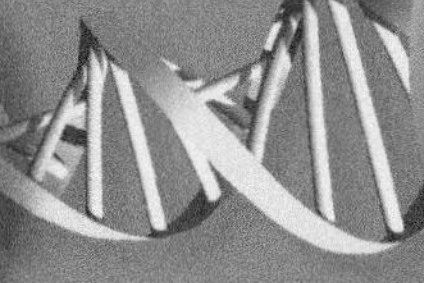

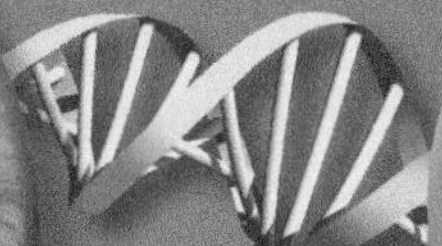

Fossil evidence indicates our primate origins date to at least 65 million years ago.

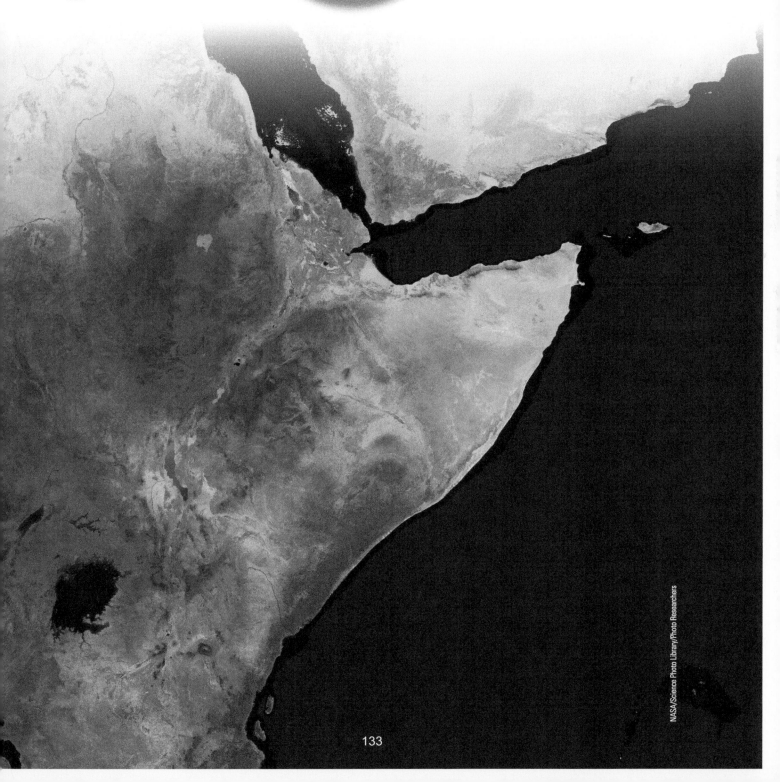

Paleoanthropology, which includes physical anthropology, archaeology, and geology, provides the scientific basis to understand hominin evolution.

The first more human-like animals (hominins) appeared in Africa around 6 mya ago and evolved into a variety of different species.

NASA/Science Photo Library/Photo Researchers

Paleoanthropology: Reconstructing Early Hominin Behavior and Ecology 6

Student Learning Objectives

After mastering the material in this chapter, you should be able to:

- Describe why paleoanthropology is necessarily a multidisciplinary science and discuss the major subdisciplines that contribute to it.
- Explain what is meant by *biocultural evolution* and provide examples of how it might have influenced the development of the earliest cultural behavior in hominins and also simultaneously influenced biological/anatomical changes in them.
- Discuss why precise dating is essential to understanding human evolution and describe some of the major techniques used.
- Discuss what the earliest tools thus far discovered looked like and explain how they may have been made.
- Describe the different hypotheses that try to account for the evolution of bipedal locomotion and discuss the strengths and weaknesses of each.

A portion of a pig's tusk, a small sample of volcanic sediment, a battered rock, a primate's molar: What do these seemingly unremarkable remains have in common, and more to the point, why are they of interest to paleoanthropologists? First of all, if they're all discovered at sites in Africa or Eurasia, they *may* be quite ancient—indeed, perhaps millions of years old. Further, some of these materials actually inform scientists directly of quite precise dating of the finds. Last and most exciting, some of these finds may have been modified, used, and discarded by bipedal creatures who looked and behaved in some ways like ourselves but were in other respects very different. And what of that molar? Is it a fossilized remnant of an ancient hominin? These are the kinds of questions asked by paleoanthropologists, and to answer them, these researchers travel to remote locales across the Old World.

How do we distinguish possible hominins from other types of animals (most notably from other primates), especially when all we have are fragmentary fossil remains from just a small portion of a skeleton? How do humans and our most distant ancestors compare with other animals? In the last three chapters, we've seen how humans are classified as primates, both structurally and behaviorally, and how our evolutionary history coincides with that of other mammals and specifically other primates. Even so, we're a unique kind of primate, and our ancestors have been adapted to a particular lifestyle for several million years. Some late Miocene fossil apes probably began this process close to 7 mya, though better-preserved fossil discoveries reveal more definitive evidence of hominins shortly after 5 mya.

We're able to determine the hominin nature of these remains by more than the structure of teeth and bones; we know that these animals were hominins also because of the way they behaved—emphasizing once again the *biocultural* nature of human evolution. In this chapter, we'll discuss the methods scientists use to explore the secrets of early hominin behavior and ecology.

Understanding Our Direct Evolutionary Connections: What's a Hominin?

The earliest evidence of hominins that has been found dates to the end of the Miocene and mainly includes dental and cranial pieces. But dental features alone don't describe the special features of hominins, and they certainly aren't distinctive of the later stages of human evolution. Modern humans, as well as our most immediate hominin ancestors, are distinguished from the great apes by more obvious features than tooth and jaw dimensions. For example, various scientists have pointed to such distinctive hominin characteristics as bipedal locomotion, large brain size, and toolmaking behavior as being significant (at some stage) in defining what makes a hominin a hominin.

It's important to recognize that all these characteristics did not develop simultaneously or at the same pace. In fact, over the last several million years of hominin evolution, a very different pattern has been evident, in which the various components (dentition, locomotion, brain size, and toolmaking) have developed at quite different rates. This pattern, in which physiological and behavioral systems evolve at different rates, is called **mosaic evolution**. As we first pointed out in Chapter 1 and will emphasize in this and the next chapter, the single most important defining characteristic of the full course of hominin evolution is bipedal locomotion. In the earliest stages of hominin emergence, skeletal evidence indicating bipedal locomotion is the only truly reliable indicator that these fossils were indeed hominins. But in later stages of hominin evolution, other features, especially those relating to brain development and behavior, become highly significant (**Fig. 9-1**).

These behavioral aspects of hominin emergence—particularly toolmaking—are what we'd like to emphasize in this chapter. Important structural attributes of the hominin brain, teeth, and especially locomotor apparatus are discussed in the next chapter, where we investigate early hominin anatomical adaptations in greater detail.

What's in a Name?

Throughout this book, we refer to members of the human family as hominins (the technical name for members of the tribe Hominini). Most professional paleoanthropologists now prefer this terminology, since it more accurately reflects evolutionary relationships. As we mentioned briefly in Chapter 6, the more traditional classification of hominoids is not as accurate and actually misrepresents key evolutionary relationships.

Over the last several years detailed molecular evidence has clearly shown that the great apes (traditionally classified as pongids and including orangutans, gorillas, chimpanzees, and bonobos) do not make up a coherent evolutionary group sharing a single common ancestor and thus are not a *monophyletic* group. Indeed, the molecular data indicate that the African great apes (gorillas, chimpanzees, and bonobos) are significantly more closely related to humans than is the orangutan. What's more, at an even closer evolutionary level, we now know that chimpanzees and bonobos are yet more closely linked to humans than is the gorilla. Hominoid classification has been significantly revised to show these more complete relationships, and two further taxonomic levels (subfamily and tribe) have been added.

We should mention a couple of important ramifications of this new classification. First, it further emphasizes the *very* close evolutionary relationship of humans with African apes and most especially with chimpanzees and bonobos. Second, the term *hominid*, which has been used for decades to refer to our specific evolutionary lineage, has a quite different meaning in the revised classification; now it refers to *all* great apes and humans together.

mosaic evolution A pattern of evolution in which the rate of evolution in one functional system varies from that in other systems. For example, in hominin evolution, the dental system, locomotor system, and neurological system (especially the brain) all evolved at markedly different rates.

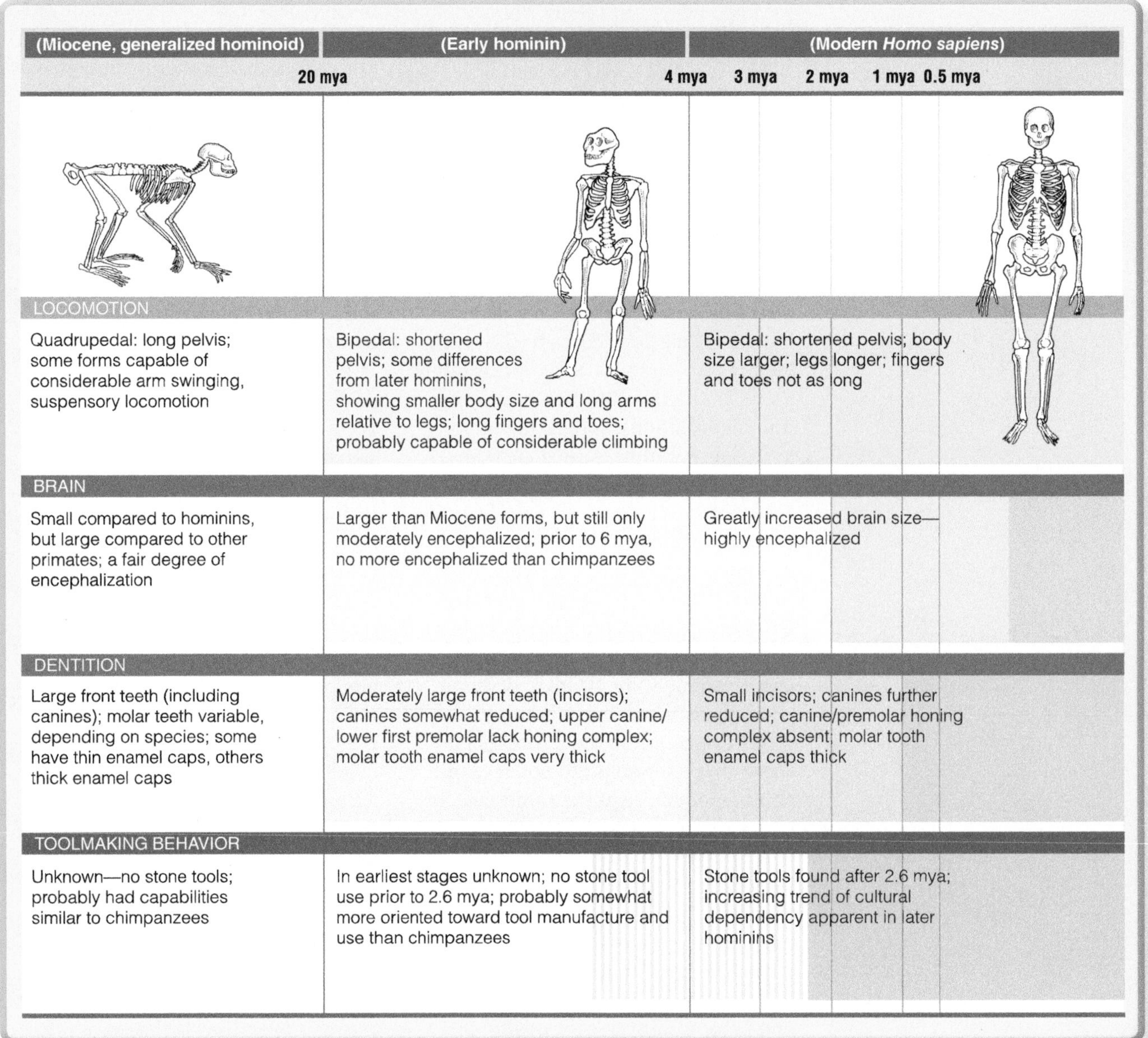

	(Miocene, generalized hominoid)	(Early hominin)	(Modern *Homo sapiens*)
	20 mya	4 mya	3 mya 2 mya 1 mya 0.5 mya
LOCOMOTION	Quadrupedal: long pelvis; some forms capable of considerable arm swinging, suspensory locomotion	Bipedal: shortened pelvis; some differences from later hominins, showing smaller body size and long arms relative to legs; long fingers and toes; probably capable of considerable climbing	Bipedal: shortened pelvis; body size larger; legs longer; fingers and toes not as long
BRAIN	Small compared to hominins, but large compared to other primates; a fair degree of encephalization	Larger than Miocene forms, but still only moderately encephalized; prior to 6 mya, no more encephalized than chimpanzees	Greatly increased brain size—highly encephalized
DENTITION	Large front teeth (including canines); molar teeth variable, depending on species; some have thin enamel caps, others thick enamel caps	Moderately large front teeth (incisors); canines somewhat reduced; upper canine/lower first premolar lack honing complex; molar tooth enamel caps very thick	Small incisors; canines further reduced; canine/premolar honing complex absent; molar tooth enamel caps thick
TOOLMAKING BEHAVIOR	Unknown—no stone tools; probably had capabilities similar to chimpanzees	In earliest stages unknown; no stone tool use prior to 2.6 mya; probably somewhat more oriented toward tool manufacture and use than chimpanzees	Stone tools found after 2.6 mya; increasing trend of cultural dependency apparent in later hominins

▲ **Figure 9-1** Mosaic evolution of hominin characteristics: a postulated time line.

Biocultural Evolution: The Human Capacity for Culture

One of the most distinctive behavioral features of humans is our extraordinary elaboration of and dependence on **culture**. Certainly other primates, and many other animals for that matter, modify their environments. As we saw in Chapter 7, chimpanzees especially are known for such behaviors as using termite sticks, and some chimpanzees as well as capuchin monkeys even carry rocks to use for crushing nuts. Because of such observations, we're on shaky ground when it comes to drawing sharp lines between early hominin toolmaking behavior and that exhibited by other animals.

Another point to remember is that human culture, at least as it's defined in contemporary contexts, involves much more than toolmaking capacity. For humans, culture integrates an entire adaptive strategy involving cognitive,

culture Behavioral aspects of human adaptation, including technology, traditions, language, religion, marriage patterns, and social roles. Culture is a set of learned behaviors transmitted from one generation to the next by nonbiological (i.e., nongenetic) means.

political, social, and economic components. *Material culture*—or the tools humans use—is but a small portion of this cultural complex.

Still, when we examine the archaeological record of earlier hominins, what's available for study is almost exclusively limited to material culture, especially the bits and pieces of broken stone left over from tool manufacture. This is why it's extremely difficult to learn anything about the earliest stages of hominin cultural development before the regular manufacture of stone tools. As you'll see, this most crucial cultural development has been traced to approximately 2.6 mya (Semaw et al., 2003). Yet because of our contemporary primate models, we can assume that hominins were undoubtedly using other kinds of tools (made of perishable materials) and displaying a whole array of other cultural behaviors long before then. But with no "hard" evidence preserved in the archaeological record, our understanding of the early development of these nonmaterial cultural components remains elusive.

The fundamental basis for human cultural success relates directly to our cognitive abilities. Again, we're not dealing with an absolute distinction but a relative one. As you've already learned, other primates, as documented in the great apes, have some of the language capabilities exhibited by humans. Even so, modern humans display these abilities in a complexity several orders of magnitude beyond that of any other animal. And only humans are so completely dependent on symbolic communication and its cultural by-products that contemporary *Homo sapiens* could not survive without them.

At this point you may be wondering when the unique combination of cognitive, social, and material cultural adaptations became prominent in human evolution. In answering that question we must be careful to recognize the manifold nature of culture; we can't expect it to always contain the same elements across species (as when comparing ourselves with nonhuman primates) or through time (when trying to reconstruct ancient hominin behavior). Richard Potts (1993) has critiqued such overly simplistic perspectives and suggests instead a more dynamic approach, one that incorporates many subcomponents (including aspects of behavior, cognition, and social interaction).

We know that the earliest hominins almost certainly didn't regularly manufacture stone tools (at least none that have been found and identified as such). These earliest members of the hominin lineage, dating back to approximately 6 to 5 mya, may have carried objects such as naturally sharp stones or stone flakes, parts of carcasses, and pieces of wood around their home ranges. At the very least, we would expect them to have displayed these behaviors to at least the same degree as exhibited by living chimpanzees.

Also, as you'll see in the next chapter, by around 6 mya, hominins had developed one crucial advantage: They were bipedal and so could more easily carry all kinds of objects from place to place. Ultimately, the efficient exploitation of resources widely distributed in time and space would most likely have led to using "central" spots where key components—especially stone objects—were cached, or collected (Potts, 1991; see "A Closer Look, What Were Early Hominins Doing, and How Do We Know?" on pages 260–261).

What we know for sure is that over a period of several million years, during the formative stages of hominin emergence, many components interacted, but not all of them developed simultaneously. As cognitive abilities developed, more efficient means of communication and learning resulted. Largely because of consequent neurological reorganization, more elaborate tools and social relationships also emerged. These, in turn, selected for greater intelligence, which in turn selected for further neural elaboration. Quite clearly these mutual dynamic interactions are at the very heart of what we call hominin *biocultural* evolution.

Discovering Human Evolution: The Science of Paleoanthropology

To adequately understand human evolution, we obviously need a broad base of information. It's the paleoanthropologist's task to recover and interpret all the clues left by early hominins. *Paleoanthropology* is defined as "the study of ancient humans." As such, it's a diverse **multidisciplinary** pursuit seeking to reconstruct every possible bit of information concerning the dating, anatomy, behavior, and ecology of our hominin ancestors. Over the past few decades, the study of early humans has marshaled the specialized skills of many different kinds of scientists. This growing and exciting adventure includes but is not limited to geologists, vertebrate paleontologists, archaeologists, physical anthropologists, and paleoecologists (**Table 9.1**).

Geologists, usually working with other paleoanthropologists, do the initial surveys to locate potential early hominin sites. Many sophisticated techniques aid in this search, including aerial and satellite imagery (**Fig. 9-2**), though the most common way to find these sites is simply to trip over fossil remains. Vertebrate paleontologists are usually involved in this early survey work, helping to find fossil beds containing faunal (animal) remains, because where conditions are favorable for the preservation of bone from such species as pigs and elephants, hominin remains may also be preserved. Paleontologists also can (through comparison with known faunal sequences) give quick and dirty approximate age estimates of fossil sites in the field without having to wait for the results of more time-consuming (though more accurate) analyses that will later be performed in a lab (**Fig. 9-3** on page 262).

Once identified, fossil beds likely to contain hominin finds are subjected to extensive field surveying. For some sites, generally those postdating 2.6 mya (roughly the age of the oldest identified human artifacts), archaeologists take over in the search for hominin material traces. We don't necessarily have to find remains of early hominins themselves to know that

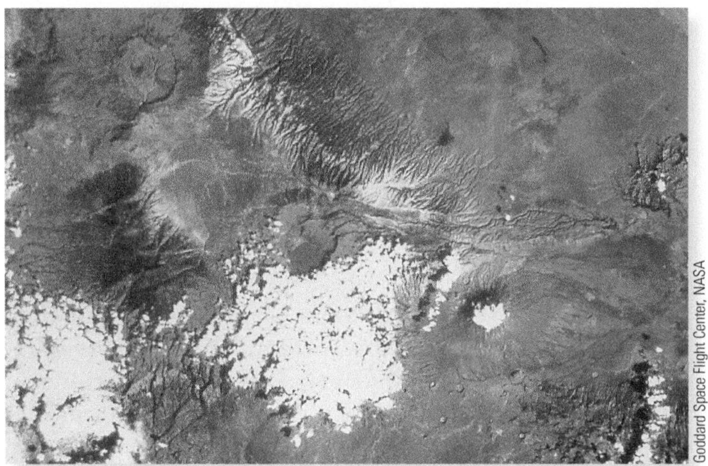

Goddard Space Flight Center, NASA

▲ **Figure 9-2** Satellite photo of geological exposures in northern Tanzania, near Olduvai Gorge. The mountainous regions are part of the Rift Valley. The lake has formed inside a volcanic crater.

Table 9.1 Subdisciplines of Paleoanthropology

Physical Sciences	Biological Sciences	Social Sciences
Geology	Physical anthropology	Archaeology
Stratigraphy	Paleoecology	Ethnoarchaeology
Petrology	Paleontology	Cultural anthropology
(rocks, minerals)	(fossil animals)	Ethnography
Pedology (soils)	Palynology	Psychology
Geomorphology	(fossil pollen)	
Geophysics	Primatology	
Chemistry		
Taphonomy		

multidisciplinary Pertaining to research involving mutual contributions and the cooperation of experts from various scientific fields, or disciplines.

A Closer Look

What Were Early Hominins Doing, and How Do We Know?

Many years ago, the popular interpretation of the bone refuse and stone tools discovered at Olduvai Gorge and other sites suggested that most or all of these materials resulted from hominin activities. However, a later and more comprehensive reanalysis of the bone remains from Olduvai localities has challenged this view (Binford, 1981, 1983). Olduvai is so important because it has the most complete and best studied paleoanthropological record of any early hominin site in the world. Archaeologist Lewis Binford criticizes those who are drawn too quickly to concluding that these bone scatters are the remnants of hominin behavior patterns while simultaneously ignoring the possibility of other explanations.

From information concerning the kinds of animals present, which body parts were found, and the differences in preservation among these skeletal elements, Binford has concluded that much of what's preserved can be explained by carnivore activity. This conclusion has been reinforced by certain details observed by Binford himself in Alaska—details on animal kills, scavenging, the transportation of elements, and preservation that are the result of wolf and dog behaviors. Binford describes his approach:

> I took as "known," then, the structure of bone assemblages produced in various settings by animal predators and scavengers; and as "unknown" the bone deposits excavated by the Leakeys at Olduvai Gorge. Using mathematical and statistical techniques I considered to what degree the finds from Olduvai Gorge could be accounted for in terms of the results of predator behavior and how much was "left over." (Binford, 1983, pp. 56–57)

Binford isn't arguing that all of the remains found at Olduvai resulted from nonhominin activity. In fact, he recognizes that "residual material" was consistently found on surfaces with high tool concentration "which could not be explained by what we know about African animals" (Binford, 1983).

Support for the idea that early hominins utilized at least some of the bone refuse has come from a totally different perspective. Researchers have analyzed (both macroscopically and microscopically) the cut marks left on fossilized bones. By experimenting with modern materials, they've been able to delineate more clearly the differences between marks left by stone tools and those left by animal teeth or other factors (Bunn, 1981; Potts and Shipman, 1981). Analyses of bones from several early localities at Olduvai have shown unambiguously that hominins used these specimens and left telltale cut marks from their stone tools. The sites investigated so far reveal a somewhat haphazard cutting and chopping, apparently unrelated to deliberate disarticulation. So the conclusion is that hominins scavenged carcasses, probably of carnivore kills, and did *not* hunt large animals themselves (Shipman, 1983). As we'll see in a moment, new evidence of possible cut marks as well as indications of pounding to get at the marrow has been found at a site in Ethiopia dating as far back as 3.4 mya.

Following and expanding on the experimental approaches pioneered by Binford, Bunn, and others, Robert Blumenschine, of Rutgers University, has more recently conducted a more detailed analysis of the Olduvai material. Like his predecessors, Blumenschine has also concluded that the cut marks on animal bones are the result of hominin processing (Blumenschine, 1995). Blumenschine and colleagues further surmise that most meat acquisition (virtually all from large animals) was the result of scavenging (from remains of carnivore kills or from animals that died from natural causes). In fact, these researchers suggest that scavenging was a crucial adaptive strategy for early hominins and considerably influenced their habitat usage, diet, and utilization of stone tools (Blumenschine and Cavallo, 1992; Blumenschine and Peters, 1998). What's more, Blumenschine and colleagues have developed a model detailing how scavenging and other early hominin adaptive strategies integrate into patterns of land use (that is, differential utilization of various niches in and around Olduvai). From this model, they formulated specific hypoth-

---

they consistently occupied a particular area. Such material clues as **artifacts** inform us directly about early hominin activities. Modifying rocks according to a consistent plan or simply carrying them around from one place to another over fairly long distances and distributing them in a manner not explicable by natural means—like movement due to streams or glaciers—is characteristic of no other animal but a hominin. So when we see such material evidence at a site, we know without a doubt that hominins were once present there.

We've suspected for a while that hominins likely used stone and other materials for a long time before they began modifying rock to a consistent (and recognizable) pattern. After all, chimpanzees carry rocks short distances and bash nuts with them (see Chapter 8). New evidence from

artifacts Objects or materials made or modified for use by hominins. The earliest artifacts are usually tools made of stone or occasionally bone.

▲ **Figure 1** Hyenas scavenging a buffalo carcass in East Africa. Early hominins also scavenged animals that had been killed by predators. In so doing, they almost certainly competed with hyenas and other scavengers.

eses concerning the predicted distribution of artifacts and animal remains in different areas at Olduvai. Subsequent excavations at Olduvai were aimed specifically at testing these hypotheses.

If early hominins (close to 2 mya) weren't hunting consistently, what did they obtain from scavenging the kills of other animals? One obvious answer is whatever meat was left behind. However, the position of the cut marks suggests that early hominins were often hacking at non-meat-bearing portions of the skeletons. Perhaps they were after bone marrow and brain, substances not fully exploited by other predators and scavengers (Binford, 1981; Blumenschine and Cavallo, 1992).

Exciting discoveries from the Bouri Peninsula of the Middle Awash of Ethiopia provide the best evidence yet for meat and marrow exploitation by early hominins. Dated to 2.5 mya (that is, as old as the oldest known artifacts), antelope and horse fossils from Bouri show telltale incisions and breaks, indicating that bones were not only smashed to extract marrow but also cut, ostensibly to retrieve meat (de Heinzelin et al., 1999). The researchers who analyzed these materials have suggested that the greater dietary reliance on animal products may have been important in stimulating brain enlargement in the lineage leading to genus *Homo*.

Another recent research twist relating to the reconstruction of early hominin diets has come from the biochemical analysis of some hominin teeth from South Africa (dating to about the same time range as hominins from Olduvai—or perhaps slightly earlier). In an innovative application of **stable carbon isotope** analysis, Matt Sponheimer and Julia Lee-Thorp found that these early hominin teeth revealed telltale chemical signatures relating to diet (Sponheimer and Lee-Thorp, 1999). In particular, the proportions of stable carbon isotopes indicated that these early hominins ate either grass products (such as seeds) or meat/marrow from animals that in turn had eaten grass products (that is, the hominins might well have derived a significant portion of their diet from meat or other animal products). What's more, newly collected stable carbon isotope data from another South African early hominin show a quite different diet from that of other South African finds and, indeed almost all other early hominins (Henry et al., 2012) (see Chapter 10). This evidence comes from an exciting new perspective that provides a more direct indicator of early hominin diets. While it's not clear how much meat these early hominins consumed, these new data do suggest that they were consistently exploiting more open regions of their environment. Moreover, a new laser technology makes it possible to detect, from a single tooth, what sorts of foods were eaten from year to year and even seasonally within the same year. Sponheimer, Thorp, and colleagues have used this new approach to show that some early hominins were able to flexibly move between different environments and exploit seasonally available foods (Sponheimer et al., 2006). To demonstrate that stable isotope data are accurate, researchers need to evaluate the influence of chemical changes (*diagenesis*) to bones and teeth that occurred during fossilization. Stable isotope methods will continue to play a prominent role in the reconstruction of hominin diets and paleoenvironments.

the Dikika site in Ethiopia might indicate that hominins were using stone in an even more sophisticated way as far back as 3.4 mya (McPherron et al., 2010). No stone tools were found, but two animal bones show cut marks (see "A Closer Look," above) as well as other marks suggesting that the bones were pounded with unmodified rocks (ostensibly to slice away meat and retrieve marrow). While it's true that this evidence doesn't mean that hominins were yet modifying rocks consistently to make tools, it potentially shows advanced behavior, including scavenging, meat eating, and marrow extraction that have not previously been considered possible for very early hominins. These finds are extremely important and have been very carefully investigated. However, just the two bones by themselves (and

stable carbon isotopes Isotopes of carbon that are produced in plants in differing proportions, depending on environmental conditions. By analyzing the proportions of the isotopes contained in fossil remains of animals (who ate the plants), it's possible to reconstruct aspects of ancient diet and environments (particularly temperature and aridity).

Institute of Human Origins, photo by Nanci Kahn

▲ **Figure 9-3** A geologist is shown making entries on a detailed map as he surveys a large area of exposures in the Hadar region of northeastern Ethiopia.

no stone tools) are not enough evidence for many paleoanthropologists to be entirely convinced that the eating of meat and marrow were yet typical behaviors of such ancient hominins (Domínguez-Rodrigo et al., 2010).

Once an area has clearly been demonstrated to be a hominin site, much more concentrated research begins (**Fig. 9-4**). We should point out that a more mundane but significant aspect of paleoanthropology not reflected in Table 9-1 is the financial one. Just the initial survey work in usually remote areas costs many thousands of dollars, and mounting a concentrated research project costs several hundred thousand dollars more. This is why many projects are undertaken in areas where promising surface finds have already been made. Massive financial support is required from government agencies and private donations; therefore, it's unrealistic just to dig at random. A great deal of a paleoanthropologist's effort and time is necessarily devoted to writing grant proposals or speaking on the lecture circuit to raise the required funds for this work.

Once the financial hurdle has been cleared, a coordinated research project can begin. Usually headed by an archaeologist or physical anthropologist, the field crew continues to survey and map the target area in great detail. In addition, field crew members begin searching carefully for bones and artifacts eroding out of the soil, taking pollen and soil samples for ecological analysis, and carefully collecting rock and other samples for use in various dating techniques. If, at this early stage of exploration, members of the field crew find fossil hominin remains, they will feel very lucky indeed. The international press usually considers human fossils the most exciting kind of discovery—a fortunate circumstance that produces wide publicity and often ensures future financial support. More likely, the crew will accumulate much information on geological setting, ecological data (particularly faunal remains), and, with some luck, artifacts and other archaeological traces.

Although paleoanthropological fieldwork is typically a long and arduous process, the detailed analyses of collected samples and other data back in the laboratory are even more time-consuming. Archaeologists must clean, sort, label, and identify all artifacts, and vertebrate paleontologists must do the same for all faunal remains. Knowing the kinds of animals represented—whether forest browsers, woodland species, or open-country forms—greatly helps in reconstructing the local *paleoecological* settings in which early hominins lived. Analysis of the fossil pollen collected from hominin sites by a scientist called a palynologist further aids in developing a detailed environmental reconstruction. All these paleoecological analyses can assist in reconstructing the diet of early humans. Also, the **taphonomy** of the site must be worked out to understand its depositional history—that is, how the site formed over time and if its present state is in a *primary* or *secondary* **context**.

In the concluding stages of interpretation, the paleoanthropologist draws together these essentials:

1. *Dating*: geological, paleontological, geophysical

taphonomy (*taphos*, meaning "tomb") The study of how bones and other materials came to be buried in the earth and preserved as fossils. Taphonomists study the processes of sedimentation, the action of streams, preservation properties of bone, and carnivore disturbance factors.

context The environmental setting where an archaeological trace is found. Primary context is the setting in which the archaeological trace was originally deposited. A secondary context is one to which it has been moved (such as by the action of a stream).

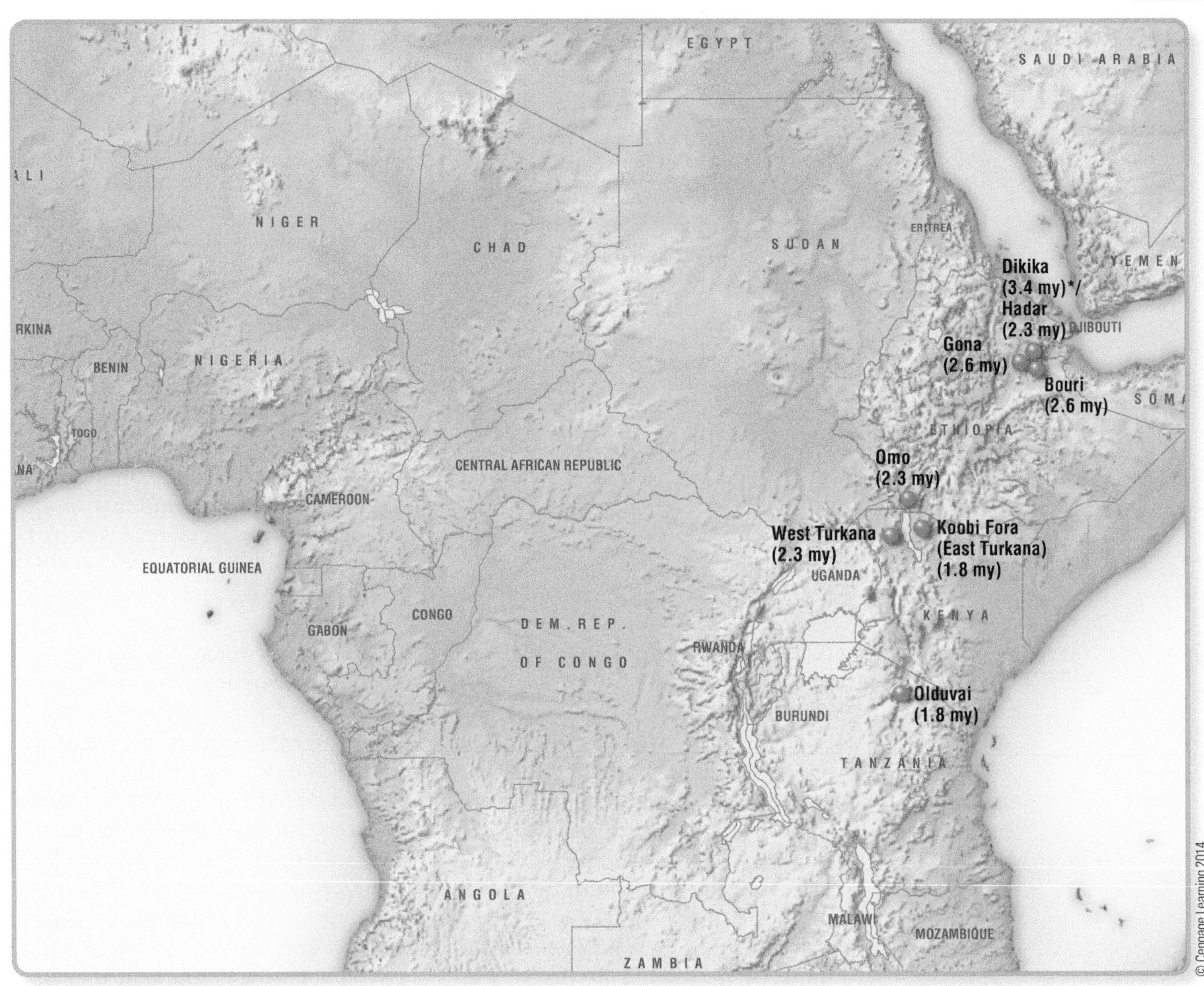

▲ **Figure 9-4** Location of sites where early evidence of stone tools has been discovered. The dates shown for each site represent the earliest dated tools found at that location.

*Interpretation of the Dikika evidence is controversial. It includes bones with presumed cut marks. However, no stone tools have been found.

2. *Paleoecology*: paleontology, palynology, geomorphology, taphonomy
3. *Archaeological traces of behavior*
4. *Anatomical evidence from hominin remains*

By analyzing all this information, scientists try to "flesh out" the kind of creature that may have been our direct ancestor (or at least a very close relative). Primatologists may assist here by showing the detailed relationships between the anatomical structure and behavior of humans and that of contemporary nonhuman primates. Cultural anthropologists and ethnoarchaeologists (who study the "archaeology" of living groups by examining their material remains) may contribute ethnographic information concerning the varied nature of modern human behavior, particularly ecological adaptations of those contemporary hunter-gatherer groups exploiting roughly similar environmental settings as those reconstructed for a hominin site.

The end result of years of research by dozens of scientists will (we hope) produce a more complete and accurate understanding of human evolution—how we came to be the way we are. Both biological and cultural aspects of our ancestors contribute to this investigation, each process developing in relation to the other.

Connecting the Dots through Time: Paleoanthropological Dating Methods

An essential objective of paleoanthropology is to place sites and fossils into a time frame. In other words, we want to know how old they are. How, then, do we date sites—or more precisely, the geological strata, or layers, in which sites are found? The question is both reasonable and important, so let's examine the dating techniques used by paleontologists, archaeologists, and other scientists involved in paleoanthropological research.

Scientists use two kinds of dating for this purpose: relative dating and **chronometric dating** (also known as *absolute dating*). Relative dating methods tell us that something is older or younger than something else but not by how much. If, for example, a cranium is found at a depth of 50 feet and another cranium at 70 feet at the same site, we usually assume that the specimen discovered at 70 feet is older. We may not know the date (in years) of either one, but we'd know that one is older (or younger) than the other. Although this may not satisfy our curiosity about the actual number of years involved, it would give us some idea of the evolutionary changes in cranial morphology (structure), especially if we found several crania at different levels and compared them.

This method of relative dating is based on **stratigraphy** and was one of the first techniques to be used by scientists working with the vast period of geological time. Stratigraphy, in turn, is based on the **principle of superposition**, which states that a lower stratum (layer) is older than a higher stratum. Because much of the earth's crust has been laid down by layer after layer of sedimentary rock, much like the layers of a cake, stratigraphy has been a valuable aid in reconstructing the history of the earth and the life upon it.

Stratigraphic dating does, however, have some problems. Earth disturbances, such as volcanic activity, river activity, and mountain building, may shift strata and the objects within them; in such cases the chronology of the material may be difficult or even impossible to reconstruct. What's more, it's impossible to accurately determine the time period of a particular stratum—that is, how long it took to accumulate (**Fig. 9-5**).

Another method of relative dating is *fluorine analysis*, which applies only to bones (Oakley, 1963). Bones in the earth are exposed to the seepage of groundwater, which usually contains fluorine. The longer a bone lies in the earth, the more fluorine it will incorporate during the fossilization process. Bones deposited at the same time in the same location thus should contain the same amount of fluorine. Professor Kenneth Oakley, of the British Museum, used this technique in the early 1950s to expose the Piltdown (England) hoax by demonstrating that a human skull was considerably older than the jaw (ostensibly also human) found with it (Weiner, 1955). When a discrepancy in the fluorine content led Oakley and others to examine the bones more closely, they found that the jaw was not that of a hominin at all but of a young adult orangutan!

Unfortunately, fluorine analysis is useful only with bones found at the same location. Because the amount of fluorine in groundwater is based on local conditions, it varies from place to place. Also, some groundwater may not contain any fluorine. For these reasons it's impossible to use fluorine analysis when comparing bones from different localities.

In both stratigraphy and fluorine analysis, it's impossible to calculate the actual age of a geological stratum and the objects within it. To determine the age in years, scientists have developed various chronometric techniques based on the phenomenon of radioactive decay. Actually, the theory is pretty simple: Certain radioactive isotopes of

chronometric dating (*chrono*, meaning "time," and *metric*, meaning "measure") A dating technique that gives an estimate in actual numbers of years; also known as absolute dating.

stratigraphy Study of the sequential layering of deposits.

principle of superposition In a stratigraphic sequence, the lower layers were deposited before the upper layers. Or, simply put, the stuff on top of a heap was put there last.

◀ **Figure 9-5** View of the main gorge at Olduvai Gorge in Tanzania. Note the clear sequence of geological beds. The discontinuity in the stratigraphic layers (to the right of the red arrow) is a major fault line. The stratigraphy at Olduvai is exceptionally well preserved, although even here you can see that it can be complicated.

Robert Jurmain

elements are unstable, causing them to decay and form an isotopic variation of another element. Since the rate of decay follows a definite mathematical pattern, the radioactive material forms an accurate geological time clock of sorts. By measuring the amount of decay in a particular sample, scientists can calculate the number of years it took for that amount of decay to accumulate. Chronometric techniques have been used for dating the immense age of the earth as well as artifacts less than 1,000 years old. Several techniques have been employed for a number of years and are now quite well known.

The most important chronometric technique used to date early hominins involves potassium-40 (^{40}K), which has a **half-life** of 1.25 billion years and produces argon-40 (^{40}Ar). Known as the K/Ar or potassium-argon method, this procedure has been extensively used by paleoanthropologists in dating materials in the 1- to 5-million-year range, especially in East Africa, where past volcanic activity makes this dating technique possible. A variant of this technique, the ^{40}Ar/^{39}Ar method, has also been used to date several hominin localities. The ^{40}Ar/^{39}Ar method permits the analysis of smaller samples (even single crystals), reduces experimental error, and is more precise than standard K/Ar dating. Consequently, it can be used to date a wide chronological range—indeed, the entire hominin record, even up to modern times. Recent applications have provided excellent dates for several early hominin sites in East Africa (discussed in Chapter 10) as well as somewhat later sites in Java (discussed in Chapter 11). In fact, the technique was used to date the famous Mt. Vesuvius eruption of A.D. 79, which destroyed the city of Pompeii, as documented by ancient historians. Remarkably, the midrange date obtained by the ^{40}Ar/^{39}Ar technique was A.D. 73, just six years from the known date (Renne et al., 1997)! And still another radiometric dating method, this one measuring the decay of uranium into lead (the U/Pb method, with a half-life of 4.47 million years), has been used recently in South Africa to date hominin sites (De Ruiter et al., 2009; Dirks et al., 2010). Organic material, such as bone, can't be directely dated by these techniques; but the rock matrix in which the bone is found can be. Scientists used K/Ar dating to obtain a minimum date for the deposit containing the *Zinjanthropus* cranium discovered at Olduvai by dating a volcanic layer above the fossil (**Fig 9-6**).

half-life The time period in which one-half the amount of a radioactive isotope is converted chemically to a daughter product. For example, after 1.25 billion years, half the potassium-40 (^{40}K) remains; after 2.5 billion years, one-fourth remains.

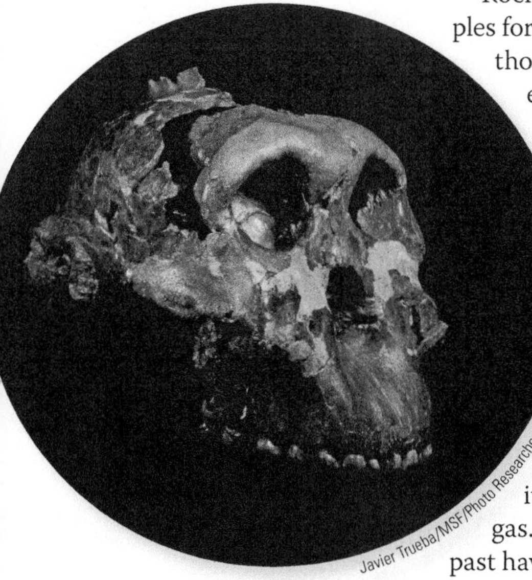

▲ **Figure 9-6** *Zinjanthropus* cranium, discovered at Olduvai Gorge and dated to 1.75 mya. This dating (using the potassium/argon method) was extraordinarily important, because previously most paleoanthropologists didn't think hominins appeared until around a million years ago.

Javier Trueba/MSF/Photo Researchers, Inc.

Rocks that provide the best samples for K/Ar and $^{40}Ar/^{39}Ar$ dating are those that have been heated to an extremely high temperature, such as that generated by volcanic activity. When the rock is in a molten state, argon, a gas, is driven off. As the rock cools and solidifies, ^{40}K continues to break down to argon; but now the gas is physically trapped in the cooled rock. To obtain the date of the rock, scientists reheat it and measure the escaping gas. Because the rock must in the past have been exposed to extreme heat, this limits these techniques to areas where sediments have been superheated, such as regions of past volcanic activity or meteorite falls.

Another well-known radiometric method popular with archaeologists makes use of carbon-14 (^{14}C), with a half-life of 5,730 years. It has been used to measure the age of organic materials (such as wood, bone, cloth, and plant remains) dating from less than 1,000 years to more than 75,000 years ago, although accuracy is reduced for materials more than 40,000 years old. Since this technique is used to study the latter stages of hominin evolution, its applications relate to material discussed in Chapters 12 and 13.

Some inorganic artifacts can be directly dated through the use of **thermoluminescence (TL)**. This method, too, relies on the principle of radiometric decay. Stone material used in manufacturing tools invariably contains trace amounts of radioactive elements, such as uranium or thorium. As the rock gets heated (perhaps by accidentally falling into a campfire or deliberately being heated to help in its production), the rapid heating releases displaced beta particles trapped within the rock. As the particles escape, they emit a dull glow known as thermoluminescence. After that, radioactive decay resumes within the fired stone, again building up electrons at a steady rate. To determine the age of an archaeological sample, the researcher must heat the sample to 500°C and measure its thermoluminescence, from which the date can be calculated. Used especially by archaeologists to date ceramic pots from recent sites, TL can also be used to date burned flint tools from earlier hominin sites.

Like TL, two other techniques used to date sites from the latter phases of hominin evolution (where neither K/Ar nor radiocarbon dating is possible) are uranium series dating and electron spin resonance (ESR) dating. Uranium series dating relies on the radioactive decay of short-lived uranium isotopes, and ESR is similar to TL because it's based on measuring trapped electrons. However, while TL is used on heated materials such as clay or stone tools, ESR is used on the dental enamel of animals. All three of these dating methods have been used to provide key dating controls for hominin sites discussed in Chapters 11 through 13.

You should realize that none of these methods is precise. Each one has problems that must be carefully considered during laboratory measurement and in collecting material to be analyzed. Because the methods aren't perfectly accurate, approximate dates are given as probability statements with an error range. For example, a date given as 1.75 ± 0.2 mya should be read as having a 67 percent chance that the actual date lies somewhere between 1.55 and 1.95 mya (see "A Closer Look, Chronometric Dating Estimates").

An important means of cross-checking dates is called **paleomagnetism**. This technique is based on the constantly shifting nature of the earth's magnetic pole. Of course, the earth's magnetic pole is now oriented in a northerly direction, but this hasn't always been so. In fact, the orientation and intensity of the geomagnetic field have undergone numerous documented changes in the last few million years. From our current viewpoint, we call a

thermoluminescence (TL) (ther-mo-loo-min-ess´-ence) A technique for dating certain archaeological materials (such as stone tools) that were heated in the past and that, upon reheating, release the stored energy of radioactive decay as light.

paleomagnetism Dating method based on the earth's shifting magnetic pole.

A Closer Look

Chronometric Dating Estimates

Chronometric dates are usually determined after testing several geological samples. The dates that result from such testing are combined and expressed statistically. For example, say that five different samples are used to give the K/Ar date 1.75 ± 0.2 mya for a particular geological bed. The individual results from all five samples are totaled together to give an average date (here, 1.75 mya), and the standard deviation is calculated (here, 0.2 million years; that is, 200,000 years). The dating estimate is then reported as the mean plus or minus (±) 1 standard deviation. Those of you who have taken statistics will realize that (assuming a normal distribution) 67 percent of a distribution of dates is included within 1 standard deviation (±) of the mean. Thus, the chronometric result, as shown in the reported range, is simply a probability statement that 67 percent of the dates from all the samples tested fell within the range of dates from 1.55 to 1.95 mya. You should carefully read chronometric dates and study the reported ranges. It's likely that the smaller the range, the more samples were analyzed. Smaller ranges mean more precise estimates; better laboratory controls will also increase precision.

northern orientation "normal" and a southern one "reversed." Paleomagnetic dating is accomplished by carefully taking samples of sediments that contain magnetically charged particles. Since these particles maintain the magnetic orientation they had when they were consolidated into rock (millions of years ago), we have a kind of "fossil compass" (**Fig. 9-7**). Then the paleomagnetic sequence is compared against the K/Ar dates to see if they agree. Some complications may arise, but once these oscillations in the geomagnetic pole are worked out, the sequence of paleomagnetic orientations can provide a valuable cross-check for K/Ar age determinations. Paleomagnetic dating has also been used recently in South Africa to confirm the U/Pb dates from a newly discovered hominin site (Dirks et al., 2010).

A final dating technique used at several African sites is based on the regular evolutionary changes in well-known groups of mammals. This technique, called *faunal correlation*, or **biostratigraphy**, provides yet another means of cross-checking the other methods. This technique employs some of the same methods used in relative stratigraphic dating, but it incorporates information on sequences of faunal remains from different sites. For instance, the presence of particular fossil pigs, elephants, antelopes, rodents, and carnivores in areas where dates are known (by K/Ar, for example) can be used to extrapolate an approximate age for other, more hard-to-date sites by noting which genera and species are present at those sites.

All these methods—K/Ar dating, paleomagnetism, and biostratigraphy—have been used in dating early hominin sites. So many different dating techniques are necessary because no single method is perfectly reliable by itself. Sampling error, contamination, and experimental error can all introduce ambiguities into our so-called absolute dates. Because the sources of error are different for each technique, however, cross-checking among several independent methods is the most reliable way of authenticating the chronology for early hominin sites.

▲ **Figure 9-7** A geologist carefully takes a sample of sediment containing magnetically charged particles for paleomagnetic dating. He must very precisely record the exact compass orientation so that it can be correlated with the sequence of magnetic orientations.

biostratigraphy A relative dating technique based on the regular changes seen in evolving groups of animals as well as the presence or absence of particular species.

Experimental Archaeology

Simply classifying artifacts into categories and types is not enough. We can learn considerably more about our ancestors by understanding how they made and used their tools. It is, after all, the artifactual traces of prehistoric tools of stone (and, to a lesser degree, bone) that provide much of our information concerning early human behavior. Tons of stone debris litter archaeological sites worldwide. A casual walk along the bottom of Olduvai Gorge could well be interrupted every few seconds by tripping over prehistoric tools!

Clearly, archaeologists are presented with a wealth of information revealing at least one part of human material culture. What do these artifacts tell us about our ancestors? How were these tools made, and how were they used? To answer these questions, contemporary archaeologists have tried to reconstruct prehistoric techniques of stone toolmaking, butchering, and so forth. In this way, experimental archaeologists are, in a sense, trying to re-create the past.

Stone Tool (Lithic) Technology

Stone is by far the most common residue of prehistoric cultural behavior. For this reason, archaeologists have long been keenly interested in this material.

When struck properly, certain types of stone will fracture in a controlled way; these nodules are called **blanks**. The smaller piece that comes off is called a **flake**, while the larger remaining chunk is called a **core** (**Fig. 9-8**). Both core and flake have sharp edges that are useful for cutting, sawing, or scraping. The earliest hominin cultural inventions probably used nondurable materials that didn't survive archaeologically (such as digging sticks or ostrich eggshells used as watertight containers). Still, a basic human invention was the recognition that stone can be fractured to produce sharp edges.

For many years, it's been assumed that in the earliest known stone tool industry (that is, the Oldowan), both core and flake tools were deliberately manufactured as final, desired products. Such core implements as "choppers" were thought to be central artifactual components of these early **lithic** assemblages (in fact, the Oldowan is often depicted as a "chopping tool industry"). However, detailed reevaluation of these artifacts has thrown these traditional assumptions into doubt. By carefully analyzing the attributes of Oldowan artifacts from Olduvai, Potts (1991, 1993) concluded that the so-called core tools really weren't tools after all. He suggests instead that early hominins were deliberately producing flake tools, and the various stone choppers were simply "incidental stopping points in the process of removing flakes from cores" (Potts, 1993, p. 60). As Potts concludes, "The flaked stones of the Oldowan thus cannot be demonstrated to constitute discrete target designs, but can be shown to represent simple by-products of the repetitive act of producing sharp flakes" (Potts, 1993, pp. 60–61).

Breaking rocks by bashing them together is one thing. Producing consistent results, even apparently simple flakes, is quite another. You might want to give it a try, just to appreciate how difficult making a stone tool can be. It takes years of practice before modern stone **knappers** learn the intricacies—the type of rock to choose, the kind of hammer to employ, the angle and velocity with which to strike, and so on. Such experience allows us to appreciate how skilled in stoneworking our ancestors truly were.

Flakes can be removed from cores in various ways. The object in making a tool, however, is to produce a usable cutting surface. By reproducing results similar to those of earlier stoneworkers, experimental archaeologists can infer

flake core

© Cengage Learning

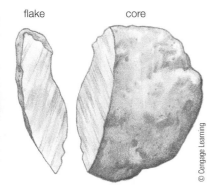

▲ **Figure 9-8** Flake and core.

blanks In archaeology, stones suitably sized and shaped to be further worked into tools.

flake A thin-edged fragment removed from a core.

core A stone reduced by flake removal. A core may or may not itself be used as a tool.

lithic (*lith*, meaning "stone") Referring to stone tools.

knappers People (frequently archaeologists) who make stone tools.

which kinds of techniques *might* have been employed.

For example, the nodules (now thought to be blanks) found in sites in Bed I at Olduvai (circa 1.85 to 1.2 mya) are flaked on one side only (that is, *unifacially*). It's possible, but by no means easy, to produce such implements by hitting one stone—the hammerstone—against another—the core—in a method called **direct percussion** (**Fig. 9-9**).

However, in later sites, particularly well studied at Olduvai (circa 400,000 ya*), most of the tools are flaked on both sides (that is, *bifacially*) and have long rippled edges. Such a result can't be reproduced by direct percussion with just a hammerstone. The edges must have been straightened ("retouched") with a "soft" hammer, such as bone or antler.

Reproducing implements similar to those found in later stages of human cultural development calls for even more sophisticated techniques. Tools such as the delicate **microliths** found in the uppermost beds at Olduvai (circa 17,000 ya), the superb Solutrean blades from Europe (circa 20,000 ya), and the expertly crafted Folsom projectile points from the New World (circa 10,000 ya) all require a mastery of stone matched by few knappers today.

To reproduce implements like those just mentioned, the knapper must remove extremely thin flakes. This can be done only through **pressure flaking**—for example, using a pointed piece of bone, antler, or hard wood and pressing firmly against the stone (**Fig. 9-10**).

Once the tools were manufactured, our ancestors used them in ways that we can infer through further experimentation. For example, archaeologists from the Smithsonian Institution successfully butchered an entire elephant (which had died in a zoo) using stone tools they had made for that purpose (Park, 1978). Other archaeologists have cut down (small) trees using stone axes they had made.

Ancient tools themselves may carry telltale signs of how they were used. Lawrence Keeley performed a series of experiments in which he manufactured flint tools and then used them in diverse ways—whittling wood, cutting bone, cutting meat, and scraping skins. Viewing these implements under a microscope at fairly high magnification revealed patterns of polishes, striations, and other kinds of **microwear**. What's most intriguing is that these patterns varied depending on how the tool was used and which material was worked. For example, Keeley was able to distinguish among tools used on bone, antler, meat, plant materials, and hides. In the last case, he was even able to determine if the hides were fresh or dried! Orientations of microwear markings also give some indication of how the tool was used (such as for cutting or scraping). Because these experiments into stone tool manufacture and use reveal valuable information about variations in microwear morphology, researchers are able to use the experimentally produced data to make inferences about specific stone tool usage in the past. For example, the 9,000-year-old Paleo-Indian flake from Nebraska shown in Figure 9-11 shows microwear polish from cutting antler or bone. Evidence of microwear polish has been examined on even the extremely early hominin stone tools from Koobi Fora (East Lake Turkana), in Kenya (Keeley and Toth, 1981).

Advances in tool use studies include the application of scanning electron microscopy (SEM). Working at 10,000× magnification, researchers have found that the edges of stone implements sometimes retain plant fibers and amino acids as well as nonorganic residues, including **phytoliths**. Because phytoliths produced by different plant species are distinctive, there is good potential for identifying the botanical materials that came in contact with the tool during its use (Rovner, 1983). Such work is most exciting; for the first time,

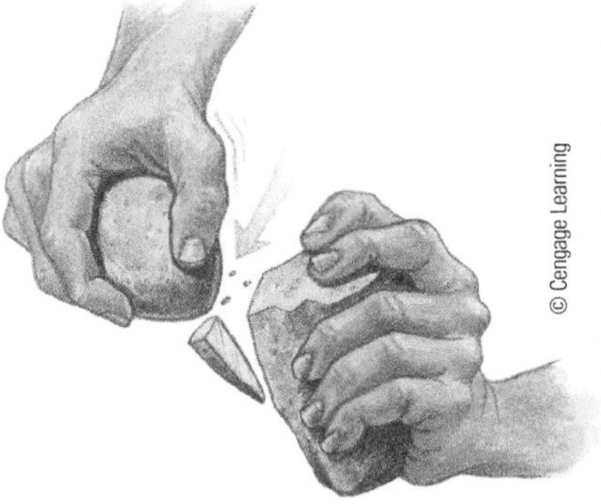

▲ **Figure 9-9** Direct percussion.

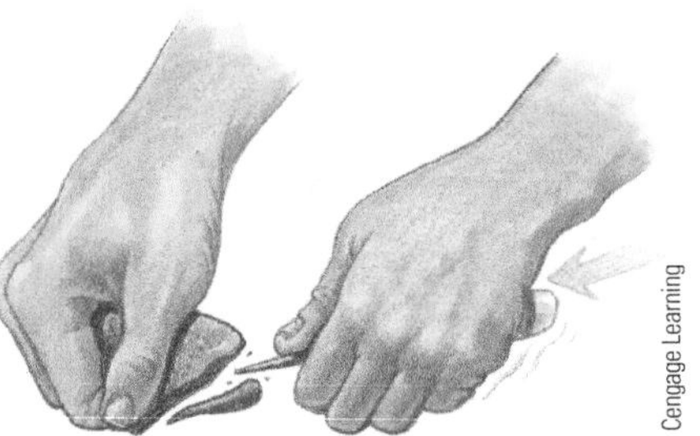

▲ **Figure 9-10** Pressure flaking.

direct percussion Striking a core or flake with a hammerstone.

microliths (*micro*, meaning "small," and *lith*, meaning "stone") Small stone tools usually produced from narrow blades punched from a core; found especially in Africa during the latter part of the Pleistocene.

pressure flaking A method of removing flakes from a core by pressing a pointed implement (e.g., bone or antler) against the stone.

microwear Polishes, striations, and other diagnostic microscopic changes on the edges of stone tools.

phytoliths (*phyto*, meaning "hidden," and *lith*, meaning "stone") Microscopic silica structures formed in the cells of many plants, particularly grasses.

* y.a. = years ago

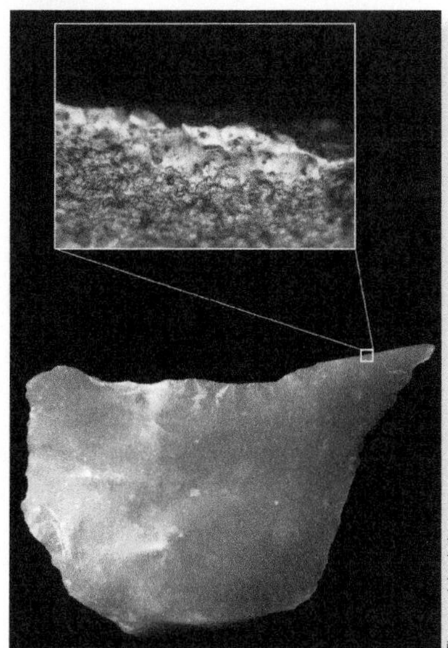

Thomas J. Loebel

▲ **Figure 9-11** Photomicrograph (200x) showing polish resulting from bone modification on a 9,000-year-old stone tool excavated from the O. V. Clary site in Nebraska by Dr. M.G. Hill, of Iowa State University.

we may be able to make definite statements concerning the uses of ancient tools. In addition, phytoliths have also been found in the dental calculus (i.e., plaque) on some Neandertal teeth as well as recently on 2-million-year-old hominins from South Africa (Henry et al., 2012). The findings for the early African hominins provided quite a surprise (see Chapter 10).

Analysis of Bone

Experimental archaeologists are also interested in the ways in which bone is altered by human and natural forces. Other scientists are vitally concerned with this process as well; in fact, it has produced an entire new branch of paleoecology—taphonomy. Taphonomists have carried out comprehensive research on how natural factors influence bone deposition and preservation. In South Africa, C. K. Brain collected data on contemporary African butchering practices, carnivore (dog) disturbances of carcasses, and so forth and then correlated these factors with the kinds and numbers of elements usually found in bone accumulations (Brain, 1981). In this way, he was able to account for the accumulation of most of the bones in South African cave sites. Likewise, in East African game parks, observations have been made on decaying animals to measure the effects of weathering, predator chewing, and trampling (Behrensmeyer et al., 1979; Perkins, 2003).

Further insight into the many ways bone is altered by natural factors has come from experimental work in the laboratory (Boaz and Behrensmeyer, 1976). In an experiment conducted at the University of California, Berkeley, human bones were put into a running-water trough. Researchers observed how far the water carried different pieces and recorded how much and what kind of damage was done. Such information is extremely useful in interpreting early hominin sites. For example, the distribution of hominin fossils at Olduvai suggests that active water transport was less prevalent there than in the Omo River Valley in southern Ethiopia.

Detailed examination of bones may also provide evidence of butchering and bone breakage by hominins, including cut and percussion marks left by stone tools. Great care must be taken to distinguish marks left on bone by carnivore or rodent gnawing, weathering processes, hoof marks, or even normal growth. High magnification of a cut made by a stone tool may reveal a minutely striated and roughened groove scored into the bone's surface. Many such finds have been recognized at early hominin sites, including Olduvai Gorge (Bunn, 1981; Potts and Shipman, 1981). (See "A Closer Look," pp. 260–261.)

Reconstruction of Early Hominin Environments and Behavior

Now that we've reviewed the many methods used by paleoanthropologists to collect their varied data, we can look at the intriguing ways in which this information is *interpreted*. Be aware that much of this interpretation is quite speculative and less amenable to scientific verification than more concrete sources of data (for example, that relating to dating, geology, or hominin anatomy). (In Chapter 1, we discussed how hypotheses are developed and tested by scientists, noting the requirement that *scientific* explanations be falsifiable.)

Paleoanthropologists are keenly interested not just in *how* early hominins evolved but also in *why* the process occurred the way it did. Accordingly, they frequently use the data available as a basis for broad, speculative scenarios that try to explain both early hominin adaptations to a changing environment and the new behaviors that these hominins adopted. Such scenarios are fascinating, and paleoanthropologists enjoy constructing them (and certainly many in the general public enjoy reading them). Without doubt, for scientists and laypersons alike, our curiosity inevitably leads to intriguing and sweeping generalizations. Still, in the following discussion, we'll focus on what is *known* from the paleoanthropological record itself and separate that from the more speculative conclusions. You, too, should evaluate these explanations with a critical eye and try to identify the empirical basis for each type of reconstruction. It's important not to accept a scenario merely because it's appealing (often because it's simple) or just because it seems plausible. We must always ask ourselves what kinds of evidence support a particular contention, how generally the explanation fits the evidence (that is, how consistent it is with different types of data from varied sources), and what types of new evidence might either help to verify or potentially falsify the interpretation.

Why Did Hominins Become Bipedal?

As we've noted several times, the adaptation of hominins to bipedal locomotion was *the* most fundamental adaptive shift among the early members of our lineage. But what were the factors that initiated this crucial change? Ecological theories have long been thought to be central to the development of bipedalism. Clearly, however, environmental influences would have to have occured *before* evidence of well-adapted bipedal behavior could appear. In other words, the major shift would have been at the end of the Miocene. Although the evidence indicates that no *sudden* wide ecological change took place at that time, locally forests probably did become patchier as rainfall became more seasonal. Given the changing environmental conditions, did hominins come to the ground to seize the opportunities offered in these more open habitats? Did bipedalism quickly ensue, stimulated somehow by this new way of life? At a very general level, the answer to these questions is yes. Obviously, hominins did at some point become bipedal, and this adaptation took place on the ground. Likewise, hominins are more adapted to mixed and open-country habitats than are our closest modern ape cousins. Successful terrestrial bipedalism probably made possible the further adaptation to more arid, open-country terrain. Still, this rendition simply tells us *where* hominins found their niche, not *why*.

As always, it's wise to be cautious in speculating about causation in evolution. It is all too easy to draw superficial conclusions. For example, scientists often surmise that the mere availability of ground niches (and perhaps that there were no direct competitors for them) inevitably led the earliest hominins to terrestrial bipedalism. But consider this: Plenty of mammalian species, including some nonhuman primates, also live mostly on the ground in open country—and they aren't bipedal. Clearly, beyond such simplistic environmental generalizations, some more complex explanation for hominin bipedalism is required. There must have been something more than just an environmental opportunity to explain this adaptation to such a unique lifestyle.

Another issue sometimes overlooked in the discussion of early hominin bipedal adaptation is that these creatures did not suddenly become completely terrestrial; but they also didn't slouch about, as illustrations of a linear progression of human evolution would suggest. We know, for example, that all terrestrial species of nonhuman primates (including savanna baboons, hamadryas baboons, and patas monkeys; see Chapter 7) regularly seek out safe sleeping sites off the ground. These safe havens help protect against predation and are usually found in trees or on cliff faces. Likewise, early hominins almost certainly sought safety at night in the trees, even after they became well adapted to terrestrial bipedalism during daytime foraging. What's more, the continued opportunities for feeding in the trees would most likely have remained significant to early hominins well after they were also utilizing ground-based resources.

Various hypotheses explaining why hominins initially became bipedal have been suggested and are summarized in **Table 9.2**. The primary influences claimed to have stimulated the shift to bipedalism include acquiring the ability to carry objects (and offspring), hunting on the ground, gathering of seeds and nuts, feeding from bushes, improved thermoregulation (that is, keeping cooler on the open savanna), having a better view of open country (to spot predators), walking long distances, and provisioning by males of females with dependent offspring.

These are all creative scenarios, but once again they're not very conducive to rigorous testing and verification. Still, two of the more ambitious scenarios proposed by Clifford Jolly (1970) and Owen Lovejoy (1981) deserve further mention. Both of these views sought to link several aspects of early hominin ecology, feeding, and social behavior and both utilized models derived from studies of contemporary nonhuman primates.

Jolly's seed-eating hypothesis used the feeding behavior and ecology of gelada baboons as an analogy for very early hominins. Seed eating is an activity that requires keen hand-eye coordination, with presumed bipedal shuffling potentially improving the efficiency of foraging. In this view, early hominins are hypothesized to have adapted to open country and bipedalism as a result of their primary adaptation to eating seeds and nuts (found on the ground). The key assumption is that early hominins were eating seeds acquired in similar ecological conditions to those of contemporary gelada baboons.

Lovejoy, meanwhile, has combined presumed aspects of early hominin ecology, feeding, pair bonding, infant care, and food sharing to devise his creative scenario. This view hinges on these assumptions: (1) that the earliest hominins had offspring at least as K-selected (see Chapter 7) as other large-bodied hominoids; (2) that hominin males ranged widely and provisioned females and their young, who remained more tied to a "home base"; and (3) that males were paired monogamously with females.

As we've noted, while not strictly testable, such scenarios do make certain predictions that can be potentially falsified or upheld. Accordingly, aspects of each scenario can be evaluated in light of more specific data (obtained from the paleoanthropological record). Regarding the seed-eating hypothesis, predictions relating to the size of the back teeth in most early hominins are met, but the proportions of the front teeth in many forms aren't what we'd expect to see in a committed seed eater. Besides, the analogy with gelada baboons is not as informative as once thought; these animals actually don't eat that many seeds and certainly aren't habitual bipeds. Finally, many of the characteristics that Jolly suggested were restricted to hominins (and geladas) are also found in several late Miocene hominoids (who weren't hominins—nor obviously bipeds). Thus, regarding the seed-eating hypothesis, the proposed dental and dietary adaptations don't appear to be linked specifically to hominin origins or bipedalism.

Further detailed analyses of data have also questioned crucial elements of Lovejoy's male-provisioning scenario. The evidence that appears to most contradict this view is that all early hominins were quite sexually dimorphic (McHenry, 1992). According to Lovejoy's model (and analogies with contemporary monogamous nonhuman primates such as gibbons), there shouldn't be such dramatic

Table 9.2 Possible Factors Influencing the Initial Evolution of Bipedal Locomotion in Hominins

Factor	Speculated Influence	Comments
Carrying (objects, tools, weapons, infants) 	Upright posture freed the arms to carry various objects (including offspring).	Charles Darwin emphasized this view, particularly relating to tools and weapons; however, evidence of stone tools is found much later in the record than first evidence of bipedalism.
Hunting 	Bipedalism allowed carrying of weapons, more accurate throwing of certain weapons, and improved long-distance walking.	Systematic hunting is now thought not to have been practiced until after the origin of bipedal hominins.
Seed and nut gathering 	Feeding on seeds and nuts occurred while standing upright.	Model initially drawn from analogy with gelada baboons (see text).
Feeding from bushes 	Upright posture provided access to seeds, berries, etc., in lower branches; analogous to adaptation seen in some specialized antelope.	Climbing adaptation already existed as prior ancestral trait in earliest hominins (i.e., bush and tree feeding already was established prior to bipedal adaptation).
Thermoregulation (cooling) 	Vertical posture exposes less of the body to direct sun; increased distance from ground facilitates cooling by increased exposure to breezes.	Works best for animals active midday on savanna; moreover, adaptation to bipedalism may have initially occurred in woodlands, not on savanna.
Visual surveillance 	Standing up provided better view of surrounding countryside (view of potential predators as well as other group members).	Behavior seen occasionally in terrestrial primates (e.g., baboons); probably a contributing factor, but unlikely as "prime mover."
Long-distance walking 	Covering long distances was more efficient for a biped than for a quadruped (during hunting or foraging); mechanical reconstructions show that bipedal walking is less energetically costly than quadrupedalism (this is not the case for bipedal running).	Same difficulties as with hunting explanation; long-distance foraging on ground also appears unlikely adaptation in earliest hominins.
Male provisioning 	Males carried back resources to dependent females and young.	Monogamous bond suggested; however, most skeletal data appear to falsify this part of the hypothesis (see text).

differences in body size between males and females. Recent studies (Reno et al., 2003, 2005) have questioned this conclusion regarding sexual dimorphism, suggesting, at least for one species (*Australopithecus afarensis*), that it was only very moderate. Further evaluation of another, even earlier hominin (*Ardipithecus*) has led Lovejoy to continue to forcefully argue for his male-provisioning model (Lovejoy, 2009). From a wider perspective, these conclusions appear at odds with most of the evidence regarding early hominins. What's more, the notions of food sharing (presumably including considerable meat), home bases, and long-distance provisioning are questioned by more controlled interpretations of the archaeological record.

Another imaginative view is also relevant to this discussion of early hominin evolution, since it relates the adaptation to bipedalism (which was first) to increased brain expansion (which came later). This interpretation, proposed by Dean Falk, suggests that an upright posture put severe constraints on brain size (since blood circulation and drainage would have been altered and cooling would consequently have been more limited than in quadrupeds). Falk thus hypothesizes that new brain-cooling mechanisms must have coevolved with bipedalism; this view is articulated in what she calls the "radiator theory" (Falk, 1990). Falk further surmises that the requirement for better brain cooling would have been particularly marked as hominins adapted to open-country ground living on the hot African savanna. Another interesting pattern observed by Falk concerns two varying cooling adaptations found in different early hominin species. She thus suggests that the type of "radiator" adapted in the genus *Homo* was particularly significant in reducing constraints on brain size—which presumably limited some other early hominins. The radiator theory works well, since it helps to explain not only the relationship of bipedalism to later brain expansion but also why only some hominins became dramatically encephalized.

The radiator theory, too, has been criticized by some paleoanthropologists. Most notably, the presumed species distinction concerning varying cooling mechanisms is not as obvious as suggested by the hypothesis. Both types of venous drainage systems can be found in contemporary *Homo sapiens* as well as within various early hominin species (that is, the variation is intraspecific, not just interspecific). Indeed, in some early hominin specimens, both systems can be found in the same individual (expressed on either side of the skull). Besides, as Falk herself has noted, the radiator itself didn't lead to larger brains; it simply helped reduce constraints on increased encephalization among hominins. It thus requires some further mechanism (prime mover) to explain why, in some hominin species, brain size increased the way it did.

As with any such ambitious effort, it's all too easy to find holes. Falk aptly reminds us that "the search for such 'prime movers' is highly speculative, and these theories do not lend themselves to hypothesis testing" (Falk, 1990, p. 334). Even so, the attempt to interrelate various lines of evidence, the use of contemporary primate models, and predictions concerning further evidence obtained from paleoanthropological contexts all conform to sound scientific methodology. All the views discussed here have contributed to this venture—one not just aimed at understanding our early ancestors but also seeking to refine its methodologies and scientific foundation.

How Do We Know?

This entire chapter is all about how we can learn about the age, behavior, and environments of our early hominin relatives. Briefly, we know the ages of most important sites by using an array of precise dating techniques. Artifacts, fossil animals, and early hominins themselves are recovered and recorded using controlled archaeological methods. How tools were made and used is discovered through experimentation in stone tool manufacture as well as the chemical study of plant residues left on tools, and early hominin diets can be revealed through chemical analysis of fossil teeth. Finally, the key hominin adaptation to bipedal locomotion can be explained by a variety of hypotheses. These are less secure and show how science continually refines its approach and tests ideas to make conclusions more rigorous.

Summary of Main Topics

- The most important subfields of paleoanthropology are geology, paleontology, archaeology, and physical anthropology.
- The two types of dating techniques are relative dating and chronometric dating. Stratigraphy and paleomagnetism are the two most important examples of relative dating; potassium-argon dating and radiocarbon (^{14}C) dating are the most important examples of chronometric dating.
- The first stone tools thus far discovered date to about 2.6 mya. These tools include mostly simple flake implements and the discarded cores from which they were struck.
- Bipedal locomotion is thought to have been significantly influenced by one or more of the following: carrying objects, seed gathering or feeding from bushes, visual spotting of predators, and long-distance walking (the latter coming more recently in human evolution).

Critical Thinking Questions

1. You are leading a paleoanthropological expedition aimed at discovering an early hominin site dating to the Pliocene. In what part of the world will you pick your site, and why? After selecting a particular region, how will you identify which area(s) to survey on foot?
2. Why is it important to have accurate dates for paleoanthropological localities? Why is it necessary to use more than one kind of dating technique?
3. What do we mean when we say that early hominins displayed cultural behavior? What types of behavior do you think this would have included? (Imagine that you've been transported back in time by a time machine, and you're sitting in a tree watching a group of hominins at Olduvai Gorge 1.5 mya.)
4. Now put yourself in the same place, this time leading an archaeological excavation. What would be left for you to detect of the cultural behavior you observed in question 3? What happened to the remainder of this behavioral repertoire?
5. What do we mean when we say that human evolution is biocultural? How do paleoanthropologists investigate early hominins using such a biocultural perspective?

Media Resources

Video

See the video "Olduvai Gorge, Tanzania" to learn more about topics covered in this chapter.

Login to your Anthropology CourseMate at www.cengagebrain.com to access videos.

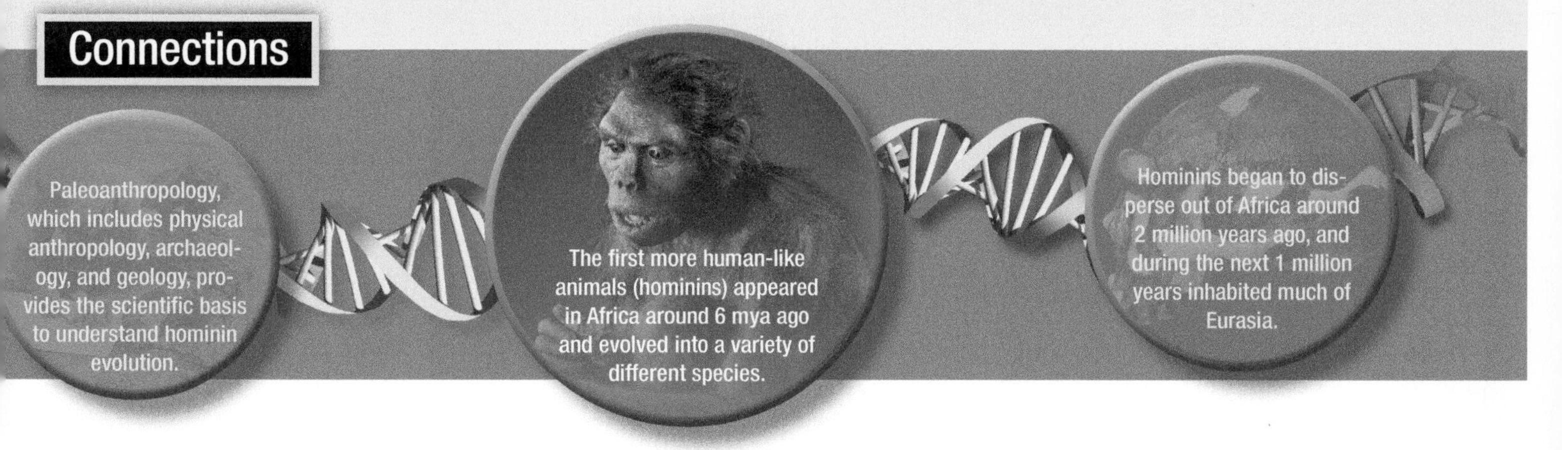

Connections

Paleoanthropology, which includes physical anthropology, archaeology, and geology, provides the scientific basis to understand hominin evolution.

The first more human-like animals (hominins) appeared in Africa around 6 mya ago and evolved into a variety of different species.

Hominins began to disperse out of Africa around 2 million years ago, and during the next 1 million years inhabited much of Eurasia.

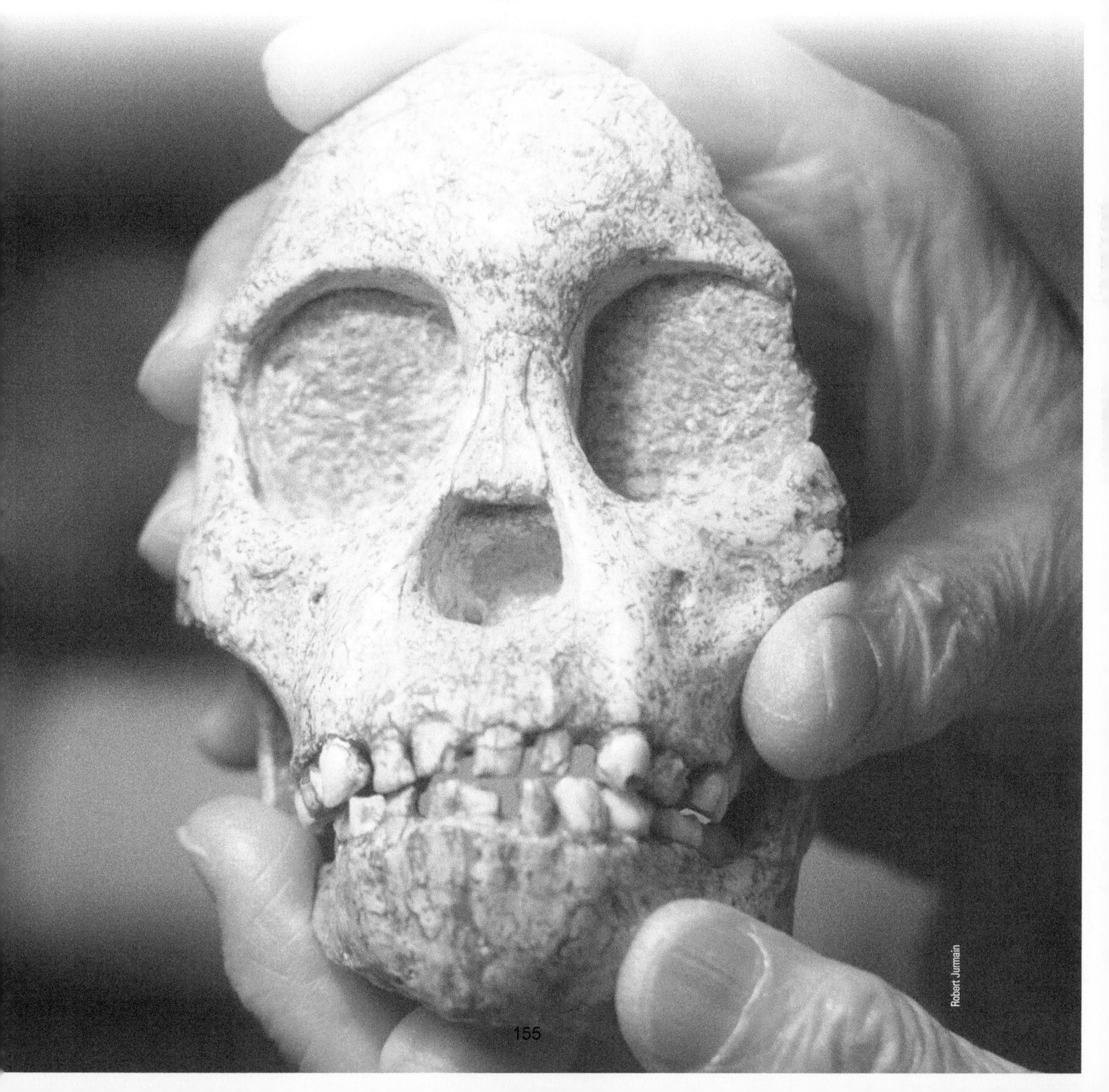

Robert Jurmain

Hominin Origins in Africa

7

Student Learning Objectives

After mastering the material in this chapter, you should be able to:

- Discuss why Africa is so central to the study of the earliest hominins and describe which portions of the continent have yielded hominin fossil remains.
- Explain why evidence of bipedal locomotion is so important in the study of fossil hominins and describe the basic mechanics of bipedal locomotion.
- Discuss what specific features indicate adaptation to bipedal locomotion and which fossil hominins display these features.
- Describe the three major groups of early hominins discussed in this chapter.
- Specifically, compare and contrast the earliest (possible) hominins (i.e., *Sahelanthropus*, *Orrorin*, and *Ardipithecus*). Also, explain why (or why not) you think they are hominins.
- Explain why we say that australopiths are diverse and some are more derived than others.
- Describe what is considered the earliest evidence of the genus *Homo*, where and when these hominins lived, and what all this tells us about human evolution.

Our species today dominates earth because we use our brains and cultural inventions to invade every corner of the planet. Yet, around 5 million years ago, our ancestors were little more than bipedal apes, confined to a few regions in Africa. What were these creatures like? When and how did they begin their evolutionary journey?

In Chapter 9, we discussed the techniques paleoanthropologists use to locate and excavate sites, as well as the multidisciplinary approaches used to interpret discoveries. In this chapter, we turn to the physical evidence of the hominin fossils themselves. The earliest fossils identifiable as hominins are all from Africa. They date from as early as 6+ mya; after 4 mya, varieties of these early hominins become more plentiful and widely distributed in Africa. It's fascinating to think about all these quite primitive early members of our family tree living side by side for millions of years, especially when we also try to figure out how they managed to coexist with their different adaptations. Most of these species became extinct. Why? And were some of these apelike animals possibly our direct ancestors?

Hominins, of course, evolved from earlier primates (dating from the Eocene to late Miocene), and in Chapter 8 we discussed the fossil evidence of prehominin primates. These fossils provide us with a context within which to understand the subsequent evolution of the human lineage. In recent years, paleoanthropologists from several countries have been excavating sites in Africa, and many exciting new finds have been uncovered. However, because many such discoveries are so recent, detailed evaluations are still in progress, and conclusions must remain tentative.

One thing is certain, however. The earliest members of the human lineage were confined to Africa. Only much later did their descendants disperse from the African continent to other areas of the Old World. (This "out of Africa" saga will be the topic of the next chapter.)

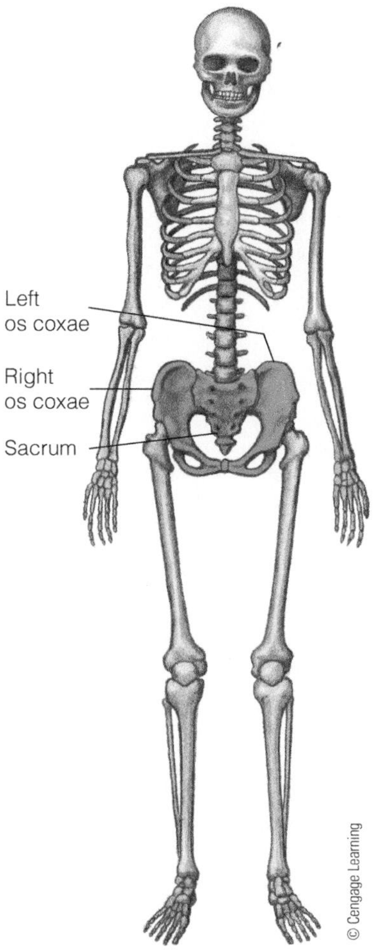

Walking the Walk: The Bipedal Adaptation

In our overview in Chapter 9 of behavioral reconstructions of early hominins, we highlighted several hypotheses that attempt to explain *why* bipedal locomotion first evolved in the hominins. Here we turn to the specific anatomical (that is, **morphological**) evidence showing us when, where, and how hominin bipedal locomotion evolved. From a broader perspective, we've noted a tendency in all primates for erect body posture and some bipedalism. Of all living primates, however, efficient bipedalism as the primary (habitual) form of locomotion is seen *only* in hominins. Functionally, the human mode of locomotion is most clearly shown in our striding gait, where weight is alternately placed on a single fully extended hind limb. This specialized form of locomotion has developed to a point where energy levels are used to near peak efficiency. Our manner of bipedal locomotion is a far cry from what we see in nonhuman primates, who move bipedally with hips and knees bent and maintain balance clumsily and inefficiently, tottering along rather than striding.

Left os coxae

Right os coxae

Sacrum

© Cengage Learning

▲ **Figure 10-1** The human pelvis: various elements shown on a modern skeleton.

From a survey of our close primate relatives, it's apparent that while still in the trees, our ancestors were adapted to a fair amount of upper-body erectness. Prosimians, monkeys, and apes all spend considerable time sitting erect while feeding, grooming, or sleeping. Presumably, our early ancestors displayed similar behavior. What caused these forms to come to the ground and embark on the unique way of life that would eventually lead to humans is still a mystery. Perhaps natural selection favored some Miocene hominoids coming occasionally to the ground to forage for food on the forest floor and forest fringe. In any case, once they were on the ground and away from the immediate safety offered by trees, bipedal locomotion could become a tremendous advantage. (For a discussion of some specific hypotheses that have tried to explain the early evolution of bipedal locomotion, see Chapter 9.)

morphological Pertaining to the form and structure of organisms.

The Mechanics of Walking on Two Legs

Our mode of locomotion is indeed extraordinary, involving, as it does, a unique kind of activity in which "the body, step by step, teeters on the edge of catastrophe" (Napier, 1967, p. 56). In this way, the act of human walking is the act of *almost falling* repeatedly! The problem is to maintain balance on the "stance" leg while the "swing" leg is off the ground. In fact, during normal walking, both feet are simultaneously on the ground only about 25 percent of the time, and this figure becomes even less as we walk (or run) faster.

Maintaining a stable center of balance in this complex form of locomotion calls for many drastic structural/anatomical alterations in the basic primate quadrupedal pattern. The most dramatic changes are seen in the pelvis. The pelvis is composed of three elements: two hip bones, or ossa coxae (*sing.*, os coxae), joined at the back to the sacrum (**Fig. 10-1**). In a quadruped, the ossa coxae are vertically elongated bones positioned along each side of the lower portion of the spine and oriented more or less parallel to it. In hominins, the pelvis is comparatively much shorter and broader and extends around to the side (**Fig. 10-2**). This configuration helps to stabilize the line of weight transmission in a bipedal posture from the lower back to the hip joint (**Fig. 10-3**).

Several consequences resulted from the remodeling of the pelvis during early hominin evolution. Broadening the two sides and extending them around to the side and front of the body produced a basin-shaped structure that helps support the abdominal organs (*pelvis* means "basin" in Latin). These alterations also repositioned the attachments of several key muscles that act on the hip and leg, changing their mechanical function. Probably

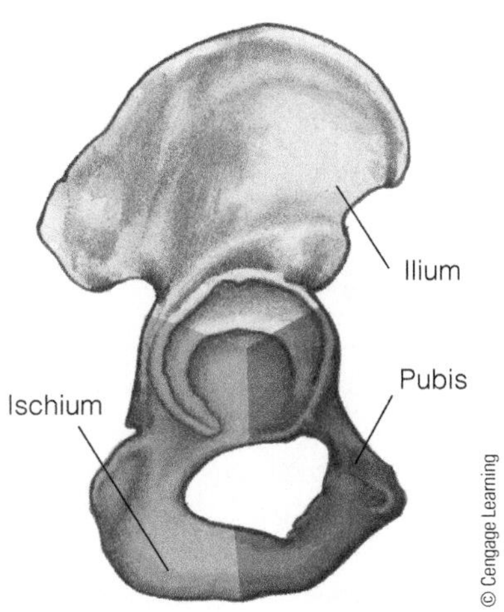

▲ **Figure 10-2** The human os coxae, composed of three bones (right side shown).

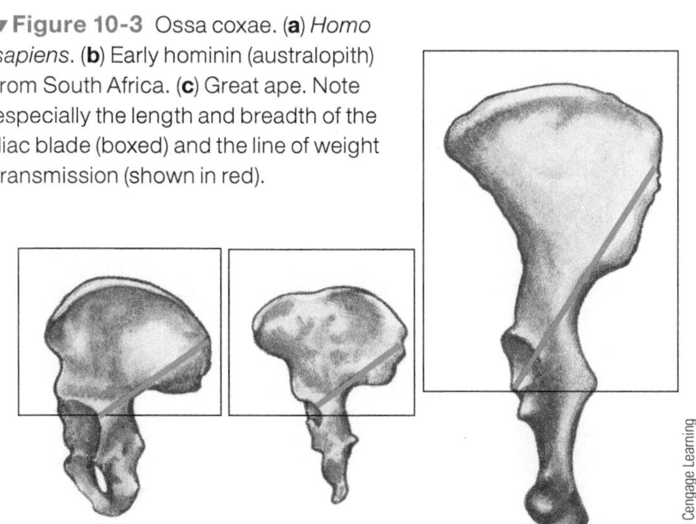

▼ **Figure 10-3** Ossa coxae. (**a**) *Homo sapiens*. (**b**) Early hominin (australopith) from South Africa. (**c**) Great ape. Note especially the length and breadth of the iliac blade (boxed) and the line of weight transmission (shown in red).

the most important of these altered relationships is that involving the gluteus maximus, the largest muscle in the body, which in humans forms the bulk of the buttocks. In quadrupeds, the gluteus maximus is positioned to the side of the hip and functions to pull the thigh to the side and away from the body. In humans, this muscle is positioned behind the hip; this arrangement allows it, along with the hamstrings, to extend the thigh, pulling it to the rear during walking and running (**Fig. 10-4**). The gluteus maximus is a truly powerful extensor of the thigh and provides additional force, particularly during running and climbing.

Modifications also occurred in other parts of the skeleton because of the shift to bipedalism. The most significant of these, summarized in "A Closer Look: Major Features of Bipedal Locomotion," (pp. 280–281) include (1) repositioning of the foramen magnum, the opening at the base of the skull through which the spinal cord emerges; (2) the addition of spinal curves which help to transmit the weight of the upper body to the hips in an upright posture; (3) shortening and broadening of the pelvis and the stabilization of weight transmission (discussed earlier); (4) lengthening of the hind limb, thus increasing stride length; (5) angling of the femur (thighbone) inward to bring the knees and feet closer together under the body; and (6) several structural changes in the foot, including the development of a longitudinal arch and realignment of the big toe in parallel with the other toes (that is, making it no longer divergent).

As you can appreciate, the evolution of hominin bipedalism required complex anatomical reorganization. For natural selection to produce anatomical change of the magnitude seen in hominins, the benefits of bipedal locomotion must have been significant indeed! We mentioned in Chapter 9 several possible adaptive advantages

▼ **Figure 10-4** Comparisons of important muscles that act to extend the hip. Note that the attachment surface (origin, shown in black) of the gluteus maximus in humans (**a**) is farther in back of the hip joint than in a chimpanzee standing bipedally (**b**). Conversely, in chimpanzees, the hamstrings are farther in back of the knee.

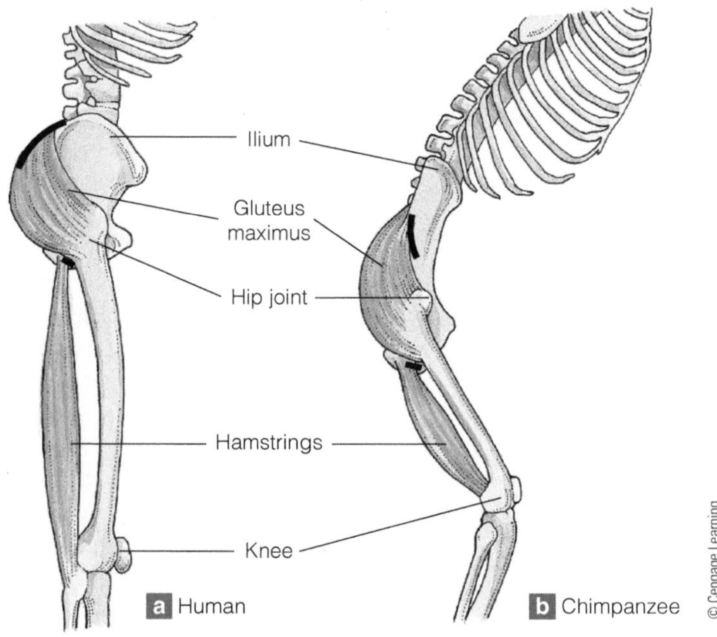

A Closer Look

Major Features of Bipedal Locomotion

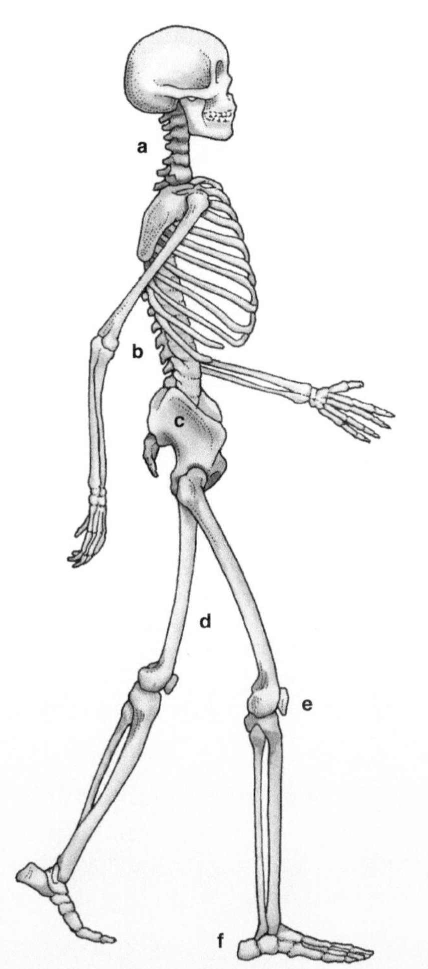

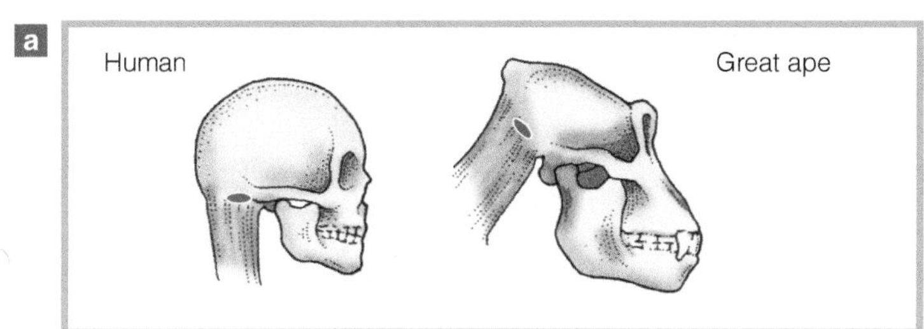

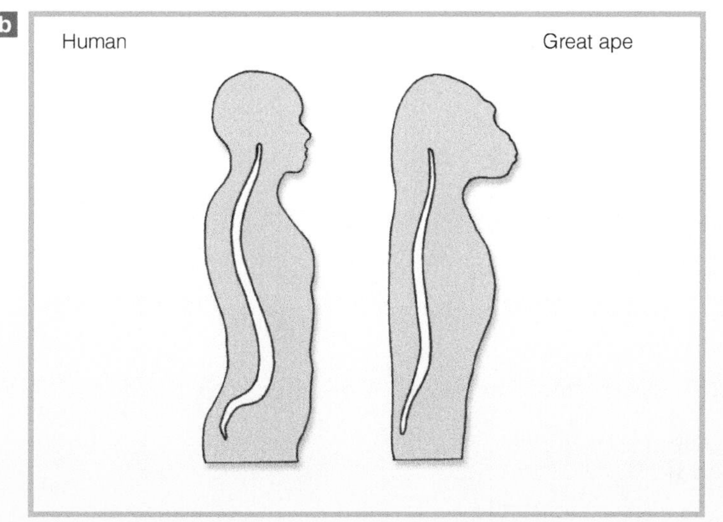

During hominin evolution, several major structural features throughout the body have been reorganized (from those seen in other primates), facilitating efficient bipedal locomotion. These are illustrated here, beginning with the head and progressing to the foot: (**a**) The foramen magnum (shown in blue) is repositioned farther underneath the skull, so that the head is more or less balanced on the spine (and thus requiring less robust neck muscles to hold the head upright). (**b**) The spine has two distinctive curves—a backward (thoracic) one and a forward (lumbar) one—that keep the trunk (and weight) centered above the pelvis. (**c**) The pelvis is shaped more in the

that bipedal locomotion may have conferred upon early hominins. But these all remain hypotheses (since they can't be tested, they could more accurately be called scenarios), and we have inadequate data for testing the various proposed models.

Still, given the anatomical alterations required for efficient bipedalism, some major behavioral stimuli must have influenced its development. When they interpret evolutionary history, biologists are fond of saying that form follows function. In other words, during evolution, organisms don't undergo significant reorganization in structure *unless* these changes—over many generations—assist individuals in some functional capacity (and in so doing increase their reproductive success). Such changes didn't necessarily occur all at once, but probably evolved over a

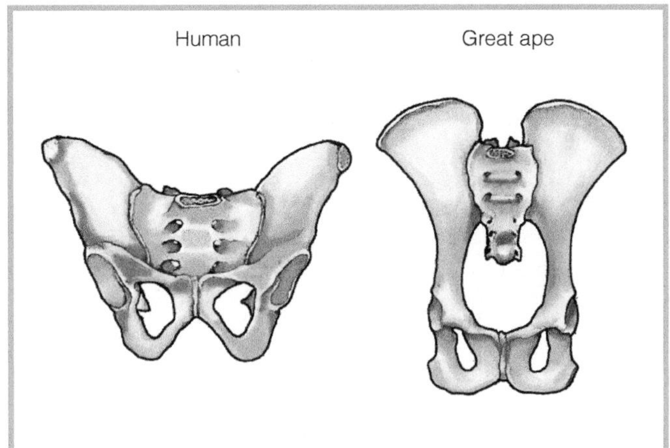

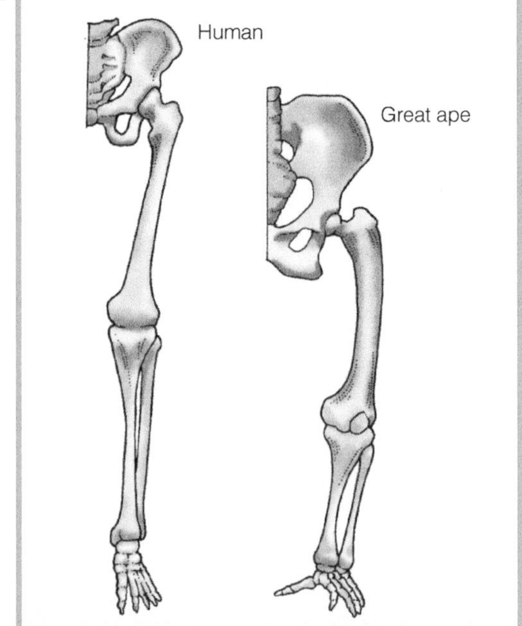

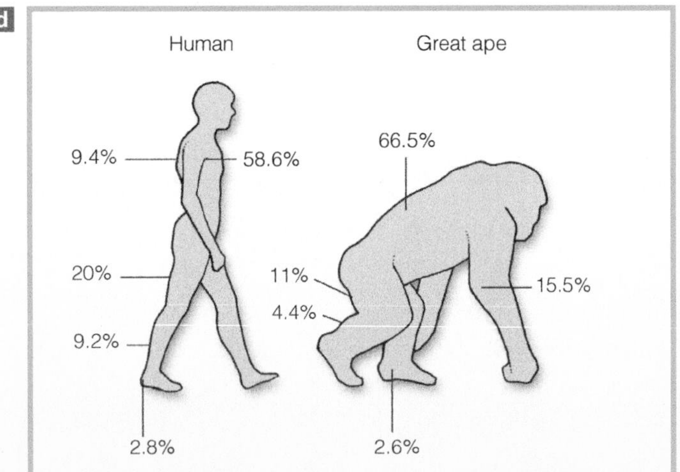

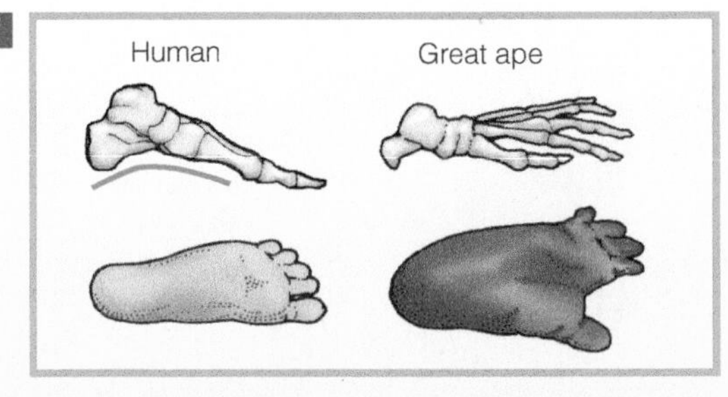

form of a basin to support internal organs; the ossa coxae (specifically, the iliac blades) are also shorter and broader, thus stabilizing weight transmission. (**d**) The lower limbs are elongated, as shown by the proportional lengths of various body segments (for example, in humans the thigh comprises 20 percent of body height, while in gorillas it comprises only 11 percent). (**e**) The femur is angled inward, keeping the legs more directly under the body; modified knee anatomy also permits full extension of this joint. (**f**) The big toe is enlarged and brought in line with the other toes; a distinctive longitudinal arch also forms, helping to absorb shock and adding propulsive spring.

fairly long period of time. Even so, once behavioral influences initiated certain structural modifications, the process gained momentum and proceeded irreversibly.

We say that hominin bipedalism is both habitual and obligate. By **habitual bipedalism**, we mean that hominins, unlike any other primate, move bipedally as their standard and most efficient mode of locomotion. By **obligate bipedalism**, we mean that hominins are committed to bipedalism and cannot locomote efficiently in any other way. For example, the loss of grasping ability in the foot makes climbing much more difficult for humans (although by no means impossible). The central task, then, in trying to understand the earliest members of the hominin lineage is to identify anatomical features that indicate

habitual bipedalism Bipedal locomotion as the form of locomotion shown by hominins most of the time.

obligate bipedalism Bipedalism as the *only* form of hominin terrestrial locomotion. Since major anatomical changes in the spine, pelvis, and lower limb are required for bipedal locomotion, once hominins adopted this mode of locomotion, other forms of locomotion on the ground became impossible.

bipedalism and to interpret to what degree these organisms were committed to this form of locomotion (that is, was it habitual and was it obligate?).

What structural patterns are observable in early hominins, and what do they imply regarding locomotor function? By at least 4 mya, all the major structural changes required for bipedalism are seen in early hominins from Africa (at least as far as the evidence permits conclusions to be drawn). In particular, the pelvis, as clearly documented by several excellently preserved specimens, was dramatically remodeled to support weight in a bipedal stance (see Fig. 10-3b).

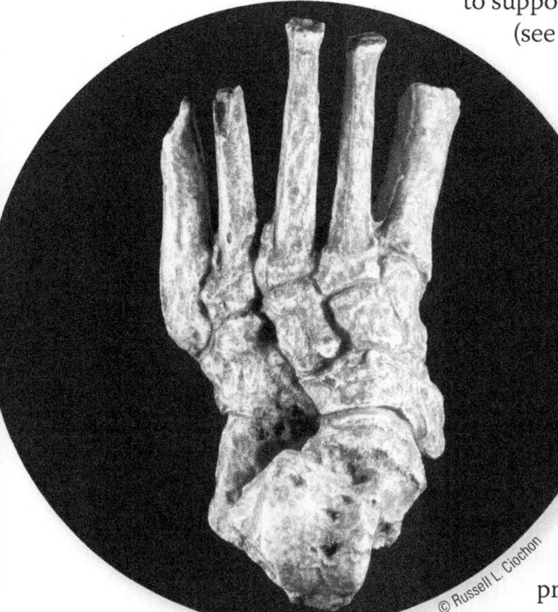

▲ **Figure 10-5** A nearly complete hominin foot (OH 8) from Olduvai Gorge, Tanzania. (See Appendix C on the Anthropology CourseMate at Cengagebrain.com for an explanation of how specimen numbers such as OH 8 are assigned.)

Other structural changes shown after 4 mya in the earliest relatively complete hominin postcranial remains further confirm the pattern seen in the pelvis. For example, the vertebral column (as known from specimens in East and South Africa) shows the same curves as in modern hominins. The lower limbs are also elongated, and they seem to be proportionately about as long as in modern humans (although the arms are longer in these early hominins). Further, the angle of weight support from the hip to the knee is very similar to that seen in *Homo sapiens*.

Fossil evidence of early hominin foot structure has come from two sites in South Africa; especially important are some fossils from **Sterkfontein** (Clarke and Tobias, 1995). These specimens, consisting of four articulating elements from the ankle and big toe, indicate that the heel and longitudinal arch were both well adapted for a bipedal gait. But the paleoanthropologists (Ron Clarke and Phillip Tobias) who analyzed these remains also suggest that the large toe was *divergent*, unlike the hominin pattern shown in "A Closer Look: Major Features of Bipedal Locomotion." If the large toe really did possess this anatomical position (and this is disputed), it most likely would have aided the foot in grasping. In turn, this grasping ability (as in other primates) would have enabled early hominins to more effectively exploit arboreal habitats. Finally, since anatomical remodeling is always constrained by a set of complex functional compromises, a foot highly capable of grasping and climbing is less useful as a stable platform during bipedal locomotion. Some researchers therefore see early hominins as perhaps not quite as fully committed to bipedal locomotion as were later hominins.

Sterkfontein (sterk′-fawn-tane)

Further evidence for evolutionary changes in the foot comes from two sites in East Africa where numerous fossilized elements have been recovered (**Fig. 10-5**). As in the remains from South Africa, the East African fossils suggest a well-adapted bipedal gait. The arches are developed, but some differences in the ankle also imply that considerable flexibility was possible (again, probably indicating some continued adaptation to climbing). From this evidence some researchers have concluded that many forms of early hominins probably spent considerable time in the trees. What's more, they may not have been quite as efficient bipedally as has previously been suggested. Nevertheless, most researchers maintain that early hominins from Africa displayed both habitual and obligate bipedalism (despite the new evidence from South Africa and the earliest traces from central and East Africa, all of which will require further study).

Digging for Connections: Early Hominins from Africa

As you are now well aware, a variety of early hominins lived in Africa, and we'll cover their comings and goings over a 5-million-year period, from at least 6 to 1 mya. It's also important to keep in mind that these hominins were geographically widely distributed, with fossil discoveries coming from central, East, and South Africa (**Fig. 10-8** on p. 284). Paleoanthropologists generally agree that there were at least six different genera among these early African fossils, which in turn comprised upward of 13 different species. At no time, in no other place were hominins ever as diverse as these very ancient members of our family tree. As you'll see in a minute, some of the earliest fossils thought by many researchers to be hominins are primitive in some ways and unusually derived in others. In fact, some paleoanthropologists remain unconvinced that they are really hominins.

As you've already guessed, there are quite a few different fossils from many sites; their formal naming can be difficult to pronounce and not easy to remember. So we'll try to discuss these fossil groups in a way that's easy to understand. Our primary focus will be to organize them by time and by major evolutionary trends. In so doing, we recognize three major groups:

- Pre-australopiths—the earliest and most primitive (possible) hominins (6.0+ to 4.4 mya)
- Australopiths—diverse forms, some more primitive, others highly derived (4.2 to 1.2 mya)
- Early *Homo*—the first members of our genus (2.0+ to 1.4 mya)

Pre-Australopiths (6.0+ to 4.4 mya)

The oldest and most surprising of these earliest hominins is represented by a cranium discovered at a central African site called Toros-Menalla in the modern nation of Chad (Brunet et al., 2002) (**Fig. 10-6**). Provisional dating using faunal correlation (biostratigraphy) suggests a date of between 7 and 6 mya (Vignaud et al., 2002). Closer examination of the evidence used in obtaining this biostratigraphic date now has led many paleoanthropologists to suggest that the later date (6 mya) is more likely.

The morphology of the fossil is unusual, with a combination of characteristics unlike that found in other early hominins. The braincase is small, estimated at no larger than a modern chimpanzee's (preliminary estimate in the range of 320 to 380 cm^3), but it is massively built, with huge browridges in front, a crest on top, and large muscle attachments in the rear. Yet, combined with these apelike features is a smallish vertical face containing front teeth very unlike an ape's. In fact, the lower face, being more tucked in under the brain vault (and not protruding, as in most other early hominins), is more of a *derived* feature more commonly expressed in much later hominins (especially members of genus *Homo*). What's more, unlike the dentition seen in apes (and some early hominins), the upper canine is reduced and is worn down from the tip (rather than shearing along its side against the first lower premolar). The lack of such a shearing canine/premolar arrangement (called a **honing complex**) (**Fig. 10-7**) is viewed by many researchers as an important derived characteristic of early hominins (White et al., 2010). Other experts are not entirely convinced and suggest that it could just as easily have evolved in both hominins and other hominoids because of homoplasy (Wood and Harrison, 2011).

In recognition of this unique combination of characteristics, paleoanthropologists have placed the Toros-Menalla remains into a new genus and species of hominin, *Sahelanthropus tchadensis* (Sahel being the region of the southern Sahara in North Africa). These new finds from Chad have forced an immediate and significant reassessment of early hominin evolution. Two cautionary comments,

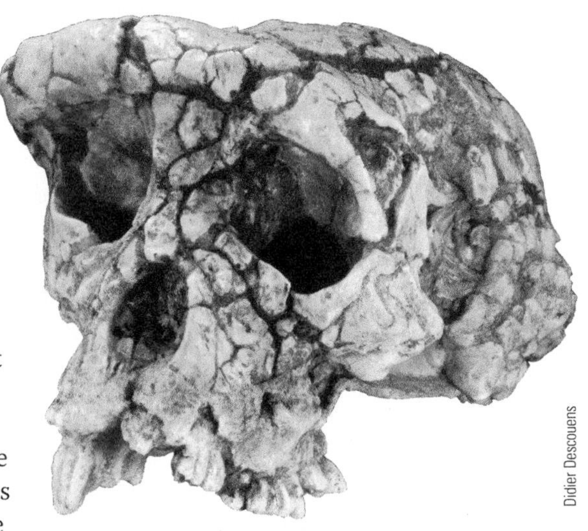
Didier Descouens

▲ **Figure 10-6** A nearly complete cranium of *Sahelanthropus* from Chad, dating to approximately 6 mya or somewhat older.

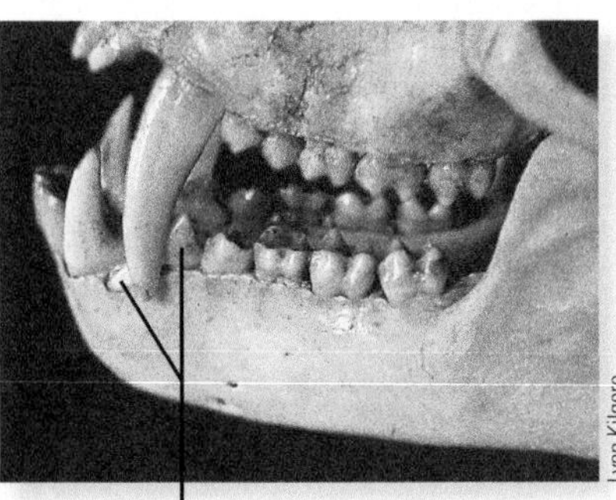
Lynn Kilgore

Sectorial lower first premolar

▲ **Figure 10-7** Canine/lower first premolar honing complex, typical of most Old World anthropoids, but lacking in most hominins (shown here in a male patas monkey). Note how the large upper canine shears against the elongated surface of the lower first premolar.

honing complex The shearing of a large upper canine with the first lower premolar, with the wear leading to honing of the surfaces of both teeth. This anatomical pattern is typical of most Old World anthropoids but is mostly absent in hominins.

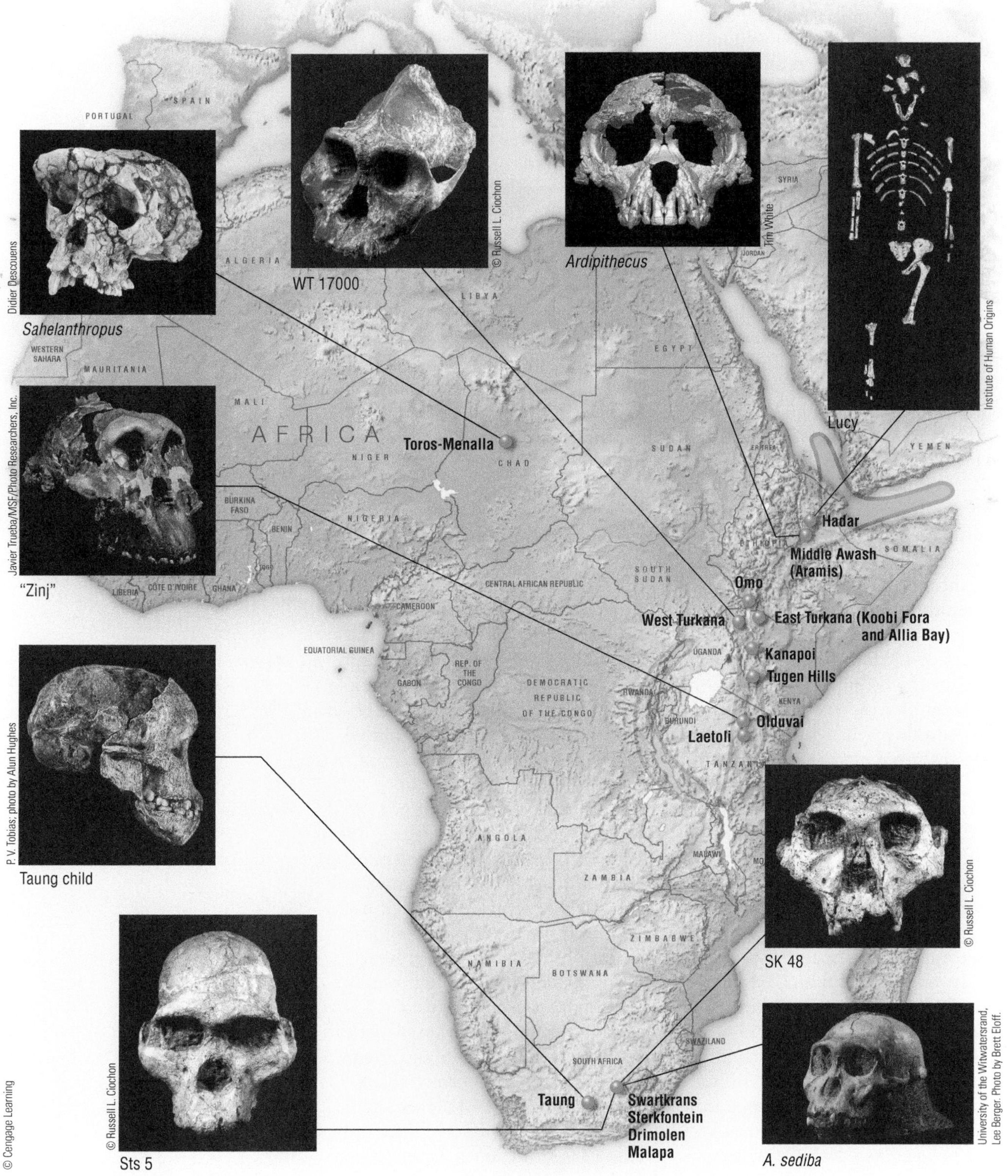

▲ **Figure 10-8** Early hominin fossil finds (pre-australopith and australopith localities). The Rift Valley in East Africa is shown in gold.

however, are in order. First, as we noted, the dating is only approximate, since it is based on biostratigraphic correlation with sites in Kenya (1,500 miles to the east). Second, and perhaps more serious, is the hominin status of the Chad fossil. Given the facial structure and dentition, it's difficult to see how *Sahelanthropus* could be anything but a hominin. However, the position of its foramen magnum is intermediate between that of a quadrupedal ape and that of a bipedal hominin (**Fig. 10-9**); for this and other reasons, some researchers (Wolpoff et al., 2002) suggest that at this time, "ape" may be a better classification for *Sahelanthropus.* As we have previously said, the best-defining anatomical characteristics of hominins relate to bipedal locomotion. Unfortunately, no postcranial elements have been recovered from Chad—at least not yet. Consequently, we do not yet know the locomotor behavior of *Sahelanthropus*, and this raises even more fundamental questions: What if further finds show this form not to be bipedal? Should we still consider it a hominin? What, then, are the defining characteristics of our lineage? For all these reasons, several paleoanthropologists have recently grown more skeptical regarding the hominin status of all the pre-australopith finds, and Bernard Wood (2010) prefers to call them "possible hominins."

Probably living at about the same time as *Sahelanthropus*, two other very early (possible) hominin genera have been found at sites in central Kenya in the Tugen Hills and from the Middle Awash area of northeastern Ethiopia. The earlier of these finds (dated by radiometric methods to around 6 mya) comes from the Tugen Hills and includes mostly dental remains, but also some quite complete lower limb bones. These fossils have been placed in a separate early hominin genus called *Orrorin.* The postcranial remains are especially important, since they seem to indicate bipedal locomotion (Pickford and Senut, 2001; Senut et al., 2001; Galik et al., 2004; Richmond and Jungers, 2008). As a result of these further analyses, *Orrorin* is the pre-australopith generally recognized as having the best evidence to establish it as a hominin (compared to less clear evidence for *Sahelanthropus* and *Ardipithecus*).

The last group of possible hominins dating to the late Miocene (that is, earlier than 5 mya) comes from the Middle Awash in the Afar Triangle of Ethiopia. Radiometric dating places the age of these fossils in the very late Miocene, 5.8 to 5.2 mya. The fossil remains themselves are very fragmentary. Some of the dental remains resemble some later fossils from the Middle Awash (discussed shortly), and Yohannes Haile-Selassie, the researcher who first found and described these earlier materials, has provisionally assigned them to the genus *Ardipithecus* (Haile-Selassie et al., 2004). (See "At a Glance: Pre-Australopith Discoveries" on p. 290.) In addition, some postcranial elements have been preserved—most informatively a toe bone, a phalanx from the middle of the foot (see Appendix A, Fig. A-8). From clues in this bone, Haile-Selassie concludes that this primate was a well-adapted biped (once again, the best-supporting evidence of hominin status).

From another million years or so later in the geological record in Ethiopia's Middle Awash region, a very large and significant assemblage of fossil hominins has been discovered at a site called **Aramis**. Radiometric dating firmly places these remains at about 4.4 mya. The site, represented by a 6-foot-thick bed of bones, has yielded more than 6,000 fossils. These abundant finds include both large and small vertebrates—birds and other reptiles and even very small mammals. Additionally, fossil wood and pollen samples have been recovered. All this information is important for understanding the environments in which these ancient hominins lived (**Fig. 10-10**).

Hominin fossil remains from Aramis include several individuals, the most noteworthy being a partial

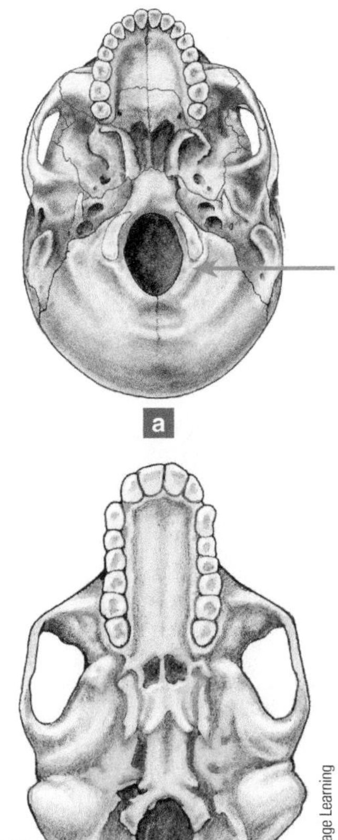

▲ **Figure 10-9** Position of the foramen magnum in (**a**) a human and (**b**) a chimpanzee. Note the more forward position in the human cranium.

Aramis (air-ah-miss)

▸ **Figure 10-10** Tim White and Yohannes Hailie-Selassie search the Aramis site, looking for even the tiniest of fossil fragments of *Ardipithecus*.

David L. Brill/Atlanta

skeleton. From this important site a total of at least 36 other hominins are represented by isolated teeth, cranial bones, and a few limb bones. All the bones were extremely fragile and fragmentary and required many years of incredibly painstaking effort to clean and reconstruct. Indeed, it took 15 years before the partial skeleton was in good enough condition to be intensively studied. But the wait was well worth it, and in 2009, Tim White and colleagues published their truly remarkable finds. By far the most informative fossil is the partial skeleton. Even though it was found crushed and fragmented, the years of work and computer imaging have now allowed researchers to interpret this 4.4-million-year-old individual. Nicknamed "Ardi," this individual has more than 50 percent of its skeleton represented; however, since it was found in such poor condition, any reconstruction must be seen as provisional and open to varying interpretations. Ardi has been sexed as female and contains several key portions, including a skull, a pelvis, and almost complete hands and feet (White et al., 2009; **Fig. 10-11**).

Ardi's brain size, estimated between 300 and 350 cm^3, is quite small, being no larger than a chimpanzee's. However, it is much like that seen in *Sahelanthropus*, and overall the skulls of the two hominins also appear to be similar. The preservation of much of the postcranial skeleton is potentially crucial, because key body elements, such as the pelvis and the foot, are only very rarely discovered. This is the *earliest* hominin for which we have so many different parts of the body represented, and it permits researchers to hypothesize more confidently about body size and proportions and, perhaps most crucially of all, the mode of locomotion.

Height is estimated at close to 4 feet, with a body weight of around 110 pounds. Compared to other early hominins, such a body size would be similar to that of a male and well above average for a female (**Table 10.1**). The pelvis and foot are preserved well enough to allow good-quality computer reconstructions. According to White and colleagues, both areas of the body show key anatomical changes indicating that *Ardipithecus* was a competent biped. For example, the ilium is short and broad (see Figs. 10-2 and 10-3), and the foot has been modified to act as a prop for propulsion during walking.

However, Ardi also presents some big surprises. While the shape of the ilium seems to show bipedal ability, other parts of the pelvis show more ancestral ("primitive") hominoid characteristics. In fact, the paleoanthropologists who analyzed the skeleton concluded that Ardi likely walked quite adequately but might well have had difficulty running (Lovejoy et al., 2009a, b). The foot is also an odd mix of features, showing a big toe that is highly divergent and capable of considerable grasping. Some researchers are not convinced that Ardi was bipedal, and considering all her other primitive characteristics, some have questioned whether *Ardipithecus* was really a hominin at all (Sarmiento, 2010). The extreme degree of reconstruction that was required (for the skull and pelvis especially) adds further uncertainty to understanding this crucial discovery. One thing that everyone agrees on is that Ardi was an able climber who likely was well adapted to walking on all fours along the tops of branches. It seems clear that she spent a lot of time in the trees.

Accepting for the moment that *Ardipithecus* was a hominin, it was a very primitive one, displaying an array of characteristics quite distinct from all later members of our lineage. In fact, its combination of characteristics is very odd and unique among our lineage. The new evidence that Ardi provides has not convinced all paleoanthropologists that *Ardipithecus* or any of the other very early pre-australopiths are hominins; indeed, Ardi's very odd anatomy has caused doubts to increase. One thing is for sure: It would take a considerable adaptive shift in the next 200,000 years to produce the more derived hominins we'll discuss in a moment. All of these considerations have not only intrigued professional anthropologists but also captured the imagination of the general public. When did the earliest member of our lineage first appear? The search goes on, and professional reputations are made and lost in this quest.

Another intriguing aspect of all these late Miocene/early Pliocene locales (that is, Toros-Menalla, Tugen Hills, early Middle Awash sites, and Aramis) relates to the ancient environments associated with these earliest hominins. Rather than the more open grassland savanna habitats so characteristic of most later hominin sites, the environment at all these early locales is more heavily forested. Perhaps at Aramis and these other ancient sites we are seeing the very beginnings of hominin divergence, not long after the division from the African apes.

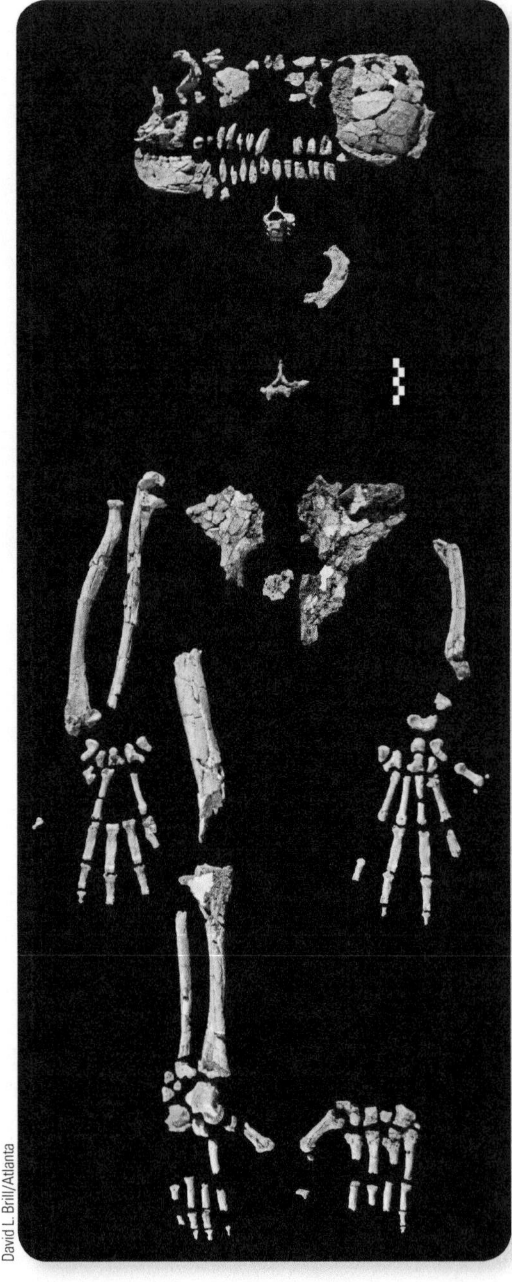

▸ **Figure 10-11** A mostly complete (but fragmented) skeleton of *Ardipithecus*. Dating to about 4.4 mya, this is the earliest hominin skeleton yet found containing so many different portions of the body.

Table 10.1 Estimated Body Weights and Stature in Plio-Pleistocene Hominins

	Body Weight		Stature	
	Male	Female	Male	Female
A. afarensis	45 kg (99 lb)	29 kg (64 lb)	151 cm (59 in.)	105 cm (41 in.)
A. africanus	41 kg (90 lb)	30 kg (65 lb)	138 cm (54 in.)	115 cm (45 in.)
A. robustus	40 kg (88 lb)	32 kg (70 lb)	132 cm (52 in.)	110 cm (43 in.)
A. boisei	49 kg (108 lb)	34 kg (75 lb)	137 cm (54 in.)	124 cm (49 in.)
H. habilis	52 kg (114 lb)	32 kg (70 lb)	157 cm (62 in.)	125 cm (49 in.)

Source: After McHenry, 1992. Note: Reno et al. (2003) conclude that sexual dimorphism in *A. afarensis* was considerably less than shown here.

At a Glance

Key Pre-Australopith Discoveries

Date	Region	Hominin	Site	Evolutionary Significance
4.4 mya	East Africa	*Ardipithecus ramidus*	Aramis	Large collection of fossils, including partial skeletons; bipedal, but derived.
5.8–5.2 mya		*Ardipithecus*	Middle Awash	Fragmentary, but possibly bipedal.
~6.0 mya		*Orrorin tugenensis*	Tugen Hills	First hominin with post-cranial remains; possibly bipedal.
~7.0–6.0 mya	Central Africa	*Sahelanthropus tchadensis*	Toros-Menalla	Oldest potential hominin; well-preserved cranium; very small-brained; bipedal?

Australopiths (4.2 to 1.2 mya)

The best-known, most widely distributed, and most diverse of the early African hominins are colloquially called **australopiths**. In fact, this varied and highly successful group of hominins is made up of two closely related genera, *Australopithecus* and *Paranthropus*. These hominins have an established time range of over 3 million years, stretching back as early as 4.2 mya and not becoming extinct until apparently close to 1 mya—making them the longest-enduring hominins yet documented. In addition, these hominins have been found in all the major geographical areas of Africa that have, to date, produced early hominin finds, namely, South Africa, central Africa (Chad), and East Africa. From all these areas combined, there appears to have been considerable complexity in terms of evolutionary diversity, with numerous species now recognized by most paleoanthropologists.

There are two major subgroups of australopiths: an earlier one that is more anatomically primitive and a later one that is much more derived. These earlier australopiths, dated 4.2 to 3.0 mya, show several more primitive (ancestral) hominin characteristics than the later australopith group, whose members are more derived, some extremely so. These more derived hominins lived after 2.5 mya and are composed of two different genera, together represented by at least five different species. (See Appendix C on the Anthropology CourseMate at Cengagebrain.com for a complete listing and more information about early hominin fossil finds.)

Given the 3-million-year time range as well as quite varied ecological niches, there are numerous intriguing adaptive differences among these varied australopith species. We'll discuss the major adaptations of the different species in a moment. But first let's emphasize the major features that all australopiths share:

1. They are all clearly bipedal (although not necessarily identical to *Homo* in this regard).
2. They all have relatively small brains (at least compared to *Homo*).

australopiths A colloquial name referring to a diverse group of Plio-Pleistocene African hominins. Australopiths are the most abundant and widely distributed of all early hominins and are also the most completely studied.

3. They all have large teeth, particularly the back teeth, with thick to very thick enamel on the molars.

In short, then, all these australopith species are relatively small-brained, big-toothed bipeds.

The earliest australopiths, dating to 4.2 to 3.0 mya, come from East Africa from a couple of sites in northern Kenya as well as two other sites in the Middle Awash region of Ethiopia (in the same area where *Ardipithecus* was discovered). Among the fossil finds of those earliest australopiths so far discovered, a few postcranial pieces clearly indicate that locomotion was bipedal. There are, however, a few primitive features in the dentition, including a large canine and a **sectorial** lower first premolar (see Fig. 10-8).

Since these particular fossils have initially been interpreted as more primitive than all the later members of the genus *Australopithecus*, paleoanthropologists have provisionally assigned them to a separate species. This important fossil species is now called *Australopithecus anamensis*, and some researchers suggest that it is a potential ancestor for many later australopiths as well as perhaps early members of the genus *Homo* (White et al., 2006) (see **Fig. 10-12**).

▲ **Figure 10-12** Fossil remains of *Australopithecus anamensis* from the Middle Awash region of Ethiopia. In addition to teeth and jaw fragments, several postcranial pieces were also found (hand and foot bones, pieces of vertebrae, and part of a thigh bone—that is, a femur).

Australopithecus afarensis

Slightly later and much more complete remains of *Australopithecus* have come primarily from the sites of Hadar (in Ethiopia) and Laetoli (in Tanzania). Much of this material has been known for over three decades, and the fossils have been very well studied; indeed, in certain instances, they are quite famous. For example, the Lucy skeleton was discovered at Hadar in 1974, and the Laetoli footprints were first found in 1978. These hominins are classified as members of the species *Australopithecus afarensis*.

Literally thousands of footprints have been found at Laetoli, representing more than 20 different kinds of animals (Pliocene elephants, horses, pigs, giraffes, antelopes, hyenas, and an abundance of hares). Several hominin footprints have also been found, including a trail more than 75 feet long made by at least two—and perhaps three—individuals (Leakey and Hay, 1979) (**Fig. 10-13**). Such discoveries of well-preserved hominin footprints are extremely important in furthering our understanding of human evolution. For the first time, we can make *definite* statements regarding the locomotor pattern and stature of early hominins.

Studies of these impression patterns clearly show that the mode of locomotion of these hominins was bipedal (Day and Wickens, 1980). Some researchers, however, have concluded that *A. afarensis* was not bipedal in quite the same way that modern humans are. From detailed comparisons with modern humans, estimates

sectorial Adapted for cutting or shearing; among primates, this term refers to the compressed (side-to-side) first lower premolar, which functions as a shearing surface with the upper canine.

▶ **Figure 10-13** Hominin footprint from Laetoli, Tanzania. Note the deep impression of the heel and the large toe (arrow) in line (adducted) with the other toes.

of stride length, cadence, and speed of walking have been ascertained, indicating that the Laetoli hominins moved in a slower ("strolling") fashion with a rather short stride.

One extraordinary discovery at Hadar is the Lucy skeleton (**Fig. 10-14**), found eroding out of a hillside by Don Johanson. This fossil is scientifically designated as Afar Locality (AL) 288-1 but is usually just called Lucy (after the Beatles song "Lucy in the Sky with Diamonds"). Representing almost 40 percent of a skeleton, this is one of the most complete individuals from anywhere in the world for the entire period before about 100,000 years ago.

Because the Laetoli area was covered periodically by ashfalls from nearby volcanic eruptions, accurate dating is possible and has provided dates of 3.7 to 3.5 mya. Dating from the Hadar region hasn't proved as straightforward; however, more complete dating calibration using a variety of techniques has determined a range of 3.9 to 3.0 mya for the hominin discoveries from this area.

Several hundred *A. afarensis* specimens, representing a minimum of 60 individuals (and perhaps as many as 100), have been removed from Laetoli and Hadar. At present, these materials represent the largest *well-studied* collection of early hominins and as such are among the most significant of the hominins discussed in this chapter.

Without question, *A. afarensis* is more primitive than any of the other later australopith fossils from South or East Africa (discussed shortly). By *primitive* we mean that *A. afarensis* is less evolved in any particular direction than are later-occurring hominin species. That is, *A. afarensis* shares more primitive features with some late Miocene apes and with living great apes than do later hominins, who display more derived characteristics.

For example, the teeth of *A. afarensis* are quite primitive. The canines are often large pointed teeth. Moreover, the lower first premolar is semisectorial (that is, it provides a shearing surface for the upper canine), and the tooth rows are parallel, even converging somewhat toward the back of the mouth (**Fig. 10-15**).

The cranial portions that are preserved also display several primitive hominoid characteristics, including a crest in the back as well as several primitive features of the cranial base. Cranial capacity estimates for *A. afarensis* show a mixed pattern compared to later hominins. A provisional estimate for the one partially complete cranium—apparently a large individual—gives a figure of 500 cm^3, but another even more fragmentary cranium is apparently quite a bit smaller and has been estimated at about 375 cm^3 (Holloway, 1983). Thus for some individuals (males?), *A. afarensis* is well within the range of other australopith species (see "A Closer Look: Cranial Capacity" on p. 293); but others (females?) may have a significantly smaller cranial capacity. However, a detailed depiction of cranial size for *A. afarensis* is not possible at this time; this part of the skeleton is unfortunately too poorly represented. One thing is clear: *A. afarensis* had a small brain, probably averaging for the whole species not much over 420 cm^3.

On the other hand, a large assortment of postcranial pieces representing almost all portions of the body of A. *afarensis* has been found. Initial impressions suggest that relative to lower limbs, the upper limbs are longer than in modern humans (also a primitive Miocene ape condition). (This statement does not mean that the arms of *A. afarensis* were longer than the legs.) In addition, the wrist, hand, and foot bones show several differences from modern humans (Susman et al., 1985). From such excellent postcranial evidence, stature can be confidently estimated: *A. afarensis* was a short hominin. From her partial skeleton, Lucy is estimated to have been only 3 to 4 feet tall. However, Lucy—as demonstrated by her pelvis—was probably a female, and there is evidence of larger individuals as well. The most economical hypothesis explaining this variation is that *A. afarensis* was quite sexually dimorphic: The larger individuals are male, and the smaller ones, such as Lucy, are female. Estimates of male stature can be approximated from the larger footprints at Laetoli, inferring a height of not quite 5 feet. If we accept this interpretation, *A. afarensis* was a very sexually dimorphic form indeed. In fact, for overall body size, this species may have been as dimorphic as *any* living primate (that is, as much as gorillas, orangutans, or baboons).

Significant further discoveries of *A. afarensis* have come from Ethiopia in the last few years, including two further partial skeletons. The first of these is a mostly complete skeleton of an *A. afarensis* juvenile discovered at the Dikika locale in northeastern Ethiopia, very near the Hadar sites mentioned earlier (**Fig. 10-16**). What's more, the juvenile skeleton comes from the same geological horizon as Hadar, with very similar dating: 3.3 to 3.2 mya (Alemseged et al., 2006).

This find of a 3-year-old hominin is remarkable because it's the first example of a very well-preserved immature

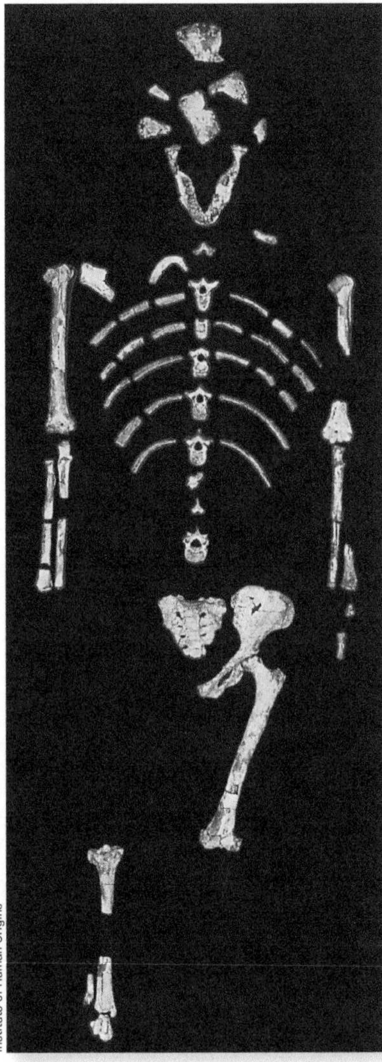

▲ **Figure 10-14** (**a**) "Lucy," a partial hominin skeleton, discovered at Hadar in 1974. This individual is assigned to *Australopithecus afarensis*. (**b**) Artist's reconstruction of a female *A. afarensis* derived from study of the Lucy skeleton.

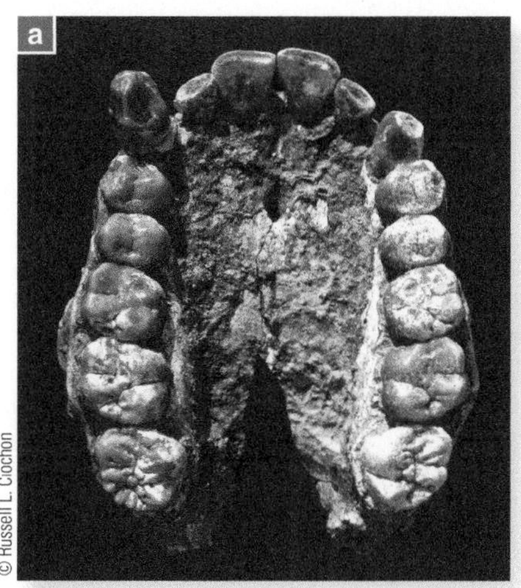

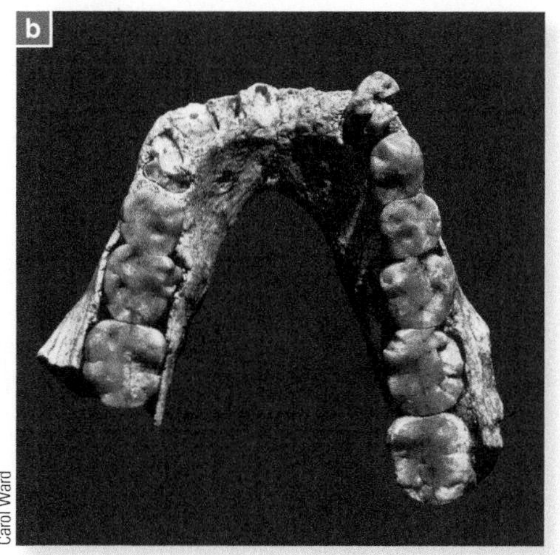

▶ **Figure 10-15** Jaws of *Australopithecus afarensis*. (**a**) Maxilla, AL 200-1a, from Hadar, Ethiopia. (Note the parallel tooth rows and large canines.) (**b**) Mandible, LH 4, from Laetoli, Tanzania. This fossil is the type specimen for the species *Australopithecus afarensis*.

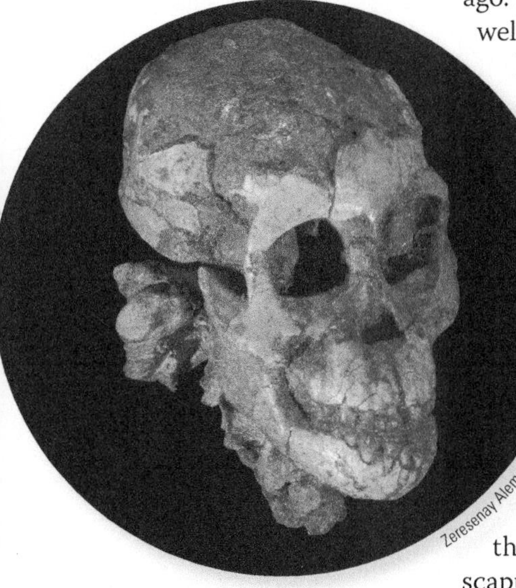

▲ **Figure 10-16** Complete skull with attached vertebral column of the juvenile skeleton from Dikika, Ethiopia (dated to about 3.3 mya).

hominin prior to about 100,000 years ago. From the individual's extremely well-preserved teeth, scientists hypothesize that she was female. A comprehensive study of her developmental biology has already begun, and many more revelations are surely in store as the Dikika fossil is more completely cleaned and studied. Initial results, accounting for her immature age, show a skeletal pattern quite similar to what we'd expect in an *A. afarensis* adult. What's more, the limb proportions, anatomy of the hands and feet, and shape of the scapula (shoulder blade) reveal a similar "mixed" pattern of locomotion. The foot and lower limb indicate that this young hominin would have been a terrestrial biped. Further analysis of her shoulder confirms that she was also capable of climbing about quite ably in the trees (Green and Alemseged, 2012).

The second recently discovered *A. afarensis* partial skeleton comes from the Woranso-Mille research area in the central Afar, only about 30 miles north of Hadar (Haile-Selassie et al., 2010). The dating places the find at close to 3.6 mya (almost 400,000 years earlier than Lucy). Moreover, this individual was considerably larger than Lucy and likely was male. Analysis of bones preserved in this new find reinforces what was previously known about *A. afarensis* as well as adding some further insights. The large degree of sexual dimorphism and well-adapted bipedal locomotion agree with prior evidence.

What makes *A. afarensis* a hominin? The answer is revealed by its manner of locomotion. From the abundant limb bones recovered from Hadar and other locales, as well as those beautiful footprints from Laetoli, we know unequivocally that *A. afarensis* walked bipedally when on the ground. (At present, we do not have nearly such good evidence concerning locomotion for *any* of the earlier hominin finds.) Whether Lucy and her contemporaries still spent considerable time in the trees and just how efficiently they walked have become topics of some controversy. Most researchers, however, agree that *A. afarensis* was an efficient habitual biped while on the ground. These hominins were also clearly *obligate* bipeds, which would have hampered their climbing abilities but would not necessarily have precluded arboreal behavior altogether.

Australopithecus afarensis is a crucial hominin group. Since it comes after the earliest, poorly known group of pre-australopith hominins, but prior to all later australopiths as well as *Homo*, it is an evolutionary bridge, linking together much of what we assume are the major patterns of early hominin evolution. The fact that there are many well-preserved fossils and that they have been so well studied also adds to the paleoanthropological significance of *A. afarensis*. The consensus among

A Closer Look

Cranial Capacity

Cranial capacity, usually reported in cubic centimeters, is a measure of brain size, or volume. The brain itself, of course, doesn't fossilize. However, the space once occupied by brain tissue (the inside of the cranial vault) is sometimes preserved, at least in those cases where fairly complete crania are recovered.

For purposes of comparison, it's easy to obtain cranial capacity estimates for contemporary species (including humans) from analyses of skeletonized specimens in museum collections. From studies of this nature, estimated cranial capacities for modern hominoids have been determined as follows (Tobias, 1971, 1983):

	Range (cm³)	**Aveage (cm³)**
Human	1,150–1,750*	1,325
Chimpanzee	285–500	395
Gorilla	340–752	506
Orangutan	276–540	411
Bonobo	—	350

*The range of cranial capacity for modern humans is very large—in fact, even greater than that shown (which approximates cranial capacity for the majority of contemporary *H. sapiens* populations).

These data for living hominoids can then be compared with those obtained for early hominins:

	Average (cm³)
Sahelanthropus	~350
Orrorin	Not currently known
Ardipithecus	~420
Australopithecus anamensis	Not currently known
Australopithecus afarensis	438
Later australopiths	410–530
Early members of genus *Homo*	631

As the tabulations indicate, cranial capacity estimates for australopiths fall within the range of most modern great apes, and gorillas actually average slightly greater cranial capacity than that seen in most early hominins. It's important to remember, however, that gorillas are very large animals, whereas most early hominins probably weighed on the order of 100 pounds (see Table 10-1). Since brain size is partially correlated with body size, comparing such different-sized animals can't be justified. Compared to living chimpanzees (most of which are slightly larger than early hominins) and bonobos (which are somewhat smaller), australopiths had *proportionately* about 10 percent bigger brains; so we would say that these early hominins were more *encephalized.*

most experts over the last several years has been that *A. afarensis* is a potentially strong candidate as the ancestor of *all* later hominins. Some ongoing analysis has recently challenged this hypothesis (Rak et al., 2007), but at least for the moment, this new interpretation has not been widely accepted. Still, it reminds us that science is an intellectual pursuit that constantly reevaluates older views and seeks to provide more systematic explanations about the world around us. When it comes to understanding human evolution, we should always be aware that things might change. So stay tuned.

A Contemporaneous and *Very* Different Kind of Hominin

From Woranso-Mille, the same site in the central Afar where researchers recently discovered a partial *A. afarensis* skeleton, they have also uncovered a partial foot dated to about 3.4 mya (Haile-Selassie et al, 2012). However, the partial foot remains, which include several nicely preserved toe bones, are very different from those of *A. afarensis* and other obligate bipeds.

The new find shows a divergent opposable big toe and other ape-like features that strongly suggesting that this animal was a good climber. At the same time there are some other characteristics suggesting that it probably could walk bipedally on the ground, although not in a manner like *A. afarensis* or any later hominin. This odd mix of characteristics looks most like that of *Ardipithecus*, which lived a full million years earlier. Without more complete fossil remains, it's impossible, for now, to assign this new find to a particular species. One thing is for sure: It isn't *A. afarensis*! So, there were two different lineages living side by side, each with very different foot anatomy and varied forms of locomotion. The researchers who have studied these new foot fossils as well as some other experts (Lieberman, 2012) think it was a hominin that was at least partially bipedal. On both counts, we'll have to wait and see.

Later More Derived Australopiths (3.0 to 1.2 mya)

Following 3.0 mya, hominins became more diverse in Africa. As they adapted to varied niches, australopiths became considerably more derived. In other words, they show physical changes making them quite distinct from their immediate ancestors.

In fact, there were at least three separate lineages of hominins living (in some cases side by side) between 2.0 and 1.2 mya. One of these is a later form of *Australopithecus*; another is represented by the highly derived three species that belong to the genus *Paranthropus*; and the last consists of early members of the genus *Homo*. Here we'll discuss *Paranthropus* and *Australopithecus*. *Homo* will be discussed in the next section.

The most derived australopiths are the various members of *Paranthropus*. While all australopiths are big-toothed, *Paranthropus* has the biggest teeth of all, especially as seen in its huge premolars and molars. Along with these massive back teeth, these hominins show a variety of other specializations related to powerful chewing (**Fig. 10-17**). For example, they all have large deep lower jaws and large attachments for muscles associated with chewing. In fact, these chewing muscles are so prominent that major anatomical alterations evolved in the architecture of their face and skull vault. In particular, the *Paranthropus* face is flatter than that of any other australopith; the broad cheekbones (to which the masseter muscle attaches) flare out; and a ridge develops on top of the skull (this is called a **sagittal crest**, and it's where the temporal muscle attaches).

All these morphological features indicating strong chewing suggest that *Paranthropus* likely was adapted for a diet emphasizing rough vegetable foods. However, this does not mean that these very big-toothed hominins did not also eat a variety of other foods, perhaps including some meat. In fact, sophisticated recent chemical analyses of *Paranthropus* teeth suggest that their diet may have been quite varied (Sponheimer et al., 2006).

The first member of the *Paranthropus* evolutionary group (clade) comes from a site in northern Kenya on the west side of Lake Turkana. This key find is that of a nearly complete skull, called the "Black Skull" (owing to the chemical staining from manganese-rich soil during fossilization), dating to approximately 2.5 mya (**Fig. 10-18**). This skull, with a cranial capacity of only 410 cm^3, is among the smallest for any hominin known, and it has other primitive traits reminiscent of *A. afarensis*. For example, there's a compound crest in the back of the skull, the upper face projects considerably, and the upper dental row converges in back (Kimbel et al., 1988).

But here's what makes the Black Skull so fascinating: Mixed into this array of distinctively primitive traits are a host of derived ones that link it to other, later *Paranthropus* species (including a broad face, a very large palate, and a large area for the back teeth). This mosaic of features seems to place this individual between earlier *A. afarensis* on the one hand and the later *Paranthropus* species on the other. Because of its unique position in hominin evolution, the Black Skull (and the population it represents) has been placed in a new species, *Paranthropus aethiopicus*.

Around 2 mya, different varieties of even more derived members of the *Paranthropus* lineage were on the scene in East Africa. As well documented by finds dated after 2 mya from Olduvai and East Turkana, *Paranthropus* continued to have a relatively small cranial capacity (ranging from 510 to 530 cm^3) and a very large, broad face with massive back teeth and lower jaws.

sagittal crest A ridge of bone that runs down the middle of the cranium like a short Mohawk. This serves as the attachment for the large temporal muscles, indicating strong chewing.

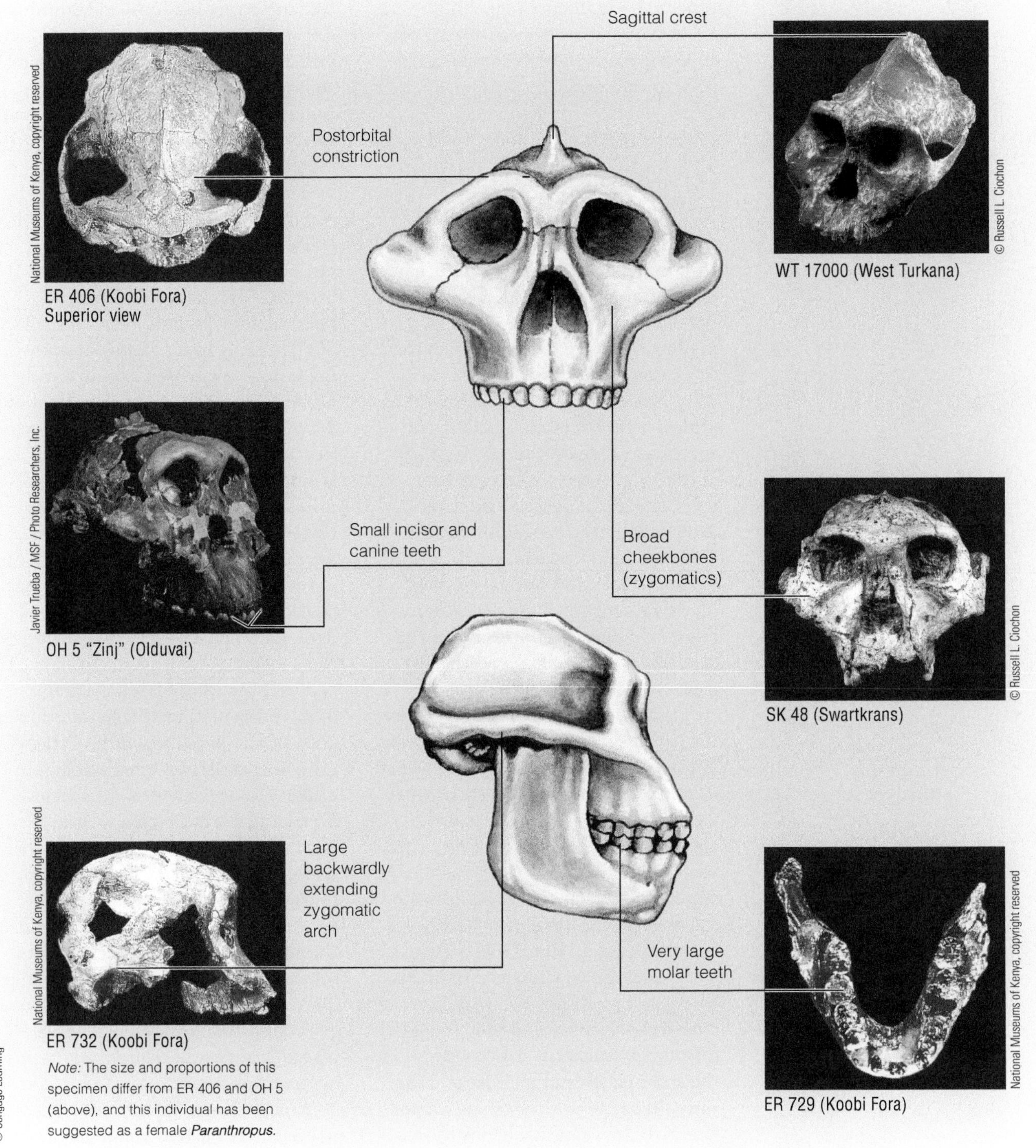

The larger (probably male) individuals also show the characteristic raised ridge (sagittal crest) along the midline of the cranium. Females are not as large or as robust as the males, indicating a fair degree of sexual dimorphism. In any case, the East African *Paranthropus* individuals are all extremely robust in terms of their teeth and jaws—although in overall body

▲ **Figure 10-17** Morphology and variation in *Paranthropus*. (Note both typical features and range of variation as shown in different specimens.)

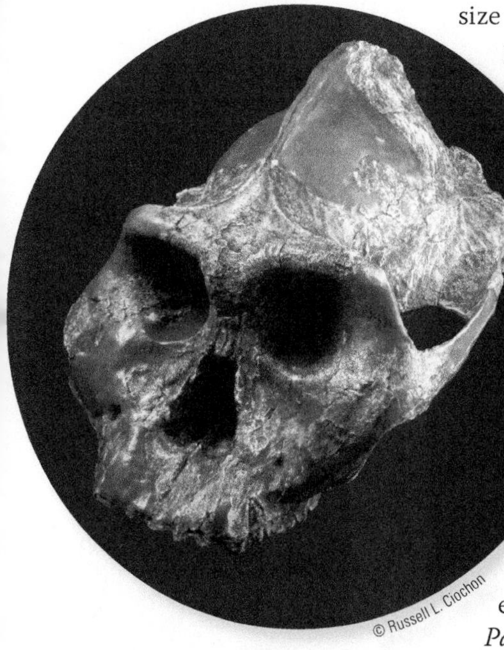

size they are much like other australopiths. Since these somewhat later East African *Paranthropus** fossils are so robust, they are usually placed in their own separate species, *Paranthropus boisei*.

Paranthropus fossils have also been found at several sites in South Africa. The geological context in South Africa usually does not allow as precise chronometric dating as is possible in East Africa. Based on less precise dating methods, *Paranthropus* in South Africa existed about 2.0 to 1.2 mya.

▲ **Figure 10-18** The "Black Skull," discovered at West Lake Turkana. This specimen is usually assigned to *Paranthropus aethiopicus*. It's called the Black Skull because of its dark color due to the fossilization (mineralization) process.

Paranthropus in South Africa is very similar to its close cousin in East Africa, but it's not quite as dentally robust. As a result, paleoanthropologists prefer to regard South African *Paranthropus* as a distinct species—one called *Paranthropus robustus*.

What became of *Paranthropus*? After 1 mya, these hominins seem to have vanished without descendants. Nevertheless, we should be careful not to think of them as "failures." After all, they lasted for 1.5 million years, during which time they expanded over a considerable area of sub-Saharan Africa. Moreover, while their extreme dental/chewing adaptations may seem peculiar to us, they represent a fascinating "evolutionary experiment" in hominin evolution. And it was an innovation that worked for a long time.

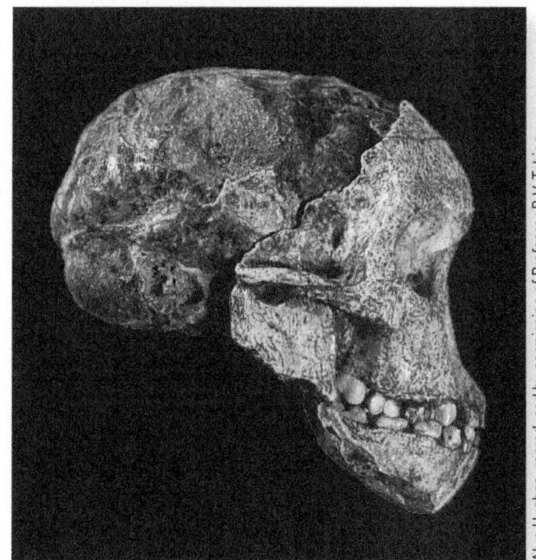

▲ **Figure 10-19** The Taung child's skull, discovered in 1924. There is a fossilized endocast of the brain in back, with the face and lower jaw in front.

Still, these big-toothed cousins of ours did eventually die out. It remains to us, the descendants of another hominin lineage, to find their fossils, study them, and ponder what these creatures were like.

No fossil finds of genus *Australopithecus* more recent than 3 mya have yet been found in East Africa. As you know, their close *Paranthropus* kin were doing quite well during this time. Whether *Australopithecus* actually did become extinct in East Africa following 3 mya or whether we just haven't yet found their fossils is impossible to say.

South Africa, however, is another story. A very well-known *Australopithecus* species has been found at four sites in southernmost Africa, in a couple of cases in limestone caves very close to where *Paranthropus* fossils have also been found.

In fact, the very first early hominin discovery from Africa (indeed, from *anywhere*) came from the Taung site and was discovered back in 1924. The story of the discovery of the beautifully preserved child's skull from Taung is a fascinating tale (**Fig. 10-19**). When first published in 1925 by a young anatomist named Raymond Dart (**Fig. 10-20**), most experts were unimpressed by the small-brained specimen of a 3- to 4-year-old child. They believed that our earliest ancestors would be easily identifiable by their larger brains and thought of Africa as an unlikely place for the origins of hominins. These skeptics, who for a long time had been focused on European and Asian hominin finds, were initially unprepared to acknowledge Africa's central place in human evolution. Only years later, following many more African discoveries from other sites, did professional opinion shift. With this admittedly slow scientific awareness came the eventual consensus that the Taung specimen (which Dart classified as *Australopithecus africanus*) was indeed an ancient member of the hominin family tree.

Like other australopiths, the "Taung child" (the type specimen) and other *A. africanus* individuals (**Fig. 10-21**) were small-brained, with an adult cranial capacity of about 440 cm^3. In fact, the Taung child is quite remarkable for its preservation of a natural **endocast**. It was this fossilized mold of the external morphology of the right side of the child's brain that led Dart to recognize it as hominin and not an ape.

endocast A solid impression of the inside of the skull vault, often preserving details relating to the size and surface features of the brain.

*Note that these later East African *Paranthropus* finds are at least 500,000 years later than the earlier species (*P. aethiopicus*, exemplified by the Black Skull).

As a recent reassessment of this brain mold has shown, *A. africanus* already had a pattern of brain development more in line with that of later hominins (Falk et al., 2012). *A africanus* was also big-toothed relative to later hominins, although not as extremely so as *Paranthropus*. Moreover, from very well-preserved postcranial remains from Sterkfontein, we know that these individuals were also were well-adapted bipeds. The ongoing excavation of the remarkably complete skeleton at Sterkfontein should tell us a lot about *A. africanus*' locomotion, body size and proportions, and much more (**Fig. 10-22**).

The precise dating of *A. africanus*, as with most other South African hominins, has been disputed. Over the last several years, it's been assumed that this species existed as far back as 3.3 mya. However, the most recent analysis suggests that *A. africanus* lived approximately between 3 and 2 mya (Walker et al., 2006; Wood, 2010) (**Fig. 10-23**).

New Connections: A Transitional Australopith?

As we'll see in the next section, almost all the evidence for the earliest appearance of our genus, *Homo*, has come from East Africa. So it's no surprise that most researchers have assumed that *Homo* probably first evolved in this region of Africa.

However, new and remarkably well-preserved fossil discoveries from South Africa may challenge this view. In 2008, paleoanthropologists discovered two partial skeletons at the Malapa Cave, located just a few miles from Sterkfontein and Swartkrans (see Fig. 10-6). Actually, the first find was made

Alun Hughes

◂ **Figure 10-20** Raymond Dart, shown working in his laboratory.

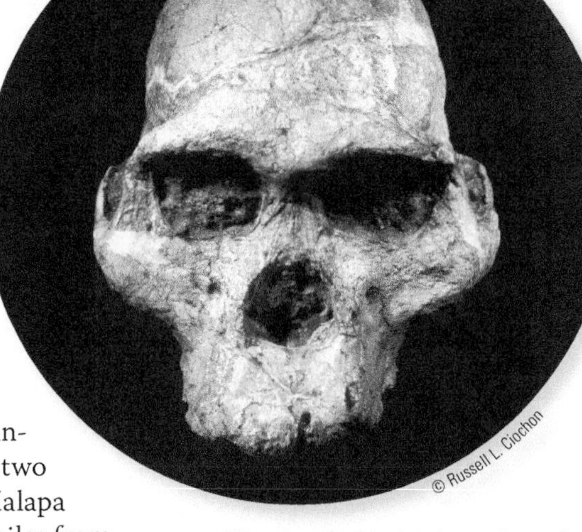

▴ **Figure 10-21** Adult cranium of *Australopithecus africanus* from Sterkfontein.

◂ **Figure 10-22** Paleoanthropologist Ronald Clarke carefully excavates a 2-million-year-old skeleton from the limestone matrix at Sterkfontein Cave. Clearly seen are the cranium (with articulated mandible) and the upper arm bone.

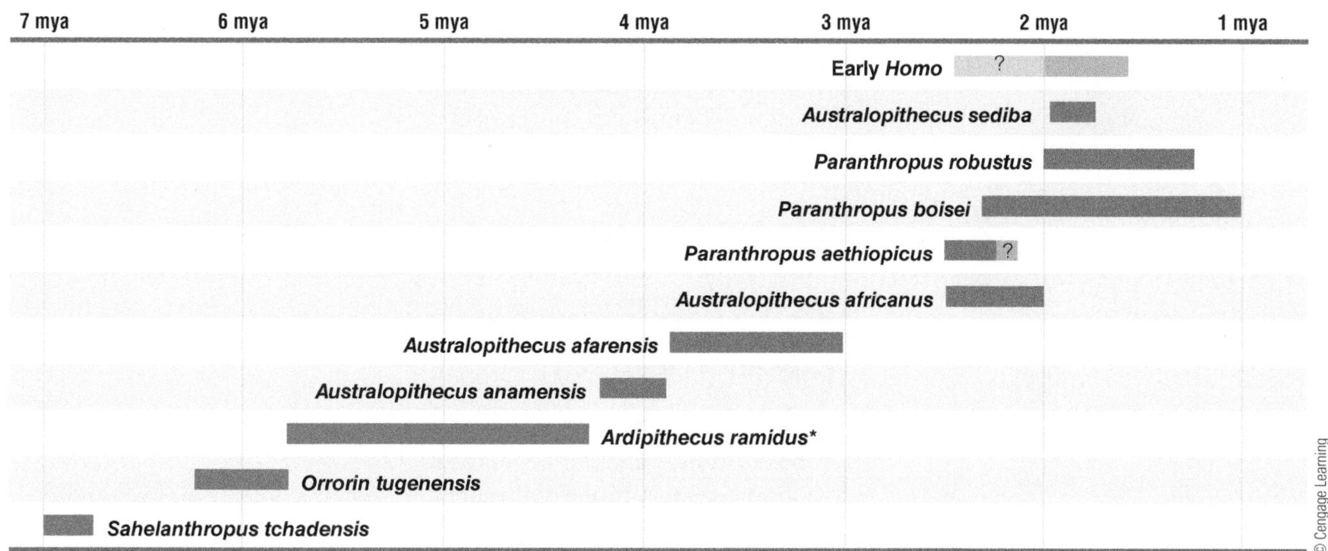

▲ **Figure 10-23** Time line of early African hominins. Note that most dates are approximations. Question marks indicate those estimates that are most tentative.

by the lead researcher's 9-year-old son, Matthew, while out walking the family dog. His father (Lee Berger, from the University of Witwatersrand) and colleagues have been further investigating inside the cave, where several skeletons may be buried; they announced and described these finds in 2010 (Berger et al., 2010).

Using paleomagnetic dating as well as more precise radiometric techniques than have been used before in South Africa (Dirks et al., 2010; Pickering et al., 2011) (see Chapter 9), the fossils are dated to just a little less than 2 mya and show a fascinating mix of australopith characteristics along with some features more suggestive of *Homo*. Because of this unique anatomical combination, these fossils have been assigned to a new species, *Australopithecus sediba* (*sediba* means "wellspring" or "fountain" in the local language). Australopith-like characteristics seen in *A. sediba* include a small brain (estimated at 420 cm^3), the australopith shoulder joint, long arms with curved fingers, and several primitive traits in the feet. In these respects *A. sediba* most resembles *A. africanus*, its potential immediate South African predecessor.

University of the Witwatersrand, Lee Berger. Photo by Brett Eloff

▲ **Figure 10-24** *A. sediba* skull, found at Malapa Cave, South Africa.

On the other hand, some other aspects of *A. sediba* more resemble *Homo*. Among these characteristics are short fingers and possible indications of brain reorganization (see **Fig. 10-24**). All this is very new and quite complex. Indeed, initial paleoanthropological interpretations are highly varied (Balter, 2010; Pickering et al., 2011; Gibbons, 2011). It will take some time for experts to figure it out.

What's more, new dental evidence shows that *A. sediba* had a surpising diet, at least one that is unusual for a hominin. Using an array of methods—including stable carbon isotopes, phytolith residues in dental calculus, and dental microwear (see Chapter 9 for discussion of all three methods)—Amanda Henry and colleagues have analyzed teeth from both skeletons thus far excavated at Malapa (Henry et al., 2012). Their results indicate that *A. sediba* primarily ate leaves, fruit, wood, and bark, along with a few grasses. Unlike that seen in most other early hominins, there is no evidence of a dietary focus on grass resources or meat, which are more typically found in more open savanna habitats. Indeed,

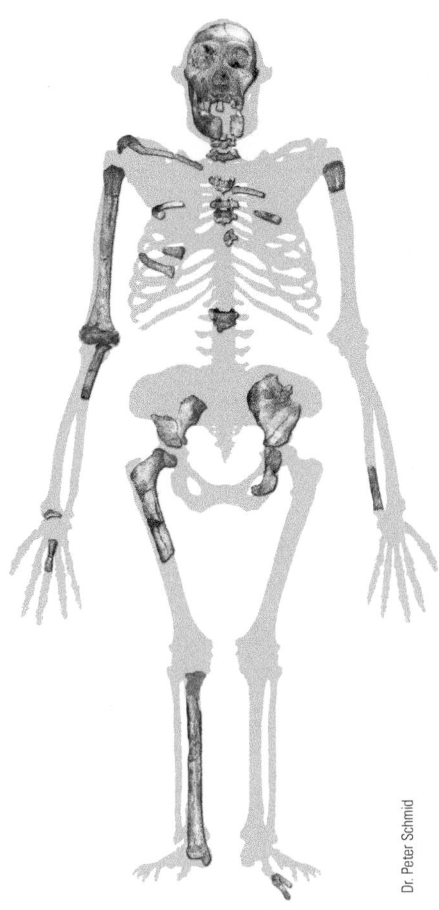

▲ **Figure 10-25** One of the two partial *A. sediba* skeletons so far discovered at Malapa Cave, showing those elements that were preserved.

A. sediba's diet appears to more closely resemble that of chimpanzees rather than that of most other hominins. The closest early hominin similarity is with *Ardipithecus*. These findings indicate that in anatomy as well as behavior, early hominins were an extremely varied group.

Remember, too, that there are more fossils still to be unearthed at Malapa. The initial consensus among paleoanthropologists is that *A. sediba* is quite different from other australopiths and shows a surprising and unique mix of primitive and derived characteristics. How it fits in with the origins of *Homo* remains to be determined. Certainly, more detailed studies of the *A. sediba* fossils, including further comparisons with other early hominins will help to further our understanding where *A. sediba* fits in (**Fig. 10-25**). For the moment, most paleoanthropologists still think that the best evidence for the origins of our genus comes from East Africa.

Closer Connections: Early *Homo* (2.0 to 1.4 mya)

In addition to the australopith remains, there's another largely contemporaneous hominin that is quite distinctive and thought to be more closely related to us. In fact, as best documented by fossil discoveries from Olduvai and East Turkana, these materials have been assigned to the genus *Homo*—and thus are different from all species assigned to either *Australopithecus* or *Paranthropus*.

The earliest appearance of genus *Homo* in East Africa may date prior to 2 mya (and thus considerably before *A. sediba*). A discovery in the 1990s from the Hadar area of Ethiopia suggested to many paleoanthropologists that early *Homo* was present in East Africa by 2.3 mya; however, we must be cautious, since the find is quite incomplete (including only one upper jaw) (Kimbel et al., 1996).

Better-preserved evidence of a **Plio-Pleistocene** hominin with a significantly larger brain than seen in australopiths was first suggested by Louis Leakey in the early 1960s on the basis of fragmentary remains found at Olduvai Gorge. Leakey and his colleagues gave a new species designation to these fossil remains, naming them *Homo habilis* (see **Fig. 10-26**). There may, in fact, have been more than one species of *Homo* living in Africa during the Plio-Pleistocene. Therefore, more generally, we'll refer to them all as "early *Homo*." The species *Homo habilis* comprises particularly those early *Homo* fossils from Olduvai and the Turkana Basin.

The *Homo habilis* material at Olduvai dates to about 1.8 mya, but

Plio-Pleistocene Pertaining to the Pliocene and first half of the Pleistocene, a time range of 5 to 1 mya. For this time period, numerous fossil hominins have been found in Africa.

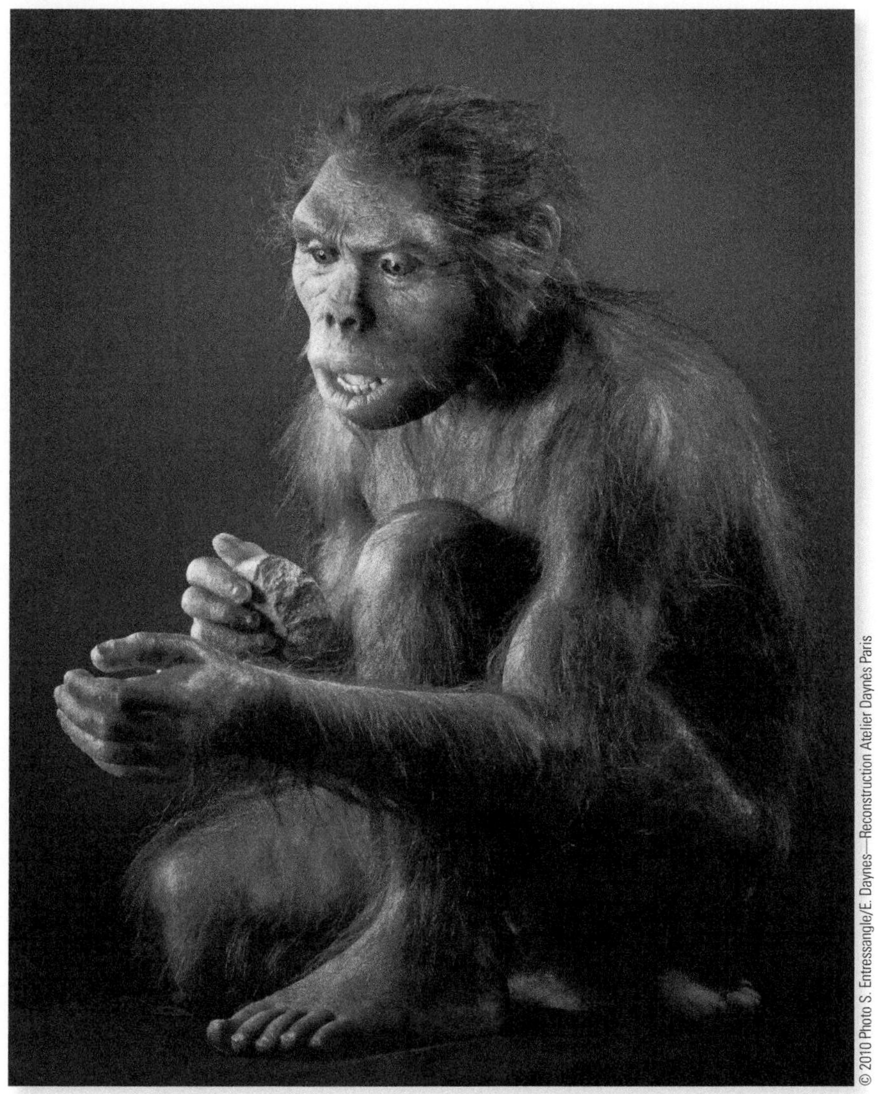

▲ **Figure 10-26** Artist's reconstruction of a female *Homo habilis* based on a cranium from East Lake Turkana. (Skull 1813; see photo of this specimen in Figure 10-28.)

owing to the fragmentary nature of the fossil remains, evolutionary interpretations have been difficult. The most immediately obvious feature distinguishing the *H. habilis* material from the australopiths is cranial size. For all the measurable early *Homo* skulls, the estimated average cranial capacity is 631 cm^3, compared to 520 cm^3 for all measurable *Paranthropus* specimens and 442 cm^3 for *Australopithecus* crania (McHenry, 1988), including *A. sediba* (see "A Closer Look: Cranial Capacity," p. 295). Early *Homo*, therefore, shows an increase in cranial size of about 20 percent over the larger of the australopiths and an even greater increase over some of the smaller-brained forms. In their initial description of *H. habilis*, Leakey and his associates also pointed to differences from australopiths in cranial shape and in tooth proportions.

The naming of this fossil material as *Homo habilis* ("handy man") was meaningful from two perspectives. First of all, Leakey argued that members of this group were the early Olduvai toolmakers. Second, and most significantly, by calling this group *Homo*, Leakey was arguing for at least *two separate branches* of hominin evolution in the Plio-Pleistocene. Clearly, only one could be on the main branch eventually leading to *Homo sapiens*. By labeling this new group *Homo* rather than *Australopithecus*, Leakey was guessing that he had found our ancestors.

Because the initial evidence was so fragmentary, most paleoanthropologists were reluctant to accept *H. habilis* as a valid species distinct from all australopiths. Later discoveries, especially from Lake Turkana, of better-preserved fossils have shed further light on early *Homo* in the Plio-Pleistocene. The most important of this additional material is a nearly complete cranium (**Fig. 10-27**). With a cranial capacity of 775 cm^3, this individual is well outside the known range for australopiths and actually overlaps the lower boundary for later species of *Homo* (that is, *H. erectus*, discussed in the next chapter). In addition, the shape of the skull vault is in many respects unlike that of australopiths. However, the face is still quite robust (Walker, 1976), and the fragments of tooth crowns that are preserved indicate that the back teeth in this individual were quite large.* The East Turkana early *Homo* material is generally contemporaneous with the Olduvai remains. The oldest date back to about 1.8 mya, but another specimen found a few years ago dates to as recently as 1.44 mya, making it by far

*In fact, some researchers have suggested that all these "early *Homo*" fossils are better classified as *Australopithecus* (Wood and Collard, 1999a).

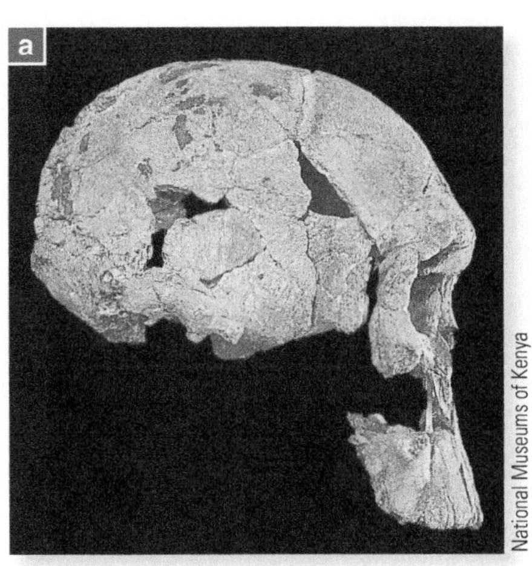

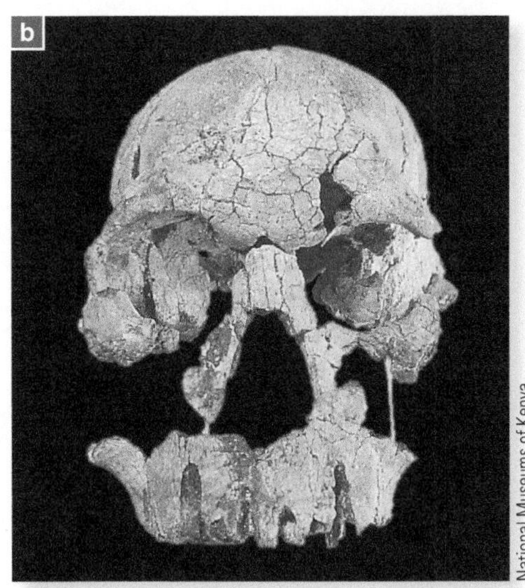

◂**Figure 10-27** A nearly complete early *Homo* cranium from East Lake Turkana (ER 1470), one of the most important single fossil hominin discoveries from East Africa. (**a**) Lateral view. (**b**) Frontal view.

the latest surviving early *Homo* fossil yet found (Spoor et al., 2007). In fact, this discovery indicates that a species of early *Homo* coexisted in East Africa for several hundred thousand years with *H. erectus*, with both species living in the exact same area on the eastern side of Lake Turkana. This new evidence raises numerous fascinating questions regarding how two closely related species existed for so long in the same region.

As in East Africa, early members of the genus *Homo* have also been found in South Africa, and these fossils are considered more distinctive of *Homo* than is the *transitional* australopith, *A. sediba*. At both Sterkfontein and Swartkrans, fragmentary remains have been recognized as most likely belonging to *Homo* (**Fig. 10-28** on p. 302).

On the basis of evidence from Olduvai, East Turkana, and Hadar, we can reasonably postulate that at least one species (and possibly two) of early *Homo* was present in East Africa perhaps before 2 mya, developing in parallel with an australopith species. These hominin lines lived contemporaneously for at least 1 million years, after which the australopiths apparently disappeared forever. One lineage of early *Homo* likely evolved into *H. erectus* about 1.8 mya. Any other species of early *Homo* became extinct sometime after 1.4 mya.

Interpretations: What Does It All Mean?

By this time, you may think that anthropologists are obsessed with finding small scraps buried in the ground and then giving them confusing numbers and taxonomic labels impossible to remember. But it's important to realize that the collection of all the basic fossil data is the foundation of human evolutionary research. Without fossils, our speculations would be largely hollow—and most certainly not scientifically testable. Several large, ongoing paleoanthropological projects are now collecting additional data in an attempt to answer some of the more perplexing questions about our evolutionary history.

The numbering of specimens, which may at times seem somewhat confusing, is an effort to keep the designations neutral and to make reference to each individual fossil as clear as possible. The formal naming of finds as *Australopithecus*, *Paranthropus*, or *Homo habilis* should come much later, since it involves a lengthy series of complex interpretations. Assigning generic and specific names to fossil finds is more than just a convenience; when we attach a particular label, such as *A. afarensis*, to a particular fossil, we should be fully

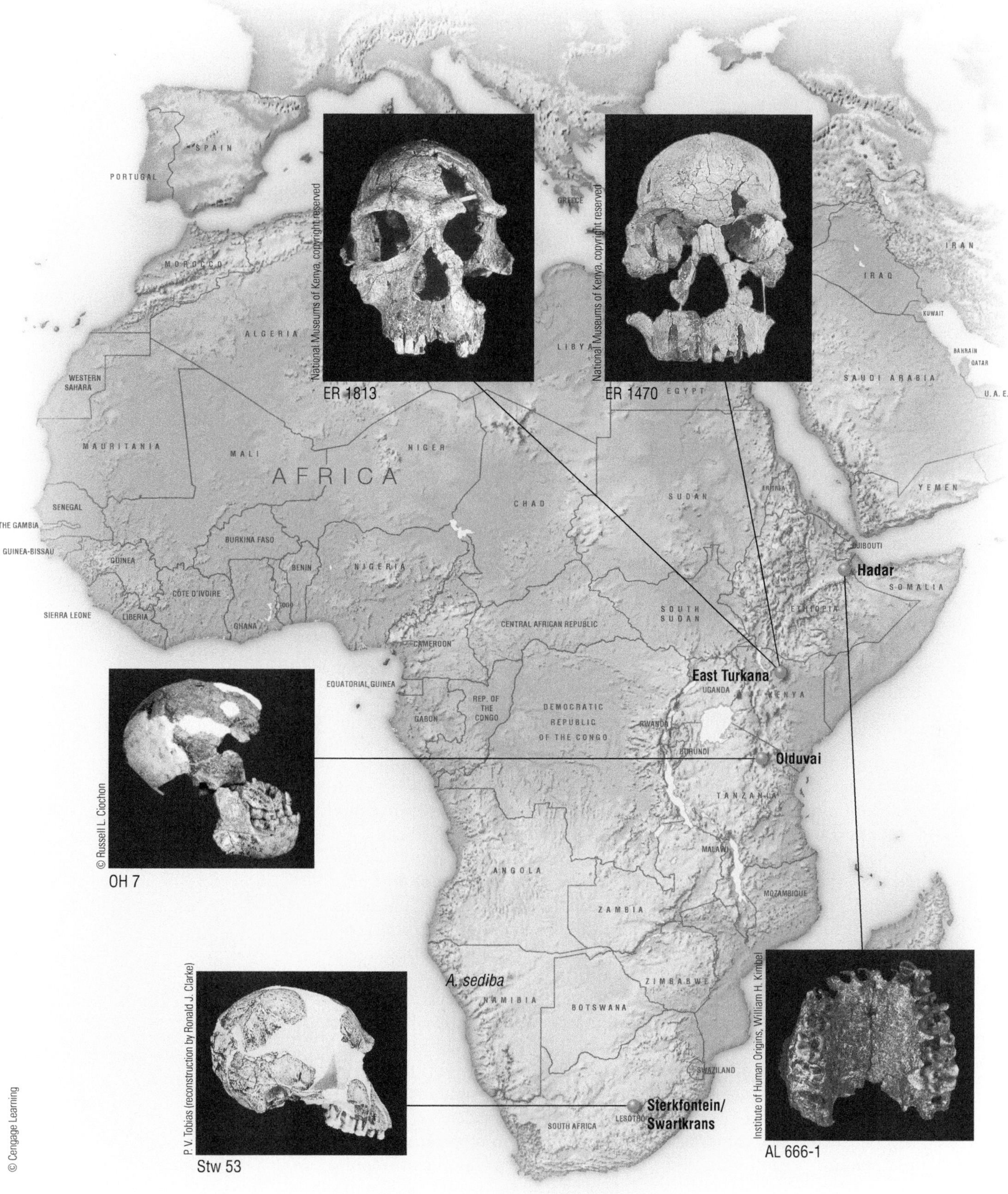

▲ **Figure 10-28** Early *Homo* fossil finds.

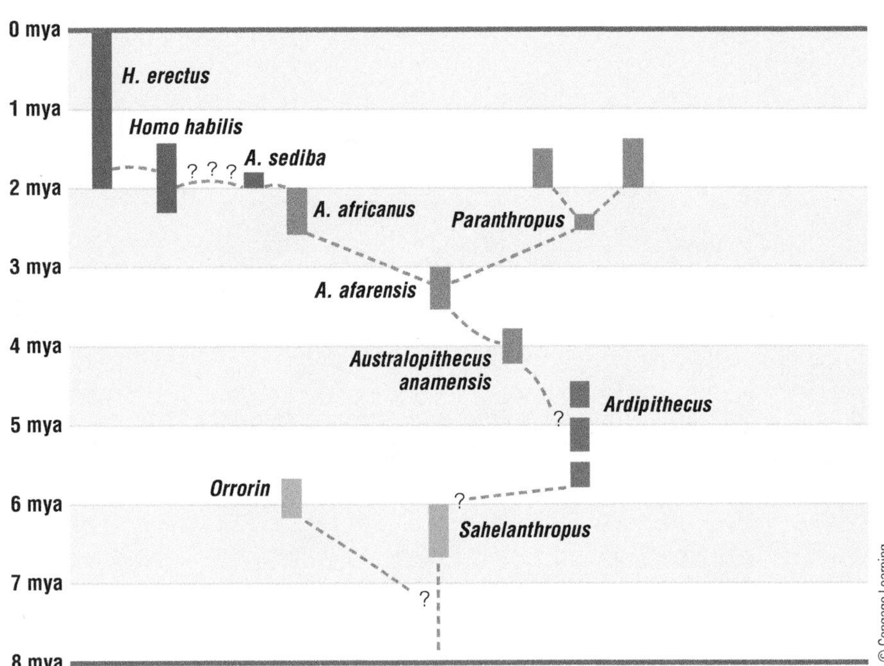

Figure 10-29 A tentative early hominin phylogeny. Note the numerous question marks, indicating continuing uncertainty regarding evolutionary relationships.

aware of the biological implications of such an interpretation.

From the time that fossil sites are first located until the eventual interpretation of hominin evolutionary patterns, several steps take place. Ideally, they should follow a logical order, for if interpretations are made too hastily, they confuse important issues for many years. Here's a reasonable sequence:

1. Selecting and surveying sites
2. Excavating sites and recovering fossil hominins
3. Designating individual finds with specimen numbers for clear reference
4. Cleaning, preparing, studying, and describing fossils
5. Comparing with other fossil material—in a chronological framework if possible
6. Comparing fossil variation with known ranges of variation in closely related groups of living primates and analyzing ancestral and derived characteristics
7. Assigning taxonomic names to fossil material

But the task of interpretation still isn't complete, for what we really want to know in the long run is what happened to the populations represented by the fossil remains. In looking at the fossil hominin record, we're actually looking for our ancestors. In the process of eventually determining those populations that are our most likely antecedents, we may conclude that some hominins are on evolutionary side branches. If this conclusion is accurate, those hominins necessarily must have become extinct. It's both interesting and relevant to us as hominins to try to find out what influenced some earlier members of our family tree to continue evolving while others died out.

Although a clear evolutionary picture is not yet possible for organizing all the early hominins discussed in this chapter, there are some general patterns that for now make good sense (**Fig. 10-29**). New finds may of course require serious alterations to this scheme. Science can be exciting, but it can also be frustrating to many in the general public looking for simple answers to complex questions. For well-informed students of human evolution, it's most important to grasp the basic principles of paleoanthropology, *how* interpretations are made, and *why* they must sometimes be revised. This way you'll be prepared for whatever shows up tomorrow.

Seeing the Big Picture: Adaptive Patterns of Early African Hominins

As you are aware by now, there are several different African hominin genera and certainly lots of species. This in itself is interesting. Speciation was occurring quite frequently among the various lineages of early hominins—more frequently, in fact, than among later hominins. What explains this pattern?

Evidence has been accumulating at a furious pace in the last decade, but it's still far from complete. What's clear is that we'll never have anything approaching a complete record of early hominin evolution, so some significant gaps will remain. After all, we're able to discover hominins only in those special environmental contexts where fossilization was likely. All the other potential habitats they might have exploited are now invisible to us.

Still, patterns are emerging from the fascinating data we do have. First, it appears that early hominin species (pre-australopiths, *Australopithecus*, *Paranthropus*, and early *Homo*) all had restricted ranges. It's therefore likely that each hominin species exploited a relatively small area with specific niches and could easily have become separated from other populations of its own species. So genetic drift (and to some extent natural selection) could have led to rapid genetic divergence and eventual speciation.

Second, most of these species appear to have been at least partially tied to arboreal habitats, although there's disagreement on this point regarding early *Homo* (see Wood and Collard, 1999b; Foley 2002). Also, *Paranthropus* was probably somewhat less arboreal than *Ardipithecus* or *Australopithecus*. These very large-toothed hominins apparently concentrated on a diet of coarse, fibrous plant foods, such as roots. Exploiting such resources may have routinely taken these hominins farther away from the trees than their dentally more gracile—and perhaps more omnivorous—cousins.

Third, except for some early *Homo* individuals, there's very little in the way of an evolutionary trend of increased body size or of markedly greater encephalization. Beginning with *Sahelanthropus*, brain size was no more than that in chimpanzees—although when accounting for body size, this earliest of all known hominins may have had a proportionately larger brain than any living ape. Close to 5 million years later (that is, the time of the last surviving australopith species), relative brain size increased by no more than 10 to 15 percent. Perhaps tied to this relative stasis in brain capacity, there's no absolute association of any of these hominins with patterned stone tool manufacture (see Chapter 9).

Although conclusions are becoming increasingly controversial, for the moment early *Homo* appears to be a partial exception. This group shows both increased encephalization and numerous occurrences of likely association with stone tools (though at many of the sites, australopith fossils were *also* found).

Last, all of these early African hominins show an accelerated developmental pattern (similar to that seen in African apes)—one quite different from the *delayed* developmental pattern characteristic of *Homo sapiens* (and our immediate precursors). This apelike development is also seen in some early *Homo* individuals (Wood and Collard, 1999a). Rates of development can be accurately reconstructed by examining dental growth markers (Bromage and Dean, 1985), and these data may provide a crucial window into understanding this early stage of hominin evolution.

These African hominin predecessors were rather small, able bipeds, but still closely tied to arboreal and/or climbing niches. They had fairly small brains and, compared to later *Homo*, matured rapidly. It would take a major evolutionary jump to push one of their descendants in a more human direction. For the next chapter in this more human saga, read on.

How Do We Know?

We know a great deal about early hominin evolution (during the time span from 6 to 1 mya), most specifically from a large number of fossils, which include thousands of individual elements—representing more than 500 individuals. What's more, some of these finds are quite complete, including some remarkable partial skeletons discovered recently in South and East Africa. By comparing these finds with contemporary primates (modern humans and great apes, especially), we can interpret the anatomy and likely function of these early hominins (for example, determining whether they were bipedal). We can also date these finds quite precisely using an array of dating techniques. Last, new research techniques (e.g., advanced computed tomography scans) allow paleoanthropologists to obtain remarkably accurate images of hominin fossils, even permitting them to actually "see inside the brain" of these ancient animals. Other new advances use very small samples of fossil teeth or even dental plaque to provide chemical evidence of diet.

Summary of Main Topics

- The earliest possible members of our lineage date back to about 6 mya, and for the next 4 million years, they stayed geographically restricted to Africa, where they diversified into many different forms.
- During this several-million-year span, at least six different hominin genera and upward of 13 species have been identified from the available fossil record.
- These early African hominins fit into three major groupings:
  - Pre-australopiths (6.0+ to 4.4 mya), including three genera of very early, and still primitive, possible hominins (*Sahelanthropus*, *Orrorin*, and *Ardipithecus*)
  - Australopiths (4.2 to 1.2 mya): Early, more primitive australopith species (4.2 to 3.0 mya), including *Australopithecus anamensis* and *Australopithecus afarensis*. These are the earliest definite hominins.

    Later, more derived australopith species (2.5 to 1.2 mya) include two genera (*Paranthropus* and later species of *Australopithecus*). A recently discovered species (*A. sediba*), shows a combination of features that some researchers hypothesize as transitional between *Australopithecus* and early *Homo* (but this view remains controversial).
  - Early *Homo* (2.0+? to 1.4 mya), including the first members of our genus, who around 2 mya likely diverged into more than one species

Critical Thinking Questions

1. In what ways are the remains of *Sahelanthropus* and *Ardipithecus* considered primitive? How do we know that these forms are hominins? How sure are we?
2. Assume that you are in the laboratory analyzing the "Lucy" *A. afarensis* skeleton. You also have complete skeletons from a chimpanzee and a modern human. (a) Which parts of the Lucy skeleton are more similar to the chimpanzee? Which are more similar to the human? (b) Which parts of the Lucy skeleton are *most informative* regarding hominin status?
3. Discuss two current disputes regarding taxonomic issues concerning early hominins. Try to give support for alternative positions.
4. What is a phylogeny? Construct one for early hominins (6.0 to 1.0 mya). Make sure you can describe the conclusions to which your scheme leads. Also, try to defend it.

Media Resources

Videos

See the videos "Biomechanics" and "Tool Time" to learn more about topics covered in this chapter. Login to your Anthropology CourseMate at www.cengagebrain.com to access videos.

Connections

The first more human-like animals (hominins) appeared in Africa around 6 mya ago and evolved into a variety of different species.

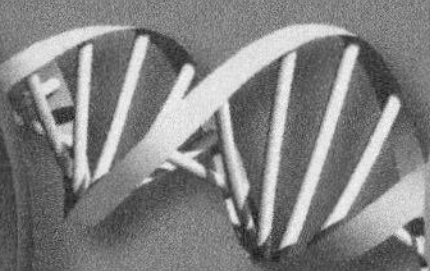

Hominins began to disperse out of Africa around 2 million years ago, and during the next 1 million years inhabited much of Eurasia.

The immediate predecessors of modern humans, including the Neandertals, were much like us, but had some anatomical and behavioral differences.

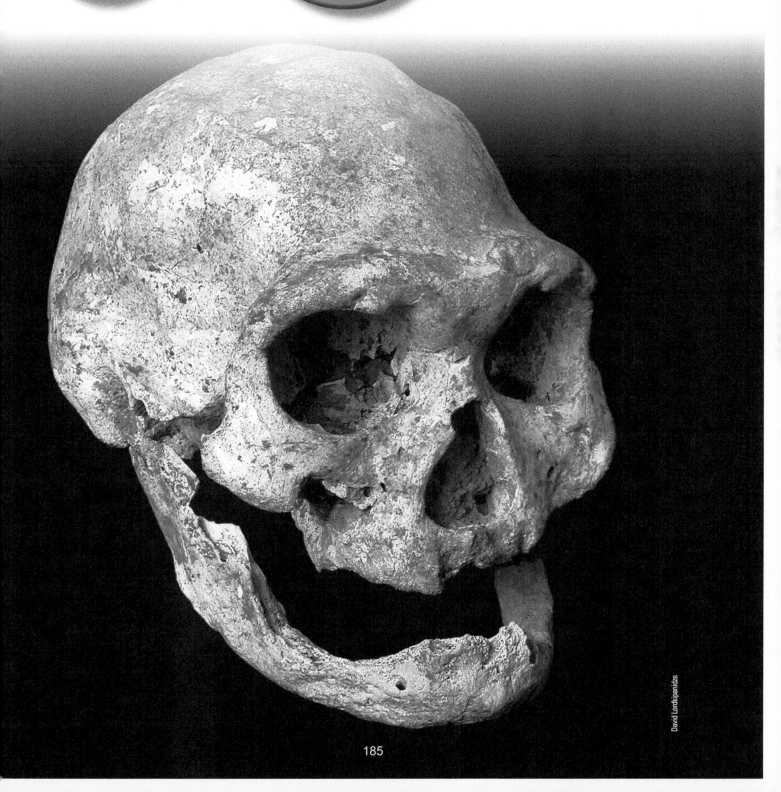

David Lordkipanidze

The First Dispersal of the Genus *Homo: Homo erectus* and Contemporaries

8

Student Learning Objectives

After mastering the material in this chapter, you should be able to:

- Discuss the geographic range of *Homo erectus* and compare it to that of earlier hominins.
- Discuss why it isn't yet fully established where the earliest *H. erectus* first evolved and describe which data you think provide the best evidence.
- Compare and contrast the morphology of *H. erectus* with that of early *Homo* as well as with *H. sapiens*.
- Compare and contrast the Dmanisi discoveries with *H. erectus* from Africa and Europe and discuss how the Dmanisi hominins complicate earlier hypotheses regarding hominin dispersal.
- Discuss what sorts of tools are associated with *H. erectus* and what they tell us about the hominins' cultural adaptations.

It's estimated that more than 1 million people now cross national borders every day. Some travel for business, some for pleasure, and others may be seeking refuge from persecution in their own countries. Regardless, it seems that modern humans have wanderlust—a desire to see distant places. Our most distant hominin ancestors were essentially homebodies, staying in fairly restricted areas, exploiting the local resources, and trying to stay out of harm's way. In this respect, they were much like other primate species.

One thing is certain: All these early hominins were restricted to Africa. When did hominins first leave Africa? What were they like, and why did they leave their ancient homeland? In what ways did they differ physically from their australopith and early *Homo* forebears, and did they have new behavioral and cultural capabilities that helped them successfully exploit new environments?

It would be a romantic misconception to think of these first hominin transcontinental emigrants as "brave pioneers, boldly going where no one had gone before." They weren't deliberately striking out to go someplace in particular. It's not as though they had a map! Still, for what they did, deliberate or not, we owe them a lot.

Sometime close to 2 mya, something decisive occurred in human evolution. As the title of this chapter suggests, for the first time, hominins expanded widely out of Africa into other areas of the Old World. Because all the early fossils have been found *only* in Africa, it seems that hominins were restricted to that continent for perhaps as long as 5 million years. The later, more widely dispersed hominins were quite different both anatomically and behaviorally from their African ancestors. They were much larger in body size, more committed to a completely terrestrial habitat, used more elaborate stone tools, and probably supplemented their diets with meat.

There is some variation among the different geographical groups of these highly successful hominins, and anthropologists still debate how to classify them. In particular, discoveries from eastern Europe over the last couple of decades have forced a major reevaluation of exactly which hominin species were the first to leave Africa (**Fig. 11-1**).

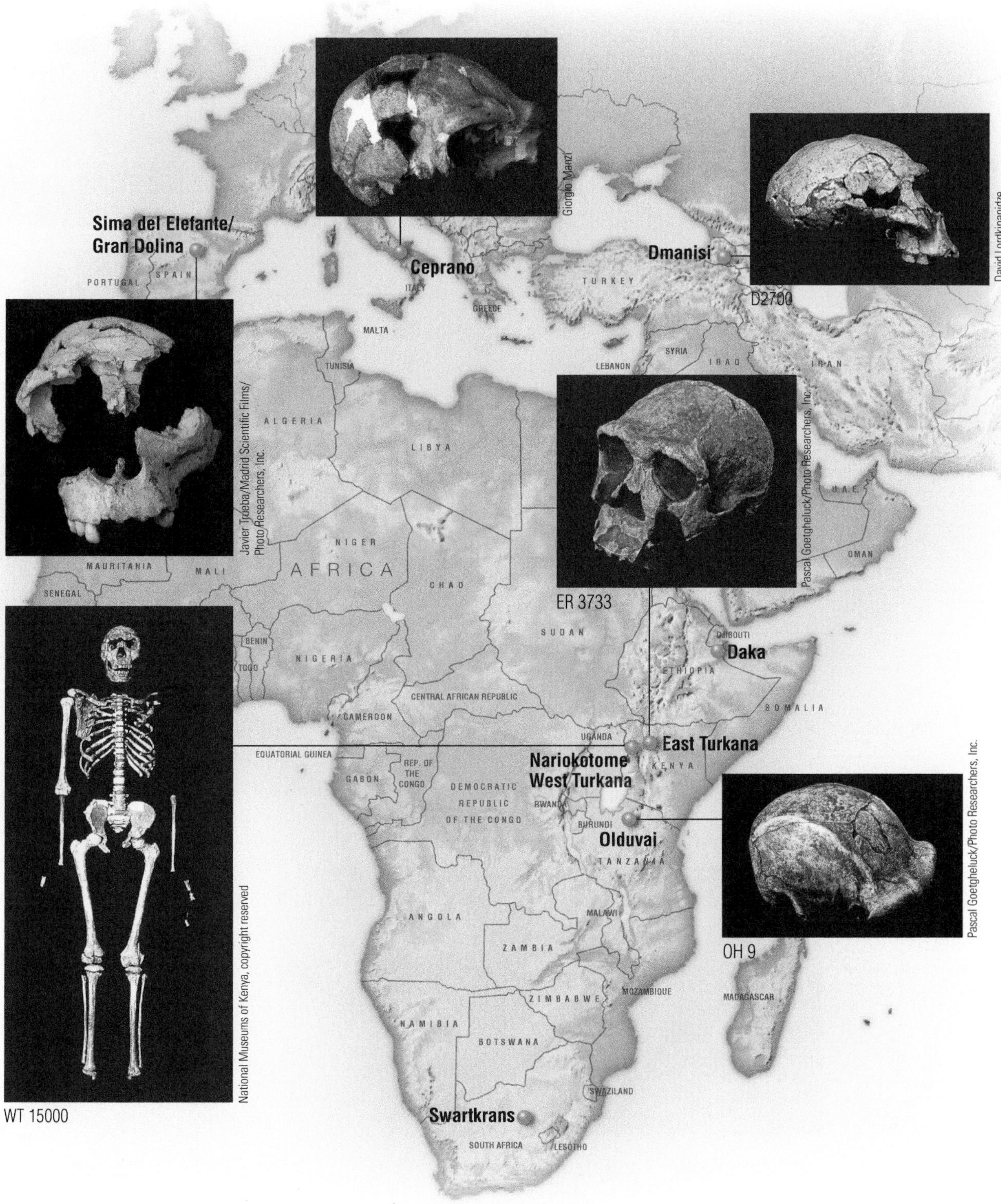

▲ **Figure 11-1** Major *Homo erectus* sites and localities of other contemporaneous hominins.

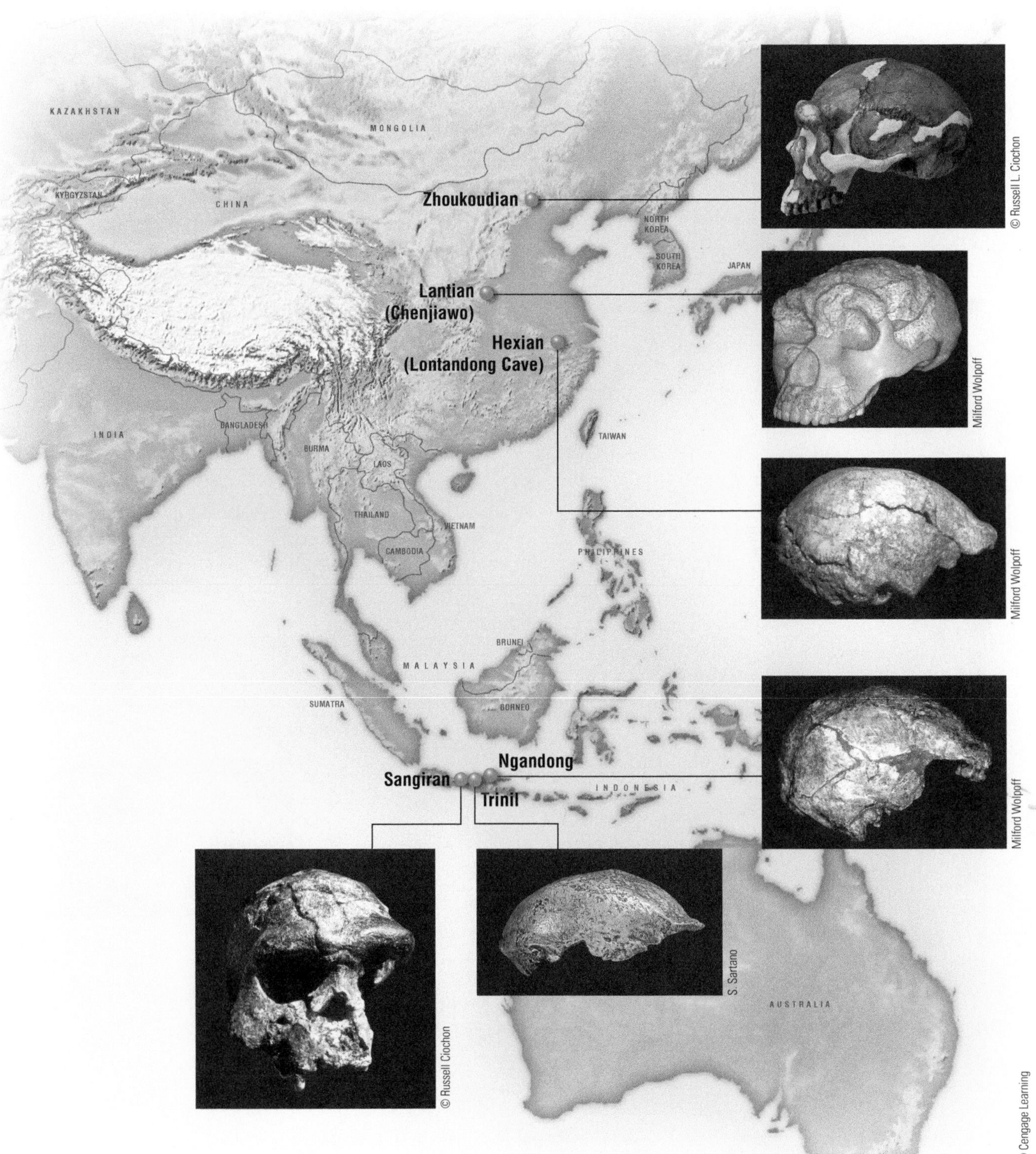

KAZAKHSTAN
MONGOLIA
KYRGYZSTAN
CHINA
Zhoukoudian
NORTH KOREA
SOUTH KOREA
JAPAN
Lantian
(Chenjiawo)
Hexian
(Lontandong Cave)
INDIA
BANGLADESH
BURMA
LAOS
TAIWAN
THAILAND
VIETNAM
CAMBODIA
PHILIPPINES
BRUNEI
MALAYSIA
SUMATRA
BORNEO
Ngandong
Sangiran
Trinil
INDONESIA
AUSTRALIA
© Russell L. Ciochon
Milford Wolpoff
Milford Wolpoff
Milford Wolpoff
© Russell Ciochon
S. Sartano
© Cengage Learning

Nevertheless, after 2 mya, there's less diversity among African hominins than is apparent in their pre-australopith and australopith predecessors. Consequently there is nearly universal agreement that the hominins found outside of Africa are all members of genus *Homo.* Thus taxonomic debates focus solely on how many species are represented. The early *Homo* species for which we have the most evidence, both physically and culturally, is called *Homo erectus*. Furthermore, this is the one group of early humans that most paleoanthropologists have recognized for decades and still agree on. Thus, in this chapter we'll focus our discussion on *Homo erectus*. We will, however, also discuss alternative interpretations that "split" the fossil sample into more species.

A New Kind of Hominin

The discovery of fossils now referred to as *Homo erectus* began in the nineteenth century. Later in this chapter, we'll discuss the historical background of these earliest discoveries in Java and the somewhat later discoveries in China. For these fossils, as well as several from Europe and North Africa, a variety of taxonomic names have been suggested.

It's important to realize that such taxonomic *splitting* was quite common during the late nineteenth century, in the early years of paleoanthropology. More systematic biological thinking came to the fore only after World War II, with the incorporation of the Modern Synthesis into paleontology. Most of the fossils that were given these varied names are now placed in the species *Homo erectus*—or at the very least have been lumped into one genus (*Homo*).

In the last few decades, discoveries from East Africa of firmly dated fossils have established the clear presence of *Homo erectus* by 1.7 mya and even a little earlier in southeastern Europe (Ferring et al., 2011). Some researchers see several anatomical differences between these African representatives of an *erectus*-like hominin and their Asian cousins (hominins that almost everybody refers to as *Homo erectus*). Thus they place the African fossils into a separate species, one they call *Homo ergaster* (Andrews, 1984; Wood, 1991).

Though, as we will discuss, there are some anatomical differences between the African specimens and those from Asia, they are all clearly *closely* related and quite possibly represent geographical varieties of a single species. We'll thus refer to them collectively as *Homo erectus.*

Most analyses show that *H. erectus* represents a quite different kind of hominin than its more ancient African predecessors. An increase in body size and robusticity, changes in limb proportions, and greater encephalization all indicate that these hominins were more like modern humans in their adaptive pattern than their African ancestors were. It's clear from most of the fossils usually classified as *Homo erectus* that a major adaptive shift had taken place—one setting hominin evolution in a distinctly more human direction.

We mentioned that there is considerable variation among different regional populations defined as *Homo erectus*. More recent discoveries show even more dramatic variation, suggesting that some of these hominins may not fit closely with this general adaptive pattern (more on this presently). For the moment, however, let's review what most of these fossils look like.

The Morphology of *Homo erectus*

Homo erectus populations lived in very different environments over much of the Old World. They all, however, shared several common physical traits.

Body Size

Anthropologists estimate that some *H. erectus* adults weighed well over 100 pounds, with an average adult height of about 5 feet 6 inches (McHenry, 1992; Ruff and Walker, 1993; Walker and Leakey, 1993). Another point to keep in mind is that *H. erectus* was quite sexually dimorphic—at least as indicated by the East African specimens.

Increased height and weight in *H. erectus* are also associated with a dramatic increase in robusticity. In fact, a heavily built body was to dominate hominin evolution not just during *H. erectus* times but through the long transitional era of premodern forms as well. Only with the appearance of anatomically modern *H. sapiens* did a more gracile skeletal structure emerge, one that still characterizes most modern populations.

Brain Size

Although *Homo erectus* differs in several respects from both early *Homo* and *Homo sapiens*, the most obvious feature is cranial size—which is closely related to brain size. Early *Homo* had cranial capacities ranging from as small as 500 cm^3 to as large as 800 cm^3. *H. erectus*, on the other hand, shows considerable brain enlargement, with a cranial capacity of about 700* to 1,250 cm^3 (and a mean of approximately 900 cm^3).

As we've discussed, brain size is closely linked to overall body size. So it's important to note that along with an increase in brain size, *H. erectus* was also considerably larger than earlier members of the genus *Homo*. In fact, when we compare *H. erectus* with the larger-bodied early *Homo* individuals, *relative* brain size is about the same (Walker, 1991). What's more, when we compare the relative brain size of *H. erectus* with that of *H. sapiens*, we see that *H. erectus* was considerably less encephalized than later members of the genus *Homo*.

*Even smaller cranial capacities are seen in recently discovered fossils from the Caucasus region of southeastern Europe at a site called Dmanisi. We'll discuss these fossils In a moment.

Cranial Shape

Homo erectus crania display a highly distinctive shape, partly because of increased brain size but probably more correlated with increased body size. The ramifications of this heavily built cranium are reflected in thick cranial bone (in most specimens), large browridges (supraorbital tori) above the eyes, and a projecting **nuchal torus** at the back of the skull (**Fig.11-2**).

The braincase is long and low, receding from the large browridges with little forehead development. Also, the cranium is wider at the base compared with earlier *and* later species of genus *Homo*. The maximum cranial breadth is below the ear opening, giving the cranium a pentagonal shape (when viewed from behind). In contrast, the skulls of early *Homo* and *H. sapiens* have more vertical sides, and the maximum width is above the ear openings.

Most specimens also have a sagittal keel running along the midline of the skull. Very different from a sagittal crest, the keel is a small ridge that runs front to back along the sagittal suture. The sagittal keel, browridges, and nuchal torus don't seem to have served an obvious function, but most likely reflect bone buttressing in a very robust skull.

The First *Homo erectus*: *Homo erectus* from Africa

Where did *Homo erectus* first appear? The answer seems fairly simple: Most likely, this species

nuchal torus (nuke´-ul) (*nucha*, meaning "neck") A projection of bone in the back of the cranium where neck muscles attach. These muscles hold up the head.

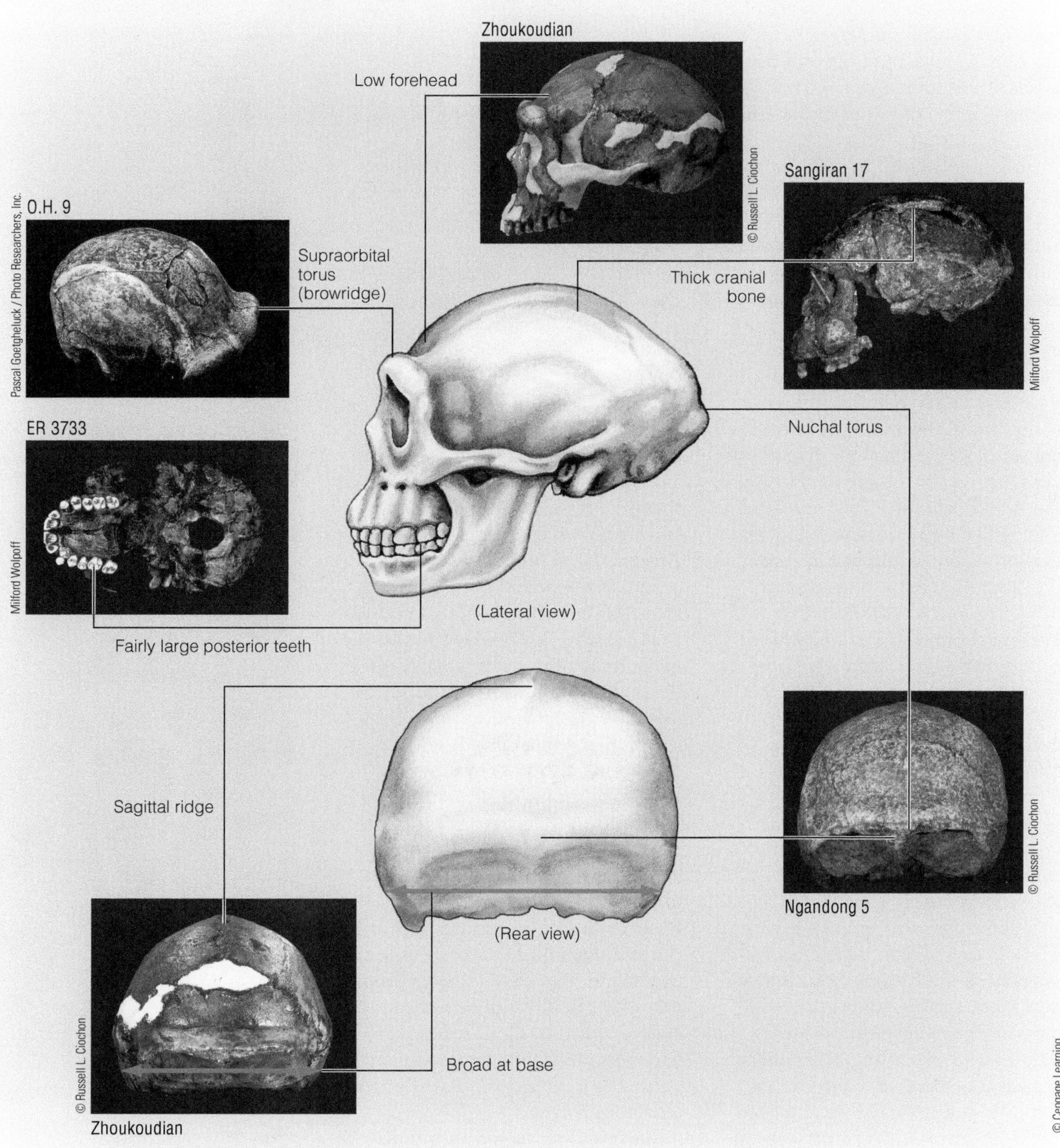

▲ **Figure 11-2** Morphology and variation in *Homo erectus*.

initially evolved in Africa. Two important pieces of evidence help to confirm this hypothesis. First, *all* of the earlier hominins prior to the appearance of *H. erectus* come from Africa. What's more, by 1.7 mya, there are well-dated fossils of this species at East Turkana, Kenya, and not long after that at other sites in East Africa.

But there's a small wrinkle in this neat view. We now know that at about 1.8 mya, similar populations were already living far away in southeastern Europe, and by 1.6 mya, in Indonesia. So, adding these pieces to our puzzle, it seems likely that *H. erectus* first arose in East Africa and then very quickly migrated to other continents; nevertheless, as we'll see shortly, the dating of sites from Africa and elsewhere does not yet clearly confirm this hypothesis. Let's first review the African *H. erectus* specimens dated at 1.7 to 1 mya, and then we'll discuss those populations that emigrated to Europe and Asia.

The earliest of the East African *H. erectus* fossils come from East Turkana, from the same area where earlier australopith and early *Homo* fossils have been found (see Chapter 10). Indeed, it seems likely that in East Africa around 2.0 to 1.8 mya, some form of early *Homo* evolved into *H. erectus*.

The most significant *H. erectus* fossil from East Turkana is a nearly complete skull (ER 3733; **Fig. 11-3**). Recently redated at 1.7 mya, this fossil is about the same age (or even just a little younger) than some other fossils outside of Africa; nevertheless, for now, it certainly is the oldest known member of this species from Africa (Lepre and Kent, 2010). The cranial capacity is estimated at 848 cm^3, in the lower range for *H. erectus* (700 to 1,250 cm^3), which isn't surprising considering its early date. A second very significant find from East Turkana is notable because it has the smallest cranium of any *H. erectus* specimen from anywhere in Africa. Dated to around 1.5 mya, the skull has a cranial capacity of only 691 cm^3. As we'll see shortly, there are a couple of crania from southeastern Europe that are even smaller. The small skull from East Turkana also shows more gracile features (such as smaller browridges) than do other East African *H. erectus* individuals, but it preserves the overall *H. erectus* vault shape. It's been proposed that perhaps this individual is a female and that the variation indicates a very high degree of sexual dimorphism in this species (Spoor et al., 2007).

Pascal Goetgheluck/Photo Researchers, Inc.

◄ **Figure 11-3** Nearly complete skull of *Homo erectus* from East Lake Turkana, Kenya, dated to approximately 1.7 mya.

Another remarkable discovery was made in 1984 by Kamoya Kimeu, a member of Richard Leakey's team known widely as an outstanding fossil hunter. Kimeu discovered a small piece of skull on the west side of Lake Turkana at a site known as **Nariokotome**. Excavations produced the most complete *H. erectus* skeleton ever found (**Fig. 11-4**). Known properly as WT 15000, the almost complete skeleton includes facial bones, a pelvis, and most of the limb bones, ribs, and vertebrae; it is chronometrically dated to about 1.6 mya.

Such well-preserved postcranial elements make for a very unusual and highly useful discovery, because these elements are scarce at other *H. erectus* sites. The skeleton is that of an adolescent about 8 years of age with an estimated height of about 5 feet 3 inches (Walker and Leakey, 1993; Dean and Smith, 2009).

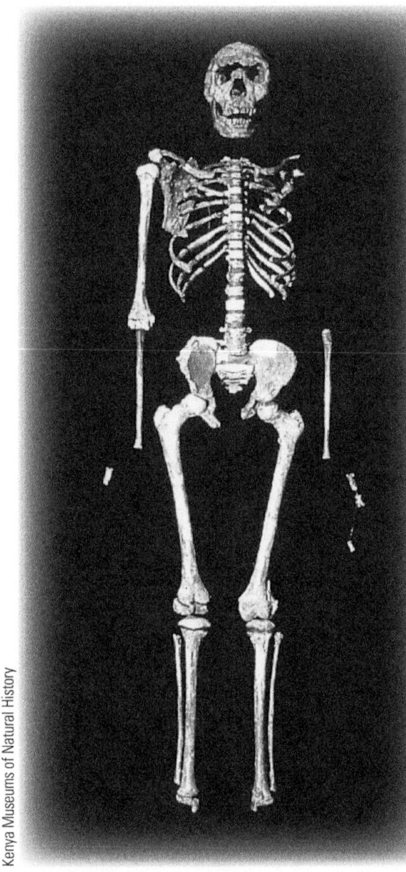
Kenya Museums of Natural History

▲ **Figure 11-4** WT 15000 from Nariokotome, Kenya: The "Nariokotome boy" is the most complete *H. erectus* specimen yet found.

Nariokotome
(nar´-ee-oh-koh´-tow-may)

Some estimates have hypothesized that the adult height of this individual could have been about 6 feet. However, this conclusion is contentious, since it assumed that the growth pattern of this species was similar to that of modern humans. But more recent and more detailed analyses find the developmental pattern in this and other *H. erectus* individuals to actually be more like that of an ape (Dean and Smith, 2009). What's more, it now seems unlikely that this individual would have experienced the typical adolescent growth spurt seen in modern humans (see Chapter 16). Indeed, the most recent estimates suggest that had he lived, the Nariokotome youth would have grown to a full adult stature of perhaps only about 64 inches (Graves et al., 2010). This may be a minimum estimate; other paleoanthropologists think that the adult stature may have been closer to 69 inches.

Nevertheless, the postcranial bones look very similar, though not quite identical, to those of modern humans. And the recent publication describing additional vertebral and rib fragments indicates that the modern human spine and rib cage shape were already present (Haeusler, Schiess, and Boeni, 2011). The cranial capacity of WT 15000 is estimated at 880 cm^3. Brain growth was nearly complete, and the adult cranial capacity would have been approximately 909 cm^3, or twice that of the australopith mean (Begun and Walker, 1993; Falk, 2012).

Other important *H. erectus* finds have come from Olduvai Gorge, in Tanzania; they include a very robust skull discovered there by Louis Leakey in 1960. The skull is dated at 1.4 mya and has a well-preserved cranial vault with just a small part of the upper face. Estimated at 1,067 cm^3, its cranial capacity is the largest of all the African *H. erectus* specimens. The browridge is huge, the largest known for any hominin, but the walls of the braincase are relatively thin. This last characteristic is seen in most East African *H. erectus* specimens; in this respect, they differ from Asian *H. erectus*, in which cranial bones are thick.

Three other sites from Ethiopia have yielded *H. erectus* fossils, the most noteworthy coming from the Gona area and the Daka locale, both in the Awash River region of eastern Africa (Gilbert and Asfaw, 2008). As you've seen, numerous remains of earlier hominins have come from this area (see Chapter 10 and Appendix C on the Anthropology CourseMate at Cengagebrain.com).

A recently discovered nearly complete female *H. erectus* pelvis comes from the Gona area in Ethiopia and is dated to approximately 1.3 mya (Simpson et al., 2008). It is a particularly interesting find because *H. erectus* postcranial remains are so rare, and this is the first *H. erectus* female pelvis yet found. The Gona pelvis is very different from the Nariokotome pelvis and is unusual for its considerable width, along with a short stature. It's possible that this may reflect considerable sexual dimorphism. This fossil also reveals some tantalizing glimpses of likely *H. erectus* growth and development. The pelvis has a very wide birth canal, indicating that quite large-brained infants could have developed *in utero* (before birth); in fact, it's possible that a newborn *H. erectus* could have had a brain that was as large as what's typical for modern human babies (DeSilva, 2011). These factors indicate a modern compromise between the demands of obligate bipedalism and that of birthing large-brained infants.

This evidence has led researchers to suggest that *H. erectus* prenatal brain growth was more like that of later humans and quite different from that found in apes or in australopiths such as Lucy. However, it's also evident that *H. erectus* brain growth after birth was more rapid than it is in modern humans. The Gona female was in some ways quite primitive, especially her unusually small body size (approximately 81 pounds, as estimated by the size of her hip joint). Some anthro-

At a Glance

Key *Homo erectus* Discoveries from Africa

Date	Site	Evolutionary Significance
1.4 mya	Olduvai	Large individual, very robust (male?) *H. erectus*
1.6 mya	Nariokotome, W. Turkana	Nearly complete skeleton; young male
1.7 mya	E. Turkana	Oldest well-dated *H. erectus* in Africa; great amount of variation seen among individuals, possibly due to sexual dimorphism

pologists conclude from this evidence that the Gona pelvis may actually have come from an australoptith rather than from *H. erectus* (or any other species of *Homo*) (Ruff, 2010).

Another recent discovery from the Middle Awash of Ethiopia of a mostly complete cranium from Daka is also important because this individual (dated at approximately 1 mya) is more like Asian *H. erectus* than are most of the earlier East African remains we've discussed (Asfaw et al., 2002). Consequently, the suggestion by several researchers that East African fossils are a different species from (Asian) *H. erectus* isn't supported by the morphology of the Daka cranium (**Fig. 11-5**).

Who Were the Earliest African Emigrants?

The fossils from East Africa imply that a new adaptive pattern in human evolution appeared in Africa not long after 2 mya. Until recently, *H. erectus* sites outside Africa all have shown dates later than the earliest finds of this species in Africa, leading paleoanthropologists to assume that the hominins who migrated to Asia and Europe descended from earlier African ancestors. Also, these travelers look like *Homo*, with longer limbs and bigger brains. Because *H. erectus* originated in East Africa, they were close to land links to Eurasia (through the Middle East) and thus were probably the first to leave the continent. We can't be sure why these hominins left—were they following animal migrations, or was it simply population growth and expansion?

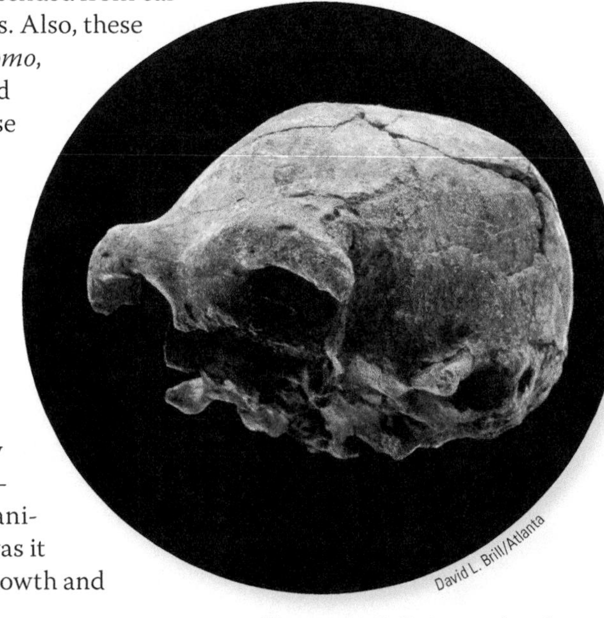

▲**Figure 11-5** Daka cranium from the Middle Awash region of Ethiopia, dated to 1.0 mya. This specimen shows many similarities with *Homo erectus* finds from Indonesia and China as well as Europe.

What we do know is that we're seeing a greater range of physical variation in the specimens outside of Africa and that the emigration out of Africa happened earlier than we had previously thought. Current evidence shows *H. erectus* in East Africa about 1.7 mya, while similar hominins were living in the Caucasus region of southeastern Europe *even a little earlier*, about

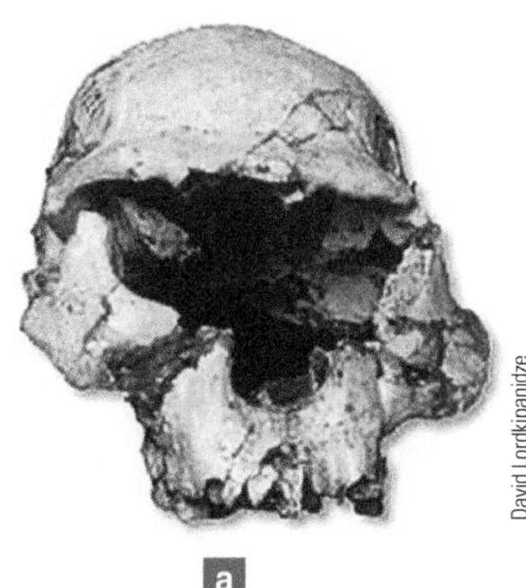

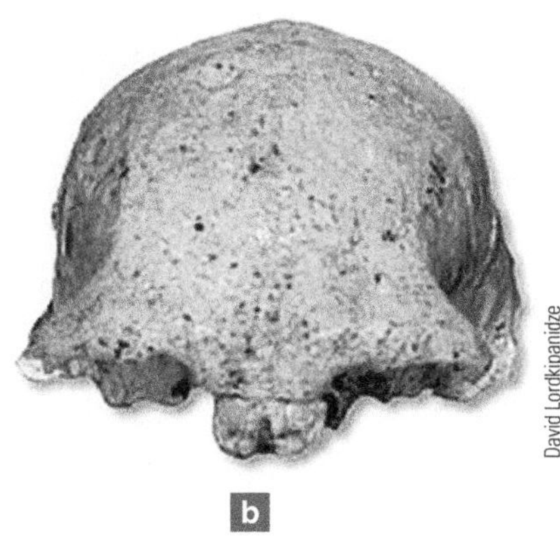

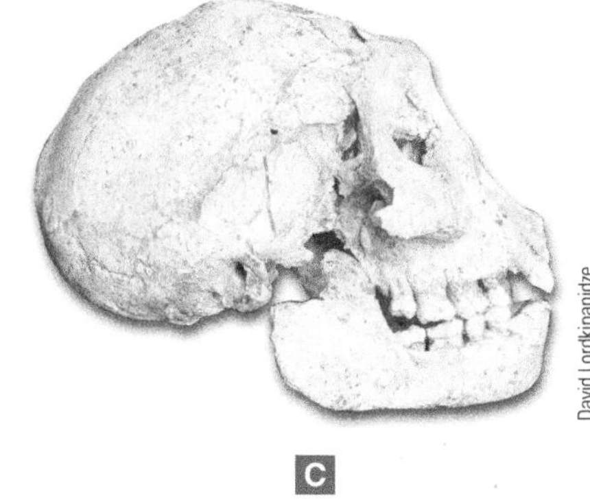

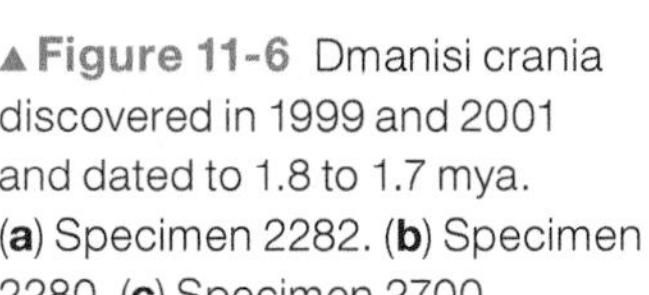

▲ **Figure 11-6** Dmanisi crania discovered in 1999 and 2001 and dated to 1.8 to 1.7 mya. (**a**) Specimen 2282. (**b**) Specimen 2280. (**c**) Specimen 2700.

1.8 mya.* Eventually hominins made it all the way to the island of Java, Indonesia, by 1.6 mya! It took *H. erectus* less than 200,000 years to travel from East Africa to Southeast Asia. Let's look at this fascinating evidence.

The site of **Dmanisi**, in the Republic of Georgia, has produced several individuals, giving us a unique look at these first possible travelers. The age of this crucial site has recently been radiometrically redated to 1.81 mya (Garcia et al., 2010). The Dmanisi crania are similar to those of *H. erectus* (for example, the long, low braincase, wide base, and sagittal keeling; see especially Fig. **11-6b**, and compare with Fig. 11-2). However, other characteristics of the Dmanisi individuals are different from other hominins outside Africa. In particular, the most complete fossil (specimen 2700; see **Fig. 11-6c**) has a less robust and thinner browridge, a projecting lower face, and a relatively large upper canine. At least when viewed from the front, this skull is more reminiscent of the smaller early *Homo* specimens from East Africa than it is of *H. erectus*. Also, specimen 2700's cranial capacity is very small—estimated at only 600 cm^3, well within the range of early *Homo*. In fact, all four Dmanisi crania so far described have relatively small cranial capacities—the other three being estimated at 630, 650, and 780 cm^3.

Probably the most remarkable find from Dmanisi is the most recently discovered skull. This nearly complete cranium is of an older adult male; and surprisingly for such an ancient find, he died with only one tooth remaining in his jaws (Lordkipanidze et al., 2006). Because his jawbones show advanced bone loss (which occurs after tooth loss), it seems that he lived for several years without being able to chew his food efficiently (**Fig. 11-7**). As a result, it probably would have been difficult for him to maintain an adequate diet.

Researchers have also recovered some stone tools at Dmanisi. The tools are similar to the Oldowan industry from Africa, as would be expected for a site dated earlier than the beginning of the **Acheulian** industry; this later and very important tool industry is first found associated with African *H. erectus* about 1.6 mya.

The most recent evidence from Dmanisi includes several postcranial bones coming from at least four individuals (Lordkipanidze et al., 2007). This evidence is especially important because it allows us to make comparisons with what is known of *H. erectus* from other areas. The Dmanisi fossils have an unusual combination of traits. They weren't especially tall, having an estimated height ranging from about 4 feet 9 inches to 5 feet 5 inches. Certainly, based on this evidence, they seem smaller than the full *H. erectus* specimens from East Africa or Asia. Yet, although very short in stature, they still show body proportions (such as leg length) like that of *H. erectus* (and *H. sapiens*) and quite different from that seen in earlier hominins.

* Note that these dates are based solely on what has been discovered so far.

Dmanisi (dim´-an-eese´-ee)

Acheulian (ash´-oo-lay-en) Pertaining to a stone tool industry from the Early and Middle Pleistocene; characterized by a large proportion of bifacial tools (flaked on both sides). Acheulian tool kits are common in Africa, Southwest Asia, and western Europe, but they're thought to be less common elsewhere. Also spelled Acheulean.

Based on the evidence from Dmanisi, we can assume that *Homo erectus* was the first hominin to leave Africa. Although the Dmanisi specimens are small in both stature and cranial capacity, they have specific characteristics that identify them as *H. erectus* (for example, a sagittal keel and low braincase). So for now, the Dmanisi hominins are thought to be *H. erectus*, although an early and quite different variety from that found almost anywhere else.

The recent evidence raises important and exciting possibilities. The Dmanisi findings suggest that the first hominins to leave Africa were quite possibly a small-bodied very early form of *H. erectus*, possessing smaller brains than later *H. erectus* and carrying with them a typical African Oldowan stone tool culture.

Also, the Dmanisi hominins had none of the adaptations hypothesized to be essential to hominin migration—that is, being tall and having relatively large brains. Another explanation may be that there were two migrations out of Africa at this time: one consisting of the small-brained, short-statured Dmanisi hominins and an almost immediate second migration that founded the well-recognized *H. erectus* populations of Java and China. The scientific community has only just recently reached a point where it is able to absorb these data, though it's still too soon to predict what further revisions may be required.

Homo erectus from Indonesia

After the publication of *On the Origin of Species*, debates about evolution were prevalent throughout Europe. While many theorists simply stayed home and debated the merits of natural selection and the likely course of human evolution, one young Dutch anatomist decided to go find evidence of it. Eugene Dubois (1858–1940) enlisted in the Dutch East Indian Army and was shipped to the island of Sumatra, Indonesia, to look for what he called "the missing link."

In October 1891, after moving his search to the neighboring island of Java, Dubois' field crew unearthed a skullcap along the Solo River near the town of Trinil—a fossil that was to become internationally famous as the first recognized human ancestor (**Fig. 11-8**). The following year, a human femur was recovered about 15 yards upstream in what Dubois claimed was the same level as the skullcap, and he assumed that the skullcap (with a cranial capacity of slightly over 900 cm^3) and the femur belonged to the same individual.

Counting the initial find plus later discoveries, so far, all the Javanese *H. erectus* fossil remains have come from six sites located in the eastern part of the island. The dating of these fossils has been hampered by the complex nature of Javanese geology, but it's generally accepted that most of the fossils belong to the Early to Middle **Pleistocene** and are between 1.6 and 1 million years old. The island of Java continues to yield new hominin fossils, with the discovery in 2001 of a *H. erectus* upper jaw at the fossil-rich Sangiran Dome (see "A Closer Look," pp. 318–319). Very well-controlled $^{40}Ar/^{39}Ar$ dating places this fossil very close to an age of 1.5 mya. Comparisons of this newly described jaw with Chinese and Western *Homo erectus* (from Georgia and Africa), as well as with *Homo habilis* reveal some interesting differences. These differences seem to indicate that there were two separate population sources for the earlier Sangiran *H. erectus* and later Zhoukoudian *H. erectus*, which

David Lordkipanidze

▲ **Figure 11-7** The most recently discovered cranium from Dmanisi, almost totally lacking in teeth (with both upper and lower jaws showing advanced bone resorption).

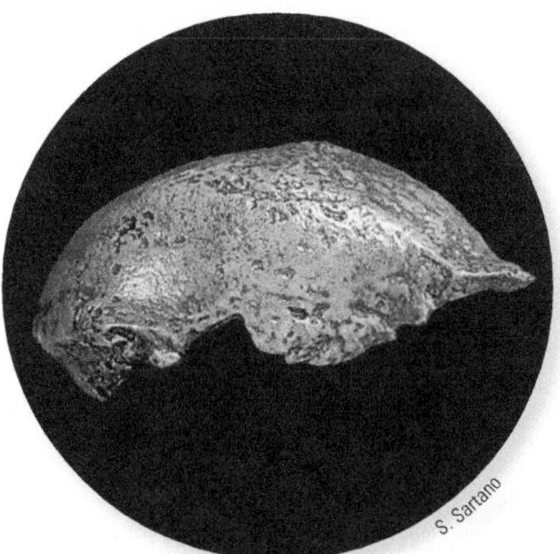
S. Sartano

▲ **Figure 11-8** The famous Trinil skullcap discovered by Eugene Dubois near the Solo River in Java. Discovered in 1891, this was the first fossil human found outside of Europe or Africa.

Pleistocene The epoch of the Cenozoic from 1.8 mya until 10,000 ya. Frequently referred to as the Ice Age, this epoch is associated with continental glaciations in northern latitudes.

A Closer Look

In Search of Ancient Human Ancestors—and a Little Shade

"Whoops!" Upon hearing this exclamation, my colleagues halt their progress along the narrow earthen walkways that outline the flooded rice paddies and make an emerald patchwork quilt on the Java landscape. They turn around and see that I've slipped. Again. Each misstep comes with some good-hearted ribbing as my comrades heave me back onto dry land. Each day we traverse the paddies by way of the thin dikes en route to our research site in central Java. Around us rise great cliffs of ancient soil, striated like an intricately layered cake. Rich green jewel tones dazzle the eye as we pass by peasants laboring in the fields under the hot sun. We, too, are in Java to work, but we toil for a different kind of produce—we seek answers about our early ancestor, Homo erectus*. As we tread across the paddies to a dusty oxcart path, our eyes comb the adjacent outcrops for darkened silhouettes of fossils—carefully, we note their locations. By the time we reach our destination, our backpacks are filled with curious remains—this one a tooth of a fossil deer, that one a piece of ancient crocodile bone—but no humans. All the fossils are stained crimson or black by the very soils in which they have lain for nearly a million years. As we begin to examine the exposed sediments, we resume our search for more fossils, our sweat-soaked shirts sticking to our skin. It's 9 a.m. and were already tired and hot, but we quickly brush these distractions away. Our search has just begun.*

For the past 12 years, my colleagues and I have been conducting fieldwork in the rice paddies of central Java. You might think it unusual to conduct scientific research in a rice paddy, but you have to "follow the fossils." Ancient sediments in our field area, the Sangiran Dome, were forced to the surface by the pressure of subterranean mud volcanoes about 120,000 years ago. What attracts us to the Sangiran Dome? It's the 1- to 2-million-year-old fossils and sediments that have been unearthed by erosion and other natural processes. This special series of events means that the Sangiran Dome is prime for both discovering the fossils of early humans in their original environmental context and for radiometrically dating them using volcanic sediments—a common occurrence in Java, an island formed by volcanoes.

If the cradle of human origins is Africa, then Asia was one of the playgrounds where our species grew and matured. Around 2 mya, *Homo erectus*, our first widely traveled ancestor, left the African savanna homeland to expand its horizons in the larger world. The first stop on this species' journey was in what is now the Republic of Georgia in southeastern Europe, where four skulls and a partial skeleton have been found. From here, we know that *Homo erectus* ventured onward to East Asia and eventually Java. We know little about the features that attracted these hominins to the Javanese landscape or when the first migration to this island occurred. We do know that over time, the descendants of original *Homo erectus* immigrants evolved, giving us both full-sized primitive peoples with thick skulls and projecting browridges and later the diminutive "Hobbits" on the island of Flores (you'll meet them in Chapter 13).

you will be introduced to in a moment (Zaim et al., 2011).

What's more, there was also a very late-surviving *H. erectus* group in Java that apparently managed to survive there until less than 100,000 years ago. These fossils from the Ngandong site are by far the most recent group of *H. erectus* fossils from Java or anywhere else. At Ngandong, an excavation along an ancient river terrace produced 11 mostly complete hominin skulls. Some estimates of the age of the Ngandong *H. erectus* fossils suggested an age of only 50,000 to 25,000 years ago (ya). These dates are quite controversial, but further evidence is establishing more strongly a *very* late survival of *H. erectus* in Java (approximately 70,000 to 40,000 ya) (Yokoyama et al., 2008). So these individuals would be contemporary with *H. sapiens*—which, by this time, had expanded widely throughout the Old World and into Australia around 60,000 to 40,000 ya. Recent work on the old excavation site of Ngandong (first excavated in the early 1930s) has led to a rediscovery of the fossil bed where all the *H. erectus* individuals had been found (Ciochon et al., 2009). New dating techniques and fossil identification will be undertaken to better understand site formation and taphonomy. As we'll see in Chapter 13, even later—and very unusual—hominins have been found not far away, apparently evolving in isolation on another Indonesian island.

Every good realtor will tell you that it's "location, location, location!" What was it about this Asian setting—particularly the island of Java—that drew these ancient immigrants to colonize, as evidenced by the nearly 100 fossils of *Homo erectus* that have been unearthed there over the past century? Was it, perhaps, the rich volcanic soils and the vegetation they fostered that attracted our distant relatives to the Sangiran Dome, or did *Homo erectus* simply follow land-loving animals to the newly emergent environment of central Java? Our research centers on this very issue, using visual and geochemical clues from soils and plant and animal fossils to reconstruct the landscape of Java when *Homo erectus* first arrived millions of years ago.

As the sun dips low on the horizon, the valley of the Sangiran Dome dims. At the end of the day, our team reassembles for the trek back to our van, joking and chatting about the day's finds. Our packs are heavy with samples of ancient soils, fossil shells and teeth, and rocks from ancient volcanic eruptions, all being hauled back for analysis. We watch our shadowy likenesses in the murky water of the paddies as we trudge out of the mists of time. In an hour we'll return to the hustle and bustle of Solo and wash away the dirt of ages. But before reentering civilization, we cast one last look into the past and wonder—"What was this place like during the time of our very ancient ancestors?" Was the landscape dominated by palms, mahogany, and cashew-bearing trees, as it is today, or was the countryside completely foreign? The full answers are just beyond our grasp. Perhaps today we carry in our backpacks the answers to these questions. Someday soon we'll be able to look at this landscape as our ancestors did, linking our common histories with modern technology.

—Russell L. Ciochon

© Russell L. Ciochon

◂ **Figure 1** The Sangiran Dome team, composed of researchers from the University of Iowa and the Bandung Institute of Technology, shown here doing a paleoecological analysis of the ancient strata of the dome.

Homo erectus from China

The story of the first discoveries of Chinese *H. erectus* is another saga filled with excitement, hard work, luck, and misfortune. Europeans had known for a long time that "dragon bones," used by the Chinese as medicine and aphrodisiacs, were actually ancient mammal bones. Scientists eventually located one of the sources of these bones near Beijing at a site called **Zhoukoudian**. Serious excavations were begun there in the 1920s, and in 1929, a fossil skull was discovered. The skull turned out to be a juvenile's, and although it was thick, low, and relatively small, there was no doubt that it belonged to an early hominin.

Zhoukoudian *Homo erectus*

The fossil remains of *H. erectus* discovered in the 1920s and 1930s, as well as some more recent excavations at Zhoukoudian (**Fig. 11-9**), are by far the largest collection of *H. erectus* material found anywhere. This excellent sample includes 14 skullcaps (**Fig. 11-10**), other cranial pieces, and more than 100 isolated teeth, but only a scattering of postcranial elements (Jia and Huang, 1990). Various interpretations to account for this unusual pattern of preservation have been offered, ranging from ritualistic treatment or cannibalism to the

Zhoukoudian (Zhoh´-koh-dee´-en)

© Russell L. Ciochon

▲ **Figure 11-9** Zhoukoudian cave.

▼ **Figure 11-10** Composite cranium of Zhoukoudian *Homo erectus*, reconstructed by Ian Tattersall and Gary Sawyer of the American Museum of Natural History in New York.

© Russell L. Ciochon

more mundane suggestion that the *H. erectus* remains are simply the leftovers of the meals of giant hyenas. The hominin remains were studied and casts were made immediately, which proved invaluable, because the original specimens were lost during the evacuation of Americans from China at the start of World War II.

The hominin remains from China belong to upward of 40 adults and children and together provide a good overall picture of Chinese *H. erectus*. Like the materials from Java, they have typical *H. erectus* features, including a large browridge and nuchal torus. Also, the skull has thick bones, a sagittal keel, and a protruding face and is broadest near the bottom. This site, along with others in China, has been difficult to date accurately. Although Zhoukoudian was previously dated to about 500,000 ya, a relatively new radiometric dating technique that measures isotopes of aluminum and beryllium shows that Zhoukoudian is actually considerably older, with a dating estimate of approximately 780,000 ya (Ciochon and Bettis, 2009; Shen et al., 2009).

Cultural Remains from Zhoukoudian

More than 100,000 artifacts have been recovered from this vast site, which was occupied intermittently for many thousands of years. The earliest tools are generally crude and shapeless, but they become more refined over time. Common tools at the site are cores, perhaps used as "choppers," but, more importantly, retouched flakes were fashioned into scrapers, points, burins, and awls (**Fig. 11-11**).

The way of life at Zhoukoudian has traditionally been described as that of hunter-gatherers who killed deer, horses, and other animals. Fragments of charred ostrich eggshells and abundant deposits of hackberry seeds unearthed in the cave seemed to suggest that these hominins supplemented their diet of meat by gathering herbs, wild fruits, tubers, and eggs. Layers of what appeared to be ash in the cave (over 18 feet deep at one point) were interpreted as indicating the use of fire by *H. erectus*.

However, with the rise of more modern techniques and the infusion of Western scientists, this idyllic picture of Zhoukoudian life was shattered. Lewis Binford and colleagues (Binford and Ho, 1985; Binford and Stone, 1986a,b) reject the description of *H. erectus* as hunters and argue that the evidence clearly points more accurately to scavenging. Using advanced archaeological analyses, Noel Boaz and colleagues have even questioned whether the *H. erectus* remains at Zhoukoudian represent evidence of hominin habitation of the cave. By comparing the types of bones, as well as the damage to the bones, with that seen in contemporary carnivore dens, Boaz and Ciochon (2001) have suggested that much of the material in the cave likely accumulated through the activities of extinct giant hyenas. In fact, they hypothesize that most of the *H. erectus* remains, too, are the leftovers of hyena meals. Boaz and his colleagues do recognize that the tools in the cave, and possibly the cut marks on some of the animal bones, provide evidence of hominin activities at Zhoukoudian.

Probably the most intriguing archaeological aspect of the presumed hominin behavior at Zhoukoudian has been the long-held assumption that *H. erectus* deliberately used fire inside the cave. Controlling fire was one of the major cultural breakthroughs of all prehistory. By providing warmth, a means of cooking, light to further modify tools, and protection, controlled fire would have been a giant technological innovation. However, in the course

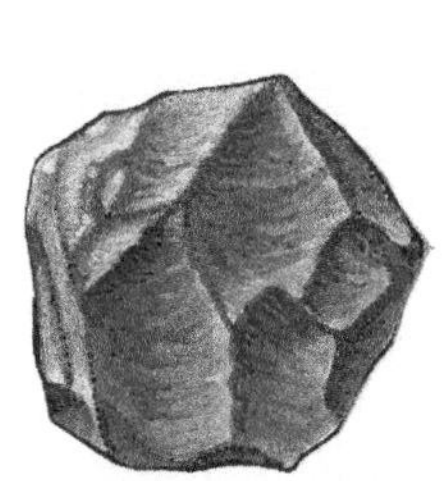

▲ **Figure 11-11** Chinese tools from Middle Pleistocene sites. (Adapted from Wu and Olsen, 1985.)

of further excavations at Zhoukoudian during the 1990s, researchers carefully collected and analyzed soil samples for distinctive chemical signatures that would show whether fire had been present in the cave (Weiner et al., 1998). They determined that burnt bone was only rarely found in association with tools. And in most cases, the burning appeared to have taken place after fossilization—that is, the bones weren't cooked. In fact, it turns out that the "ash" layers aren't actually ash but naturally accumulated organic sediment. This last conclusion was derived from chemical testing that showed absolutely no sign of wood having been burnt inside the cave. Finally, the "hearths" that have figured so prominently in archaeological reconstructions of presumed fire control at this site apparently aren't hearths at all. They are simply round depressions formed in the past by water.

Despite this debunking of some long-held beliefs, some potential early African sites have yielded evidence suggesting hominin control of fire, though many of these finds are controversial. However, a newly discovered cave site in South Africa, dated to 1 mya, has shown the best evidence yet of likely fire use based on archaeological finds of ash and burnt bone associated with Acheulian tools. Not only that, but it suggests that our ancestors controlled fire much earlier than we had thought (Berna et al., 2012). (See A Closer Look on pp. 322–323.)

Another provisional interpretation of Zhoukoudian's cave geology suggests that the cave wasn't open to the outside, as a habitation site would be, but was accessed only through a vertical shaft. This theory has led archaeologist Alison Brooks to remark, "It wouldn't have been a shelter, it would have been a trap" (quoted in Wuethrich, 1998). These serious doubts about control of fire, coupled with the suggestive evidence of bone accumulation by carnivores, have led anthropologists Boaz and Ciochon to conclude that the "Zhoukoudian cave was neither hearth nor home" (Boaz and Ciochon, 2001).

Other Chinese Sites

More work has been done at Zhoukoudian than at any other Chinese site. Even so, there are other paleoanthropological sites worth mentioning. Three of the more important regions outside of Zhoukoudian are Lantian County (including two sites, often simply referred to as Lantian), Yunxian County, and several discoveries in Hexian County (usually referred to as the Hexian finds).

Dated to 1.15 mya, Lantian is older than Zhoukoudian (Zhu et al., 2003). The cranial remains of two adult *H. erectus* females have been found at the Lantian sites (Woo, 1966; **Fig. 11-12a** on p. 324). One of the specimens, an almost complete mandible containing several teeth, is quite similar to those from Zhoukoudian.

Two badly distorted crania were discovered in Yunxian County, Hubei Province, in 1989 and 1990 (Li and Etler, 1992). A combination

A Closer Look

Dragon Bone Hill: Cave Home or Hyena Den?

About 30 miles southwest of Beijing, near Zhoukoudian, is the locality known as Dragon Bone Hill. In the 1920s and 1930s, this cave site yielded the first (and still the largest) cache of fossils of *Homo erectus*, historically known as Peking Man. The remains of about 45 individuals, along with thousands of stone tools, debris from tool manufacture, and thousands of animal bones, were contained within the 100-foot-thick deposits that once completely filled the original cave. Some evidence unearthed at the site suggests to many researchers that these creatures, who lived from about 800,000 to 400,000 ya, had mastered the use of fire and practiced cannibalism. Still, despite years of excavation and analysis, little is certain about what occurred here long ago.

To most of the early excavators, the likely scenario was that these particular early humans lived in the cave where their bones and stone tools were found. The animal bones were likely the remains of meals—proof of their hunting expertise. A more sensational view, first advanced in 1929, was that the cave contained evidence of cannibalism. Skulls were conspicuous among the remains, suggesting to Chinese paleoanthropologist Jia Lanpo that these might be the trophies of headhunters.

But another Chinese paleoanthropologist—Pei Wenzhong, who codirected the early Zhoukoudian excavations—believed that hyenas , not human killers, were responsible for the presence and condition of the skulls and other accompanying damage. In 1939, his views were bolstered by the emerging science of taphonomy, which is the study of how, after death, animal and plant remains become modified, moved, buried, and fossilized (see Chapter 9). Published observations on the way hyenas at

▲ **Figure 1** These illustrations demonstrate the two interpretations of the remains from Dragon Bone Hill: (**a**) the more traditional cave home model and (**b**) the newer, and probably more accurate, hyena den model.

of ESR and paleomagnetism dating methods (see Chapter 9) gives us an average dating estimate of 800,000 to 580,000 ya. If the dates are correct, this would place Yunxian at a similar age to Zhoukoudian in the Chinese sequence. Due to extensive distortion of the crania from ground pressure, it was very difficult to compare these crania with other *H. erectus* fossils; more recently, however, French paleoanthropologist Amélie Vialet has restored the crania using sophisticated imaging techniques (Vialet et al., 2005). And from a recent analysis of the fauna and paleoenvironment at Yunxian, the *H. erectus* inhabitants are thought to have had limited hunting capabilities, since they appear to have been restricted to the most vulnerable prey, namely, the young and old animals.

In 1980 and 1981, the remains of several individuals, all bearing some resemblance to similar fossils from Zhoukoudian, were recovered from Hexian County, in southern China (Wu and Poirier, 1995; see **Fig. 11-12b**). A close relationship has been postulated between the *H. erectus* specimens from the Hexian finds the Vienna zoo fed on cow bones led later scientists to reject the idea of cannibalism, although they continued to look upon the cave as a shelter used by early humans equipped with stone tools and fire (as reflected in the title of *The Cave Home of Peking Man*, published in 1975).

In the mid- to late 1970s, however, Western scientists began to better appreciate and develop the field of taphonomy. One assumption of taphonomy is that the most common species at a fossil site and/or the best-preserved animal remains at the site are most likely the ones to have inhabited the area in life. Of all the mammal fossils from the cave, very few belonged to *H. erectus*—perhaps only 0.5 percent, suggesting that most of the time, this species did not live in the cave. What's more, none of the *H. erectus* skeletons are complete. There's a lack of limb bones—especially of forearms, hands, lower leg bones, and feet—indicating that these individuals died somewhere else and that their partial remains were later carried to the cave. But how?

The answer is suggested by the remains of the most common and complete animal skeletons in the cave deposit—those of the giant hyena, *Pachycrocuta brevirostris*. Had *H. erectus*, instead of being the mighty hunter of anthropological lore, simply met the same unhappy fate as the deer and other prey species in the cave? To test the giant hyena hypothesis, scientists reexamined the fossil casts and a few actual fossils of *H. erectus* from Zhoukoudian for evidence of carnivore damage. Surprisingly, two thirds of the *H. erectus* fossils displayed puncture marks from a carnivore's large, pointed front teeth, most likely the canines of a hyena. What's more, there were long, scraping bite marks, typified by U-shaped grooves along the bone, and fracture patterns comparable to those modern hyenas make when they chew bone. One of the *H. erectus* bones, part of a femur, even reveals telltale surface etchings from stomach acid, indicating it was swallowed and then regurgitated.

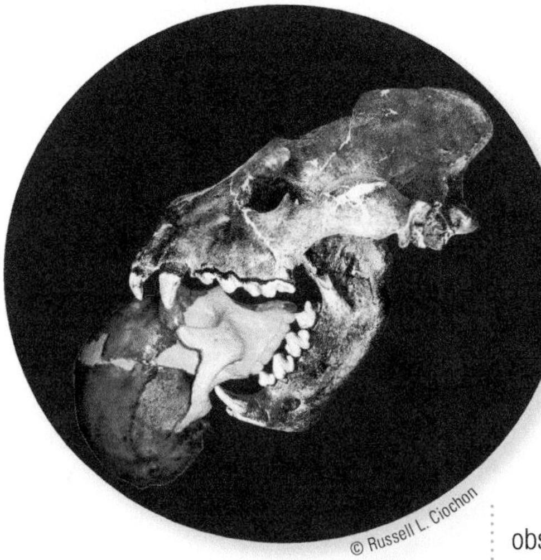

◀ **Figure 2** A composite image of the skulls of *Pachycrocuta* and *Homo erectus* that shows how the giant hyena may have attacked the face. Recent studies have shown that many of the *Homo erectus* remains from Zhoukoudian show hyena damage.

Cut marks (made by stone tools) observed on several mammal bones from the cave suggest that early humans did sometimes make use of Zhoukoudian, even if they weren't responsible for accumulating most of the bones. Stone tools left near the cave entrance also attest to their presence. Given its long history, the cave may have served a variety of occupants or at times have been configured as several separate, smaller shelters. Another possibility is that, in a form of time sharing, early humans ventured part way into the cave during the day to scavenge on what the hyenas had not eaten and to find temporary shelter. They might not have realized that the animals, which roamed at twilight and at night, were sleeping in the dark recesses a couple of hundred feet away.

and from Zhoukoudian (Wu and Dong, 1985). Dating of the Hexian remains is unclear, but they appear to be later than Zhoukoudian, perhaps by several hundred thousand years.

The Asian crania from Java and China share many similar features, which could be explained by *H. erectus* migration from Java to China perhaps around 1 mya. Asia has a much longer *H. erectus* habitation than Africa (1.8 mya to 40,000 or 70,000 ya versus 1.7 to 1 mya), and it's important to understand the variation seen in this geographically dispersed species.

Asian and African *Homo erectus*: A Comparison

The *Homo erectus* remains from East Africa show several differences from the Javanese and Chinese fossils. Some African cranial specimens—particularly ER 3733, presumably a female, and WT 15000, presumably a male—aren't as strongly buttressed at the browridge and nuchal torus, and their cranial bones aren't as

▶ **Figure 11-12** (**a**) Reconstructed cranium of *Homo erectus* from Lantian, China, dated to approximately 1.15 mya. (**b**) Hexian cranium.

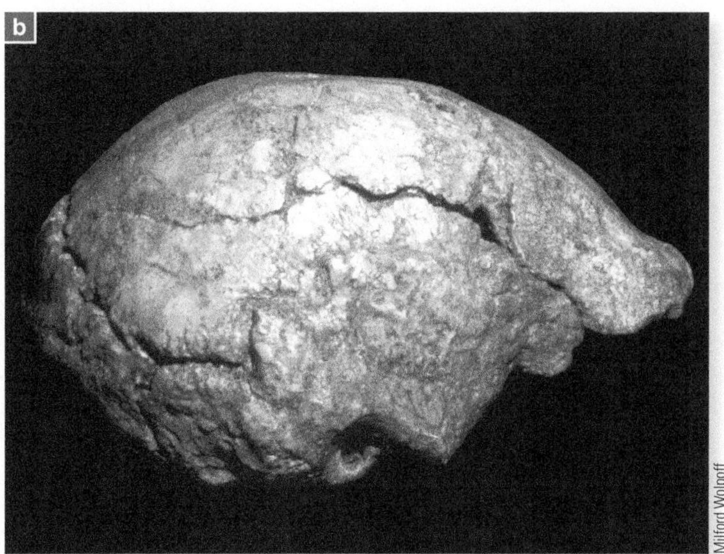

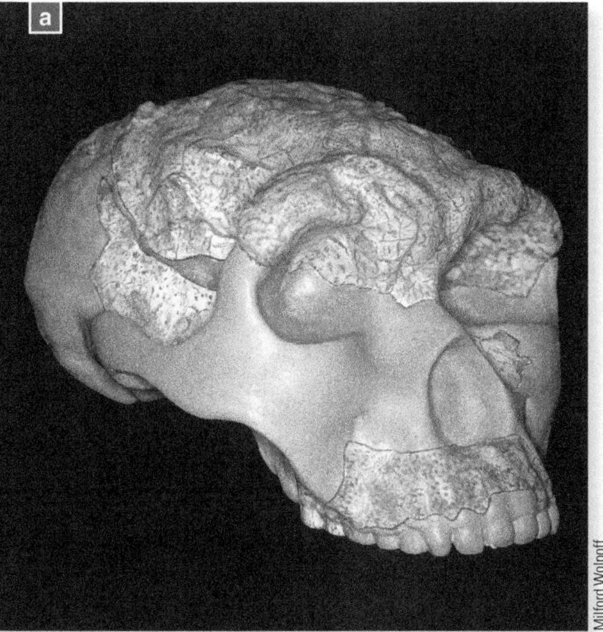

thick. Indeed, some researchers are so impressed by these differences, as well as others in the postcranial skeleton, that they're arguing for a separate species status for the African material, to distinguish it from the Asian samples. Bernard Wood, the leading proponent of this view, has suggested that the name *Homo ergaster* be used for the African remains and that *H. erectus* be reserved solely for the Asian material (Wood, 1991). In addition, the very early dates now postulated for the dispersal of *H. erectus* into Asia (Java) would argue that the Asian and African populations were separate (distinct) for more than 1 million years.

As a result of the discovery of the Daka cranium in Ethiopia and continued comparison of these specimens, this species division has not been fully accepted; the current consensus (and the one we prefer) is to continue referring to all these hominins as *Homo*

At a Glance

Key *Homo erectus* Discoveries from Asia

Date	Site	Evolutionary Significance
70,000–40,000 ya	Ngandong (Java)	Very late survival of *H. erectus* in Java
780,000 ya	Zhoukoudian (China)	Large sample; most famous *H. erectus* site; shows some *H. erectus* populations well adapted to temperate (cold) environments
1.6 mya	Sangiran (Java)	First discovery of *H. erectus* from anywhere; shows dispersal out of Africa into southeast Asia by 1.6 mya

erectus (Kramer, 1993; Conroy, 1997; Rightmire, 1998; Asfaw et al., 2002). Therefore, as with some earlier hominins, our interpretation of *H. erectus* requires us to recognize a considerable degree of variation within this species. This high degree of variability is likely related to the vast differences in climatic and environmental conditions encountered by ancient humans in the West and in the East. Additionally, the vast distances and island dynamics encountered by *Homo erectus* in the East increased genetic drift, perhaps in some cases producing large enough biological differences to cause speciation (Larick and Ciochon, in press). We will explore this topic further in later chapters.

Later *Homo erectus* from Europe

We've talked about *H. erectus* in Africa, the Caucasus region, and Asia, but there are European specimens as well, found in Spain and Italy. Though not as old as the Dmanisi material, fossils from the Atapuerca region in northern Spain are significantly extending the antiquity of hominins in western Europe. There are several caves in the Atapuerca region, two of which (Sima del Elefante and Gran Dolina) have yielded hominin fossils contemporaneous with *H. erectus.*

The earliest find from Atapuerca (from Sima del Elefante) was discovered recently and dates to 1.2 mya, making it clearly the oldest hominin specimen yet found in western Europe (Carbonell et al., 2008). So far, just one specimen has been found here, a partial jaw with a few teeth. Very provisional analysis suggests that it most closely resembles the Dmanisi fossils. There are also tools and animal bones from the site. As at the Dmanisi site, the implements are simple flake tools similar to those of the Oldowan. Some of the animal bones also bear the scars of hominin activity, with cut marks indicating butchering.

Gran Dolina is a later site, and based on specialized techniques discussed in Chapter 9, it's dated to approximately 850,000 to 780,000 ya (Parés and Pérez-González, 1995; Falguères et al., 1999). Because all the remains so far identified from both these caves at Atapuerca are fragmentary, assigning these fossils to particular species poses something of a problem. Spanish paleoanthropologists who study the Atapuerca hominins have placed them into another (separate) species, which may represent a link between early *Homo* and the later hominins (Bermúdez de Castro et al., 1997; Arsuaga et al., 1999; Bermúdez de Castro et al., 2011). And though they may exhibit some modern features, there is speculation that the hominins of Gran Dolina engaged in a most startling behavior: cannibalism. What's most unsettling about this practice is that the evidence suggests that this was not for ritual purposes or as a last resort. Cut and percussion marks on the hominin bones in question indicate that the bodies were processed much in the same way as any other animal (Carbonell et al., 2010).

Finally, the southern European discovery of a well-preserved cranium from the Ceprano site in central Italy may be the best evidence yet of *H. erectus* in Europe (Ascenzi et al., 1996). Provisional dating suggested a date between 900,000 and 800,000 ya (**Fig. 11-13**), but a recent

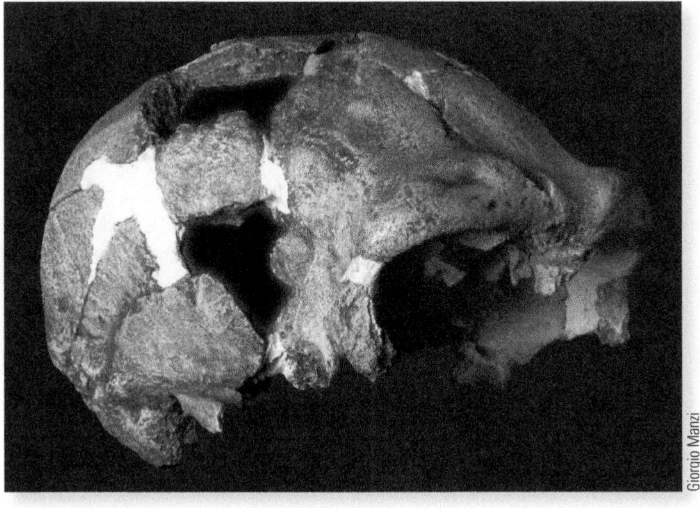

▾ **Figure 11-13** The Ceprano *Homo erectus* cranium from central Italy, recently dated to 450,000 ya. This is the best evidence for *Homo erectus* in Europe.

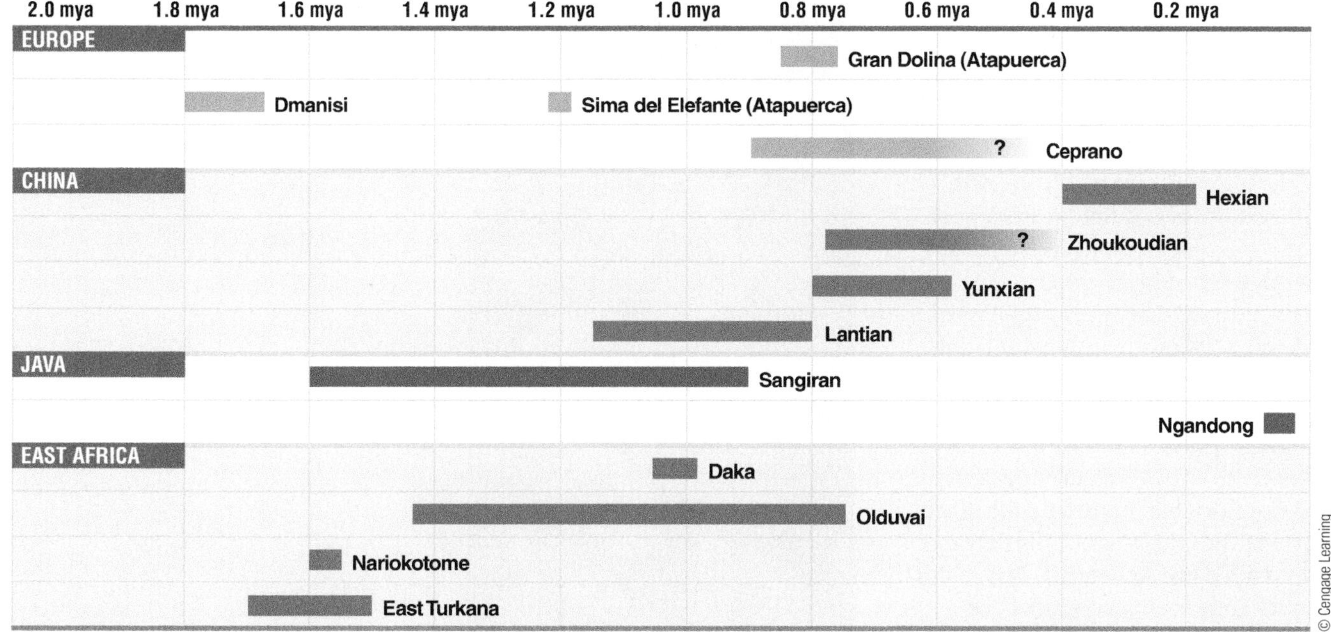

▲**Figure 11-14** Time line for *Homo erectus* discoveries and other contemporary hominins. (*Note:* Most dates are only imprecise estimates. However, the dates from East African sites are chronometrically determined and are thus much more secure. The early dates from Java are also radiometric and are gaining wide acceptance.)

$^{40}Ar/^{39}Ar$ study has indicated that it more likely dates only as far back as 353,000 ya (Nomade et al., 2011). Philip Rightmire (1998) has concluded that cranial morphology places this specimen quite close to *H. erectus*. Italian researchers have proposed a different interpretation, which classifies the Ceprano hominin as a species separate from *H. erectus*. For the moment, the exact relationship of the Ceprano find to *H. erectus* remains to be fully determined.

After about 400,000 ya, the European fossil hominin record becomes increasingly abundant. More fossils mean more variation, so it's not surprising that interpretations regarding the proper taxonomic assessment of many of these remains have been debated, in some cases for decades. In recent years, several of these somewhat later "premodern" specimens have been regarded either as early representatives of *H. sapiens* or as a separate species, one immediately preceding *H. sapiens*. These enigmatic premodern humans are discussed in Chapter 12. A time line for the *H. erectus* discoveries discussed in this chapter as well as other finds of more uncertain status is shown in **Figure 11-14**.

At a Glance

Key *Homo erectus* and Contemporaneous Discoveries from Europe

Date	Site	Evolutionary Significance
??900,000–350,000 ya	Ceprano (Italy)	Well-preserved cranium; best evidence of full *H. erectus* morphology from any site in Europe
1.2 mya	Sima del Elefante (Atapuerca, Spain)	Oldest evidence of hominins in western Europe, possibly not *H. erectus*
1.80 mya	Dmanisi (Republic of Georgia)	Oldest well-dated hominins outside of Africa; not like full *H. erectus* morphology, but are small-bodied and small-brained

Technological Trends During *Homo erectus* Times

The temporal span of *H. erectus* includes two different stone tool industries, one of which was probably first developed by *H. erectus*. Earlier finds indicate that *H. erectus* started out using Oldowan tools, which the *H. erectus* emigrants took with them to Dmanisi, Java, and Spain. The newer industry was invented (about 1.6 mya) after these early African emigrants left their original homeland for other parts of the Old World. This new tool kit is called the Acheulian. The important change in this kit was a core worked on both sides, called a biface (known widely as a hand axe or cleaver; **Fig. 11-15**). The biface had a flatter shape than seen in the rounder earlier Oldowan cores (which were worked to make quick and easy flakes and were soon discarded). Beginning with the Acheulian culture, we find the first evidence that raw materials were being transported more consistently and for longer distances. When Acheulian tool users found a suitable piece of stone, they would often take it with them as they traveled from one place to another. This behavior suggests foresight: They likely knew that they might need to use a stone tool in the future and that this chunk of rock could later prove useful. This is a major change from the Oldowan, where all stone tools are found very close to their raw-material sources. With the biface as a kind of "Acheulian Swiss army knife," these tools served to cut, scrape, pound, and dig. This most useful tool has been found in Africa, parts of Asia, and later in Europe. Take note as well that Acheulian tool kits also include several types of small tools (**Fig. 11-16**).

For many years, scientists thought that a cultural "divide" separated the Old World, with Acheulian technology found only in Africa, the Middle East, and parts of Europe (elsewhere, the Acheulian was presumed to be absent). But more recently reported excavations from many sites in southern China have forced reevaluation of this hypothesis (Hou et al., 2000). The archaeological assemblages from southern China are securely dated at about 800,000 ya and contain numerous bifaces, very similar to contemporaneous Acheulian bifaces from Africa (see Fig. 11-15). New evidence from India dates the Acheulian in southern Asia to at least 1 mya (Pappu et al., 2011). It now appears likely that cultural traditions relating to stone tool technology were largely equivalent over the *full* geographical range of *H. erectus* and its contemporaries.

William Turnbaugh

◂ **Figure 11-15** Acheulian biface ("hand axe"), a basic tool of the Acheulian tradition.

Evidence of butchering is widespread at *H. erectus* sites; in the past, such evidence has been cited in arguments for consistent hunting (researchers formerly interpreted any association of bones and tools as evidence of hunting). But some studies now suggest that cut marks on bones from the *H. erectus* time period often overlie carnivore tooth marks. This would mean that hominins weren't necessarily hunting large animals but were scavenging meat from animals killed by carnivores. It's also crucial to mention

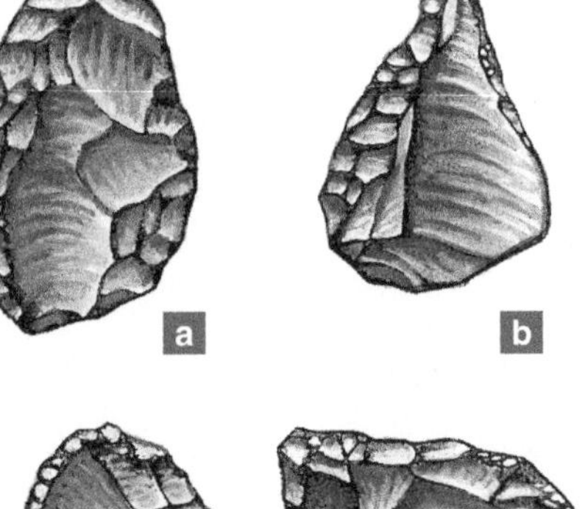

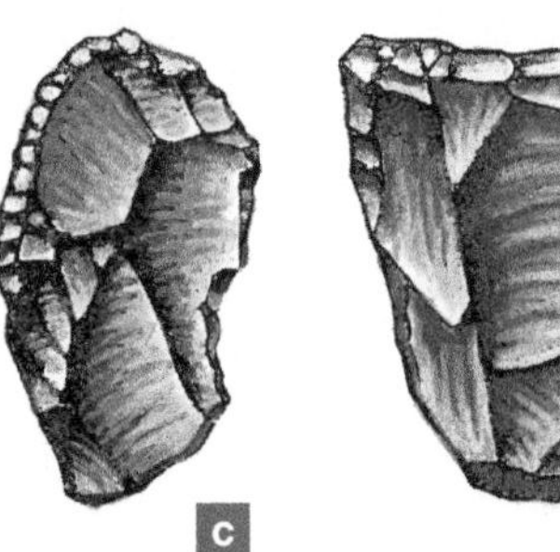

▴ **Figure 11-16** Small tools of the Acheulian industry. (**a**) Side scraper. (**b**) Point. (**c**) End scraper. (**d**) Burin.

that they obtained a large amount of their daily calories from gathering wild plants, tubers, and fruits. Like hunter-gatherers of modern times, *H. erectus* individuals were most likely consuming most of their daily calories from plant materials.

Seeing the Connections: Interpretations of *Homo erectus*

Several aspects of the geographical, physical, and behavioral patterns shown by *Homo erectus* seem clear. But new discoveries and more in-depth analyses are helping us to reevaluate our prior ideas. The fascinating Dmanisi hominins are perhaps the most challenging piece of this puzzle.

Early scenarios suggested that *H. erectus* was able to emigrate from Africa owing to more advanced tools and a more modern anatomy (longer legs, larger brains) compared to earlier African predecessors. Yet, now we see that what really happened was not this straightforward. Much like the Taung child changed our perspectives on early hominin evolution, the Dmanisi hominins surprisingly reveal that these very early Europeans still had small brains; moreover, in Dmanisi, Java, and Spain, these hominins were also still using Oldowan-style tools.

What becomes clear is that at least some of the earliest emigrants from Africa didn't yet show the entire suite of *H. erectus* physical and behavioral traits. Additionally, the Dmanisi hominins exhibit a very wide range of variability, making it tempting to conclude that more than one type of hominin is represented; but this is not likely, because all the fossils were found in the same geological context. This degree of apparent intraspecific variation is biologically noteworthy, and it's influencing how paleoanthropologists interpret all of these fossil samples.

This growing awareness of the broad intraspecific variation among some hominins brings us to our second consideration: Is *Homo ergaster* in Africa a separate species from *Homo erectus*, as strictly defined in Asia? Although this interpretation was popular in the last decade, it's now losing support. The finds from Dmanisi raise fundamental issues of interpretation. For example, among four crania from one locality (see Fig. 11-6), we see more variation than between the African and Asian forms, which many researchers have interpreted as different species. Also, the discovery from Daka (Ethiopia) of a young African specimen with Asian traits further weakens the separate-species interpretation of *H. ergaster.*

The separate-species status of the early European fossils from Spain (Sima del Elefante and Gran Dolina) is also not yet clearly established. Recall also that no other western European hominin fossils are known until at least 500,000 years later. Nevertheless, it's quite apparent that later in the Pleistocene, well-established hominin populations were widely dispersed in both Africa and Europe. These later premodern humans are the topic of the next chapter.

In looking back at the evolution of *H. erectus*, we realize how significant this early human was. *H. erectus* had greater limb length and thus more efficient bipedalism; was the first species with a cranial capacity approaching the range of *H. sapiens*; became a more efficient scavenger and exploited a wider range of nutrients, including meat; and ranged across the Old World, from Spain to Indonesia. In short, it was *H. erectus* that transformed hominin evolution to human evolution. As Richard Foley states, "The appearance and expansion of *H. erectus* represented a major change in adaptive strategy that influenced the subsequent process and pattern of human evolution" (1991, p. 425).

How Do We Know?

We know about the dispersal of early hominins out of Africa from a large number of fossils found in Africa, Asia, and Europe. Fairly recently, more discoveries have been made in East Africa, Asia (Indonesia), and Europe (Republic of Georgia and Spain). Accurate radiometric dating techniques have been used in Africa, Indonesia, and Georgia, and new methods have recently established more accurate dating for early Chinese fossils. Archaeological as well paleoecological studies have shown the variety of stone tools used by *H. erectus* as well as aspects of their behavioral adaptations (e.g., were they mostly hunters or scavengers? It seems they were mostly the latter).

Summary of Main Topics

- *Homo erectus* remains have been found in Africa, Europe, and Asia dating from about 1.8 mya to at least 100,000 ya and probably even later; thus this species spanned a period of more than 1.5 million years.
- *Homo erectus* likely first appeared in East Africa and later migrated to other areas. This widespread and highly successful hominin displays a new and more modern pattern of human evolution.
- *Homo erectus* differs from early *Homo*, with a larger brain, taller stature, robust build, and changes in facial structure and cranial buttressing.
- *Homo erectus* and contemporaries introduced more sophisticated tools (as part of the Acheulian industry) and probably ate novel foods processed in new ways. By using these new tools—and at later sites possibly fire as well—they were also able to move into different environments and successfully adapt to new conditions.

Critical Thinking Questions

1. Why is the nearly complete skeleton from Nariokotome so important? What kinds of evidence does it provide?
2. Assume that you're in the laboratory and have the Nariokotome skeleton as well as a skeleton of a modern human. First, given a choice, what age and sex would you choose for the comparative human skeleton, and why? Second, what similarities and differences do the two skeletons show?
3. What fundamental questions of interpretation do the fossil hominins from Dmanisi raise? Does this evidence completely overturn the earlier views (hypotheses) concerning *H. erectus* dispersal from Africa? Explain why or why not.
4. How has the interpretation of *H. erectus* behavior at Zhoukoudian been revised in recent years? What kinds of new evidence from this site have been used in this reevaluation, and what does that tell you about modern archaeological techniques and approaches?

Connections

Hominins began to disperse out of Africa around 2 million years ago, and during the next 1 million years inhabited much of Eurasia.

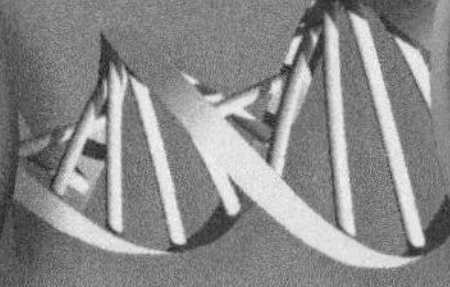

The immediate predecessors of modern humans, including the Neandertals, were much like us, but had some anatomical and behavioral differences.

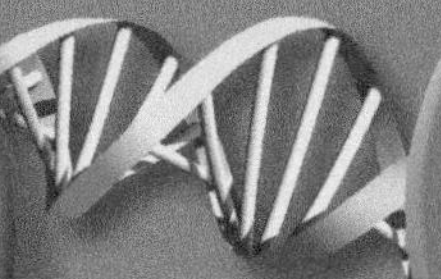

Modern humans first evolved in Africa and later spread to other areas of the world, where they occasionally interbred with Neandertals and other premodern humans.

Javier Trueba/Madrid Scientific Films/Photo Researchers

Premodern Humans

9

Student Learning Objectives

After mastering the material in this chapter, you should be able to:

- Describe the general time frame when earlier premodern humans (mostly classified as *Homo heidelbergensis*) lived and in what areas of the world they have been found.
- Compare and contrast the physical characteristics of *H. heidelbergensis* with *H. erectus*.
- Describe the time frame during which Neandertals lived and where their remains have been found.
- Compare and contrast the physical characteristics of Neandertals with those of modern humans.
- Explain what the information from the whole genome sequencing of Neandertals tells us and why this is important.
- Discuss some of the major cultural innovations displayed by Neandertals and how these compare with those of earlier hominins.

What do you think of when you hear the term *Neandertal*? Most people think of imbecilic hunched-over brutes. Yet Neandertals had brains at least as large as ours, and they showed many sophisticated cultural capabilities. What's more, they definitely weren't hunched over but stood fully erect (as hominins had for millions of years). In fact, Neandertals and their immediate predecessors could easily be called human.

That brings us to possibly the most basic of all questions: What does it mean to be human? The meaning of this term is highly varied, encompassing religious, philosophical, and biological considerations. As you know, physical anthropologists primarily concentrate on the biological aspects of the human organism. All living people today are members of one species, sharing a common anatomical pattern and similar behavioral potentials. We call hominins like us "modern" *Homo sapiens*, and in the next chapter, we'll discuss the origin of forms that were essentially identical to people living today.

When in our evolutionary past can we say that our predecessors were obviously human? Certainly, the further back we go in time, the less hominins look like modern *Homo sapiens*. This is, of course, exactly what we'd expect in an evolutionary sequence.

We saw in Chapter 11 that *Homo erectus* took crucial steps in the human direction and defined a new adaptive level in human evolution. In this chapter, we'll discuss the hominins who continued this journey. Both physically and behaviorally, they're much like modern *Homo sapiens*, though they still show several significant differences. So while most paleoanthropologists are comfortable referring to these hominins as "human," we must qualify this recognition a bit to set them apart from fully modern people. Thus, in this text, we'll refer to these fascinating immediate predecessors as "premodern humans."

When, Where, and What

Most of the hominins discussed in this chapter lived during the **Middle Pleistocene**, a period beginning 780,000 ya and ending 125,000 ya. In addition, some of the later premodern humans, especially the Neandertals, lived well into the **Late Pleistocene** (125,000 to 10,000 ya).

The Pleistocene

The Pleistocene has been called the Ice Age because, as had occurred before in geological history, it was marked by periodic advances and retreats of massive continental **glaciations**. During glacial periods, when temperatures dropped dramatically, ice accumulated because more snow fell each year than melted, causing the advance of massive glaciers. As the climate fluctuated, it sometimes became much warmer. During these **interglacials**, the ice that had built up during the glacial periods melted and the glaciers retreated back toward the earth's polar regions. The Pleistocene was characterized by numerous advances and retreats of ice, with at least 15 major and 50 minor glacial advances documented in Europe alone (Delson et al., 2000).

These glaciations, which enveloped huge swaths of Europe, Asia, and North America as well as Antarctica, were mostly confined to northern latitudes. Hominins living at this time—all still restricted to the Old World—were severely affected as the climate, flora, and animal life shifted during these Pleistocene oscillations. The most dramatic of these effects were felt in Europe and northern Asia—less so in southern Asia and Africa.

Still, the climate also fluctuated in the south. In Africa, the main effects were changing rainfall patterns. During glacial periods, the climate in Africa became more arid, while during interglacials, rainfall increased. The changing availability of food resources affected not only the hominins permanently residing in Africa; but probably even more importantly, also their migration routes, which swung back and forth. For example, during glacial periods (**Fig. 12-1**), the Sahara Desert expanded, blocking migration in and out of sub-Saharan Africa (Lahr and Foley, 1998).

In Eurasia, glacial advances also greatly affected migration routes. As the ice sheets expanded, sea levels dropped, making more northern regions uninhabitable, and some

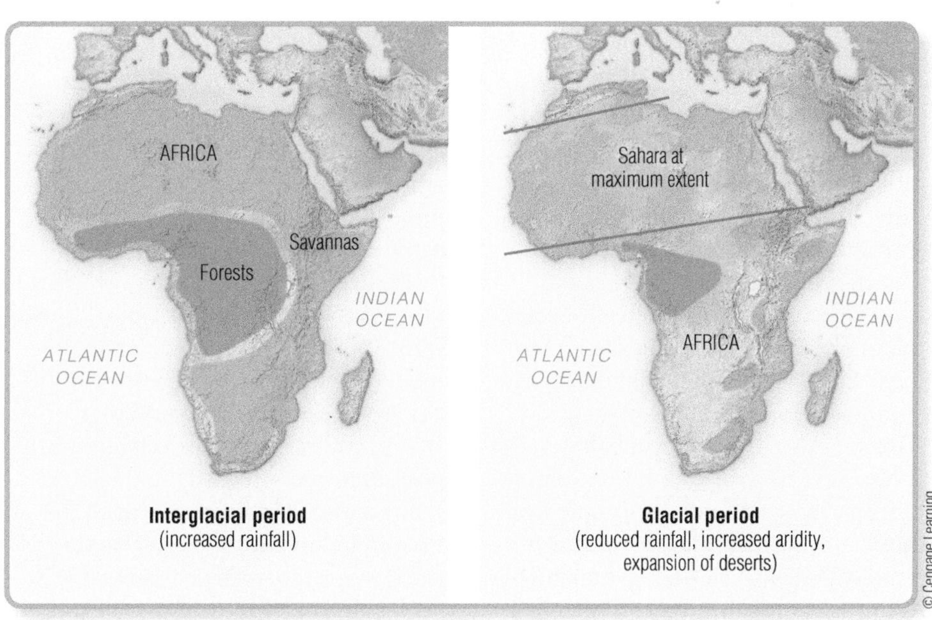

▲ **Figure 12-1** Changing Pleistocene environments in Africa.

Middle Pleistocene The portion of the Pleistocene epoch beginning 780,000 ya and ending 125,000 ya.

Late Pleistocene The portion of the Pleistocene epoch beginning 125,000 ya and ending approximately 10,000 ya.

glaciations Climatic intervals when continental ice sheets cover much of the northern continents. Glaciations are associated with colder temperatures in northern latitudes and more arid conditions in southern latitudes, most notably in Africa.

interglacials Climatic intervals when continental ice sheets are retreating, eventually becoming much reduced in size. Interglacials in northern latitudes are associated with warmer temperatures, while in southern latitudes the climate becomes wetter.

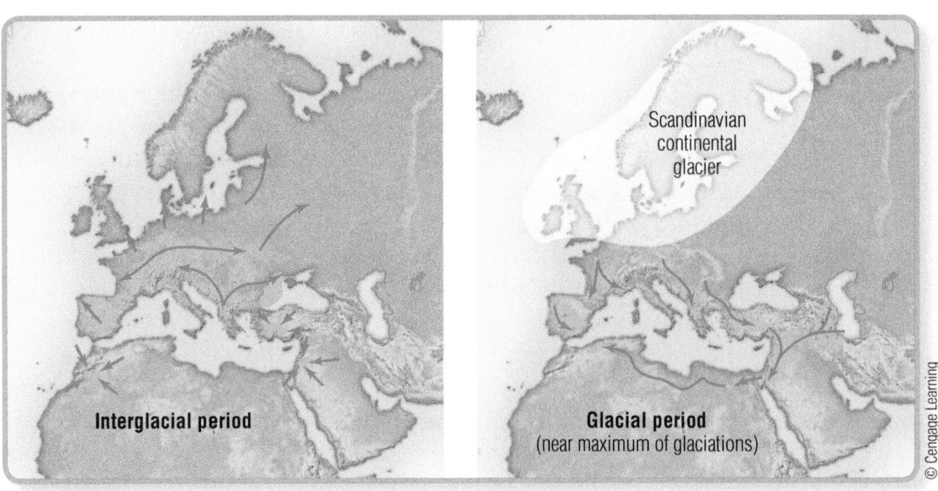

◄ **Figure 12-2** Changing Pleistocene environments in Eurasia. Orange areas show regions of likely hominin occupation. White areas are major glaciers. Arrows indicate likely migration routes.

key passages between areas became blocked by glaciers. For example, during glacial peaks, much of western Europe would have been cut off from the rest of Eurasia (**Fig. 12-2**).

During the warmer—and in the south wetter—interglacials, the ice sheets shrank, sea levels rose, and certain migration routes reopened (for example, from central Europe into western Europe). Clearly, to understand Middle Pleistocene hominins, it's crucial to view them within their shifting Pleistocene world. As we will see, this had important implications for gene flow, causing some populations to become isolated, leading to genetic drift.

Dispersal of Middle Pleistocene Hominins

Like their *Homo erectus* predecessors, later hominins were widely distributed in the Old World. Discoveries of their presence have come from three continents—Africa, Asia, and Europe. For the first time, Europe became more permanently and densely occupied, with evidence of Middle Pleistocene hominins from England, France, Spain, Germany, Italy, Hungary, and Greece. Africa, as well, probably continued as a central area of hominin occupation, and finds have come from northern, eastern, and southern Africa. Finally, Asia has yielded several important finds, especially from China. We should point out, though, that these Middle Pleistocene premodern humans didn't vastly extend the geographical range of *Homo erectus*, but rather largely replaced the earlier hominins in previously exploited habitats. One exception appears to be the more successful occupation of Europe, a region where earlier hominins have only sporadically been found.

Middle Pleistocene Hominins: Terminology

The premodern humans of the Middle Pleistocene (that is, after 780,000 ya) generally succeeded *H. erectus*. Still, in some areas—especially in Southeast Asia—there apparently was a long period of coexistence, lasting 300,000 years or longer; you'll recall the very late dates for the Javanese Ngandong *H. erectus* (see Chapter 11).

The earliest premodern humans exhibit several *H. erectus* characteristics: The face is large, the brows are projected, the forehead is low, and in some cases the cranial vault is still thick. Even so, some of their other features show that they had some derived traits more closely approximating the modern condition than their *H. erectus* predecessors. Compared with *H. erectus*, these premodern humans possessed an increased brain size, a more rounded braincase (that is, the maximum breadth is higher up on the sides), a more vertical nose, and a less angled back of the skull (occipital). We should note that the time span encompassed by Middle Pleistocene premodern humans is at least 500,000 years, so it's no surprise that over time we can observe certain trends. Later Middle Pleistocene hominins, for example, show even more brain expansion and an even less angled occipital than do earlier forms.

We know that premodern humans were a diverse group dispersed over three continents. Deciding how to classify them has been disputed for decades, and anthropologists still have disagreements. However, a growing consensus has recently emerged. Beginning perhaps as early as 850,000 ya and extending to about 200,000 ya, the fossils from Africa and Europe are placed within *Homo heidelbergensis*, named after a fossil found in Germany in 1907. What's more, some Asian specimens possibly represent a regional variant of *H. heidelbergensis.*

Until recently, many researchers regarded these fossils as early but more primitive members of *Homo sapiens.* In recognition of this somewhat transitional status, the fossils were called "archaic *Homo sapiens,*" with all later humans also belonging to the species *Homo sapiens.* However, most paleoanthropologists now find this terminology unsatisfactory. For example, Phillip Rightmire concludes that "simply lumping diverse ancient groups with living populations obscures their differences" (1998, p. 226). In our own discussion, we recognize *H. heidelbergensis* as a transitional species between *H. erectus* and later hominins (that is, primarily *H. sapiens*). Keep in mind, however, that this species was probably an ancestor of both modern humans and Neandertals. It's debatable whether *H. heidelbergensis* actually represents a fully separate species in the biological sense, that is, following the biological species concept (see Chapter 5). Still, it's useful to give this group of premodern humans a separate name to make this important stage of human evolution more easily identifiable. (We'll return to this issue later in the chapter when we discuss the theoretical implications in more detail.)

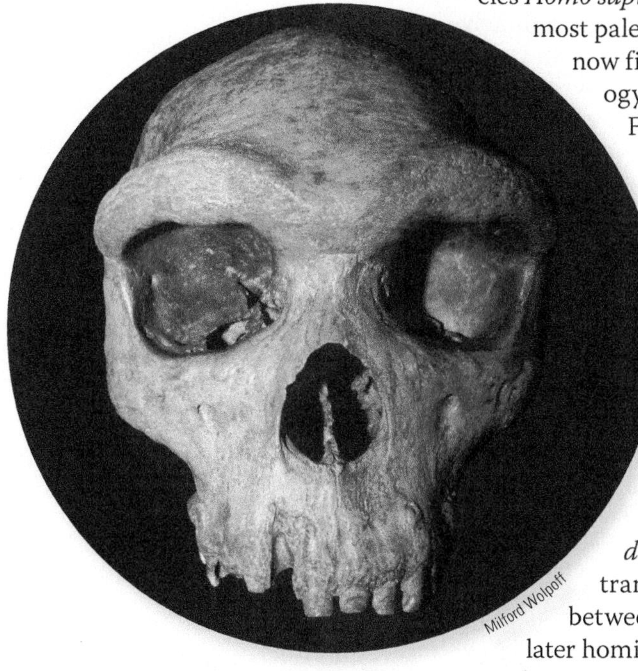

▲ **Figure 12-3** The Kabwe (Broken Hill) Homo heidelbergensis skull from Zambia. Note the very robust browridges.

Premodern Humans of the Middle Pleistocene

Africa

In Africa, premodern fossils have been found at several sites. One of the best known is Kabwe (Broken Hill). At this site in Zambia, fieldworkers discovered a complete cranium (**Fig. 12-3**) together with other cranial and postcranial elements belonging to several individuals. In this and other African premodern specimens, we can see a mixture of primitive and more derived traits. The skull's massive browridge (one of the largest of any hominin), low vault, and prominent occipital torus recall those of *H. erectus.* On the other hand, the occipital region is less angulated, the cranial vault bones are thinner, and the cranial base is essentially modern. Dating estimates of Kabwe and most of the other premodern fossils from Africa have ranged throughout the Middle and Late Pleistocene, but recent estimates have given dates for most of the sites in the range of 600,000 to 125,000 ya.

Bodo is another significant African premodern fossil (**Fig. 12-4**). A nearly complete cranium, Bodo has been dated to relatively early in the Middle Pleistocene (estimated at 600,000 ya), making it one of the oldest specimens of *H. heidelbergensis* from the African continent. The Bodo cranium is particularly interesting because it shows a distinctive pattern of cut marks, similar to modifications seen on butchered animal bones. Researchers have thus hypothesized that the Bodo individual was defleshed by other hominins, but for what purpose is not clear. The defleshing may have been related to cannibalism, though it also may have been for some other purpose, such as ritual. In any case, this is the earliest evidence of deliberate bone processing of hominins *by* hominins (White, 1986).

A number of other crania from South and East Africa also show a combination of retained ancestral with more derived (modern) characteristics, and they're all mentioned in the literature as being similar to Kabwe. The most important of these African finds come from the sites of Florisbad and Elandsfontein (in South Africa) and Laetoli (in Tanzania).

The general similarities among all these African premodern fossils indicate a close relationship between them, almost certainly representing a single species (most commonly referred to as *H. heidelbergensis*). These African premodern humans are also quite similar to those found in Europe.

Europe

More fossil hominins of Middle Pleistocene age have been found in Europe than in any other region—maybe because more archaeologists have been searching longer in Europe than anywhere else. In any case, during the Middle Pleistocene, Europe was more widely and consistently occupied than it was earlier in human evolution.

The time range of European premodern humans extends the full length of the Middle Pleistocene and beyond. At the earlier end, the Gran Dolina finds from northern Spain (discussed in Chapter 11) are definitely not *Homo erectus*. The Gran Dolina remains may, as proposed by Spanish researchers, be members of a new

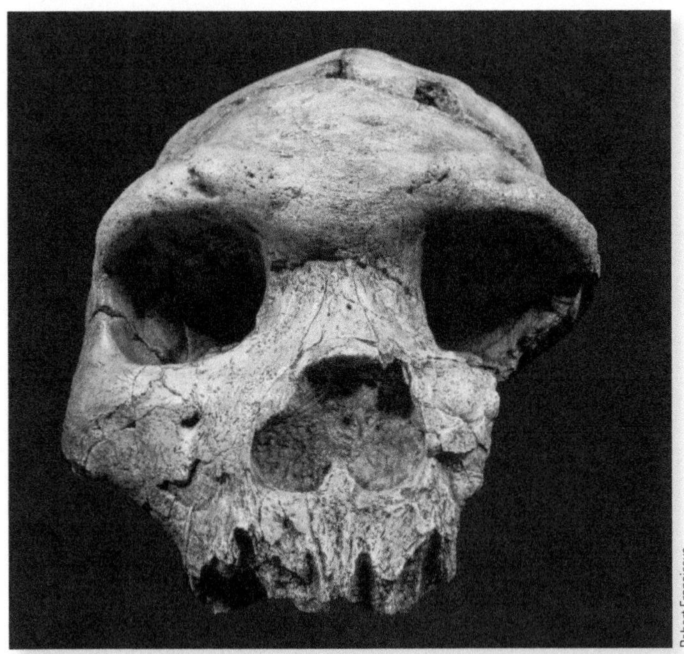

▲**Figure 12-4** Bodo cranium, the earliest evidence of *Homo heidelbergensis* in Africa.

At a Glance

Key Premodern Human (*H. heidelbergensis*) Fossils from Africa

Date	Site	Evolutionary Significance
130,000 ya	Kabwe (Broken Hill, Zambia)	Nearly complete skull; mosaic of features (browridge very robust, but braincase expanded)
600,000 ya	Bodo (Ethiopia)	Earliest example of African *H. heidelbergensis*; likely evidence of butchering

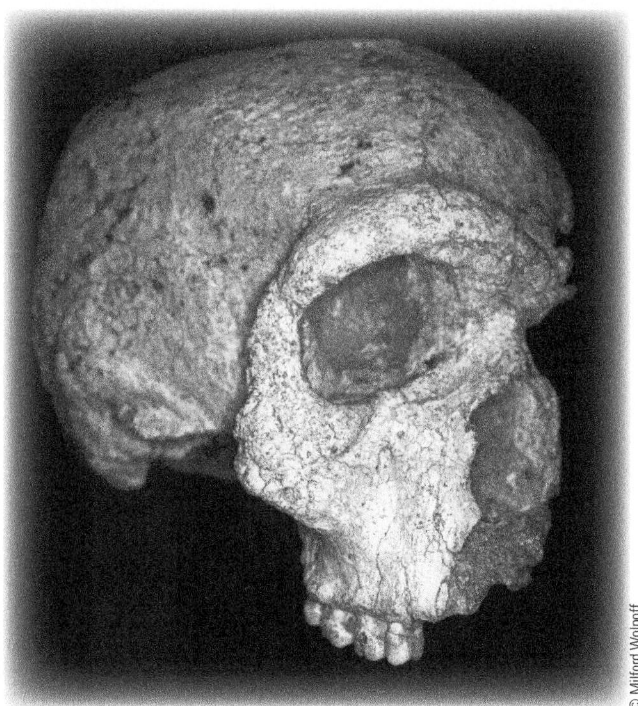

© Milford Wolpoff

▶ **Figure 12-5** Steinheim cranium, a representative of *Homo heidelbergensis* from Germany.

hominin species. However, Rightmire (1998) has suggested that the Gran Dolina hominins may simply represent the earliest well-dated occurrence of *H. heidelbergensis*, possibly dating as early as 850,000 ya.

More recent and more completely studied *H. heidelbergensis* fossils have been found throughout much of Europe. Examples of these finds come from Steinheim (Germany), Petralona (Greece), Swanscombe (England), Arago (France), and another cave site at Atapuerca (Spain), known as Sima de los Huesos. Like their African counterparts, these European premoderns have retained certain *H. erectus* traits, but they're mixed with more derived ones—for example, increased cranial capacity, less angled occiput, parietal expansion, and reduced tooth size (**Figs. 12-5** and **12-7** on pp. 338–339).

The hominins from the Atapuerca site of Sima de los Huesos are especially interesting. These finds come from another cave in the same area as the Gran Dolina discoveries, but are slightly younger, likely dating to between 500,000 and 400,000 ya. Using a different dating method, a date as early as 600,000 ya has been proposed (Bischoff et al., 2007), but most researchers prefer the more conservative later dating (Green et al., 2010; Wood, 2010). A total of at least 28 individuals have been recovered from Sima de los Huesos, which literally means "pit of bones." In fact, with more than 4,000 fossil fragments recovered, Sima de los Huesos contains more than 80 percent of all Middle Pleistocene hominin remains in the world (Bermúdez de Castro et al., 2004). Excavations continue at this remarkable site, where bones have somehow accumulated within a deep chamber inside a cave. From initial descriptions, paleoanthropologists interpret the hominin morphology as showing several indications

At a Glance

Key Premodern Human (*H. heidelbergensis*) Fossils from Europe

Date	Site	Evolutionary Significance
300,000?–259,000? ya	Swanscombe (England)	Partial skull, but shows considerable brain expansion
?600,000–400,000 ya	Sima de los Huesos (Atapuerca, northern Spain)	Large sample; very early evidence of Neandertal ancestry (>500,000 ya); earliest evidence of deliberate body disposal of the dead anywhere

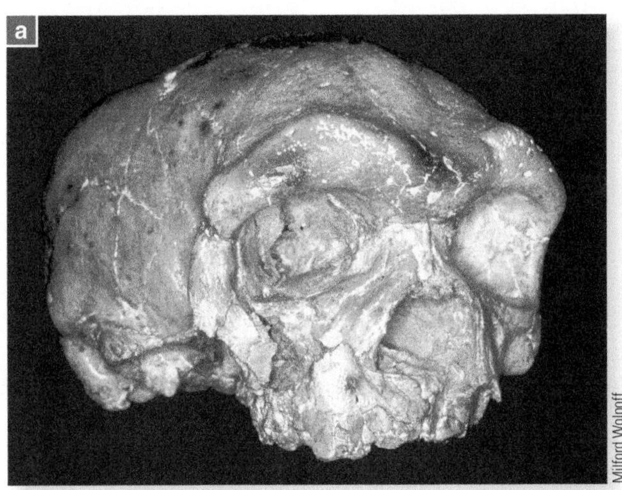

Milford Wolpoff

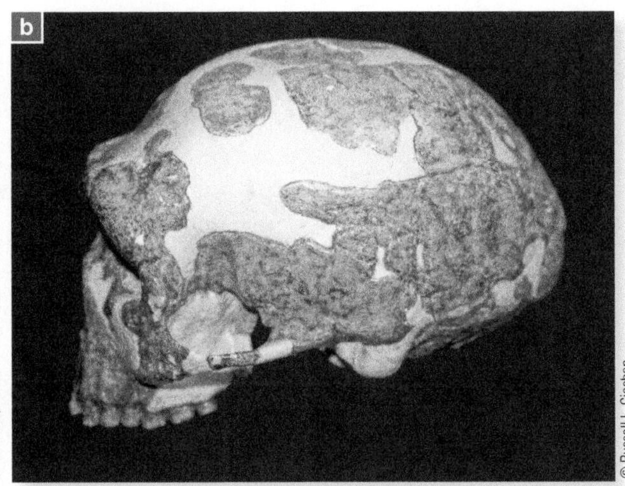

© Russell L. Ciochon

▲ **Figure 12-6** (**a**) Dali skull and (**b**) Jinniushan skull, both from China. These two crania are considered by some to be Asian representatives of *Homo heidelbergensis*.

of an early Neandertal-like pattern, with arching browridges, a projecting midface, and other Neandertal features (Rightmire, 1998).

Asia

Like their contemporaries in Europe and Africa, Asian premodern specimens discovered in China also display both earlier and later characteristics. Chinese paleoanthropologists suggest that the more ancestral traits, such as a sagittal ridge and flattened nasal bones, are shared with *H. erectus* fossils from Zhoukoudian. They also point out that some of these features can be found in modern *H. sapiens* in China today, indicating substantial genetic continuity. That is, some Chinese researchers have argued that, anatomically, modern Chinese didn't evolve from *H. sapiens* in either Europe or Africa; instead, they evolved locally in China from a separate *H. erectus* lineage. Whether such regional evolution occurred or whether anatomically modern migrants from Africa displaced local populations is the subject of a major ongoing debate in paleoanthropology. This important controversy will be a central focus of the next chapter.

Dali, the most complete skull of the later Middle or early Late Pleistocene fossils in China, displays *H. erectus* and *H. sapiens* traits, with a cranial capacity of 1,120 cm^3 (**Fig. 12-6**). Like Dali, several other Chinese specimens combine both earlier and later traits. In addition, a partial skeleton from Jinniushan, in northeast China, has been given a provisional date of 200,000 ya (Tiemel et al., 1994). The cranial capacity is fairly large (approximately 1,260 cm^3), and the walls of the braincase are thin. These are both modern features, and they're somewhat unexpected in an individual this ancient—if the dating estimate is indeed correct. Just how to classify these Chinese Middle Pleistocene hominins has been a subject of debate and controversy. More recently, though, a leading paleoanthropologist has concluded that they're regional variants of *H. heidelbergensis* (Rightmire, 2004).

At a Glance

Key Premodern Human (*H. heidelbergensis*) Fossils from Asia

Date	Site	Evolutionary Significance
230,000–180,000 ya	Dali (China)	Nearly complete skull; best evidence of *H. heidelbergensis* in Asia
200,000 ya	Jinniushan (China)	Partial skeleton with cranium showing relatively large brain size; some Chinese scholars suggest it as possible ancestor of early Chinese *H. sapiens*

© Cengage Learning

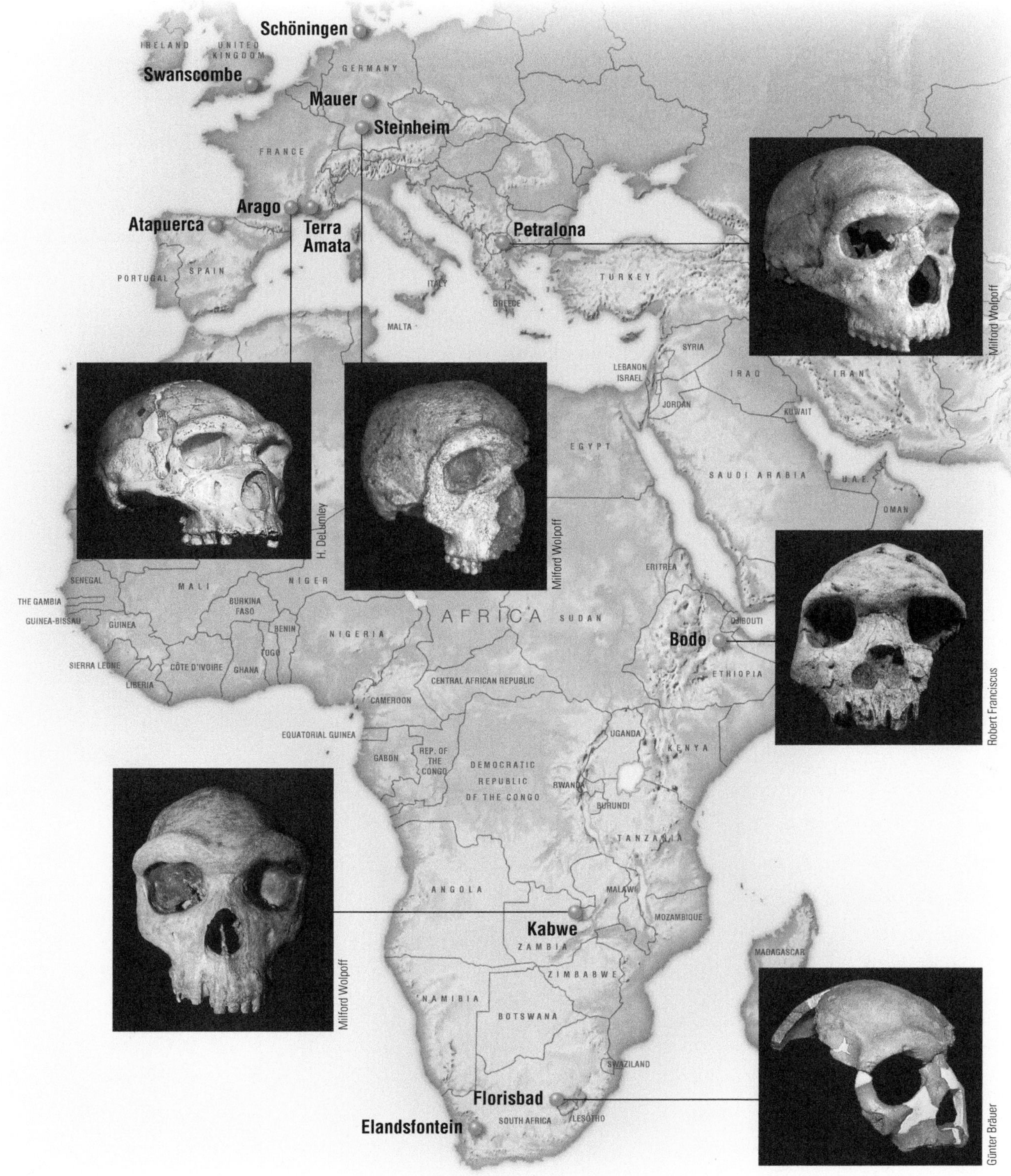

▲ **Figure 12-7** Fossil discoveries and archaeological localities of Middle Pleistocene premodern hominins.

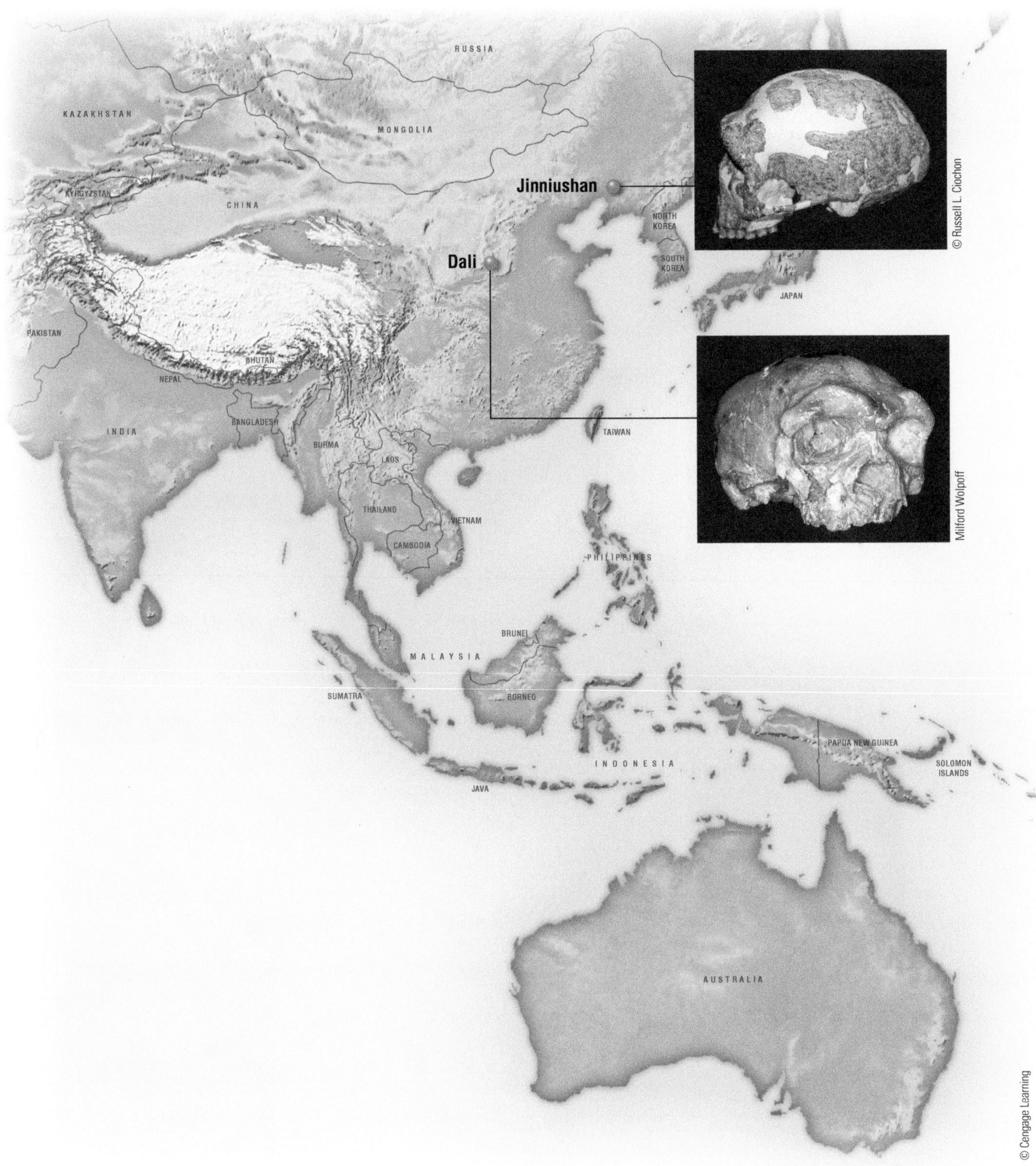
RUSSIA
KAZAKHSTAN
MONGOLIA
KYRGYZSTAN
CHINA
Jinniushan
NORTH KOREA
SOUTH KOREA
Dali
JAPAN
PAKISTAN
BHUTAN
NEPAL
BANGLADESH
INDIA
BURMA
LAOS
TAIWAN
THAILAND
VIETNAM
CAMBODIA
PHILIPPINES
BRUNEI
MALAYSIA
SUMATRA
BORNEO
PAPUA NEW GUINEA
SOLOMON ISLANDS
INDONESIA
JAVA
AUSTRALIA
© Russell L. Ciochon
Milford Wolpoff
© Cengage Learning

A Review of Middle Pleistocene Evolution

Premodern human fossils from Africa and Europe resemble each other more than they do the hominin fossils from Asia. The mix of some ancestral characteristics—retained from *Homo erectus* ancestors—with more derived features gives the African and European fossils a distinctive look; thus Middle Pleistocene hominins from these two continents are usually referred to as *H. heidelbergensis.*

The situation in Asia isn't so tidy. To some researchers, the remains, especially those from Jinniushan, seem more modern than do contemporary fossils from either Europe or Africa. This observation explains why Chinese paleoanthropologists and some American colleagues conclude that the Jinniushan remains are early members of *H. sapiens.* Other researchers (for example, Rightmire, 1998, 2004) suggest that they represent a regional branch of *H. heidelbergensis.*

The Pleistocene world forced many small populations into geographical isolation; most of these regional populations no doubt died out. Some, however, did evolve, and their descendants are likely a major part of the later hominin fossil record. In Africa, *H. heidelbergensis* is hypothesized to have evolved into modern *H. sapiens.* In Europe, *H. heidelbergensis* evolved into Neandertals. Meanwhile, the Chinese premodern populations may all have met with extinction. Right now, though, there's no consensus on the status or the likely fate of these enigmatic Asian Middle Pleistocene hominins (**Fig. 12-8**).

Middle Pleistocene Culture

The Acheulian technology of *H. erectus* carried over into the Middle Pleistocene with relatively little change until near the end of the period, when it became slightly more sophisticated. Bone, a high-quality tool material, remained practically unused during this time. Stone flake tools similar to those of the earlier era persisted, possibly in greater variety. Some of the later premodern humans in Africa and Europe invented a method—the Levallois technique (**Fig. 12-9**)—for controlling flake size and shape, resulting in a "turtle back" profile. The Levallois technique required several complex and coordinated steps, suggesting increased cognitive abilities in later premodern populations.

Premodern human populations continued to live in both caves and open-air sites, but they may have increased their use of caves. Did these hominins control fire? Klein (1999), in interpreting archaeological evidence from

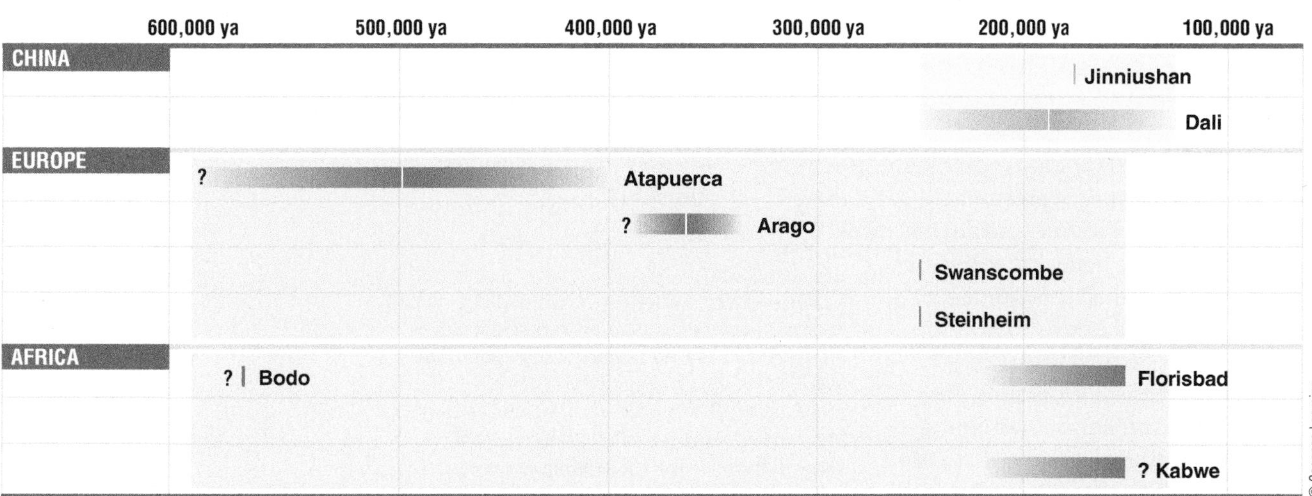

▼**Figure 12-8** Time line of Middle Pleistocene hominins. Note that most dates are approximations. Question marks indicate those estimates that are most tentative.

Nodule

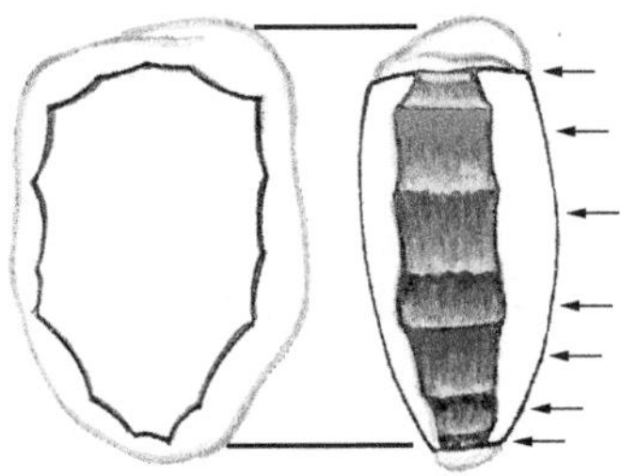

The nodule is chipped on the perimeter.

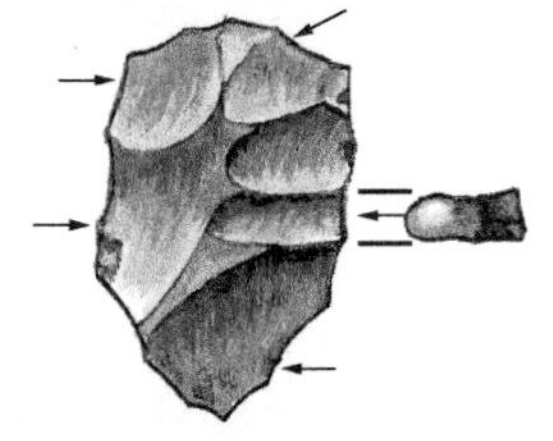

Flakes are radially removed from top surface.

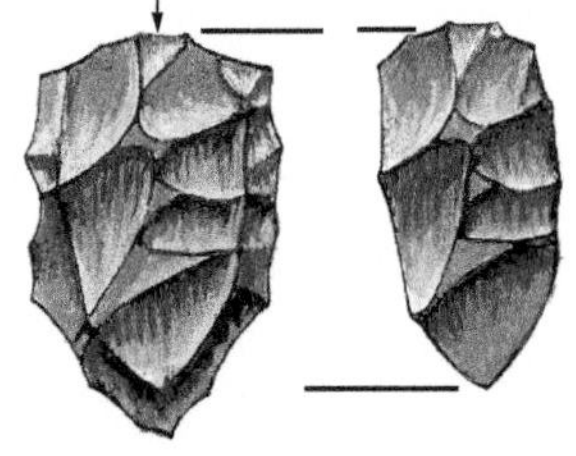

A final blow struck at one end removes a large flake. The flake on the right is the goal of the whole process and is the completed tool.

▲ **Figure 12-9** The Levallois technique.

France, Germany, and Hungary, suggests that they did. What's more, Chinese archaeologists insist that many Middle Pleistocene sites in China contain evidence of human-controlled fire. However, the best (and earliest) documented evidence has recently been found in South Africa (Berna et al., 2012). (This new discovery was discussed in Chapter 11.)

We know that Middle Pleistocene hominins built temporary structures, because researchers have found concentrations of bones, stones, and artifacts at several sites. We also have evidence that they exploited many different food sources—fruits, vegetables, seeds, nuts, and bird eggs, each in its own season. Importantly, they also exploited marine life, a new innovation in human biocultural evolution.

The hunting capabilities of premodern humans, as for earlier hominins, are still greatly disputed. Most researchers have found little evidence supporting widely practiced advanced hunting. Some more recent finds, however, are beginning to change this view—especially the discovery in 1995 of remarkable wood spears from the Schöningen site in Germany (Thieme, 1997). These large, extremely well-preserved weapons (provisionally dated to about 400,000 to 300,000 ya) were most likely used as throwing spears, presumably to hunt large animals. Also interesting in this context, the bones of numerous horses were recovered at Schöningen.

As documented by the fossil remains as well as artifactual evidence from archaeological sites, the long period of transitional hominins in Europe continued well into the Late Pleistocene (after 125,000 ya). But with the appearance and expansion of the Neandertals, the evolution of premodern humans took a unique turn.

Neandertals: Premodern Humans of the Late Pleistocene

Since their discovery more than a century ago, the Neandertals have haunted the minds and foiled the best-laid theories of paleoanthropologists. They fit into the general scheme of human evolution, and yet they're misfits. Classified variously either as *H. sapiens* or as belonging to a separate species, they are like us and yet different. It's not easy to put them in their place. Many anthropologists classify Neandertals within *H. sapiens*, but as a distinctive subspecies, *Homo sapiens neanderthalensis*,* with modern *H. sapiens* designated as *Homo sapiens sapiens*. However, not all experts agree with this interpretation. The most recent genetic evidence of interbreeding between Neandertals and early modern humans (Green et al., 2010) suggests that complete speciation was never attained. This argues against a clear designation of Neandertals as a species separate from *H. sapiens*. We'll discuss this important evidence in more detail in a moment.

* *Thal*, meaning "valley," is the old spelling; due to rules of taxonomic naming, this spelling is retained in the formal species designation *Homo neanderthalensis* (although the *h* was never pronounced). The modern spelling, *tal*, is used today in Germany; we follow contemporary usage in the text with the spelling of the colloquial *Neandertal*.

Neandertal fossil remains have been found at dates approaching 130,000 ya; but in the following discussion of Neandertals, we'll focus on those populations that lived especially during the last major glaciation, which began about 75,000 ya and ended about 10,000 ya (**Fig. 12-10**). We should also note that the evolutionary roots of Neandertals apparently reach quite far back in western Europe, as evidenced by the 400,000+-year-old remains from Sima de los Huesos. Some researchers conclude that these hominins are derived enough to be considered members of the Neandertal clade (Stringer, 2012).

The majority of fossils have been found in Europe, where they've been most studied. Our description of Neandertals is based primarily on those specimens, usually called classic Neandertals, from western Europe. Not all Neandertals—including others from eastern Europe and western Asia and those from the interglacial period just before the last glacial one—exactly fit our description of the classic morphology. They tend to be less robust, possibly because the climate in which they lived was not as cold as in western Europe during the last glaciation.

One striking feature of Neandertals is brain size, which was actually larger than that of *H. sapiens* today. The average for contemporary *H. sapiens* is between 1,300 and 1,400 cm^3, while for Neandertals it was 1,520 cm^3. The larger size may be associated with the metabolic efficiency of a larger brain in cold weather. The Inuit (Eskimo), also living in very cold areas, have a larger average brain size than most other modern human populations. We should also point out that the larger brain size in both premodern and contemporary human populations adapted to cold climates is partially correlated with larger body size, which has also evolved among these groups (see Chapter 15).

The classic Neandertal cranium is large, long, low, and bulging at the sides. Viewed from the side, the occipital bone is somewhat bun-shaped, but the marked occipital angle typical of many *H. erectus* crania is absent. The forehead rises more vertically than that of *H. erectus*, and the browridges arch over the orbits instead of forming a straight bar (see **Fig. 12-11**).

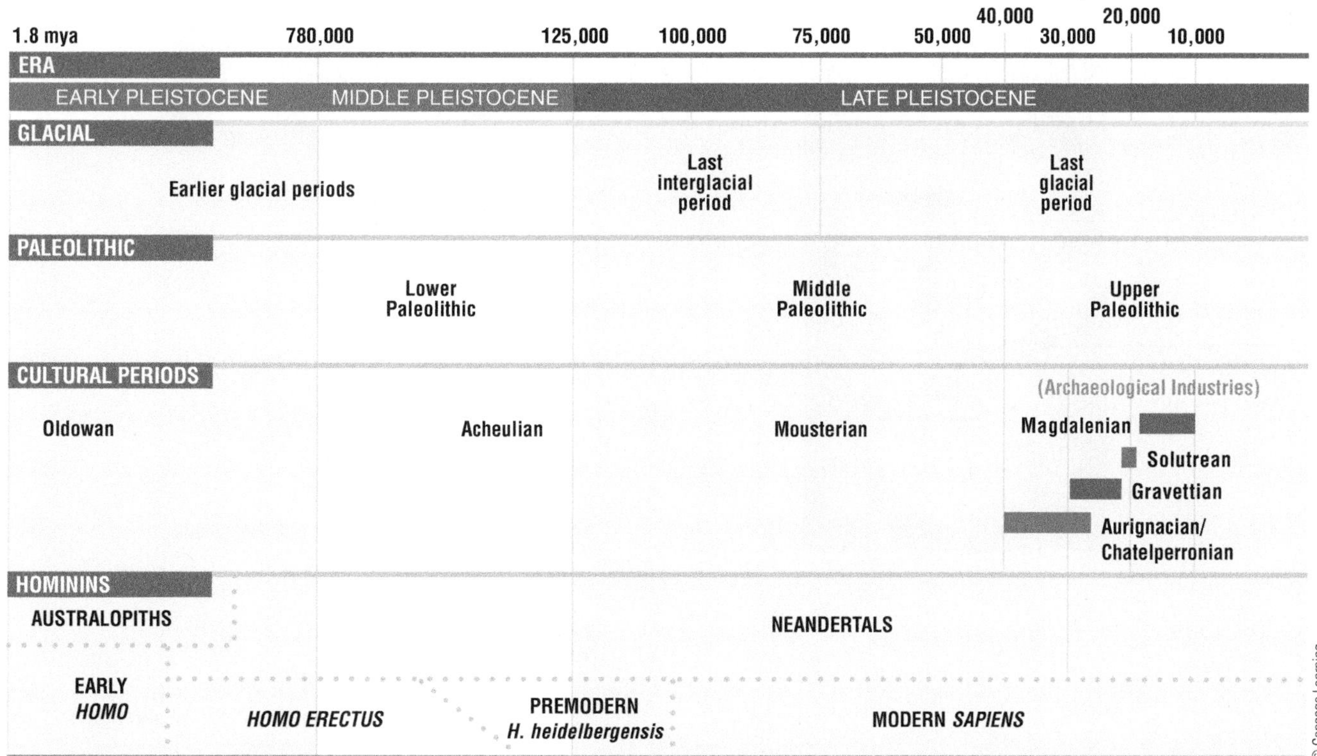

▼ **Figure 12-10** Correlation of Pleistocene subdivisions with archaeological industries and hominins. Note that the geological divisions are separate and different from the archaeological stages (e.g., Late Pleistocene is not synonymous with Upper Paleolithic).

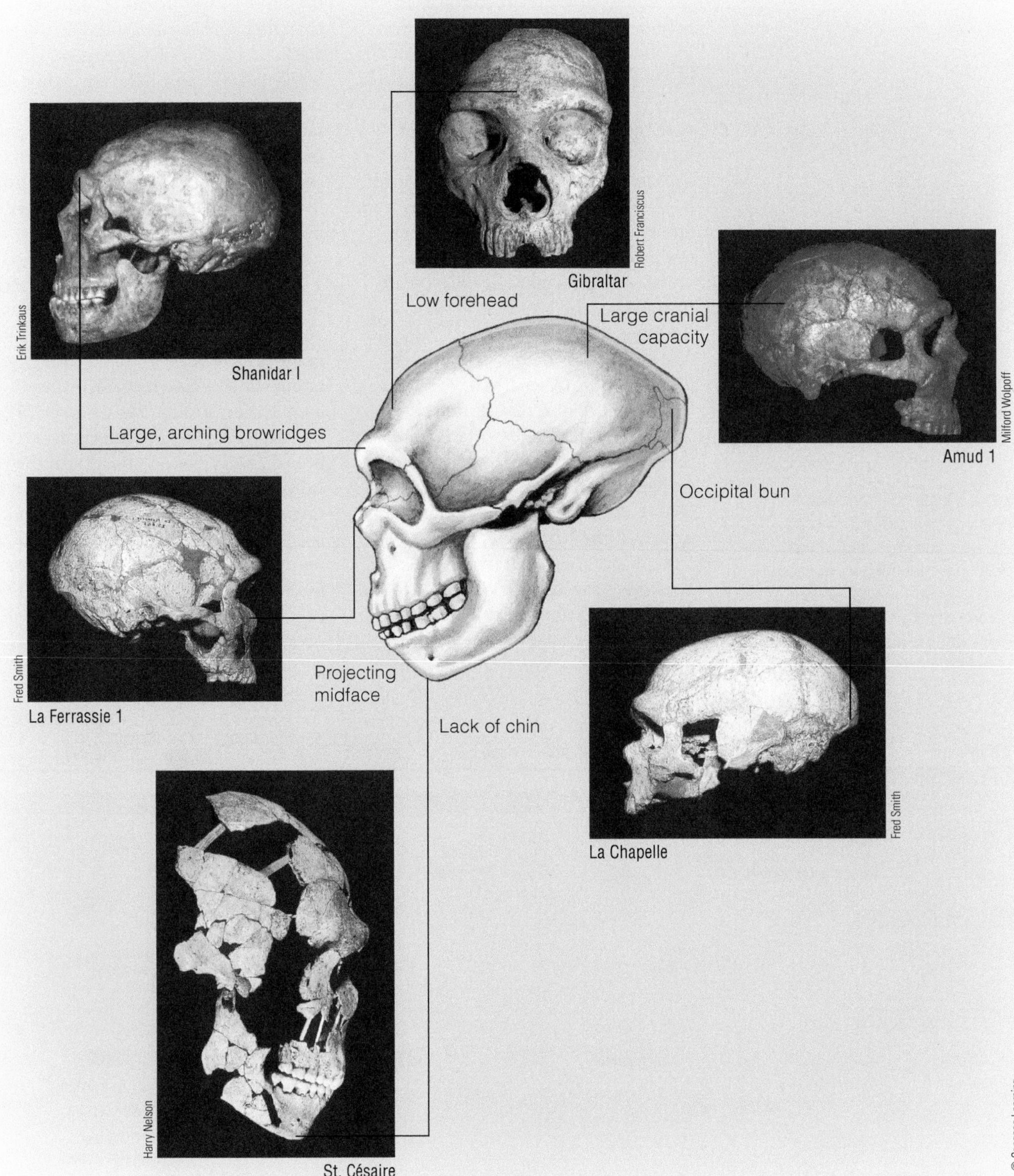

▲ **Figure 12-11** Morphology and variation in Neandertal crania.

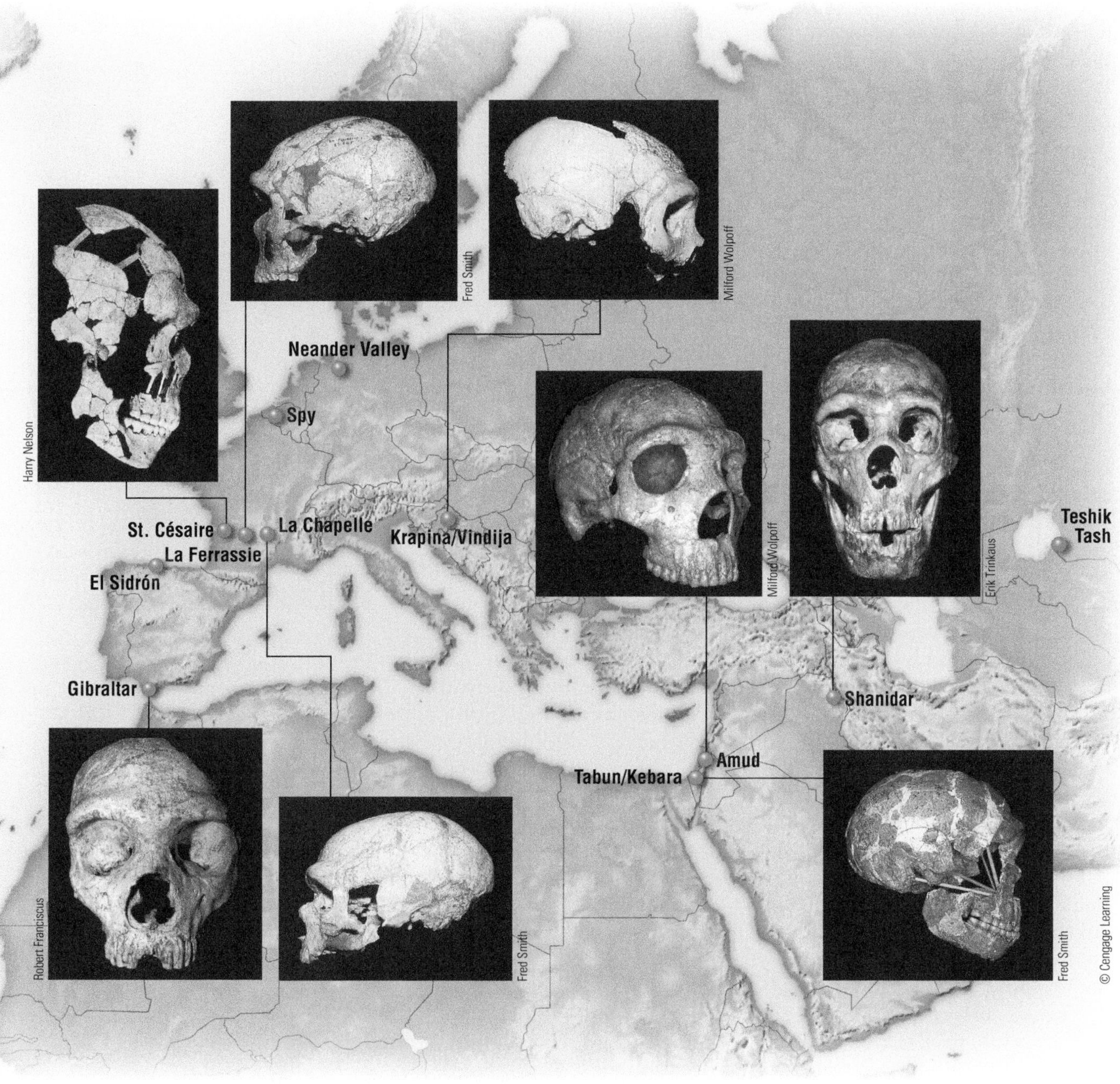

▲ **Figure 12-12** Fossil discoveries of Neandertals.

Compared with anatomically modern humans, the Neandertal face stands out. It projects almost as if it were pulled forward. Postcranially, Neandertals were very robust, barrel-chested, and powerfully muscled. This robust skeletal structure, in fact, dominates hominin evolution from *H. erectus* through all premodern forms. Still, the Neandertals appear particularly robust, with shorter limbs than seen in most modern *H. sapiens* populations. Both the facial anatomy and the robust postcranial structure of Neandertals have been interpreted by Erik Trinkaus, of Washington University in St. Louis, as adaptations to rigorous living in a cold climate.

For about 100,000 years, Neandertals lived in Europe and western Asia (see **Fig. 12-12**), and their coming and going have raised more questions and controversies than for any other hominin group. As we've noted, Neandertal forebears were transitional forms dating to the later Middle Pleistocene. However, it's not until the Late Pleistocene that Neandertals become fully recognizable.

Western Europe

One of the most important Neandertal discoveries was made in 1908 at La Chapelle-aux-Saints, in southwestern France. A nearly complete skeleton was found buried in a shallow grave in a **flexed** position (**Fig. 12-13**). Several fragments of nonhuman long bones had been placed over the head, and over them, a bison leg. Around the body were flint tools and broken animal bones.

The skeleton was turned over for study to Marcellin Boule, a well-known French paleontologist, who subsequently depicted the La Chapelle Neandertal as a brutish, bent-kneed, not fully erect biped. Because of this exaggerated interpretation, some scholars, and certainly the general public, concluded that all Neandertals were highly primitive creatures.

Why did Boule draw these conclusions from the La Chapelle skeleton? Today, we think he misjudged the Neandertal posture because this adult male skeleton had arthritis of the spine. Also, and probably more importantly, Boule and his contemporaries found it difficult to accept an individual who appeared in any way to depart from the modern pattern as a human ancestor.

The skull of this male, who was possibly at least 40 years of age when he died, is very large, with a cranial capacity of 1,620 cm^3. Typical of western European classic forms of Neandertal, the vault is low and long; the browridges are immense, with the typical Neandertal arched shape; the forehead is low and retreating; and the face is long and projecting. The back of the skull is protuberant and bun-shaped (see Figs. 12-11 and **12-14**).

The La Chapelle skeleton actually isn't a typical Neandertal but an unusually robust male who "evidently represents an extreme in the Neandertal range of variation" (Brace et al., 1979, p. 117). Unfortunately, this skeleton, which Boule claimed didn't even walk completely erect, was widely accepted as "Mr. Neandertal." But few other Neandertal individuals possess such an exaggerated expression of Neandertal traits as the "Old Man of La Chapelle-aux-Saints."

Dramatic new evidence of Neandertal behavior comes from the El Sidrón site in northern Spain. Dated to about 49,000 ya, fragmented remains of 12 individuals show bone changes indicating that they were smashed, butchered, and likely cannibalized—presumably by other Neandertals (Lalueza-Fox et al., 2011).

Because the remains of all 12 individuals were found together in a cave where their remains had accidentally fallen, they all probably died (were killed) at about the same time. Lying there undisturbed for almost 50,000 years, these individuals reveal several secrets about Neandertals. First, they are hypothesized to all have belonged to the same social group, representing a band of hunter-gatherers. Their ages and sex support this interpretation: three adult males, three adult females, five children/adolescents, and one infant.

What's more, genetic evidence shows that the adult males were all closely related, but the females weren't. It seems that Neandertals practiced a patrilocal form of mating, in which related males stay together and mate with females from other groups (see **Fig. 12-15**).

Some of the most recent of the western European Neandertals come from St. Césaire, in southwestern France, and are dated at about 35,000 ya

▲ **Figure 12-13** Artist's reconstruction of an adult male Neandertal based on skeletal remains from La Chapelle, France.

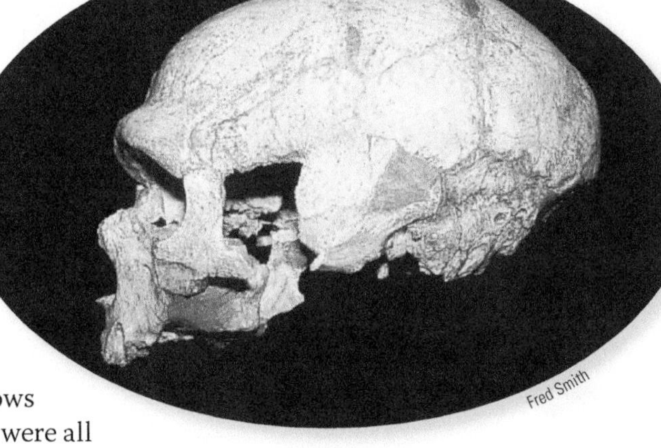

▲ **Figure 12-14** Specimen from La Chapelle-aux-Saints. Note the occipital bun, projecting face, and low vault.

flexed The position of the body in a bent orientation, with arms and legs drawn up to the chest.

▲ **Figure 12-15** "Clean" excavations at the El Sidrón cave in Spain, where special precautions are used to prevent contamination and allow more controlled later DNA analyses. From this site recent evidence from mtDNA analyses suggests that males likely practiced a patrilocal mating pattern.

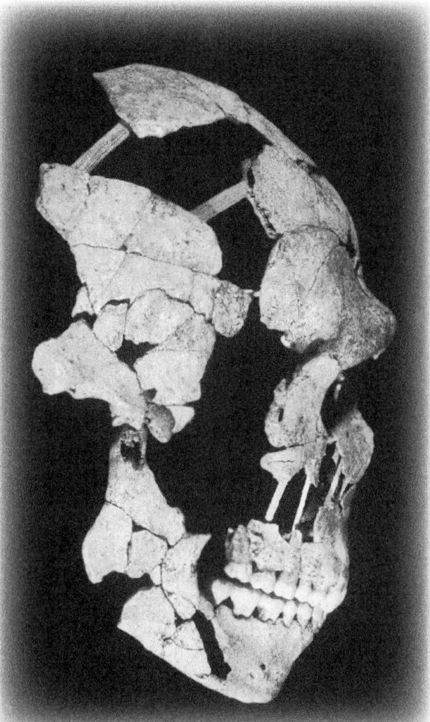

▲ **Figure 12-16** Specimen from St. Césaire, among the "last" Neandertals.

Upper Paleolithic A cultural period usually associated with modern humans but also found with some Neandertals and distinguished by technological innovation in various stone tool industries. Best known from western Europe, similar industries are also known from central and eastern Europe and Africa.

(**Fig. 12-16**). At St. Césaire, Neandertal remains were recovered from an archaeological level that also included discarded chipped blades, hand axes, and other stone tools of an **Upper Paleolithic** tool industry associated with Neandertals.

Central Europe

There are quite a few other European classic Neandertals, including significant finds from central Europe (see Fig. 12-12). At Krapina, Croatia, researchers have recovered an abundance of bones—1,000 fragments representing up to 70 individuals—and 1,000 stone tools or flakes (Trinkaus and Shipman, 1992). Krapina is an old site, possibly the earliest showing the full suite of classic Neandertal morphology (**Fig. 12-17**) dating back to the beginning of the Late Pleistocene (estimated at 130,000 to 110,000 ya). Krapina is also important as an intentional burial site—one of the oldest on record.

About 30 miles from Krapina, Neandertal fossils have also been discovered at Vindija. This site is an excellent source of faunal, cultural, and hominin materials stratified in *sequence* throughout much of the Late Pleistocene. Neandertal fossils from Vindija consist of some 35 specimens dated to between 42,000 and 32,000 ya, making them some of the most recent Neandertals ever discovered (Higham et al., 2006). Given these dates, it seems that the most recent Neandertal remains yet recovered come from Vindija.

As we've seen, the Neandertals from St. Césaire are only slightly older than those from Vindija, making these two sites important for several reasons. Anatomically modern humans were living in both western and central Europe by about 35,000 ya or a bit earlier. So it's possible that Neandertals and modern *H. sapiens* were living quite close to each other for several thousand years (**Fig. 12-18**). How did these two groups interact? Evidence from a number of French sites indicates that Neandertals may have borrowed

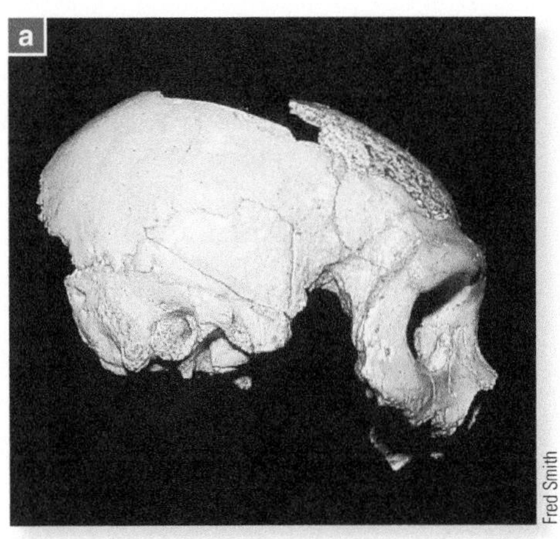

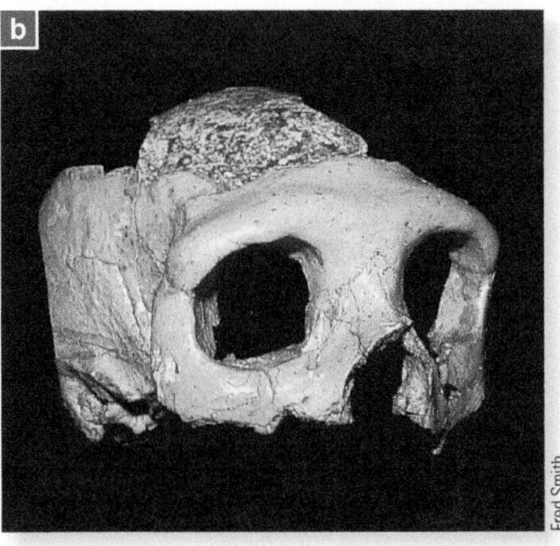

◄ **Figure 12-17** Krapina cranium. (**a**) Lateral view showing characteristic Neandertal traits. (**b**) Three-quarters view.

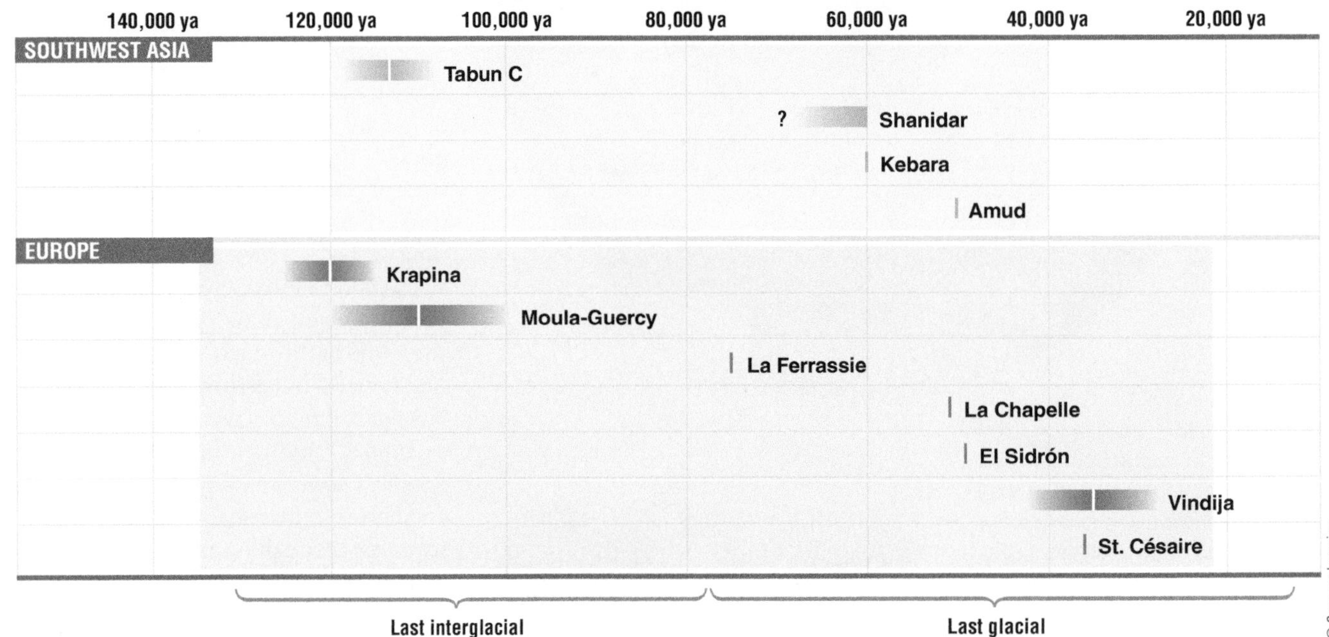

▲ **Figure 12-18** Time line for Neandertal fossil discoveries.

technological methods and tools (such as blades) from the anatomically modern populations and thereby modified their own tools, creating a new industry, the **Chatelperronian**. It's also possible, of course, that early modern *H. sapiens* borrowed cultural innovations from the Neandertals (who, as we'll soon see, were in many ways also quite sophisticated). What's more, we now know that they very likely were *interbreeding* with each other!

Western Asia

Israel Many important Neandertal discoveries have also been made in southwest Asia. Neandertal specimens from Israel are less robustly built than the classic Neandertals of Europe, though again the overall pattern is clearly Neandertal. One of the best known of these discoveries is from Tabun (**Fig. 12-19**). Tabun, excavated in the early 1930s, yielded a female skeleton dated by thermoluminescence (TL) at about 120,000 to 110,000 ya. (TL dating is discussed in Chapter 9.) If this dating is accurate, Neandertals at Tabun were generally contemporary with early modern *H. sapiens* found in nearby caves.

A more recent Neandertal burial of a large male comes from Kebara, a neighboring cave at Mt. Carmel. A partial skeleton, dated to 60,000 ya, it contains the most complete Neandertal thorax and pelvis yet found. Also

Chatelperronian Pertaining to an Upper Paleolithic industry found in France and Spain, containing blade tools and associated with Neandertals.

▶ **Figure 12-19** Excavation of the Tabun Cave, Mt. Carmel, Israel.

recovered at Kebara is a hyoid—a small bone located in the throat, and the first ever found from a Neandertal; this bone is especially important because of its usefulness in reconstructing language capabilities.*

Iraq A most remarkable site is Shanidar Cave, in the Zagros Mountains of northeastern Iraq, where fieldworkers found partial skeletons of nine individuals, four of them deliberately buried. One of the more interesting skeletons recovered from Shanidar is that of a male (Shanidar 1) who lived to be approximately 30 to 45 years old, a considerable age for a prehistoric human (**Fig. 12-20**). He is estimated to have stood 5 feet 7 inches tall, with a cranial capacity of 1,600 cm^3. The skeletal remains of Shanidar 1 also exhibit several other fascinating features.

> There had been a crushing blow to the left side of the head, fracturing the eye socket, displacing the left eye, and probably causing blindness on that side. He also sustained a massive blow to the right side of the body that so badly damaged the right arm that it became withered and useless; the bones of the shoulder blade, collar bone, and upper arm are much smaller and thinner than those on the left. The right lower arm and hand are missing, probably not because of poor preservation . . . but

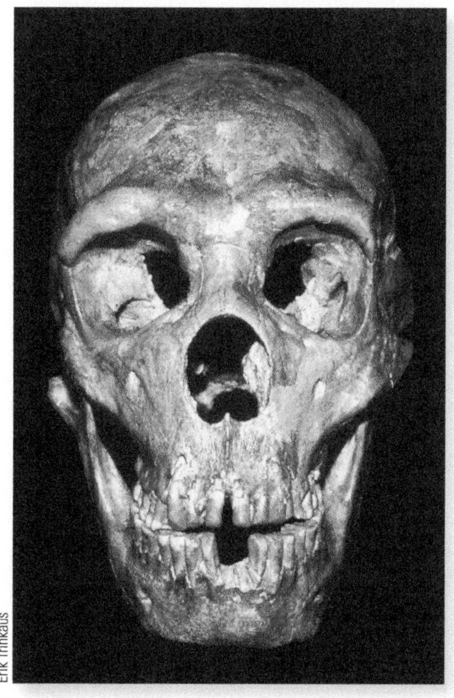

▲ **Figure 12-20** Shanidar 1. Does he represent Neandertal compassion for the disabled?

*The Kebara hyoid is identical to that of modern humans, suggesting that Neandertals did not differ from modern *H. sapiens* in this key element.

> because they either atrophied and dropped off or because they were amputated. (Trinkaus and Shipman, 1992, p. 340)

Besides these injuries, the man had further trauma to both legs, and he probably limped. It's hard to imagine how he could have performed day-to-day activities without assistance. This is why Erik Trinkaus, who has studied the Shanidar remains, suggests that to survive, Shanidar 1 must have been helped by others: "A one-armed, partially blind, crippled man could have made no pretense of hunting or gathering his own food. That he survived for years after his trauma was a testament to Neandertal compassion and humanity" (Trinkaus and Shipman, 1992, p. 341).

Central Asia

Neandertals extended their range even farther to the east, far into central Asia. A discovery made in the 1930s at the site of Teshik-Tash, in Uzbekistan, of a Neandertal child associated with tools of the Mousterian industry suggested that this species had dispersed a long way into Asia. However, owing to poor archaeological control during excavation and the young age of the individual, the find was not considered by all paleoanthropologists as clearly that of a Neandertal. New finds and molecular evaluation have provided crucial evidence that Neandertals did in fact extend their geographical range far into central Asia and perhaps even farther east.

DNA analysis of the Teshik-Tash remains shows that they are clearly Neandertal. What's more, other fragments from southern Siberia also show a distinctively Neandertal genetic pattern (Krause et al., 2007a). As we'll see shortly, researchers have recently been able to identify and analyze DNA from several Neandertal specimens. It's been shown that Neandertals and modern humans differ in both their mitochondrial DNA (mtDNA) and nuclear DNA; these results are extremely significant in determining the evolutionary status of the Neandertal lineage. Moreover, in the case of the fragmentary remains from southern Siberia (dating to 44,000 to 37,000 ya), it was the DNA findings that provided the key evidence in determining whether the hominin is even a Neandertal. In a sense, this is analogous to doing forensic analysis on our ancient hominin predecessors.

Surprising Connections: Another Contemporary Hominin? In 2000, 2008, and 2010 researchers found more fragmentary hominin remains in another cave (Denisova Cave) in the Altai Mountains of southern Siberia. Only a finger bone and two teeth were found, and these are dated to as old as 80,000–60,000 ya (Meyer et al., 2012). From such incomplete skeletal remains, accurate anatomical species identification is impossible. In prior years, this seemingly meager find would have been stashed away in a cabinet in a museum or a university laboratory and mostly forgotten. But in the twenty-first century, we have new ways to study bits and pieces of ancient hominins. So the finger bone was sent to the Max-Planck Institute for Evolutionary Biology in Germany to see if DNA analysis could determine to which species it belongs.

Initially, mitochondrial DNA analysis was performed and provided a big surprise: The mtDNA from the hominin at Denisnova Cave did not match that of either a modern *H. sapiens* or a Neandertal!

Lying in a cool, dry, stable environment inside the cave, the Denisnova remains stood a good chance of preserving even more complete ancient DNA. So, the Max Planck team, along with many colleagues from around the world, decided to attempt to sequence the nuclear genome derived from DNA in the finger bone (in which DNA preservation was exceptionally good).

Within less than 2 years they successfully sequenced the *entire* genome from this one small bone, in other words, more than three billion base pairs—a truly amazing scientific accomplishment (Reich et al., 2010). In

At a Glance

Key Neandertal Fossil Discoveries

Date	Site	Evolutionary Significance
42,000––28,000 ya	Vindija (Croatia)	Large sample (best evidence of Neandertals in eastern Europe); latest well-dated Neandertal site
50,000 ya	La Chapelle (France)	Most famous Neandertal site; historically provided early, but distorted, interpretation of Neandertals
70,000–60,000 ya	Shanidar (Iraq)	Several well-preserved skeletons; good example of Neandertals from southwestern Asia; one individual with multiple injuries
110,000 ya; date uncertain	Tabun (Israel)	Well-preserved and very well-studied fossils showing early evidence of Neandertals in southwestern Asia

2012 they went even further doing a far more precise sequencing (up to 30× more accurate than the one two years earlier) of the entire genome from the same finger bone. (Meyer et al., 2012). These far more complete data confirmed the earlier findings, most notably that the "Denisovans" were a separate branch of hominins living side by side in central Asia with two other lineages of hominins (Neandertals and modern humans).

The most recent whole genome analysis has also been able to identify the sex of the individual (as female) and reveal that her skin was dark along with brown hair and brown eyes. What's more it was possible to sequence separately the two DNA strands and thus to tell which genes were inherited from the girl's mother and which ones from her father. Lastly, up to 34 genes that are known to cause disease were found to be different in the Denisovans as compared to modern humans (Meyer et al., 2012). The complete genome also provided another big surprise regarding how these ancient Denisovans are genetically connected to some living human populations (see "Molecular Connections" below).

Culture of Neandertals

Anthropologists almost always associate Neandertals, who lived in the cultural period known as the Middle Paleolithic, with the **Mousterian** industry—although they don't always associate the Mousterian industry with just Neandertals (since it is sometimes also found with modern humans). Early in the last glacial period, Mousterian culture extended across Europe and North Africa into the former Soviet Union, Israel, Iran, and as far east as central Asia and possibly even China. Also, in sub-Saharan Africa, the contemporaneous Middle Stone Age industry is broadly similar to the Mousterian.

Technology

Neandertals extended and diversified traditional methods of making tools, and there's some indication that they developed specialized tools for skinning and preparing meat, hunting, woodworking, and hafting (**Fig. 12-21**).

Even so, in strong contrast to the following cultural period, the Upper

Mousterian Pertaining to the stone tool industry associated with Neandertals and some modern *H. sapiens* groups; also called Middle Paleolithic. This industry is characterized by a larger proportion of flake tools than is found in Acheulian tool kits.

Randall White

◄ **Figure 12-21** Examples of the Mousterian tool kit, including (from left to right) a Levallois point, a perforator, and a side scraper.

Paleolithic, there's almost no evidence that they used bone tools. Still, Neandertals advanced their technology well beyond that of earlier hominins. It's possible that their technological advances helped provide part of the basis for the remarkable changes of the Upper Paleolithic, which we'll discuss in the next chapter. What's more, Neandertals also were quite advanced in exploiting new food resources as well as fashioning personal adornments.

Subsistence

We know, from the abundant remains of animal bones at their sites, that Neandertals were successful hunters. But though it's clear that Neandertals could hunt large mammals, they may not have been as efficient at this task as Upper Paleolithic modern humans. For example, it wasn't until the beginning of the Upper Paleolithic that the spear-thrower, or atlatl, came into use (see Chapter 13). Soon after that, in Upper Paleolithic groups, the bow and arrow greatly increased efficiency (and safety) in hunting large mammals by putting distance between the hunters and the hunted. Because Neandertals had no long-distance weaponry and were mostly limited to thrusting spears, they may have been more prone to serious injury—a hypothesis supported by paleoanthropologists Thomas Berger and Erik Trinkaus. Berger and Trinkaus (1995) analyzed the pattern of trauma, particularly fractures, in Neandertals and compared it with that seen in contemporary human samples. Interestingly, the pattern in Neandertals, especially the relatively high proportion of head and neck injuries, was most similar to that seen in contemporary rodeo performers. Berger and Trinkaus concluded that "the similarity to the rodeo distribution suggests frequent close encounters with large ungulates unkindly disposed to the humans involved" (Berger and Trinkaus, 1995, p. 841).

Recent archaeological discoveries have shown that Neandertals also expanded their range of available foods to include marine resources—a subsistence strategy previously thought to have been developed later by modern humans during the Upper Paleolithic. From the island of Gibraltar, new evidence has shown that some Neandertals gathered shellfish and hunted seals and dolphins, displaying no difference in their hunting behavior from modern humans of the same region (Stringer et al., 2008).

Speech and Symbolic Behavior

There are a variety of hypotheses concerning the speech capacities of Neandertals, and many of these views

A Closer Look

The Evolution of Language

One of the most distinctive behavioral attributes of all modern humans is our advanced ability to use highly sophisticated symbolic language. Indeed, it would be impossible to imagine human social relationships or human culture without language.

When did language evolve? First, we should define what we mean by full human language. As we discussed in Chapter 7, nonhuman primates have shown some elements of language. For example, some chimpanzees, gorillas, and bonobos display the ability to manipulate symbols and a rudimentary understanding of grammar. Still, the full complement of skills displayed by humans includes the extensive use of arbitrary symbols; sophisticated grammar; and a complex, open system of communication.

Most scholars are comfortable attributing such equivalent skills to early members of *H. sapiens*, as early as 200,000 to 100,000 ya. In fact, some researchers have hypothesized that the elaborate technology and artistic achievements, as well as the rapid dispersal, of modern humans were a direct result of behavioral advantages—particularly full language capabilities. More recently, we have come to appreciate that Neandertal cultural abilities were also quite advanced and that the transition to the more elaborate Upper Paleolithic associated with modern humans was not instantaneous.

Clearly, earlier hominins had some form of complex communication; almost everyone agrees that even the earliest hominins did communicate (and the form was at least as complex as that seen in living apes). What's not generally agreed upon is just when the full complement of human language capacity first emerged. Indeed, the controversy relating to this process will continue to ferment, since there's no clear answer to the question. At present, there's not enough evidence available to fully establish the language capabilities of any fossil hominin. We said in Chapter 7 that there are neurological foundations for language and that these features relate more to brain reorganization than to simple increase in brain size. Also, as far as spoken language is concerned, alterations within several anatomical structures—including the brain, tongue and vocal tract—must have occurred at some time during hominin evolution.

Yet, because it's soft tissue, we have no complete record of fossil hominin brains or their vocal tracts. We do have endocasts, which preserve a few external features of the brain. For example, there are several preserved endocasts of australopiths from South Africa. However, the information is incomplete and thus subject to varying interpretations. (For example, did these hominins possess language? If not, what form of communication did they display?) Evidence from the vocal tract has been even more elusive, although recent finds are helping to fill in at least some of the gaps.

In such an atmosphere of fragmentary data, a variety of conflicting hypotheses have been proposed. Some paleoanthropologists argue that early australopiths (3 mya) had language. Others think that such capabilities were first displayed by early *Homo* (perhaps 2 mya). Still others suggest that language didn't emerge fully until

are contradictory. Although some researchers argue that Neandertals were incapable of human speech, the prevailing consensus has been that they *were* capable of articulate speech and possibly capable of producing the same range of sounds as modern humans.

Recent genetic evidence likely will help us to determine when fully human language first emerged (Enard et al., 2002; Fisher and Scharff, 2009). In humans today, mutations in a particular gene (locus) are known to produce serious language impairments. From an evolutionary perspective, what is perhaps most significant is the greater variability seen in the alleles at this locus in modern humans as compared with other primates. One explanation for this increased variation is intensified selection acting on human populations. And, as we'll see shortly, DNA evidence from Neandertal fossils shows that these hominins had already made this transformation.

Many researchers are convinced that Upper Paleolithic *H. sapiens* had some significant behavioral advantages over Neandertals and other premodern humans. Was it some kind of new and expanded ability to symbolize, communicate, organize social activities, elaborate technology, obtain a wider range of food resources, or care for the sick or injured? Or was it some other factor? Compared with modern *H. sapiens*, were the Neandertals limited by neurological differences that may have contributed to their demise?

the time of *Homo erectus* (2 to 1 mya), or perhaps it was premodern humans (such as the Neandertals) who first displayed such skills. And finally, some researchers assert that language first developed only with the appearance of fully modern *H. sapiens.*

Because the question of language evolution is so fundamental to understanding human evolution (indeed, what it means *to be* human), a variety of creative techniques have been applied to assess the (limited) evidence that's available. We've already mentioned the analysis of endocasts.

To reconstruct speech capabilities in fossil hominins, the physiology of the vocal tract can also provide some crucial hints, especially the position of the voice box (larynx) within the throat. In adult modern humans, the larynx is placed low in the throat, where it can better act as a resonating chamber. Unfortunately, since all the crucial structures within the vocal tract are soft tissue, they decompose after death, leaving paleoanthropologists to their own imaginations to speculate about the relative positions of the larynx in life. One way to determine the position of the larynx in long-dead hominins is to look at the degree of flexion at the base of the cranium. This flexion can be directly linked to the placement of the larynx in life, since "it shapes the roof of the voice box" (Klein, 1999). In comparisons of fossil hominin crania, it's been determined that full cranial base flexion similar to that found in modern *sapiens* is not found before *Homo heidelbergensis*.

The tongue is, of course, another crucial structure influencing speech. Because it's a site of attachment for one of the muscles of the tongue, the shape and position of the hyoid bone (**Fig. 1**) can tell us a lot about speech capabilities in earlier hominins. A hyoid located higher up and farther back in the throat allows modern humans to control their tongues much more efficiently and precisely. In the *Australopithecus afarensis* child's skeleton (from Dikika, Ethiopia; see Chapter 10), the hyoid is shaped more like that in a chimpanzee than in a modern human. So it seems most likely that these early hominins weren't able to fully articulate human speech. The only other hyoid found in a fossil hominin comes from the Neandertal skeleton found at Kebara (Israel); quite unlike the australopith condition, it resembles modern hyoids in all respects. We thus have some basis for concluding that the tongue musculature of Neandertals may have been much like our own.

Also potentially informative are possible genetic differences between humans and apes in regard to language. As the human genome is fully mapped (especially identifying functional regions and their specific actions) and compared with ape DNA (the chimpanzee genome is now also completely sequenced at a structural level), we might at long last begin to find a key to solving this great mystery.

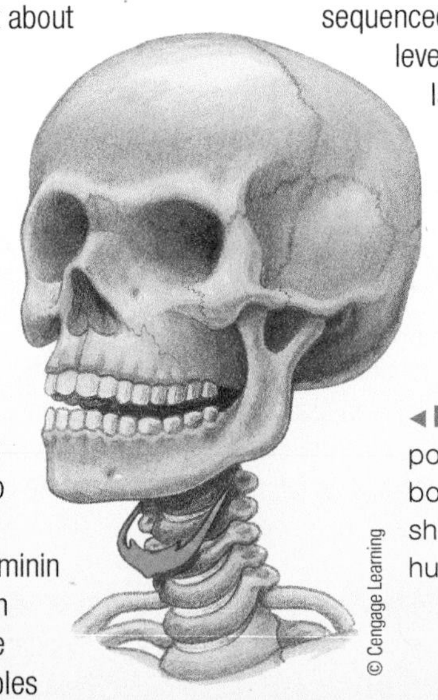

◀**Figure 1** The position of the hyoid bone in the throat, shown in a modern human skeleton.

The direct anatomical evidence derived from Neandertal fossils isn't much help in answering these questions. Ralph Holloway (1985) has maintained that Neandertal brains—at least as far as the fossil evidence suggests (from endocasts—both natural and artificial)—aren't significantly different from those of modern *H. sapiens.* What's more, the positioning of the Neandertal vocal tract (determined by the shape of the hyoid bone), as well as other morphological features, doesn't appear to have seriously limited them.

Most of the reservations about advanced cognitive abilities in Neandertals have been based on archaeological data. However, as more archaeological data have been collected and better dating controls applied to a large number of sites bridging the Mousterian–Upper Paleolithic transition, many of the proposed behavioral differences between Neandertals and early modern humans have blurred. For example, it is now known that, like early *H. sapiens,* Neandertals sometimes used pigment (probably as body ornamentation) and wore jewelry. The most significant recent finds come from two sites in Spain dating to 50,000 to 37,000 ya, and both have a Mousterian stone tool industry. Since these sites were occupied *before* modern *H. sapiens* reached this part of Europe, the most likely conclusion is that the objects found were made by Neandertals (Zilhão et al., 2010). The finds include perforated shells, ostensibly drilled to be used as jewelry, as

▲ **Figure 12-22** Upper portion of a bivalve shell that has been perforated and stained with pigment, from the Antón rock-shelter site in Spain (dated around 44,000 to 37,000 ya). The reddish inner surface (left) is natural, but the yellow colorant on the outer whitish surface (right) was the result of an added pigment.

well as natural pigments that were deliberately brought to the site and applied to the shells and some animal bones (see **Fig. 12-22**).

Neandertals and modern humans coexisted in some parts of Europe for up to 15,000 years, so Neandertals didn't vanish suddenly. Nevertheless, shortly after 30,000 ya, they disappear from the fossil and archaeological record. At some point, as a recognizable human group, Neandertals became an evolutionary dead end. Right now, we can't say exactly what caused their disappearance and ultimate replacement by anatomically modern Upper Paleolithic peoples. Indeed, Neandertals didn't really disappear altogether, since a few of their genes can still be found today in many human groups.

Burials

Anthropologists have known for some time that Neandertals deliberately buried their dead. Undeniably, the spectacular discoveries at La Chapelle, Shanidar, and elsewhere were the direct results of ancient burial, which permits preservation that's much more complete. Such deliberate burial treatment goes back at least 90,000 years at Tabun. From a much older site, some form of consistent "disposal" of the dead—not necessarily below-ground burial—is evidenced. As previously discussed, at the site of Sima de los Huesos in Spain, archaeologists found thousands of fossilized bone fragments in a cave at the end of a deep vertical shaft. From the nature of the site and the accumulation of hominin remains, Spanish researchers are convinced that the site demonstrates some form of human activity involving deliberate disposal of the dead (Arsuaga et al., 1997).

The recent dating of Sima de los Huesos to more than 400,000 ya suggests that Neandertal precursors were already handling their dead in special ways during the Middle Pleistocene. Such behavior was previously thought to have emerged only much later, in the Late Pleistocene. As far as current data indicate, this practice is seen in western European contexts well before it appears in Africa or eastern Asia. For example, in the premodern sites at Kabwe and Florisbad (discussed earlier), deliberate disposal of the dead is not documented, nor is it seen in African early modern sites—for example, the Klasies River Mouth, dated at 120,000 to 100,000 ya (see Chapter 13).

Yet, in later contexts (after 35,000 ya), where modern *H. sapiens* remains are found in clear burial contexts, their treatment is considerably more complex than in Neandertal burials. In these later (Upper Paleolithic) sites, grave goods, including bone and stone tools as well as animal bones, are found more consistently and in greater concentrations. Because many Neandertal sites were excavated in the nineteenth or early twentieth century, before more rigorous archaeological methods were developed, many of these supposed burials are now in question. Still, the evidence seems quite clear that deliberate burial was practiced not only at La Chapelle, La Ferrassie (eight graves), Tabun, Amud, Kebara, Shanidar, and Teshik-Tash, but also at several other localities, especially in France. In many cases, the body's position was deliberately modified, having been placed in the grave in a flexed posture. This flexed position has been found in 16 of the 20 best-documented Neandertal burial contexts (Klein, 1999).

Molecular Connections: The Genetic Evidence

With the revolutionary advances in molecular biology (discussed in Chapter 3), fascinating new avenues of research have become possible in the study of earlier hominins. It's becoming fairly commonplace to extract, amplify, and sequence ancient DNA from contexts spanning the last 10,000 years or so. For example, researchers have analyzed the entire nuclear genome from a 4,000-year-old Inuit (Eskimo) from Greenland (Rasmussen et al., 2010) and recently the 5,000-year-old "Iceman" found in the Italian Alps. The last of these analyses has provided us with surprisingly complete information about the Iceman. For example, he most likely had brown eyes and was blood-type O; it was even determined that he couldn't digest lactose (Keller et al., 2012).

It's much harder to find usable DNA in even more ancient remains because the organic components, often including the DNA, have been destroyed during the mineralization process. Nevertheless, in the past few years exciting results have been announced about DNA found in more than a dozen different Neandertal fossils dated between 50,000 and 32,000 ya. These fossils come from sites in France (including La Chapelle), Germany (from the original Neander Valley locality), Belgium, Italy, Spain, Croatia, and Russia (Krings et al., 1997, 2000; Ovchinnikov et al., 2000; Schmitz et al., 2002; Serre et al., 2004; Green et al., 2006). As we previously mentioned, recently ascertained ancient DNA evidence strongly suggests that other fossils from central Asia (Uzbekistan and two caves in southern Siberia), dated at 48,000 to 30,000 ya, are also Neandertals (Krause et al., 2007b) or even an entirely different species (Krause et al., 2010; Reich et al., 2010).

The technique most often used in studying most Neandertal fossils involves extracting mitochondrial DNA (mtDNA), amplifying it through polymerase chain reaction (PCR; see Chapter 3), and sequencing nucleotides in parts of the molecule. Initial results from the Neandertal specimens show that these individuals are genetically more different from contemporary *Homo sapiens* populations than modern human populations are from each other—in fact, about three times as much.

Major advances in molecular biology have allowed much more of the Neandertal genetic pattern to be determined, with the ability to now sequence the entire mtDNA sequence in several individuals (Briggs et al., 2009) as well as big chunks of the *nuclear* DNA (which, as you may recall, contains more than 99 percent of the human genome). In fact, the most exciting breakthrough yet in ancient DNA studies was achieved in 2010 with the completion of the *entire* nuclear genome of European Neandertals (Green et al., 2010). Just a handful of years ago, this sort of achievement would have seemed like science fiction.

This new information has already allowed for crucial (as well as quite surprising) revisions in our understanding of Neandertal and early modern human evolution. First of all, Neandertal DNA is remarkably similar to modern human DNA, with 99.84 percent of it being identical. However, to detect those few (but possibly informative) genes that do differ, the team sequenced the entire genome of five modern individuals (two from Africa and one each from China, France, and New Guinea). To the surprise of almost everyone, the researchers found that many people today still have Neandertal genes! What's more, these Neandertal genes are found only in non-Africans, strongly suggesting that interbreeding occurred between Neandertals and modern *H. sapiens* after the latter had emigrated out of Africa. In fact, the three modern non-African individuals used for comparison in this study all had the same amount of Neandertal DNA. What makes this finding even more startling is the fact that the modern non-African humans evaluated come from widely scattered regions (western Europe, China, and the far South

A Closer Look

Are They Human?

At the beginning of this chapter, we posed the question "What does it mean to be human?" Applying the term *human* to our extinct hominin predecessors is somewhat tricky. Various prior hominin species share with contemporary *Homo sapiens* a mosaic of physical features. For example, they're all bipedal, most (but not all) have fairly small canine teeth, some are completely terrestrial, and some are moderately encephalized (while others are much more so). Thus, the *physical* characteristics that define humanity appear at different times during hominin evolution.

Even more tenuous are the *behavioral* characteristics frequently identified as signifying human status. The most significant of these proposed behavioral traits include major dependence on culture, innovation, cooperation in acquiring food, full language, and elaboration of symbolic representations in art and body adornment. Once again, these characteristics become apparent at different stages of hominin evolution. But distinguishing when and how these behavioral characteristics became established in our ancestors is even more problematic than analyzing anatomical traits. While the archaeological record provides considerable information regarding stone tool technology, it's mostly silent on other aspects of material culture. The social organization and language capabilities of earlier hominins are as yet almost completely invisible.

From the available evidence, we can conclude that *H. erectus* took significant steps in the human direction—well beyond that of earlier hominins. *H. erectus* vastly expanded hominin geographical ranges, achieved the full body size and limb proportions of later hominins, had increased encephalization, and became considerably more dependent on culture for their survival, unlike previous forms, which relied more upon physical adaptations.

H. heidelbergensis (in the Middle Pleistocene) and, to an even greater degree, Neandertals (in the Late Pleistocene) maintained several of these characteristics—such as body size and proportions—while also showing further evolution in the human direction. Most particularly, relative brain size increased further, expanding on average about 22 percent beyond that of *H. erectus* (**Fig. 1**). Notice, however, that the largest jump in proportional brain size occurs very late in hominin evolution—only with the appearance of fully modern humans.

In addition to brain enlargement, cranial shape also was remodeled in *H. heidelbergensis* and Neandertals, producing a more globular shape of the vault as well as suggesting further neurological reorganization. Stone tool technology also became more sophisticated during the Middle Pleistocene, with the manufacture of tools requiring a more complicated series of steps. Also, for the first time, fire was definitely controlled and widely used; caves were routinely occupied; hominin ranges were successfully expanded throughout much of Europe as well as into northern Asia (that is, colder habitats were more fully exploited); structures were built; the dead were deliberately buried; and more systematic hunting took place.

Some premoderns also were like modern humans in another significant way. Analysis of teeth from a Neandertal shows that these hominins had the same *delayed maturation* found in modern *H. sapiens* (Dean et al., 2001). We don't yet have similar data for

Pacific). Further evidence, including complete genomes from another seven modern people from even more dispersed populations, has further confirmed these findings (Reich et al., 2010).

The best (and simplest) hypothesis for this genetic pattern is that shortly after modern *H. sapiens* migrants left Africa, a few of them interbred with Neandertals *before* these people and their descendants dispersed to other areas of the world. The best guess is that this intermixing between the two groups occurred in the Middle East, likely sometime between 80,000 and 50,000 ya. DNA data from more individuals, both within and outside of Africa, will help to substantiate this hypothesis. For the moment, the degree of interbreeding appears to be small but still significant—about 1 to 4 percent of the total genome for living non-Africans.

More astonishing molecular findings also came in 2010 and 2012 during the analysis of the Denisovan DNA from Siberia (see above). These ancient hominins, called "Denisovans," from central Asia quite possibly represent a different branch of recent human evolution (Reich et al., 2010). They are also more closely related to just *some* populations of modern humans, sharing about 4% to 5% of genes with contemporary people from Melanesia (a region of islands in the south Pacific, including New Guinea, located north and east of Australia). We will focus much more on the ancestral connections of modern humans in the next chapter. As you'll

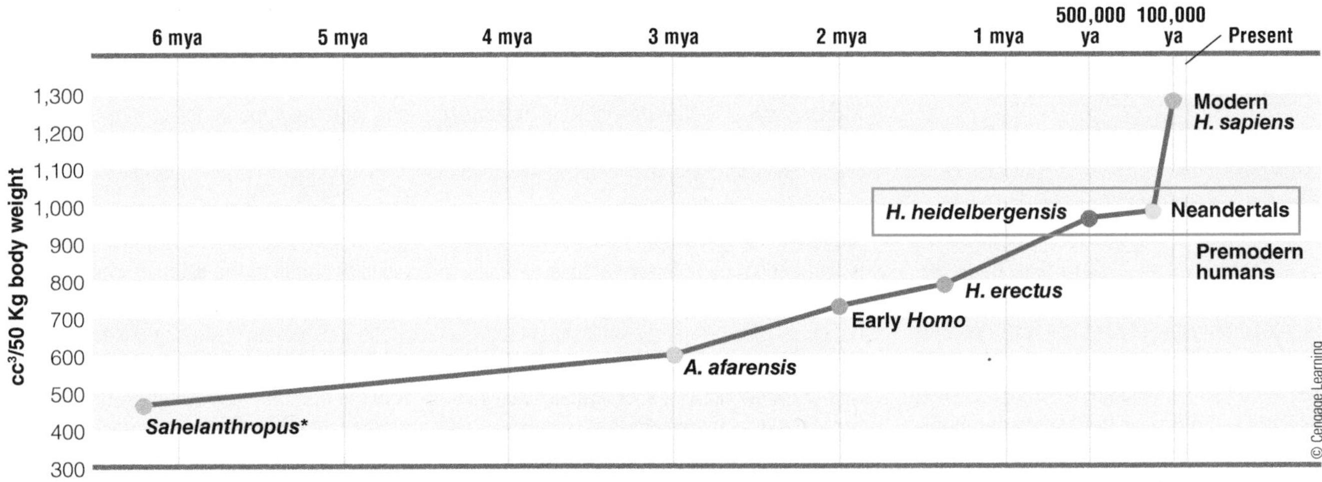

*There are no direct current data for body size in *Sahelanthropus*. Body size is estimated from tooth size in comparison with *A. afarensis*. Data abstracted from McHenry (1992), Wood and Collard (1999), Brunet (2002), and Carroll (2003).

▲ **Figure 1** Relative brain size in hominins. The scale shows brain size as cm³ per 50 kg of body weight. Premodern humans have a more than 20 percent increase in relative brain size compared to *H. erectus*, but modern humans show another 30 percent expansion beyond that seen in premodern humans.

earlier *H. heidelbergensis* individuals, but it's possible that they, too, showed this distinctively human pattern of development.

Did these Middle and Late Pleistocene hominins have the full language capabilities and other symbolic and social skills of living peoples? It's impossible to answer this question completely, given the types of fossil and archaeological evidence available. Yet, it does seem quite possible that neither *H. heidelbergensis* nor the Neandertals had the entire array of *fully* human attributes. That's why we call them premodern humans.

So, to rephrase our initial question: "Were these hominins human?" We can answer conditionally: They were human—at least mostly so.

see, all of us derive mostly from fairly recent African ancestors. But when these African migrants came into contact with premodern humans living in Eurasia, some interbreeding occurred with at least two of these premodern groups. We can tell this by distinctive genetic "signatures" that can still be found in living people.

What's more, we've already had tantalizing clues of how we differ from Neandertals as well as from Denisovans in terms of specific genes. As the data are further analyzed and expanded, we will surely learn more about the evolutionary development of human anatomy *and* human behavior. In so doing, we'll be able to answer far more precisely the age-old question of "What does it mean to be human?"

Seeing Close Human Connections: Understanding Premodern Humans

As you can see, the Middle Pleistocene hominins are a very diverse group, broadly dispersed through time and space. There is considerable variation among them, and it's not easy to get a clear evolutionary picture. We know that regional populations were small and frequently isolated. As environmental conditions changed, hominin populations were likely pushed into smaller and smaller habitable areas, often referred to by biologists as "refugia" (Stewart and Stringer, 2012).

As conditions became harsher, these refugia supported fewer people, leading to a dramatic decrease in population size. In turn, such circumstances accelerated the effects of genetic drift as well as intensifying natural selection. Biologist John Stewart and anthropologist Chris Stringer (2012) have recently developed a comprehensive model employing environmental (specifically glacial/interglacial cycles), genetic, and fossil data to explain how in Ice Age Eurasia the development and fate of refuge populations of both premodern and modern humans help explain species distributions, extinctions, and potential opportunities for interbreeding (e.g., Neandertals or Denisovans with modern humans).

We must remember, though, that it's virtually certain that many premodern human populations died out, leaving no descendants. So it's a mistake to see an "ancestor" in every fossil find. Still, as a group, these Middle Pleistocene premoderns do reveal some general trends. In many ways, for example, it seems that they were *transitional* between the hominins that came before them (*H. erectus*) and the ones that followed them (modern *H. sapiens*). It's not a stretch to say that all the Middle Pleistocene premoderns derived from *H. erectus* forebears and that some of them, in turn, were probably ancestors of the earliest fully modern humans.

Paleoanthropologists are certainly concerned with such broad generalities as these, but they also want to focus on meaningful anatomical, environmental, and behavioral details as well as the underlying processes. So they consider the regional variability displayed by particular fossil samples as significant—but just how significant is debatable. In addition, increasingly sophisticated theoretical and technological approaches are being used to better understand the processes that shaped the evolution of later *Homo* at both macroevolutionary and microevolutionary levels.

Scientists, like all humans, assign names or labels to phenomena—a point we addressed in discussing classification in Chapter 5. Paleoanthropologists are certainly no exception. Yet, working from a common evolutionary foundation, paleoanthropologists still come to different conclusions about the most appropriate way to interpret the Middle/Late Pleistocene hominins. Consequently, a variety of species names have been proposed in recent years.

Paleoanthropologists who advocate an extreme lumping approach recognize only one species for all the premodern humans discussed in this chapter. These premoderns are classified as *Homo sapiens* and are thus lumped together with modern humans, although they're partly distinguished by such terminology as "archaic *H. sapiens*." As we've noted, this degree of lumping is no longer supported by most researchers. Alternatively, a second, less extreme view postulates modest species diversity and labels the earlier premoderns as *H. heidelbergensis* (**Fig. 12-23a**).

At the other end of the spectrum, more enthusiastic paleontological splitters have identified at least two (or more) species distinct from *H. sapiens*. The most important of these, *H. heidelbergensis* and *H. neanderthalensis*, have been discussed earlier. This more complex evolutionary interpretation is shown in **Figure 12-23b**.

We addressed similar differences of interpretation in Chapters 10 and 11, and we know that disparities such as these can be frustrating to students who are new to paleoanthropology. The proliferation of new names is confusing, and it might seem that experts in the field are endlessly arguing about what to call the fossils.

Fortunately, it's not quite that bad. There's actually more agreement than you might think. No one doubts that all these hominins are closely related to each other as well as to modern humans. And everyone agrees that only some of the fossil samples represent populations that left descendants. Where paleoanthropologists disagree is when they start discussing which hominins are the most likely to be closely related to later hominins. The grouping of hominins into evolution-

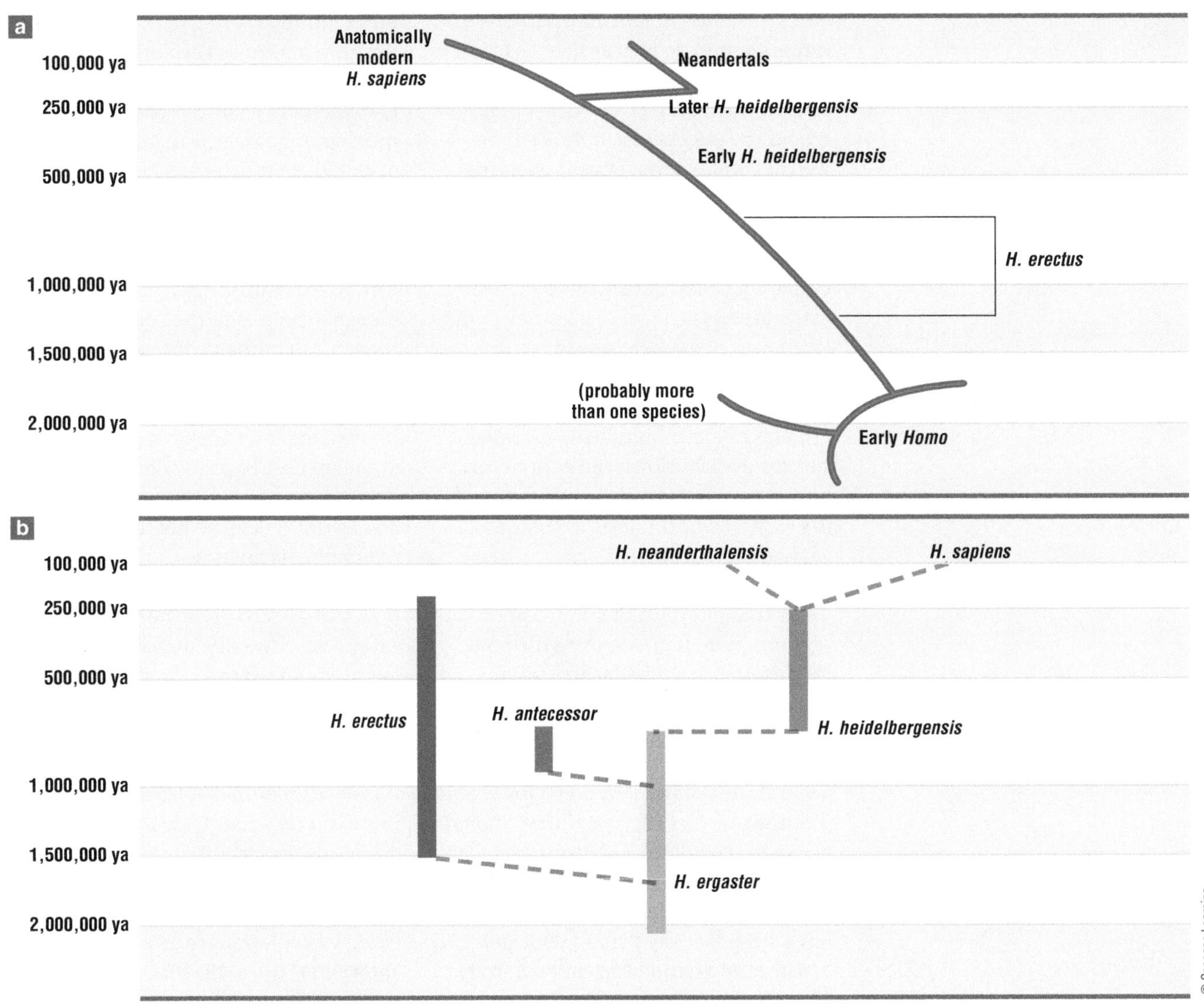

▲ **Figure 12-23** (**a**) Phylogeny of the genus *Homo*. Only very modest species diversity is implied. (**b**) Phylogeny of genus *Homo* showing considerable species diversity (after Foley, 2002).

ary clusters (clades) and assignment of different names to them is a reflection of differing interpretations—and, more fundamentally, of somewhat differing philosophies.

But we shouldn't emphasize these naming and classification debates too much. Most paleoanthropologists recognize that a great many of these disagreements result from simple, practical considerations. Even the most enthusiastic splitters acknowledge that the fossil "species" are not true species as defined by the biological species concept (see Chapter 5) (Holliday, 2003). As prominent paleoanthropologist Robert Foley puts it, "It is unlikely they are all biological species. . . . These are probably a mixture of real biological species and evolving lineages of subspecies. In other words, they could potentially have interbred, but owing to allopatry [that is, geographical separation] were unlikely to have had the opportunity" (Foley, 2002, p. 33).

Even so, Foley, along with an increasing number of other professionals, distinguishes these different fossil samples with species names to highlight their distinct position in hominin evolution. That is, these hominin groups are more loosely defined as a type of paleospecies (see Chapter 5) rather than as fully biological species. Giving distinct hominin samples a separate (species) name makes them more easily identifiable to other researchers and makes various cladistic hypotheses more explicit and, equally important, more directly testable.

The hominins that best illustrate these issues are the Neandertals. Fortunately they're also the best known, represented by dozens of well-preserved individuals and also a complete genome. With all this evidence, researchers can systematically test and evaluate many of the differing hypotheses.

Are Neandertals very closely related to modern *H. sapiens*? Certainly. Are they physically and behaviorally somewhat distinct from both ancient and fully modern humans? Yes. Does this mean that Neandertals are a fully separate biological species from modern humans and therefore theoretically incapable of fertilely interbreeding with modern people? Almost certainly not. Finally, then, should Neandertals really be placed in a separate species from *H. sapiens*? For most purposes, it doesn't matter, since the distinction at some point is arbitrary, like looking at a spectrum of colors that grade from red to orange to yellow. Where does one color definitely begin and end? Is that reddish-orange or is it orangey-red? Speciation is, after all, a *dynamic* process and fossil groups such as the Neandertals represent just one point in this process (see Chapter 5), which continues even today.

We can view Neandertals as a distinctive side branch of later hominin evolution. It is not unreasonable to say that Neandertals were likely an incipient species. The much less well-known "Denisovans" from Siberia also likely represent another partially distinct incipient species, separate from both Neandertals and early modern humans. Given enough time and enough isolation, Neandertals and Denisovans likely would have separated completely from their modern human contemporaries. The new DNA evidence suggests that they were partly on their way but had not yet reached full speciation from *Homo sapiens*. Their fate, in a sense, was decided for them as more successful competitors expanded into their habitats. These highly successful hominins were fully modern humans, and in the next chapter we'll focus on their story.

How Do We Know?

We know a great deal about premodern humans, based both on fossil finds as well as new and highly informative DNA data. Not only have a large number of fossils been discovered but, for the first time, many are quite complete (as a result of deliberate burial). In addition, more complete archaeological remains make it possible to test much more specific hypotheses about their behavior than is possible for any earlier group of hominins. Last, the detailed DNA data, obtained from skeletal remains dated from as early as 60,000 years ago, allow far-reaching scientific study and rigorous conclusions regarding exactly how similar these hominins were to us. Indeed, new studies have shown that they interbred with early modern humans, and we can still see traces of this gene exchange in living human populations.

Summary of Main Topics

- Premodern humans from the Middle Pleistocene show similarities both with their predecessors (*H. erectus*) and with their successors (*H. sapiens*). They've also been found in many areas of the Old World—in Africa, Asia, and Europe.
- Most paleoanthropologists call the majority of Middle Pleistocene fossils *H. heidelbergensis*. Similarities between the African and European Middle Pleistocene hominin samples suggest that they can all reasonably be seen as part of this same species, but contemporaneous Asian fossils don't fit as neatly into this model.
- Some of the later *H. heidelbergensis* populations in Europe likely evolved into Neandertals, and abundant Neandertal fossil and archaeological evidence has been collected from the Late Pleistocene time span of Neandertal existence, about 130,000 to 30,000 ya.
- Neandertals are more geographically restricted than earlier premoderns and are found in Europe, southwest Asia, and central Asia.
- Neandertals have been considered quite distinct from modern *H. sapiens*, but recent genetic evidence confirms that some interbreeding took place between these hominins (likely 80,000 to 50,000 ya).

Critical Thinking Questions

1. Why are the Middle Pleistocene hominins called premodern humans? In what ways are they human?
2. What is the general popular conception of Neandertals? Based on what you have just learned, would you agree with this view? (Cite both anatomical and archaeological evidence to support your conclusion.)
3. What evidence suggests that Neandertals deliberately buried their dead? Do you think the fact that they buried their dead is important? Why? How would you interpret this behavior (remembering that Neandertals were not identical to us)?
4. How are species defined, both for living animals and for extinct ones? Use the Neandertals to illustrate the problems encountered in distinguishing species among extinct hominins. Contrast specifically the interpretation of Neandertals as a distinct species with the interpretation of Neandertals as a subspecies of *H. sapiens*.

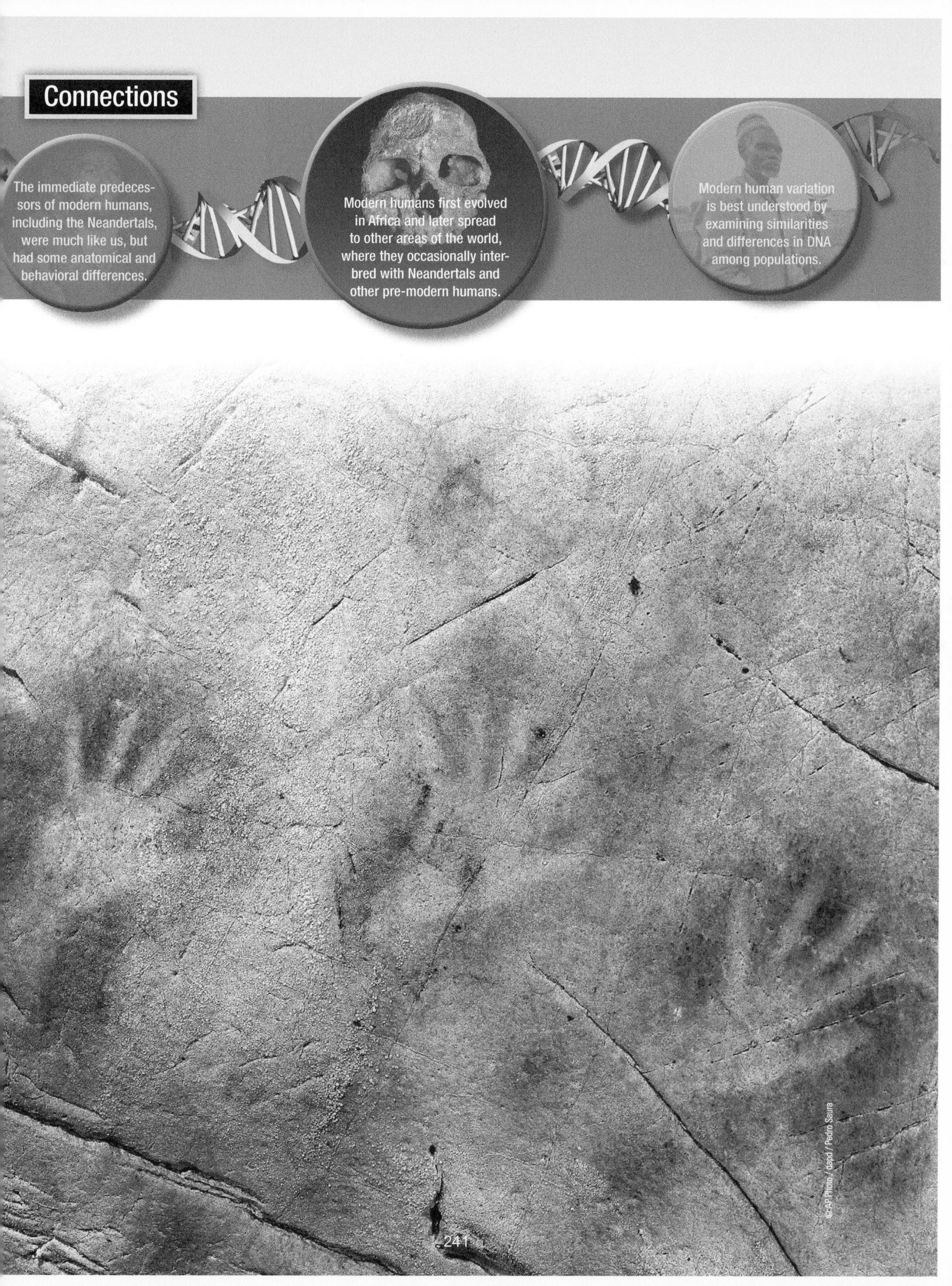
Connections
The immediate predecessors of modern humans, including the Neandertals, were much like us, but had some anatomical and behavioral differences.
Modern humans first evolved in Africa and later spread to other areas of the world, where they occasionally interbred with Neandertals and other pre-modern humans.
Modern human variation is best understood by examining similarities and differences in DNA among populations.
© AP Photo / dapd / Pedro Saura

The Origin and Dispersal of Modern Humans

10

Student Learning Objectives

After mastering the material in this chapter, you should be able to:

- Compare and contrast the two major models that seek to explain modern human origins.
- Explain the evidence that supports each model and critically evaluate why recent molecular evidence has largely solved this issue.
- Describe the major geographical areas and general dating of the key early fossil evidence of modern humans.
- Describe the major physical features of *Homo floresiensis* and explain why the discovery of this hominin was such a surprise.
- Discuss the cultural developments that characterize the Upper Paleolithic as well as contemporaneous cultures in other parts of the world (e.g., Africa) and contrast these with cultural/technological practices of earlier periods.

Today, our species numbers more than 7 billion individuals spread all over the globe, and there are no other living hominins but us. Our last hominin cousin disappeared several thousand years ago. Perhaps about 80,000 ya, modern peoples in the Middle East encountered beings that walked on two legs, hunted large animals, made fire, lived in caves, and fashioned complex tools. These beings were the Neandertals, and imagine what it would have been like to be among a band of modern people following game into what is now Israel and coming across these other *humans*, so like yourself in some ways, yet so different in others. It's almost certain that such encounters took place, perhaps many times. How strange would it have been to look into the face of a being sharing so much with you, yet being a total stranger both culturally and, to some degree, biologically? What would you think seeing a Neandertal for the first time? What do you imagine a Neandertal would think seeing you? If a similar encounter had occurred in southern Siberia, modern people would quite likely have been staring into the eyes of a Denisovan. What would that have been like?

At some time, probably close to 200,000 ya, the first modern *Homo sapiens* populations appeared in Africa. Within 150,000 years or so, their descendants had spread across most of the Old World, even expanding as far as Australia (and somewhat later to the Americas).

Who were they, and why were these early modern people so successful? What was the fate of the other hominins, such as the Neandertals, who were already long established in areas outside Africa? Did they continue to evolve as well, leaving descendants among some living human populations? Or did they go extinct, completely swept aside and replaced by African emigrants?

In this chapter, we'll discuss the origin and dispersal of modern *H. sapiens sapiens*. All contemporary populations are placed within this species and subspecies. Most paleoanthropologists agree that several fossil forms of *Homo sapiens*, dating back as far as 100,000 ya, should also be included in the same *fully* modern group as ourselves. In addition, some recently discovered fossils from Africa are also clearly *H. sapiens,* though they show some (minor) differences from living people and could thus be more accurately described as *near*-modern. Still, we can think of these early African humans as well as their somewhat later relatives as "us."

These first modern humans, who had evolved by 195,000 ya, were probably descendants of some of the premodern humans we discussed in Chapter 12. In particular, African populations of *H. heidelbergensis* are the most likely ancestors of the earliest modern *H. sapiens*. The evolutionary events that took place as modern humans made the transition from more ancient premodern forms and then dispersed throughout most of the Old World were relatively rapid, and they raise several basic questions:

1. When (approximately) did modern humans first appear?
2. Where did the transition take place? Did it occur in just one region or in several?
3. What was the pace of evolutionary change? How quickly did the transition occur and was it uniform across regions?
4. How did the dispersal of modern humans to other areas of the Old World (outside their area of origin) take place?

These questions concerning the origins and early dispersal of modern *Homo sapiens* continue to fuel much controversy among paleoanthropologists. And it's no wonder, for at least some early *H. sapiens* populations are the direct ancestors of all contemporary humans. They were much like us skeletally, genetically, and (most likely) behaviorally. In fact, it's the various hypotheses regarding the behaviors and abilities of our most immediate predecessors that have most fired the imaginations of scientists and laypeople alike. In every major respect, these are the first hominins that we can confidently refer to as *fully* human.

In this chapter, we'll also discuss archaeological evidence coming from the Upper Paleolithic cultures. This evidence will give us a better understanding of the technological and social developments during the period when modern humans arose and quickly came to dominate the planet.

The evolutionary story of *Homo sapiens* is really the biological autobiography of all of us. It's a story that still has many unanswered questions, but some general theories can help us organize the many lines of evidence that are now available.

Approaches to Understanding Modern Human Origins

In attempting to organize and explain modern human origins, paleoanthropologists have proposed a few major hypotheses that can be summarized into two contrasting views: the *multiregional continuity* model and various versions of *replacement* models. These two views are quite distinct, and in some ways they're completely opposed to each other. Since so much of our contemporary view of modern human origins is influenced by the debates linked to these differing models, we'll start by briefly reviewing them. Then we'll turn to the fossil evidence and emerging genetic analyses to see what morphology and molecules can contribute to answering the four questions we've posed.

The Regional Continuity Model: Multiregional Evolution

The multiregional continuity model is most closely associated with paleoanthropologist Milford Wolpoff of the University of Michigan and his associates (Wolpoff et al., 1994, 2001). They suggest that local populations—not all, of course—in Europe, Asia, and Africa continued their indigenous evolutionary development from premodern Middle Pleistocene forms to anatomically modern humans. But if that's true, we have to ask how so many different local populations around the globe happened to evolve with such similar morphology. In other words, how could anatomically modern humans arise separately in different continents and end up so much alike, both physically and genetically? The multiregional model answers this question by (1) denying that the earliest modern *H. sapiens* populations originated *exclusively* in Africa and (2) asserting that significant levels of gene flow (migration and interbreeding) between various geographically dispersed premodern populations were extremely likely throughout the Pleistocene.

Through gene flow and natural selection, according to the multiregional hypothesis, local populations would *not* have evolved totally independently from one another, and such mixing would have "prevented speciation between the regional lineages and thus maintained human beings as a single, although obviously *polytypic* [see Chapter 14], species throughout the Pleistocene" (Smith et al., 1989). Thus, under a multiregional model, there are no taxonomic distinctions between modern and premodern hominins. That is, all hominins following *Homo erectus* are classified as a single species: *Homo sapiens*.

In light of emerging evidence over the last few years, advocates of the multiregional model tend not to be dogmatic about the degree of regional continuity. They recognize that a strong influence from modern humans evolving *first* in Africa has left an imprint on populations throughout the world that is still genetically detectable today. Nevertheless, the most recent data suggest that multiregional models no longer tell us much that is useful about the origins of modern humans, nor do they seem to provide much information regarding the dispersal of modern *H. sapiens*.

Replacement Models

Replacement models all emphasize that modern humans first evolved in Africa and only later dispersed to other parts of the world, where they replaced those hominins already living in these other regions. In recent years, two versions of such replacement models have been proposed, the first emphasizing *complete* replacement. The complete replacement model proposes that anatomically modern populations arose in Africa within the last 200,000 years and then migrated from Africa, completely replacing populations in Europe and Asia (Stringer and Andrews, 1988). It's important to note that this model doesn't account for a transition from premodern forms to modern *H. sapiens* anywhere in the world except Africa. Stringer and Andrews' original hypothesis argued that anatomically modern humans appeared as the result of a biological speciation event. So in this view, migrating African modern *H. sapiens* could not have successfully interbred with local non-African populations producing fertile offspring because the African modern humans were a *biologically* different species. Under this model, all of the premodern populations outside Africa would be taxonomically classified as belonging to different species of *Homo*. For example, the Neandertals would be classified as *H. neanderthalensis*. This explanation of nonhybridizing speciation would fit nicely with, and, in fact, help explain *complete* replacement; but Stringer has more recently stated that he isn't insistent on this issue. He does suggest that even though there may have been potential for interbreeding, apparently very little actually took place (Stewart and Stringer, 2012).

Interpretations of the latter phases of human evolution have recently been greatly extended and aided by newly available genetic techniques that have been applied to the question of modern human origins. Drawing genetic data from numerous geographically diverse contemporary human populations, geneticists have precisely determined and compared a wide variety of DNA sequences in order to gain a better understanding of current human variation. The theoretical basis of this approach assumes that at least some of the genetic patterning seen today can act as a kind of window into the past. In particular, the genetic patterns observed today between geographically widely dispersed humans are thought to partly reflect migrations occurring in the Late Pleistocene. This hypothesis can be further tested as contemporary and archaic population genetic patterning becomes better documented.

As these new data have accumulated and are being assimilated, reliable relationships are emerging, especially those showing that indigenous African populations have far greater diversity than do populations from elsewhere in the world. The consistency of the results is highly significant because it strongly supports an African origin for modern humans and some subsequent mode of replacement across other regions. What's more, as we will discuss in Chapter 14, new, even more complete nuclear genomic data on contemporary population patterning further confirm these observations.

Certainly, most molecular data come from contemporary individuals, since ancient DNA is not *usually* preserved. Even so, exceptions do occur; for example, the Ice Man and two very recently sequenced 7,000-year-old Iberian hunter-gatherers (Sánchez-Quinto et al., 2012). These cases open another genetic window—one that can directly illuminate the past. As discussed in Chapter 12, mtDNA has been recovered from more than a dozen Neandertal fossils.

In addition, researchers have recently sequenced the mtDNA of nine ancient fully modern *H. sapiens* skeletons from sites in Italy, France, the Czech Republic, and Russia (Caramelli et al., 2003; Kulikov et al., 2004; Serre et al., 2004). MtDNA data, however, are somewhat limited because mtDNA is a fairly small segment of DNA, and since it is transmitted between generations without recombination with male DNA, it only provides information regarding the maternal lineage. Indeed, in just the last few years, comparisons of Neandertal and early modern mtDNA have led to some significant misinterpretations. It should be no surprise, though, that data from the vastly larger nuclear genome are far more informative.

As we discussed in Chapter 12, a giant leap forward occurred in 2010 when sequencing of the entire Neandertal nuclear genome was completed. Researchers immediately compared the Neandertal genome with that of people living today and discovered that some populations still retain some Neandertal genes (Green et al., 2010; Reich et al., 2011). Without doubt, we can now conclude that some interbreeding took place between Neandertals and modern humans, arguing against *complete* replacement and supporting some form of *partial* replacement.

Partial Replacement Models For a number of years, several paleoanthropologists, such as Günter Bräuer, of the University of Hamburg, suggested that very little interbreeding occurred—a view supported more recently by John Relethford (2001) in what he described as "mostly out of Africa." The DNA analysis done in 2010 by Green and colleagues confirms that the degree of interbreeding was modest, ranging from 1 to 4 percent in modern populations outside Africa, while also revealing that contemporary Africans have no trace of Neandertal genes, suggesting that the interbreeding occurred *after* modern humans migrated out of Africa. Another fascinating discovery is that among the modern people so far sampled for these comparisons (five individuals: two African, one European, one Asian and one Pacific Islander), the three non-Africans all have some Neandertal DNA. The tentative conclusion from these preliminary findings suggests that the interbreeding occurred soon after modern humans emigrated out of Africa. The most likely scenario suggests that the intermixing occurred around 80,000 to 50,000 ya, quite possibly in the Middle East and only later in Europe and then Asia.

These results are very new and are partly based on very limited samples of living people. Technological innovations in DNA sequencing are occurring at an amazing pace, making it faster and cheaper. But it is still a challenge to sequence all the 3 billion nucleotides each of us has in our nuclear genome. When we have full genomes from more individuals living in many more geographical areas, the patterns of modern human dispersal should become clearer. Did the modern human-Neandertal interbreeding occur primarily in one area, or did it happen in several regions? Moreover, did some modern human populations several thousand years ago interbreed with their Neandertal cousins more than others did?

We can ask yet another question, which is perhaps even most interesting: Were there still other premodern human groups still around when modern humans emigrated from Africa—and did they interbreed with modern humans too? As we discussed in Chapter 12, the answer is yes! Detailed DNA evidence from the fragmentary remains from Denisova Cave in southern Siberia show that these hominins had also interbred with modern humans. What's more, these Denisovans may have been quite widespread, since we can today still see a few of their genes in Southeast Asian, Pacific islands, and Australian populations (Reich et al., 2011; Rasmussen et al., 2011).

This recent research has helped to support what appears to have been (at least) a two-stage migration of modern humans into Asia (after an earlier initial migration of modern humans out of Africa). The earlier of these migrations took place through parts of Southeast Asia and eventually reached the South Pacific (including New Guinea and Australia). In fact, the recent whole genome sequencing using the hair from an Australian Aboriginal man who lived 100 years ago shows that he had Denisovan genes and that Aboriginal populations diverged from other groups 75,000 to 62,000 ya. The second migration occurred considerably later (38,000 to 25,000 ya), and it led to the peopling of eastern Asia (Rasmussen et al., 2011).

From his study of fossil remains, Fred Smith of Illinois State University has proposed an "assimilation" model hypothesizing that more interbreeding did take place, at least in some regions (Smith, 2002). To test these hypotheses and answer all the fascinating questions associated with them, we will also need more whole-genome DNA from ancient remains, particularly from early modern human skeletons. New technology applied just in the last year allows far faster DNA sequencing; so at least some of our questions may soon be answered. However, we also need to be aware that DNA thousands of years old can be obtained from hominin remains found in environments that have been persistently cold (or at least cool). In tropical areas, DNA degrades rapidly, so it seems a long shot that any usable DNA can be obtained from hominins that lived in many extremely large and significant regions (for example, Africa and Southeast Asia). Nevertheless, another alternative and very useful approach to partly answer these questions uses the genetic patterning still visible in contemporary humans. From such studies we know that there was more interbreeding and eventual gene flow of Denisovan genes in Asia (and the Pacific) than there was in Europe.

The Earliest Discoveries of Modern Humans

Africa

In Africa, several early (around 200,000 to 100,000 ya) fossils have been interpreted as fully anatomically modern forms (**Fig. 13-2**). The earliest of these specimens comes from Omo Kibish, in southernmost Ethiopia. Using radiometric techniques, the redating of a fragmentary skull (Omo 1) demonstrated that this is the earliest modern human—originating 195,000 ya—yet found in Africa or, for that matter, anywhere (McDougall et al., 2005). An interesting aspect of fossils from this site concerns the variation shown between the two individuals. Omo 1 (**Fig. 13-1**) is essentially modern in most respects (note the presence of a chin; see **Fig. 13-3**, where a variety of modern human cranial characteristics are shown). But another ostensibly contemporary cranium (Omo 2) is much more robust and less modern in morphology.

▾ Figure 13-1 Reconstructed skull of Omo 1, an early modern human from Ethiopia, dated to 195,000 ya. Note the clear presence of a chin.

© Milford Wolpoff

Somewhat later modern human fossils come from the Klasies River Mouth on the south coast of Africa and from Border Cave, just slightly to the north. Using relatively new techniques, paleoanthropologists have dated both sites to about 120,000 to 80,000 ya. The original geological context at Border Cave is uncertain, and the fossils may be younger than those at Klasies River Mouth. Although a recent reevaluation of the Omo site has provided much more dependable dating, there are still questions about some of the other early African modern fossils. Nevertheless, it now seems very likely that early modern humans appeared in East Africa by shortly after 200,000 ya and had migrated to southern Africa by approximately 100,000 ya. More recently discovered fossils are helping to confirm this view.

Herto The announcement in 2003 of well-preserved *and* well-dated *H. sapiens* fossils from Ethiopia has gone a long way toward filling gaps in the African fossil record. As a result, these fossils are helping to resolve key issues regarding modern human origins. Tim White of the University of California, Berkeley, and his colleagues have been working for three decades in the Middle Awash area of Ethiopia. They've discovered a remarkable array of early fossil hominins (*Ardipithecus* and *Australopithecus*) as well as somewhat later forms (*H. erectus*). From this same area in the Middle Awash, further highly significant discoveries came to light in 1997. For simplicity, these new hominins are referred to as the Herto remains.

These Herto fossils include a mostly complete adult cranium, an incomplete adult cranium, a fairly complete (but heavily reconstructed) child's cranium, and a few other cranial fragments. Following lengthy reconstruction and detailed comparative studies, White and colleagues were prepared to announce their findings in 2003.

What they said caused quite a sensation among paleoanthropologists, and it was reported in the popular press as well. First, well-controlled radiometric dating ($^{40}Ar/^{39}Ar$) securely places the remains at between 160,000 and 154,000 ya, making these the best-dated hominin fossils from this time period from anywhere in the world. Note that this date is clearly *older* than for any other equally modern *H. sapiens* from anywhere else in the world. Moreover, the preservation and morphology of the remains leave little doubt about their relationship to modern humans. The mostly complete adult cranium (**Fig. 13-4**) is very large, with an extremely

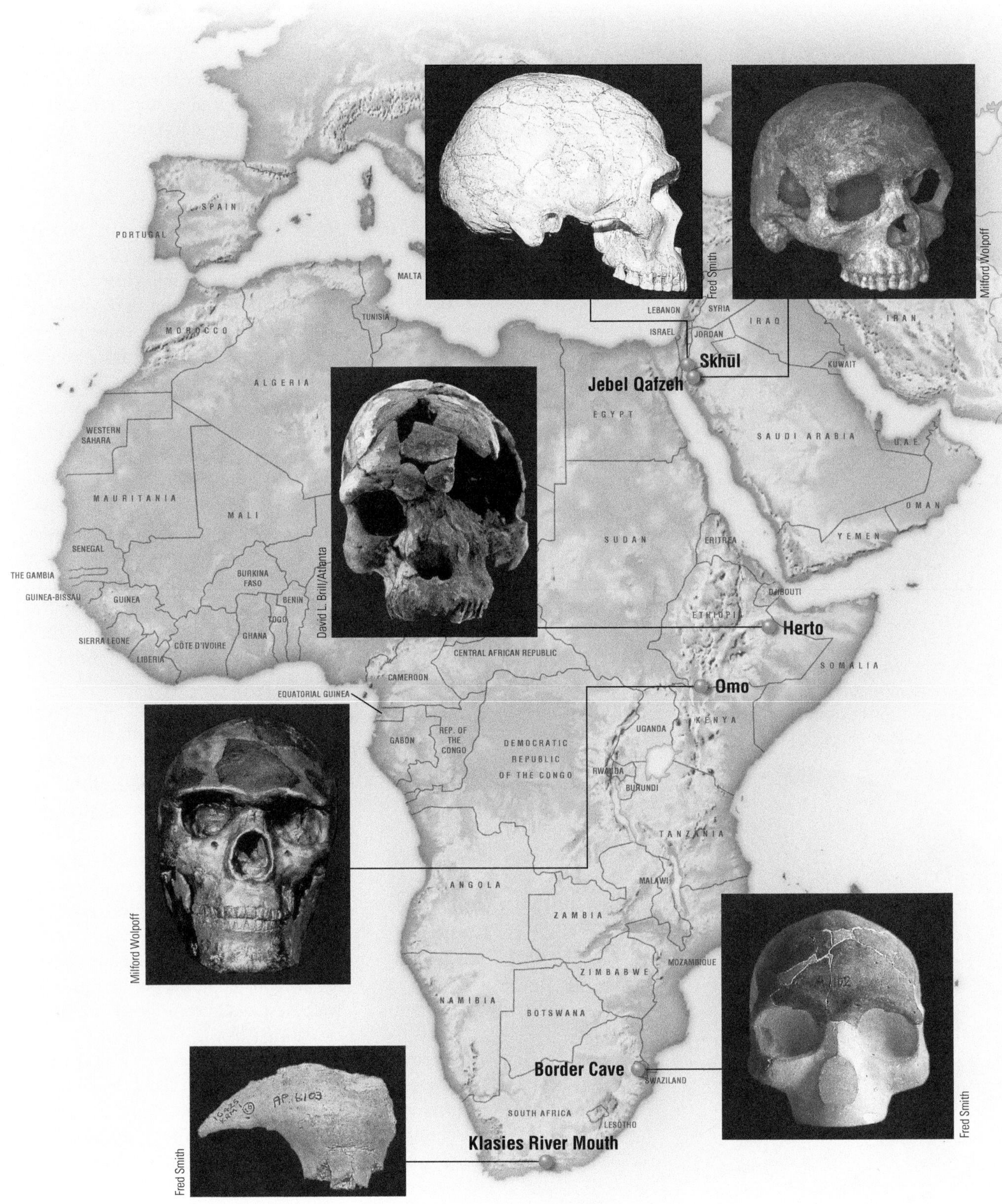

▲**Figure 13-2** Modern humans from Africa and the Near East.

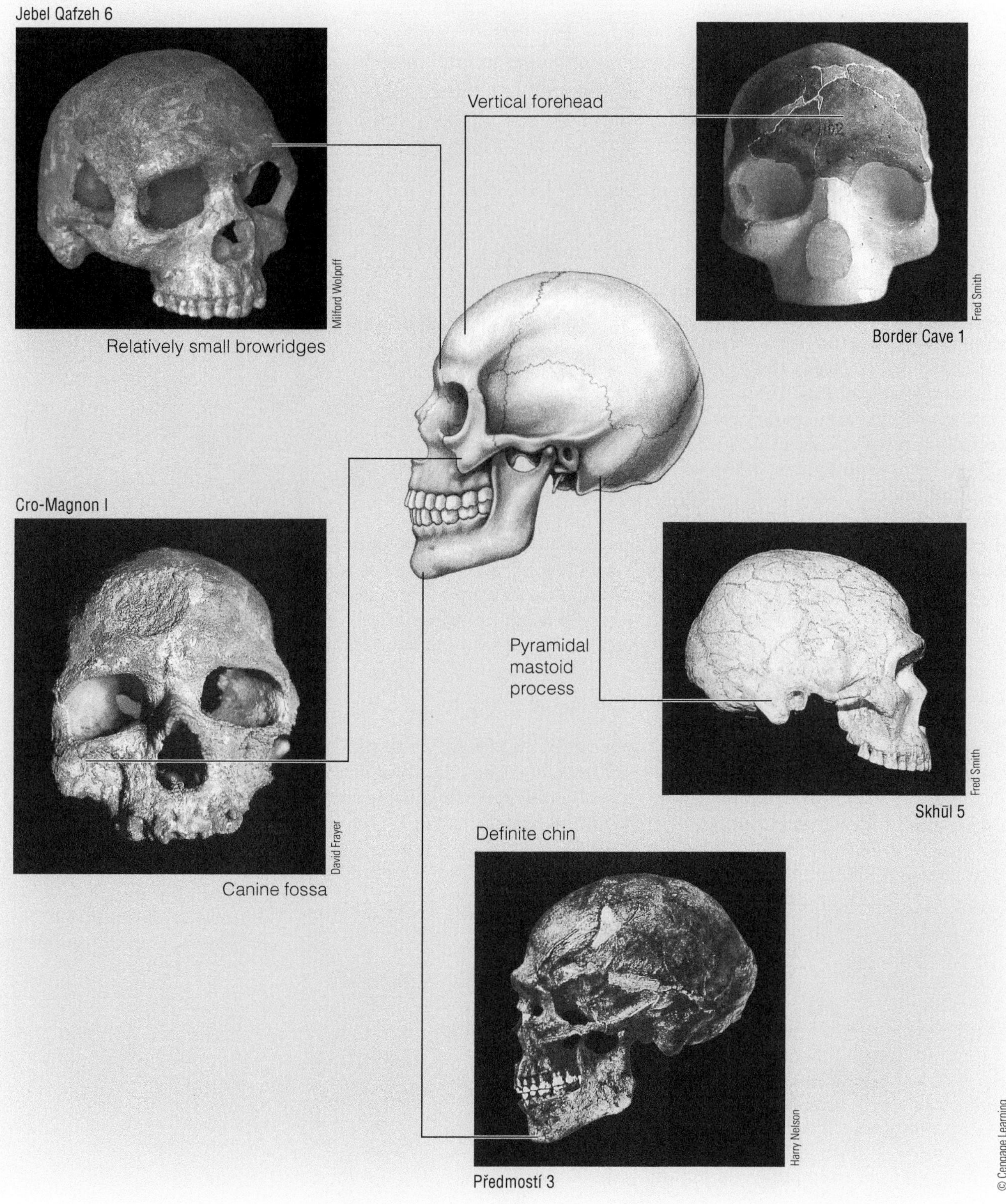

▲**Figure 13-3** Morphology and variation in early specimens of modern *Homo sapiens*.

long cranial vault. The cranial capacity is 1,450 cm^3, well within the range of contemporary *H. sapiens* populations. The skull is also in some respects heavily built, with a large, arching browridge in front and a large, projecting occipital protuberance in back. The face does not project, in stark contrast to Eurasian Neandertals.

The overall impression is that this individual is clearly *Homo sapiens*—as are the other fossils from the site. Following comprehensive statistical studies, Tim White and colleagues concluded that, though not identical to modern people, the Herto fossils are near-modern. That is, these fossils "sample a population that is on the verge of anatomical modernity but not yet fully modern" (White et al., 2003, p. 745). To distinguish these individuals from fully modern humans (*H. sapiens sapiens*), the researchers have placed them in a newly defined subspecies: *Homo sapiens idaltu*. The word *idaltu*, from the Afar language, means "elder."

What, then, can we conclude? First, we can say that these new finds strongly support an African origin of modern humans. The Herto fossils are the right age, and they come from the right place. Besides that, they look much like what we might have predicted. Considering all these facts, they're the most conclusive fossil evidence yet indicating an African origin of modern humans. What's more, this fossil evidence is compatible with a great deal of strong genetic data indicating some form of replacement model for human origins.

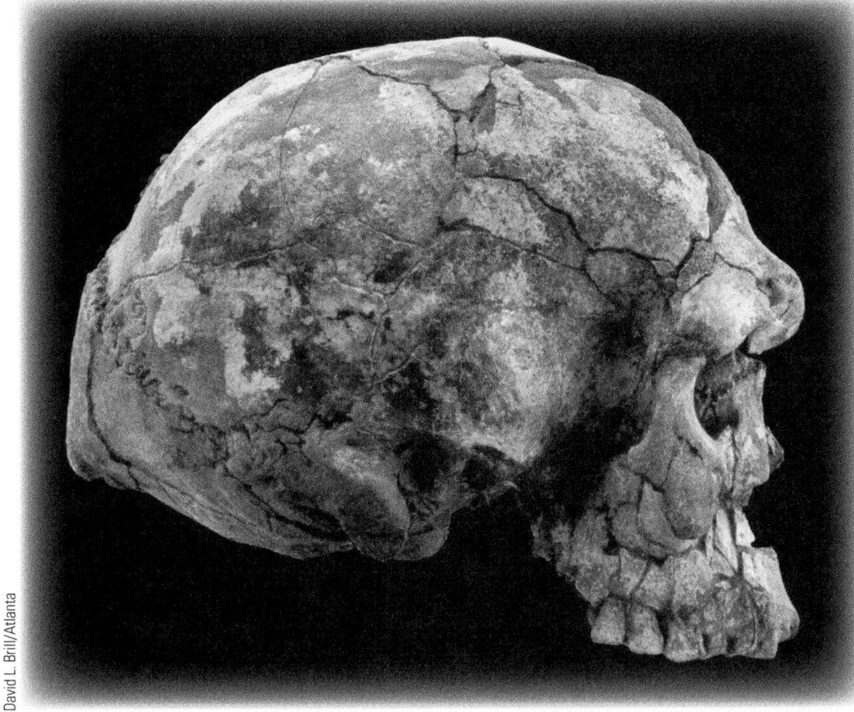
David L. Brill/Atlanta

▲ **Figure 13-4** Herto cranium from Ethiopia, dated 160,000 to 154,000 ya. This is the best-preserved early modern *H. sapiens* cranium yet found.

The Near East

In Israel, in the Skhūl Cave at Mt. Carmel, researchers found early modern *H. sapiens* fossils, including the remains of at least 10 individuals (**Figs. 13-5** and

David Frayer

◄ **Figure 13-5** Mt. Carmel, studded with caves, was home to *H. sapiens sapiens* at Skhūl (and to Neandertals at Tabun and Kebara).

▶ **Figure 13-6** (**a**) Skhūl 5. (**b**) Qafzeh 6. These specimens from Israel are thought to be representatives of early modern *Homo sapiens*. The vault height, forehead, and lack of prognathism are modern traits.

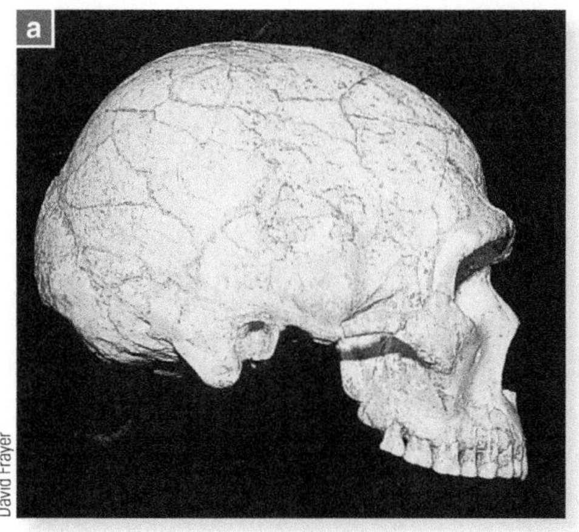

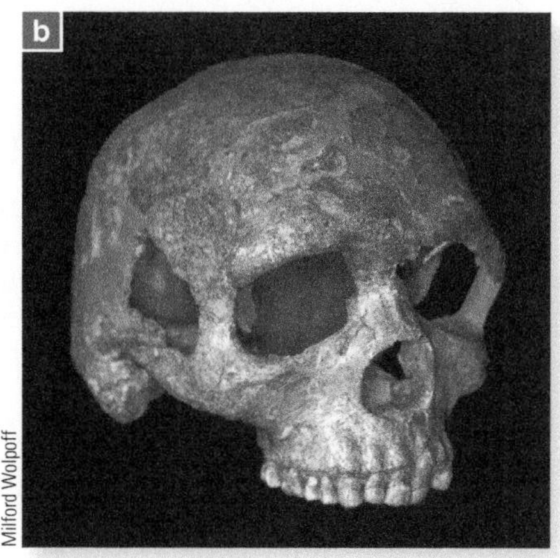

13-6a). Also from Israel, the Qafzeh Cave has yielded the remains of at least 20 individuals (**Fig. 13-6b**). Although their overall configuration is definitely modern, some specimens show certain premodern features. Skhūl has been dated to between 130,000 and 100,000 ya (Grün et al., 2005), while Qafzeh has been dated to around 120,000 to 92,000 ya (Grün and Stringer, 1991). The time line for these fossil discoveries is shown in **Figure 13-7**.

Such early dates for modern specimens pose some problems for those advocating the influence of local evolution as proposed by the multiregional model. How far back do the premodern populations—that is, Neandertals—appear in the Near East? A chronometric calibration for the Tabun Cave suggests a date as early as 120,000 ya. This dating for these sites, all located *very* close to each other, suggests that there's considerable chronological overlap in the occupation of the Near East by Neandertals and modern humans. This chronological overlap in such a small area (as well as in close proximity to Africa) has led anthropologists to suggest this region as a likely place where Neandertals and modern humans might well have interbred.

▼ **Figure 13-7** Time line of modern *Homo sapiens* discoveries. Note that most dates are approximations. Question marks indicate those estimates that are most tentative.

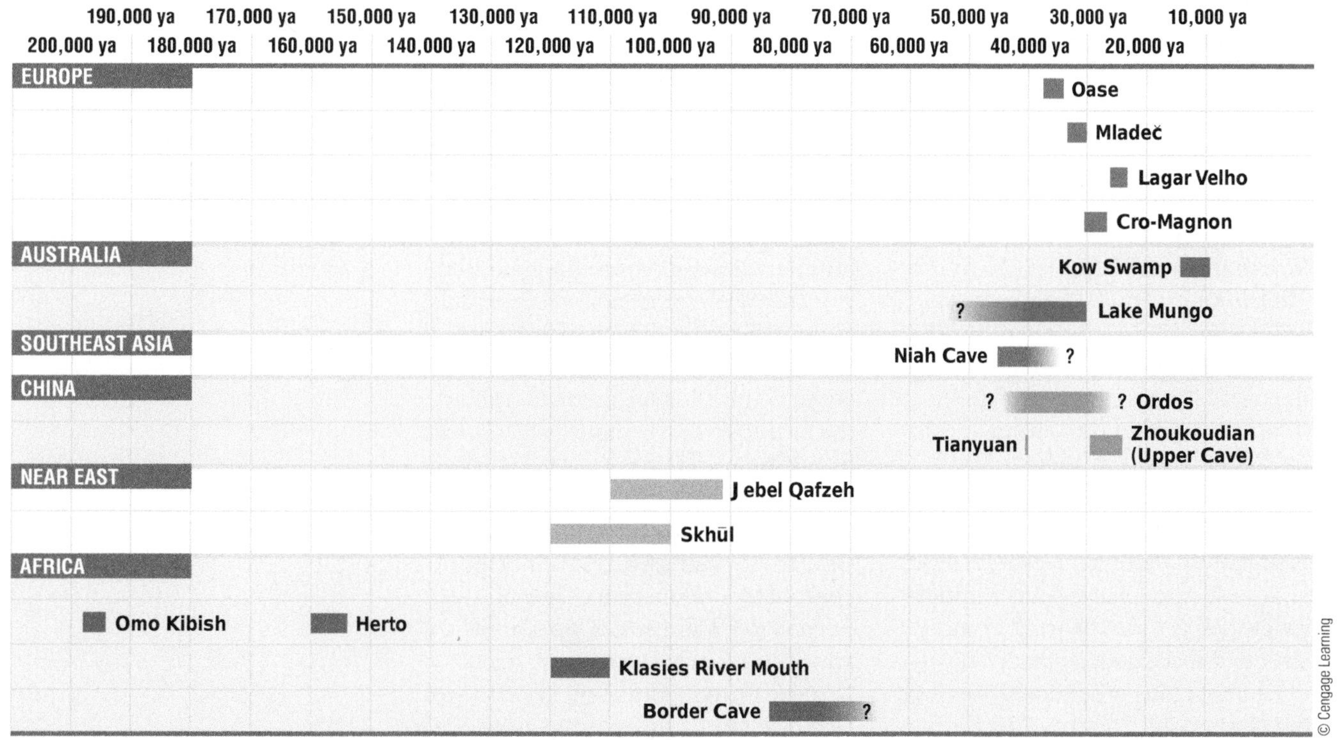

At a Glance

Key Early Modern *Homo sapiens* Discoveries from Africa and the Near East

Date	Site	Hominin	Evolutionary Significance
110,000 ya	Qafzeh (Israel)	*H. sapiens sapiens*	Large sample (at least 20 individuals); definitely modern, but some individuals fairly robust; early date (>100,000 ya)
115,000 ya	Skhūl (Israel)	*H. sapiens sapiens*	Minimum of 10 individuals; like Qafzeh modern morphology, but slightly earlier date (and earliest modern humans known outside of Africa)
160,000–154,000 ya	Herto (Ethiopia)	*H. sapiens idaltu*	Very well-preserved cranium; date >150,000 ya, the best-preserved early modern human found anywhere
195,000 ya	Omo (Ethiopia)	*H. sapiens*	Dated almost 200,000 ya and the oldest modern human found anywhere; two crania found, one more modern looking than the other

Asia

There are seven early anatomically modern human localities in China, the most significant of which are Upper Cave at Zhoukoudian, Tianyuan Cave (very near Zhoukoudian), and Ordos, in Mongolia (**Fig. 13-8**). The fossils from these Chinese sites are all fully modern, and all are considered to be from the Late Pleistocene, with dates probably later than 40,000 ya. Many of these dates are controversial and not very precise; for example, Upper Cave at Zhoukoudian has been dated variously to between 10,000 and 29,000 ya (Cunningham and Wescott, 2002).

In addition, some researchers (e.g., Tiemel et al., 1994) have suggested that the Jinniushan skeleton discussed in Chapter 12 hints at modern features in China as early as 200,000 ya. If this date—as early as that proposed for direct antecedents of modern *H. sapiens* in Africa—should prove accurate, it would cast doubt on replacement models. This position, however, is a minority view and is not supported by more recent and more detailed analyses.

Just about four miles down the road from the famous Zhoukoudian Cave is another cave called Tianyuan, the source of an important find in 2003. Consisting of a fragmentary skull, a few teeth, and several postcranial bones, this fossil is accurately dated by radiocarbon at close to 40,000 ya (Shang et al., 2007). The skeleton shows mostly modern features but has a few archaic characteristics as well. The Chinese and American team that analyzed the remains from Tianyuan proposes that they indicate an African origin of modern humans, but there is also evidence of at least some interbreeding in China with resident archaic (that is, premodern) populations. More complete analysis and (with some luck) further finds at this new site will help to provide a better picture of early modern *H. sapiens* in China. For the moment, this is the best-dated early modern *H. sapiens* from China and one of the two earliest from anywhere in Asia.

The other early fossil is a partial skull from Niah Cave on the north coast of the Indonesian island of Borneo (see Fig. 13-8). This is actually not a new find and was, in fact, first excavated more than 50 years ago. However, until recent, more extensive

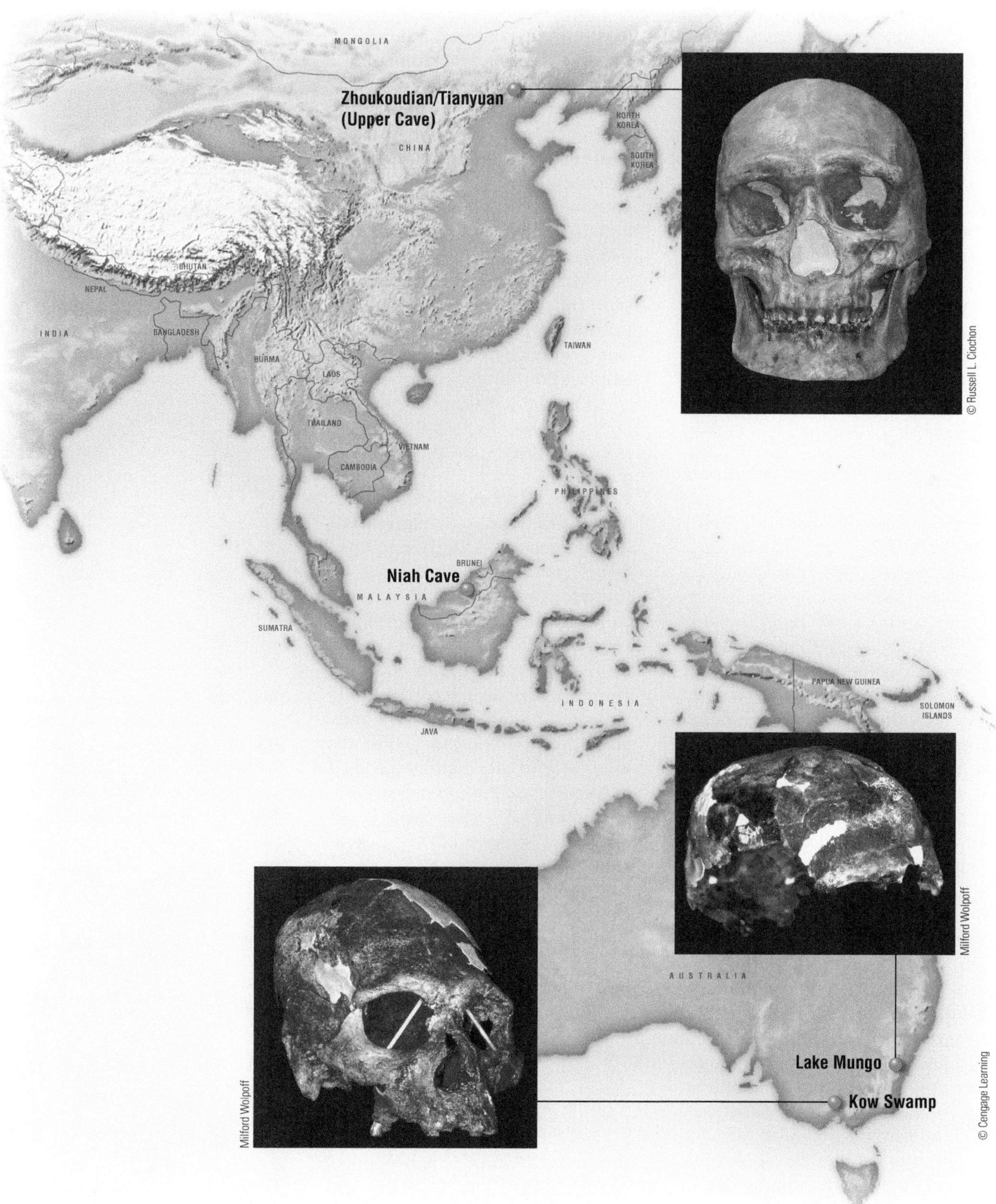

▲**Figure 13-8** Anatomically modern *Homo sapiens* in Asia and Australia.

analysis, it had been relegated to the paleoanthropological back shelf owing to uncertainties regarding its archaeological context and dating. Now all this has changed with a better understanding of the geology of the site and new dates strongly supporting an age of more than 35,000 ya—most likely even 45,000 to 40,000 ya, making it perhaps older than Tianyuan (Barker et al., 2007). Like its Chinese counterparts, the Niah skull is modern in morphology. It's hypothesized that some population contemporaneous with Niah or somewhat earlier inhabitants of Indonesia was perhaps the first group to colonize Australia.

Australia

During glacial times, the Indonesian islands were joined to the Asian mainland, but Australia wasn't. It's likely that by 50,000 ya, modern humans inhabited Sahul—the area including New Guinea and Australia. Bamboo rafts may have been used to cross the ocean between islands, though this would certainly have been dangerous and difficult. It's not known just where the ancestral Australians came from, but as noted, Indonesia has been suggested.

Human occupation of Australia occurred quite early, as indicated by several types of evidence. Some archaeological sites have been dated 55,000 ya. There's some controversy about the dating of the earliest Australian human remains, which are all modern *H. sapiens*. The earliest finds so far discovered have come from Lake Mungo, in southeastern Australia (see Fig. 13-8). In agreement with archaeological context and radiocarbon dates, the hominins from this site have been dated at approximately 30,000 to 25,000 ya.

Fossils from a site called Kow Swamp suggest that the people who lived there between about 14,000 and 9,000 ya were different from the more gracile early Australian forms from Lake Mungo (see Fig. 13-8). The Kow Swamp fossils display certain archaic cranial traits—such as receding foreheads, heavy supraorbital tori, and thick bones—that are difficult to explain, since these features contrast with the postcranial anatomy, which matches that of living indigenous Australians. Regardless of the different morphology of these later Australians, recent genetic evidence indicates that all native Australians are descendants of a *single* migration dating back to at least 50,000 ya (Hudjashou et al., 2007). Even newer research using the whole genome analysis of an Aboriginal Australian male (mentioned earlier) suggests that the divergence of native Australian populations occurred sometime between 75,000 and 62,000 ya.

Central Europe

Central Europe has been a source of many fossil finds, including the earliest anatomically modern *H. sapiens* yet discovered anywhere in Europe. Dated to approximately 40,000 ya, these early *H. sapiens* fossils come from discoveries at the Oase Cave in Romania (**Fig. 13-9**). Here cranial remains of three individuals were recovered, including a complete mandible and a partial skull. While quite robust, they are similar to later modern specimens, as seen in the clear presence of both a chin and a canine fossa (see Fig. 13-3) (Trinkaus et al., 2003; Crevecoeur et al., 2009).

▼ **Figure 13-9** Excavators at work within the spectacular cave at Oase, in Romania. The floor is littered with the remains of fossil animals, including the earliest dated cranial remains of *Homo sapiens* in Europe.

Mircea Gherase

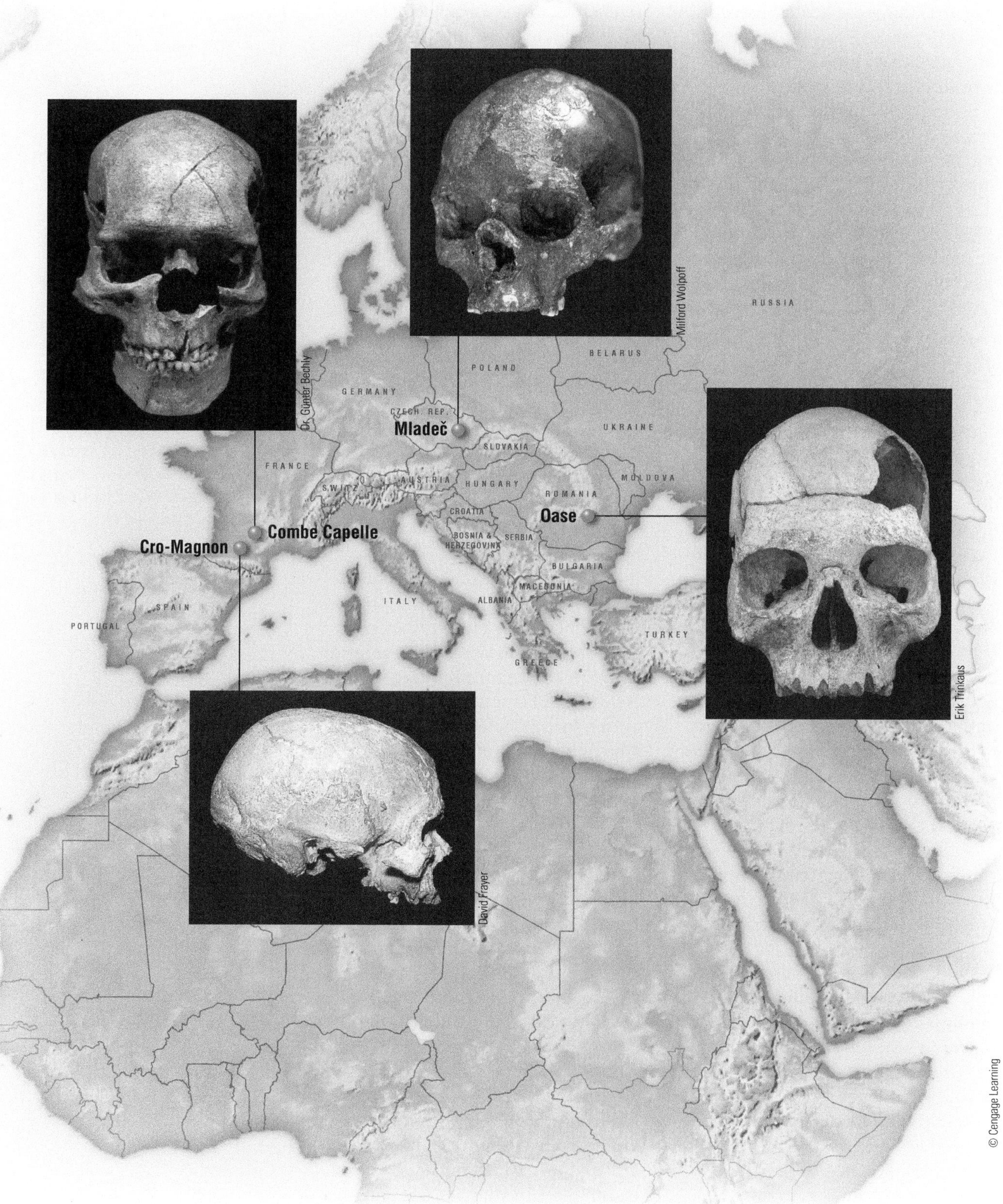

▲**Figure 13-10** Anatomically modern humans in Europe.

Another early modern human site in central Europe is Mladeč in the Czech Republic (Fig. 13-10). Several individuals have been excavated here and are dated to approximately 31,000 ya. Although there's some variation among the crania, including some with big browridges, Fred Smith (1984) is confident that they're all best classified as modern *H. sapiens* (Fig. 13-11). It's clear that by 28,000 ya, modern humans were widely dispersed in central and western Europe (Trinkaus, 2005).

Western Europe

For several reasons, western Europe (and its fossils) has received more attention than other regions. Over the last 150 years, many of the scholars doing this research happened to live in western Europe, and the southern region of France turned out to be a fossil treasure trove.

As a result of this scholarly interest, a great deal of data accumulated beginning back in the nineteenth century, with little reliable comparative information available from elsewhere in the world. Consequently, theories of human evolution were based almost exclusively on the western European material. It's only been in more recent years, with growing evidence from other areas of the world and the application of new dating techniques, that recent human evolutionary dynamics are being seriously considered from a worldwide perspective.

Western Europe has yielded many anatomically modern human fossils, but by far the best-known sample of western European *H. sapiens* is from the **Cro-Magnon** site, a rock shelter in southern France. At this site, the remains of eight individuals were discovered in 1868.

The Cro-Magnon materials are associated with an **Aurignacian** tool assemblage, an Upper Paleolithic industry. Dated at about 28,000 ya, these individuals represent the earliest of France's anatomically modern humans. The so-called Old Man (Cro-Magnon 1) became the original model for what was once termed the Cro-Magnon, or Upper Paleolithic, "race" of Europe (Fig. 13-12). Actually, of course, there's no such valid biological category, and Cro-Magnon 1 is not typical of Upper Paleolithic western Europeans—and not even all that similar to the other two male skulls found at the site.

Most of the genetic evidence, as well as the newest fossil evidence from Africa, argues against continuous local evolution producing modern groups directly from any Eurasian premodern population (in Europe, these would be Neandertals). Still, for some researchers, the issue isn't completely settled. With all the latest evidence, there's no longer much debate that a *large* genetic contribution from migrating early modern Africans influenced other groups throughout the Old World. What's being debated is just how much admixture might have occurred between these migrating Africans and the resident premodern groups. For those paleoanthropologists (for example, Trinkaus, 2005) who hypothesize that significant admixture (assimilation) occurred in western Europe as well as elsewhere, a recently discovered child's skeleton from Portugal provides some of the best skeletal evidence of possible interbreeding between Neandertals and anatomically modern *H. sapiens*. This important discovery from the Abrigo do Lagar Velho site was excavated in late 1998 and is dated to 24,500 ya—that's at least 5,000 years more recent than the last clearly identifiable Neandertal fossil. Associated with an Upper Paleolithic industry and buried with red ocher and pierced shell is a fairly complete skeleton of a 4-year-old child (Duarte et al., 1999). In studying the remains, Cidália Duarte, Erik Trinkaus, and their colleagues found a highly mixed set of anatomical features. From this

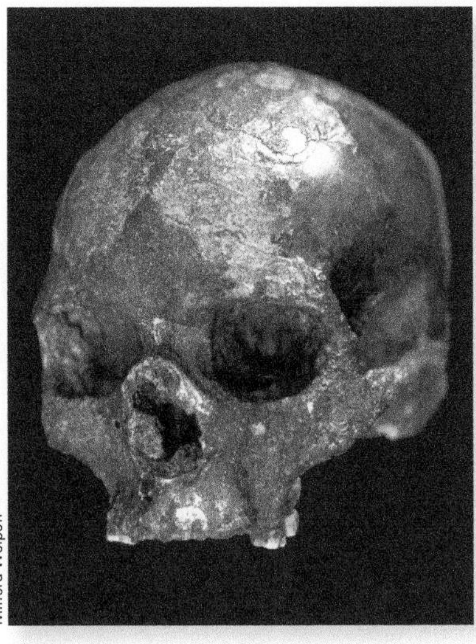

▲**Figure 13-11** The Mladeč cranium from the Czech Republic represents a good example of early modern *Homo sapiens* in central Europe. Along with Oase, in Romania, the evidence for early modern *Homo sapiens* appears first in central Europe before the later finds in western Europe.

Cro-Magnon (crow-man´-yon)

Aurignacian Pertaining to an Upper Paleolithic stone tool industry in Europe beginning at about 40,000 ya.

▶ **Figure 13-12** Cro-Magnon 1 (France). In this specimen, modern traits are quite clear. (**a**) Lateral view. (**b**) Frontal view.

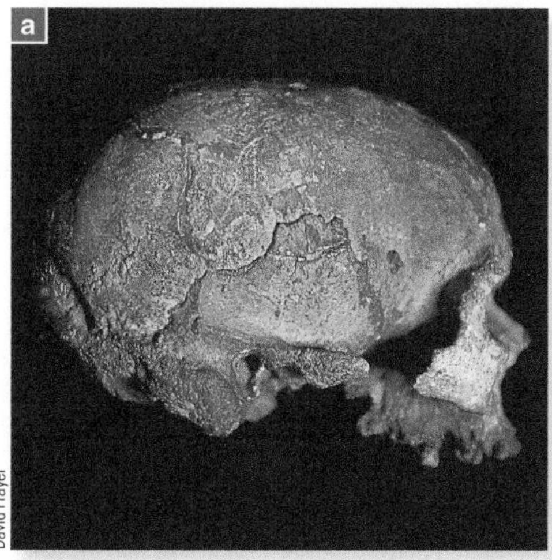

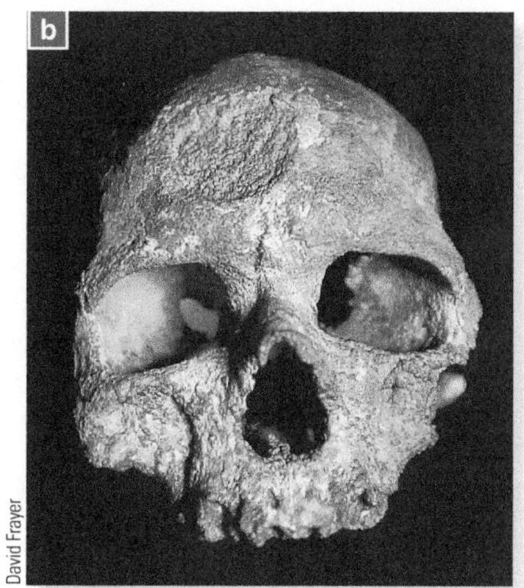

evidence they concluded that the young child was the result of interbreeding between Neandertals and modern humans and thus supports a partial replacement model of human origins. It's still debatable from this fossil evidence whether interbreeding with Neandertals took place in Portugal this late in time. Nevertheless, the genetic evidence is unequivocal: Neandertals and modern humans *did* interbreed at some point, though the extent and frequency are presently unknown.

Something New and Different: The "Little People"

As we've seen, by 25,000 years ago, modern humans had dispersed to all major areas of the Old World, and they would soon journey to the New World as well. But at about the same time, remnant populations of earlier hominins still survived in a few remote and isolated corners. We mentioned in

At a Glance

Key Early Modern *Homo sapiens* Discoveries from Europe and Asia

Date	Site	Hominin	Evolutionary Significance
24,500 ya	Abrigo do Lagar Velho (Portugal)	*H. sapiens sapiens*	Child's skeleton; some suggestion of possible hybrid between Neandertal and modern human—but is controversial
30,000 ya	Cro-Magnon (France)	*H. sapiens sapiens*	Most famous early modern human find in world; earliest evidence of modern humans in France
40,000 ya	Tianyuan Cave (China)	*H. sapiens sapiens*	Partial skull and a few postcranial bones; oldest modern human find from China
45,000–40,000 ya	Niah Cave (Borneo, Indonesia)	*H. sapiens sapiens*	Partial skull recently redated more accurately; oldest modern human find from Asia

Chapter 11 that populations of *Homo erectus* in Java managed to survive on that island long after their cousins had disappeared from other areas (for example, China and East Africa). What's more, even though they persisted well into the Late Pleistocene, these Javanese hominins were still physically similar to other *H. erectus* individuals.

Even more surprising, it seems that other populations possibly branched off from some of these early inhabitants of Indonesia and either intentionally or accidentally found their way to other, smaller islands to the east. There, under even more extreme isolation pressures, they evolved in an astonishing direction. In late 2004, the world awoke to the startling announcement that an extremely small-bodied, small-brained hominin had been discovered in Liang Bua Cave on the island of Flores, east of Java (**Fig. 13-13**). Dubbed the "Little Lady of Flores" or simply "Flo," the remains consist of an incomplete skeleton of an adult female (LB1) as well as additional pieces from approximately 13 other individuals, which the press has collectively nicknamed "hobbits." The female skeleton is remarkable in several ways (**Fig. 13-14**), though in some aspects similar to the Dmanisi hominins. First, she was barely 3 feet tall—as short as the smallest australopith—and her brain, estimated at a mere 417 cm^3 (Falk et al., 2005), was no larger than that of a chimpanzee (Brown et al., 2004). Possibly most startling of all, these extraordinary hominins were still living on Flores just 13,000 ya (Morwood et al., 2004, 2005; Wong, 2009)!

Where did they come from? As we said, their predecessors were perhaps *H. erectus* populations like those found on Java. How they got to Flores—some 400 miles away, partly over open ocean—is a mystery. There are several connecting islands, and to get from one to another these hominins may have drifted across on rafts; but there's no way to be sure of this. What's more, these little hominins were apparently living on Flores for a very long time; recently discovered stone tools have been radiometrically dated to at least 1 mya (Brumm et al., 2010). Such an ancient date, as well as the overall similarities to the Dmanisi hominins, suggests to some researchers that *Homo floresiensis* may derive from an early migration of early *Homo* to Southeast Asia (Jungers et al., 2009; Wong, 2009). In other words, this highly unusual hominin might have evolved from ancestors who left Africa even before *H. erectus* did.

How did they get to be so physically different from all other known hominins? Here we're a little more certain of the answer. Isolated island populations can quite rapidly diverge from their relatives elsewhere. Among such isolated animals, natural selection frequently favors reduced body size. For example, remains of dwarfed elephants have been found on islands in the Mediterranean as well as on some channel islands off the coast of southern California. And perhaps most interesting of all, dwarf elephants *also*

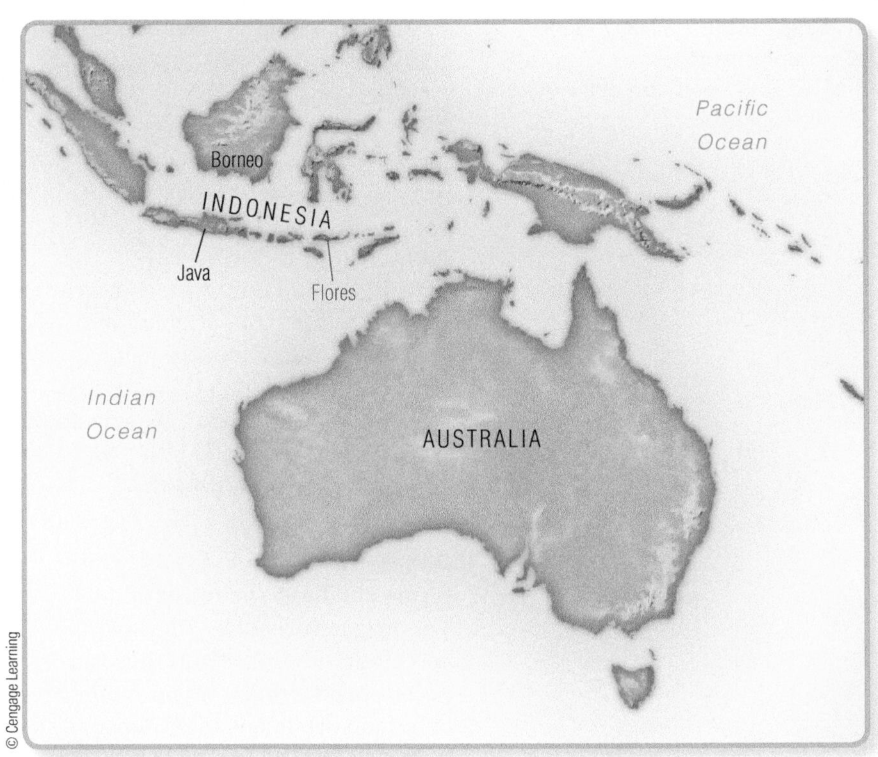

© Cengage Learning

▲ **Figure 13-13** Location of the Flores site in Indonesia.

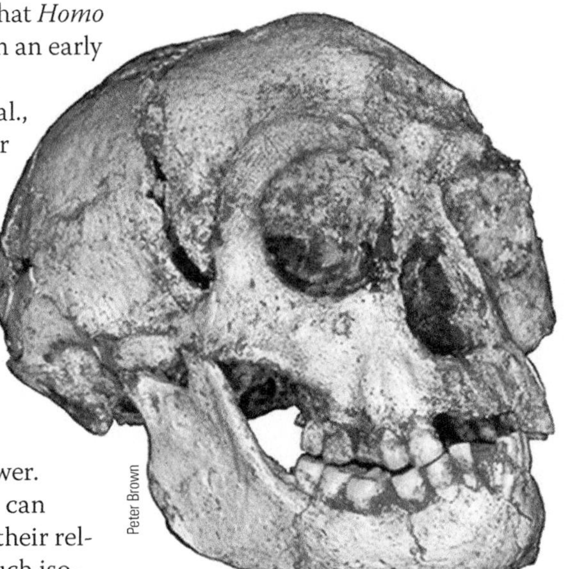

Peter Brown

▲ **Figure 13-14** Cranium of an adult female *Homo floresiensis* from Flores, Indonesia, dated 18,000 ya.

evolved on Flores; they were found in the same geological beds with the little hominins. The evolutionary mechanism (called "insular dwarfing") thought to explain such extreme body size reduction in both the elephants and the hominins is an adaptation to reduced resources, with natural selection favoring smaller body size (Schauber and Falk, 2008).

Other than short stature, what did the Flores hominins look like? In their cranial shape, thickness of cranial bone, and dentition, they most resemble *H. erectus*. Still, they have some derived features that also set them apart from all other hominins. For that reason, many researchers have placed them in a separate species, *Homo floresiensis*.

Immediately following the first publication of the Flores remains, intense controversy arose regarding their interpretation (Jacob et al., 2006; Martin et al., 2006). Some researchers have argued that the small-brained hominin (LB1) is actually a pathological modern *H. sapiens* afflicted with a severe disorder (microcephaly, and others have been proposed). The researchers who did most of the initial work reject this conclusion and provide some further details to support their original interpretation (for example, Dean Falk and colleagues' further analysis of microcephalic endocasts; Falk et al., 2009).

The conclusion that among this already small-bodied island population the one individual found with a preserved cranium happened to be afflicted with a severe (and rare) growth defect is highly unlikely. Yet, it must also be recognized that long-term, extreme isolation of hominins on Flores, leading to a new species showing dramatic dwarfing and even more dramatic brain size reduction, is quite unusual.

So where does this leave us? Because a particular interpretation is unlikely, it's not necessarily incorrect. We do know, for example, that such "insular dwarfing" has occurred in other mammals. For the moment, most analyses strongly indicate that this hominin species (*H. floresiensis*) did, in fact, evolve on Flores (Nevell et al., 2007; Tocheri et al., 2007; Falk et al., 2008; Schauber and Falk, 2008; Jungers et al., 2009). The more detailed studies of hand and foot anatomy suggest that in several respects the morphology is like that of *H. erectus* (Nevell et al., 2007; Tocheri et al., 2007) or even early *Homo* (Jungers et al., 2009). The most comprehensive recent analysis reviews all the available data relating to the well-preserved cranium of LB1 (Kaifu et al., 2011). In most respects the cranium most resembles early *Homo erectus* from Java—which, after all, is very close to Flores. In any case, the morphology of the Flores hominins is different in several key respects from that of *H. sapiens*, including even those rare individuals who show pathological conditions.

Technology and Art in the Upper Paleolithic

Europe

The cultural period known as the Upper Paleolithic began in western Europe approximately 40,000 ya (**Fig. 13-15**). Upper Paleolithic cultures are usually divided into five different industries based on stone tool technologies: Chatelperronian, Aurignacian, Gravettian, Solutrean, and Magdalenian. Major environmental shifts were also apparent during this period. During the last glacial period, about 30,000 ya, a warming trend lasting several thousand years par-

▾ **Figure 13-15** Cultural periods of the European Upper Paleolithic and their approximate beginning dates.

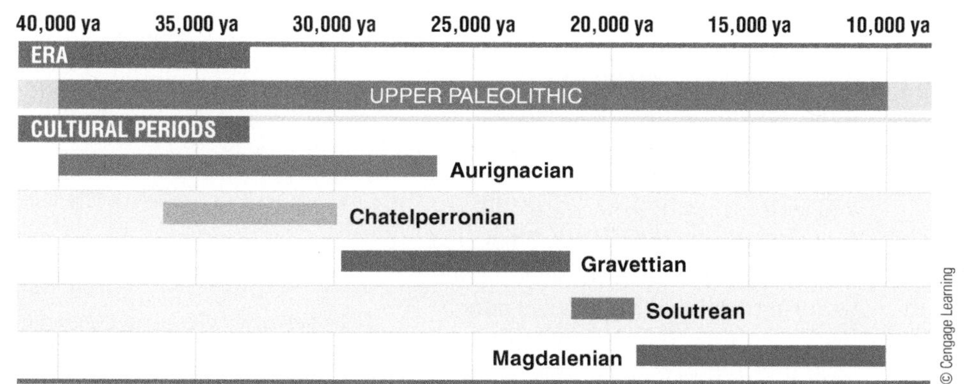

tially melted the glacial ice. The result was that much of Eurasia was covered by tundra and steppe, a vast area of treeless country dotted with lakes and marshes. In many areas in the north, permafrost prevented the growth of trees but permitted the growth, in the short summers, of flowering plants, mosses, and other kinds of vegetation. This vegetation served as an enormous pasture for herbivorous animals large and small, and carnivorous animals fed off the herbivores. It was a hunter's paradise, with millions of animals dispersed across expanses of tundra and grassland from Spain through Europe and into the Russian steppes.

Large herds of reindeer roamed the tundra and steppes, along with mammoths, bison, horses, and a host of smaller animals that served as a bountiful source of food. In addition, humans exploited fish and fowl systematically, apparently for the first time. It was a time of relative abundance, and ultimately Upper Paleolithic people spread out over Eurasia, living in caves and open-air camps and building large shelters. We should recall that many of the cultural innovations seen in the Upper Paleolithic had begun with Neandertals (see Chapter 12). Nevertheless, in looking at the entire Upper Paleolithic, there are notable differences. For example, far more elaborate burials are found, most spectacularly at the 24,000-year-old Sungir site near Moscow (**Fig. 13-16**), where grave goods included a bed of red ocher, thousands of ivory beads, long spears made of straightened mammoth tusks, ivory engravings, and jewelry (Formicola and Buzhilova, 2004). During this period, either western Europe or perhaps portions of Africa achieved the highest population density in human history up to that time.

Humans and other animals in most of Eurasia had to cope with shifts in climate conditions, some of them quite rapid. For example, at 20,000 ya, another climatic "pulse" caused the weather to become noticeably colder in Europe and Asia as the continental glaciations reached their maximum extent for this entire glacial period, which is called the Würm in Eurasia.

As a variety of organisms attempted to adapt to these changing conditions, *Homo sapiens* had a major advantage: the elaboration of increasingly sophisticated technology and probably other components of culture as well. In fact, one of the greatest challenges facing numerous Late Pleistocene mammals was the ever more dangerously equipped humans—a trend that continues today.

The Upper Paleolithic was an age of innovation that can be compared to the past few hundred years in our recent history of amazing technological change. Anatomically modern humans of the Upper Paleolithic not only invented new and specialized tools (**Fig. 13-17**) but, as we've seen, also experimented with and greatly increased the use of new materials such as bone, ivory, and antler.

Solutrean tools are good examples of Upper Paleolithic skill and likely aesthetic appreciation as well (see Fig. 13-17b). In this lithic (stone) tradition, skill in modifying rock (called "knapping") developed to the finest degree ever known. Using specialized flaking techniques, the artist/technicians made beautiful parallel-flaked lance heads, expertly flaked on both surfaces. The lance points are so delicate that they can be considered works of art that quite possibly never served, nor were intended to serve, a utilitarian purpose.

The last stage of the Upper Paleolithic, known as the **Magdalenian**, saw even more advances in technology. The spear-thrower, or atlatl, was a hooked rod made of bone or wood that extended the hunter's arm, enhancing the force and distance of a spear throw (**Fig. 13-18**). For catching salmon and other fish, the barbed harpoon is a good example of skillful craftsmanship. There's also evidence that bows and arrows may have been used for the first time during this period. The introduction of much more efficient manufacturing methods, such as the punch blade technique (**Fig. 13-19**), provided an abundance of standardized stone

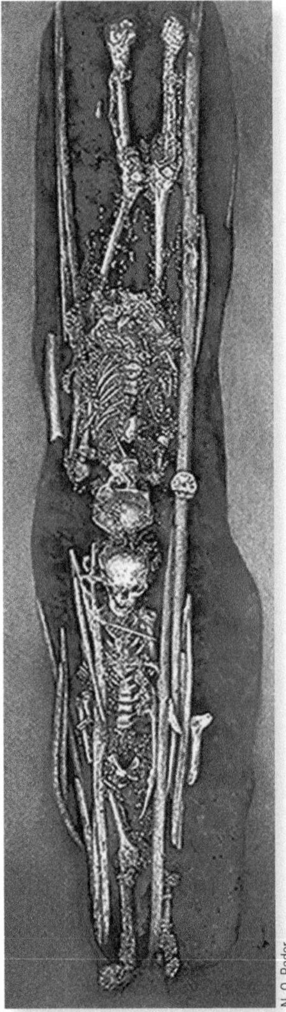

N. O. Bader

▲ **Figure 13-16** Skeletons of two teenagers, a male and a female, from Sungir, Russia. Dated 24,000 ya, this is the richest find of any Upper Paleolithic grave.

Magdalenian Pertaining to the final phase of the Upper Paleolithic stone tool industry in Europe.

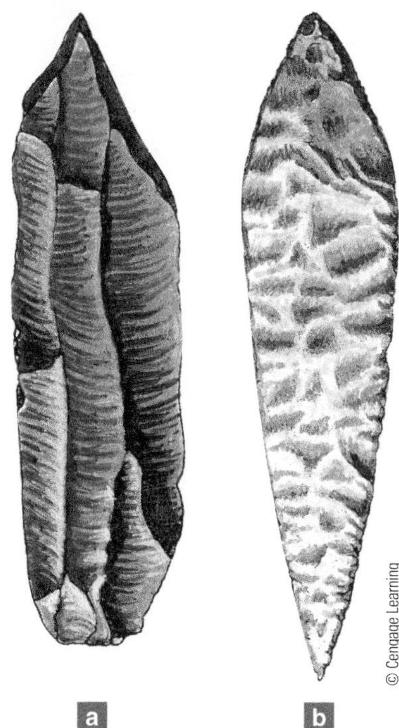

▲ **Figure 13-17** (**a**) A burin, a very common Upper Paleolithic tool. (**b**) A Solutrean blade. This is the best-known work of the Solutrean tradition. Solutrean stonework is considered the most highly developed of any Upper Paleolithic industry.

blades. These could be fashioned into **burins** (see Fig. 13-17a) for working wood, bone, and antler; borers for drilling holes in skins, bones, and shells; and knives with serrated or notched edges for scraping wooden shafts into a variety of tools.

By producing many more specialized tools, Upper Paleolithic peoples probably had more resources available to them; moreover, these more effective tools may also have had an impact on the biology of these populations. Emphasizing a biocultural interpretation, C. Loring Brace of the University of Michigan has suggested that with more effective tools as well as the use of fire, allowing for more efficient food processing, modern *H. sapiens* wouldn't have required the large teeth and facial skeletons seen in earlier populations.

In addition to their reputation as hunters, western Europeans of the Upper Paleolithic are even better known for their symbolic representation (what we today recognize as art). There's an extremely wide geographical distribution of symbolic images, best known from many parts of Europe but now also well documented from Siberia, North Africa, South Africa, and Australia. Given a 25,000-year time depth of what we call Paleolithic art, along with its nearly worldwide distribution, we must appreciate that it showed a remarkable range of expression.

Besides cave art, there are many examples of small sculptures excavated from sites in western, central, and eastern Europe. Perhaps the most famous of these are the female figurines, popularly known as "Venuses," found at such sites as Brassempouy in France and Grimaldi in Italy. Some of these figures were realistically carved, and the faces appear to be modeled after actual women. Other figurines may seem grotesque, with sexual characteristics exaggerated, perhaps to promote fertility or serve some other ritual purpose.

Beyond these quite well-known figurines, there are numerous other examples of what's frequently called portable art, including elaborate engravings on tools and tool handles (see Fig. 13-18). Such symbolism can be found in many parts of Europe and was already well established early in the Aurignacian, by perhaps as early as 40,000 ya. Recently improved carbon dating used at Geissenklösterle Cave in southwest Germany shows what are thought to be the earliest musical instruments found anywhere (eight flutes made of bone). In addition, sophisticated carved figures were also found, all dating to *at least* 40,000 ya (Higham et al., 2012). Improved dating methods also show early painted representations in several caves in Spain. From the famous cave site at Altamira (dating to 35 kya*) as well as at El Castillo (dating to about 41 kya) come the earliest examples of cave painting from anywhere yet discovered. These new, surprisingly early dates derive from advancements in a radiometric technique called uranium-series dating (see Chapter 9). By using tiny samples of accumulated calcite deposits that form on top of painted or engraved images, archaeologists now have much more accurate ideas of when these images were made (Pike et al., 2012). Remember too that the dates are *minimum* ones: The calcite formed after (perhaps long after) the images were completed.

Innovations in symbolic representations also benefited from and probably further stimulated technological advances. New methods of mixing pigments and applying them were important in rendering painted or drawn images. Engraving and carving on bone and ivory were made easier with the use of special stone tools (see Fig. 13-17). At two sites in the Czech Republic, Dolní Věstonice and Předmostí (both dated at approximately 27,000 to 26,000 ya), small animal figures were fashioned from fired clay. This is the first documented use of ceramic technology anywhere; in fact, it precedes the

*kya = thousand years ago

burins Small, chisel-like tools with a pointed end; thought to have been used to engrave bone, antler, ivory, or wood.

later invention of pottery by more than 15,000 years.

But it wasn't until the final phases of the Upper Paleolithic, particularly during the Magdalenian, that European prehistoric art reached its climax. Cave art is now known from more than 150 separate sites, the vast majority from southwestern France and northern Spain. Apparently in other areas the rendering of such images did not take place in deep caves. People in central Europe, China, Africa, and elsewhere certainly may have painted or carved representations on rock faces in the open, but these images long since would have disappeared. So we're fortunate that the people of at least one of the many sophisticated cultures of the Upper Paleolithic chose to journey below ground to create their artwork, preserving it not just for their immediate descendants but for us as well. The most spectacular and famous of the cave art sites are Lascaux and Grotte Chauvet in France and Altamira in Spain.

In Lascaux Cave, for example, immense wild bulls dominate what's called the Great Hall of Bulls; also horses, deer, and other animals drawn with remarkable skill adorn the walls in black, red, and yellow. Equally impressive, the walls and ceiling of an immense cave at Altamira are filled with superb portrayals of bison in red and black. The artist even took advantage of bulges in the walls to create a sense of relief (that is, three-dimensionality) in the paintings.

Inside the cave called Grotte Chauvet, preserved unseen for thousands of years, are a multitude of images including dots, stenciled human handprints, and, most dramatically, hundreds of animal representations. Radiocarbon dating has placed the paintings during the Aurignacian,

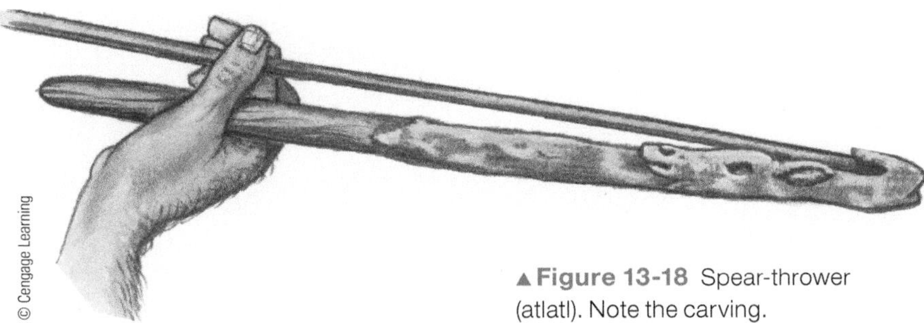

▲ **Figure 13-18** Spear-thrower (atlatl). Note the carving.

▼ **Figure 13-19** The punch blade technique.

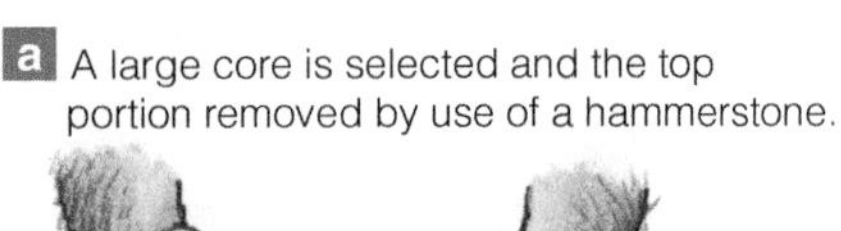

a A large core is selected and the top portion removed by use of a hammerstone.

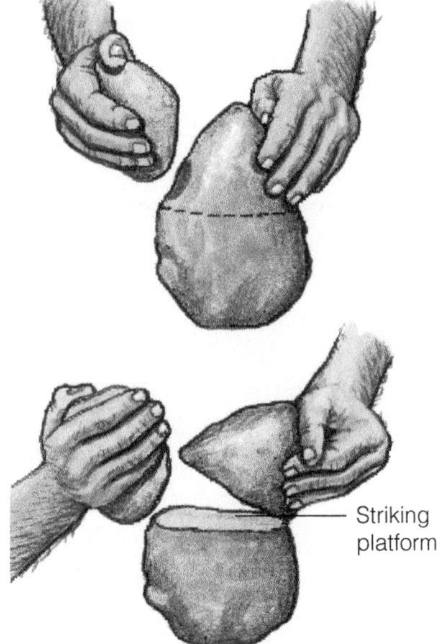

b The objective is to create a flat surface called a striking platform.

c Next, the core is struck by use of a hammer and punch (made of bone or antler) to remove the long narrow flakes (called blades).

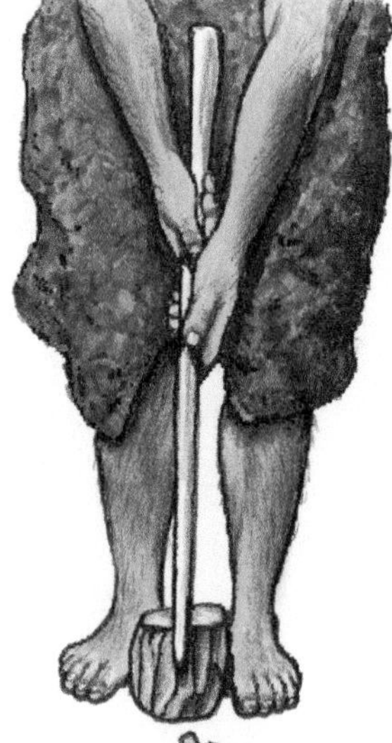

d Or the blades can be removed by pressure flaking.

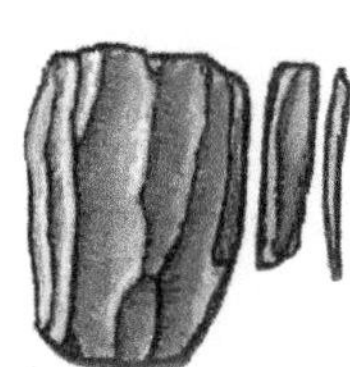

e The result is the production of highly consistent sharp blades, which can be used, as is, as knives; or they can be further modified (retouched) to make a variety of other tools (such as burins, scrapers, and awls).

A Closer Look

Maybe You *Can* Take It with You

The practice of deliberately burying the dead is an important and distinctive aspect of later human biocultural evolution. We saw in Chapter 12 that Neandertals buried their dead at a number of sites; but we also noted that the assortment of grave goods found in Neandertal burials was pretty sparse.

Something remarkable happened with the appearance and dispersal of modern humans. Suddenly—at least in archaeological terms—graves became much more elaborate. And it wasn't just that many more items were placed with the deceased; it was also the kinds of objects. Neandertal graves sometimes contain a few stone tools and some unmodified animal bones, such as cave bear. But fully modern humans seem to have had more specialized and far more intensive cultural capacities. For example, from 40,000 ya at Twilight Cave, in Kenya, researchers have found 600 fragments of carefully drilled ostrich eggshell beads (Klein and Edgar, 2002). These beads aren't directly associated with a human burial, but they do show an intensification of craft specialization and possibly a greater interest in personal adornment (although Neandertals in Spain at about the same time were doing similar things, but to a somewhat lesser extent; see Chapter 12)

A locale where such elaborate grave goods (including beads) have been found in association with Upper Paleolithic modern human burials is the famous Cro-Magnon site in southwestern France. Likewise, numerous elaborate grave goods were found with human burials at Grimaldi, in Italy.

No doubt the richest Upper Paleolithic burial sites are those at Sungir, in Russia. Parts of several individuals have been recovered there, dating to about 24,000 ya. Most dramatically, three individuals were found in direct association with thousands of ivory beads and other elaborate grave goods. Two of the individuals, a girl about 9 or 10 years of age and a boy about 12 or 13 years of age, were buried together head to head in a spectacular grave (see Fig. 13-16). The more than 10,000 beads excavated here were probably woven into clothing, a task that would have been extraordinarily time-consuming. The two individuals were placed directly on a bed of red ocher, and with them were two magnificent spears made of straightened mammoth tusks—one of them more than 6 feet (240 cm) long! What's more, there were hundreds of drilled fox canine teeth, pierced antlers, and ivory carvings of animals as well as ivory pins and pendants (Formicola and Buzhilova, 2004).

The production of all of these items, which were so carefully placed with these two young individuals, took thousands of hours of labor. Indeed, one estimate suggests that it took 10,000 hours just to make the beads (Klein and Edgar, 2002). What were the Magdalenian people who went to all this trouble thinking? The double burial is certainly the most extravagant of any from the Upper Paleolithic, but another at Sungir is almost as remarkable. Here, the body of an adult male—perhaps about 40 years old when he died—was also found with thousands of beads, and he, too, was carefully laid out on a bed of red ocher.

Sungir is likely a somewhat extraordinary exception; still, far more elaborate graves are often found associated with early modern humans than was ever the case in earlier cultures. At Sungir, and to a lesser extent at other sites, it took hundreds or even thousands of hours to produce the varied and intricate objects.

The individuals who were buried with these valuable goods must have been seen as special. Did they have unique talents? Were they leaders or the children of leaders? Or did they have some special religious or ritual standing? To be sure, this evidence is the earliest we have from human history revealing highly defined social status. Thousands of years later, the graves of the Egyptian pharaohs express the same thing—as do the elaborate monuments seen in most contemporary cemeteries. The Magdalenians and other Upper Paleolithic cultures were indeed much like us. They, too, may have tried to defy death and "take it with them"!

likely more than 35,000 ya, making Grotte Chauvet considerably earlier than the Magdalenian sites of Lascaux and most of the images at Altamira (Balter, 2006). However, as we mentioned above, Altamira and a couple of other Spanish caves contain some images that are now dated even earlier.

Africa

Early accomplishments in rock art, possibly as early as in Europe, are seen in southern Africa (Namibia) at the Apollo 11 rock shelter site, where painted slabs have been identified as dating to between 28,000 and 26,000 ya (Freundlich et al., 1980; Vogelsang, 1998). At Blombos Cave, farther to the south, remarkable bone tools, beads, and decorated ocher fragments are all dated to 73,000 ya (Henshilwood et al., 2004; Jacobs et al., 2006). The most recent and highly notable discovery from South Africa comes from another cave located at Pinnacle Point, not far from Blombos. At Pinnacle Point, ocher has been found (perhaps used for personal adornment) as well as clear evidence of systematic exploitation of shellfish and the use of very small stone blades (microliths). What is both important and surprising is that the site is dated to approximately 165,000 ya, providing the earliest evidence from anywhere of these behaviors, which are thought by many to be characteristic of modern humans (Marean et al., 2007). The microliths also show evidence that the stone had been carefully heated, making it easier to modify into such small tools (Brown et al., 2009; Marean, 2010). Other recent finds from Sibudu, another cave site in South Africa dated to around 70,000 ya, show what archaeologist Lyn Wadley and colleagues have identified as traces of compound adhesives made from red ocher and plant gum, which were then used to haft stone tools to handles (Wadley et al., 2009). Wadley and colleagues conclude that such traces of behavior show evidence of what she terms "complex cognition," since they appear to indicate an understanding of basic chemical reactions.

In central Africa there was also considerable use of bone and antler, some of it possibly quite early. Excavations in the Katanda area of the eastern portion of the Democratic Republic of the Congo (**Fig. 13-20**) have shown remarkable development of bone craftwork. Dating of the site is quite early, with initial ESR and TL dating results indicating an age of 80,000 ya (Feathers and Migliorini, 2001). Preliminary reports have demonstrated that these technological achievements rival those of the more renowned European Upper Paleolithic (Yellen et al., 1995).

Summary of Upper Paleolithic Culture

In looking back at the Upper Paleolithic, we can see it as the culmination of 2 million years of cultural development. Change proceeded incredibly slowly for most of the Pleistocene; but as cultural traditions and materials accumulated, and the brain—as well as, we assume, intelligence—expanded and reorganized, the rate of change quickened.

Cultural evolution continued with the appearance of early premodern humans and moved a bit faster with later premodern humans. Neandertals in Eurasia and their contemporaries elsewhere added deliberate burials, body ornamentation, technological innovations, and much more.

Building on existing cultures, Late Pleistocene populations attained sophisticated cultural and material heights in a seemingly short (by previous standards) burst of exciting activity. In Europe and southern and central Africa, particularly, there seem to have been dramatic cultural innovations, among them big game hunting with new weapons, such as harpoons, spear-throwers, and eventually bows and arrows. Other innovations included needles, "tailored" clothing, hafting of tools, and burials with elaborate grave goods—a practice that may indicate some sort of status hierarchy.

This dynamic age was doomed, or so it seems, by the climate changes of about 10,000 ya. As the temperature slowly rose and the glaciers retreated, animal and plant species were seriously affected, and these changes, in turn, affected humans. As traditional prey animals were depleted or disappeared altogether, humans had to seek other means of obtaining food.

The grinding of hard seeds or roots became important, and as humans grew more familiar with propagating plants, they began to domesticate both plants and animals. Human dependence on domestication became critical, and with it came permanent settlements, new technology, and more complex social organization. This continuing story of human biocultural evolution will be the topic of the remainder of this text.

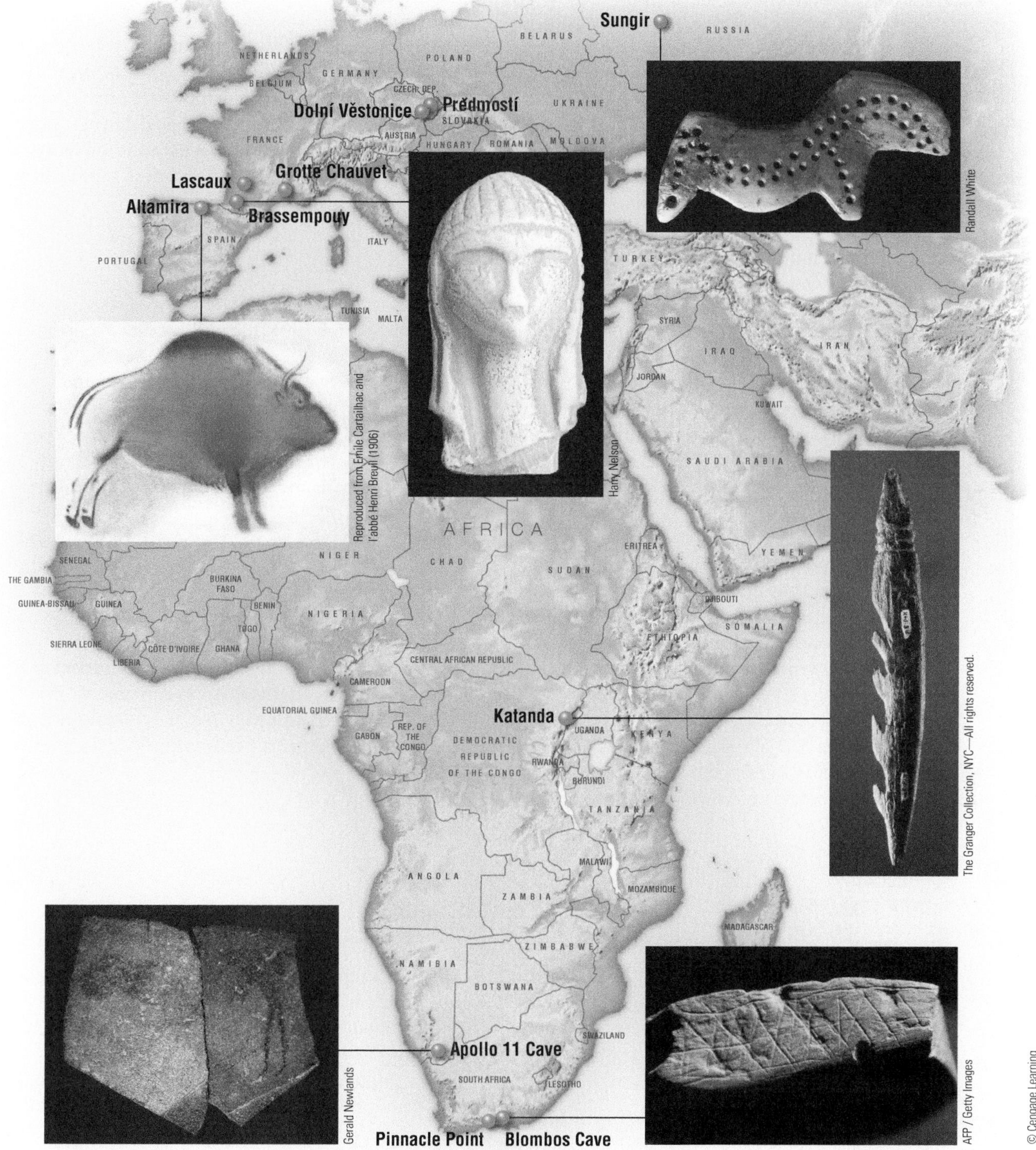

▲ **Figure 13-20** Symbolic artifacts from the Middle Stone Age of Africa and the Upper Paleolithic in Europe. It is notable that evidence of symbolism is found in Blombos Cave (77,000 ya) and Katanda (80,000 ya), both in Africa, about 45,000 years before any comparable evidence is known from Europe.

How Do We Know?

As with the previous discussions of early hominins, our main basis of information comes from a well-dated and quite complete fossil record (including dozens of skeletons) from Africa, Europe, and Asia as well as the first finds from Australia. In addition, new ancient DNA data, especially the sequencing of the full Neandertal and Denisovan genomes, has shed crucial new light on the age, location, and aspects of gene flow, all relating to the dispersal of modern human populations. Last, abundant archaeological discoveries of tools as well as symbolic representations tell us a great deal about the behavior of early modern human beings.

Summary of Main Topics

- Two main hypotheses have been used to explain the origin and dispersal of modern humans:
  —The regional continuity model suggests that different groups of modern people evolved from local populations of premodern humans.
  —Various replacement models, especially those emphasizing partial replacement, suggest that modern humans originated in Africa and migrated to other parts of the world. However, when they came into contact with premodern human groups, they did not completely replace them, but interbred with them to some extent.
- New DNA evidence from ancient Neandertals as well as from modern people demonstrates that some modest interbreeding did take place, probably between 80,000 and 50,000 ya. These findings clearly support a partial replacement model.
- Archaeological finds and some fossil evidence (although the latter is not as well established) also support the view that intermixing occurred between modern *H. sapiens* and Neandertals.
- The earliest finds of modern *H. sapiens* come from East Africa (Ethiopia), with the oldest dating to about 200,000 ya. Another find from Herto is very well dated (160,000 ya) and is the best evidence of an early modern human from anywhere at this time.
- Modern humans are found in South Africa beginning around 100,000 ya, and the first anatomical modern *H. sapiens* are found in the Middle East, dating to perhaps more than 100,000 ya.
- The Upper Paleolithic is a cultural period showing many innovations in technology, development of more sophisticated (cave) art, and, in many cases, very elaborate burials rich in grave goods. Similar cultural developments occurred in both Eurasia and Africa.

Critical Thinking Questions

1. What anatomical characteristics define *modern* as compared with *premodern* humans? Assume that you're analyzing an incomplete skeleton that may be early modern *H. sapiens*. Which portions of the skeleton would be most informative, and why?
2. What recent evidence supports a partial replacement model for an African origin and later dispersal of modern humans? Do you find this evidence convincing? Why or why not? Can you propose an alternative that has better data to support it?
3. Why are the fossils discovered from Herto so important? How does this evidence influence your conclusions in question 2?
4. What archaeological evidence shows that modern human behavior during the Upper Paleolithic was significantly different from that of earlier hominins? Do you think that early modern *H. sapiens* populations were behaviorally superior to the Neandertals? Be careful to define what you mean by *superior*.
5. Why do you think some Upper Paleolithic people painted in caves? Why don't we find such evidence of cave painting from a wider geographical area?

4

A

B

C

D

E

F

G

H

I

J

K

L

M

N

O

P

Q

R

S

T

U

W

X

Y

Z